Mike Holt's Illustrated Guide to

Changes to THE NEC® 2014

Mike Holt Enterprises, Inc.
888.NEC.CODE (632.2633) www.MikeHolt.com

Mike Holt's Illustrated Guide to Changes to the NEC® 2014

First Printing: October 2013

Technical Illustrator: Mike Culbreath
Cover Design: Madalina Iordache-Levay
Layout Design and Typesetting: Cathleen Kwas

ISBN 978-1-932685-79-4

Produced and Printed in the USA

For more information, call 888.NEC.CODE (632.2633), or e-mail Info@MikeHolt.com.

I dedicate this book to the
Lord Jesus Christ, my mentor and teacher

Our Commitment

We are committed to serving the electrical industry with integrity and respect by always searching for the most accurate interpretation of the *NEC*® and creating the highest quality instructional material that makes learning easy.

We are invested in the idea of changing lives, and build our products with the goal of not only helping you meet your licensing requirements, but also with the goal that this knowledge will improve your capability in the field and help you throughout your career.

We are committed to building a life-long relationship with you, and to helping you in each stage of your electrical career. Whether you are an apprentice just getting started in the industry, or an electrician preparing to take an exam, we are here to help you. When you need Continuing Education credits to renew your license, we will do everything we can to get our online courses and seminars approved in your state. Or if you are a contractor looking to train your team, we have a solution for you. And if you have advanced to the point where you are now teaching others, we are here to help you build your program and provide tools to make that task easier.

We genuinely care about providing quality electrical training that will help you take your skills to the next level.

Thanks for choosing Mike Holt Enterprises for your electrical training needs. We are here to help you every step of the way and encourage you to contact us so we can be a part of your success.

God Bless,

TABLE OF CONTENTS

About This Textbook xi

About the *National Electrical Code* xv

About the Authors and Illustrator xix

About the Team xxi

Article 90—Introduction to the *National Electrical Code* 1

90.1 Purpose of the *NEC* 2

CHAPTER 1—GENERAL 5

Article 100—Definitions 7

Accessible, Readily (Readily Accessible) 8

Adjustable Speed Drive 8

Adjustable Speed Drive System 9

Cable Routing Assembly 9

Communications Equipment 10

Communications Raceway 10

Concealed 11

Control Circuit 11

Coordination (Selective) 12

Device 13

Effective Ground-Fault Current Path 13

Electric-Discharge Lighting 14

Exposed (as applied to live parts) 15

Ground-Fault Current Path 15

Grounding Conductor, Equipment (EGC) 16

Hermetic Refrigerant Motor-Compressor 17

Intersystem Bonding Termination 17

Lighting Track (Track Lighting) 17

Location, Damp 18

Premises Wiring 18

Raceway 19

Retrofit Kit 20

Sealable Equipment 20

Separately Derived System 20

Voltage, Nominal 21

Article 110—Requirements for Electrical Installations 23

110.1 Scope 23

110.14 Conductor Termination and Splicing 24

110.16 Arc-Flash Hazard Warning 25

110.21 Markings 26

110.22 Identification of Disconnecting Means 27

110.24 Available Fault Current 27

110.25 Lockable Disconnecting Means 28

110.26 Spaces About Electrical Equipment 29

110.27 Guarding 36

CHAPTER 2—WIRING AND PROTECTION 37

Article 200—Use and Identification of Grounded [Neutral] Conductors 39

200.4 Neutral Conductors 40

200.6 Neutral Conductor Identification 41

Article 210—Branch Circuits 43

210.4 Multiwire Branch Circuits 44

210.8 GFCI Protection 45

210.12 Arc-Fault Circuit-Interrupter Protection 49

210.17 Electric Vehicle Branch Circuit 51

210.19 Conductor Sizing 52

210.22 Permissible Loads, Individual Branch Circuits 53

210.50 General 53

210.52 Dwelling Unit Receptacle Outlet Requirements 54

210.62 Show Windows 58

210.64 Electrical Service Areas 58

Article 215—Feeders 61

215.2 Minimum Rating 61

Article 220—Branch-Circuit, Feeder, and Service Calculations 65
220.3 Application of Other Articles 65
220.12 General Lighting 66
220.14 Other Loads—All Occupancies 67

Article 225—Outside Branch Circuits and Feeders 69
225.17 Masts as Supports 69
225.27 Raceway Seal 71
225.36 Type 71

Article 230—Services 73
230.6 Conductors Considered Outside a Building 74
230.26 Point of Attachment 75
230.28 Service Masts Used as Supports 75
230.42 Size and Rating 77

Article 240—Overcurrent Protection 79
240.21 Overcurrent Protection Location in Circuit 80

Article 250—Grounding and Bonding 83
250.8 Termination of Grounding and Bonding Conductors 83
250.10 Protection of Fittings 84
250.21 Ungrounded Systems—50V to 1,000V 84
250.24 Service Equipment—Grounding and Bonding 85
250.62 Grounding Electrode Conductor 85
250.64 Grounding Electrode Conductor Installation 86
250.66 Sizing Grounding Electrode Conductor 89
250.68 Termination to the Grounding Electrode 90
250.100 Bonding in Hazardous (Classified) Locations 92
250.102 Bonding Conductors and Jumpers 92
250.119 Identification of Equipment Grounding Conductors 94
250.121 Use of Equipment Grounding Conductors 96
250.122 Sizing Equipment Grounding Conductor 97
250.130 Replacing Nongrounding Receptacles 98

Article 285—Surge Protective Devices (SPDs) 101
285.1 Scope 102
285.13 Type 4 and Other Component Type SPDs 102

CHAPTER 3—WIRING METHODS AND MATERIALS 103

Article 300—General Requirements for Wiring Methods and Materials 107
300.1 Scope 107
300.5 Underground Installations 108
300.6 Protection Against Corrosion and Deterioration 109
300.22 Wiring in Ducts Not for Air Handling, Fabricated Ducts for Environmental Air, and Other Spaces for Environmental Air (Plenums) 109

Article 310—Conductors for General Wiring 113
310.15 Conductor Ampacity 114

Article 312—Cabinets, Cutout Boxes, and Meter Socket Enclosures 125
312.5 Enclosures 125
312.8 Enclosures With Splices, Taps, and Feed-Through Conductors 126

Article 314—Outlet, Device, Pull, and Junction Boxes; Conduit Bodies; and Handhole Enclosures 129
314.15 Damp or Wet Locations 129
314.17 Conductors That Enter Boxes or Conduit Bodies 130
314.23 Support of Boxes and Conduit Bodies 130
314.25 Covers and Canopies 131
314.27 Outlet Box 132
314.29 Wiring to be Accessible 134

Article 320—Armored Cable (Type AC) 135
320.23 In Accessible Attics or Roof Spaces 135

Article 330—Metal-Clad Cable (Type MC) 137
330.10 Uses Permitted 137
330.30 Securing and Supporting 138

Article 334—Nonmetallic-Sheathed Cable (Types NM and NMC) 141
334.10 Uses Permitted 141
334.12 Uses Not Permitted 142

Article 338—Service-Entrance Cable (Types SE and USE) 145
338.10 Uses Permitted 145

Article 344—Rigid Metal Conduit (Type RMC) 147
344.30 Securing and Supporting 147
344.100 Construction 148

Article 348—Flexible Metal Conduit (Type FMC) 149
348.30 Securing and Supporting 149

Article 350—Liquidtight Flexible Metal Conduit (Type LFMC) 151
350.30 Securing and Supporting 151
350.42 Fittings 152

Article 352—Rigid Polyvinyl Chloride Conduit (Type PVC) 153
352.2 Definition—Rigid Polyvinyl Chloride Conduit (PVC) 153

Article 356—Liquidtight Flexible Nonmetallic Conduit (Type LFNC) 155
356.30 Securing and Supporting 155

Article 376—Metal Wireways 157
376.22 Number of Conductors and Ampacity 157
376.56 Splices, Taps, and Power Distribution Blocks 158

Article 386—Surface Metal Raceways 161
386.30 Securing and Supporting 161

Article 392—Cable Trays 163
392.60 Equipment Grounding Conductor 163

Article 393—Low Voltage Suspended Ceiling Power Distribution Systems 165

CHAPTER 4—EQUIPMENT FOR GENERAL USE 167

Article 400—Flexible Cords and Flexible Cables 169
400.23 Equipment Grounding Conductor Identification 169

Article 404—Switches 171
404.2 Switch Connections 171
404.10 Mounting Snap Switches 173

Article 406—Receptacles, Cord Connectors, and Attachment Plugs (Caps) 175
406.3 Receptacle Rating and Type 175
406.4 General Installation Requirements 176
406.5 Receptacle Mounting 177
406.9 Receptacles in Damp or Wet Locations 178
406.12 Tamper-Resistant Receptacles 180
406.15 Dimmer-Controlled Receptacles 181

Article 408—Switchboards and Panelboards 183
408.4 Field Identification 183

Article 410—Luminaires, Lampholders, and Lamps 185
410.6 Listing Required 185
410.10 Luminaires in Specific Locations 186
410.130 General 186
410.151 Installation 187

Article 411—Lighting Systems Operating at 30V or Less and Lighting Equipment Connected to Class-2 Power Sources 189

Article 422—Appliances 191
422.5 Ground-Fault Circuit-Interrupter (GFCI) Protection 191
422.16 Flexible Cords 191
422.19 Space for Conductors 192
422.20 Outlet Boxes to Be Covered 192
422.21 Covering of Combustible Material at Outlet Boxes 192
422.23 Tire Inflation and Automotive Vacuum Machines 193
422.51 Vending Machines 193

Article 430—Motors, Motor Circuits, and Controllers 195
430.102 Disconnect Requirement 195

Article 440—Air-Conditioning and Refrigeration Equipment 197
440.14 Location 197

Article 445—Generators 199
445.11 Marking 199
445.16 Bushings 200
445.20 Ground-Fault Circuit Interrupter Protection for Receptacles on 15 kW or Smaller Portable Generators 201

Article 450—Transformers 203
450.10 Grounding and Bonding 203
450.11 Marking 204
450.14 Disconnecting Means 204

CHAPTER 5—SPECIAL OCCUPANCIES 207

Article 500—Hazardous (Classified) Locations 211
500.8 Equipment 212

Article 501—Class I Hazardous (Classified) Locations 213
501.10 Wiring Methods 213
501.15 Raceway and Cable Seals 216
501.30 Grounding and Bonding 221
501.145 Receptacles and Attachment Plugs 222

Article 502—Class II Hazardous (Classified) Locations 225
502.10 Wiring Methods 225
502.130 Luminaires 226
502.140 Flexible Cords 227
502.145 Receptacles and Attachment Plugs 228

Article 503—Class III Hazardous (Classified) Locations 229
503.10 Wiring Methods 229

Article 514—Motor Fuel Dispensing Facilities 231
514.3 Classification of Locations 231

Article 517—Health Care Facilities 233
517.2 Definitions—Patient Care Space 234
517.16 Isolated Ground Receptacles 235
517.18 General Care Areas 235

Article 525—Carnivals, Circuses, Fairs, and Similar Events 237
525.32 Equipment Grounding Conductor Continuity Assurance 237

Article 547—Agricultural Buildings 239
547.2 Definitions—Equipotential Plane 239
547.5 Wiring Methods 240

Article 555—Marinas and Boatyards 241
555.2 Definitions—Marine Power Outlet 241
555.15 Grounding 242

Article 590—Temporary Installations 243
590.4 General 243
590.6 Ground-Fault Protection for Personnel 244

CHAPTER 6—SPECIAL EQUIPMENT 245

Article 600—Electric Signs and Outline Lighting 247
600.3 Listing 247
600.4 Markings 248
600.6 Disconnecting Means 248
600.7 Grounding and Bonding 250
600.21 Ballasts, Transformers, Class 2 Power Sources, and Electronic Power Supplies 250

Article 620—Elevators, Escalators, and Moving Walks 253
620.51 Disconnecting Means 254

Article 640—Audio Signal Processing, Amplification, and Reproduction Equipment 255
640.1 Scope 255
640.10 Audio Systems Near Bodies of Water 256

Article 645—Information Technology Equipment 257
645.14 System Grounding 257

Article 646 Modular Data Centers 259

Article 680—Swimming Pools, Spas, Hot Tubs, Fountains, and Similar Installations 261

680.2 Definitions—Storable Swimming Pool 262
680.8 Overhead Conductor Clearance 262
680.11 Equipment Rooms and Pits 263
680.12 Maintenance Disconnecting Means 263
680.21 Motors 264
680.22 Lighting, Receptacles, and Equipment 264
680.26 Equipotential Bonding 266
Part III. Storable Swimming Pools, Storable Spas, and Storable Hot Tubs 267
680.42 Outdoor Installations 267
680.43 Indoor Installations 268
680.57 Signs in or Adjacent to Fountains 269
680.74 Equipotential Bonding 269

CHAPTER 7—SPECIAL CONDITIONS 271

Article 700—Emergency Systems 273

700.8 Surge Protection 273
700.12 General Requirements 274
700.16 Emergency Illumination 276
700.19 Multiwire Branch Circuits 276
700.27 Ground-Fault Protection of Equipment 277
700.28 Selective Coordination 277

Article 701—Legally Required Standby Systems 279

701.12 General Requirements 279
701.26 Ground-Fault Protection of Equipment 280
701.27 Selective Coordination 280

Article 702—Optional Standby Systems 281

702.7 Signs 281
702.12 Outdoor Generator Sets 282

Article 725—Remote-Control, Signaling, and Power-Limited Circuits 285

725.3 Other Articles 285
725.135 Installation of Class 2, Class 3, and PLTC Cables 286
725.139 Conductors of Different Circuits in the Same Cable, Enclosure, Cable Tray, Raceway, or Cable Routing Assembly 287
725.154 Applications of Class 2 and Class 3 Cables 289

Article 760—Fire Alarm Systems 291

760.3 Other Articles 291
760.32 Fire Alarm Circuit Cables Extending Beyond a Building 291
760.135 Installation of PLFA Cables in Buildings 292
760.139 Power-Limited Fire Alarm Circuits, Class 2, Class 3, and Communications Circuits 292
760.154 Applications of Power-Limited Fire Alarm Cables (PLFA) 293

Article 770—Optical Fiber Cables and Raceways 295

770.2 Definitions—Innerduct 295
770.2 Definitions—Optical Fiber Cable 296
770.2 Definitions—Point of Entrance 296
770.12 Innerduct 296
770.24 Mechanical Execution of Work 297
770.48 Unlisted Cables Entering Buildings 298
770.49 Metallic Entrance Conduit Grounding 299
770.110 Raceways and Cable Routing Assemblies for Optical Fiber Cables 299
770.113 Installation of Optical Fiber Cables 300
770.133 Installation of Optical Fiber Cables 301

CHAPTER 8—COMMUNICATIONS SYSTEMS 303

Article 800—Communications Circuits 305

800.2 Definitions—Innerduct 306

800.2 Definitions—Point of Entrance 306

800.12 Innerduct 307

800.24 Mechanical Execution of Work 307

800.49 Metallic Entrance Conduit Grounding 308

800.110 Raceways and Cable Routing Assemblies for Communications Wires and Cables 309

800.113 Installation of Communications Cables, Communications Raceways, and Cable Routing Assemblies 310

800.133 Installation of Communications Cables 311

800.154 Applications of Communications Cables, Communications Raceways, and Cable Routing Assemblies 312

Article 810—Radio and Television Equipment 315

810.6 Antenna Lead-In Protectors 315

810.7 Grounding Devices 315

Article 820—Community Antenna Television (CATV) and Radio Distribution Systems 317

820.2 Definitions—Point of Entrance 317

820.24 Mechanical Execution of Work 318

820.49 Metallic Entrance Conduit Grounding 319

820.110 Raceways for Coaxial Cables 319

ANNEX J— ADA STANDARDS FOR ACCESSIBLE DESIGN 321

FINAL EXAM FOR *CHANGES TO THE NEC 2014* 323

INDEX 341

ABOUT THIS TEXTBOOK

Mike Holt's Illustrated Guide to Changes to the NEC® 2014

Mike Holt's Illustrated Guide to Changes to the NEC® 2014 is intended to provide you with the tools necessary to understand the changes made to the 2014 *National Electrical Code® (NEC).* There were literally thousands of proposals to change the *Code.* As a result, hundreds of rules were changed that will affect us all.

The writing style of this textbook is meant to be informative, practical, useful, easy to read, and applicable for today's electrical professional. Just like all of Mike Holt's textbooks, this one contains hundreds of full-color illustrations showing the safety requirements of the *National Electrical Code* in practical use, helping you visualize the *Code* in today's electrical installations.

This illustrated textbook contains cautions regarding possible conflicts or confusing *NEC* requirements, tips on proper electrical installations, and warnings of dangers related to improper electrical installations. In spite of this effort, some rules may still seem unclear or need additional editorial improvement.

We can't eliminate confusing, conflicting, or controversial *Code* requirements, but we do try to put them into sharper focus to help you understand their intended purpose. Sometimes a requirement is confusing and it might be hard to understand its actual application. When this occurs, this textbook will point the situation out in an upfront and straightforward manner. We apologize in advance if that ever seems disrespectful, but our intention is to help the industry understand the current *NEC* as best as possible, point out areas that need refinement, and encourage *Code* users to be a part of the change process that creates a better *NEC* for the future.

The Scope of this Textbook

This textbook, *Illustrated Guide to Changes to the NEC 2014,* covers those installation requirements that we consider to be of critical importance, excluding Article 690 (which is covered in a separate textbook, *Changes to the NEC 2014—Solar PV Systems Edition),* and is based on the following conditions:

1. Power Systems and Voltage. All power-supply systems are assumed to be one of the following, unless identified otherwise:
    - 2-wire, single-phase, 120V
    - 3-wire, single-phase, 120/240V
    - 4-wire, three-phase, 120/240V Delta
    - 4-wire, three-phase, 120/208V or 277/480V Wye
2. **Electrical Calculations.** Unless the question or example specifies three-phase, they're based on a single-phase power supply. In addition, all amperage calculations are rounded to the nearest ampere in accordance with Section 220.5(B).
3. **Conductor Material.** Conductors are considered copper, unless aluminum is identified or specified.
4. **Conductor Sizing.** Conductors are sized based on a THHN/THWN copper conductor terminating on a 75°C terminal in accordance with 110.14(C), unless the question or example indicates otherwise.
5. **Overcurrent Device.** The term "overcurrent device" refers to a molded-case circuit breaker, unless specified otherwise. Where a fuse is specified, it's a single-element type fuse, also known as a "one-time fuse," unless the text specifies otherwise.

This textbook is to be used along with the *NEC,* not as a replacement for it. Be sure to have a copy of the 2014 *National Electrical Code* handy. Compare what's being explained in this textbook to what the *Code* book says, and discuss any topics that you find difficult to understand with others.

You'll notice that we've paraphrased a great deal of the *NEC* wording, and some of the article and section titles appear different from the text in the actual *Code* book. We believe doing so makes it easier to understand the content of the rule, so keep this in mind when comparing this textbook to the actual *NEC.*

This textbook follows the *NEC* format, but it doesn't cover every *Code* requirement. For example, it doesn't include every article, section, subsection, exception, or Informational Note. So don't be concerned if you see that the textbook contains Exception 1 and Exception 3, but not Exception 2.

We hope that as you read through this textbook, you'll allow sufficient time to review the text along with the outstanding graphics and examples, which are invaluable to your understanding.

How to Use This Textbook

The layout of this textbook incorporates special features designed not only to help you navigate easily through the material but to enhance your understanding as well.

A gray bar contains a summary of the change, and is followed by the *NEC* rule affected by it.

2014 CC **Graphics with an icon and green border** contain a 2014 *Code* change. *NEC* text changes will be underlined in green in all graphics. Green-bordered graphics with no green underlined text most likely indicate that the change is the removal of some text. Graphics without a colored border support the concept being discussed, but nothing in the graphic was affected by a change for 2014.

Yellow "sticky notes" contain an analysis of the change.

Text that's underlined in the chapter color denotes a change in the 2014 *Code*.

Bolded Author's Comments are intended to help you understand the *NEC* material and background information on the change.

Italicized Question and Answer sections show practical application questions with their solutions.

Danger, Caution, and Warning icons highlight areas of concern.

Color coding and a modular format make it easy to navigate through each section of the textbook.

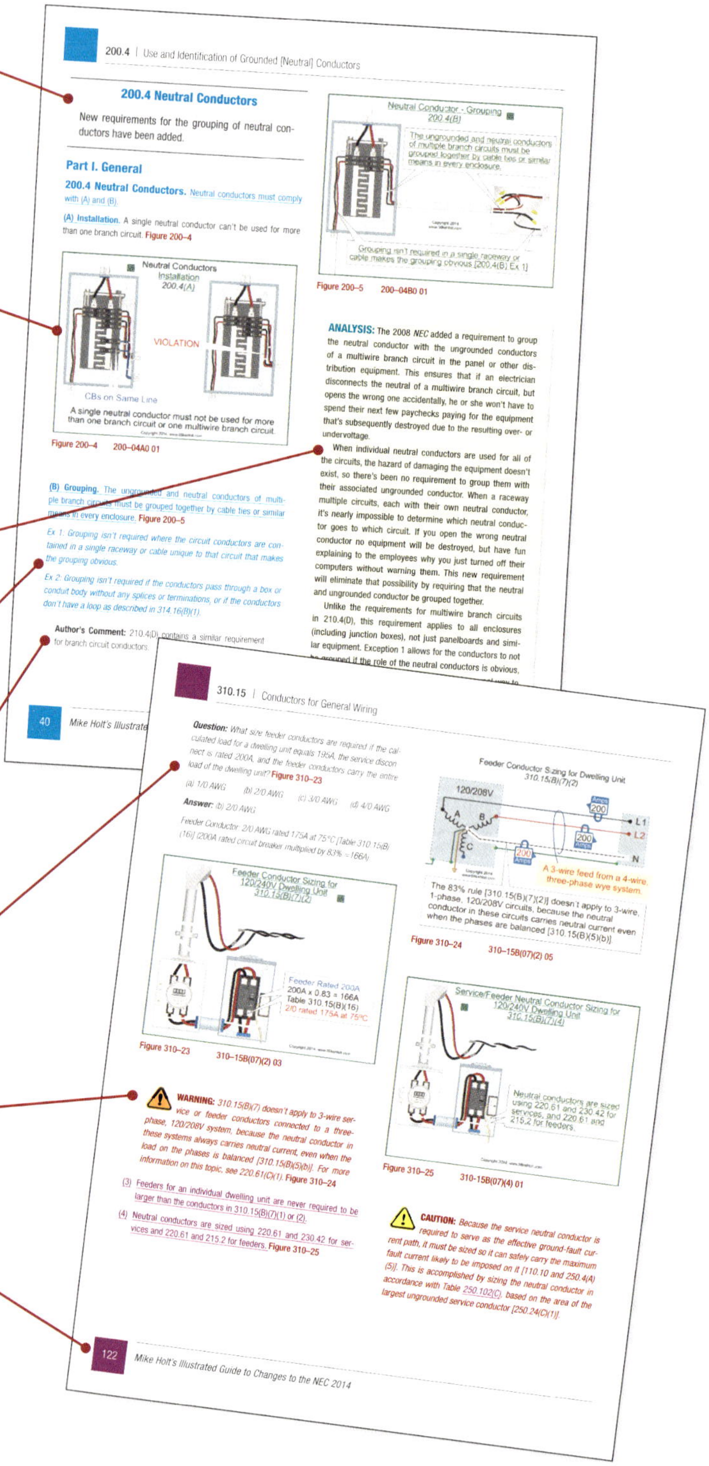

Cross-References, Notes, and Exceptions

Cross-References. This textbook contains several *NEC* cross-references to other related *Code* requirements to help you develop a better understanding of how the *NEC* rules relate to one another. These cross-references are indicated by *Code* section numbers in brackets, an example of which is "[90.4]."

Informational Notes. Informational Notes contained in the *NEC* will be identified in this textbook as "Note," except when that phrase is used in the change summary (gray background) or analysis (yellow background).

Exceptions. Exceptions contained in this textbook will be identified as "Ex" and not spelled out.

Textbook Corrections

We're committed to providing you the finest product with the fewest errors. We take great care in researching the *NEC* requirements to ensure this textbook is correct, but we're realistic and know that there'll be errors found and reported after this textbook is printed. This can occur because the *NEC* is dramatically changed each *Code* cycle; new articles are added, some are deleted, some are relocated, and many are renumbered.

The last thing we want is for you to have problems finding, communicating, or accessing this information. Any errors found after printing are listed on our website, so if you find an error, first check to see if it's already been corrected by going to www.MikeHolt.com, click on "Books," and then click on "Corrections" (www.MikeHolt.com/bookcorrections.htm).

If you believe that there's an error of any kind (typographical, grammatical, technical, or anything else) in this textbook or in the Answer Key and it isn't already listed on the website, e-mail Corrections@MikeHolt. com. Be sure to include the textbook title, page number, and any other pertinent information.

If you have adopted Mike Holt textbooks for use in your classroom you can register for up-to-date answer keys that can be downloaded from our website. To register and receive a log-in password, go to our website www.MikeHolt.com, click on "Instructors" in the sidebar of links, and then click on "Answer Keys." On this same page you'll also find instructions for accessing and downloading these answer keys. Please note that this feature will only work after you've received a log-in password.

Technical Questions

As you progress through this textbook, you might find that you don't understand every explanation, example, calculation, or comment. Don't become frustrated, and don't get down on yourself. Remember, this is the *National Electrical Code*, and sometimes the best attempt to explain a concept isn't enough to make it perfectly clear. If you're still confused, visit www.MikeHolt.com, and post your question on our free Code Forum for help. The forum is a moderated community of electrical professionals where you can exchange ideas and post technical questions that will be answered by your peers.

QR Codes

What's this symbol? It's a QR code and gives you the ability to use your smartphone to scan the image (using a barcode reader app) and be directed to a website. For example, the QR code to the right (when captured) will direct your smartphone to the Mike Holt Enterprises website. We've included these in various places in our textbook to make it easier for you to go directly to the website page referenced. In order to use a QR code, you'll need an app for your phone that allows it to read this barcode. Your phone may already have the ability to scan QR codes, but if it doesn't then visit the website or the Apps store on your smartphone to look for a QR Code Reader.

Additional Products to Help You Learn the *Code*

Changes to the NEC 2014 DVDs

One of the best ways to get the most out of this textbook is to use it in conjunction with the corresponding DVDs. Mike Holt's DVDs provide a 360° view of each topic with specialized commentary from Mike Holt and his panel of industry experts. Whether you're a visual or an auditory learner, watching the DVDs will enhance your knowledge and understanding.

To order a copy of the DVDs at a discounted price, call our office at 888.632.2633.

Changes to the NEC 2014—Solar PV Systems Edition

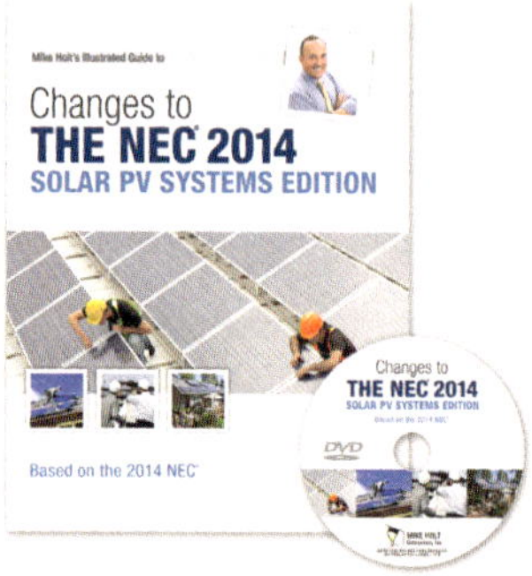

Want to know the Changes to the *Code* as they relate to Solar PV installations? Order Mike's newest book, *Changes to the NEC 2014— Solar PV Systems Edition*. This new title will review all of the major changes that have impacted Article 690 and supporting articles.

For more information visit www.mikeholt.com/14solar.

Detailed *Code* Library

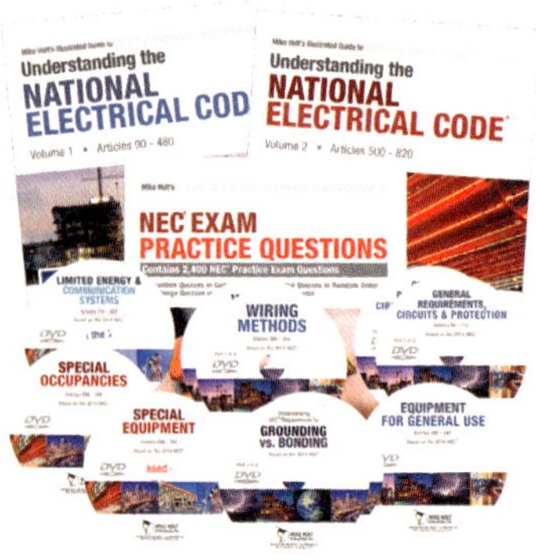

When you really need to understand the *NEC*, there's no better way to learn it than with Mike's Detailed *Code* Library. It takes you step-by-step through the *NEC*, in *Code* order with detailed illustrations, great practice questions, and in-depth DVD analysis. This library is perfect for engineers, electricians, contractors, and electrical inspectors.

- **Understanding the National Electrical Code - Volume 1**
- **Understanding the National Electrical Code - Volume 2**
- ***NEC* Exam Practice Questions workbook**
- *General Requirements DVDs (2)*
- *Grounding versus Bonding DVDs (2)*
- *Wiring Methods DVDs (2)*
- *Equipment for General Use DVD*
- *Special Occupancies DVD*
- *Special Equipment DVD*
- *Limited Energy and Communications Systems DVD*

Order Mike Holt's Detailed *Code* Library by calling 888.NEC.CODE (632.2633) or going to our website at www.MikeHolt.com/14DECO.

2014 *Code* Book

Whether you prefer the softbound, spiral bound or the loose-leaf version, everyone should have an updated *Code* book for accurate reference.

To order yours, visit www.mikeholt.com/14code.

Tabs

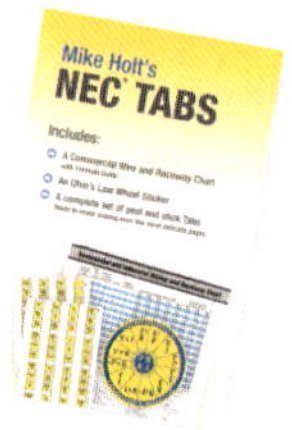

To navigate your *Code* book correctly, it helps to have it tabbed. Mike's best-selling tabs make this easy.

Visit www.MikeHolt.com/14tabs.

ABOUT THE *NATIONAL ELECTRICAL CODE*

The *National Electrical Code* is written for persons who understand electrical terms, theory, safety procedures, and electrical trade practices. These individuals include electricians, electrical contractors, electrical inspectors, electrical engineers, designers, and other qualified persons. The *Code* isn't written to serve as an instructional or teaching manual for untrained individuals [90.1(A)].

Learning to use the *NEC* can be likened to learning the strategy needed to play the game of chess well; it's a great game if you enjoy mental warfare. When learning to play chess, you must first learn the names of the game pieces, how they're placed on the board, and how each one is moved.

Once you understand the fundamentals, you're ready to start playing the game. Unfortunately, at this point all you can do is make crude moves, because you really don't understand how all the information works together. To play chess well, you'll need to learn how to use your knowledge by working on subtle strategies before you can work your way up to the more intriguing and complicated moves.

The *Code* is updated every three years to accommodate new electrical products and materials, changing technologies, improved installation techniques, and to make editorial refinements to improve readability and application. While the uniform adoption of each new edition of the *NEC* is the best approach for all involved in the electrical industry, many inspection jurisdictions modify the *Code* when it's adopted. To further complicate this situation, the *NEC* allows the authority having jurisdiction, typically the "Electrical Inspector," the flexibility to waive specific *Code* requirements, and to permit alternative methods. This is only allowed when he or she is assured the completed electrical installation is equivalent in establishing and maintaining effective safety [90.4].

Keeping up with requirements of the *Code* should be the goal of everyone involved in the safety of electrical installations. This includes electrical installers, contractors, owners, inspectors, engineers, instructors, and others concerned with electrical installations.

About the 2014 *NEC*

The actual process of changing the *Code* takes about two years, and it involves thousands of individuals making an effort to have the *NEC* as current and accurate as possible. Let's review how this process works:

Step 1. Proposals—November, 2011. Anybody can submit a proposal to change the *Code* before the proposal closing date. Thousands of proposals were submitted to modify the 2011 *NEC* and create the 2014 *Code*. Of these proposals, several hundred rules were revised that significantly affect the electrical industry. Some changes were editorial revisions, while others were more significant, such as new articles, sections, exceptions, and Informational Notes.

Step 2. *Code*-Making Panel(s) Review Proposals—January, 2012. All *Code* change proposals were reviewed by *Code*-Making Panels. There were 19 panels in the 2014 revision process who voted to accept, reject, or modify proposals.

Step 3. Report on Proposals (ROP)—July, 2012. The voting of the *Code*-Making Panels on the proposals was published for public review in a document called the "Report on Proposals," frequently referred to as the "ROP."

Step 4. Public Comments—October, 2012. Once the ROP was available, public comments were submitted asking the *Code*-Making Panel members to revise their earlier actions on change proposals, based on new information. The closing date for "Comments" was October, 2012.

Step 5. Comments Reviewed by *Code* Panels—December, 2012. The *Code*-Making Panels met again to review, discuss, and vote on public comments.

Step 6. Report on Comments (ROC)—March, 2013. The voting on the "Comments" was published for public review in a document called the "Report on Comments," frequently referred to as the "ROC."

Step 7. Electrical Section—June, 2013. The NFPA Electrical Section discussed and reviewed the work of the *Code*-Making Panels. The Electrical Section developed recommendations on last-minute motions to revise the proposed *NEC* draft that would be presented at the NFPA's annual meeting.

Step 8. NFPA Annual Meeting—June, 2013. The 2014 *NEC* was voted by the NFPA members to approve the action of the *Code*-Making Panels at the annual meeting, after a number of motions (often called "floor actions" or "NITMAMs") were voted on.

Step 9. Standards Council Review Appeals and Approves the 2014 *NEC*—July, 2013. The NFPA Standards Council reviewed the record of the *Code*-making process and approved publication of the 2014 *NEC*.

Step 10. 2014 *NEC* Published—September, 2013. The 2014 *National Electrical Code* was published, following the NFPA Board of Directors review of appeals.

> **Author's Comment:** Proposals and comments can be submitted online at the NFPA website (www.nfpa.org). From the homepage, click on "Codes and Standards", then find NFPA 70 (*National Electrical Code*). From there, follow the on screen instructions to download the proposal form. The deadline for proposals to create the 2017 *National Electrical Code* will be around November of 2014. If you would like to see something changed in the *Code*, you're encouraged to participate in the process.

Not a Game

Electrical work isn't a game, and it must be taken very seriously. Learning the basics of electricity, important terms and concepts, as well as the basic layout of the *NEC* gives you just enough knowledge to be dangerous. There are thousands of specific and unique applications of electrical installations, and the *Code* doesn't cover every one of them. To safely apply the *NEC*, you must understand the purpose of a rule and how it affects the safety aspects of the installation.

NEC Terms and Concepts

The *NEC* contains many technical terms, so it's crucial for *Code* users to understand their meanings and their applications. If you don't understand a term used in a *Code* rule, it will be impossible to properly apply the *NEC* requirement. Be sure you understand that Article 100 defines the terms that apply to two or more *Code* articles. For example, the term "Dwelling Unit" is found in many articles; if you don't know what a dwelling unit is, how can you apply the requirements for it?

In addition, many articles have terms unique for that specific article and definitions of those terms are only applicable for that given article. For example, Section 250.2 contains the definitions of terms that only apply to Article 250—Grounding and Bonding.

Small Words, Grammar, and Punctuation

It's not only the technical words that require close attention, because even the simplest of words can make a big difference to the application of a rule. The word "or" can imply alternate choices for wiring methods, while "and" can mean an additional requirement. Let's not forget about grammar and punctuation. The location of a comma can dramatically change the requirement of a rule.

Slang Terms or Technical Jargon

Electricians, engineers, and other trade-related professionals use slang terms or technical jargon that isn't shared by all. This makes it very difficult to communicate because not everybody understands the intent or application of those slang terms. So where possible, be sure you use the proper word, and don't use a word if you don't understand its definition and application. For example, lots of electricians use the term "pigtail" when describing the short conductor for the connection of a receptacle, switch, luminaire, or equipment. Although they may understand it, not everyone does.

NEC Style and Layout

Before we get into the details of the *NEC*, we need to take a few moments to understand its style and layout. Understanding the structure and writing style of the *Code* is very important before it can be used and applied effectively. The *National Electrical Code* is organized into ten major components.

1. Table of Contents
2. Article 90 (Introduction to the *Code*)
3. Chapters 1 through 9 (major categories)
4. Articles 90 through 840 (individual subjects)
5. Parts (divisions of an article)
6. Sections and Tables (*NEC* requirements)
7. Exceptions (*Code* permissions)
8. Informational Notes (explanatory material)
9. Annexes (information)
10. Index

1. Table of Contents. The Table of Contents displays the layout of the chapters, articles, and parts as well as the page numbers. It's an excellent resource and should be referred to periodically to observe the interrelationship of the various *NEC* components. When attempting to locate the rules for a particular situation, knowledgeable *Code* users often go first to the Table of Contents to quickly find the specific *NEC* Part that applies.

2. Introduction. The *NEC* begins with Article 90, the introduction to the *Code*. It contains the purpose of the *NEC*, what's covered and what isn't covered along with how the *Code* is arranged. It also gives information on enforcement and how mandatory and permissive rules are written as well as how explanatory material is included. Article 90 also includes information on formal interpretations, examination of equipment for safety, wiring planning, and information about formatting units of measurement.

3. Chapters. There are nine chapters, each of which is divided into articles. The articles fall into one of four groupings: General Requirements (Chapters 1 through 4), Specific Requirements (Chapters 5 through 7), Communications Systems (Chapter 8), and Tables (Chapter 9).

Chapter 1—General
Chapter 2—Wiring and Protection
Chapter 3—Wiring Methods and Materials
Chapter 4—Equipment for General Use
Chapter 5—Special Occupancies
Chapter 6—Special Equipment
Chapter 7—Special Conditions
Chapter 8—Communications Systems (Telephone, Data, Satellite, Cable TV and Broadband)
Chapter 9—Tables–Conductor and Raceway Specifications

4. Articles. The *NEC* contains approximately 140 articles, each of which covers a specific subject. For example:

Article 110—General Requirements
Article 250—Grounding and Bonding
Article 300—General Requirements for Wiring Methods and Materials
Article 430—Motors and Motor Controllers
Article 500—Hazardous (Classified) Locations
Article 680—Swimming Pools, Fountains, and Similar Installations
Article 725—Remote-Control, Signaling, and Power-Limited Circuits
Article 800—Communications Circuits

5. Parts. Larger articles are subdivided into parts. Because the parts of a *Code* article aren't included in the section numbers, we have a tendency to forget what "part" the *NEC* rule is relating to. For example, Table 110.34(A) contains working space clearances for electrical equipment. If we aren't careful, we might think this table applies to all electrical installations, but Table 110.34(A) is located in Part III, which only contains requirements for "Over 600 Volts, Nominal" installations. The rules for working clearances for electrical equipment for systems 600V, nominal, or less are contained in Table 110.26(A)(1), which is located in Part II—600 Volts, Nominal, or Less.

6. Sections and Tables.

Sections. Each *NEC* rule is called a "*Code* Section." A *Code* section may be broken down into subsections by letters in parentheses (A), (B), and so on. Numbers in parentheses (1), (2), and so forth, may further break down a subsection, and lowercase letters (a), (b), and so on, further break the rule down to the third level. For example, the rule requiring all receptacles in a dwelling unit bathroom to be GFCI protected is contained in Section 210.8(A)(1). Section 210.8(A)(1) is located in Chapter 2, Article 210, Section 8, Subsection (A), Sub-subsection (1).

Many in the industry incorrectly use the term "Article" when referring to a *Code* section. For example, they say "Article 210.8," when they should say "Section 210.8." Section numbers in this textbook are shown without the word "Section," unless they begin a sentence. For example, Section 210.8(A) is shown as simply 210.8(A).

Tables. Many *NEC* requirements are contained within tables, which are lists of *Code* rules placed in a systematic arrangement. The titles of the tables are extremely important; you must read them carefully in order to understand the contents, applications, limitations, and so forth, of each table in the *NEC*. Many times notes are provided in or below a table; be sure to read them as well since they're also part of the requirement. For example, Note 1 for Table 300.5 explains how to measure the cover when burying cables and raceways, and Note 5 explains what to do if solid rock is encountered.

7. Exceptions. Exceptions are *Code* requirements or permissions that provide an alternative method to a specific rule. There are two types of exceptions—mandatory and permissive. When a rule has several exceptions, those exceptions with mandatory requirements are listed before the permissive exceptions.

Mandatory Exceptions. A mandatory exception uses the words "shall" or "shall not." The word "shall" in an exception means that if you're using the exception, you're required to do it in a particular way. The phrase "shall not" means it isn't permitted.

Permissive Exceptions. A permissive exception uses words such as "shall be permitted," which means it's acceptable (but not mandatory) to do it in this way.

8. Informational Notes. An Informational Note contains explanatory material intended to clarify a rule or give assistance, but it isn't a *Code* requirement.

9. Annexes. Annexes aren't a part of the *NEC* requirements, and are included in the *Code* for informational purposes only.

Annex A. Product Safety Standards
Annex B. Application Information for Ampacity Calculation
Annex C. Raceway Fill Tables for Conductors and Fixture Wires of the Same Size
Annex D. Examples
Annex E. Types of Construction
Annex F. Critical Operations Power Systems (COPS)

Annex G. Supervisory Control and Data Acquisition (SCADA)
Annex H. Administration and Enforcement
Annex I. Recommended Tightening Torques
Annex J. ADA Standards for Accessible Design

10. Index. The Index at the back of the *Code* book is helpful in locating a specific rule.

Changes to the *NEC* since the previous edition(s), are identified by shading, but rules that have been relocated aren't identified as a change. A bullet symbol "•" is located on the margin to indicate the location of a rule that was deleted from a previous edition. New articles contain a vertical line in the margin of the page.

Different Interpretations

Some electricians, contractors, instructors, inspectors, engineers, and others enjoy the challenge of discussing the *NEC* requirements, hopefully in a positive and productive manner. This give-and-take is important to the process of better understanding the *Code* requirements and application(s). However, if you're going to participate in an *NEC* discussion, please don't spout out what you think without having the actual *Code* book in your hand. The professional way of discussing an *NEC* requirement is by referring to a specific section, rather than talking in vague generalities.

How to Locate a Specific Requirement

How to go about finding what you're looking for in the *Code* book depends, to some degree, on your experience with the *NEC*. *Code* experts typically know the requirements so well they just go to the correct rule without any outside assistance. The Table of Contents might be the only thing very experienced *NEC* users need to locate the requirement they're looking for. On the other hand, average *Code* users should use all of the tools at their disposal, including the Table of Contents and the Index.

Table of Contents. Let's work out a simple example: What *NEC* rule specifies the maximum number of disconnects permitted for a service? If you're an experienced *Code* user, you'll know Article 230 applies to "Services," and because this article is so large, it's divided up into multiple parts (actually eight parts). With this knowledge, you can quickly go to the Table of Contents and see it lists the Service Equipment Disconnecting Means requirements in Part VI.

Author's Comment: The number 70 precedes all page numbers because the *NEC* is NFPA Standard Number 70.

Index. If you use the Index, which lists subjects in alphabetical order, to look up the term "service disconnect," you'll see there's no listing. If you try "disconnecting means," then "services," you'll find that the Index indicates that the rule is located in Article 230, Part VI. Because the *NEC* doesn't give a page number in the Index, you'll need to use the Table of Contents to find it, or flip through the *Code* book to Article 230, then continue to flip through pages until you find Part VI.

Many people complain that the *NEC* only confuses them by taking them in circles. As you gain experience in using the *Code* and deepen your understanding of words, terms, principles, and practices, you'll find the *NEC* much easier to understand and use than you originally thought.

Customizing Your *Code* Book

One way to increase your comfort level with the *Code* book is to customize it to meet your needs. You can do this by highlighting and underlining important *NEC* requirements, and by attaching tabs to important pages. Be aware that if you're using your *Code* book to take an exam, some exam centers don't allow markings of any type.

Highlighting. As you read through this textbook, be sure you highlight those requirements in the *Code* that are the most important or relevant to you. Use yellow for general interest and orange for important requirements you want to find quickly. Be sure to highlight terms in the Index and the Table of Contents as you use them.

Underlining. Underline or circle key words and phrases in the *NEC* with a red pen (not a lead pencil) and use a 6-inch ruler to keep lines straight and neat. This is a very handy way to make important requirements stand out. A small 6-inch ruler also comes in handy for locating specific information in the many *Code* tables.

Tab Your *Code* Book

Placing tabs on *Code* articles, sections, and tables will make it easier for you to use the *NEC*. However, too many tabs will defeat the purpose. You can order a set of *Code* book tabs designed by Mike Holt online at www.MikeHolt.com/14code, or by calling 1.888.NEC.CODE (632.2633).

ABOUT THE AUTHORS AND ILLUSTRATOR

Ryan Jackson—Author

Electrical Inspector
Draper City, UT

Ryan Jackson is a combination inspector in the Salt Lake City, Utah, area. He began his career as a carpenter while in high school. At 23, Ryan landed his first job as an electrical inspector and subsequently became certified in building, plumbing, and mechanical inspection (commercial and residential), as well as building and electrical plan review. Two years after becoming an inspector, he was approached by a friend in the area asking him to fill in for him at an electrical seminar. After his first class Ryan was hooked, and is now a highly sought after seminar instructor. He's taught in several states, and loves helping people increase their understanding of the *Code*.

Ryan met Mike in 2005 and helped with his 2005 *Understanding the NEC, Volume 2* videos and textbooks. He believes there are only a few opportunities that can change a person's life and career—and meeting Mike was one of them.

When Ryan isn't working, he can often be found in his garage turning wood on his lathe, or in the kitchen where he enjoys wine making. Ryan married his high school sweetheart, Sharie, and they have two beautiful children together: Kaitlynn and Aaron.

Special Acknowledgments—I want to first thank my amazing wife and my children for putting up with me for all of these years, which is often a difficult task, particularly when I'm writing.

Professionally, I'm indebted to Gary Beckstrand for getting me started in my teaching career, and Noel Williams who inspired me to do it in the first place. Mark Ode is one of the finest men that I've ever met, and has always been there for me. Dick Loyd and Mike Johnston have been patient with me, and I appreciate it very much.

Last, and most certainly not least, I want to thank my mother, Donna Jackson. She was one of the very first certified electrical inspectors in the state of Utah, and she did an amazing job raising three boys on her own. Mom, I love you very much, and I wouldn't have made it very far without you.

Dedication—I dedicate my contributions to this textbook to my loving and supportive wife Sharie.

Mike Holt—Co-Author

Founder, President, Mike Holt Enterprises
Groveland, FL
www.MikeHolt.com

Mike Holt worked his way up through the electrical trade. He began as an apprentice electrician and became one of the most recognized experts in the world as it relates to electrical power installations. He's worked as a journeyman electrician, master electrician, and electrical contractor. Mike's experience in the real world gives him a unique understanding of how the *NEC* relates to electrical installations from a practical standpoint. You'll find his writing style to be direct, nontechnical, and powerful.

Did you know Mike didn't finish high school? So if you struggled in high school or didn't finish at all, don't let it get you down. Since Mike understood the importance of education, he immediately attained his GED, and attended the University of Miami's Graduate School for a MBA.

Mike resides in Central Florida, is the father of seven children, has five grandchildren, and enjoys many outside interests and activities. He's a nine-time National Barefoot Water-Ski Champion (1988, 1999, 2005–2009, 2012–2013). He's set many national records and continues to train year-round at a World competition level (www.barefootwaterskier.com). What sets him apart from some is his commitment to living a balanced lifestyle; placing God first, family, career, then self.

Special Acknowledgments—First, I want to thank God for my godly wife who's always by my side and my children, Belynda, Melissa, Autumn, Steven, Michael, Meghan, and Brittney.

A special thank you must be sent to the staff at the National Fire Protection Association (NFPA), publishers of the *NEC*—in particular Jeff Sargent for his assistance in answering my many *Code* questions over the years. Jeff, you're a "first class" guy, and I admire your dedication and commitment to helping others understand the *NEC*. Other former NFPA staff members I would like to thank include John Caloggero, Joe Ross, and Dick Murray for their help in the past.

A personal thank you goes to Sarina, my long-time friend and office manager. It's been wonderful working side-by-side with you for over 25 years nurturing this company's growth from its small beginnings.

Mike Culbreath—Illustrator

Graphic Illustrator
Alden, MI
www.MikeHolt.com

Mike Culbreath devoted his career to the electrical industry and worked his way up from an apprentice electrician to master electrician. He started in the electrical field doing residential and light commercial construction. He later did service work and custom electrical installations. While working as a journeyman electrician, he suffered a serious on-the-job knee injury. As part of his rehabilitation, Mike completed courses at Mike Holt Enterprises, Inc. and then passed the exam to receive his Master Electrician's license. In 1986, with a keen interest in continuing education for electricians, he joined the staff to update material and began illustrating Mike Holt's textbooks and magazine articles.

He started with simple hand-drawn diagrams and cut-and-paste graphics. When frustrated by the limitations of that style of illustrating, he took a company computer home to learn how to operate some basic computer graphic software. Becoming aware that computer graphics offered a lot of flexibility for creating illustrations, Mike took every computer graphics class and seminar he could to help develop his computer graphic skills. He's now worked as an illustrator and editor with the company for over 25 years and, as Mike Holt has proudly acknowledged, has helped to transform his words and visions into lifelike graphics.

Originally from South Florida, Mike now lives in northern lower Michigan where he enjoys kayaking, photography, and cooking, but his real passion is playing with his horses.

Mike loves spending time with his children Dawn and Mac and his grandchildren Jonah and Kieley.

Special Acknowledgments—I would like to thank Ryan Jackson, an outstanding and very knowledgeable *Code* guy, and Eric Stromberg, an electrical engineer and super geek (and I mean that in the most complimentary manner, this guy is brilliant), for helping me keep our graphics as technically correct as possible.

I also want to give a special thank you to Cathleen Kwas for making me look good with her outstanding layout design and typesetting skills and Toni Culbreath who proofreads all of my material. I would also like to acknowledge Belynda Holt Pinto, our Chief Operations Officer and the rest of the outstanding staff at Mike Holt Enterprises, for all the hard work they do to help produce and distribute these outstanding products.

And last but not least, I need to give a special thank you to Mike Holt for not firing me over 25 years ago when I "borrowed" one of his computers and took it home to begin the process of learning how to do computer illustrations. He gave me the opportunity and time needed to develop my computer graphic skills. He's been an amazing friend and mentor since I met him as a student many years ago. Thanks for believing in me and allowing me to be part of the Mike Holt Enterprises family.

ABOUT THE TEAM

Editorial and Production Team

We want to thank **Toni Culbreath** who worked tirelessly to proofread and edit the final stages of this publication. Her attention to detail and dedication to this project is greatly appreciated.

Many thanks to **Cathleen Kwas** who did the design, layout, and production of this book. Her desire to create the best possible product for our customers is greatly appreciated.

Also, thanks to **Paula Birchfield** who was the Production Coordinator of the textbook. She helped keep everything flowing and tying up all the loose ends.

Thanks to **Bruce Marcho** for doing such an excellent job recording, editing, and producing our DVDs. Bruce has been a vital part of our video products for over 25 years.

Video Team Members

Ryan Jackson and **Mike Culbreath** provided outstanding technical advice in serving on the video team along with **Mike Holt** and the following highly qualified professionals.

Daniel Brian House

Dan House Electric, Inc
Ocala, FL
www.DanHouseElectric.com

Brian House is a high-energy entrepreneur with a passion for doing business the right way. Brian is currently the CEO of Dan House Electric, Inc., an unlimited electrical contracting company based in Florida and working throughout the Southeast United States.

He's been involved in varying aspects of electrical contracting and energy conservation since the 1990s. He has a passion for constantly improving the combinations of technology offered to his customers, whether it is designing energy-efficient lighting retrofits, exploring "green" biomass generators, or partnering with solar energy companies as their preferred installer. Brian has experienced the ups and downs of electrical contracting and enjoys the challenges of design build projects.

Passionate about helping others, he regularly engages with the youth of the local community to motivate them into exploring their future.

Brian and his wife Carissa have shared the joy of their four children and over 30 foster children during a happy 16 years of marriage. When not at work or church, he can be found racing mountain bikes with his kids or on the action-packed intercoastals as an avid fly fisherman.

Lee Jolley

Electrical Inspector II, Baltimore County, MD
Instructor, Harford County, MD
Airville, PA

Lee Jolley began in the trade over 30 years ago, working for several companies in many aspects of the field. He feels fortunate to have worked with some great guys that taught him *NEC* requirements as much as the skills to do the work. Special thanks to Chad, Ronn, Dennis, and Eddie for keeping me straight and arguing *Code* with me.

Lee went to work for the Baltimore County, Maryland government in 1990 as an electrical inspector. With great respect for the position, he strived to learn as much as he could about all the codes that are pertinent to our industry. In 1997 Lee started teaching at the Harford County Electrical Contractors Association apprenticeship program. There he learned how much he loved teaching. Leading electricians to doing their jobs in the safest methods possible was very rewarding. Lee also began doing seminars for electrical contractors several years ago. His seminars covered many of topics including the *NEC* changes since 2002, Grounding vs. Bonding, PV Systems changed by the NFPA 1, and many more. By using Mike Holt material, building power point programs from scratch, and adding his own sense of humor, he's become a well-respected instructor and *Code* official in the area.

Lee is first and foremost a very proud dad and grandfather. He loves his children as much as a man can. His daughter Lauren and granddaughter Ava are the lights of his life. His son Elijah joined the Marines in 2012 and works on F-18s and has his dad's utmost respect. He also loves his Lord and Savior with all his heart.

Michael P. Pillarella

Owner, Pillarella School of Electrical Code & Theory
Assonet, MA
www.pillarellaschool.com

Mike Pillarella holds a Master's Degree in Education, a BS in Industrial Arts, and an AE in Electric and Electronics Engineering Technology. He became a Certified Electrical Related & Shop Instructor in the Massachusetts School system. In 1988, Mike established EMI Electrical Contractors, Inc. providing electrical maintenance and installation services in the New England South Shore area.

In 2007, Mike established the proprietary Pillarella School of Electrical Code & Theory. While serving as an electrical inspector, he became increasingly aware of the areas in which more education was needed and structured his curriculum accordingly. His proudest moment as an instructor was when his son, Tim, earned his Master's license—the first attendee of the school to do so.

Mike holds master licenses in Massachusetts, Rhode Island, New Hampshire, Vermont and Maine, and is an approved CEU provider and OSHA Outreach Construction instructor in these states. He's President of the Massachusetts Electrical Contractors Association, Bristol Chapter, and President and Education Chairman of the International Association of Electrical Inspectors, Roger Williams Chapter. Mike served for several years as an instructor for the Massachusetts Firefighters' Academy teaching Electrical Safety, Fire, and Arson Investigation. He served his community for 17 years as a firefighter, EMT, and finished as Fire Chief.

Mike is extremely proud of his wife, Valerie, and their three children, Amy, Michael, and Tim.

Eric Stromberg

Electrical Engineer/Instructor
Stromberg Engineering, Inc.
Los Alamos, NM
www.strombergengineering.com.

Eric Stromberg worked as a journeyman electrician, before and during the time he attended college. When he graduated with a degree in Electrical Engineering in 1982, he took a job as an electronics technician. Eric became a licensed fire alarm installation superintendent and spent the next seven years installing and maintaining life safety systems in high-rise buildings.

In 1989, he went to work for Dow Chemical, where he designed power distribution systems for world-class industrial facilities. Eric began teaching *National Electrical Code* classes to engineers in 1997. He received his professional engineering license, for the State of Texas, in 2003 and, in 2005, started Stromberg Engineering.

In 2013, Eric retired from Dow Chemical and now lives in the mountains of Northern New Mexico. Eric's oldest daughter, Ainsley, lives in Boston, Massachusetts with her husband Nathan. His son, Austin, is in the Air Force and is stationed at Minot, North Dakota. His youngest daughter, Brieanna, is a singer/songwriter who lives in Austin, Texas.

ARTICLE 90 INTRODUCTION TO THE *NATIONAL ELECTRICAL CODE*

Introduction to Article 90—Introduction to the *National Electrical Code*

Many *NEC* violations and misunderstandings wouldn't occur if people doing the work simply understood Article 90. For example, many people see *Code* requirements as performance standards. In fact, the *NEC* requirements are bare minimums for safety. This is exactly the stance electrical inspectors, insurance companies, and courts take when making a decision regarding electrical design or installation.

Article 90 opens by saying the *NEC* isn't intended as a design specification or instruction manual. The *National Electrical Code* has one purpose only, and that's the "practical safeguarding of persons and property from hazards arising from the use of electricity." The necessity of carefully studying the *NEC* rules can't be overemphasized, and the role of textbooks such as this one is to help in that undertaking. Understanding where to find the rules in the *Code* that apply to the installation is invaluable. Rules in several different articles often apply to even a simple installation.

Article 90 then describes the scope and arrangement of the *NEC*. The balance of this article provides the reader with information essential to understanding the *Code* rules.

Typically, electrical work requires you to understand the first four chapters of the *NEC* which apply generally, plus have a working knowledge of the Chapter 9 tables. That understanding begins with Article 90. Chapters 5, 6, and 7 make up a large portion of the *Code*, but they apply to special occupancies, special equipment, or other special conditions. They build on, modify, or amend the rules in the first four chapters. Chapter 8 contains the requirements for communications systems, such as telephone systems, antenna wiring, CATV, and network-powered broadband systems. Communications systems aren't subject to the general requirements of Chapters 1 through 4, or the special requirements of Chapters 5 through 7, unless there's a specific reference in Chapter 8 to a rule in Chapters 1 through 7.

90.1 Purpose of the *NEC*

This section has been condensed to make the purpose of the *Code* more obvious.

90.1 Purpose of the *NEC*.

(A) Practical Safeguarding. The purpose of the *NEC* is to ensure that electrical systems are installed in a manner that protects people and property by minimizing the risks associated with the use of electricity.

The *Code* is intended to be used by those skilled and knowledgeable in electrical theory, electrical systems, construction, and the installation and operation of electrical equipment.

It isn't a design specification standard or instruction manual for the untrained and unqualified.

(B) Adequacy. The *Code* contains requirements considered necessary for a safe electrical installation. If an electrical system is installed in compliance with the *NEC*, it will be essentially free from electrical hazards. The *Code* is a safety standard, not a design guide.

NEC requirements aren't intended to ensure the electrical installation will be efficient, convenient, adequate for good service, or suitable for future expansion. Specific items of concern, such as electrical energy management, maintenance, and power quality issues aren't within the scope of the *Code*. Figure 90–1

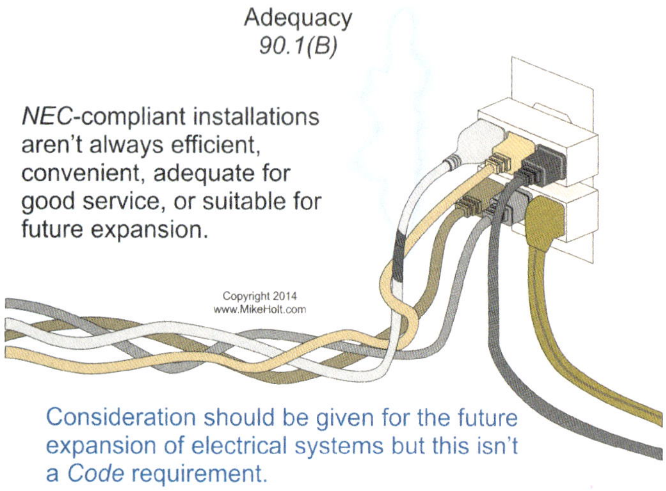

Figure 90–1

Note: Hazards in electrical systems often occur because circuits are overloaded or not properly installed in accordance with the *NEC*. These often occur if the initial wiring didn't provide reasonable provisions for system changes or for the increase in the use of electricity.

Author's Comments:

- See the definition of "Overload" in Article 100.
- The *NEC* doesn't require electrical systems to be designed or installed to accommodate future loads. However, the electrical designer (typically an electrical engineer) is concerned with not only ensuring electrical safety (*Code* compliance), but also with ensuring the system meets the customers' needs, both of today and in the near future. To satisfy customers' needs, electrical systems are often designed and installed above the minimum requirements contained in the *NEC*. But just remember, if you're taking an exam, licensing exams are based on your understanding of the minimum *Code* requirements.

(C) Relation to International Standards. The requirements of the *NEC* address the fundamental safety principles contained in the International Electrotechnical Commission (IEC) standards, including protection against electric shock, adverse thermal effects, overcurrent, fault currents, and overvoltage. Figure 90–2

Figure 90–2

Author's Comment: The *NEC* is used in Chile, Ecuador, Peru, and the Philippines. It's also the Electrical *Code* for Colombia, Costa Rica, Mexico, Panama, Puerto Rico, and Venezuela. Because of these adoptions, it's available in Spanish from the National Fire Protection Association, 617.770.3000, or www.NFPA.Org.

ANALYSIS: 90.1 is the first statement in the *NEC*, and it's an important one. Quite often *Code* users need to determine whether or not what they're installing, inspecting, or specifying meets the intent of the *NEC*, and this section tells them what that intent is.

90.1(C) was deleted from the *Code* and moved into the last sentence of subsection (A). This sentence can be a bit intimidating for newer *NEC* users, but it's important to remember that the *Code* is intended to be used by people who understand the electrical industry. The *NEC* doesn't use slang terms, it doesn't dance around a subject, and it doesn't sugar coat difficult topics. A person reading the *Code* needs to have a good understanding of the principals involved or they'll find themselves confused, frustrated, and angry.

The remainder of the section was renumbered due to the removal of 90.1(C).

Notes

CHAPTER 1 GENERAL

Introduction to Chapter 1—General

Before you can make sense of the *Code*, you must become familiar with a few basic rules, concepts, definitions, and requirements. As you study the *NEC*, you'll see that these are the foundation for a proper understanding of the *Code*.

Chapter 1 consists of two topics. Article 100 provides definitions so people can understand one another when trying to communicate about *Code*-related matters and Article 110 provides the general requirements needed to correctly apply the rest of the *NEC*.

Time spent learning this general material is a great investment. After understanding Chapter 1, some of the *Code* requirements that seem confusing to other people—those who don't understand Chapter 1—will become increasingly clear to you. The requirements will strike you as being "common sense," because you'll have the foundation from which to understand and apply them. When you read the *NEC* requirements in later chapters, you'll understand the principles upon which many of them are based, and not be surprised at all. You'll read them and feel like you already know them.

- **Article 100—Definitions.** Part I of Article 100 contains the definitions of terms used throughout the *Code* for systems that operate at 600V, nominal, or less. The definitions of terms in Part II apply to systems that operate at over 600V, nominal.

  Author's Comment: This textbook covers the requirements for systems that operate at 600V, nominal, or less.

Definitions of standard terms, such as volt, voltage drop, ampere, impedance, and resistance, aren't listed in Article 100. If the *NEC* doesn't define a term, then a dictionary suitable to the authority having jurisdiction should be consulted. A building code glossary might provide better definitions than a dictionary found at your home or school.

Definitions located at the beginning of an article apply only to that specific article. For example, the definition of a swimming "pool" is contained in 680.2, because this term applies only to the requirements contained in Article 680—Swimming Pools, Fountains, and Similar Installations. As soon as a defined term is used in two or more articles, its definition should be included in Article 100.

- **Article 110—Requirements for Electrical Installations.** This article contains general requirements for electrical installations for the following:

  - Part I. General
  - Part II. 600V, Nominal, Or Less

ARTICLE 100 DEFINITIONS

Introduction to Article 100—Definitions

Have you ever had a conversation with someone, only to discover that what you said and what he or she heard were completely different? This often happens when people in a conversation don't understand the definitions of the words being used, and that's why the definitions of key terms are located right at the beginning of the *NEC* (Article 100), or at the beginning of each article.

If we can all agree on important definitions, then we speak the same language and avoid misunderstandings. Because the *Code* exists to protect people and property, it's very important to know the definitions presented in Article 100.

Now, here are a couple of things you may not know about this article:

Article 100 contains many, but not all, of the terms defined by the *NEC*. In general, only those terms used in two or more articles are defined in this article. Those terms used only within one article are located within that article, often near the beginning of it.

- **Part I** of Article 100 contains the definitions of terms used throughout the *Code* for systems that operate at 600V, nominal, or less.
- **Part II** of Article 100 contains only terms that apply to systems that operate at over 600V, nominal.

Here are a few tips for learning the many definitions in the *Code*:

- Break the task down. Study a few words at a time, rather than trying to learn them all at one sitting.
- Review the graphics in the textbook. These will help you see how a term is applied.
- Relate the definitions to your work. As you read a word, think about how it applies to the work you're doing. This will provide a natural reinforcement to the learning process.

Article 100—Accessible, Readily (Readily Accessible)

The definition of "readily accessible" has been revised to address the use of tools.

Accessible, Readily (Readily Accessible). Capable of being reached quickly without having to climb over or remove obstacles, resort to portable ladders, or use tools. Figures 100–1 and 100–2

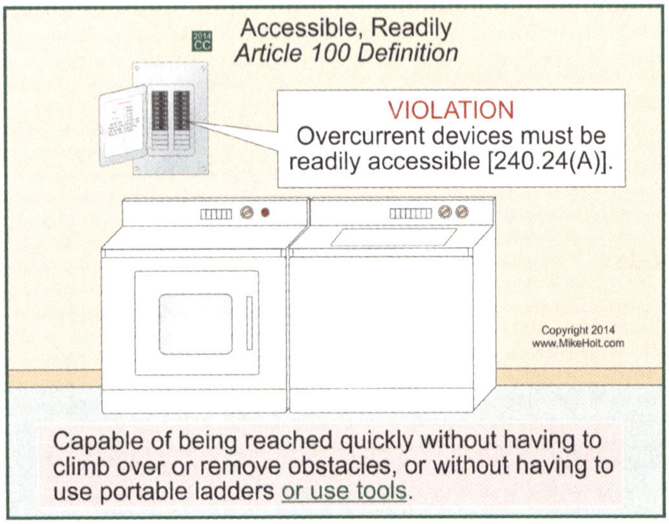

Figure 100–1

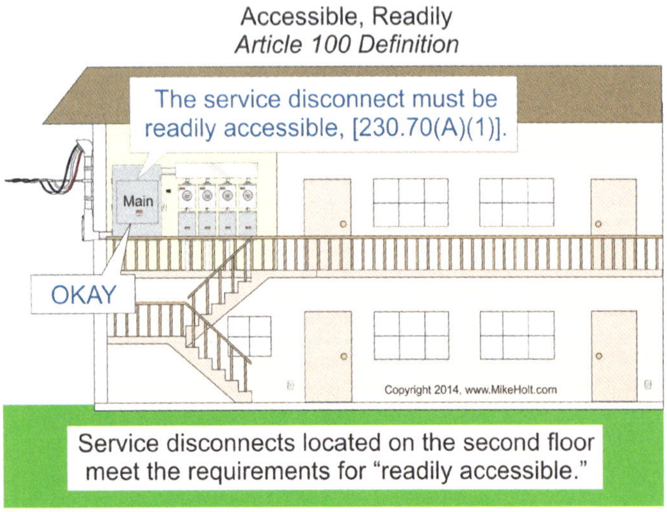

Figure 100–2

ANALYSIS: Many items in the *Code* are required to be readily accessible, including GFCI devices [210.8], building and service disconnects [225.32 and 230.70(A)(1)], and overcurrent devices [240.24(A)]. These are required to be readily accessible so they can be reached quickly, such as in an emergency. In an emergency, a person shouldn't have to run to the garage and drag out a ladder so that he or she can shut power off to the house. The same idea holds true as it relates to the use of tools. Do you really want to dig through the toolbox and find a 5⁄16" socket to open your service disconnect to shut it off?

Is a key a tool? A literal analysis of the word "tool" would indicate that yes, a key is a tool. If that approach is taken, the *Code* will be unusable. Would that mean panels can't have locks on them? What about doors to equipment rooms that require a key? For that matter, what if your panel is in your house? Does that mean that your front door can't have a lock on it? This change is going to have unintended consequences, and I would implore anyone reading this to not consider a key to be a tool.

Article 100—Adjustable Speed Drive

The definition of "adjustable speed drive" has been relocated from Article 430 (motors) to Article 100, and a new Informational Note has been added.

Adjustable Speed Drive. A piece of equipment that provides a way to adjust the speed of an electric motor.

Author's Comment: Adjustable-speed drives are often referred to as "variable-speed drives" or "variable-frequency drives (VFDs)."

Note: A variable frequency drive is one type of electronic adjustable speed drive that controls the speed of an AC motor by changing the frequency and voltage of the motor's power supply.

ANALYSIS: Because this term is used in more than one article, the definition should be in Article 100. It was formerly located in 430.2, which meant that the definition could only apply within the context of Article 430. While that may not seem to be a problem (Article 430 covers motors after all), adjustable speed drives are being introduced into Article 440, which covers air conditioners. When the term is used in more than one article, it needs to be in the proper location for the sake of consistency if nothing else.

The new Informational Note describes one of the most common types of adjustable speed drives, the variable frequency drive (VFD). As the note says, a VFD works by changing the frequency (hence the name) as well as the voltage to a motor. This in turn changes the motor's speed.

Article 100—Adjustable Speed Drive System

The definition for "adjustable speed drive system" has been relocated from Article 430 (motors) to Article 100.

Adjustable Speed Drive System. A combination of an adjustable speed drive, its associated motor(s), and any other equipment associated with the two.

ANALYSIS: Like the definition of "adjustable speed drive," this definition has been relocated to Article 100 because it's used in more than just one *Code* article. It's used in Part X of Article 430, which covers adjustable speed drive systems, but is also used in Article 110.

Article 100—Cable Routing Assembly

The definition of Cable Routing Assembly is now in Article 100 instead of 770 (optical fiber cables).

Cable Routing Assembly. A channel or channels, with their fittings, that support and route communications wires and cables, optical fiber cables, data cables, Class 2 and Class 3 cables, and power-limited fire alarm cables. Figure 100–3

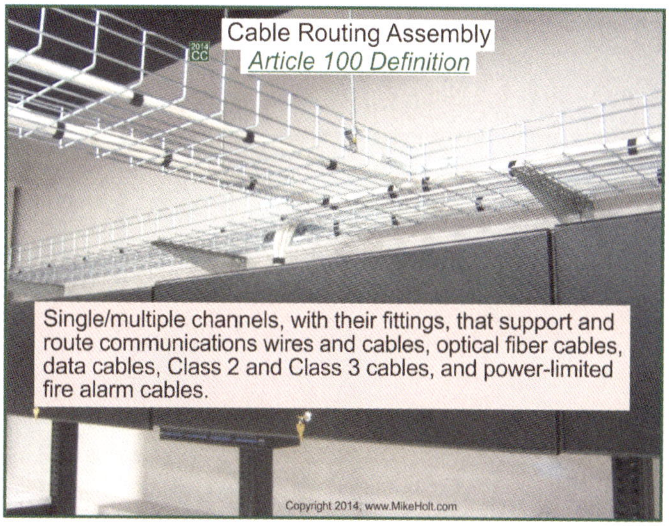

Figure 100–3

Author's Comment: A cable routing assembly is typically a "U" shaped trough, with or without covers, designed to hold cables, and it isn't a raceway.

ANALYSIS: The term "cable routing assembly" was defined in the 2011 *Code* in 770.2, which defines terms used in the optical fiber cable article. This term is (and was) used in many articles of the *NEC*, including 770, 800 for communications systems, and 820 for coaxial cables. By defining this term in Article 770, the *Code* was incredibly difficult to use, particularly if you, like most other *NEC* users, don't use Article 770. Imagine reading Article 800 (which is read much more often than 770) and trying to find the definition for this term. In the 2014 *Code* change process, the original idea was to place this definition in several articles of the *NEC*, but fortunately sanity prevailed and it's now found in Article 100.

Article 100—Communications Equipment

The definition of "Communications Equipment" was revised to include associated wiring.

Communications Equipment. Electronic telecommunications equipment used for the transmission of audio, video, and data, including support equipment such as computers, as well as the conductors that are used solely for the operation of the equipment. Figure 100–4

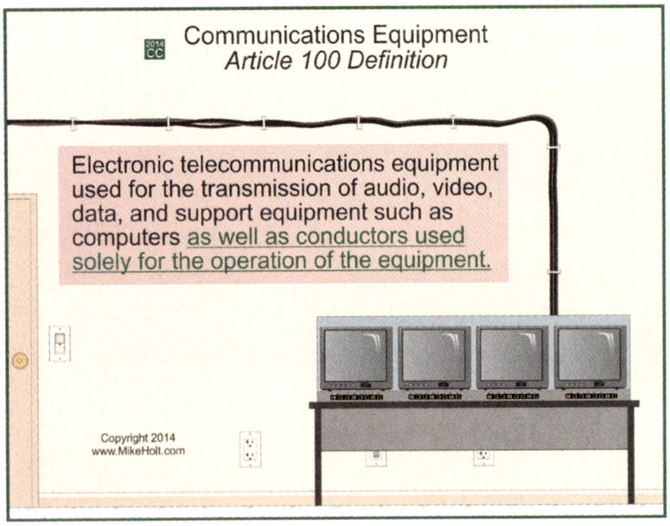

Figure 100–4

Article 100—Communications Raceway

The definition of "communications raceway" has been relocated from Article 800 (communications circuits) to Article 100.

Communications Raceway. An enclosed channel of nonmetallic materials designed for holding communications wires and cables in plenum, riser, and general-purpose applications. Figure 100–5

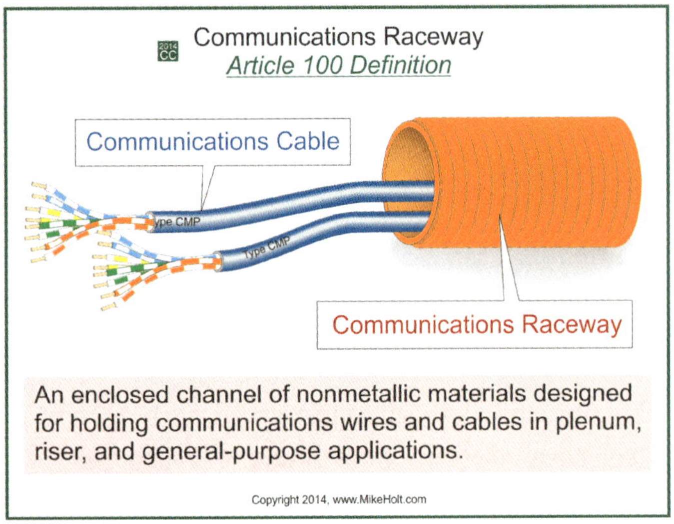

Figure 100–5

ANALYSIS: It may seem that some terms don't need to be defined at all, like "communications equipment." The word "equipment" is already defined, and it includes all aspects of installation, right down to the smallest fitting. One could infer that any equipment having to do with communications is, by default, communications equipment. The problem with that logic is that communications equipment is found in Chapter 8, and, unfortunately, some people who use Chapter 8 use it exclusively, without ever opening Chapters 1 through 7 unless Chapter 8 tells them to. By revising the definition of communications equipment, the *Code* user doesn't have to put two and two together to come up with a solid understanding of what communications equipment actually is.

ANALYSIS: The term "communications raceway" is used in several articles of the *Code*, and as such should be defined in Article 100. The previous edition of the *NEC* had the definition in 800.2, which is fine if your world is communications systems and you dwell in Article 800, but not if you focus on optical fiber installations and spend most of your time in Article 770.

Previous editions of the *Code* contained different names for the same raceway, depending on what was inside of it. For example, 770, 800, and 820 contained rules for optical fiber raceways, communications raceways, and coaxial cable raceway, respectively, despite the fact that they are all the same raceway. By changing the definition and relocating it to Article 100, there is no need to have (at least) three different definitions and sets of rules for the same piece of equipment

Article 100—Concealed

Part of the definition of "Concealed" has been moved to an Informational Note.

Concealed. Rendered inaccessible by the structure or finish of the building.

Note: Conductors in a concealed raceway are considered concealed, even though they may be made accessible by withdrawing them from the raceway. Figure 100–6

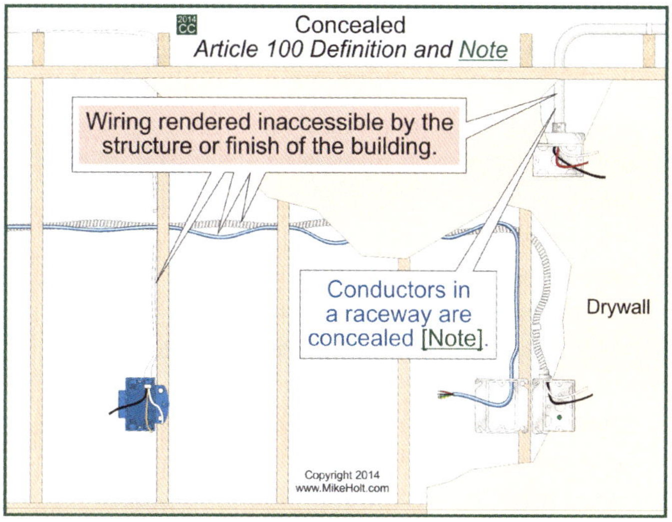

Figure 100–6

Author's Comment: Wiring behind panels designed to allow access, such as removable ceiling tile, is considered exposed.

ANALYSIS: The definition of "concealed" confuses many *Code* users. If wiring is located behind a wall, or above a drywall ceiling, it's considered "concealed." It isn't concealed simply by the fact that you can't see it. Wiring above a suspended ceiling isn't concealed; it's exposed, even though you can't see it either.

The real meaning of this definition is that you can't get to the wiring (or equipment) without removing part of building or structure, such as tearing a hole in the wall to get to the wiring supplying a receptacle. Wires in a raceway are still considered concealed, even though you don't need to tear down walls to get to them, which seems to be a contradiction of this definition. You may have to make a hole in the wall to get to the raceway containing the conductors, but you don't need to do that to get to the conductors themselves.

Moving this part of the definition into an Informational Note may be viewed as a step backwards for some. Informational Notes aren't enforceable portions of the *NEC* [90.5(C)], and therefore putting the language regarding raceways into a note makes the statement invalid from a technical perspective. Without the language regarding raceways in the main text of the definition, ask yourself whether or not conductors in a raceway are "inaccessible by the structure or finish of the building." Most will argue that they aren't, and therefore this is a major change to some people. Others may argue the contrary, and with text being moved to a note it seems to open the door for new arguments.

Article 100—Control Circuit

The definition of "Control Circuit" has been relocated from 409.2 (industrial control panels) to Article 100.

Control Circuit. The circuit of a control apparatus or system that carries the electric signals directing the performance of the controller but doesn't carry the main power current. Figure 100–7

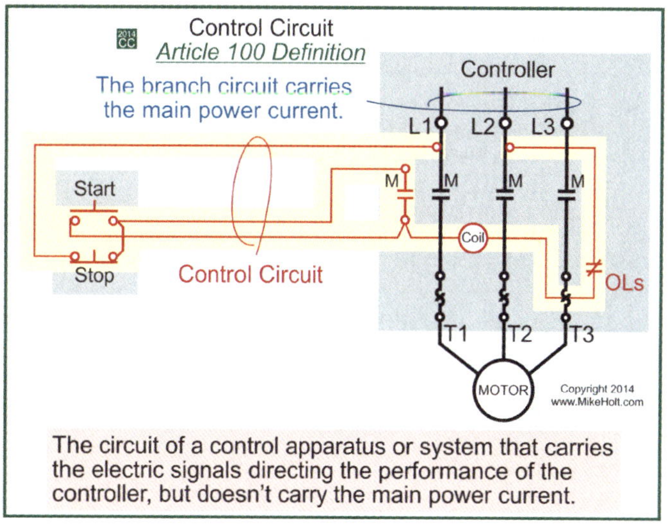

Figure 100–7

ANALYSIS: Terms used in more than one Article are supposed to be defined in Article 100 so that the definition can be applied to the term uniformly throughout the *Code*. The term "control circuit" is found in the *NEC* over 100 times, and certainly not just in Article 409 (the former location of the definition).

It's important to note that there's also a definition for "remote-control circuit" in Article 100, and they aren't the same. A remote-control circuit is governed by Article 725. There are also motor control circuits, which are governed by Part VI of Article 430.

Article 100—Coordination (Selective)

This definition has been revised to address arguments about selective coordination.

Coordination (Selective). Localization of an overcurrent condition to restrict outages to the circuit or equipment affected, accomplished by the choice of overcurrent devices. Selective coordination includes all currents, from overloads to short circuits. Figure 100–8

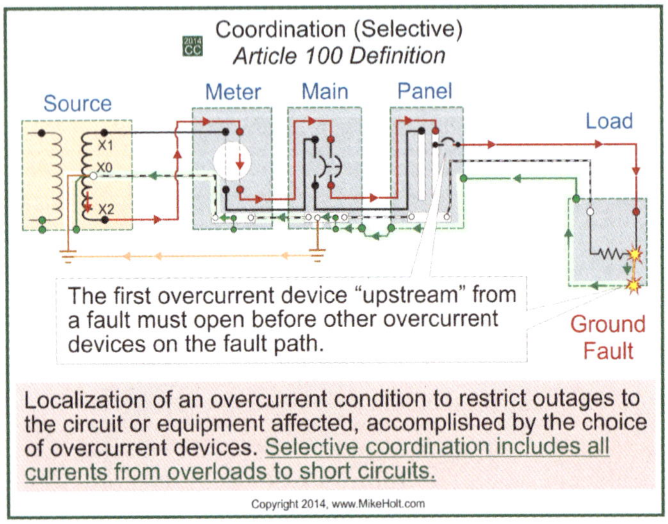

Figure 100–8

Author's Comment: Selective coordination means the overcurrent protection scheme confines the interruption to a particular area rather than to the whole system. For example, if someone plugs in a space heater and raises the total demand on a 20A circuit to 25A, or if a short circuit or ground fault occurs with selective coordination, the only breaker or fuse that will open is the one protecting just that branch circuit. Without selective coordination, an entire building can go dark!

ANALYSIS: Ever since its introduction into the *Code*, few rules have created more arguments than selective coordination. Selectively coordinating a system isn't a walk in the park if circuit breakers are involved, but it can be done. In order to allow a wider range of products to be in a given installation, many jurisdictions have created legal definitions of the term by providing a numerical value to the time involved to clear a fault. For example, "systems shall be selectively coordinated to within 0.0xx seconds." That has never been the intent of the *NEC*, and reading the dozens and dozens of rejected proposals to 700.27 and 701.27 only confirms that fact. The change to the definition doesn't technically change anything, but it may help people who aren't aware of the fact that selective coordination is intended to apply to the full gamut of currents, not just overloads, but ground-faults and short-circuits too.

The *Code* only requires selective coordination for the most important systems, such as emergency and legally required standby systems and health care facilities (see 517.17, 700.27, and 701.27). Due to the importance of these systems, the electrical installation must be a complete, 100-percent coordinated system. There's no time limit or allowance for short overlaps of the overcurrent devices. A selectively coordinated system must ensure no possibility whatsoever of an upstream overcurrent device such as the main breaker for the building, opening before the overcurrent device closest to the fault opens.

Article 100—Device

The definition of "device" has been revised, again.

Device. A component of an electrical installation, other than a conductor, intended to carry or control electric energy as its principal function. Figure 100–9

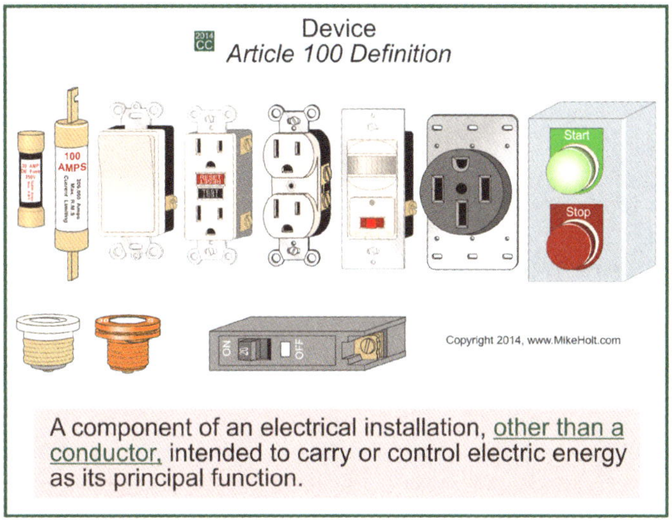

Figure 100–9

Author's Comment: Devices include busbars, receptacles, switches, illuminated switches, circuit breakers, fuses, time clocks, controllers, and so forth, but not locknuts or other mechanical fittings. A device may consume very small amounts of energy, such as an illuminated switch, but still be classified as a device based on its principal function.

ANALYSIS: Ask any electrician in the world what a "device" is and you'll get some pretty predictable answers. A receptacle. A breaker. A fuse. What you probably won't hear is "a conductor." This definition was revised a few years ago to create a nice, simple definition. For years, there were arguments about whether or not a switch with a pilot light was a device or utilization equipment. In an attempt to answer this question, the definition became much simpler. As is often the case, when a definition changes it's changed again three years later to answer a new question. That question was, "Is a conductor a device?" It was certainly never intended to be a device, but creating a good definition is one of the most difficult things to do when it comes to writing *Code.* This change clarifies the intent by answering this newest question. Stay tuned in three years to see if it's revised again as new questions come up.

Article 100—Effective Ground-Fault Current Path

This definition has been relocated from 250.2 (grounding and bonding definitions) to Article 100.

Effective Ground-Fault Current Path. An intentionally constructed low-impedance conductive path designed to carry fault current from the point of a ground fault on a wiring system to the electrical supply source. Figure 100–10

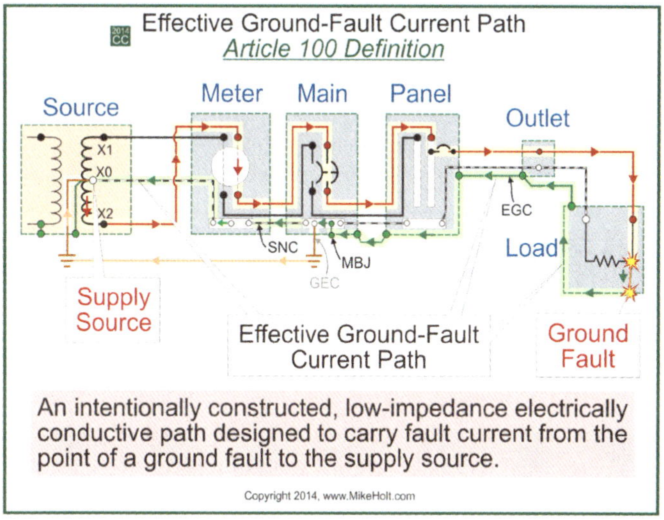

Figure 100–10

Author's Comment: In Figure 100–12, "EGC" represents the equipment grounding conductor [259.118], "MBJ" represents the main bonding jumper, "SNC" represents the service neutral conductor (grounded service conductor), and "GEC" represents the grounding electrode conductor.

The current path shown between the supply source grounding electrode and the grounding electrode at the service main shows that some current will flow through the earth but the earth isn't part of the effective ground-fault current path.

The effective ground-fault current path is intended to help remove dangerous voltage from a ground fault by opening the circuit overcurrent device. Figure 100–11

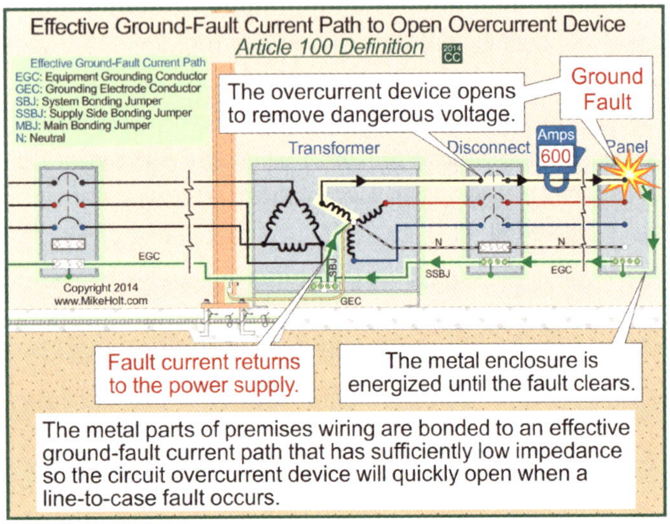

Figure 100–11

ANALYSIS: Terms used in more than one Article are supposed to be defined in Article 100. Although this one is mainly used in Article 250, it's used in other locations as well. By moving the definition here, the layout of the *NEC* becomes more consistent.

In addition to be being relocated, the language regarding high-impedance grounded systems was deleted from the definition. Previous editions of the *Code* stated that the effective ground-fault current path works to operate the ground-fault detectors on a high-impedance system. While that's true, it can be said of ungrounded systems as well. Should the *NEC* discuss both systems in the definition, or should it just remove the one example? The *Code*-Making panel opted to remove the example altogether.

Article 100—Electric-Discharge Lighting

This definition has been relocated from Article 600 (signs) to Article 100.

Electric-Discharge Lighting. Systems of illumination utilizing fluorescent lamps, high-intensity discharge (HID) lamps, or neon tubing. Figure 100–12

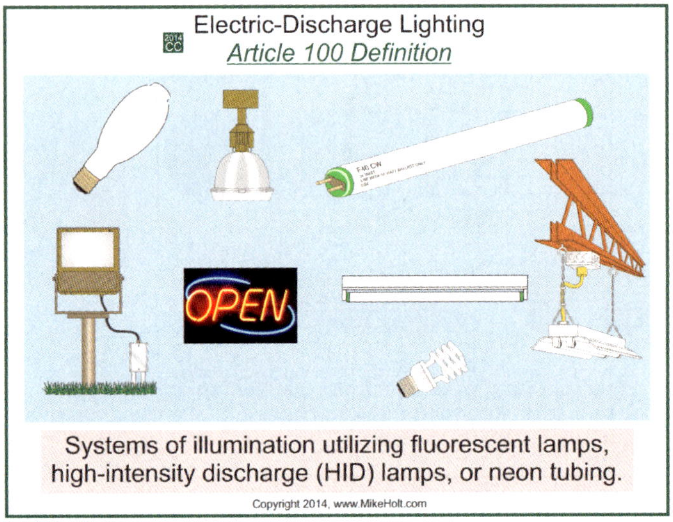

Figure 100–12

ANALYSIS: Electric-discharge luminaires are discussed in several *Code* articles, but where was the definition in the last edition of the *NEC*? Considering that Article 410 covers luminaires, one would think that this term would be defined there. You may be surprised to find that it was actually defined in Article 600, which covers signs! By placing the definition where a *Code* user can actually find it (Article 100), the *NEC* becomes a much better document.

Article 100—Exposed (as applied to live parts)

Part of this definition is now in Informational Note.

Exposed (as applied to live parts). Capable of being accidentally touched or approached to an unsafe distance.

Note: This term applies to parts that aren't suitably guarded, isolated, or insulated.

ANALYSIS: "Exposed (live parts)." "Exposed (wiring methods)." "Concealed." "Accessible (wiring methods)." "Accessible (equipment)." Where does it end? These can be some of the most difficult, yet important, terms found in Article 100. They must all be used together if any of them are to make sense at all. Add "guarded," "isolated," and "insulated" to the list as well. Exposed live parts are those that aren't covered by fences, shields, enclosures, casings, and so forth (guarded), aren't readily accessible (isolated), and aren't insulated.

This isn't a technical change, because the definition already provided this information. By moving it to an Informational Note the definition becomes a more concise, single sentence.

Article 100—Ground-Fault Current Path

This definition has been moved from 250.2 to Article 100.

Ground-Fault Current Path. An electrically conductive path from a ground fault to the electrical supply source.

Note: The ground-fault current path could be metal raceways, cable sheaths, electrical equipment, or other electrically conductive materials, such as metallic water or gas piping, steel-framing members, metal ducting, reinforcing steel, or the shields of communications cables. Figure 100–13

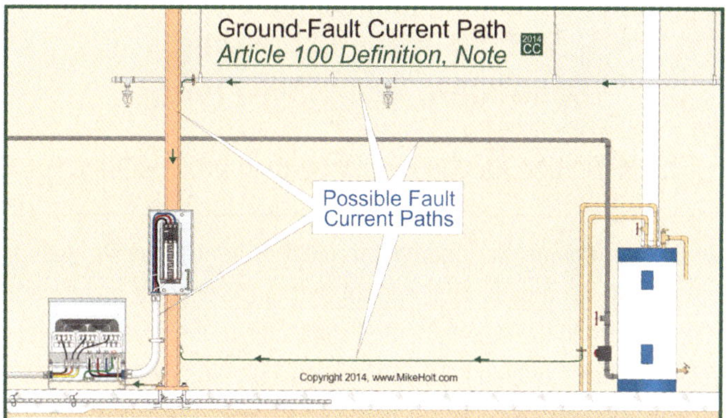

The ground-fault current path can consist of bonding conductors, metal raceways, metal cable sheaths, metal enclosures, and other electrically conductive materials, such as metallic water or gas piping, steel-framing members, metal ducting, reinforcing steel, the shields of communications cables, and the earth itself.

Figure 100–13

Author's Comment: The difference between an "effective ground-fault current path" and a "ground-fault current path" is the effective ground-fault current path is "intentionally" constructed to provide a low-impedance fault current path to the electrical supply source for the purpose of clearing a ground fault. A ground-fault current path is all of the available conductive paths over which fault current flows on its return to the electrical supply source during a ground fault.

ANALYSIS: This term is used very sparingly in the *Code* (compared to the term "effective ground-fault current path"), but it's used in more places than just Article 250. In order to comply with the *NEC* Style Manual, the definition has been moved to Article 100.

Article 100—Grounding Conductor, Equipment (EGC)

This definition has been revised to improve clarity.

Grounding Conductor, Equipment (EGC). The conductive path(s) that provides a ground-fault current path and connects metal parts of equipment to the system neutral conductor, to the grounding electrode conductor, or both [250.110 through 250.126]. **Figure 100–14**

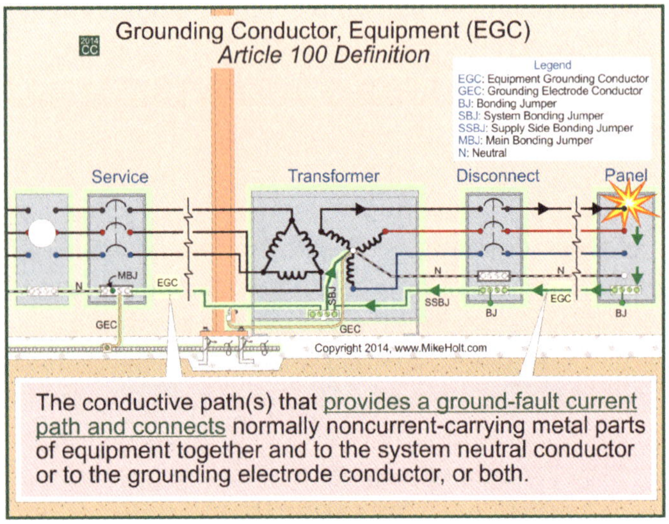

Figure 100–14

Note 1: The circuit equipment grounding conductor also performs bonding.

Author's Comment: To quickly remove dangerous touch voltage on metal parts from a ground fault, the equipment grounding conductor must be connected to the system neutral conductor at the source, and have low enough impedance so that fault current will quickly rise to a level that will open the circuit's overcurrent device [250.2 and 250.4(A)(3)].

Note 2: An equipment grounding conductor can be any one or a combination of the types listed in 250.118. **Figure 100–15**

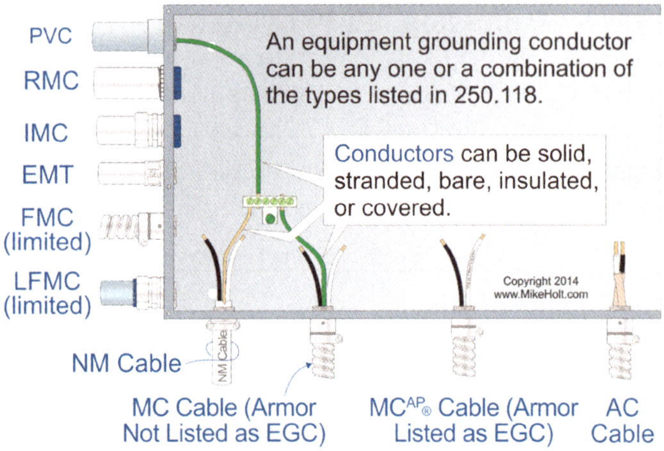

Figure 100–15

Author's Comment: Equipment grounding conductors include:

- A bare or insulated conductor
- Rigid Metal Conduit
- Intermediate Metal Conduit
- Electrical Metallic Tubing
- Listed Flexible Metal Conduit as limited by 250.118(5)
- Listed Liquidtight Flexible Metal Conduit as limited by 250.118(6)
- Armored Cable
- Copper metal sheath of Mineral Insulated Cable
- Metal-Clad Cable as limited by 250.118(10)
- Metallic cable trays as limited by 250.118(11) and 392.60
- Electrically continuous metal raceways listed for grounding
- Surface Metal Raceways listed for grounding

ANALYSIS: Anyone who has used a *Code* book for more than ten years or so will certainly agree that the *NEC* deals with grounding and bonding better now than it ever has before. As a continuation of the effort to solidify the concepts, this definition was revised to more fully describe the role of an equipment grounding conductor. Despite its name, this conductor serves much more of a bonding role than a grounding role, and this change shows that. The main function of this conductor is to create a ground-fault current path that will be a major component of the effective ground-fault current path. The effective ground-fault current path is a system of ground-fault current paths, including the EGCs, the system or main bonding jumper, the utility neutral conductor, and even small things like raceway fittings and terminations that, when installed correctly, come together to create a low-impedance fault current path that's capable of opening the circuit's overcurrent device.

Article 100—Hermetic Refrigerant Motor-Compressor

This term has been relocated from 440.2 to Article 100.

Hermetic Refrigerant Motor-Compressor. A compressor and motor enclosed in the same housing, operating in the refrigerant.

ANALYSIS: Terms used in more than one article are supposed to be defined in Article 100. This particular term is used in several different articles, such as 220, 422, 424, 430, and 400. The definition was in 440.2, but has been relocated to Article 100 without being changed.

Article 100—Intersystem Bonding Termination

A revision to this definition makes it more accurate.

Intersystem Bonding Termination. A device that provides a means to connect intersystem bonding conductors for communications systems to the grounding electrode system, in accordance with 250.94. Figure 100–16

ANALYSIS: While it may seem obvious that an intersystem bonding termination is used to connect intersystem bonding conductors, the definition didn't exactly say that. It said that the termination was for any bonding conductor used in a communications system.

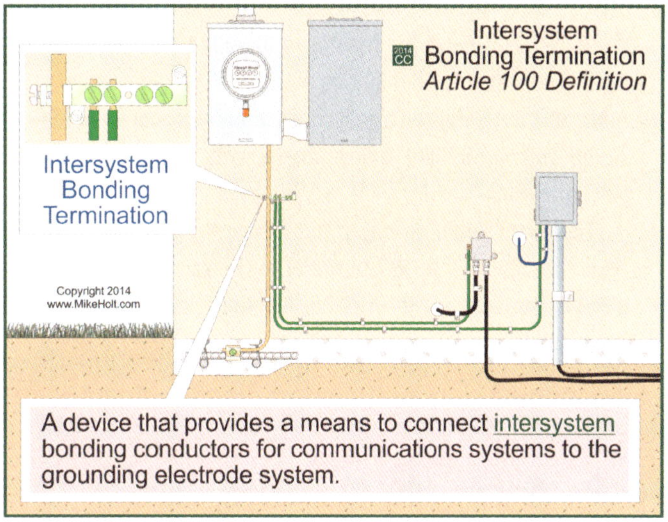

Figure 100–16

Article 100—Lighting Track (Track Lighting)

This definition has been relocated from Article 410 (luminaires) to Article 100, and name of the term has been expanded.

Lighting Track (Track Lighting). This is a manufactured assembly designed to support and energize luminaires that can be readily repositioned on the track, and whose length may be altered by the addition or subtraction of sections of track. Figure 100–17

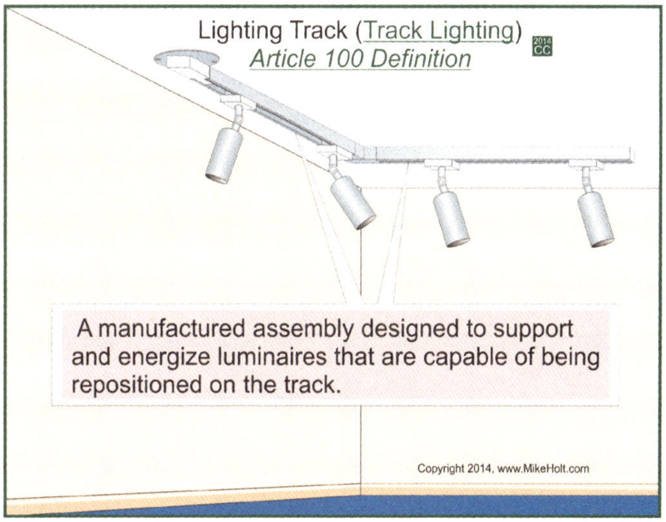

Figure 100–17

ANALYSIS: One of the themes in the 2014 *NEC* seems to be the relocation of definitions. While it may seem tedious and not worthwhile, it really does create a more usable *Code*. This term, like many others, was defined in the wrong article.

The terms "lighting track" and "track lighting" are both used throughout the *NEC*, but refer to the same thing. Most electricians use the term "track lighting" as well, so it's been added as part of the definition.

ANALYSIS: Definitions seem to work better when they're short and to the point. This definition has always been a rather lengthy one, but necessarily so. A damp location is somewhere between a dry location and a wet location, and some explanatory material in the *Code* helps to point that out. By removing the explanatory material from the actual definition, however, some *NEC* users may ignore it. Informational Notes aren't enforceable [90.5(C)], which means some *Code* users don't read them, don't care about them, and see no value in them.

Article 100—Location, Damp

Parts of the definition for "Location, Damp" are now an Informational Note.

Location, Damp. Locations protected from weather and not subject to saturation with water or other liquids.

Note: This includes locations partially protected under canopies, marquees, roofed open porches, and interior locations subject to moderate degrees of moisture, such as some basements, barns, and cold-storage warehouses. Figure 100–18

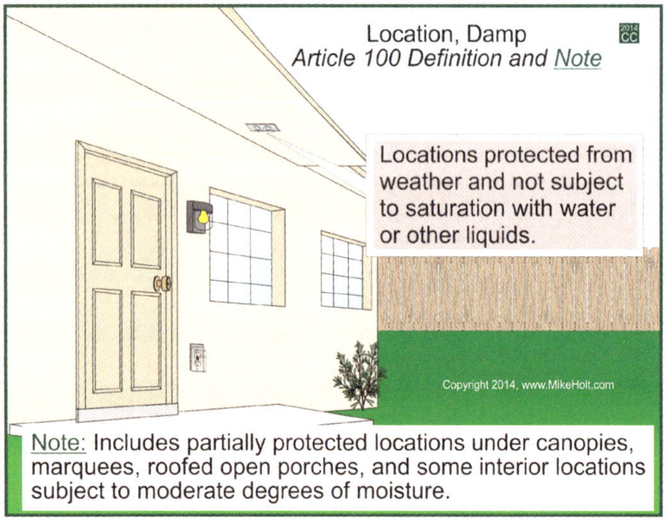

Figure 100–18

Article 100—Premises Wiring

An Informational Note has been added to include different sources of electricity.

Premises Wiring. The interior and exterior wiring, including power, lighting, control, and signal circuits, and all associated hardware, fittings, and wiring devices. This includes both permanently and temporarily installed wiring from the service point to the outlets, or where there's no service point, wiring from and including the power source, such as a generator, transformer, or PV system to the outlets. Figure 100–19

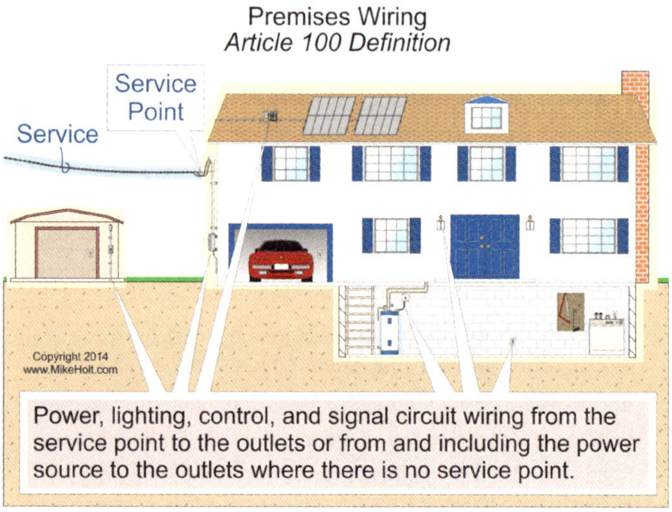

Figure 100–19

Premises wiring doesn't include the internal wiring of electrical equipment and appliances, such as luminaires, dishwashers, water heaters, motors, controllers, motor control centers, air-conditioning equipment, and so on [90.7 and 300.1(B)]. Figure 100–20

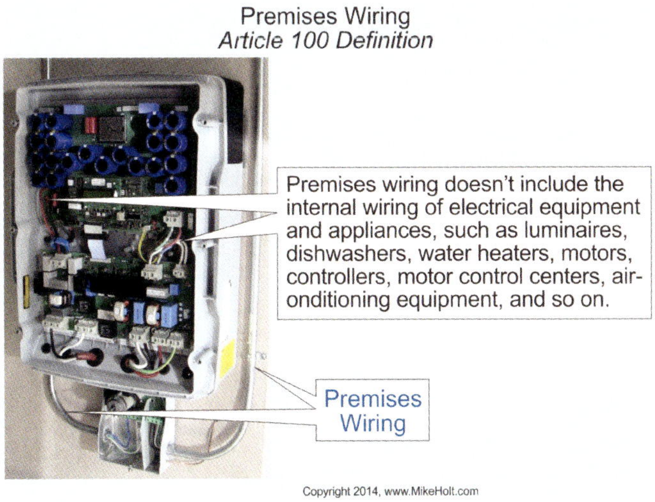

Figure 100–20

Note: Power sources include, but aren't limited to, interconnected or stand-alone batteries, PV systems, other distributed generation systems, or generators.

ANALYSIS: The more things change the more they stay the same. Experienced *Code* users might be asking themselves "didn't we just delete this last *Code* cycle?" A list similar to this used to be in the Article 100 definitions of "premises wiring system" and "separately derived system," but was removed because it was becoming so long it was no longer manageable.

Time will only tell how long this Informational Note is left alone before people want to start adding all of the stuff that was deleted from the definition in 2005, like wind, fuel cells, and converter windings.

Article 100—Raceway

An Informational Note has been added to direct *Code* users to other definitions.

Raceway. An enclosure designed for the installation of conductors, cables, or busbars. Raceways in the *NEC* include:

Note: Each raceway is defined in the 3xx.2 section of its own article.

Author's Comments: A cable tray system isn't a raceway; it's a support system for cables and raceways [392.2].

Raceway Type	Article
Busways	368
Electrical Metallic Tubing	358
Electrical Nonmetallic Tubing	362
Flexible Metal Conduit	348
Intermediate Metal Conduit	342
Liquidtight Flexible Metal Conduit	350
Liquidtight Flexible Nonmetallic Conduit	356
Metal Wireways	376
Multioutlet Assembly	380
Rigid Metal Conduit	344
PVC Conduit	352
Surface Metal Raceways	386
Surface Nonmetallic Raceways	388

ANALYSIS: There are many different types of raceways discussed in the *NEC*, and yes, technically they should all be defined in Article 100 because they're discussed throughout the *Code*. The problem with that concept is that it would probably make the *Code* worse instead of better. As currently written, the definitions of the wiring methods discussed in Chapter 3 are all found in their respective articles. (Well, almost. Multioutlet assembly is still in Article 100, and for whatever reason proposals to move it have been rejected!). While this style doesn't meet the *NEC* Style Manual, most people agree that it's better this way. By adding the Informational Note the overall intent of the *NEC* Style Manual is satisfied, thereby creating a more user-friendly document.

Article 100—Retrofit Kit

A new term and definition have been added.

Retrofit Kit. An assembly of parts for the field conversion of utilization equipment.

ANALYSIS: As LED luminaires become more and more popular, so does the act of changing existing luminaires into LED luminaires. When this occurs, a listed retrofit kit must be used [410.6 and 600.3]. Several changes have been made in Articles 410 and 600 to address this practice, so a definition has been added here to help *Code* users agree on what a retrofit kit is.

Article 100—Sealable Equipment

An Informational Note was added to create a shorter definition.

Sealable Equipment. Equipment enclosed with a means of sealing or locking so that live parts can't be made accessible without opening the enclosure.

Note: The equipment may or may not be operable without opening the enclosure.

ANALYSIS: Definitions are typically more effective when they're one sentence long. Moving the second sentence of the existing definition into an Informational Note accomplishes that. Of course, the text doesn't go away, and nothing really changes, but on the bright side, it gives *Code* Change book authors something to write about!

Article 100—Separately Derived System

This definition has been changed to increase simplicity and accuracy.

Separately Derived System. An electrical source, other than a service, having no direct connection(s) to circuit conductors of any other electrical source other than those established by grounding and bonding connections. Figures 100–21 and 100–22

Author's Comment: Separately derived systems are actually much more complicated than the above definition suggests, and understanding them requires additional study. For more information, see 250.30.

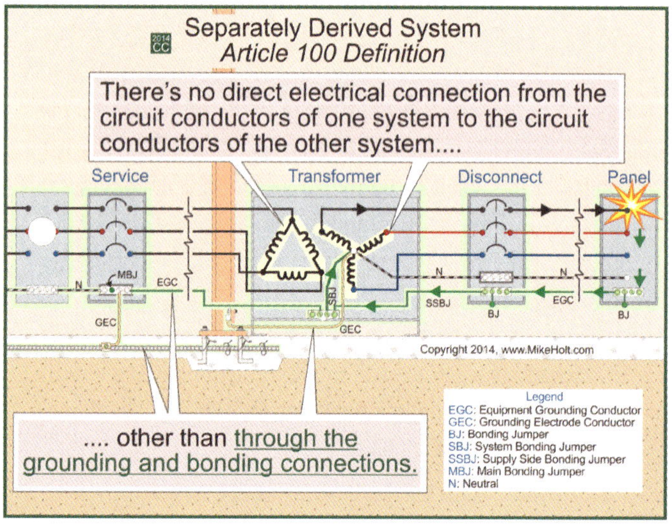

Figure 100–21

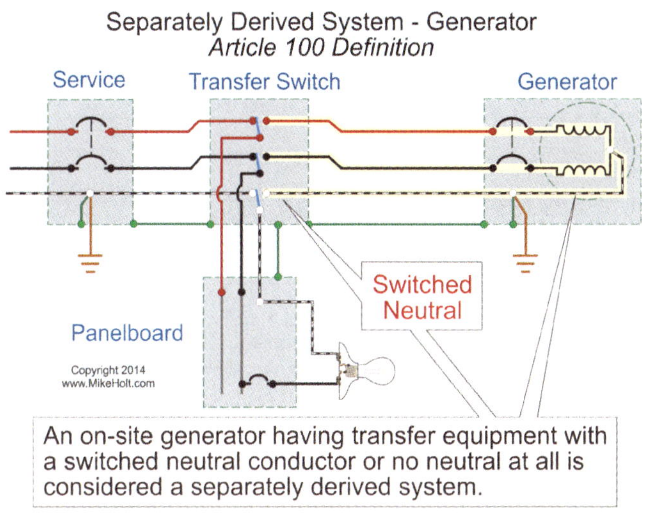

Figure 100–22

ANALYSIS: *The Elements of Style* by Strunk and White is considered by many to be the best book on the subject of writing. Rule number 17 in this wonderful book provides this gem, "Omit needless words." The phrase "whose power is derived from a source of electric energy or equipment other than a service" was reduced to "other than a service." Kudos to the submitter of this change for making things simpler.

The last sentence was revised to become more accurate. The 2011 edition of the *Code* added the language about the incidental interconnections through grounding and bonding connections that are permitted, and that was a welcome change. This change removes the list of incidental connections that are allowed and simplifies things by just referring to "grounding and bonding connections."

Article 100—Voltage, Nominal

This definition has been revised to include a new Informational Note.

Voltage, Nominal. A value assigned for the purpose of conveniently designating voltage classes, such as 120/240V, 120/208V, or 277/480V [220.5(A)]. Figure 100–23

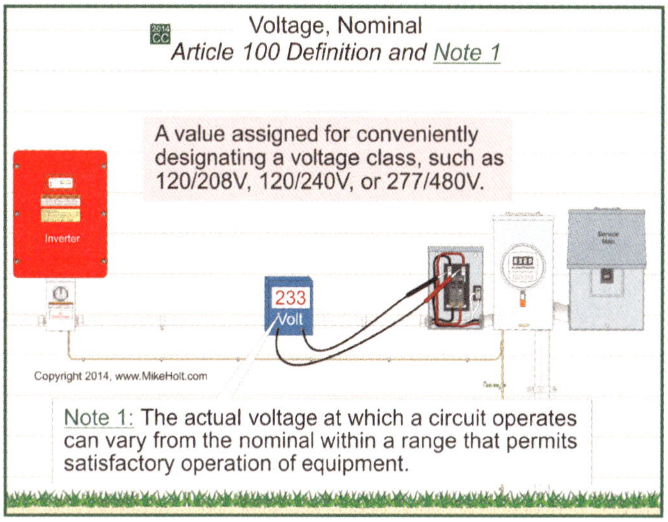

Figure 100–23

Note 1: The actual voltage at which a circuit operates can vary from the nominal within a range that permits satisfactory operation of equipment.

Author's Comment: Common voltage ratings of electrical equipment are 115V, 200V, 208V, 230V, and 460V. The electrical power supplied might be at the 240V, nominal voltage, but the voltage at the equipment will be less. Therefore, electrical equipment is rated at a value less than the nominal system voltage.

ANALYSIS: In an effort to make this definition one sentence, a portion of it was cut and pasted into a new Informational Note. This information may be useful, so it wasn't removed from the *Code* altogether, but it's not really part of the definition either.

Notes

ARTICLE 110 REQUIREMENTS FOR ELECTRICAL INSTALLATIONS

Introduction to Article 110—Requirements for Electrical Installations

Article 110 sets the stage for how you'll implement the rest of the *NEC*. This article contains a few of the most important and yet neglected parts of the *Code*. For example:

- How should conductors be terminated?
- What kinds of warnings, markings, and identification does a given installation require?
- What's the right working clearance for a given installation?
- What do the temperature limitations at terminals mean?
- What are the *NEC* requirements for dealing with flash protection?

110.1 Scope

An Informational Note was added to refer *Code* users to a new Annex.

110.1 Scope. Article 110 covers the general requirements for the examination and approval, installation and use, access to and spaces about electrical equipment; as well as general requirements for enclosures intended for personnel entry (manholes, vaults, and tunnels).

Note: See Annex J for information regarding ADA accessibility design.

Author's Comment: Requirements for people with disabilities include things like mounting heights for switches and receptacles, and requirements for the distance that objects such as wall sconces protrude from a wall.

ANALYSIS: Most commercial buildings and some multifamily dwellings need to be constructed to meet the Americans with Disabilities Act. This can be done by following the *Americans with Disabilities Act Accessibility Guidelines* (ADAAG), or the ICC/ANSI A117.1 *Accessible and Usable Buildings and Facilities.* Municipalities typically choose one or the other to adopt and enforce. Both documents meet the "safe harbor" provision of ADA. They're nearly identical, and both contain information that's pertinent to electrical installations. This includes mounting heights for things such as receptacles, switches, and thermostats, as well as limitations on protruding objects like wall sconce luminaires.

If you're in a wheelchair, you're obviously limited by how far you can reach. Due to this, receptacles and switches must be mounted between 15 in. and 48 in. above the floor, generally speaking (see Annex J for more detailed requirements). What if you're visually impaired and use a cane to assist you? One of the more dangerous things that you could encounter is an object that sticks out from the wall (like a wall sconce) that's mounted high enough that your cane won't detect it, but low enough your face will! For this reason, objects must only stick out from the wall 4 in. if that object is mounted between 27 in. and 80 in. above the floor (next time you're in a commercial building look at how many things violate this, like drinking fountains and fire extinguishers).

Annex J was added to let *Code* users know of some of these requirements. Annex J is certainly not an all-inclusive list of the requirements for accessibility for disabled persons, but it does include the most common requirements about which electricians and electrical engineers need to know.

110.14 Conductor Termination and Splicing

The Informational Note was revised for accuracy.

110.14 Conductor Termination and Splicing. Conductor terminal and splicing devices must be identified for the conductor material and they must be properly installed and used. Figure 110–1

Conductor Termination - Terminal Conductor Marking
110.14

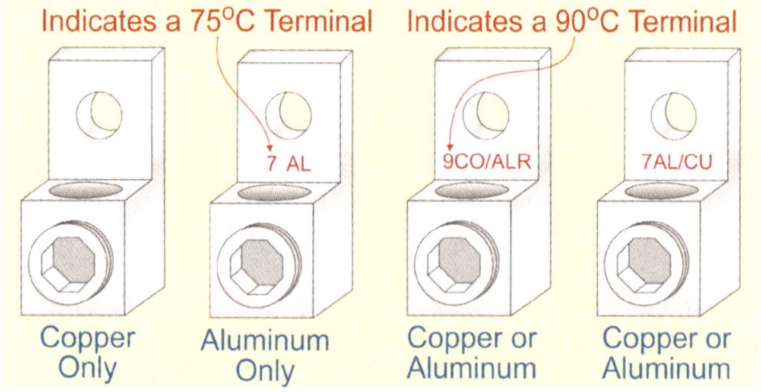

Terminals that are suitable only for aluminum must be marked AL. Terminals suitable for both copper and aluminum must be marked CO/ALR or AL/CU.

Figure 110–1

Author's Comment: Switches and receptacles marked CO/ALR are designed to ensure a good connection through the use of a larger contact area and compatible materials. The terminal screws are plated with the element called "Indium." Indium is an extremely soft metal that forms a gas-sealed connection with the aluminum conductor.

Connectors and terminals for conductors more finely stranded than Class B and Class C, as shown in Table 10 of Chapter 9, must be identified for the conductor class. Figure 110–2

Author's Comment: According to UL Standard 486 A-B, a terminal/lug/connector must be listed and marked for use with other than Class B stranded conductors. With no marking or factory literature/instructions to the contrary, terminals may only be used with Class B stranded conductors.

Finely Stranded Flexible Conductor Termination
110.14

Connectors and terminations for conductors more finely stranded than Class B and Class C stranding must be identified for the conductor Class [Chapter 9, Table 10].

Figure 110–2

Author's Comments:

- See the definition of "Identified" in Article 100.
- Conductor terminations must comply with the manufacturer's instructions as required by 110.3(B). For example, if the instructions for the device state "Suitable for 18-12 AWG Stranded," then only stranded conductors can be used with the terminating device. If the instructions state "Suitable for 18-12 AWG Solid," then only solid conductors are permitted, and if the instructions state "Suitable for 18-12 AWG," then either solid or stranded conductors can be used with the terminating device.

Copper and Aluminum Mixed. Copper and aluminum conductors must not make contact with each other in a device unless the device is listed and identified for this purpose.

Author's Comment: Few terminations are listed for the mixing of aluminum and copper conductors, but if they are, that will be marked on the product package or terminal device. The reason copper and aluminum shouldn't be in contact with each other is because corrosion develops between the two different metals due to galvanic action, resulting in increased contact resistance at the splicing device. This increased resistance can cause the splice to overheat and cause a fire.

Note: Many terminations and equipment are either marked with a tightening torque or have the torque values included in the product's instructions.

Author's Comment: Conductors must terminate in devices that have been properly tightened in accordance with the manufacturer's torque specifications included with equipment instructions. Failure to torque terminals can result in excessive heating of terminals or splicing devices due to a loose connection. A loose connection can also lead to arcing which increases the heating effect and may also lead to a short circuit or ground fault. Any of these can result in a fire or other failure, including an arc-flash event. In addition, this is a violation of 110.3(B), which requires all equipment to be installed in accordance with listing or labeling instructions. Figure 110–3

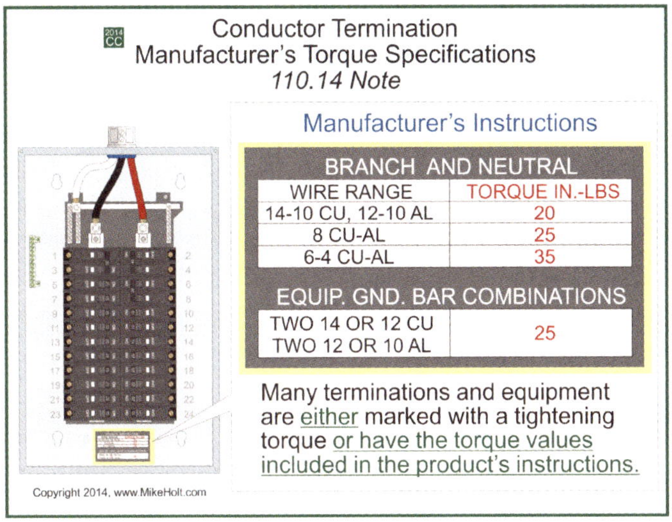

Figure 110–3

Question: *What do you do if the torque value isn't provided with the device?*

Answer: *Call the manufacturer, visit the manufacturer's Website, or have the supplier make a copy of the installation instructions.*

Author's Comment: Terminating conductors without a torque tool can result in an improper and unsafe installation. If a torque screwdriver isn't used, there's a good chance the conductors aren't properly terminated.

ANALYSIS: Many pieces of equipment are, in fact, marked with their tightening torque. This isn't, however, the only place that one might expect to find this information. The instructions that come with the product may contain this information as well, and, if it's listed equipment, these instructions must be followed [110.3(B)]. Although it wouldn't be a *Code* violation to ignore torque values on equipment that isn't listed, it probably wouldn't be a good idea to do so. Most electrical fires don't start in the middle of a raceway; they start at a termination of some sort. The importance of properly torquing terminatlons can't possibly be overstated.

110.16 Arc-Flash Hazard Warning

Marking requirements have been relaxed and changes have been made to correlate with other *Code* changes.

110.16 Arc-Flash Hazard Warning. Electrical equipment such as switchboards, panelboards, industrial control panels, meter socket enclosures, and motor control centers in other than dwelling units that are likely to require examination, adjustment, servicing, or maintenance while energized must be marked to warn qualified persons of the danger associated with an arc flash from short circuits or ground faults. The marking can be made in the field or the factory, but it must meet the requirements of 110.21(B), and be clearly visible to qualified persons before they examine, adjust, service, or perform maintenance on the equipment. Figure 110–4

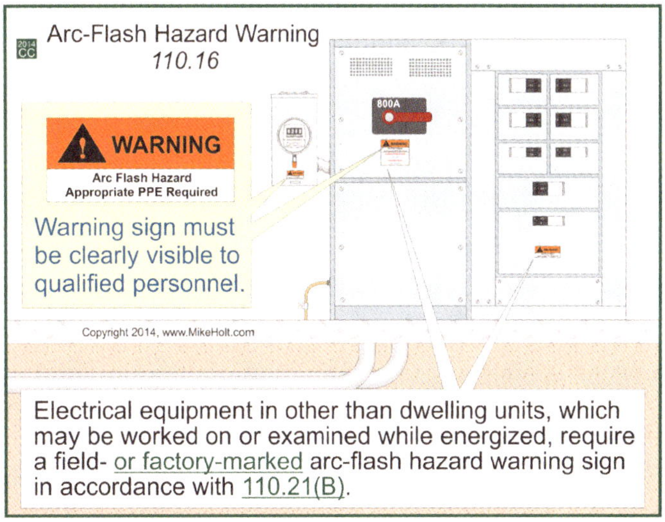

Figure 110–4

Author's Comments:

- See the definition of "Qualified Person" in Article 100.
- This rule is meant to warn qualified persons who work on energized electrical systems that an arc flash hazard exists so they'll select proper personal protective equipment (PPE) in accordance with industry accepted safe work practice standards.

Note 1: NFPA 70E, *Standard for Electrical Safety in the Workplace*, provides assistance in determining the severity of potential exposure, planning safe work practices, arc-flash labeling, and selecting personal protective equipment.

ANALYSIS: Since the introduction of this section in 2002, it's been changed every single *Code* cycle. The upside is that it seems to improve every three years.

The requirement for the marking to take place in the field has been removed. It seems a bit silly that an installation can pass or fail an inspection based on who put the sticker on the equipment. If the sticker is present, and it provides the necessary information, why should it be noncompliant?

A reference to the new 110.21(B) has also been added. This new requirement contains information about signage in general, and will be discussed further in that section of this textbook.

Lastly, Informational Note 1 has been revised to make the *Code* user aware of the fact NFPA 70E contains requirements for arc-flash labeling as well.

110.21 Markings

New requirements for field-applied labels have been added.

110.21 Markings.

(A) Manufacturer's Markings. The manufacturer's name, trademark, or other descriptive marking must be placed on all electrical equipment and, where required by the *Code*, markings such as voltage, current, wattage, or other ratings must be provided. All marking must have sufficient durability to withstand the environment involved.

(B) Field-Applied Hazard Markings. Where caution, warning, or danger signs or labels are required, the labels must meet the following:

(1) The markings must use words, colors, or symbols that effectively warn personnel. **Figure 110–5**

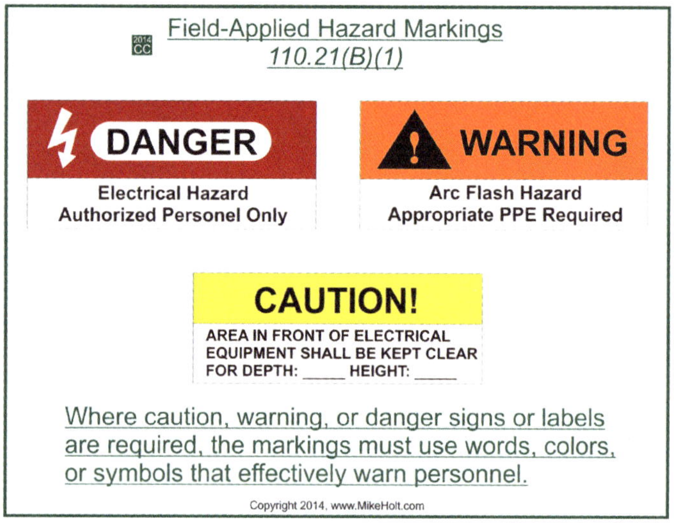

Figure 110–5

Note: ANSI Z535.4, *Product Safety Signs and Labels*, provides guidelines for the design and durability of signs and labels.

(2) The label can't be handwritten, and it must be permanently affixed to the equipment. **Figure 110–6**

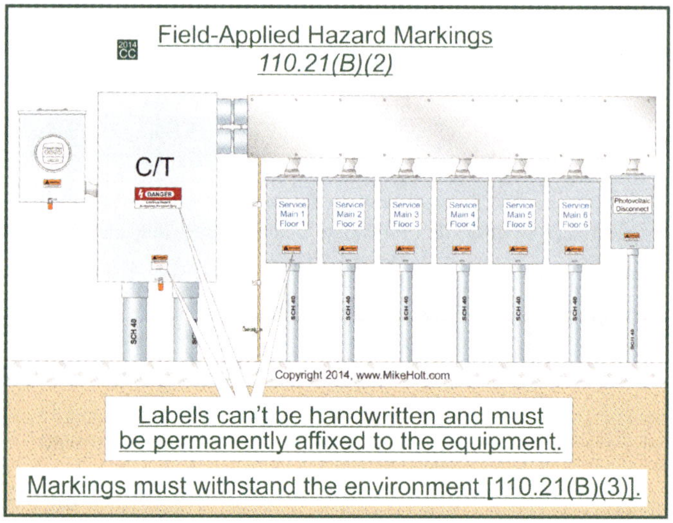

Figure 110–6

Ex to (2): Labels that contain information that's likely to change can be handwritten, if it's legible.

Author's Comment: A permanently affixed sign would include a sticker, but not a piece of paper taped to the equipment.

(3) The marking must be of sufficient durability to withstand the environment involved.

ANALYSIS: In an effort to standardize the marking requirements found in the *NEC*, this requirement has been added. Certainly most will agree that a typed sign is better than a handwritten one.

There are several changes to the *Code* that require compliance with this section, but even without those changes this rule still applies. For example, 110.16 includes a statement requiring compliance with this section. If that statement weren't in 110.16, it wouldn't make this rule optional.

Some of the locations in which this rule applies are 110.16, 110.22, 250.20 (although there's no reference in that section) 312.8, 404.6, 408.3, and many, many others.

110.22 Identification of Disconnecting Means

This section was revised to require compliance with 110.21(B).

110.22 Identification of Disconnecting Means.

(A) General. Each disconnecting means must be legibly marked to indicate its purpose unless located and arranged so the purpose is evident. The marking must be of sufficient durability to withstand the environment involved. Figure 110–7

(C) Tested Series Combination Systems. Tested series-rated installations must be legibly field-marked in accordance with 240.86(B) and 110.21(B) to indicate the equipment has been applied with a series combination rating.

Identification of Disconnecting Means
110.22(A)

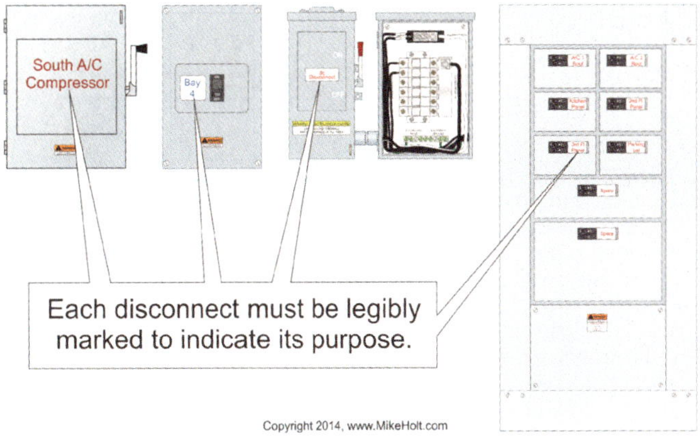

Figure 110–7

ANALYSIS: With the addition of 110.21(B), several *Code* requirements such as this one have been revised. Section 110.21(B) requires that field-applied labels be permanently affixed, be suitable for the environment, and can't be handwritten. Because there are so many changes that are similar to this, not all of them will be covered in this textbook.

110.24 Available Fault Current

An Informational Note has been added to inform the user of the intent of this requirement.

110.24 Available Fault Current.

(A) Field Marking. Service equipment in other than dwelling units must be legibly field-marked with the maximum available fault current, including the date the fault current calculation was performed, and be of sufficient durability to withstand the environment involved. Figure 110–8

Note: The fault current markings required by this section are to ensure compliance with 110.9 and 110.10. They're not intended to be used for arc flash analysis. Arc flash hazard information is available in NFPA 70E, *Standard for Electrical Safety in the Workplace.*

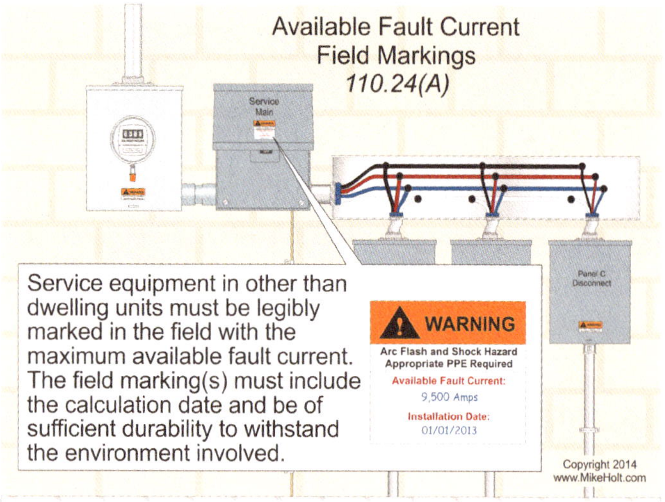

Figure 110–8

(B) Modifications. When modifications to the electrical installation affect the maximum available fault current at the service, the maximum available fault current must be recalculated to ensure the service equipment ratings are sufficient for the maximum available fault current at the line terminals of the equipment. The required field marking(s) in 110.24(A) must be adjusted to reflect the new level of maximum available fault current.

Ex: Field markings aren't required for industrial installations where conditions of maintenance and supervision ensure that only qualified persons service the equipment.

ANALYSIS: This section requires that the service equipment be marked with the maximum available fault current. This value is often determined by employing the "Infinite Buss Primary" method, which is based on having no impedance from the utility's point of generation all the way to the transformer serving the building. This method will ensure that the equipment will be rated to handle any dramatic rise in current from a ground fault or a short circuit, because the value will be artificially high (there's obviously impedance between the point of generation and the transformer supplying the building). Having an artificially high value is perfectly acceptable for sizing equipment, but it's dangerous if a person is trying to determine what level of Personal Protective Equipment (PPE) they need to use in order to work on the equipment. By using an artificially high value of available fault current, the results of the calculations used for determining PPE will be wrong. This is because a false (higher than reality) value of available fault current means the breaker would trip faster than it really would (the higher the fault current, the faster the overcurrent device opens). This false value could ultimately result in a lower level of PPE, and put workers in a dangerous situation.

110.25 Lockable Disconnecting Means

A new section provides the rules for lockable disconnecting means.

110.25 Lockable Disconnecting Means. Where the *Code* requires that a disconnecting means is lockable in the open position, the provisions for locking must remain in place whether the lock is installed or not. Figure 110–9

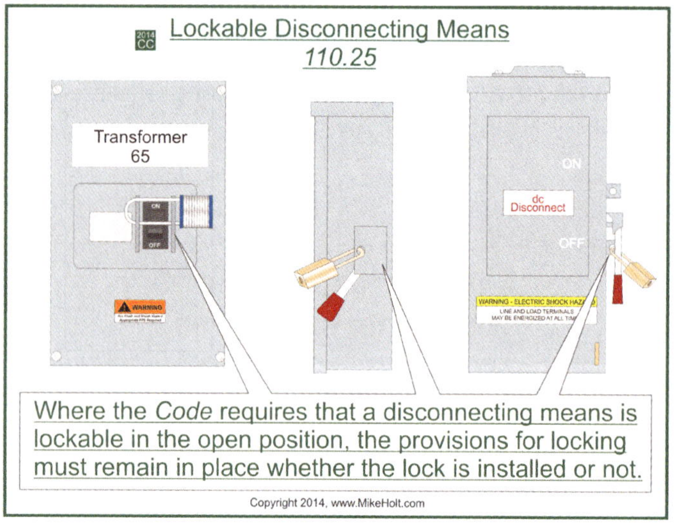

Figure 110–9

Ex: Locking provisions for cord-and-plug connected equipment don't need to remain in place without the lock installed.

ANALYSIS: When different *Code* articles have the same requirements it's nearly impossible to make them all say the same thing. This is due to the fact that there isn't just one group of a bunch of guys smoking cigars in a dark room choosing which *NEC* change proposals pass and which fail. They're groups of professionals in 19 different *Code*-Making Panels (CMPs), each of which is responsible for a few *NEC* articles. For example, CMP-4 reviews all of the proposals for Articles 225 and 230, while CMP-9 covers 312, 314, 404, 408, 450, and 490. It makes sense that the rules in Part II of Article 225 are almost identical to those in Article 230—the same people are responsible for both articles. The rule requiring a disconnect in Article 450 (CMP-9) is probably not going to say the same thing as the rule in Article 210 (CMP-2). The rules for equipment requiring a disconnect run the entire gamut of the *Code*-Making Panels. In order for all of the rules to say the same thing, you have to have one rule, and it has to cover everything. This new rule will hopefully satisfy this goal.

The exception to this rule is a rather obvious one, but I guess the *NEC* has to include it. A lock installed over the end of a cord is an effective way to ensure worker safety. It obviously can't remain in place at all times, unless you never want to use the equipment again!

110.26 Spaces About Electrical Equipment

Changes have been made to the door hardware requirements for large equipment, and outdoor dedicated electrical space provisions have been added.

Part II. 600V, Nominal, or Less

110.26 Spaces About Electrical Equipment. For the purpose of safe operation and maintenance of equipment, access and working space must be provided about all electrical equipment.

(A) Working Space. Equipment that may need examination, adjustment, servicing, or maintenance while energized must have working space provided in accordance with (1), (2), and (3):

Author's Comment: The phrase "while energized" is the root of many debates. As always, check with the AHJ to see what equipment he or she believes needs a clear working space.

(1) Depth of Working Space. The working space, which is measured from the enclosure front, must not be less than the distances contained in Table 110.26(A)(1). Figure 110–10

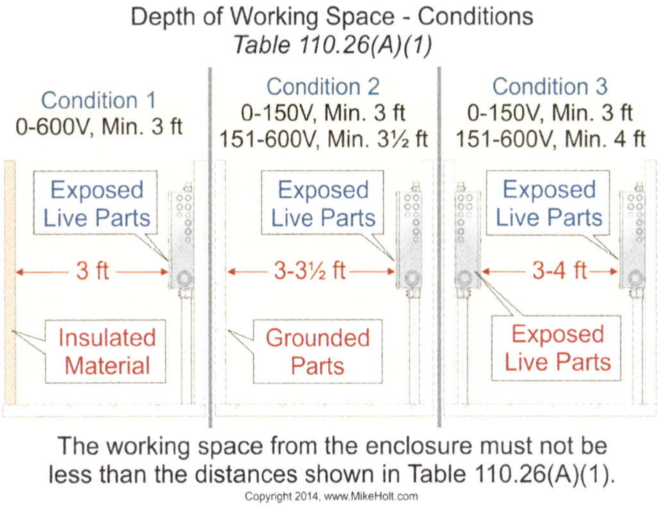

Figure 110–10

Table 110.26(A)(1) Working Space

Voltage-to-Ground	Condition 1	Condition 2	Condition 3
0–150V	3 ft	3 ft	3 ft
151–600V	3 ft	3½ft	4 ft

- **Condition 1**—*Exposed live parts on one side of the working space and no live or grounded parts, including concrete, brick, or tile walls are on the other side of the working space.*
- **Condition 2**—*Exposed live parts on one side of the working space and grounded parts, including concrete, brick, or tile walls are on the other side of the working space.*
- **Condition 3**—*Exposed live parts on both sides of the working space.*

(a) Rear and Sides. Working space isn't required for the back or sides of assemblies where all connections and all renewable or adjustable parts are accessible from the front. Figure 110–11

(b) Low Voltage. If special permission is granted in accordance with 90.4, working space for equipment that operates at not more than 30V ac or 60V dc can be less than the distance in Table 110.26(A)(1). Figure 110–12

Author's Comment: See the definition of "Special Permission" in Article 100.

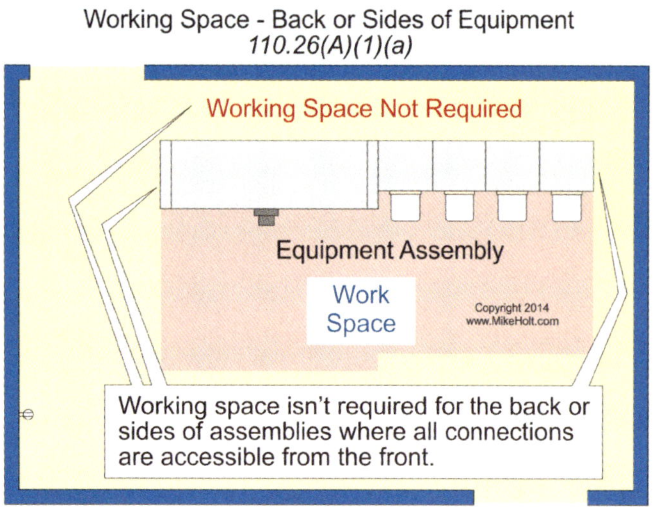

Figure 110–11

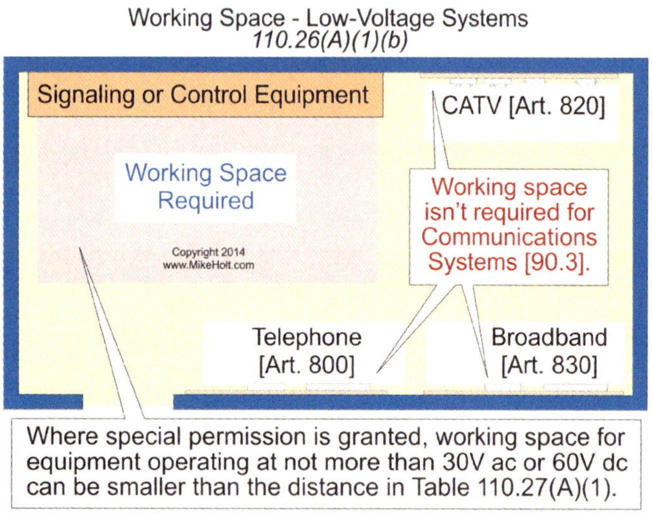

Figure 110–12

(c) Existing Buildings. If electrical equipment is being replaced, Condition 2 working space is permitted between dead-front switchboards, panelboards, or motor control centers located across the aisle from each other where conditions of maintenance and supervision ensure that written procedures have been adopted to prohibit equipment on both sides of the aisle from being open at the same time, and only authorized, qualified persons will service the installation.

> **Author's Comment:** The working space requirements of 110.26 don't apply to equipment included in Chapter 8—Communications Circuits [90.3].

(2) Width of Working Space. The width of the working space must be a minimum of 30 in., but in no case less than the width of the equipment. Figure 110–13

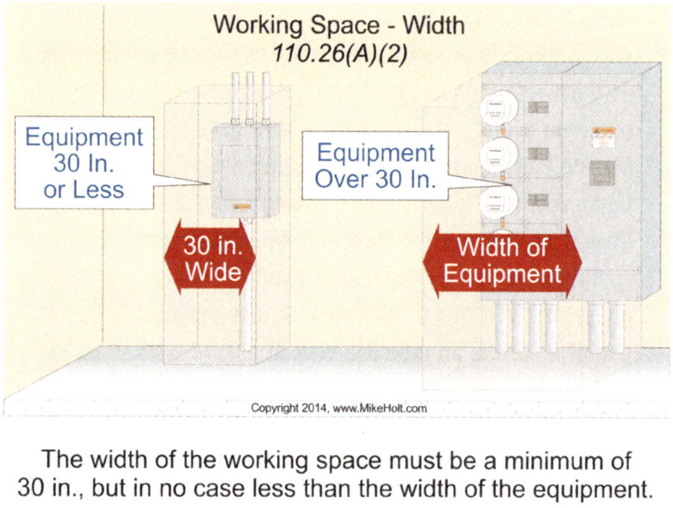

Figure 110–13

> **Author's Comment:** The width of the working space can be measured from left-to-right, from right-to-left, or simply centered on the equipment, and the working space can overlap the working space for other electrical equipment. Figure 110–14

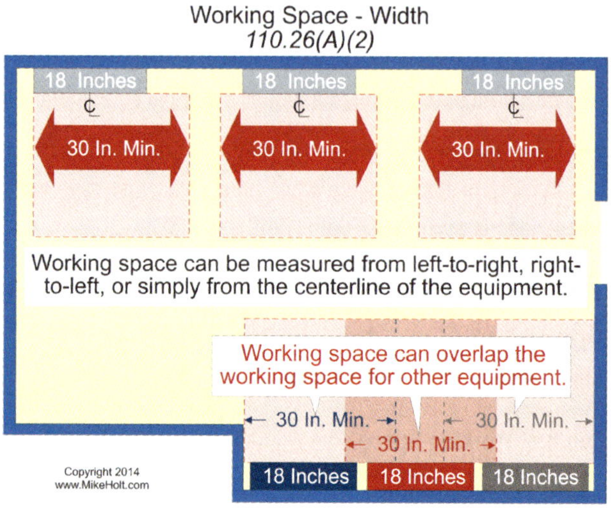

Figure 110–14

In all cases, the working space must be of sufficient width, depth, and height to permit all equipment doors to open 90 degrees. Figure 110–15

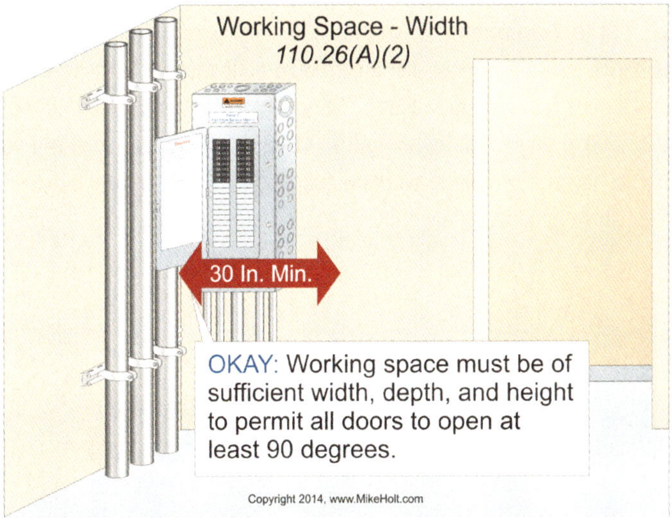

Figure 110–15

(3) Height of Working Space (Headroom). The height of the working space in front of equipment must not be less than 6½ ft, measured from the grade, floor, platform, or the equipment height, whichever is greater. Figure 110–16

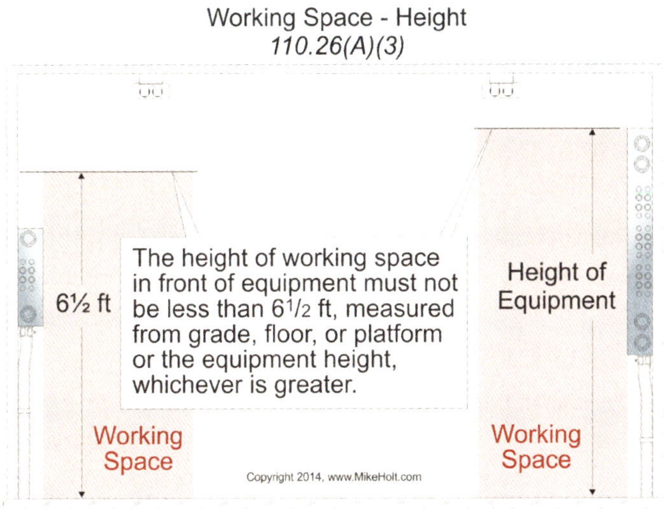

Figure 110–16

Equipment such as raceways, cables, wireways, cabinets, panels, and so on, can be located above or below electrical equipment, but must not extend more than 6 in. into the equipment's working space. Figure 110–17

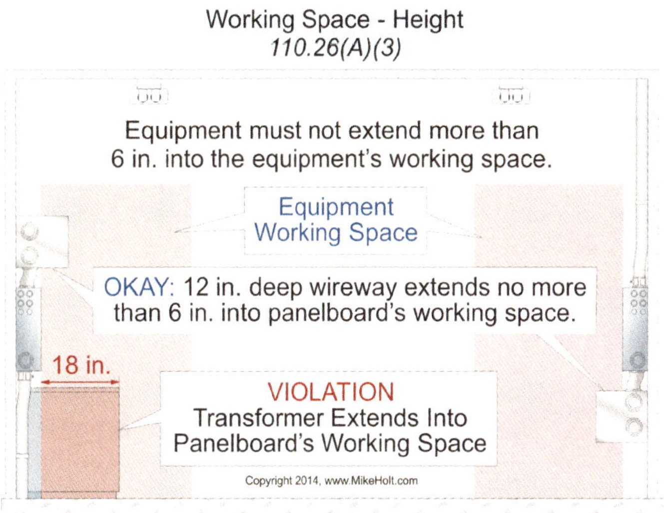

Figure 110–17

Ex 1: The minimum headroom requirement doesn't apply to service equipment or panelboards rated 200A or less located in an existing dwelling unit.

> **Author's Comment:** See the definition of "Dwelling Unit" in Article 100.

Ex 2: Meters are permitted to extend beyond the other equipment.

(B) Clear Working Space. The working space required by this section must be clear at all times. Therefore, this space isn't permitted for storage, Figure 110–18. When normally enclosed live parts are exposed for inspection or servicing, the working space, if in a passageway or general open space, must be suitably guarded.

> **Author's Comment:** When working in a passageway, the working space should be guarded from occupants using it. When working on electrical equipment in a passageway one must be mindful of a fire alarm evacuation with numerous occupants congregated and moving through the area.

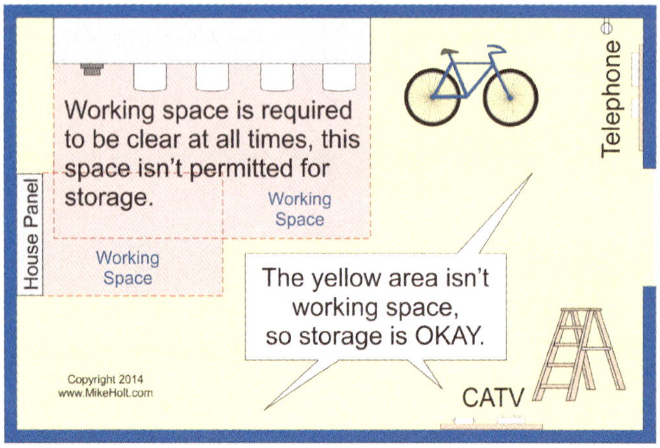

Figure 110–18

CAUTION: *It's very dangerous to service energized parts in the first place, and it's unacceptable to be subjected to additional dangers by working around bicycles, boxes, crates, appliances, and other impediments.*

Author's Comment: Signaling and communications equipment must not be installed in a manner that encroaches on the working space of the electrical equipment. Figure 110–19

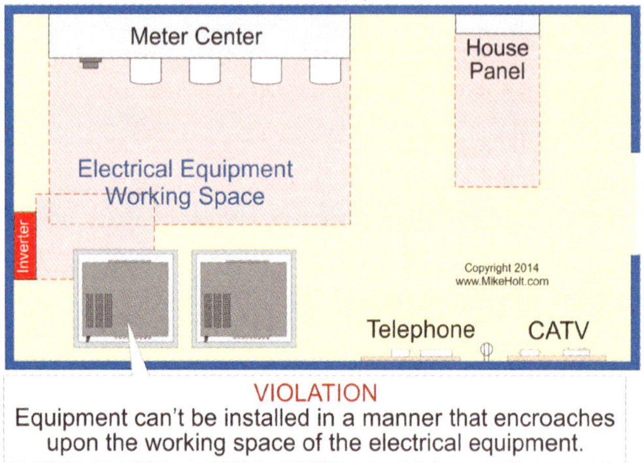

Figure 110–19

(C) Entrance to and Egress from Working Space.

(1) Minimum Required. At least one entrance of sufficient area must provide access to and egress from the working space.

Author's Comment: Check to see what the authority having jurisdiction considers "Sufficient Area." Building codes contain minimum dimensions for doors and openings for personnel travel.

(2) Large Equipment. An entrance to and egress from each end of the working space of electrical equipment rated 1,200A or more that's over 6 ft wide is required. The opening must be a minimum of 24 in. wide and 6½ ft high, Figure 110–20. A single entrance to and egress from the required working space is permitted where either of the following conditions is met:

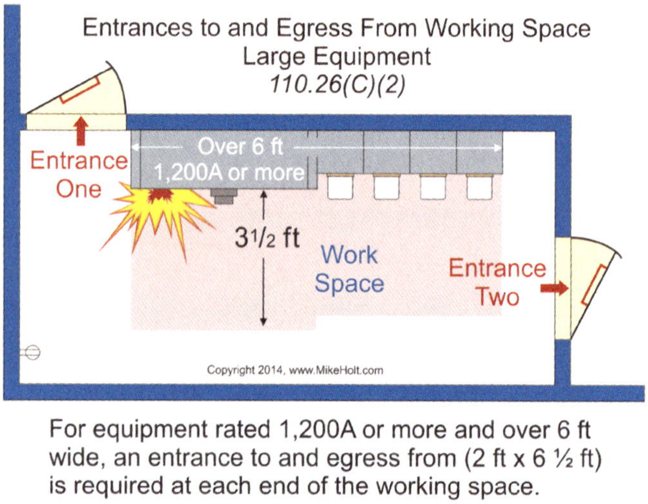

Figure 110–20

(a) Unobstructed Egress. Only one entrance is required where the location permits a continuous and unobstructed way of egress travel. Figure 110–21

(b) Double Workspace. Only one entrance is required where the required working space depth is doubled, and the equipment is located so the edge of the entrance is no closer than the required working space distance. Figure 110–22

(3) Personnel Doors. If equipment with overcurrent or switching devices rated 800A or more is installed, personnel door(s) for entrance to and egress from the working space located less than 25 ft from the nearest edge of the working space must have the door(s) open in the direction of egress and be equipped with listed panic hardware. Figure 110–23

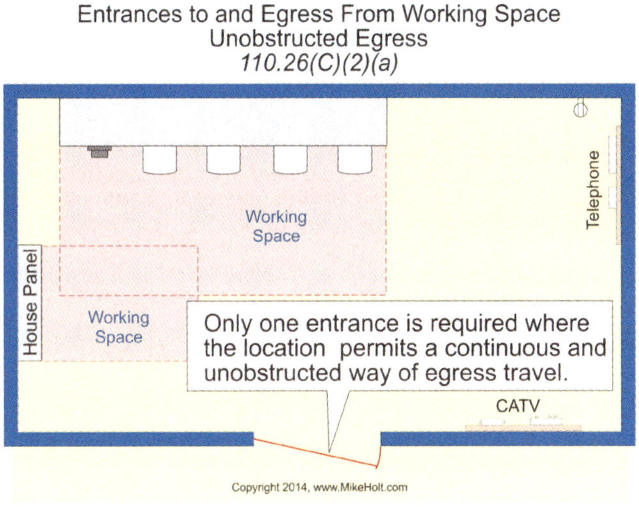

Figure 110–21

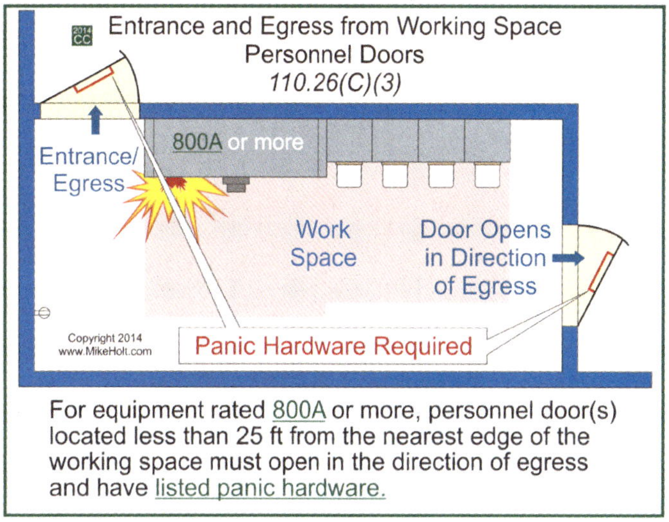

Figure 110–23

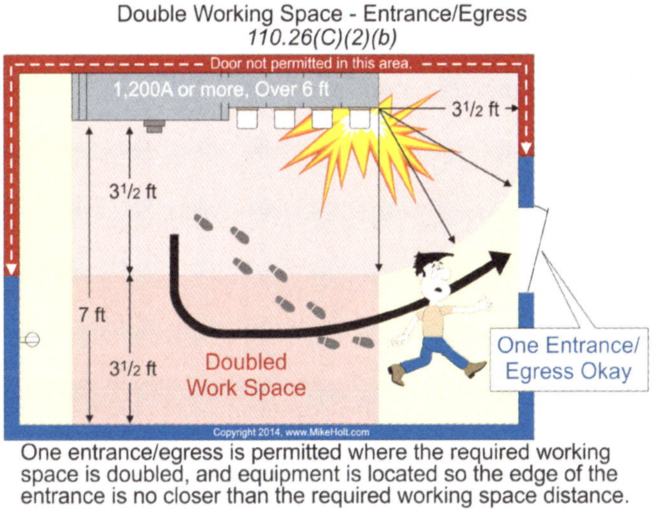

Figure 110–22

Author's Comments:

- History has shown that electricians who suffer burns on their hands in electrical arc flash or arc blast events often can't open doors equipped with knobs that must be turned.
- Since this requirement is in the *NEC*, the electrical contractor is responsible for ensuring that panic hardware is installed where required. Some electrical contractors are offended at being held liable for nonelectrical responsibilities, but this rule is designed to save the lives of electricians. For this and other reasons, many construction professionals routinely hold "pre-construction" or "pre-con" meetings to review potential opportunities for miscommunication—before the work begins.

ANALYSIS: The requirements for door swings and hardware in equipment rooms containing large equipment are among the most important safety provisions for electricians in the entire *NEC*. When an electrical accident occurs, particularly an arc flash or arc blast, the victim is rendered incapable of opening a door if the door swings in or has hardware that must be operated. Because the victim's hands and eyes are the two parts of the body most often affected, this issue is even more important. These incidents occur at currents much, much less than 1,200A. By decreasing the current threshold of this requirement to 800A, more electrical rooms will be equipped with outward swinging doors with panic hardware.

The requirements for the door hardware itself have also changed. Since the inception of this rule in 2002, the hardware requirements for the outward swinging door have allowed for panic hardware or similar devices that open without the victim having to manipulate a knob or similar hardware. In this new edition of the *Code*, there's no longer any option. Panic hardware must be used, and it must be listed. Most people will agree that a safety feature like panic hardware probably should be a listed piece of equipment, but now that's the only option. Hardware like a push/pull plate is no longer allowed, despite the fact that it's even easier to use than the required panic hardware.

(D) Illumination. Service equipment, switchboards, and panelboards, as well as motor control centers located indoors must have illumination located indoors and must not be controlled by automatic means only. Figure 110–24

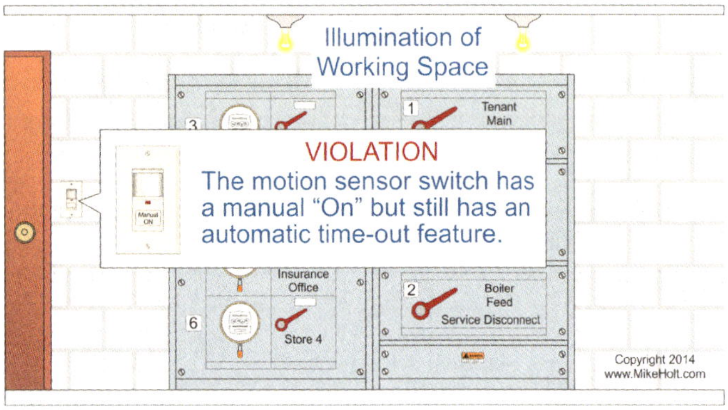

Service equipment, switchboards, and panelboards, and motor control centers located indoors must have illumination not controlled by automatic means only.

Figure 110–24

Author's Comment: The *Code* doesn't provide the minimum foot-candles required to provide proper illumination. Proper illumination of electrical equipment rooms is essential for the safety of those qualified to work on such equipment.

(E) Dedicated Equipment Space. Switchboards, panelboards, and motor control centers must have dedicated equipment space as follows:

(1) Indoors.

(a) Dedicated Electrical Space. The footprint space (width and depth of the equipment) extending from the floor to a height of 6 ft above the equipment or to the structural ceiling, whichever is lower, must be dedicated for the electrical installation, Figure 110–25. No piping, ducts, or other equipment foreign to the electrical installation can be installed in this dedicated footprint space. Figure 110–26

Ex: Suspended ceilings with removable panels can be within the dedicated footprint space [110.26(E)(1)(d)].

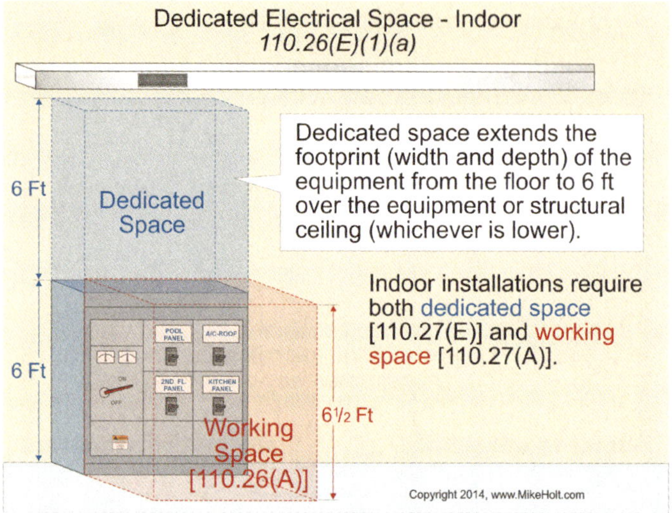

Figure 110–25

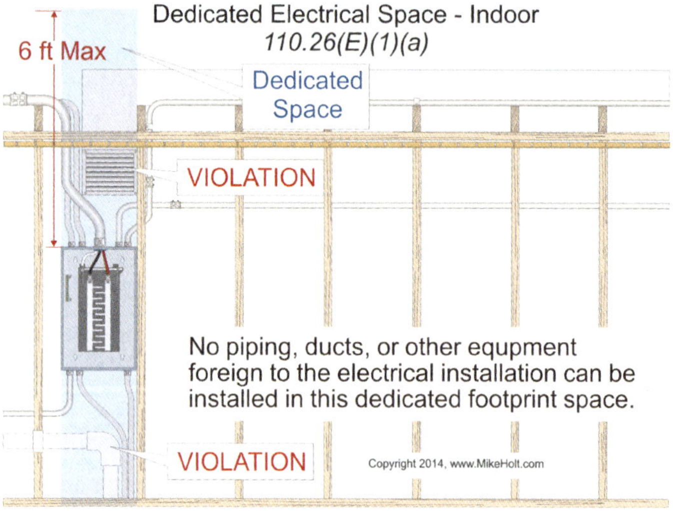

Figure 110–26

Author's Comment: Electrical raceways and cables not associated with the dedicated space can be within the dedicated space. These aren't considered "equipment foreign to the electrical installation." Figure 110–27

(b) Foreign Systems. Foreign systems can be located above the dedicated space if protection is installed to prevent damage to the electrical equipment from condensation, leaks, or breaks in the foreign systems, which can be as simple as a drip-pan. Figure 110–28

(c) Sprinkler Protection. Sprinkler protection piping isn't permitted in the dedicated space, but the *NEC* doesn't prohibit sprinklers from spraying water on electrical equipment.

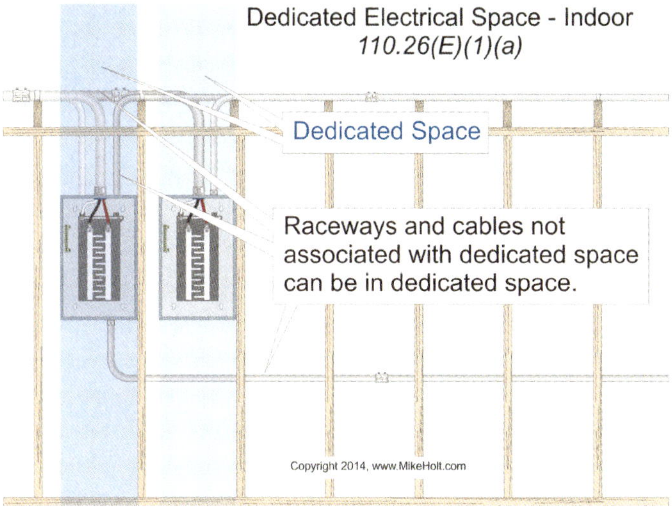

Figure 110–27

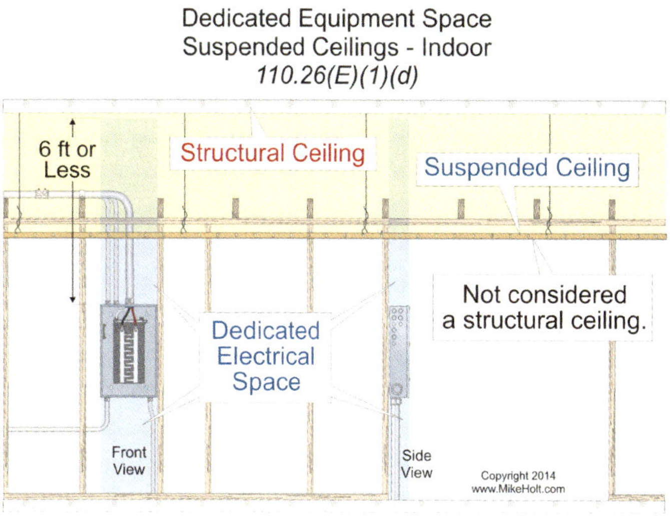

Figure 110–29

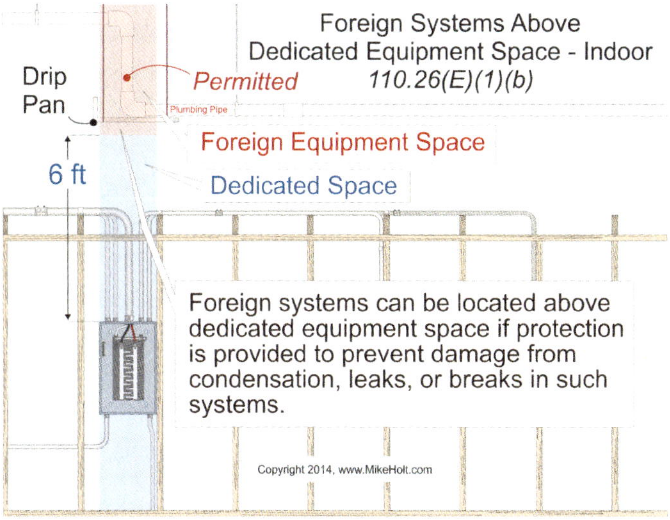

Figure 110–28

(d) Suspended Ceilings. A dropped, suspended, or similar ceiling isn't considered a structural ceiling. **Figure 110–29**

(2) Outdoor. Outdoor installations must comply with 110.26(E)(2)(a) and (b).

(a) Installation Requirements. Outdoor electrical equipment must be installed in suitable enclosures and be protected from accidental contact by unauthorized personnel, or by vehicular traffic, or by accidental spillage or leakage from piping systems.

(b) Dedicated Electrical Space. The footprint space (width and depth of the equipment) extending from the floor to a height of 6 ft above the equipment must be dedicated for the electrical installation. No piping, ducts, or other equipment foreign to the electrical installation can be installed in this dedicated footprint space. **Figure 110–30**

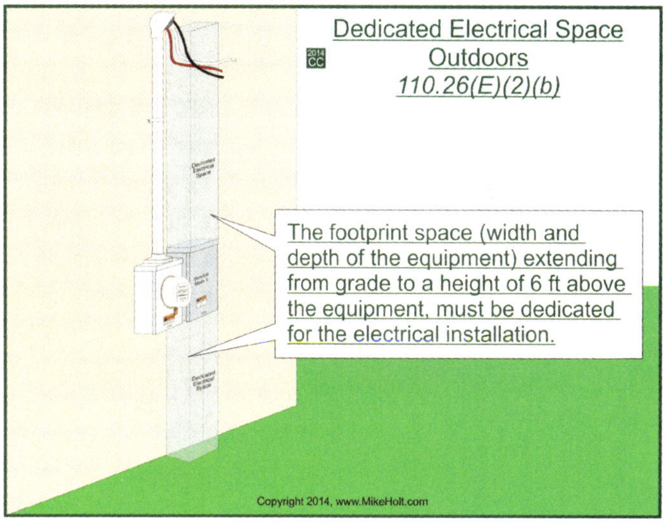

Figure 110–30

(F) Locked Electrical Equipment Rooms or Enclosures. Electrical equipment rooms and enclosures housing electrical equipment can be controlled by locks because they're still considered to be accessible to qualified persons who require access. Figure 110–31

Figure 110–31

Author's Comment: See the definition of "Accessible as it applies to equipment" in Article 100.

ANALYSIS: New to this edition of the *NEC* is a requirement for outdoor equipment to have dedicated space above and below it, similar to the requirements for indoor installations. The intent of the dedicated space rule for indoor equipment is to allow the installer enough space to install raceways and cables. This is just as important outdoors as it is indoors.

110.27 Guarding

The height requirements for the guarding of equipment have been clarified and increased.

110.27 Guarding.

(A) Guarding Live Parts. Live parts of electrical equipment operating at 50V or more must be guarded against accidental contact. This can be done by:

(1) Locating them in a separate room, vault, or enclosure.

(2) Guarding with a partition or screen.

(3) Locating them on a balcony or platform.

(4) Elevating them above the floor or working surface, in accordance with the following:

(a) 8 ft for 50V through 300V.

(b) 8½ ft for 301V through 600V.

ANALYSIS: The requirements for guarding live parts have been revised in order to correlate with the *National Electrical Safety Code* (*NESC*). It's typically used by utility companies as the document that regulates their installations. In many instances there's no need to correlate the *NEC* and the *NESC*, since they're intended to have different rules. In this case, however, it was determined that the *NESC* has the better rule for elevation requirements, so it's been copied and pasted here.

CHAPTER 2 WIRING AND PROTECTION

Introduction to Chapter 2—Wiring and Protection

Chapter 2 provides general rules for wiring and for the protection of conductors. The rules in this chapter apply to all electrical installations covered by the *NEC*—except as modified in Chapters 5, 6, and 7 [90.3]. Communications systems (Chapter 8 systems) aren't subject to the general requirements of Chapters 1 through 4, or the special requirements of Chapters 5 through 7, unless there's a specific reference in Chapter 8 to a rule in Chapters 1 through 7 [90.3].

As you go through Chapter 2, remember its purpose. It's primarily concerned with correctly sizing and protecting circuits. Every article in this chapter deals with a different aspect of this purpose. This differs from the purpose of Chapter 3, which is to correctly install the conductors that make up those circuits.

Chapter 1 introduced you to the *NEC* and provided a solid foundation for understanding the *Code*. Chapters 2 (Wiring and Protection) and 3 (Wiring Methods and Materials) continue building the foundation for applying the *NEC*. Chapter 4 applies the preceding chapters to general equipment. It's beneficial to learn the first four chapters of the *Code* in a sequential manner because each of the first four chapters builds on the one before it. Once you've mastered the first four chapters, you can learn the next four in any order you wish.

- **Article 200—Use and Identification of Grounded [Neutral] Conductors.** This article contains the requirements for the use and identification of the grounded conductor and its terminals.

  Author's Comment: Throughout this textbook, we'll use the term "neutral" when referring to the grounded conductor when the application isn't related to PV systems or corner-grounded delta-connected systems.

- **Article 210—Branch Circuits.** Article 210 contains the requirements for branch circuits, such as conductor sizing, identification, and GFCI protection, as well as receptacle and lighting outlet requirements.
- **Article 215—Feeders.** This article covers the requirements for the installation and ampacity of feeders.
- **Article 220—Branch-Circuit, Feeder, and Service Calculations.** Article 220 provides the requirements for calculating the minimum size for branch circuits, feeders, and services. This article also aids in determining related factors such as the number of receptacles on a circuit in nondwelling installations, and the minimum number of branch circuits required.

- **Article 225—Outside Branch Circuits and Feeders.** This article covers the installation requirements for equipment, including branch circuits and feeders located outside (overhead and underground) that run on or between buildings, poles, and other structures on the premises.
- **Article 230—Services.** Article 230 covers the installation requirements for service conductors and equipment. It's very important to know where the service begins and ends when applying Article 230.

  Author's Comment: Conductors from a battery, uninterruptible power supply, solar PV system, generator, or transformer aren't service conductors; they're feeder conductors.

- **Article 240—Overcurrent Protection.** This article provides the requirements for overcurrent protection and overcurrent devices. Overcurrent protection for conductors and equipment is provided to open the circuit if the current reaches a value that will cause an excessive or dangerous temperature on the conductors or conductor insulation.
- **Article 250—Grounding and Bonding.** Article 250 covers the grounding requirements for providing a low-impedance path to the earth to reduce overvoltage from lightning, and the bonding requirements for a low-impedance fault current path necessary to facilitate the operation of overcurrent devices in the event of a ground fault.
- **Article 285—Surge Protective Devices (SPDs).** This article covers the general, installation, and connection requirements for surge protective devices (SPDs) permanently installed on both the line side and load side of service equipment.

ARTICLE 200 USE AND IDENTIFICATION OF GROUNDED [NEUTRAL] CONDUCTORS

Introduction to Article 200—Use and Identification of Grounded [Neutral] Conductors

This article contains the requirements for the identification of the grounded [neutral] conductor and its terminals. Article 100 contains definitions for both "Grounded Conductor" and "Neutral Conductor." In some cases, both of these terms apply to the same conductor. Figures 200–1 and 200–2

In a system that produces direct current, such as a PV system, the "grounded conductor" isn't a neutral conductor. Figure 200–3

> **Author's Comment:** Throughout this textbook, we'll use the term "neutral" when referring to the grounded conductor when the application isn't related to PV systems or corner-grounded delta-connected systems.

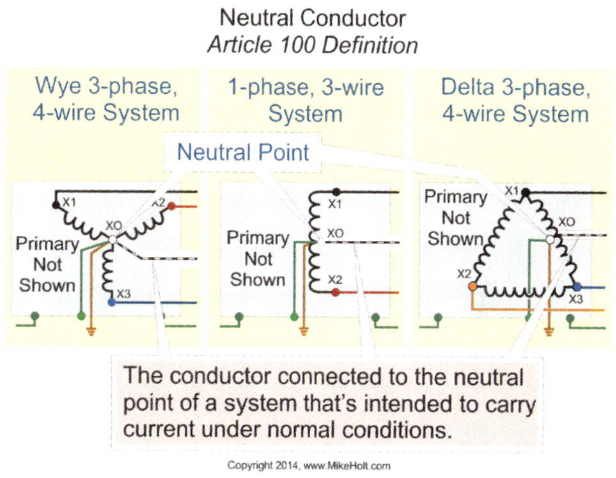

Figure 200–2

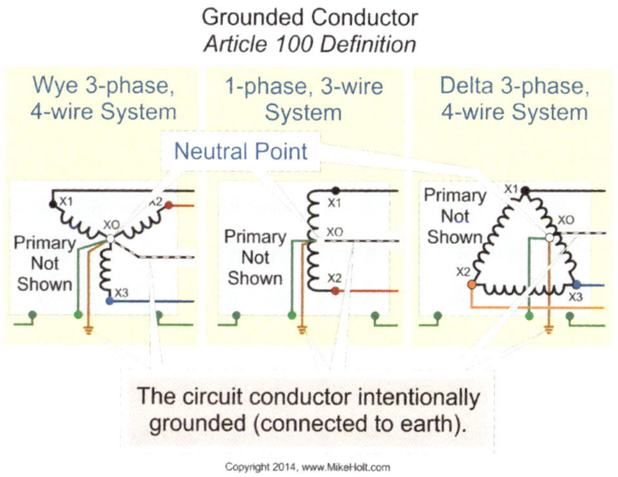

Figure 200–1

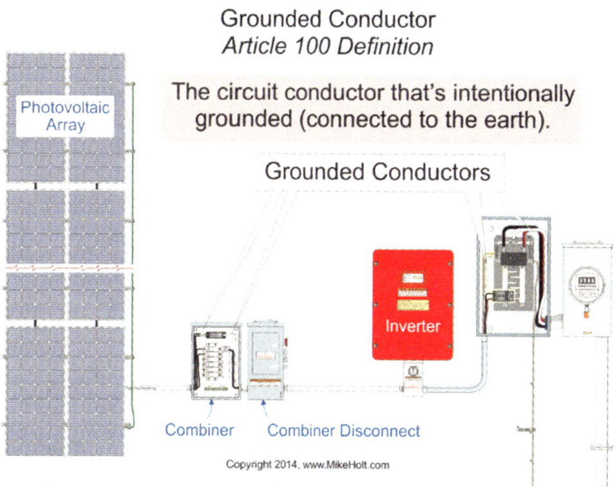

Figure 200–3

200.4 Neutral Conductors

New requirements for the grouping of neutral conductors have been added.

Part I. General

200.4 Neutral Conductors. Neutral conductors must comply with (A) and (B).

(A) Installation. A single neutral conductor can't be used for more than one branch circuit. Figure 200–4

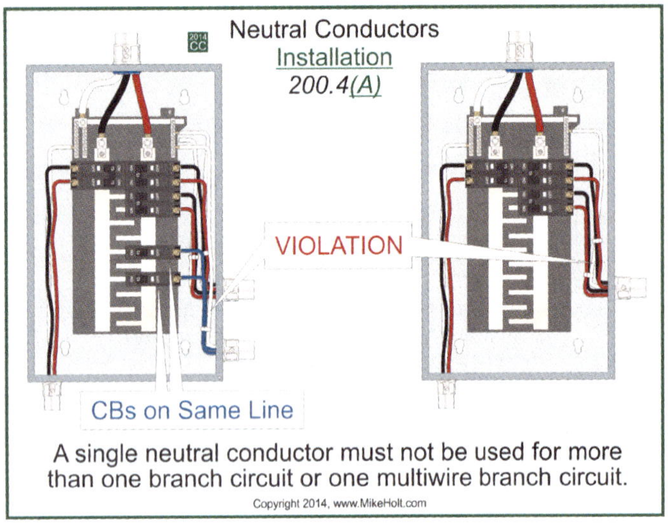

Figure 200–4

(B) Grouping. The ungrounded and neutral conductors of multiple branch circuits must be grouped together by cable ties or similar means in every enclosure. Figure 200–5

Ex 1: Grouping isn't required where the circuit conductors are contained in a single raceway or cable unique to that circuit that makes the grouping obvious.

Ex 2: Grouping isn't required if the conductors pass through a box or conduit body without any splices or terminations, or if the conductors don't have a loop as described in 314.16(B)(1).

Author's Comment: 210.4(D) contains a similar requirement for branch circuit conductors.

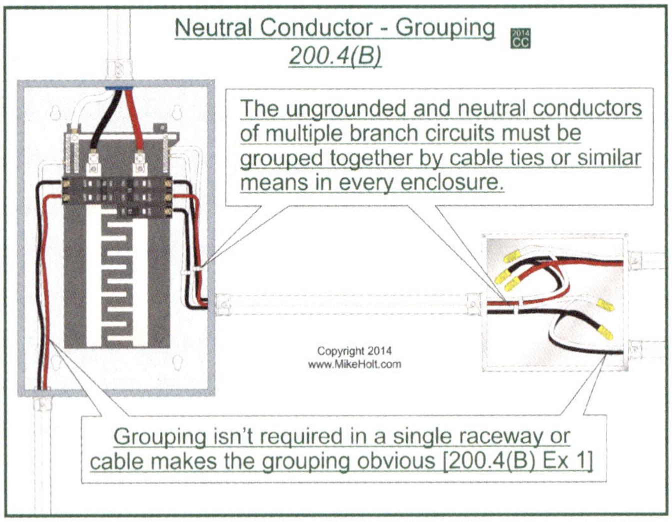

Figure 200–5

ANALYSIS: The 2008 *NEC* added a requirement to group the neutral conductor with the ungrounded conductors of a multiwire branch circuit in the panel or other distribution equipment. This ensures that if an electrician disconnects the neutral of a multiwire branch circuit, but opens the wrong one accidentally, he or she won't have to spend their next few paychecks paying for the equipment that's subsequently destroyed due to the resulting over- or undervoltage.

When individual neutral conductors are used for all of the circuits, the hazard of damaging the equipment doesn't exist, so there's been no requirement to group them with their associated ungrounded conductor. When a raceway multiple circuits, each with their own neutral conductor, it's nearly impossible to determine which neutral conductor goes to which circuit. If you open the wrong neutral conductor no equipment will be destroyed, but have fun explaining to the employees why you just turned off their computers without warning them. This new requirement will eliminate that possibility by requiring that the neutral and ungrounded conductor be grouped together.

Unlike the requirements for multiwire branch circuits in 210.4(D), this requirement applies to all enclosures (including junction boxes), not just panelboards and similar equipment. Exception 1 allows for the conductors to not be grouped if the role of the neutral conductors is obvious, and Exception 2 provides relief when there's no real way to splice or terminate the conductors in the future.

200.6 Neutral Conductor Identification

Revisions to the requirements for marking neutral conductors have been made.

200.6 Neutral Conductor Identification.

(A) Size 6 AWG or Smaller. Neutral conductors 6 AWG and smaller must be identified by one of the following means: Figure 200–6

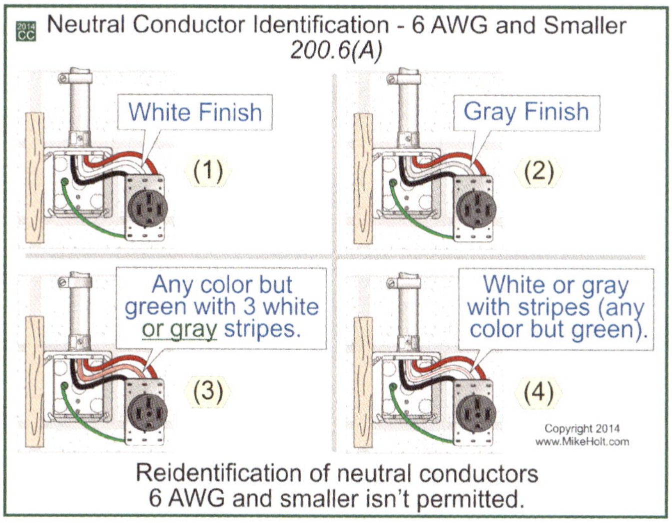

Figure 200–6

(1) A continuous white outer finish.

(2) A continuous gray outer finish.

(3) Three continuous white or gray stripes along its entire length on other than green insulation.

(4) Wires that have their outer covering finished to show a white or gray color but have colored tracer threads in the braid identifying the source of manufacture are considered to meet the provisions of this section.

Author's Comment: The use of white tape, paint, or other methods of identification aren't permitted for neutral conductors 6 AWG and smaller. Figure 200–7

(6) A single-conductor, sunlight-resistant, outdoor-rated cable used as the grounded conductor in PV power systems as permitted by 690.31(B) can be identified by distinctive white marking at all terminations. Figure 200–8

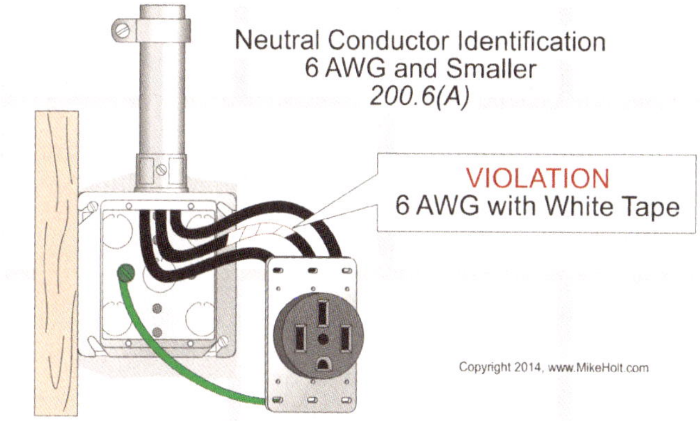

White tape, paint, or other methods of identification aren't permitted for neutral conductors 6 AWG and smaller.

Figure 200–7

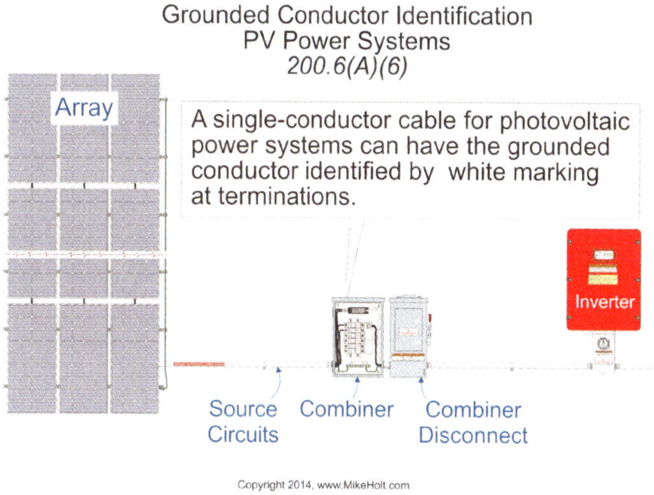

Figure 200–8

(B) Size 4 AWG or Larger. Neutral conductors 4 AWG or larger must be identified by one of the following means: Figure 200–9

(1) A continuous white outer finish along its entire length.

(2) A continuous gray outer finish along its entire length.

(3) Three continuous white or gray stripes along its length.

(4) White or gray tape or markings at the terminations.

(D) Neutral Conductors of Different Systems. If neutral conductors of different voltage systems are installed in the same raceway, cable, or enclosure, each system neutral conductor must be identified by:

(1) A continuous white or gray outer finish along its entire length. Figure 200–10

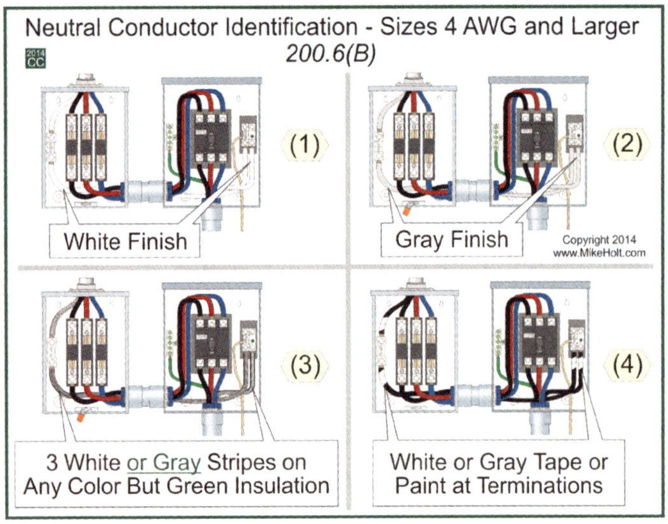

Figure 200–9

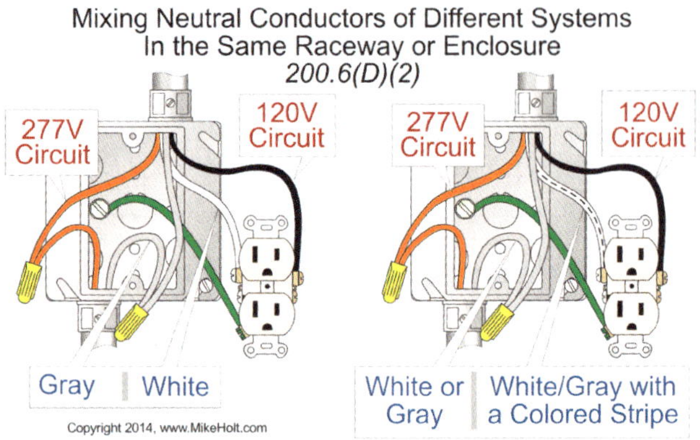

The neutral conductor of the different systems must have an outer covering of continuous white or gray finish along its entire length or by an outer covering of white or gray with a readily distinguishable colored stripe (other than green) along its entire length.

Figure 200–11

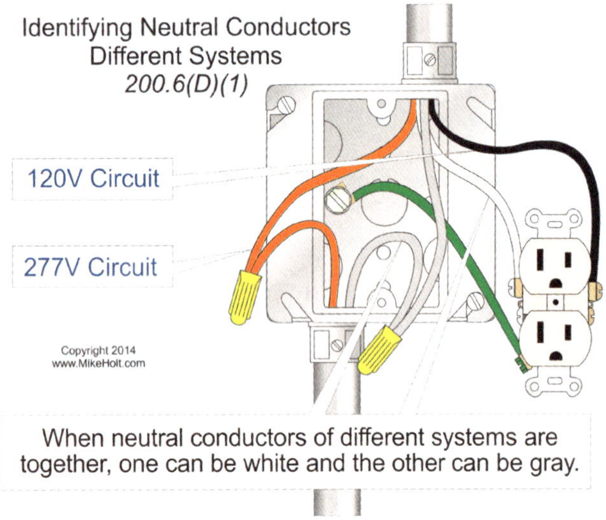

When neutral conductors of different systems are together, one can be white and the other can be gray.

Figure 200–10

(2) The neutral conductor of the other system must have a different outer covering of continuous white or gray outer finish along its entire length or by an outer covering of white or gray with a readily distinguishable color stripe (other than green) along its entire length. **Figure 200–11**

(3) Other identification allowed by 200.6(A) or (B) that distinguishes the neutral conductor from other systems.

ANALYSIS: It's interesting that the *NEC* can have an obvious error in it that nobody catches for several *Code* cycles. Neutral conductors have long been required to be either white or gray in color or to have white stripes on them (or the other methods discussed here). It seems that the *NEC* never intended to prohibit gray stripes, but interestingly that practice wasn't recognized in the *Code*. Since most people never noticed the omission, most people won't consider this a substantial change.

A similar change has been made to 200.7.

ARTICLE 210 BRANCH CIRCUITS

Introduction to Article 210—Branch Circuits

This article contains the requirements for branch circuits, such as conductor sizing and identification, GFCI protection, and receptacle and lighting outlet requirements. It consists of three parts:

- **Part I. General Provisions**
- **Part II. Branch-Circuit Ratings**
- **Part III. Required Outlets**

Table 210.2 of this article identifies specific-purpose branch circuits. The provisions for branch circuits that supply equipment listed in Table 210.2 amend or supplement the provisions given in Article 210 for branch circuits, so it's important to be aware of the contents of this table.

The following sections contain a few key items on which to spend extra time as you study Article 210:

- **210.4—Multiwire Branch Circuits.** The conductors of these circuits must originate from the same panel.
- **210.8—GFCI Protection.** Crawl spaces, unfinished basements, and boathouses are just some of the many locations that require GFCI protection.
- **210.11—Branch Circuits Required.** With three subheadings, 210.11 gives summarized requirements for the number of branch circuits in certain situations, states that a load calculated on a VA per area basis must be evenly proportioned, and covers some minimum branch circuit rules for dwelling units.
- **210.12—Arc-Fault Circuit-Interrupter Protection.** An arc-fault circuit interrupter (AFCI) is a device intended to de-energize a circuit when it detects the current waveform characteristics unique to an arcing fault. The purpose of an AFCI is to protect against a fire hazard, whereas the purpose of a GFCI is to protect people against electrocution.
- **210.19—Conductors—Minimum Ampacity and Size.** This section covers the basic rules for sizing branch-circuit conductors, including continuous and noncontinuous loads.
- **210.21—Outlet Devices.** Outlet devices must have an ampere rating at least as large as the load to be served, as well as following the other rules of this section.
- **210.22** and **210.23—Permissible Loads.** This is intended to prevent a circuit overload from occurring because of an improper design and planning of circuitry.
- **210.52—Dwelling Unit Receptacle Outlets.** There are some specific receptacle spacing rules and branch-circuit requirements for dwelling units that don't apply to other occupancies.

Mastering the branch-circuit requirements in Article 210 will give you a jump-start toward completing installations that are free of *Code* violations.

210.4 Multiwire Branch Circuits

The requirement for grouping multiwire branch-circuit neutral conductors has been lessened.

Part I. General Provisions

210.4 Multiwire Branch Circuits.

(D) Grouping. The ungrounded and neutral conductors of a multiwire branch circuit must be grouped together by cable ties or similar means at the point of origination. Figure 210–1

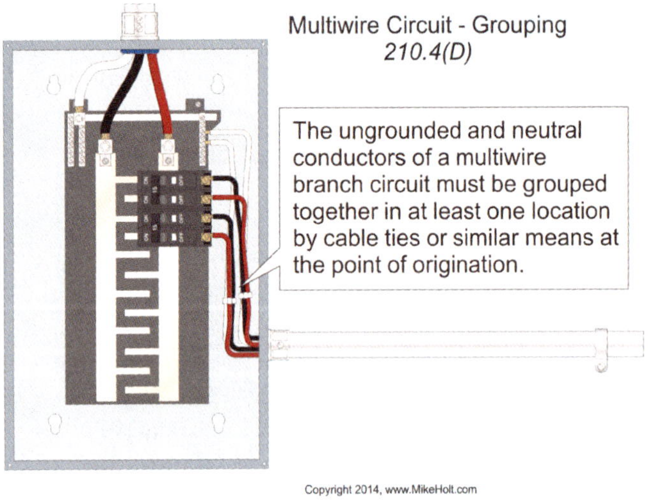

Figure 210–1

Ex: Grouping isn't required where the circuit conductors are contained in a single raceway or cable unique to that circuit that makes the grouping obvious, or if the conductors have circuit number tags on them. Figure 210–2

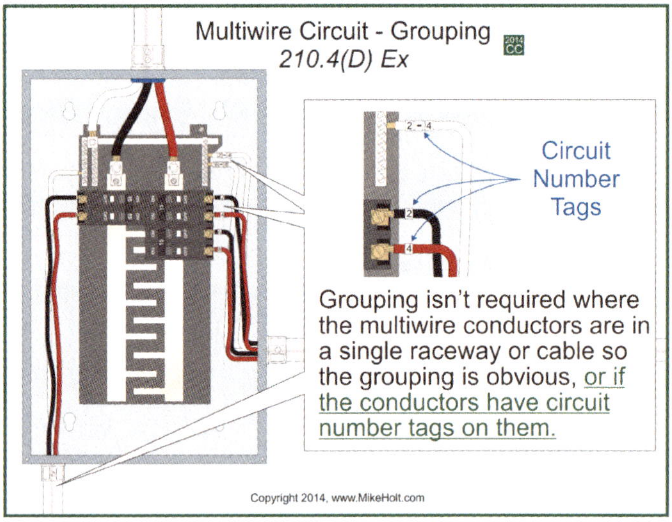

Figure 210–2

Author's Comment: Grouping all associated conductors of a multiwire branch circuit together by cable ties or other means within the point of origination makes it easier to visually identify the conductors of the multiwire branch circuit. The grouping will assist in making sure that the correct neutral is used at junction points and in connecting multiwire branch-circuit conductors to circuit breakers correctly, particularly where twin breakers are used. If proper diligence isn't exercised when making these connections, two circuit conductors can be accidentally connected to the same phase or line.

CAUTION: *If the ungrounded conductors of a multiwire circuit aren't terminated to different phases or lines, the currents on the neutral conductor won't cancel, which can cause an overload on the neutral conductor.* Figure 210–3

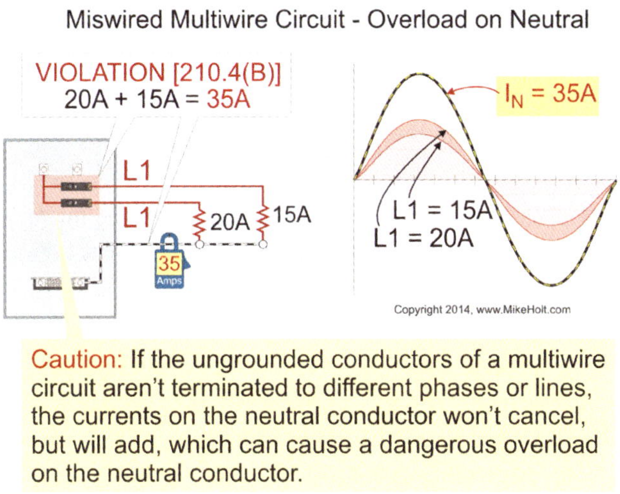

Figure 210–3

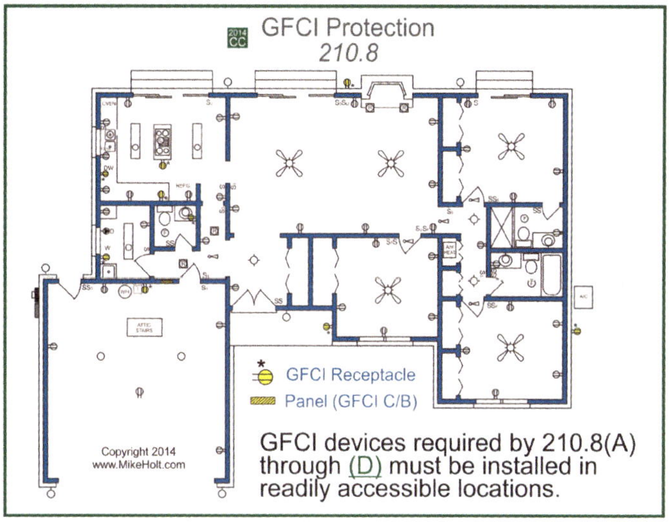

Figure 210–4

ANALYSIS: The requirement for grouping the neutral of a multiwire branch circuit was added in the 2008 *NEC*. It allows for cable ties or "similar means." This "similar means" is the subject of debate among many. Is electrical tape "similar means"? Is identifying the neutral conductor with numbered tags, corresponding to the ungrounded conductors, "similar means"? With this change, it becomes clear that placing circuit number tags on the neutral conductors is a suitable method and can be used instead of cable ties.

210.8 GFCI Protection

The requirements for GFCI protection have been greatly expanded.

210.8 GFCI Protection. Ground-fault circuit interruption for personnel must be provided as required in 210.8(A) through (D). The ground-fault circuit-interrupter device must be installed at a readily accessible location. Figure 210–4

Author's Comment: According to Article 100, "readily accessible" means capable of being reached quickly without having to climb over or remove obstacles, or resort to portable ladders.

(A) Dwelling Units. GFCI protection is required for all 15A and 20A, 125V receptacles installed in the following locations:

Author's Comment: See the definitions of "GFCI" and "Dwelling Unit" in Article 100.

(7) Sinks. GFCI protection is required for all 15A and 20A, 125V receptacles located within an arc measurement of 6 ft from the outside edge of a sink. Figure 210–5

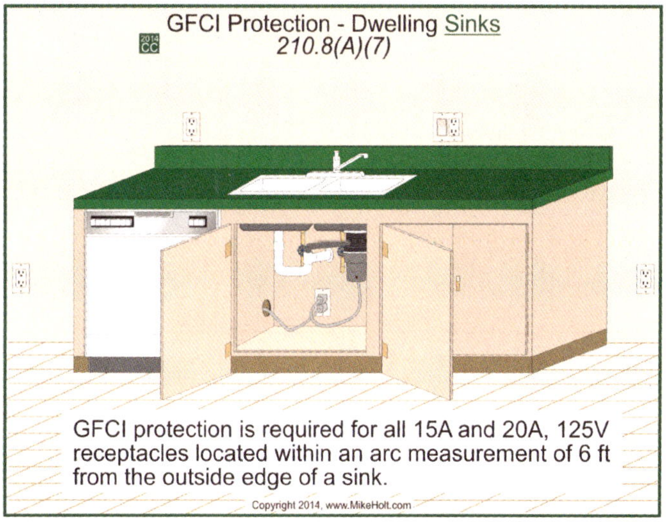

Figure 210–5

ANALYSIS: Previous editions of the *Code* required that, in a dwelling unit kitchen, only the receptacles serving the countertop needed to be GFCI protected. For all other sinks, most notably wet bar sinks, the receptacles within 6 ft of the sink needed to be protected. Consider, for example, a disposal receptacle under the sink. If we're discussing a wet bar (that isn't in a kitchen), GFCI protection will be required. If, however, the wet bar is in a kitchen, protection isn't required because it isn't a countertop receptacle. The safety concern is exactly the same in both installations, so why were the rules different? They're more similar now with this change, although kitchens will still have more GFCI requirements than wet bars. Kitchens now require GFCI protection for the countertop receptacles [210.8(A)(6)], and for receptacles within 6 ft of the sink.

(9) Bathtubs or Shower Stalls. GFCI protection is required for all 15A and 20A, 125V receptacles located within 6 ft of the outside edge of a bathtub or shower stall. Figure 210–6

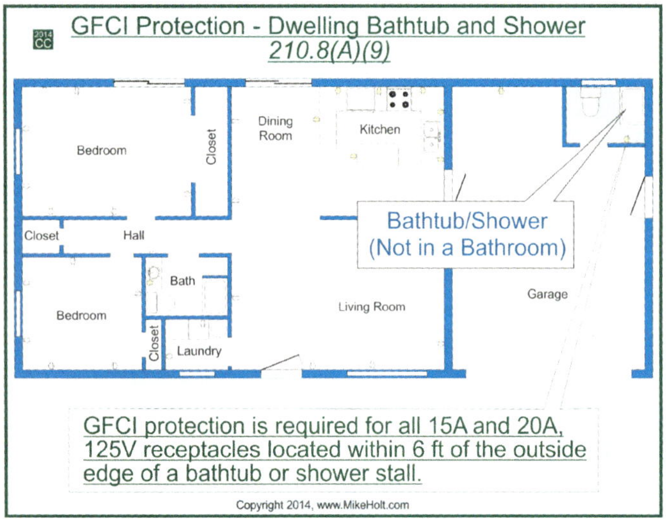

Figure 210–6

ANALYSIS: GFCI protection for 125V, 15A and 20A receptacles in bathrooms is required by 210.8(A)(1). Although it's rare, there are instances where a shower or bathtub is located remote from the other plumbing fixtures and therefore isn't in the bathroom. In cases such as this GFCI protection has never been required, despite having (more or less) the same dangers as a bathroom. Obviously both bathrooms and shower rooms involve water, but they also might involve tile floors, which significantly increase the risk of electrical shock. Although this change doesn't specify the fact that it applies only to showers and bathtubs that aren't in a bathroom, 210.8(A)(1) still requires GFCI protection for all 15A and 20A, 125V receptacles in a bathroom, not just those within 6 ft of the shower or bathtub.

(10) Laundry Areas. All 15A and 20A, 125V receptacles installed in laundry areas of a dwelling unit must be GFCI protected. Figure 210–7

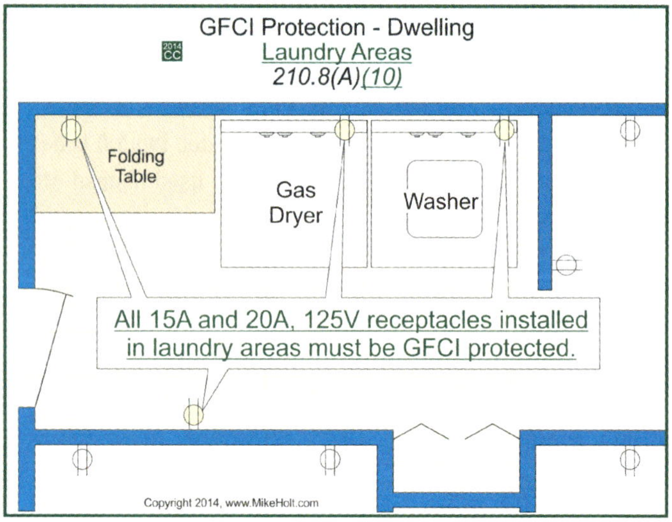

Figure 210–7

ANALYSIS: Nobody can argue the fact that GFCI protection has significantly decreased the number of electrocutions in the United States. Despite having no examples of deaths or injuries to point out in this *Code* change proposal, the *NEC* has now incorporated laundry areas into the list of locations requiring GFCI protection. In previous editions of the *Code* this was only required if the receptacle was within 6 ft of a sink.

When the laundry sink rule first came into the *NEC* many people were nervous thinking that a washing machine wouldn't work on a GFCI-protected circuit (which, of course, it will). This new requirement for laundry areas was submitted by one of the leading manufacturers of appliances in the United States, so perhaps that will silence those who think GFCIs and motors don't play well together.

It's worth noting that the *Code* uses the term "laundry area," not "laundry room." If the laundry equipment is in a very large laundry room, perhaps the AHJ will only require the GFCI protection within 6 ft of the washing machine. Maybe they'll require protection for the entire room. As always, when in doubt, check with the inspector if you think this rule is going to create a problem in the field.

(B) Other than Dwelling Units. GFCI protection is required for all 15A and 20A, 125V receptacles installed in the following commercial/industrial locations:

(3) Rooftops. All 15A and 20A, 125V receptacles installed on rooftops must be GFCI protected. Figure 210–8

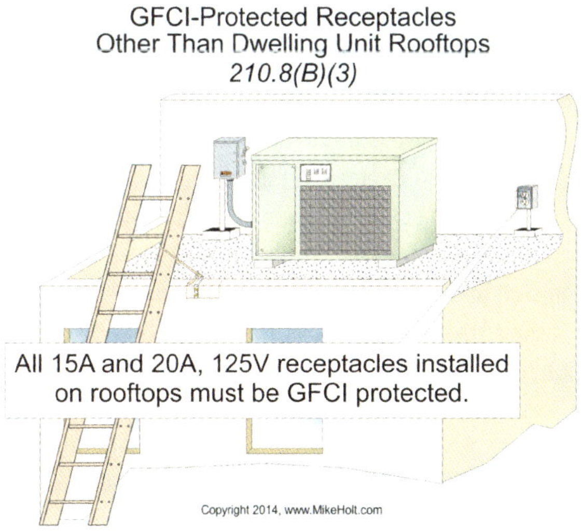

Figure 210–8

Author's Comment: A 15A or 20A, 125V receptacle outlet must be installed within 25 ft of heating, air-conditioning, and refrigeration equipment [210.63].

Ex 1 to (3): Receptacles on rooftops aren't required to be readily accessible other than from the rooftop. Figure 210–9

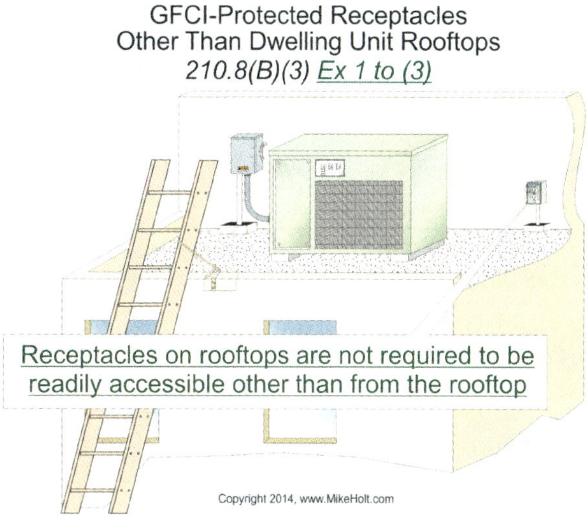

Figure 210–9

ANALYSIS: 210.8 requires that GFCI devices discussed in this section must be readily accessible, which means that they are capable of being reached quickly by those who need to access the equipment. Climbing over or removing obstacles, or having to use a portable ladder, also violates this rule [Article 100 accessible, readily]. In a commercial building, there doesn't need to be a permanent ladder to the roof unless the roof is over 16 ft in height (refer to the International Mechanical Code). A rooftop without a permanent ladder obviously requires a portable ladder, and is therefore not readily accessible, according to Article 100.

Because GFCI devices must be installed in readily accessible locations [210.8], a rooftop without a permanent ladder can't have a GFCI device. While that doesn't sound like a major issue at first, you probably wouldn't want to be the person on the roof that has to go on an Easter egg hunt through the building trying to find the reset button.

Interestingly, it could be argued that this exception isn't required at all. A close read of the definition says that those "to whom ready access is requisite" aren't required to use a portable ladder. If a GFCI is on the roof, then who needs the ready access? It will probably the person who's already on the roof to begin with. It will be he or she that might trip the GFCI, and they're the ones who need access to it. It can even be argued that having a GFCI in the building instead of on the roof violates this rule, since you're now forced to use a portable ladder to get back down and reset it!

(8) Garages. All 15A and 20A, 125V receptacles installed in garages, service bays, and similar areas must be GFCI protected, unless they're in show rooms or exhibition halls. Figure 210–10

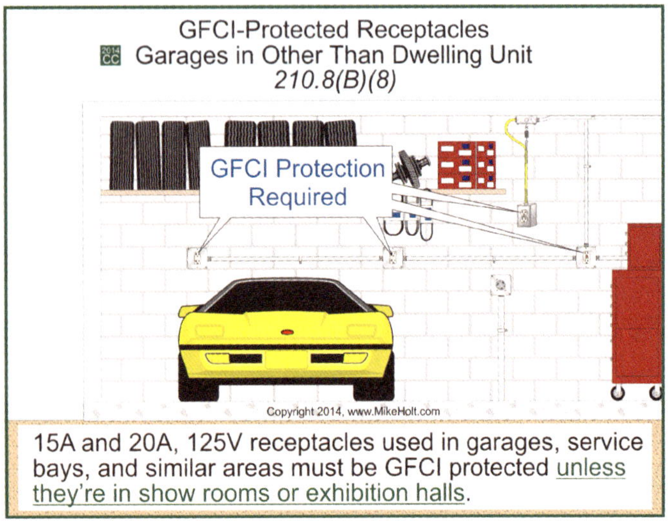

Figure 210–10

ANALYSIS: The 2011 version of the *Code* added requirements for commercial garages, but only in the areas where electrical diagnostic equipment, electrical hand tools, or portable lighting were being used. The rules for GFCI protection are typically governed by location, not by specific equipment usage. GFCIs are required in commercial garages because the floor is conductive, not because "electrical diagnostic equipment, electrical hand tools, or portable lighting" are more hazardous than other electrical equipment. By removing this text from the rule, GFCI protection is now required for things like engine block heaters, which are very common in some parts of the country. These block heaters aren't always listed, and therefore may have more leakage current than product standards allow, which greatly increases the possibility of electrocution. Eliminating the list of equipment also helps the enforcement community in a major way, as inspectors are no longer required to try to figure out what each receptacle in the garage is for and make GFCI requirements based on what is often complete guesswork.

(D) Dwelling Unit Dishwashers. Outlets supplying dishwashers in a dwelling unit must be GFCI protected. Figure 210–11

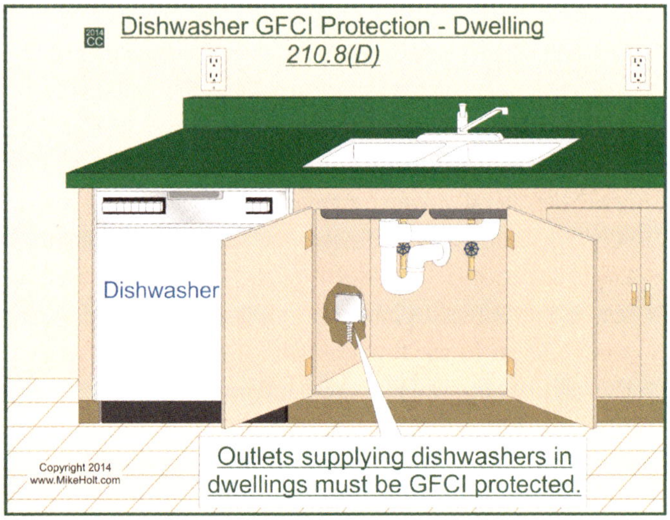

Figure 210–11

ANALYSIS: No one will argue that GFCIs reduce the likelihood of a fatal electrical shock, and have greatly reduced the number of electrocutions since their inception. New to this edition, we have a rule for dwelling unit dishwashers. This change was warranted, according to the submitter of the proposal, because of the track record of GFCIs and the data showing the decrease in electrocutions in this country. According to some members of the *Code*-Making Panel, "any electrical appliance combined with the use of water should be GFCI protected."

It may seem odd that this rule isn't found in 210.8(A), since that's the location for dwelling units. The reason that it's found here in (D) is because (A) only applies to receptacle outlets, whereas this new rule requires GFCI protection for dwelling unit dishwashers, even if the equipment is hardwired.

210.12 Arc-Fault Circuit-Interrupter Protection

Numerous revisions have been made to the AFCI requirements.

210.12 Arc-Fault Circuit-Interrupter Protection.

Arc-fault circuit-interrupter protection must be provided in accordance with 210.12(A), (B) and (C). AFCI devices must be installed in readily accessible locations.

(A) Where Required. All 15A or 20A, 120V branch circuits in dwelling units supplying outlets or devices in kitchens, family rooms, dining rooms, living rooms, parlors, libraries, dens, bedrooms, sunrooms, recreation rooms, closets, hallways, laundry areas, or similar rooms or areas must be protected by one of the following: Figure 210–12

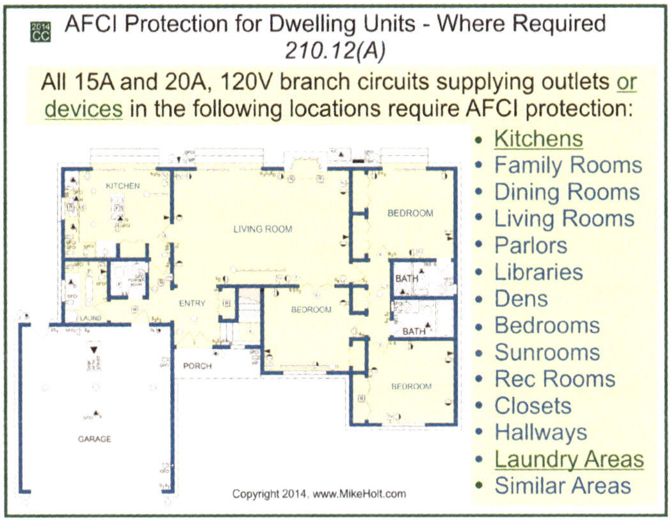

Figure 210–12

(1) A listed combination type AFCI, installed to provide protection of the entire branch circuit.

(2) A listed branch/feeder type AFCI at the origin of the branch circuit, plus a listed outlet branch-circuit AFCI installed at the first outlet box of the branch circuit. The outlet box must be marked to indicate that it's the first outlet box of the circuit.

(3) A listed supplemental arc protection circuit breaker installed at the origin of the branch circuit, plus a listed outlet branch-circuit type AFCI installed at the first outlet box on the branch circuit. When using this option, the following must be met:

(a) The branch-circuit wiring must be continuous from the branch circuit overcurrent device to the AFCI device.

(b) The maximum length of the branch circuit to the AFCI is 50 ft for 14 AWG conductors or 70 ft for 12 AWG conductors.

(c) The first outlet box in the circuit must be marked.

(4) A regular fuse or circuit breaker, plus a listed outlet branch-circuit type AFCI installed at the first outlet of the branch circuit. When using this option, the following must be met:

(a) The branch-circuit wiring must be continuous from the branch-circuit overcurrent device to the AFCI device.

(b) The maximum length of the branch circuit to the AFCI is 50 ft for 14 AWG conductors or 70 ft for 12 AWG conductors.

(c) The first outlet box in the circuit must be marked.

(d) The combination of the branch-circuit overcurrent device and the AFCI must be listed and identified as meeting the requirements for a "System Combination" type AFCI.

(5) A listed outlet branch-circuit type AFCI at the first outlet can be used, if the wiring between the overcurrent device and the AFCI contains all metal boxes and is installed using any (or a combination) of the following: RMC, IMC, EMT, Type MC, Type AC cables meeting the requirements of 250.118, metal wireways, or metal auxiliary gutters.

(6) A listed outlet branch-circuit type AFCI at the first outlet of the circuit can be used, if the wiring between the overcurrent device and the AFCI is in a raceway with 2 in. of concrete encasement.

Author's Comments:

- The combination AFCI is a circuit breaker that protects downstream branch-circuit wiring as well as cord sets and power-supply cords; an outlet branch-circuit AFCI (receptacle) is installed as the first outlet in a branch circuit to protect downstream branch-circuit wiring, cord sets, and power-supply cords.
- The 120V circuit limitation means AFCI protection isn't required for equipment rated 230V, such as a baseboard heater or room air conditioner. For more information, visit www.MikeHolt.com, click on the "Search" link, and then search for "AFCI."

Ex: AFCI protection can be omitted for an individual branch circuit to a fire alarm system in accordance with 760.41(B) and 760.121(B), if the circuit conductors are installed in metal wireways, metal auxiliary gutters, RMC, IMC, EMT, or steel sheath Type AC or MC cable that qualifies as an equipment grounding conductor in accordance with 250.118, with metal outlet and junction boxes.

Note 3: See 760.41(B) and 760.121(B) for power-supply requirements for fire alarm systems.

Author's Comment: Smoke alarms connected to a 15A or 20A circuit in a dwelling unit must be AFCI protected if the smoke alarm is located in one of the areas specified in 210.12(A). The exemption from AFCI protection for the "fire alarm circuit" contained in 760.41(B) and 760.121(B) doesn't apply to the single- or multiple-station smoke alarm circuit typically installed in dwelling unit bedroom areas. This is because a smoke alarm circuit isn't a fire alarm circuit as defined in NFPA 72, *National Fire Alarm Code*. Unlike single- or multiple-station smoke alarms, fire alarm systems are managed by a fire alarm control panel. **Figure 210–13**

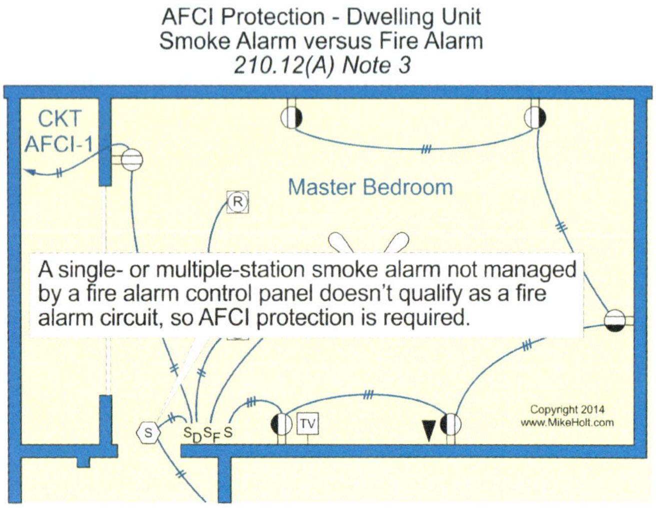

Figure 210–13

ANALYSIS: Since the introduction of AFCIs to the *NEC* in 1999, this section has changed every single *Code* cycle. Changes have included expanding the locations where they're required, adding exceptions and then changing them every three years, addressing existing wiring as well as extending the wiring, and allowing for devices other than circuit breakers.

The option of using devices other than circuit breakers is no longer written as an exception, but that doesn't mean that it became any easier to use them. A total of six different options now exist for AFCI protection, including various combinations of circuit breakers and receptacles. Obviously option one is the easiest to follow (and understand), but depending on the prices of the various devices now on the market, it may not be the most economical.

Kitchens and laundry areas have been added to the locations where AFCIs are required. Because a combination AFCI trips on both parallel and series arcs, this seems to make sense. The series arcs that are detected by an AFCI are only those that exceed 5A of current. Because the amount of current in a series arc is limited by the load, few circuits include equipment that will experience this kind of load. Refrigerators and washing machines are some of the first pieces of 120V equipment that come to mind when thinking of energy-consuming appliances, yet they weren't required to be protected until now.

The *NEC* now requires AFCI protection for devices as well as outlets. This probably won't have any real impact, but there've been questions about whether or not a switch that's located in an area requiring AFCIs needs to have the protection if its load is located in an area that doesn't require protection (consider a bathroom light whose switch is in the hallway next to the door, which was a common practice in the 1950s). Most people agree that a switch box isn't an outlet, because the switch doesn't meet the definition of "outlet" as it relates to the "current is taken" portion of the definition. This change removes that issue, and will force *Code* geeks to find another point to argue about.

Metal wireways and auxiliary gutters have been added to exceptions one and three, although it's very doubtful that you'll ever see a house with an auxiliary gutter.

MC Cable is now allowed to be used with concrete encasement as an option for using an AFCI device. It's probably not often that someone will go to the expense of using a concrete-encased wiring method just to eliminate having to use a breaker, as it hardly seems cost effective, but from a safety perspective there's no real reason it shouldn't be allowed

(B) Branch-Circuit Extensions or Modifications—Dwelling Units. Where branch-circuit wiring is modified, replaced, or extended in any of the areas specified in 210.12(A), the branch circuit must be protected by:

(1) A listed combination AFCI located at the origin of the branch circuit; or

(2) A listed outlet branch circuit AFCI located at the first receptacle outlet of the existing branch circuit.

Ex: AFCI protection isn't required for extensions less than 6 ft long, as long as there are no outlets or devices added.

ANALYSIS: The requirement for adding AFCI protection to existing branch circuits that are extended received a bit of relief. If outlets or devices are being added as part of the extension of the circuit, AFCI protection is still required. If a person is doing a panel change on an older house, it's not uncommon for the existing conductors to be a little too short when it's time to put the new panel in. In these instances the electrician can add up to six feet of conductor length (to each circuit) and not have to burden the homeowner with a few hundred dollars of AFCI breakers.

(C) Dormitory Units. All 120V, single phase, 15A and 20A branch circuits supplying outlets installed in dormitory unit bedrooms, living rooms, hallways, closets, and similar rooms must be AFCI protected by one of the methods discussed in 210.12(A)(1) through (6).

ANALYSIS: New to this edition of the *Code* is subsection (C), which requires AFCI protection for dormitories. Dormitories aren't defined in the *NEC*, but if you look up the definition in a dictionary, you will find that is a residence for students. Dormitories have more or less the same hazards as a dwelling unit, so the *Code*-Making Panel decided to give college kids the same protection that they had growing up at home.

210.17 Electric Vehicle Branch Circuit

A new section has been added for electric vehicle charging circuits.

210.17 Electric Vehicle Branch Circuit. Electric vehicle charging outlets must be supplied by a circuit that has no other outlets. Figure 210–14

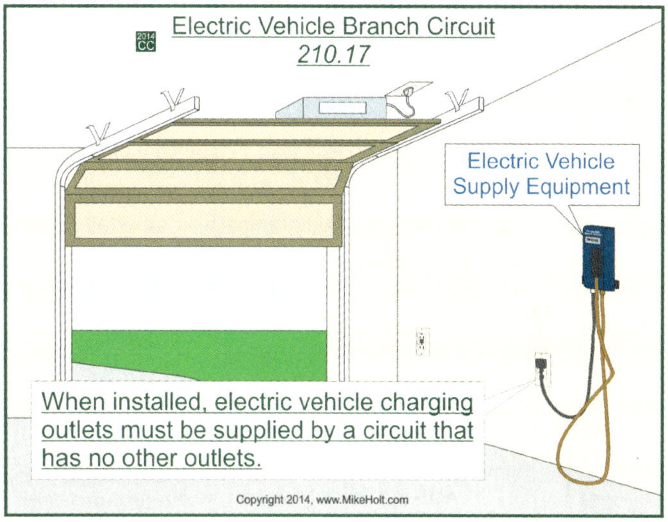

Figure 210–14

Note: See 625.2 for the definition of "Electrical Vehicle."

ANALYSIS: This change requires that a circuit for electric vehicle charging systems must serve no other outlets. There was no technical substantiation whatsoever for this requirement. According to the Report on Proposals, which details all of the proposals submitted to the *NEC Code*-Making Panels, "The panel has added a provision to require a separate branch circuit when outlets are installed for the purposes of charging an electric vehicle." There was no data submitted showing any real-world problems with these systems, but the change passed regardless. Perhaps the reason was because this type of equipment will be a continuous load, but there's no evidence that this is the reason. There's also a new Information Note that tells the *Code* user that these systems are defined in 625.2.

210.19 Conductor Sizing

The section regarding branch-circuit conductor sizing has been simplified.

Part II. Branch-Circuit Ratings

210.19 Conductor Sizing.

(A) Branch Circuits.

(1) General. Branch-circuit conductors must have an ampacity of not less than the maximum load to be served. The conductor must be the larger of (a) or (b).

(a) Conductors must be sized no less than 125 percent of the continuous loads, plus 100 percent of the noncontinuous loads, based on the terminal temperature rating ampacities as listed in Table 310.15(B)(16). **Figure 210–15**

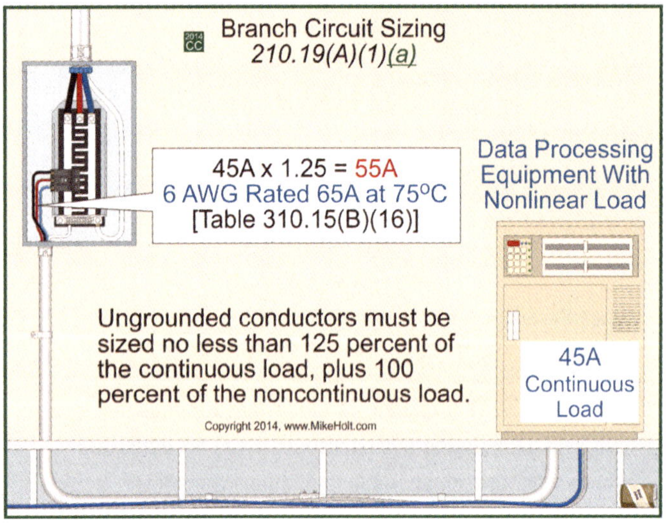

Figure 210–15

(b) Conductors must be sized to the maximum load to be served after the application of any adjustment or correction factors. **Figure 210–16**

Ex 1: If the assembly and the overcurrent device are both listed for operation at 100 percent of its rating, the conductors can be sized at 100 percent of the continuous load.

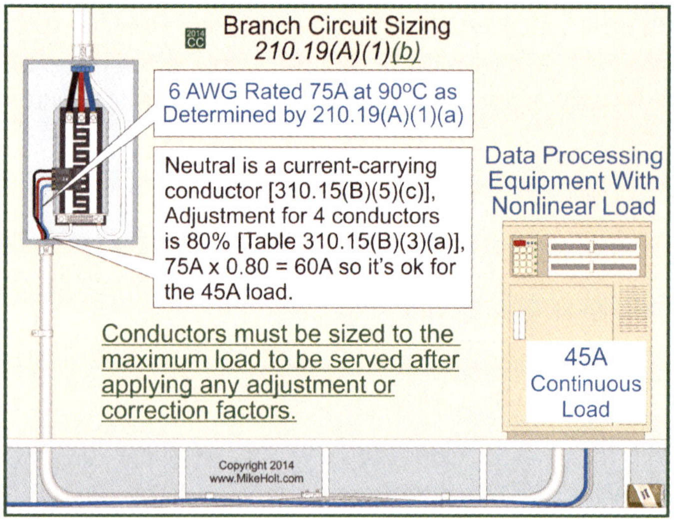

Figure 210–16

Author's Comments:

- Equipment suitable for 100 percent continuous loading is rarely available in ratings under 400A.
- See the definition of "Continuous Load" in Article 100.
- See 210.20 for the sizing requirements for the branch-circuit overcurrent device for continuous and noncontinuous loads.

Question: *What size branch-circuit conductors are required for a 4-wire circuit of a 45A nonlinear continuous load, if the equipment terminals are rated 75°C?*

(a) 10 AWG (b) 8 AWG (c) 6 AWG (d) 4 AWG

Answer: *(c) 6 AWG*

Since the load is 45A continuous, the conductors must be sized to have an ampacity of not less than 56A (45A x 1.25). According to the 75°C column of Table 310.15(B)(16), a 6 AWG conductor is suitable, because it has an ampere rating of 65A at 75°C. This satisfies the portion of the calculation discussed in 210.19(A)(1)(a).

For 210.19(A)(1)(b), we have to address ambient temperature and conductor bundling.

Because the neutral in this example is considered a current-carrying conductor [310.15(B)(5)(c)], there are four current-carrying conductors. Table 310.15(B)(3)(a) requires an adjustment factor of 80% for this example.

6 AWG rated 75A at 90°C x 0.80 = 60A after adjustment factors which is adequate for the 45A load, **Figure 210–17.** *If we had selected an 8 AWG rated 55A at 90°C, based on the 45A load, it would be too small for the load after applying the adjustment factor (55A x 0.80 = 44A).*

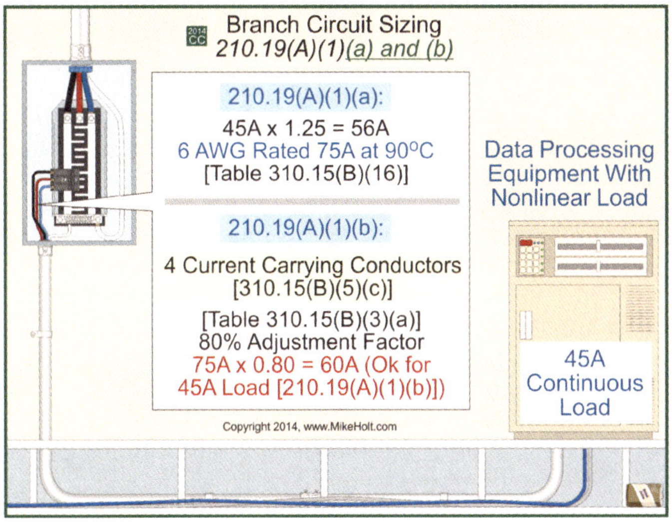

Figure 210–17

ANALYSIS: The hardest thing to understand in the entire *Code* book might be how to properly size a conductor, and it seems that every time you get it all figured out you read this section again and realize you're wrong. This change should go a long way toward clearing up the issue. Refer to the example above for further information.

210.22 Permissible Loads, Individual Branch Circuits

A new section has been created to deal with individual branch circuits.

210.22 Permissible Loads, Individual Branch Circuits. An individual branch circuit is permitted to supply any load that doesn't exceed the ampere rating of the branch-circuit. **Figure 210–18**

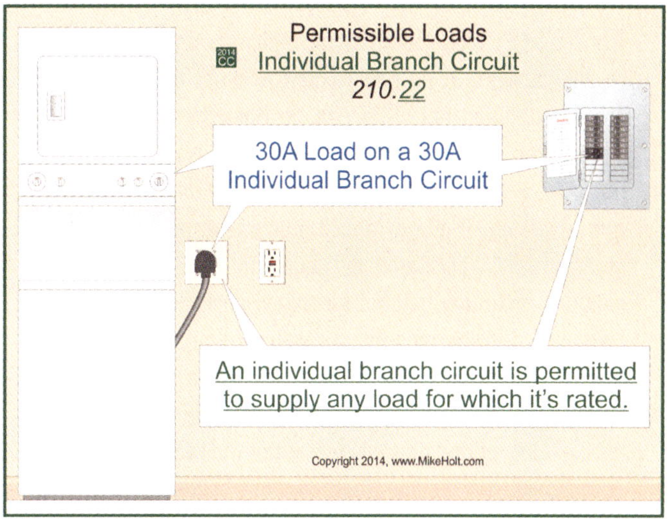

Figure 210–18

ANALYSIS: This text was cut from 210.23 and pasted here. 210.23 dealt with two different types of circuits, but it wasn't clear at first glance. With this new section the ratings of branch circuits should be easier to find, as you now look here for individual circuits and in 210.23 for multioutlet branch circuits.

210.50 General

An Informational Note was added to refer to a new Annex.

Part III. Required Outlets

210.50 General. Receptacle outlets must be installed in accordance with 210.52 through 210.64.

Note: See Annex J for information regarding ADA accessibility design.

Author's Comment: Many places don't use the *Americans with Disabilities Act Accessibility Guidelines* (ADAAG); they use ICC A117.1 *Accessible and Usable Buildings and Facilities.* These documents are very similar, and both are ways of satisfying the Americans with Disabilities Act (ADA).

ANALYSIS: Most commercial buildings and multifamily dwellings need to be constructed to meet the Americans with Disabilities Act. This can be done by following the *Americans with Disabilities Act Accessibility Guidelines* (ADAAG), or the ICC A117.1 *Accessible and Usable Buildings and Facilities*. Both of these documents contain information that's pertinent to electrical installations. This includes mounting heights for things such as receptacles, switches, and thermostats, as well as limitations on protruding objects like wall sconce luminaires. Annex J was added to let *Code* users know some of these requirements. It's certainly not an all-inclusive list of the requirements for accessibility for disabled persons, but it does include the most common ones about which electricians and electrical engineers need to know.

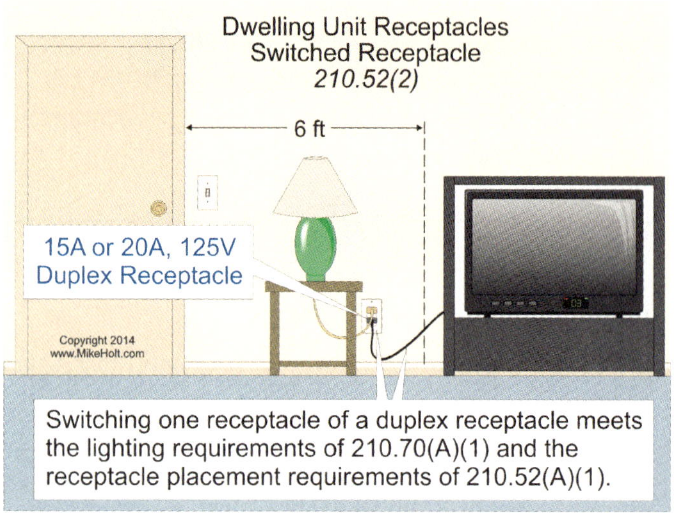

Figure 210–19

210.52 Dwelling Unit Receptacle Outlet Requirements

Many changes, as usual, have been made to the rules on dwelling unit receptacles.

210.52 Dwelling Unit Receptacle Outlet Requirements. This section provides requirements for 15A and 20A, 125V receptacle outlets. The receptacles required by this section are in addition to any receptacle that's:

(1) Part of a luminaire or appliance,

(2) Controlled by a wall switch in accordance with 210.70(A)(1), Ex 1. Figure 210–19

(3) Located within cabinets or cupboards, or

(4) Located more than 5½ ft above the floor.

(D) Dwelling Unit Bathroom Receptacles. In dwelling units, not less than one 15A or 20A, 125V receptacle outlet must be installed within 3 ft from the outside edge of each bathroom basin, Figure 210–20. The receptacle outlet must be located on a wall or partition adjacent to the basin counter surface, or on the side or face of the basin cabinet. In no case can the receptacle be located more than 12 in. below the top of the basin. Figure 210–21

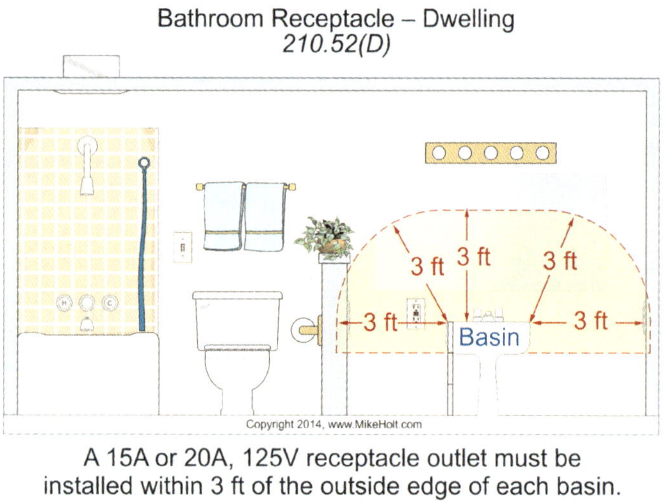

Figure 210–20

Receptacle outlet assemblies listed for the application can be installed in countertops.

Note: Receptacles must not be installed in a face-up position in countertops or similar work surface areas [406.5(E)].

Author's Comments:

- One receptacle outlet can be located between two basins to meet this requirement, but only if it's located within 3 ft of the outside edge of each basin. Figure 210–22
- The bathroom receptacles must be GFCI protected [210.8(A)(1)].

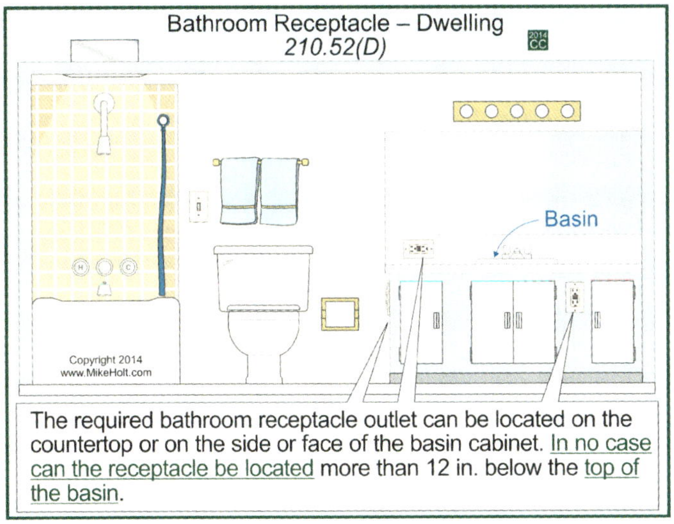

Figure 210–21

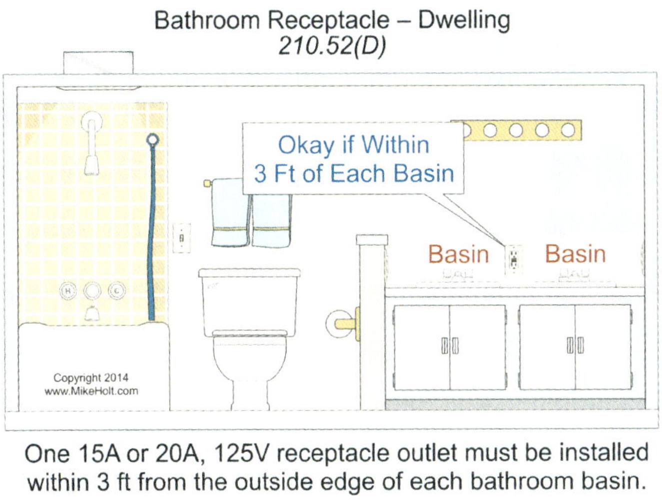

Figure 210–22

ANALYSIS: A grammatical error in the 2011 *NEC* required that the bathroom receptacle be installed within 12 in. of the countertop, but only if the receptacle was mounted on the cabinet. If the receptacle was mounted on an adjacent wall, it could be mounted an inch above the floor and the result would be a compliant installation. Obviously that wasn't the intent of the *Code* rule, so this change closes that loophole.

(E) Dwelling Unit Outdoor Receptacles. Outdoor receptacles must comply with the following:

Note: See 210.8(A)(3).

(1) One- and Two-Family Dwellings. Two GFCI-protected 15A or 20A, 125V receptacle outlets that are readily accessible from grade must be installed outdoors for each dwelling unit, one at the front and one at the back, no more than 6½ ft above grade. Figure 210–23

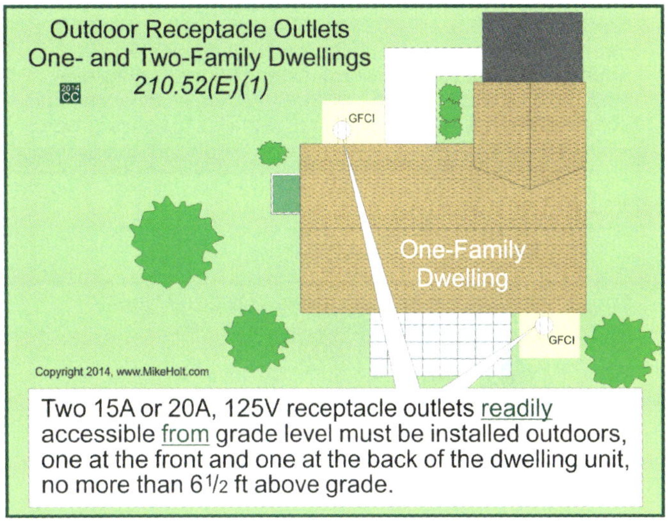

Figure 210–23

(2) Multifamily Dwelling. Each dwelling unit of a multifamily dwelling that has an individual entrance at grade level must have at least one GFCI-protected 15A or 20A, 125V receptacle outlet readily accessible from grade located not more than 6½ ft above grade. Figure 210–24

(3) Balconies, Decks, and Porches. At least one 15A or 20A, 125V receptacle outlet must be installed not more than 6½ ft above any balcony, deck, or porch surface that's attached to, and accessible from, the inside of a dwelling unit. The receptacle must be accessible from the deck, balcony, or porch surface. Figure 210–25

Author's Comment: These receptacles must be GFCI protected [210.8(A)(3)].

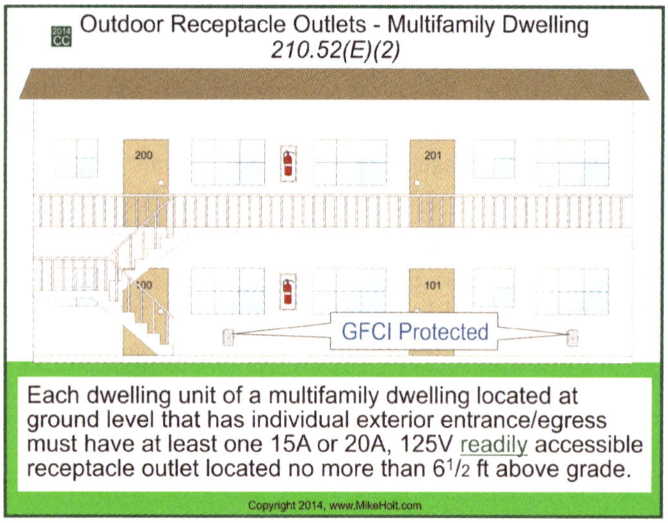

Figure 210–24

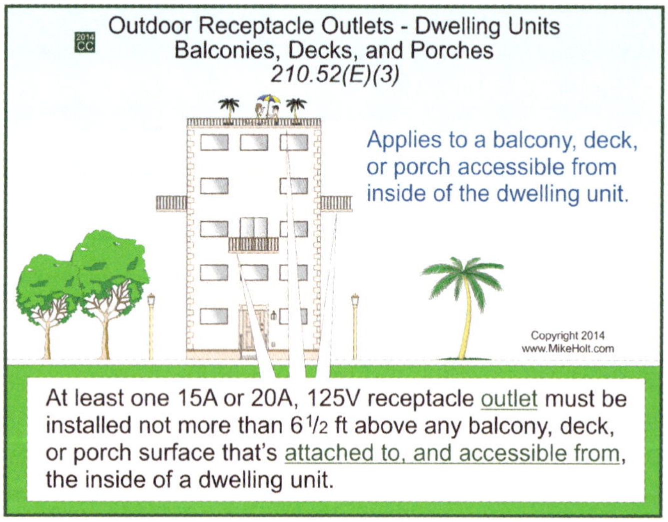

Figure 210–25

ANALYSIS: 210.52(E) was extensively revised for the 2008 *NEC* edition, and again for 2011. This edition of the *Code* fixes some mistakes that were made during that process. With the change to items (1) and (2) a receptacle installed on a small deck of a dwelling can now serve as the required outdoor receptacle, without having to install another receptacle that's not on the deck. This applies only if the receptacle is readily accessible from grade, meaning that a person doesn't have to use a ladder to reach it and doesn't have to climb over or remove obstacles either.

Item (3) was changed to provide an allowance for very small decks and balconies. The 2011 edition of the *NEC* required that a receptacle for a deck or balcony be installed within the physical perimeter of the deck or balcony. Some balconies are so small that they're basically unusable and are for aesthetics only. These balconies have a guardrail surrounding them that's no bigger than the balcony itself, and the balcony is no bigger than the door that serves it (these are often called "Juliet balconies," since the only real use for them is for Juliet to stand on while listening to Romeo speak/sing to her from below). The only ways that *Code* compliance could be achieved for these balconies was to install a floor outlet (bad idea for outdoor applications) or to have a box above the door and dangle a pendant cord with a receptacle from it! At first glance, it seems that requiring a receptacle for these balconies is rather silly, but often times they're covered with decorative lighting during holiday seasons and the *NEC* doesn't want people powering these lights from a receptacle indoors, forcing a cord to be run through the doorway. The required receptacle can now be installed next to the balcony and still be compliant.

(G) Dwelling Unit Garage, Basement, and Accessory Building Receptacles. For single family dwellings, at least one receptacle must be installed in accordance with (1) through (3). The receptacle must be in addition to any receptacles supplied for specific equipment.

(1) Garages. A 15A or 20A, 125V receptacle is required in each attached garage and in each detached garage with electric power. The branch circuit supplying this receptacle(s) must not supply outlets outside of the garage. At least one receptacle must be provided for each car space. Figure 210–26

Author's Comment: The required garage receptacle circuit can't supply other loads commonly seen on this circuit, such as the exterior lights and receptacles for the house.

(2) Accessory Buildings. A 15A or 20A, 125V receptacle is required in each accessory building with electric power. Figure 210–27

Author's Comment: GFCI protection is required for all 15A or 20A, 125V receptacles installed in unfinished basements [210.8(A)(5)], garages, and accessory buildings [210.8(A)(2)] of dwelling units.

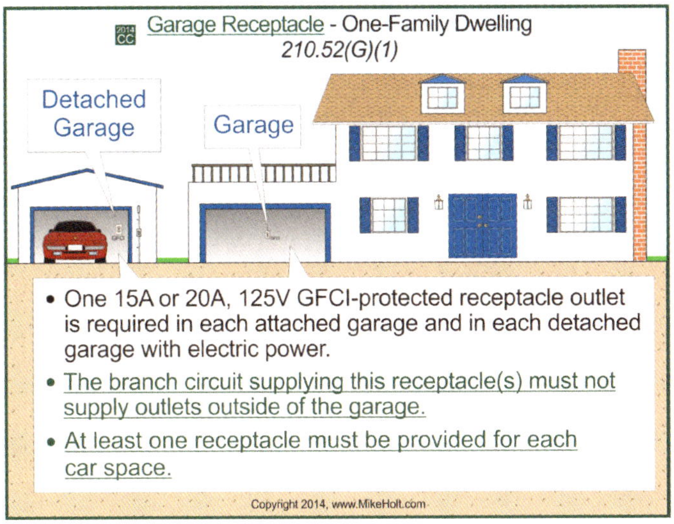

Figure 210–26

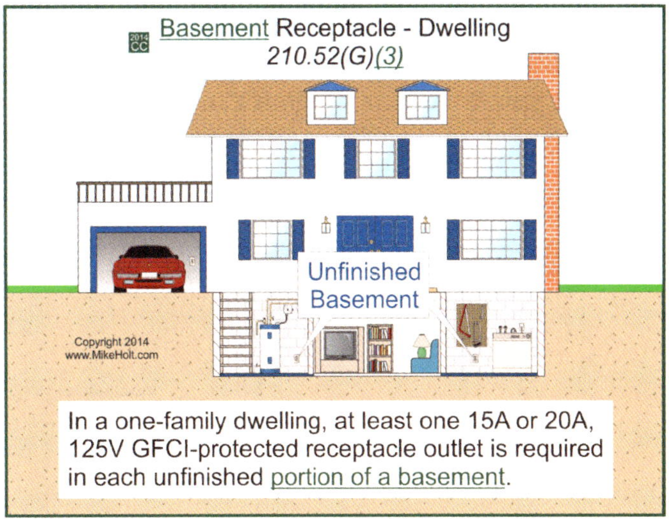

Figure 210–28

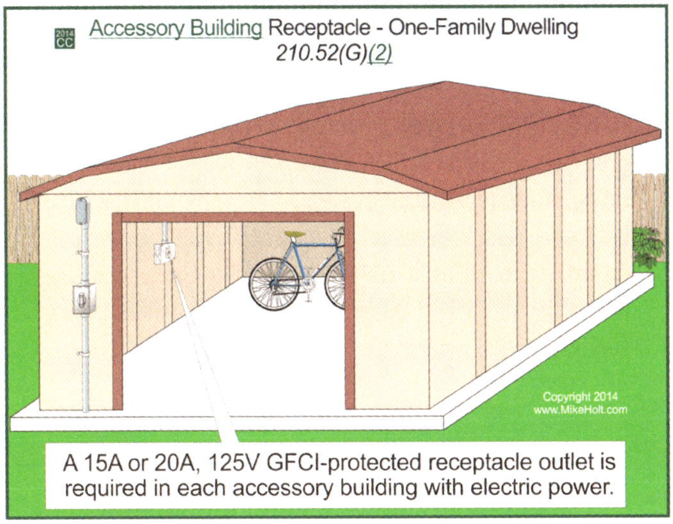

Figure 210–27

(3) Basements. Each unfinished portion of a basement must. have a 15A or 20A, 125V receptacle outlet installed. Figure 210–28

Author's Comments:

- One 15A or 20A, 125V receptacle outlet is required in a dwelling unit basement even if no portion has been finished into a habitable room.
- The purpose of this requirement is to prevent an extension cord from a non-GFCI-protected receptacle from being used to supply power to loads in the unfinished portion of the basement.

ANALYSIS: This section was revised to add language to the opening statement of (G) that states that the required receptacle for these areas be in addition to any receptacle installed for a specific piece of equipment. By placing the language here it's clear that the provision applies to items (1) through (3).

Item (1) was revised to require that the garage receptacle(s) circuit serve no other loads beyond the garage. This is a fairly substantial change, because many dwellings use the "house" GFCI circuit to provide power for the outdoor receptacles, garage, and unfinished basement. This proposal was accepted based on the argument that this receptacle can be used for electric vehicle charging and therefore should be restricted. This would make sense, but the opening statement of (G) mandates that the required garage receptacle can't be used for a specific piece of equipment (like a vehicle charger). The new 210.17 also covers electric vehicle charging circuits, and requires that they be a dedicated circuit. With these changes, it seems that garages will now have a lot of ampacity dedicated to them. Additionally, the *Code* requires a receptacle for each "car space" in a garage, although this doesn't seem like a very clear requirement. If a house has a two-car garage, it seems that a duplex receptacle installed anywhere in the garage would meet this requirement, since a duplex contains two receptacles.

(I) Foyer Receptacles. Foyers that aren't part of a hallway [210.52(H)] having an area greater than 60 sq ft must have a receptacle located on any wall space 3 ft or more in width and unbroken by doorways, windows next to doors that extend to the floor, and similar openings. Figure 210–29

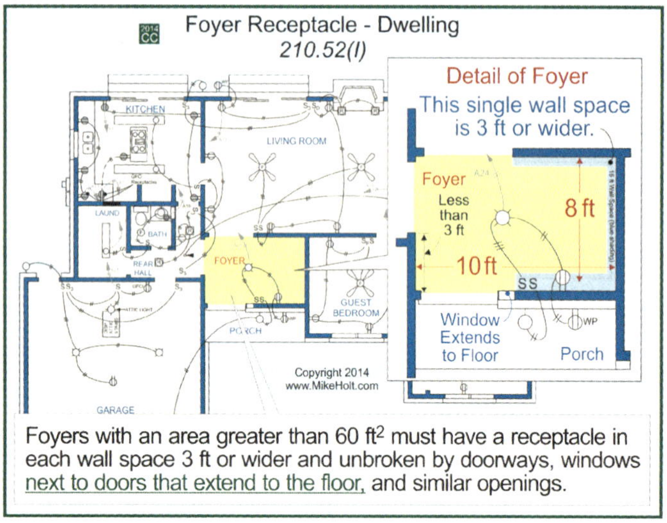

Figure 210–29

ANALYSIS: When this rule was added in 2011 it was clear that side lights (tall windows next to doors) weren't to be included in the wall space measurement. The literal text, however, only omitted these side lights if they extended from the floor to the ceiling. Even the most formal doorways typically don't have sidelights that literally extend to the ceiling (they end at the top of the door). This change recognizes that fact by removing the language regarding the ceiling.

210.62 Show Windows

The voltage and current rating of the required show window receptacle(s) is now specified.

210.62 Show Windows. At least one 125V, 15A or 20A receptacle outlet must be installed within 18 in. of the top of a show window for each 12 linear feet or major fraction thereof measured horizontally at its maximum width. Figure 210–30

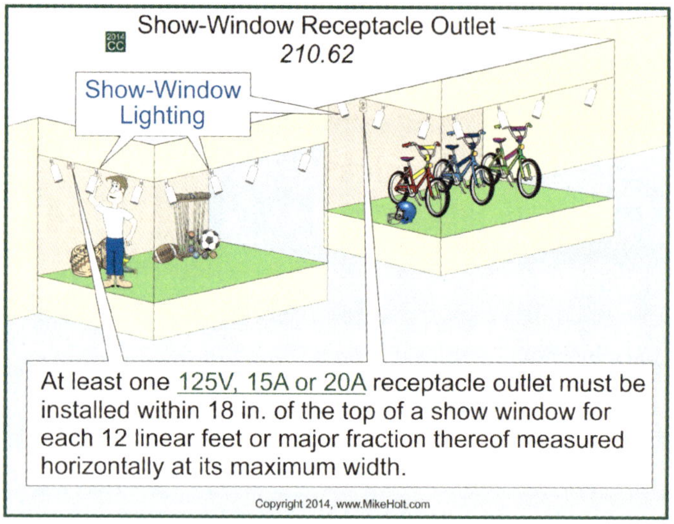

Figure 210–30

Author's Comment: See the definition of "Show Window" in Article 100.

ANALYSIS: In order to provide consistency with other *Code* requirements in this article, the voltage and current rating of the receptacle(s) required for show windows has been specified. In previous editions of the *NEC*, any obscure receptacle, such as a 208V, 50A, locking type receptacle, would have satisfied this requirement, but wouldn't have served much of a purpose.

210.64 Electrical Service Areas

A new requirement for a receptacle near the service disconnect has been added.

210.64 Electrical Service Areas. At least one 15A or 20A, 125V receptacle outlet must be installed within 50 ft of the electrical service equipment. Figures 210–31 and 210–32

Ex: The receptacle outlet isn't required for one- and two-family dwellings.

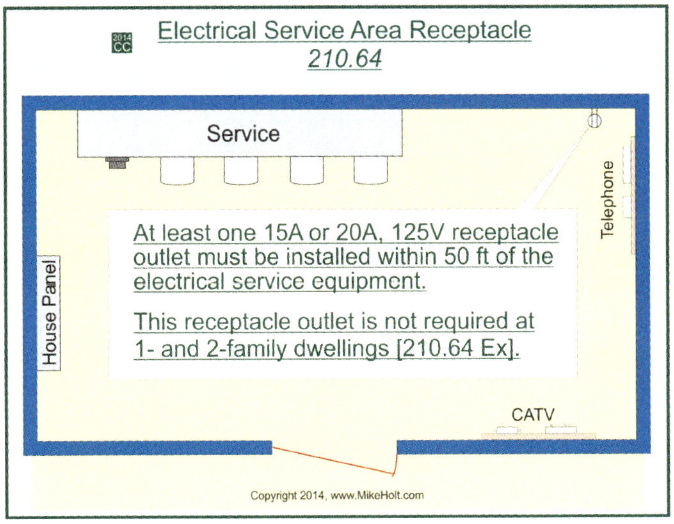

Figure 210–31

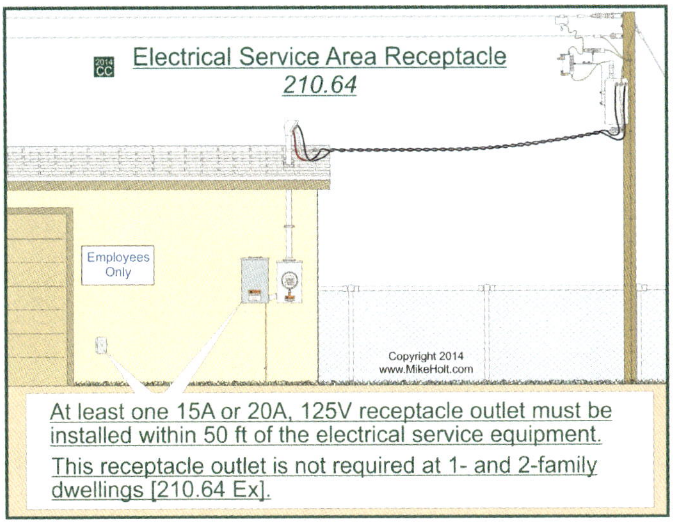

Figure 210–32

ANALYSIS: The *Code* has long required a receptacle outlet near heating, air-conditioning, and refrigeration equipment for servicing such equipment [210.63], but has never required one near electrical service equipment. Adding a requirement for a receptacle near the service equipment now gives service personnel a means to connect not only electric hand tools, but data acquisition equipment as well, such as a meter that records power usage.

Notes

ARTICLE 215 FEEDERS

Introduction to Article 215—Feeders

Article 215 covers the rules for the installation and ampacity of feeders. The requirements for feeders have some similarities to those for branch circuits, but in some ways, feeders bear a resemblance to service conductors. It's important to understand the distinct differences between these three types of circuits in order to correctly apply the *Code* requirements.

Feeders are the conductors between the service equipment, the separately derived system, or other supply source, and the final branch-circuit overcurrent device. Conductors past the final overcurrent device protecting the circuit and the outlet are branch-circuit conductors and fall within the scope of Article 210 [Article 100 Definitions].

Service conductors are the conductors from the service point of the electric utility to the service disconnecting means [Article 100 Definition]. If there's no serving utility, and the electrical power is derived from a generator or other on-site power source, then the conductors from the supply source are defined as feeders and there are no service conductors.

It's easy to be confused between feeder, branch circuit, and service conductors, so it's important to evaluate each installation carefully using the Article 100 Definitions to be sure the correct *NEC* rules are followed.

215.2 Minimum Rating

The procedure used for feeder circuit sizing has been clarified, and the text about dwellings and mobile homes has been removed.

215.2 Minimum Rating.

(A) Feeder Conductor Size.

(1) General. Feeders must be sized to carry the calculated load from Parts III, IV, and V of Article 220. The feeder conductors must be the larger of (a) or (b):

(a) The minimum feeder conductor ampacity must be no less than 125 percent of the continuous load, plus 100 percent of the noncontinuous load, based on the terminal temperature rating ampacities as listed in Table 310.15(B)(16) [110.14(C)(1)]. Figure 215–1

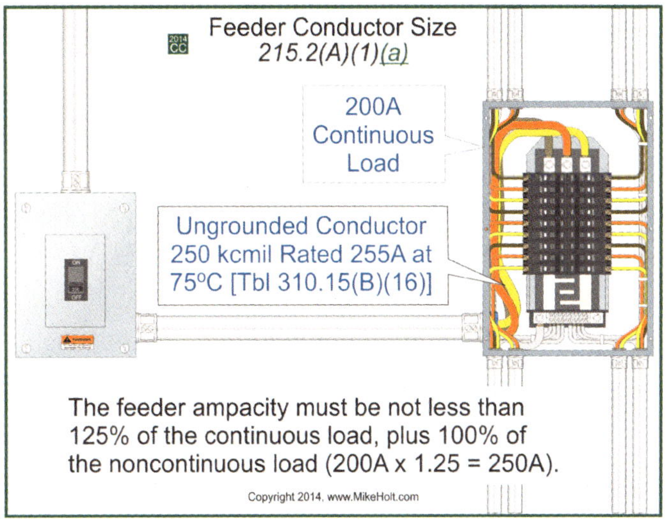

Figure 215–1

(b) The feeder ampacity must be not less than the maximum load to be served after the application of any adjustment or correction factors. Figure 215–2

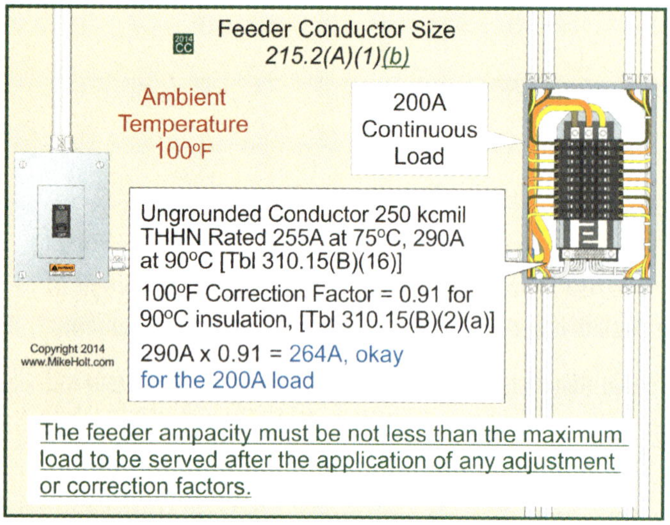

Figure 215–2

Author's Comment: See 215.3 for the feeder overcurrent device sizing requirements for continuous and noncontinuous loads.

Note 2: To provide reasonable efficiency of operation of electrical equipment, feeder conductors should be sized to prevent a voltage drop not to exceed 3 percent. In addition, the maximum total voltage drop on both feeders and branch circuits shouldn't exceed 5 percent.

Note 3: See 210.19(A), Note 4, for voltage drop for branch circuits.

Ex 1: If the assembly and the overcurrent device are both listed for operation at 100 percent of their rating, the conductors can be sized at 100 percent of the continuous load.

Author's Comment: Equipment suitable for 100 percent continuous loading is rarely available in ratings under 400A.

Ex 2: Neutral conductors can be sized at 100 percent of the continuous and noncontinuous load.

Question: *What size feeder conductors are required for a 200A continuous load if the terminals are rated 75°C?* Figure 215–3

(a) 2/0 AWG ungrounded conductors and a 1/0 AWG neutral conductor

(b) 3/0 AWG ungrounded conductors and a 1/0 AWG neutral conductor

(c) 4/0 AWG ungrounded conductors and a 1/0 AWG neutral conductor

(d) 250 kcmil ungrounded conductors and a 3/0 AWG neutral conductor

Answer: *(d) 250 kcmil AWG ungrounded conductors and a 3/0 AWG neutral conductor*

Since the load is 200A continuous, the feeder conductors must have an ampacity of not less than 250A (200A x 1.25). The neutral conductor is sized to the 200A continuous load according to the 75°C column of Table 310.15(B)(16). According to the 75°C column of Table 310.15(B)(16), 250 kcmil has an ampacity of 255A, and 3/0 has an ampacity of 200A.

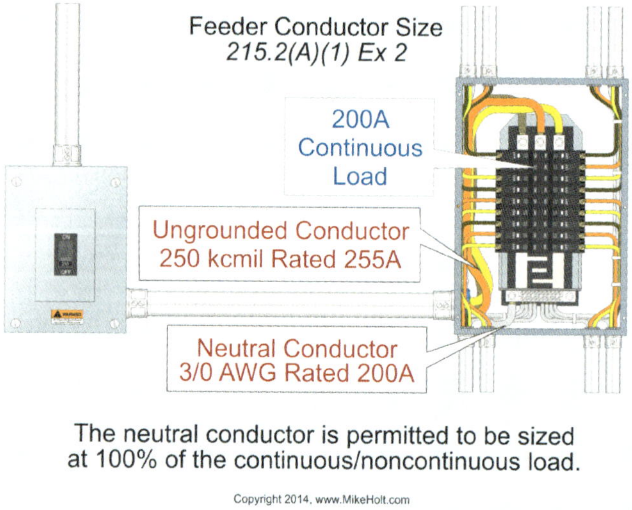

Figure 215–3

(2) Neutral Conductor Size. The feeder neutral conductor must be sized to carry the maximum unbalanced load in accordance with 220.61, and must not be smaller than the size listed in 250.122, based on the rating of the feeder overcurrent device. The sizing requirements of 250.122(F) for parallel conductors don't apply.

Question: *What size neutral conductor is required for a feeder consisting of 250 kcmil ungrounded conductors and one neutral conductor protected by a 250A overcurrent device, where the unbalanced load is only 50A, with 75°C terminals?* **Figure 215–4**

(a) 6 AWG *(b) 4 AWG* *(c) 1/0 AWG* *(d) 3/0 AWG*

Answer: *(b) 4 AWG [based on Table 250.122]*

Table 310.15(B)(16) and 220.61 permit an 8 AWG neutral conductor, rated 50A at 75°C to carry the 50A unbalanced load, but the neutral conductor isn't permitted to be smaller than 4 AWG, as listed in Table 250.122, based on the 250A overcurrent device.

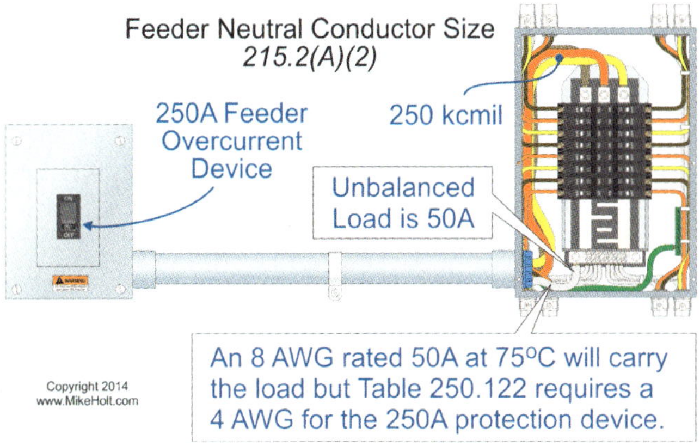

The size of the neutral conductor must carry the maximum unbalanced load and not be smaller than required by 250.122, based on the rating of the feeder overcurrent device.

Figure 215–4

(3) Ampacity Relative to Service Conductors. The feeder conductor ampacity must not be less than that of the service conductors where the feeder conductors carry the total load supplied by service conductors with an ampacity of 55A or less.

ANALYSIS: Sizing circuit conductors is, without question, one of the most difficult things to deal with in the *NEC*. I have personally been involved in e-mail discussions with some of the top *Code* experts in the country that have been several pages long, with the end result of nobody agreeing on how to size a conductor! This change clarifies the procedure by affirming that the continuous vs. noncontinuous issue (and the terminal ratings) are dealt with in their own calculations, and any ampacity or correction factors (such as the number of current-carrying conductors in a raceway) are dealt with in a separate calculation. The more restrictive (bigger conductor) is then used for the final conductor size.

Additionally, the text regarding conductor sizing for dwellings and mobile homes has been removed from this section, as it's dealt with adequately in Article 310.

Notes

ARTICLE 220 BRANCH-CIRCUIT, FEEDER, AND SERVICE CALCULATIONS

Introduction to Article 220—Branch-Circuit, Feeder, and Service Calculations

This five-part article focuses on the requirements for calculating the minimum size of branch circuit, feeder, and service conductors.

Part I describes the layout of Article 220 and provides a table of where other types of load calculations can be found in the *NEC*. Part II provides requirements for branch-circuit calculations and for specific types of branch circuits. Part III covers the requirements for feeder and service calculations, using what's commonly called the "standard method of calculation." Part IV provides optional calculations that can be used in place of the standard calculations provided in Parts II and III—if your installation meets certain requirements. Farm Load Calculations are discussed in Part V of the article.

In many cases, either the standard method (Part III) or the optional method (Part IV) can be used; however, these two methods don't yield identical results. In fact, sometimes these two answers may be diverse enough to call for different service sizes. There's nothing to say that either answer is right or wrong. If taking an exam, read the instructions carefully to be sure which method the test wants you to use. As you work through Article 220, be sure to study the illustrations to help you fully understand it. Also be sure to review the examples in Annex D of the *NEC* to provide more practice with these calculations.

220.3 Application of Other Articles

This section has been revised to remind *Code* users that Article 625 contains load calculation information for electric vehicles.

Part I. General

220.3 Application of Other Articles. Other articles contain calculations that are in addition to, or modify, those contained within Article 220. Take a moment to review the following additional calculation requirements found in these sections:

- Air-Conditioning and Refrigeration Equipment, 440.6, 440.21, 440.22, 440.31, 440.32, and 440.62
- Appliances, 422.10 and 422.11
- Branch Circuits, 210.19 and 210.20(A)
- Computers (Data Processing Equipment), 645.4 and 645.5(A)
- Conductors, 310.15
- Electric Vehicle Charging Systems, 625.14
- Feeders, 215.2(B) and 215.3
- Fire Pumps, 695.7
- Fixed Electric Space-Heating Equipment, 424.3(B)
- Marinas, 555.12, 555.19(A)(4), and 555.19(B)
- Mobile Homes and Manufactured Homes, 550.12 and 550.18
- Motors, 430.6(A), 430.22, 430.24, 430.52, and 430.62
- Overcurrent Protection, 240.4 and 240.15
- Refrigeration (Hermetic), 440.6 and Part IV of Article 440
- Recreational Vehicle Parks, 551.73(A)
- Electronic Equipment, 647.4(D)
- Services, 230.42(A) and 230.79
- Signs, 600.5
- Transformers, 450.3

ANALYSIS: Electric vehicle chargers have been added to table 220.3. Electric vehicle chargers are considered continuous loads in accordance with 625.14. Due to this, calculations for conductor sizes and overcurrent devices must use 125% of the actual load [210.19, 210.20, 215.2, and 215.3]. 220.3 provides the *Code* user with a nice reference to other articles that have calculation requirements, so it's worth ensuring that it's kept up to date. With this change that goal is met.

220.12 General Lighting

A new exception to the lighting load calculations has been made to more closely reflect reality.

Part II. Branch-Circuit Load Calculations

220.12 General Lighting. The general lighting load specified in Table 220.12 must be calculated from the outside dimensions of the building or area involved. Figure 220–1

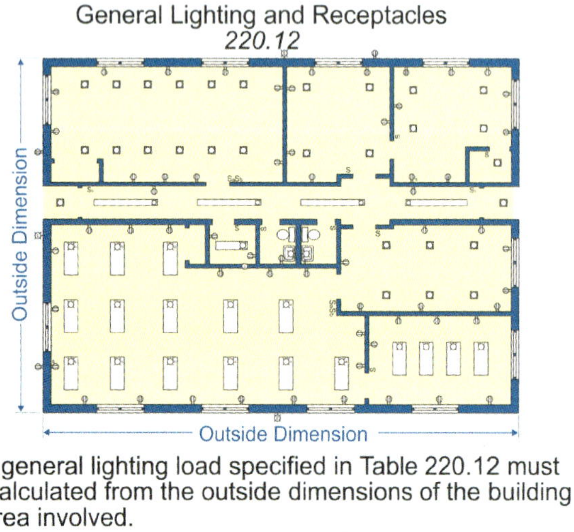

Figure 220–1

Table 220.12 General Lighting VA per Square Foot

Occupancy	VA/Sq. Ft
Armories and auditoriums	1
Assembly halls and auditoriums	1
Banks	3½[b]
Barber shops and beauty parlors	3
Churches	1
Clubs	2
Courtrooms	2
Dwelling units	3[a]
Garages—commercial (storage)	½
Halls, corridors, closets, stairways	½
Hospitals	2
Hotels and motels without cooking facilities	2
Industrial commercial (loft buildings)	2
Lodge rooms	1½
Office buildings	3½[b]
Restaurants	2
Schools	3
Storage spaces	¼
Stores	3
Warehouses (storage)	¼

Table Note a: *The VA load for general-use receptacles, bathroom receptacles [220.14(J)(1) and 210.11(C)(3)], outside receptacles, as well as garage, basement receptacles [220.14(J)(2), 210.52(E) and (G)], and lighting outlets [220.14(J)(3), 210.70(A) and (B)] in a dwelling unit are included in the 3 VA per-square-foot general lighting [220.14(J)].*

Table Note b: *The receptacle calculated load for banks and office buildings is the largest calculation of either (1) or (2) [220.14(K)].*

Ex: Where the adopted energy code requires a smaller value for lighting loads, the energy code values can be used if the following requirements are met:

(1) A power monitoring system that provides continuous information on the lighting load of the building must be installed.

(2) The power monitoring system must have an alarm that alerts the building owner or manager if the lighting load exceeds the values set by the energy code.

(3) The lighting load demand factors in 220.42 can't be used.

ANALYSIS: Office buildings require a calculation of 3½ VA per square foot, despite the fact that many energy codes don't allow more than 1½ VA to be connected. With the *NEC* calculation being twice as much as energy codes allow, something has to give eventually. There've been many proposals to the *NEC* to change this section to reflect energy code requirements, but they've all been soundly rejected. This proposal stands out as it requires a monitoring system to be installed that warns the building owner or manager if the lighting load is exceeding the value that was allowed for with this exception. Members of the *Code*-Making Panel (CMP 2) had very differing views on this change. Some said this change shouldn't require any sort of monitoring at all, while others said the change doesn't take into account task lighting, such as desk lamps, that are often used when energy codes are very restrictive. It should be interesting to see how this evolves over the next few years, as this is the first time an exception like this has been introduced. Perhaps the *NEC* will include more exceptions like this once there's a track record of its effectiveness.

220.14 Other Loads—All Occupancies

The odds of you getting an obscure test question wrong have been reduced.

220.14 Other Loads—All Occupancies. The minimum VA load for each outlet must comply with (A) through (L).

(B) Electric Dryers and Electric Cooking Appliances in Dwelling Units **and Household Cooking Appliances used in Instructional Programs.** The branch-circuit VA load for household electric dryers must comply with 220.54, and household electric ranges and other cooking appliances must comply with 220.55.

ANALYSIS: Have you ever read Note 5 to Table 220.55? Few have (it says that household cooking appliances in instructional programs can use the table), and that's why the title of this section has been changed. This change doesn't result in any real-world ramifications, but it does make the *Code* a bit easier to use, and that's almost always worth pursuing.

ARTICLE 225 OUTSIDE BRANCH CIRCUITS AND FEEDERS

Introduction to Article 225—Outside Branch Circuits and Feeders

This article covers the installation requirements for equipment, including branch circuit and feeder conductors (overhead and underground), located outdoors on or between buildings, poles, and other structures on the premises. Conductors installed outdoors can serve many purposes such as area lighting, power for outdoor equipment, or providing power to a separate building or structure. It's important to remember that the power supply for buildings or structures isn't always a service conductor, but in many cases may be feeders or branch-circuit conductors originating in another building. Be careful not to assume that the conductors supplying power to a building are service conductors until you've identified where the utility service point is and reviewed the Article 100 Definitions for feeders, branch circuits, and service conductors. If they're service conductors, use Article 230. For outside branch-circuit and feeder conductors, whatever they feed, use this article.

Table 225.3 shows other articles that may furnish additional requirements, then Part I of Article 225 goes on to address installation methods intended to provide a secure installation of outside conductors while providing sufficient conductor size, support, attachment means, and maintaining safe clearances.

Part II of this article limits the number of supplies (branch circuits or feeders) permitted to a building or structure and provides rules regarding disconnects for them. These rules include the disconnect rating, construction characteristics, labeling, and where to locate the disconnecting means and the grouping of multiple disconnects.

Outside branch circuits and feeders over 1,000V are the focus of Part III of Article 225.

225.17 Masts as Supports

The requirements for overhead masts were revised to more clearly address conduit fittings.

Part I. General

225.17 Masts as Supports. Only branch-circuit or feeder conductors can be attached to the mast, Figure 225–1. Masts used for the support of final spans of feeders or branch circuits must be installed in accordance with (A) and (B).

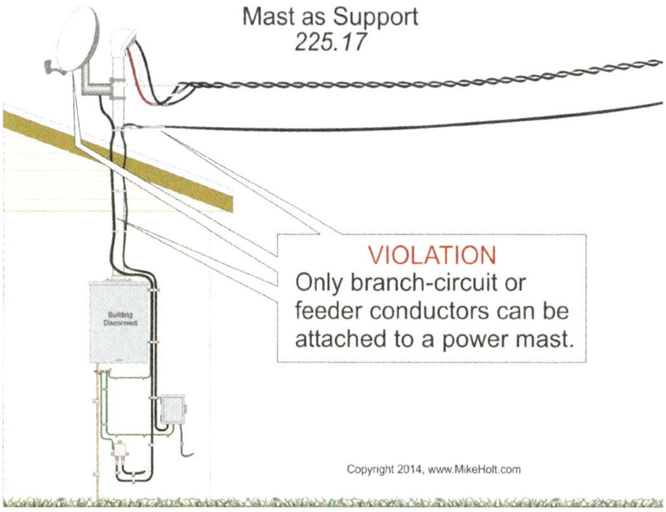

Figure 225–1

Author's Comment: Aerial cables and antennas for radio and TV equipment must not be attached to the feeder or branch-circuit mast [810.12]. In addition, 800.133(B) prohibits communications cables from being attached to raceways, including a mast for power conductors.

(A) Strength. If a mast is used for overhead conductor support, it must have adequate mechanical strength, braces, or guy wires to withstand the strain caused by the conductors. Conduit hubs must be identified for use with a mast. Figure 225–2

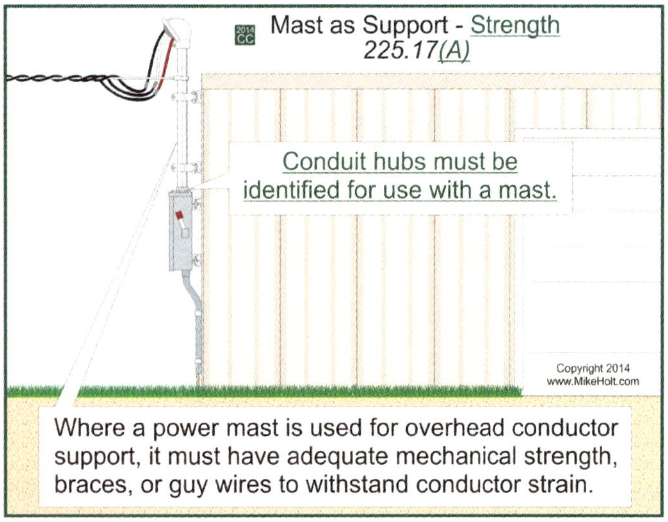

Figure 225–2

(B) Attachment. Conductors can't be attached to a mast between a weatherhead or end of the conduit and a coupling if the coupling is above the last conduit support, or if the coupling is above the building or structure. Figure 225–3

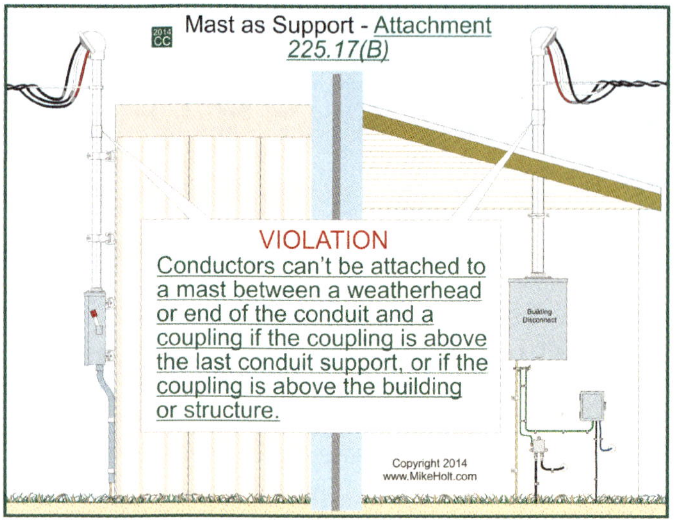

Figure 225–3

ANALYSIS: The *Code* has never provided much guidance on the strength requirements for overhead masts. While it still requires some judgment (what does "adequate strength" mean?), the new language regarding couplings provides at least some prescriptive requirements for inspectors to hang their hats on and for installers to follow. Previous editions of the *NEC* stated that all fittings used in a mast must be identified for such use. This was problematic because some fittings, such as rigid couplings, aren't specifically identified for such use (see the UL White Book, category DWTT), although they're certainly strong enough to be used. Conduit hubs that meet the requirements are marked on either the fittings themselves or on the carton that they come in as being suitable for use on a mast.

225.27 Raceway Seal

Conductor insulation integrity is now addressed in this requirement.

225.27 Raceway Seal. Underground raceways (used or unused) entering buildings or structures must be sealed or plugged to prevent moisture from contacting energized live parts [300.5(G)]. To ensure that the conductors or cables aren't damaged, sealants must be identified for use with the conductor or cable in the raceway. Figure 225–4

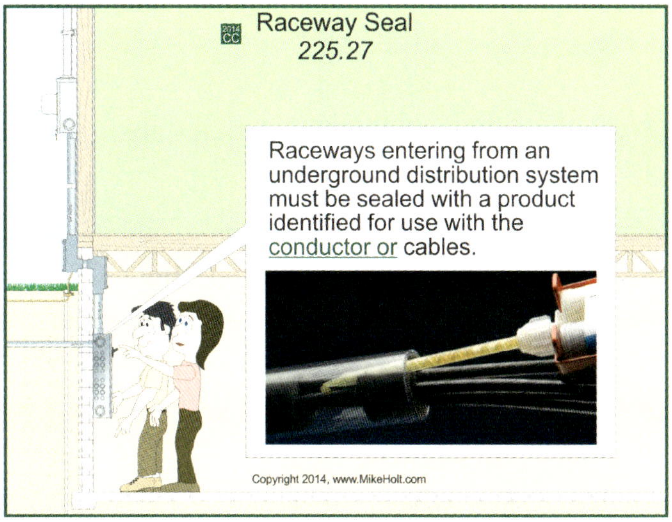

Figure 225–4

ANALYSIS: As is often the case, new *Code* rules are changed three years after they're created so they can say what they were supposed to say all along. This rule was added to the 2011 *NEC*, and it required that the sealing material be of a type that doesn't damage cable insulation. The only problem is that conductors are installed in raceways far more often than cables, yet they weren't discussed in this section.

225.36 Type

The rule requiring building disconnects to be "suitable for use as service equipment" has been extensively revised.

Part II. Buildings or Other Structures Supplied by a Feeder(s) or Branch Circuit(s)

225.36 Type. The building/structure disconnecting means can be comprised of a circuit breaker, molded case switch, general-use switch, snap switch, or other approved means. If an existing building uses the neutral conductor for the bonding of metal parts [250.32(B) Ex], the disconnect must be listed as suitable for use as service equipment. Figure 225–5

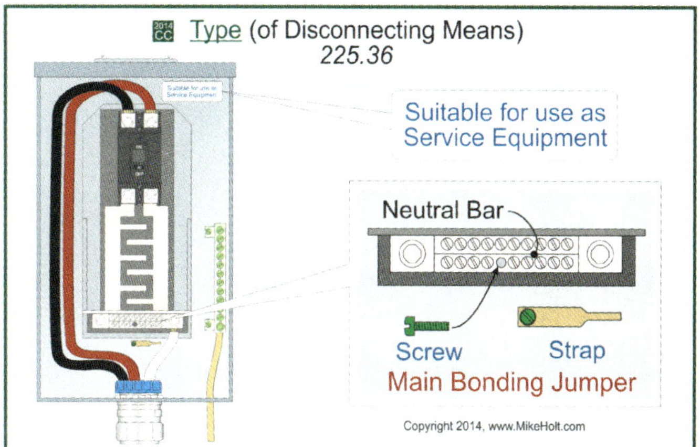

Figure 225–5

Author's Comment: "Suitable for use as service equipment" means, among other things, that the service disconnecting means is supplied with a main bonding jumper so a neutral-to-case connection can be made, as required in 250.24(C) and 250.142(A).

ANALYSIS: Previous editions of the *Code* required a switch that was "suitable for use as service equipment" as the disconnect for a building supplied by a feeder or branch circuit. The main difference between a disconnect that's "suitable for use as service equipment" and one that isn't is the ability to connect the neutral to the frame of the disconnect enclosure. This practice is only allowed for buildings supplied by a service [250.24], not those supplied by a feeder or branch circuit (except for existing buildings discussed in 250.32(B) Ex). Because this article only deals with branch circuits and feeders, there's no real need for this requirement. The exception allowing snap switches for residential garages was removed from this rule, since now any building supplied by a branch circuit can use a snap switch as a disconnect if it can handle the load.

ARTICLE 230 SERVICES

Introduction to Article 230—Services

This article covers the installation requirements for service conductors and service equipment. The requirements for service conductors differ from those for other conductors. For one thing, service conductors for one building/structure can't pass through the interior of another building or structure [230.3], and you apply different rules depending on whether a service conductor is inside or outside a building/structure. When are they "outside" as opposed to "inside"? The answer may seem obvious, but 230.6 should be consulted before making this decision.

Let's review the following definitions in Article 100 to understand when the requirements of Article 230 apply:

- **Service Point.** The point of connection between the serving utility and the premises wiring.
- **Service Conductors.** The conductors from the service point to the service disconnecting means. Service-entrance conductors can either be overhead or underground.
- **Service Equipment.** The necessary equipment, usually consisting of circuit breakers or switches and fuses and their accessories, connected to the load end of service conductors at a building or other structure, and intended to constitute the main control and cutoff of the electrical supply. Service equipment doesn't include individual meter socket enclosures [230.66].

After reviewing these definitions, you should understand that service conductors originate at the serving utility (service point) and terminate on the line side of the service disconnecting means. Conductors and equipment on the load side of service equipment are considered feeder conductors or branch circuits, and must be installed in accordance with Articles 210 and 215. They must also comply with Article 225 if they're outside branch circuits and feeders, such as the supply to a building/structure. Feeder conductors include: Figures 230–1 and 230–2

- Secondary conductors from customer-owned transformers,
- Conductors from generators, UPS systems, or PV systems, and
- Conductors to remote buildings or structures

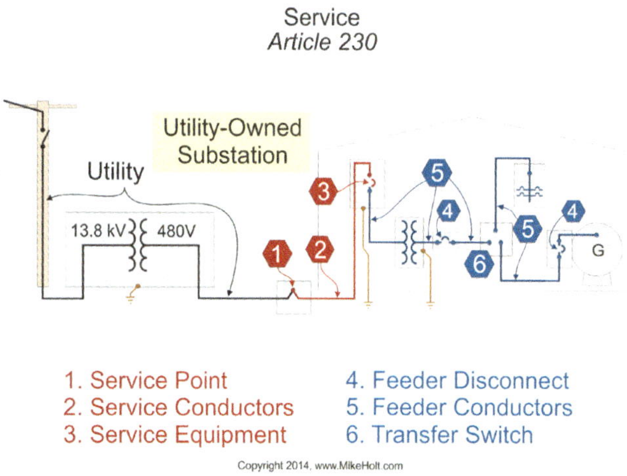

Figure 230–1

Article 230 consists of seven parts:

- **Part I. General**
- **Part II. Overhead Service Conductors**
- **Part III. Underground Service Conductors**
- **Part IV. Service-Entrance Conductors**
- **Part V. Service Equipment**
- **Part VI. Disconnecting Means**
- **Part VIII. Overcurrent Protection**

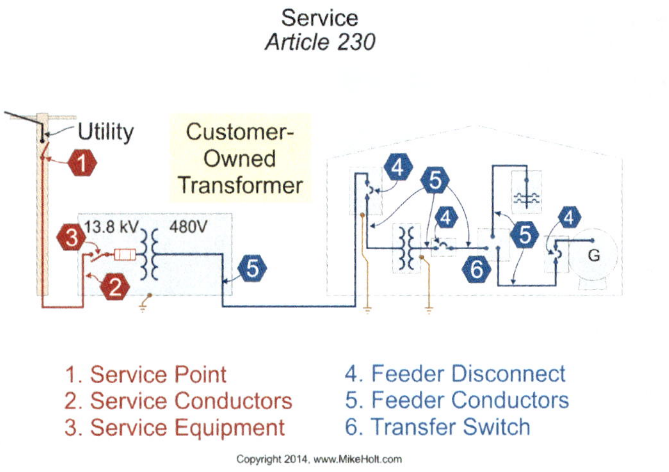

Figure 230–2

230.6 Conductors Considered Outside a Building

The requirements for overhead masts considered outside of a building have been revised.

Part I. General

230.6 Conductors Considered Outside a Building.

Conductors are considered outside of a building when they're installed:

(1) Under not less than 2 in. of concrete beneath a building/structure. **Figure 230–3**

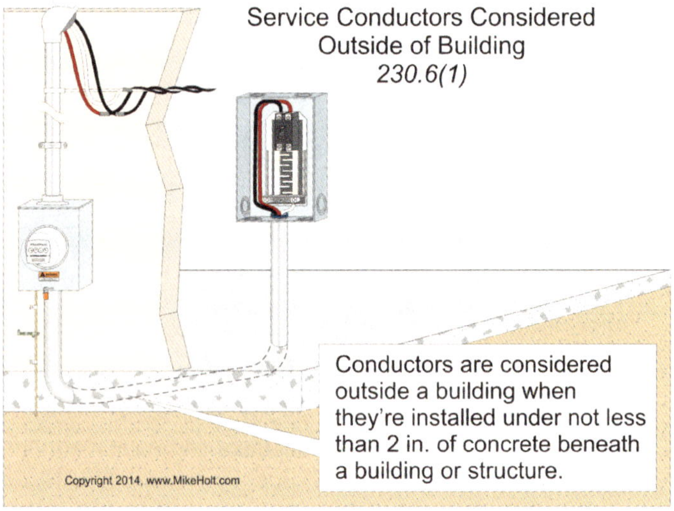

Figure 230–3

(2) Within a building/structure in a raceway encased in not less than 2 in. of concrete or brick.

(3) In a vault that meets the construction requirements of Article 450, Part III.

(4) In a raceway under not less than 18 in. of the earth beneath a building/structure.

(5) Within rigid or intermediate metal conduit that passes directly through an eave but not a wall of a building. **Figure 230–4**

ANALYSIS: Item (5) has been revised to clarify that the conductors inside of a raceway mast are considered outside of the building when they travel through the eaves of a building. The word "mast" was removed because, while most people think of raceways as the only type of mast, a mast can literally be a large piece of wood with SE cable attached to it. Obviously such a mast doesn't provide the protection given by rigid or intermediate metal conduit, so the *Code* was changed to clarify the issue. The *NEC* is also

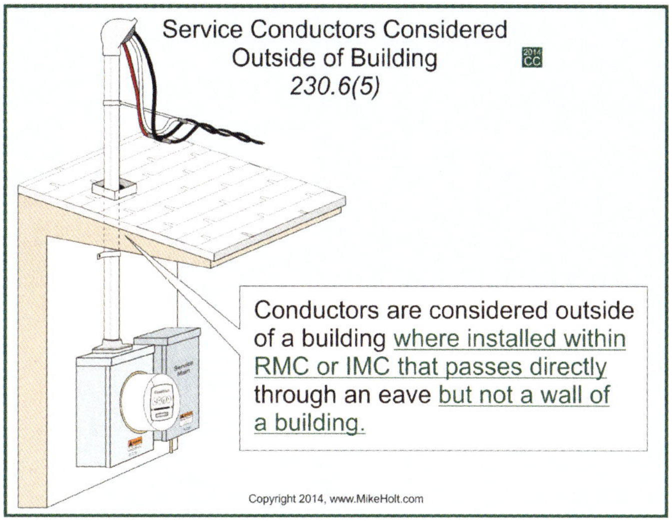

Figure 230–4

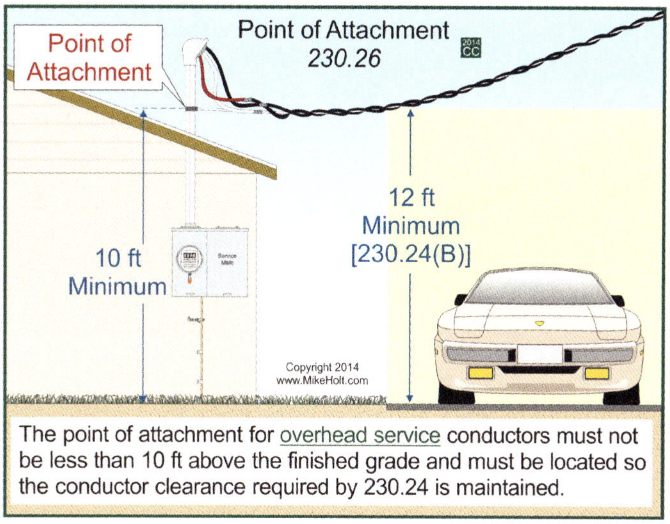

Figure 230–5

very clear that this allowance is intended only to apply to a short length of raceway that travels vertically through the eave. There have been installations where the raceway penetrates the eave, travels horizontally for 10 ft or more inside of the eave, then turns vertically to penetrate the roof. This type of installation wasn't intended to be allowed under previous editions of the *Code*, and is now specifically discussed.

230.26 Point of Attachment

This section was revised to reflect changes made in 2011.

Part II. Overhead Service Conductors

230.26 Point of Attachment. The point of attachment for overhead service conductors must not be less than 10 ft above the finished grade, and it must be located so that the minimum service conductor clearances required by 230.9 and 230.24 can be maintained.

CAUTION: *The point of attachment for conductors might need to be raised so the overhead service conductors will comply with the clearances from building openings required by 230.9 and from other areas by 230.24.* **Figure 230–5**

ANALYSIS: The 2011 *NEC* contained many, many changes to "service" related terms (service point, service drop, overhead service conductors, and so on) in Articles 100 and 230. With that many changes, some instances of incorrect usage are bound to remain, as it's nearly impossible to make that many changes and not miss something. Service-drop conductors are utility conductors and therefore have no requirements in the *Code*. This section has been revised to use the correct term, overhead service conductors, as those are the conductors regulated by the *NEC*.

230.28 Service Masts Used as Supports

The requirements for service masts have been extensively revised.

230.28 Service Masts Used as Supports. Masts used for the support of overhead service conductors or service drops must be installed in accordance with (A) and (B). Only these conductors can be attached to the mast.

Author's Comment: Sections 810.12 and 820.44(C) specify that aerial cables for radio, TV, or CATV must not be attached to the service mast, and 810.12 prohibits antennas from being attached to the service mast. In addition, 800.133(B) and 830.133(B) prohibit broadband communications cables from being attached to raceways, including a service mast. **Figure 230–6**

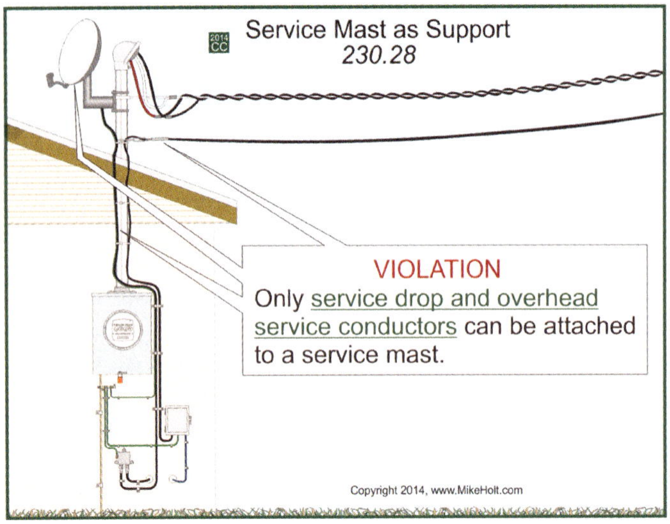

Figure 230–6

(A) Strength. If a mast is used for overhead conductor support, it must have adequate mechanical strength, braces, or guy wires to withstand the strain caused by the conductors. Conduit hubs must be identified for use with a mast. Figure 230–7

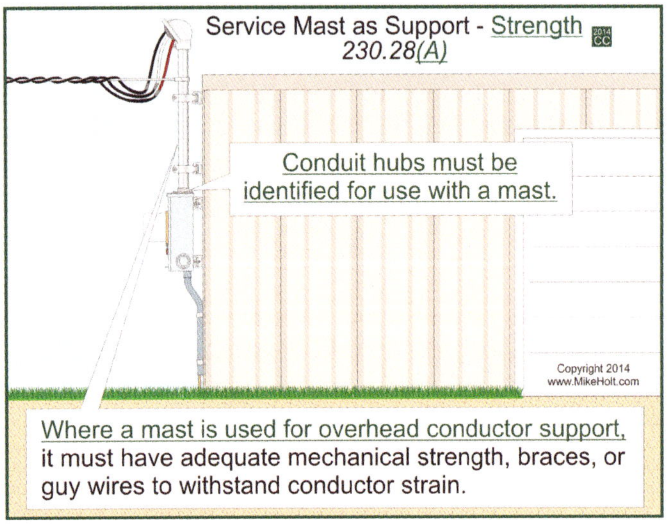

Figure 230–7

(B) Attachment. Conductors can't be attached to a mast between a weatherhead or end of the conduit and a coupling if the coupling is above the last conduit support, or if the coupling is above the building or structure. Figure 230–8

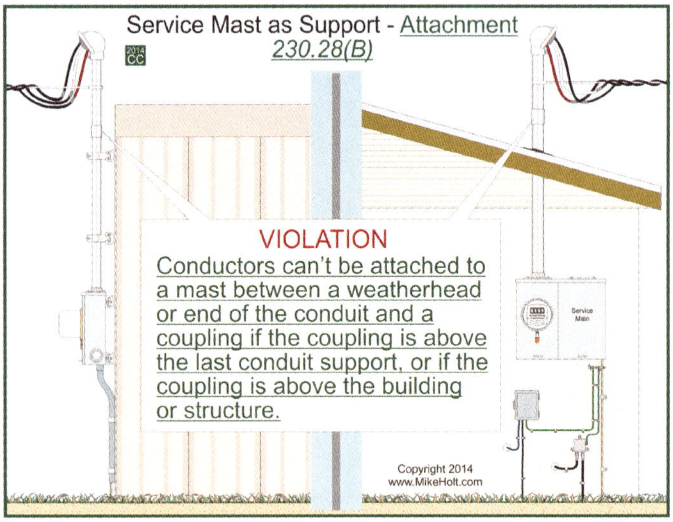

Figure 230–8

Author's Comment: Some local codes require a minimum trade size 2 rigid metal conduit for the service mast. In addition, many electric utilities contain specific requirements for the installation of the service mast.

ANALYSIS: The *Code* has never provided much guidance on the strength requirements for overhead masts. While it still requires some judgment (what does "adequate strength" mean?), the new language regarding couplings provides at least some prescriptive requirements for inspectors to hang their hats on and for installers to follow. Previous editions of the *Code* stated that all fittings used in a mast must be identified for such use. This was problematic because some fittings, such as rigid couplings, aren't specifically identified for such use (see the UL White Book, category DWTT), although they're certainly strong enough to be used. Conduit hubs that meet the requirements are marked on either the fittings themselves or on the carton in which they come as being suitable for use on a mast.

230.42 Size and Rating

The sizing requirements for service conductors have been clarified.

Part IV. Service-Entrance Conductors

230.42 Size and Rating.

(A) Load Calculations. Service-entrance conductors must have sufficient ampacity for the loads to be served in accordance with Parts III, IV, or V of Article 220. The ampacity must not be less than (1), (2), or (3).

(1) 125 percent of the continuous loads, plus 100 percent of the noncontinuous loads.

Author's Comment: See 215.3 for the sizing requirements of feeder overcurrent devices for continuous and noncontinuous loads.

Question: *What size service-entrance conductors are required for a 200A continuous three-phase load, if the terminals are rated 75°C?* **Figure 230–9**

(a) 2/0 AWG (b) 3/0 AWG (c) 4/0 AWG (d) 250 kcmil

Answer: *(d) 250 kcmil*

Since the load is 200A continuous, the service-entrance conductors must have an ampacity not less than 250A (200A x 1.25). According to the 75°C column of Table 310.15(B)(16), 250 kcmil conductors are suitable because they have an ampere rating of 255A at 75°C.

(2) The sum of the noncontinuous load plus the continuous load after the application of any adjustment of correction factors. **Figure 230–10**

(3) 100 percent of the continuous and noncontinuous load, if the conductors terminate to an overcurrent device listed for 100 percent of its rating.

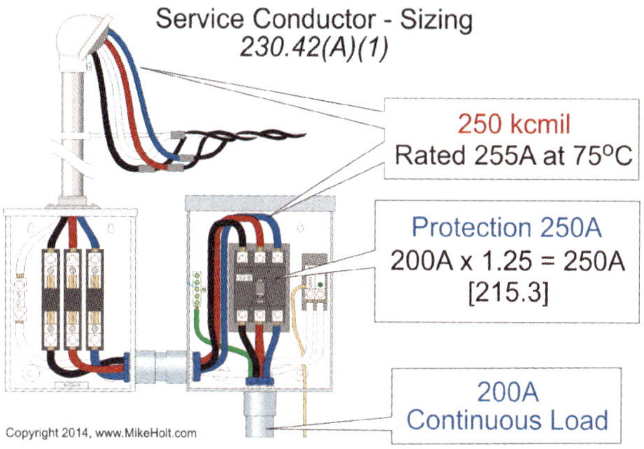

Figure 230–9

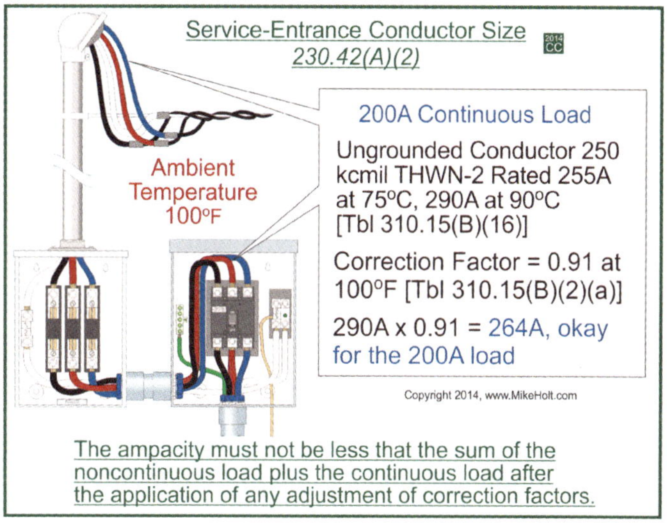

Figure 230–10

(C) Neutral Conductor Size. The service neutral conductor must be sized to carry the maximum unbalanced load in accordance with 220.61, and must not be sized smaller than required by 250.24(C).

WARNING: *In all cases the service neutral conductor size must not be smaller than required by 250.24(C) to ensure that it has sufficiently low impedance and current-carrying capacity to safely carry fault current in order to facilitate the operation of the overcurrent device.*

ANALYSIS: This change, like the changes in 210.19 and 215.3, has been made in order to clarify the mathematical procedure used to size conductors. Questions regarding when (in the mathematical process) the adjustment and correction factors are supposed to be factored in have been long unanswered, but hopefully these changes will fix that glaring problem.

ARTICLE 240 OVERCURRENT PROTECTION

Introduction to Article 240—Overcurrent Protection

This article provides the requirements for selecting and installing overcurrent devices. Overcurrent exists when current exceeds the rating of equipment or the ampacity of a conductor. This can be due to an overload, short circuit, or ground fault [Article 100].

- **Overload.** An overload is a condition where equipment or conductors carry current exceeding their current rating [Article 100]. A fault, such as a short circuit or ground fault, isn't an overload. An example of an overload is plugging two 12.50A (1,500W) hair dryers into a 20A branch circuit.
- **Short Circuit.** A short circuit is the unintentional electrical connection between any two normally current-carrying conductors of an electrical circuit, either line-to-line or line-to-neutral.
- **Ground Fault.** A ground fault is an unintentional, electrically conducting connection between an ungrounded conductor of an electrical circuit and the normally noncurrent-carrying conductors, metallic enclosures, metallic raceways, metallic equipment, or the earth [Article 100]. During the period of a ground fault, dangerous voltages will be present on metal parts until the circuit overcurrent device opens.

Overcurrent devices protect conductors and equipment. Selecting the proper overcurrent protection for a specific circuit can become more complicated than it sounds. The general rule for overcurrent protection is that conductors must be protected in accordance with their ampacities at the point where they receive their supply [240.4 and 240.21]. There are many special cases that deviate from this basic rule, such as the overcurrent protection limitations for small conductors [240.4(D)] and the rules for specific conductor applications found in other articles, as listed in Table 240.4(G). There are also a number of rules allowing tap conductors in specific situations [240.21(B)]. Article 240 even has limits on where overcurrent devices are allowed to be located [240.24].

An overcurrent protection device must be capable of opening a circuit when an overcurrent situation occurs, and must also have an interrupting rating sufficient to avoid damage in fault conditions [110.9]. Carefully study the provisions of this article to be sure you provide sufficient overcurrent protection in the correct location.

240.21 Overcurrent Protection Location in Circuit

An exception for listed equipment, such as surge protective devices, has been added to the 10-ft tap rule.

Part II. Location

240.21 Overcurrent Protection Location in Circuit.

Except as permitted by (A) through (H), overcurrent devices must be placed at the point where the branch-circuit or feeder conductors receive their power. Taps and transformer secondary conductors aren't permitted to supply another conductor (tapping a tap isn't permitted). Figure 240–1

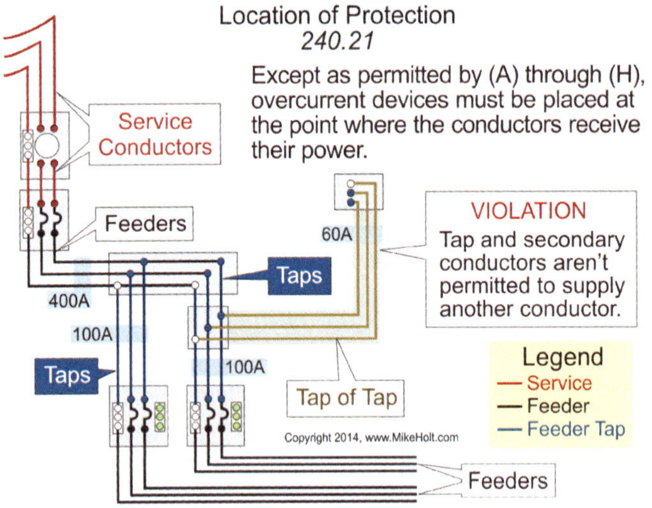

Figure 240–1

(B) Feeder Taps. Conductors can be tapped to a feeder as specified in 240.21(B)(1) through (B)(5). The "next size up protection rule" of 240.4(B) isn't permitted for tap conductors. Figure 240–2

(1) 10-Foot Feeder Tap. Feeder tap conductors up to 10 ft long are permitted without overcurrent protection at the tap location if the tap conductors comply with the following:

(1) The ampacity of the tap conductor must not be less than: Figure 240–3

a. The calculated load in accordance with Article 220, and

b. The rating of the overcurrent device supplied by the tap conductors.

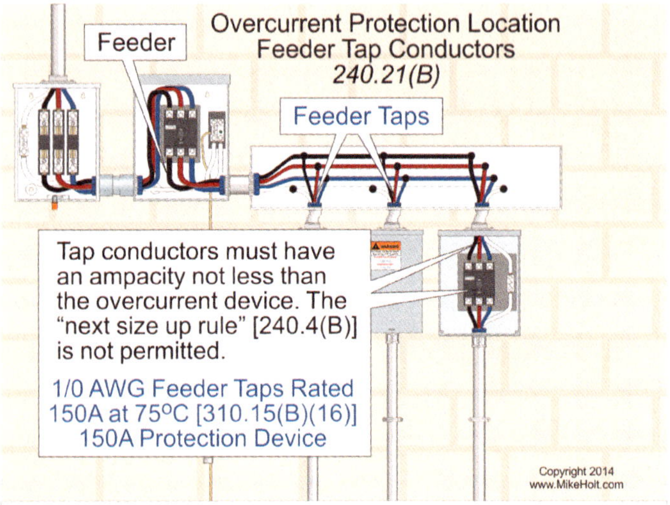

Figure 240–2

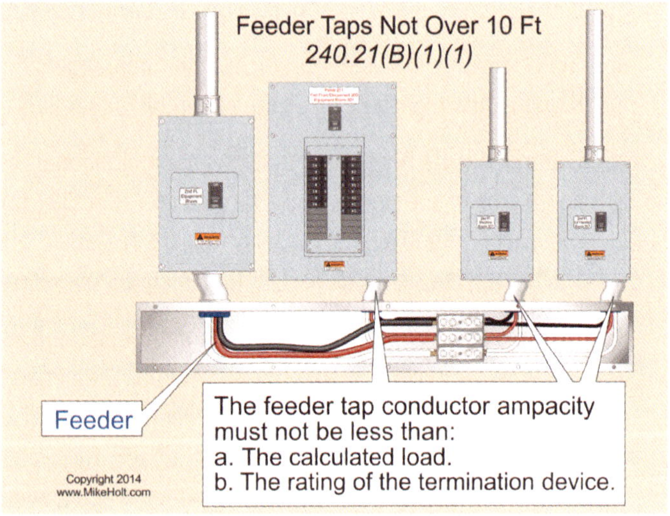

Figure 240–3

Ex: Listed equipment, such as a surge protection device, can have their conductors sized in accordance with the manufacturer's instructions.

(2) The tap conductors must not extend beyond the equipment they supply.

(3) The tap conductors are installed in a raceway if they leave the enclosure.

(4) If the tap conductors leave the enclosure or vault in which the tap is made, the tap conductors must have an ampacity not less than 10 percent of the rating of the overcurrent device that protects the feeder. Figure 240–4

Note: See 408.36 for the overcurrent protection requirements for panelboards.

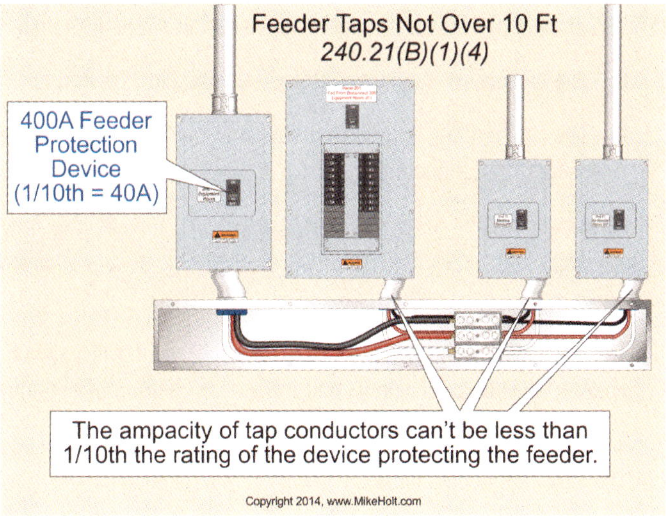

Figure 240–4

Example: *A 400A breaker protects a set of 500 kcmil feeder conductors. There are three taps fed from the 500 kcmil feeder that supply disconnects with 200A, 150A, and 30A overcurrent devices. What are the minimum size conductors for these taps?* Figure 240–5

- *200A: 3/0 AWG is rated 200A at 75°, and is greater than 10 percent of the rating of the overcurrent device (400A).*
- *150A: 1/0 AWG is rated 150A at 75°, and is greater than 10 percent of the rating of the overcurrent device (400A).*

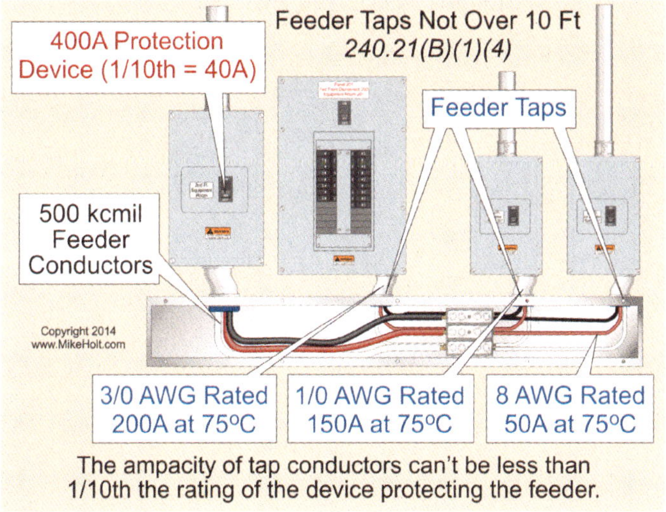

Figure 240–5

- *30A: 8 AWG is rated 50A at 75°, and is greater than 10 percent of the rating of the overcurrent device (400A). Anything smaller than 8 AWG can't be used, as it will have an ampacity of less than 10 percent of the rating of the overcurrent device (400A).*

ANALYSIS: Surge protection devices (SPDs) often have very specific instructions regarding conductor sizing and installation. These instructions frequently include not only what size conductor to use, but the length and bending radius of the conductors as well. These conductor sizes are a result of investigation and engineering by the manufacturer, and are reviewed during the listing process by third parties as well. Due to the unique natures of the different SPDs, it would be nearly impossible to write *Code* language that applies to all of them. By having this exception, the *NEC* defers to the manufacturer and third party listing to ensure safety.

240.21 Overcurrent Protection Location in Circuit

An exception for listed equipment, such as surge protective devices, has been added to the 10-ft secondary conductor rule.

240.21 Overcurrent Protection Location in Circuit. Except as permitted by (A) through (H), overcurrent devices must be placed at the point where the branch-circuit or feeder conductors receive their power. Taps and transformer secondary conductors aren't permitted to supply another conductor (tapping a tap isn't permitted).

(C) Transformer Secondary Conductors. A set of conductors supplying single or separate loads is permitted to be connected to a transformer secondary without overcurrent protection in accordance with (1) through (6).

Author's Comment: The permission of the "next size up" protection rule when the conductor ampacity doesn't correspond with the standard size overcurrent protection device of 240.4(B) doesn't apply to transformer secondary conductors. Figure 240–6

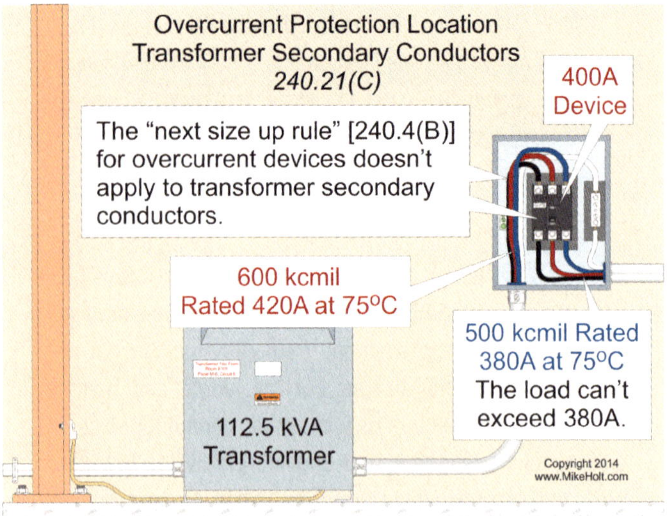

Figure 240–6

(2) 10 Ft Secondary Conductors. Secondary conductors can be run up to 10 ft without overcurrent protection if installed as follows: Figure 240–7

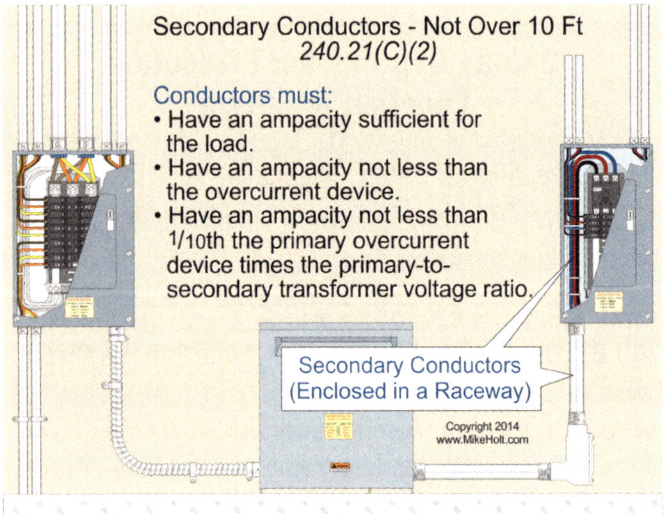

Figure 240–7

(1) The ampacity of the secondary conductor must not be less than:

a. The calculated load in accordance with Article 220, and

b. The rating of the overcurrent device at the termination of the secondary conductors

Ex: Listed equipment, such as a surge protection device, can have their conductors sized in accordance with the manufacturer's instructions.

(2) The secondary conductors must not extend beyond the switchboard, panelboard, disconnecting means, or control devices they supply.

(3) The secondary conductors are enclosed in a raceway.

(4) Not less than 10 percent of the rating of the overcurrent device protecting the primary of the transformer, multiplied by the primary-to-secondary transformer voltage ratio.

ANALYSIS: Surge protection devices (SPDs) often have very specific instructions regarding conductor sizing and installation. These instructions frequently include not only what size of conductor to use, but the length, bending radius, and voltage drop as well. These conductor sizes are a result of investigation and engineering by the manufacturer, and are reviewed during the listing process by third parties as well. Due to the unique natures of the different SPDs, it would be nearly impossible to write *Code* language that applies to all of them. By having this exception, the *NEC* defers to the manufacturer and third party listing to ensure safety.

ARTICLE 250 GROUNDING AND BONDING

Introduction to Article 250—Grounding and Bonding

No other article can match Article 250 for misapplication, violation, and misinterpretation. Terminology used in this article has been a source for much confusion, but that has improved during the last few *NEC* revisions. It's very important to understand the difference between grounding and bonding in order to correctly apply the provisions of Article 250. Pay careful attention to the definitions that apply to grounding and bonding both here and in Article 100 as you begin the study of this important article. Article 250 covers the grounding requirements for providing a path to the earth to reduce overvoltage from lightning, and the bonding requirements for a low-impedance fault current path back to the source of the electrical supply to facilitate the operation of overcurrent devices in the event of a ground fault.

Over the past several *Code* cycles, this article was extensively revised to organize it better and make it easier to understand and implement. It's arranged in a logical manner, so it's a good idea to just read through Article 250 to get a big picture view—after you review the definitions. Next, study the article closely so you understand the details. The illustrations will help you understand the key points.

250.8 Termination of Grounding and Bonding Conductors

The requirements for terminating equipment grounding conductors (EGCs), grounding electrode conductors (GECs), and bonding jumpers have been editorially revised.

Part I. General

250.8 Termination of Grounding and Bonding Conductors.

(A) Permitted Methods. Equipment grounding conductors, grounding electrode conductors, and bonding jumpers must terminate in one or more of the following methods:

(1) Listed pressure connectors

(2) Terminal bars

(3) Pressure connectors listed for direct burial or concrete encasement [250.70]

(4) Exothermic welding

(5) Machine screws that engage at least two threads or are secured with a nut. Figure 250–1

(6) Self-tapping machine screws that engage at least two threads

(7) Connections that are part of a listed assembly

(8) Other listed means

(B) Methods Not Permitted. Connection devices or fittings that depend solely on solder aren't allowed.

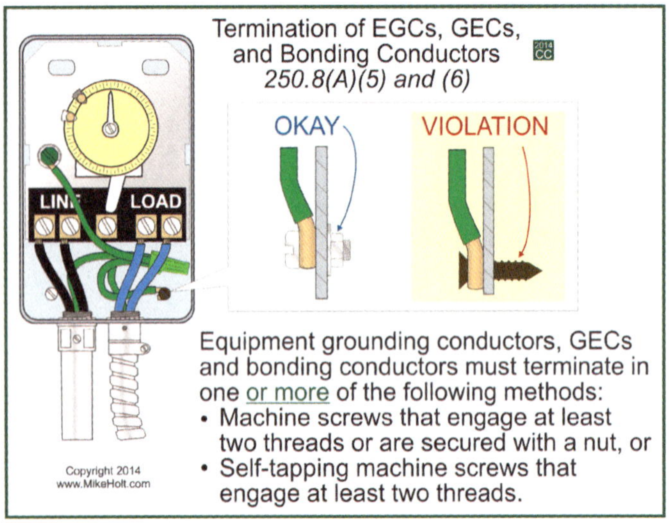

Figure 250–1

ANALYSIS: While this change is completely obvious, it's an important enough section of the *Code* to make sure that the language is completely accurate. One can argue that in 2011 one (and only one) of the methods discussed could be used. This certainly wasn't the intent of this section, so the text has been changed to eliminate the argument.

250.10 Protection of Fittings

The protection of grounding and bonding fittings has been editorially revised.

250.10 Protection of Fittings. Where subject to physical damage, grounding and bonding fittings must be protected by enclosing the fittings in metal, wood, or an equivalent protective covering.

Author's Comment: Grounding and bonding fittings can be buried or encased in concrete if they're installed in accordance with 250.53(G), 250.68(A) Ex 1, and 250.70.

ANALYSIS: Over the last few *Code* development cycles there's been a real effort to use lists when there are multiple requirements or options in a paragraph. Most of the time this is a change for the better, but sometimes it doesn't really make any sense. The previous edition of this section had a two-item list that was unnecessary since item one was so incredibly obvious (protecting the equipment from damage by putting it somewhere that it can't be harmed).

250.21 Ungrounded Systems—50V to 1,000V

The signage requirement for ungrounded systems was revised to require more information.

Part II. System Grounding and Bonding

250.21 Ungrounded Systems—50V to 1,000V.

(B) Ground Detectors.

(1) Systems that aren't required to be grounded in accordance with 250.20(B) [250.21(A)(4)] must have ground detectors installed.

(2) The ground detection sensing equipment must be connected as close as practicable to where the system receives its supply.

(C) Marking. Ungrounded systems must be legibly marked "Caution Ungrounded System Operating — _____ Volts Between Conductors" at the source or first disconnecting means of the system, with sufficient durability to withstand the environment involved. Figure 250–2

ANALYSIS: The 2011 *NEC* added a requirement for marking ungrounded systems in order to alert electricians to the fact that they're dealing with a system that's uncommon. While that change was great and provided for a safer workplace, it would be even better if the voltage was indicated. The voltage of the ungrounded system is now required to be marked, similar to the requirements in 408.3(F) for a high-leg system.

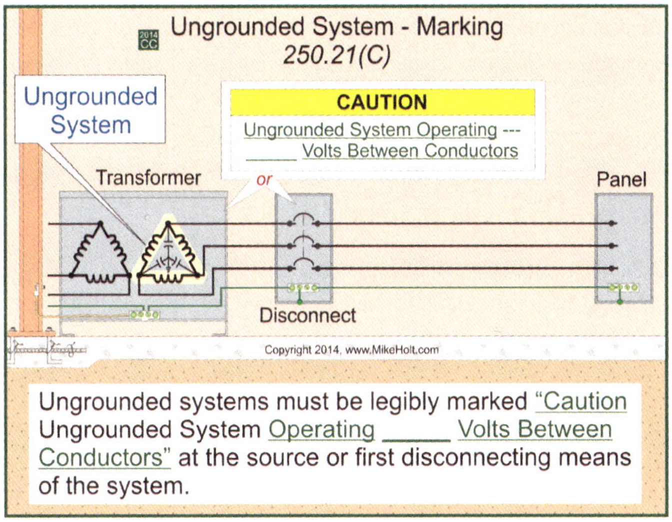

Figure 250–2

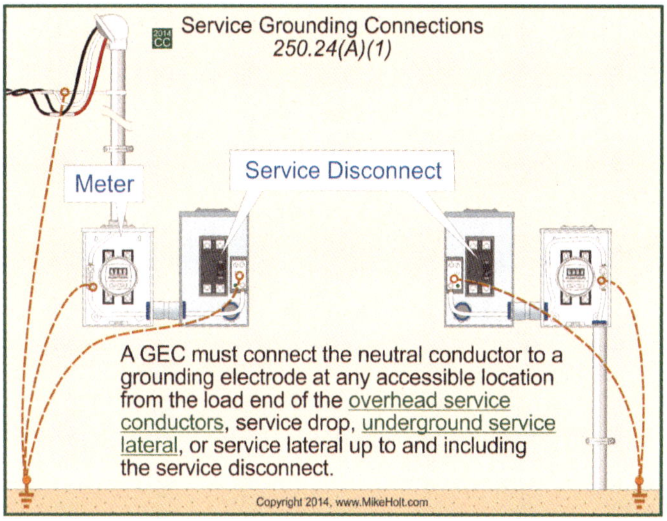

Figure 250–3

250.24 Service Equipment—Grounding and Bonding

The permitted locations for the grounding electrode conductor have been revised to correlate with changes made in 2011.

250.24 Service Equipment—Grounding and Bonding.

(A) Grounded System. Service equipment supplied from a grounded system must have the neutral conductor terminate in accordance with (1) through (5).

(1) Grounding Location. A grounding electrode conductor must connect the service neutral conductor to the grounding electrode at any accessible location, from the load end of the overhead service conductors, service drop, underground service lateral, or service lateral, up to and including the service disconnecting means. Figure 250–3

Author's Comment: Some inspectors require the service neutral conductor to be grounded (connected to the earth) from the meter socket enclosure, while other inspectors insist that it be grounded (connected to the earth) only from the service disconnect.

ANALYSIS: The 2011 *NEC* contained many, many changes in Articles 100 and 230 to "service" related terms (service point, service drop, overhead service conductors, and so on). With that many changes, some instances of incorrect usage are bound to remain, as it's nearly impossible to make that many changes and not miss something. This section has been revised to reflect the fact that service laterals and service drops aren't the only two ways electricity can get to a building that's supplied by a utility.

250.62 Grounding Electrode Conductor

This section has been revised for accuracy.

Part III. Grounding Electrode System and Grounding Electrode Conductor

250.62 Grounding Electrode Conductor.

Grounding electrode conductors of the wire type must be solid or stranded, insulated or bare, and must be copper if within 18 in. of the earth [250.64(A)]. Grounding electrode conductors can also be a water pipe, concrete-encased electrode, or structural metal, in accordance with 250.68(C). Figure 250–4

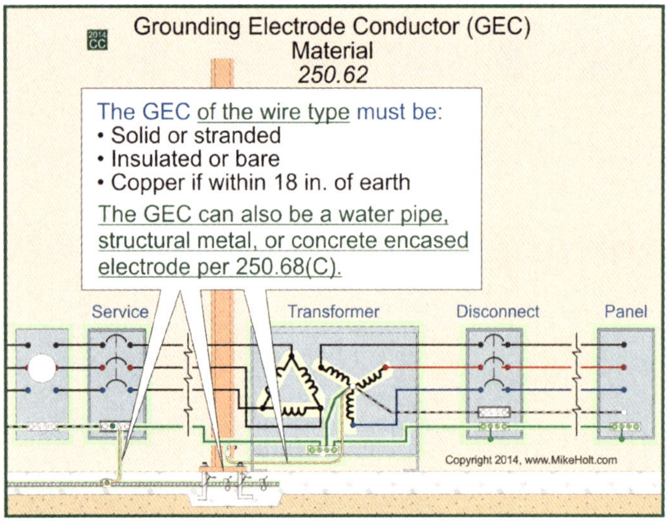

Figure 250–4

ANALYSIS: Changes made in the 2011 *NEC* to 250.68 had the ultimate effect of calling interior water pipe and structural metal "grounding electrode conductors" without coming right out and saying it. While there's no problem within the context of 250.68(C), it does create a bit of a conflict with this section (250.62). By stating that grounding electrode conductors must be copper, aluminum, or copper-clad aluminum, the structural metal of a building can't be used unless it's made of one of these materials. Since buildings aren't typically built out of copper, this section was tweaked to resolve the conflict that only the keenest of *Code*-reading eyes noticed to begin with.

250.64 Grounding Electrode Conductor Installation

Changes to this section address underground grounding electrode conductors (GECs), as well as buildings supplied by feeder circuits and the requirements for ferrous metal enclosures containing a GEC.

250.64 Grounding Electrode Conductor Installation.

Grounding electrode conductors must be installed as specified in (A) through (F).

(B) Conductor Protection. Where installed exposed, grounding electrode conductors must be protected where subject to physical damage and are permitted to be installed on or through framing members. Grounding electrode conductors 6 AWG copper and larger can be installed exposed along the surface of the building if securely fastened and not subject to physical damage.

Grounding electrode conductors sized 8 AWG must be protected by installing them in rigid metal conduit, intermediate metal conduit, PVC conduit, electrical metallic tubing, or reinforced thermosetting resin conduit.

Author's Comment: A ferrous metal raceway containing a grounding electrode conductor must be made electrically continuous by bonding each end of that type of raceway to the grounding electrode conductor [250.64(E)], so it's best to use PVC conduit or reinforced thermosetting resin conduit.

The cover requirements found in 300.5 don't apply to grounding electrode conductors or their bonding jumpers. Figure 250–5

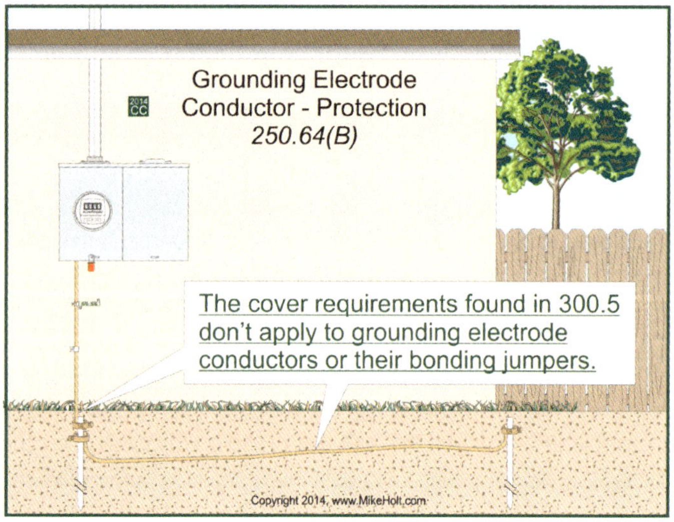

Figure 250–5

ANALYSIS: Table 300.5 gives the cover (also known as burial depth) requirements for underground installations. Nothing in that table, or section, indicates whether or not it applies to grounding electrode conductors or bonding jumpers. While it wouldn't be good to hit one of these conductors with a shovel, you probably wouldn't get electrocuted.

(D) Grounding Electrode Conductor for Multiple Building or Structure Disconnects. If a service or building/structure disconnect consists of more than a single enclosure, grounding electrode connections must be made in one of the following methods:

(1) Common Grounding Electrode Conductor and Taps. A grounding electrode conductor tap must extend to the inside of each disconnecting means enclosure.

The common grounding electrode conductor must be sized in accordance with 250.66, based on the sum of the circular mil area of the largest ungrounded conductor supplying the equipment. Figure 250–6

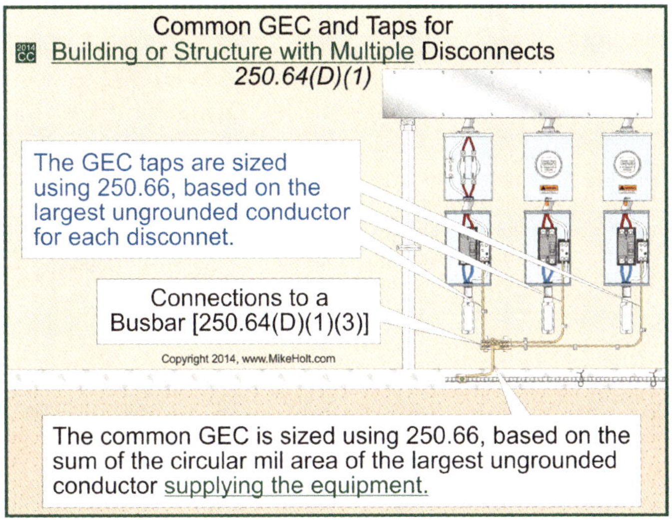

Figure 250–6

A grounding electrode conductor must extend from each disconnecting means, sized not smaller than specified in Table 250.66, based on the area of the largest ungrounded conductor for each disconnecting means.

The grounding electrode tap conductors must be connected to the common grounding electrode conductor, without splicing the common grounding electrode conductor, by one of the following methods:

(1) Exothermic welding.

(2) Connectors listed as grounding and bonding equipment.

(3) Connections to a busbar of sufficient length and not less than ¼ in. thick × 2 in. wide that's securely fastened and installed in an accessible location. Figure 250–7

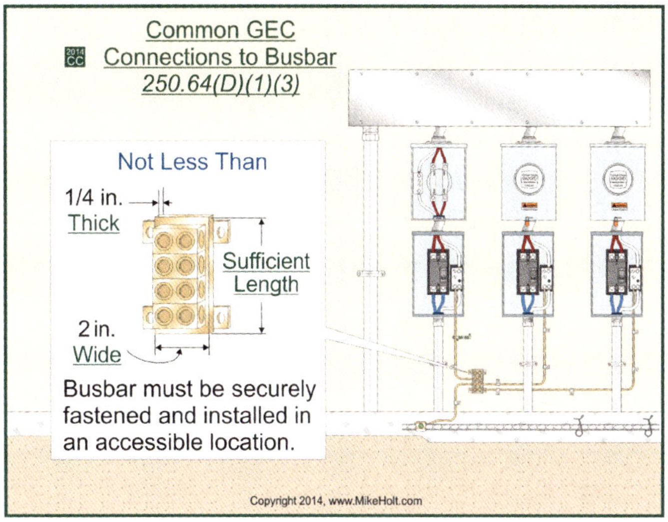

Figure 250–7

(2) Individual Grounding Electrode Conductors. A grounding electrode conductor, sized in accordance with 250.66 based on the ungrounded conductor(s) supplying the individual disconnecting means, must be connected between the grounding electrode system and one or more of the following:

(1) the service neutral conductor, Figure 250–8

(2) the equipment grounding conductor of the feeder circuit,

(3) the supply-side bonding jumper.

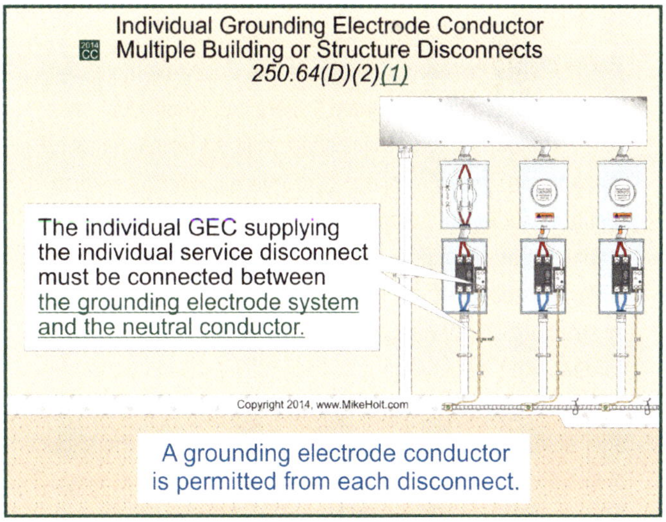

Figure 250–8

(3) Common Location. A single grounding electrode conductor is permitted from a common location, sized not smaller than specified in Table 250.66, based on the area of the ungrounded conductor at the location where the connection is made. The grounding electrode conductor must connect the grounding electrode system to one or more of the following: Figure 250–9

(1) the service neutral conductor,

(2) the equipment grounding conductor of the feeder circuit,

(3) the supply-side bonding jumper.

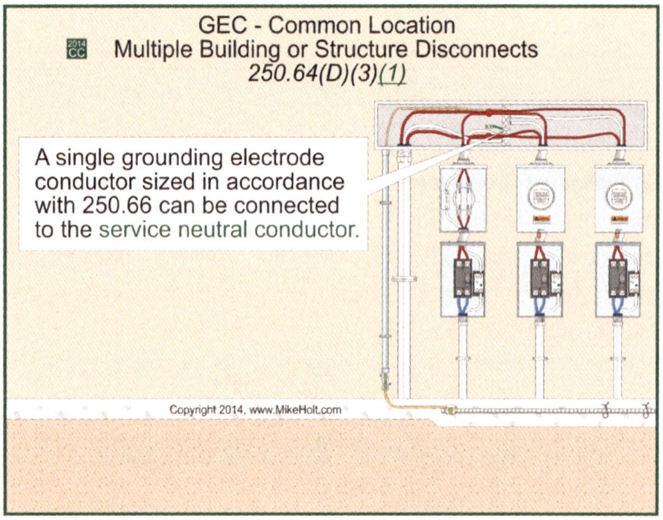

Figure 250–9

ANALYSIS: Previous versions of this *Code* rule have used the terms "service equipment," "service disconnect," "service conductors," and other service related terms. By using these terms, the *NEC* paints itself into a corner by inadvertently excluding buildings or structures that are fed by a feeder circuit. It makes sense that the rules would be the same regardless of the type of circuit feeding the building or structure, as the intent and purpose of the rules are the same in both instances.

The size of the busbar discussed in this section has also been cleared up. By only providing two of the three dimensions of the busbar, some *Code* users were misunderstanding and misusing this section. A typical ground bar that's found in nearly every panel has two dimensions that are ¼" and 2"...it just so happens that they're the wrong dimensions. Considering that this busbar is connecting multiple grounding electrode conductors and their bonding jumpers, it needs to have considerable mass. This change makes it clear the ground bar in a small panel doesn't meet the requirements.

(E) Ferrous Metal Enclosures and Raceways Containing Grounding Electrode Conductors.

(1) General. To prevent inductive choking of grounding electrode conductors, ferrous raceways and enclosures containing grounding electrode conductors must have each end of the raceway or enclosure bonded to the grounding electrode or grounding electrode conductor. Figures 250–10 and 250–11

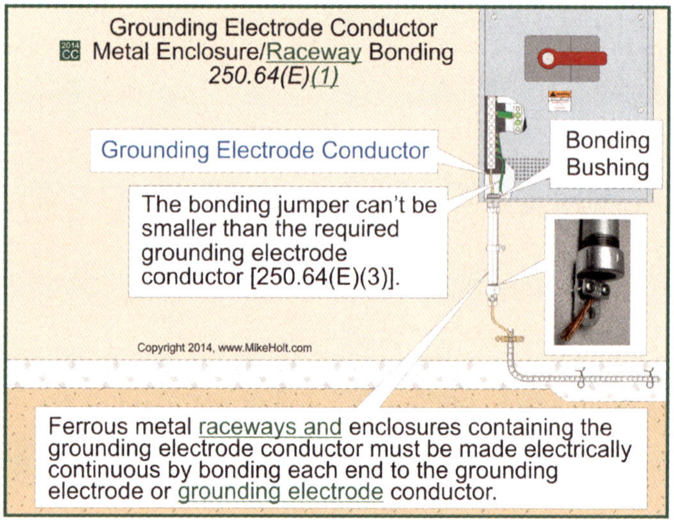

Figure 250–10

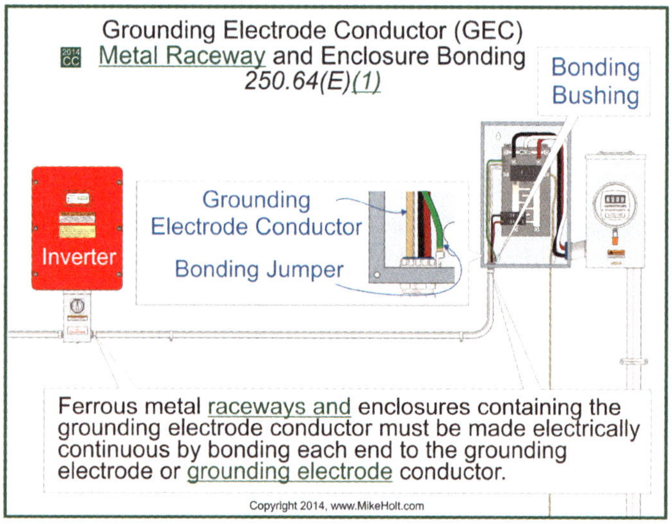

Figure 250–11

(2) Methods. Bonding must be done by one of the methods discussed in 250.92(B)(2) through (B)(4).

(3) Size. Bonding jumpers must be the same size or larger than the required size of the grounding electrode conductor in the raceway or other enclosure. **Figure 250–12**

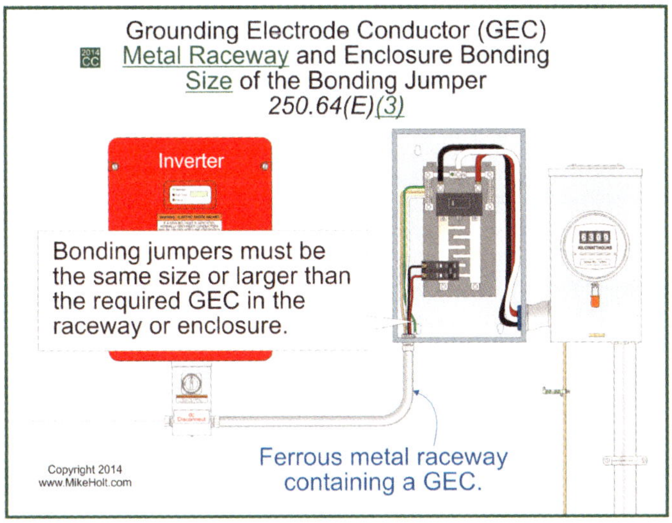

Figure 250–12

(4) Wiring Methods. When a raceway is used for a grounding electrode conductor, it must meet all of the requirements for the raceway, such as securing and supporting, number of bends, conductor fill, and so forth.

> **Author's Comment:** Nonferrous metal raceways, such as aluminum rigid metal conduit, enclosing the grounding electrode conductor aren't required to meet the "bonding each end of the raceway to the grounding electrode conductor" provisions of this section.

> **CAUTION:** *The effectiveness of a grounding electrode is significantly reduced if a ferrous metal raceway containing a grounding electrode conductor isn't bonded to the ferrous metal raceway at both ends. This is because a single conductor carrying high-frequency induced lightning current in a ferrous raceway causes the raceway to act as an inductor, which severely limits (chokes) the current flow through the grounding electrode conductor. ANSI/IEEE 142—Recommended Practice for Grounding of Industrial and Commercial Power Systems (Green Book) states: "An inductive choke can reduce the current flow by 97 percent."*

> **Author's Comment:** To save a lot of time and effort, install the grounding electrode conductor exposed if it's not subject to physical damage [250.64(B)], or enclose it in PVC conduit suitable for the application [352.10(F)].

> **ANALYSIS:** In 2011 250.64(E) was a remarkably long paragraph. When rules are written in overly long paragraphs they tend to be misread, misunderstood, or ignored altogether. While there are no real technical changes to the requirements of bonding these raceways, few will argue that the list format the *NEC* is using more and more often is a better method here.

250.66 Sizing Grounding Electrode Conductor

The sizing requirements for grounding electrode conductors terminating at ground rods and concrete-encased electrodes were changed to address a loophole.

250.66 Sizing Grounding Electrode Conductor. Except as permitted in (A) through (C), a grounding electrode conductor must be sized in accordance with Table 250.66.

(A) Ground Rod. If the grounding electrode conductor is connected to one or more ground rods as permitted in 250.52(A)(5), that portion of the grounding electrode conductor that's the sole connection to the ground rods isn't required to be larger than 6 AWG copper. **Figure 250–13**

(B) Concrete-Encased Grounding Electrode. If the grounding electrode conductor is connected to one or more concrete-encased electrodes, the portion of the grounding electrode conductor that's the sole connection to the concrete-encased electrodes isn't required to be larger than 4 AWG copper. **Figure 250–14**

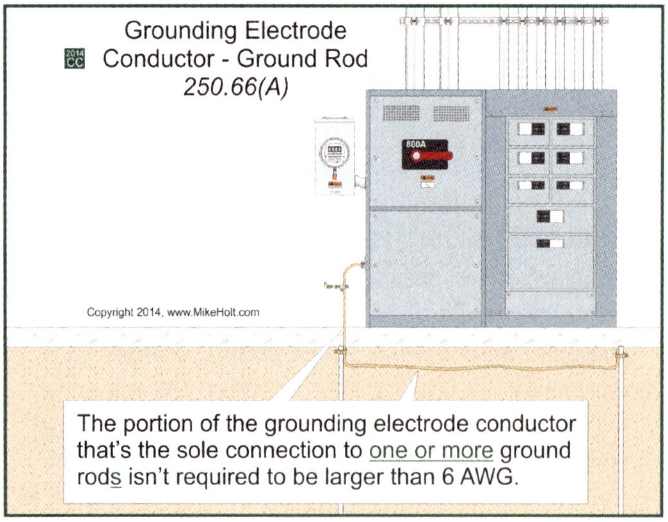

Figure 250–13

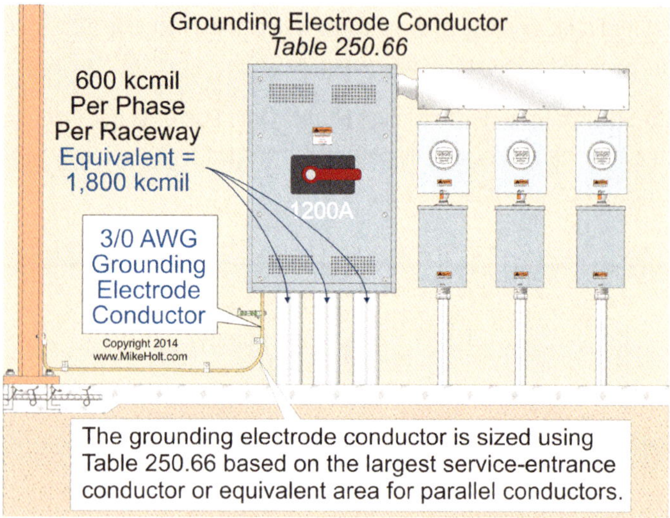

Figure 250–15

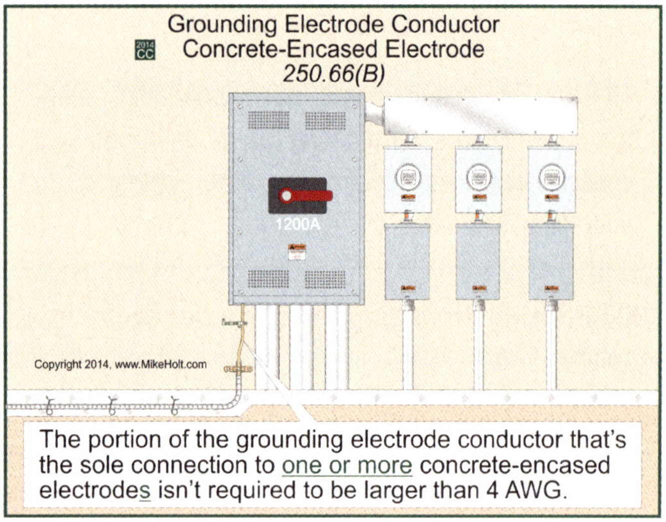

Figure 250–14

Author's Comment: Table 250.66 is used to size the grounding electrode conductor when the conditions of 250.66(A), (B), or (C) don't apply. Figure 250–15

ANALYSIS: The *Code* has long allowed for smaller grounding electrode conductors for ground rods and concrete-encased electrodes. Unfortunately, there was a subtle omission that's been addressed by this change. If a person can use 6 AWG to one ground rod, why not allow it for two ground rods that are in parallel? This practice has been used by installers and allowed by inspectors who either didn't realize the error in the *NEC* or realized the error and recognized that it was just that—an error.

250.68 Termination to the Grounding Electrode

The objects that grounding electrode conductors and bonding jumpers can connect to have been clarified.

250.68 Termination to the Grounding Electrode.

(C) Grounding Electrode Connections. Grounding electrode conductors and grounding electrode bonding jumpers are permitted to terminate to:

(1) Interior metal water piping located not more than 5 ft from the point of entrance to the building/structure.

Ex: In industrial, institutional, and commercial buildings where conditions of maintenance and supervision ensure only qualified persons service the installation, the entire length of the metal water piping system can be used for grounding purposes, provided the entire length, other than short sections passing through walls, floors, or ceilings, is exposed.

(2) The metal frame of a building/structure. Figure 250–16

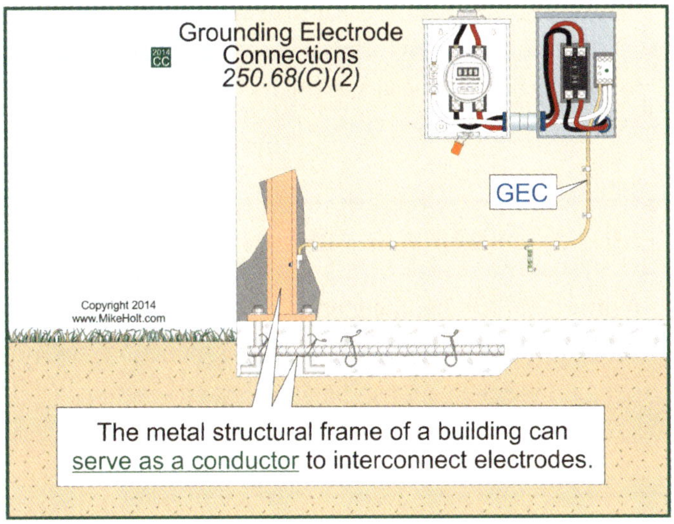

Figure 250–16

(3) A concrete-encased electrode can be extended from the concrete to an accessible location above the concrete. Figure 250–17

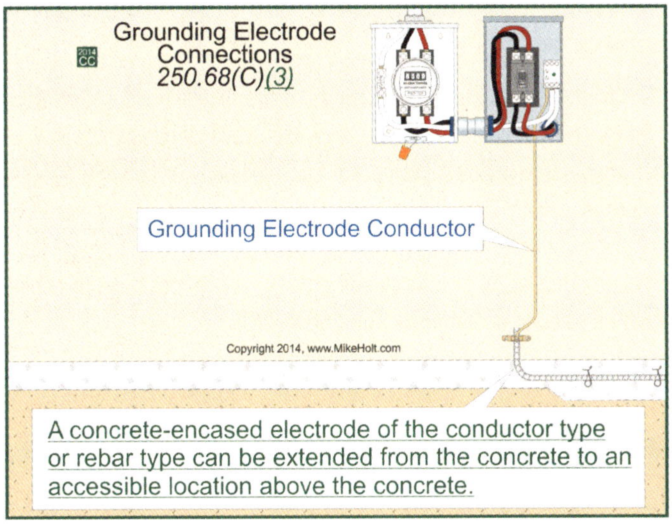

Figure 250–17

ANALYSIS: These welcome changes answer many questions that *Code* users have had in the past. It's important to remember that this section isn't telling us when structural metal or water pipe is an electrode...that's handled in 250.52. This section is simply telling us when we can use these items as conductors to connect other items together. The structural metal of a building may or may not be a grounding electrode, but it's certainly conductive, so it can be used to connect different electrodes together.

Consider a metal frame of a building that doesn't meet the definition of a grounding electrode, because it doesn't meet the criteria of 250.52(A)(2). This same building has a water pipe that meets 250.52(A)(1) and therefore must be used as a grounding electrode. The water pipe enters the building three hundred feet away from the service disconnect. Is it okay to use the metal of the building as a conductor to connect the water pipe to the service equipment? This will allow me to use a short piece of wire from the service equipment to the structural metal, then walk three hundred feet to the water pipe and connect the pipe to the structural metal with another short piece of wire. The answer is now clearly yes, as it should be. The structural metal of the building is not only conductive, it has low impedance (probably lower impedance than a copper conductor would be, given the size of the metal). Previous editions of the *Code* only allowed this practice if the structural metal met the criteria of being a grounding electrode.

A new item (3) has also been added to this list, which many people will see as a welcome change. The *NEC* has been silent on the issue of having a piece of rebar (that meets the criteria of a concrete-encased electrode) exit the concrete and enter the building. That piece of steel couldn't be called a grounding electrode, because that portion of the steel wasn't in the concrete and therefore didn't meet the requirements of 250.52(A)(3). This shouldn't matter, and most installers and inspectors have installed and passed it for years, but now the argument can end.

250.100 Bonding in Hazardous (Classified) Locations

An Informational Note has been added to this section to advise *Code* users of other requirements.

ANALYSIS: Where two different *Code* articles cover the same installation requirements problems are sure to ensue. This is because the entire *NEC* isn't written by the same group of people. The people who decide on proposals to Article 250 aren't the same ones who decide on proposals to the hazardous location rules in Chapter 5. When two different groups of people are deciding what the rules for the same installation should be, there will almost surely be differences. This Informational Note reminds *Code* users that Article 250 doesn't contain every requirement about grounding and bonding in a hazardous location.

Part V. Bonding

250.100 Bonding in Hazardous (Classified) Locations.

Regardless of the circuit voltage, electrical continuity of metal parts of equipment and raceways in hazardous (classified) locations must be ensured by bonding-type locknuts, bushings, wedges, or bushings with bonding jumpers [250.92(B)(4)]; whether or not equipment grounding conductors of the wire type are installed in the raceway. Figure 250–18

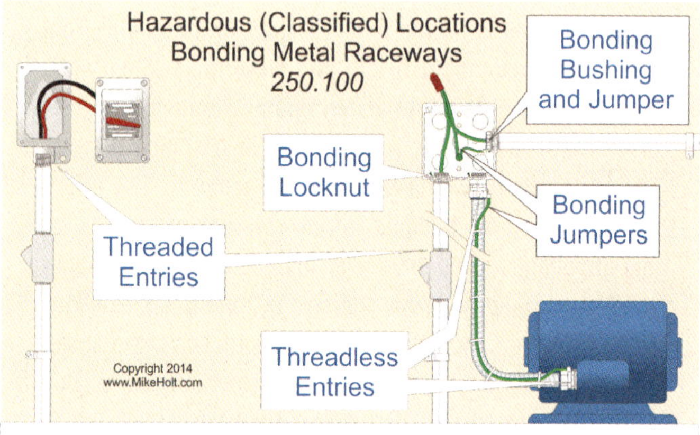

One or more of the above bonding methods [250.92(B)(2) through (B)4)] are required whether or not equipment grounding conductors of the wire type are installed.

Figure 250–18

Note: See 501.30, 502.30, or 503.30 for specific bonding requirements.

250.102 Bonding Conductors and Jumpers

A new table has been added to deal with supply-side bonding jumpers, main bonding jumpers, system bonding jumpers, and service neutral conductors.

250.102 Bonding Conductors and Jumpers.

(C) Size for Supply-Side Bonding Jumper.

(1) Single Raceway Installations. The supply-side bonding jumper is sized in accordance with Table 250.102(C)(1), based on the largest ungrounded conductor within the raceway, Figure 250–19. If the ungrounded supply conductors are larger than 1,100 kcmil copper or 1,750 kcmil aluminum, the supply-side bonding jumper must be sized not less than 12½ percent of the area of the largest set of ungrounded supply conductors.

(2) Parallel Conductor Installations. If the ungrounded supply conductors are paralleled in two or more raceways or cables, the size of the supply-side bonding jumper for each raceway or cable is sized in accordance with Table 250.102(C)(1), based on the size of the largest ungrounded conductors in each raceway or cable. A single supply-side bonding jumper for bonding two or more raceways or cables must be sized in accordance with 250.102(C)(1).

Table 250.102(C)(1). Grounded Conductor, Main Bonding Jumper, System Bonding Jumper, and Supply-Side Bonding Jumper for Alternating-Current Systems

Size of Largest Ungrounded Conductor or Equivalent Area for Parallel Conductors (AWG/kcmil)		Size of Grounded Conductor or Bonding Jumper (AWG/kcmil)	
Copper	Aluminum or Copper-Clad Aluminum	Copper	Aluminum or Copper-Clad Aluminum
2 or smaller	1/0 or smaller	8	6
1 or 1/0	2/0 or 3/0	6	4
2/0 or 3/0	4/0 or 250	4	2
4/0 through 350	300 through 500	2	1/0
400 through 600	600 through 900	1/0	3/0
700 through 1,100	1,000 through 1,750	2/0	4/0
Over 1,100	Over 1,750	See Notes	

[a] *In this table, "bonding jumper" includes main bonding jumpers, system bonding jumpers, and supply-side bonding jumpers.*

Table Notes:

1. *If the ungrounded conductors are larger than 1,100 kcmil copper or 1,750 kcmil aluminum, the neutral conductor or bonding jumper must be not less than 12½ percent of the area of the largest ungrounded conductor or equivalent area for parallel conductors. The neutral conductor or bonding jumper isn't required to be larger than the largest ungrounded conductor or set of parallel ungrounded conductors.*

4. *If there are no service-entrance conductors, the supply conductor size is determined by the equivalent size of the conductor that would be required for the load.*

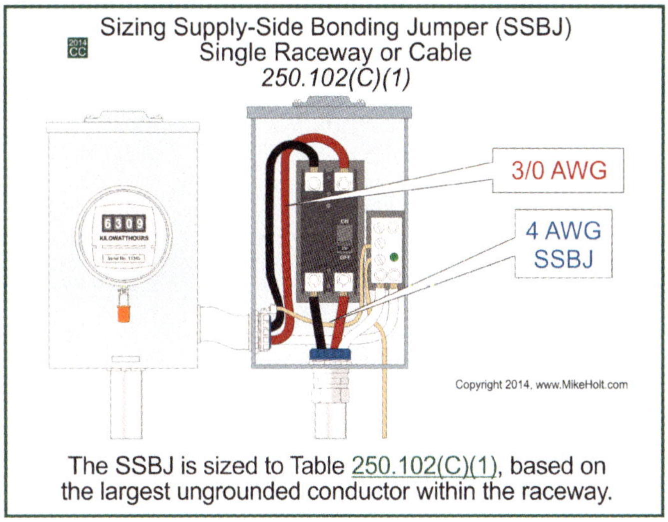

Figure 250–19

Question 1: *What size supply-side bonding jumper is required for a metal raceway containing 700 kcmil service conductors?* Figure 250–20

(a) 1 AWG (b) 1/0 AWG (c) 2/0 AWG (d) 3/0 AWG

Answer: *(c) 2/0 AWG [Table 250.102(C)(1)]*

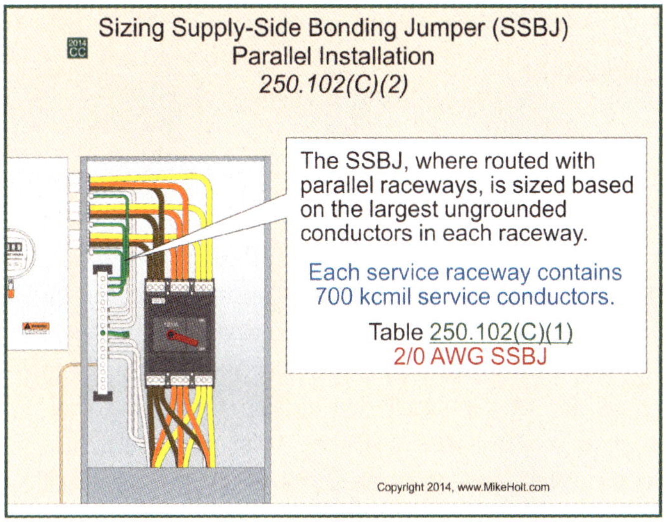

Figure 250–20

Question 2: *What size single supply-side bonding jumper is required for three metal raceways containing 700 kcmil service conductors?* **Figure 250–21**

(a) 1 AWG (b) 1/0 AWG (c) 2/0 AWG (d) 300 AWG

Answer: *(d) 300 kcmil [Table 250.102(C)(1)]*

700 kcmil x 3 = 2,100 kcmil
2,100 kcmil x 0.125 = 263 kcmil
Chapter 9, Table 8, use 300 kcmil

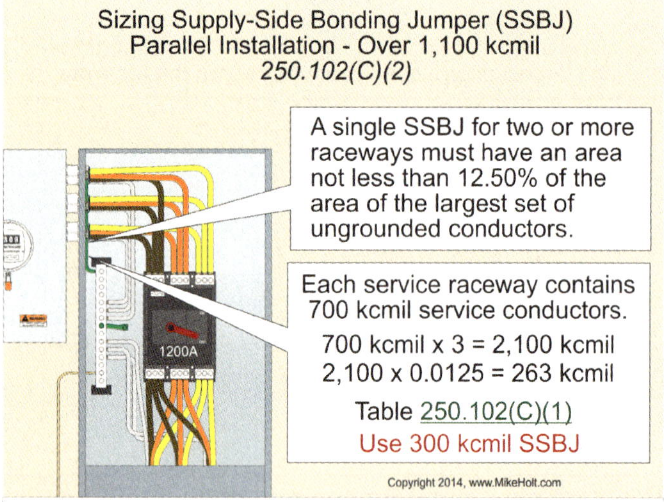

Figure 250–21

ANALYSIS: Experienced *Code* users will recognize this table as a near perfect reproduction of Table 250.66. Despite being named "Grounding Electrode Conductor for AC Systems," Table 250.66 always served many different roles, including sizing the main bonding jumper, system bonding jumper, supply-side bonding jumper, and minimum service neutral conductor. All of these (other than the grounding electrode conductor [GEC]) must carry fault current back to the source, and therefore are very different from the GEC. It makes sense to create a new table for these items, and anyone who has tried to teach Article 250 (especially to a new *Code* user) will almost certainly agree.

250.119 Identification of Equipment Grounding Conductors

Two exceptions and an Informational Note have been added to the identification requirements for equipment grounding conductors.

Part VI. Equipment Grounding and Equipment Grounding Conductors

250.119 Identification of Equipment Grounding Conductors.

Unless required to be insulated, equipment grounding conductors can be bare, covered, or insulated. Insulated equipment grounding conductors must have a continuous outer finish that's either green or green with one or more yellow stripes.

Conductors with insulation that's green, or green with one or more yellow stripes must not be used for an ungrounded or neutral conductor. **Figure 250–22**

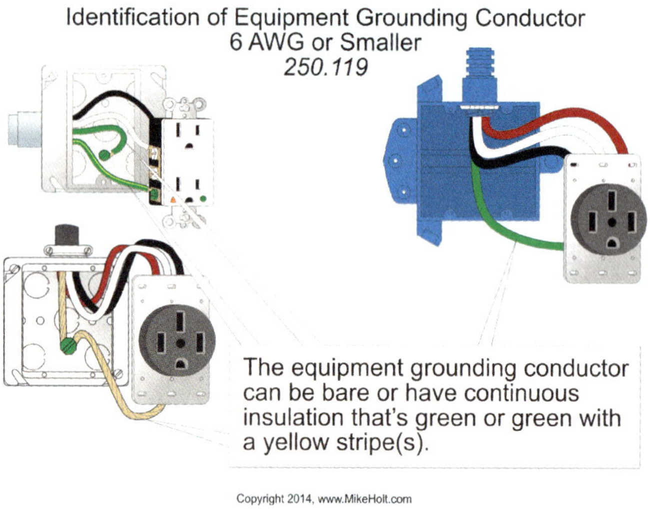

Figure 250–22

Author's Comment: The *NEC* neither requires nor prohibits the use of the color green for the identification of grounding electrode conductors. **Figure 250–23**

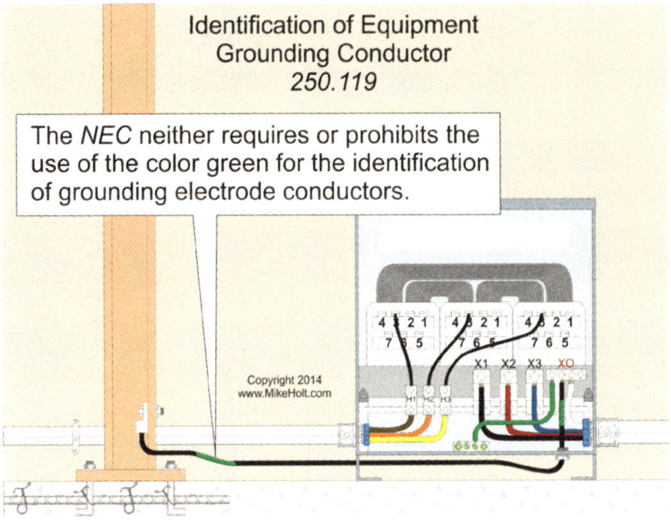

Figure 250–23

Ex 1: Power-limited, Class 2 or Class 3 cables, power-limited fire alarm cables, or communications cables containing circuits operating at less than 50V can use conductors with insulated green or green with one or more yellow stripes for other than equipment grounding conductors [250.20(A) and 250.112(I)]. **Figure 250–24**

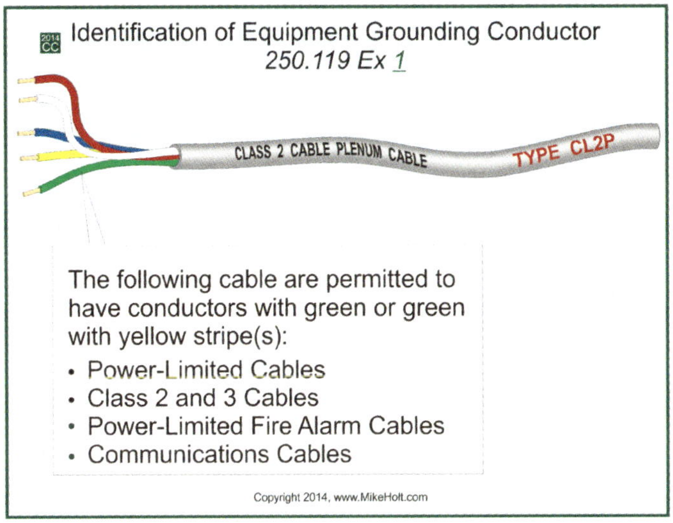

Figure 250–24

Ex 2: Flexible cords, without an equipment grounding conductor, that use the outer jacket of the cord as the conductor insulation can be green.

Note: An example of such a cord is a green colored 2-conductor Type SPT-2 cord.

Ex 3: Conductors with green insulation can be used as ungrounded signal conductors for traffic signal control and traffic signal indicating heads. The circuit must still include an equipment grounding conductor, and if it's of the wire type it must be bare or green with one or more yellow stripes.

(A) Conductors 4 AWG and Larger.

(1) Identified if Accessible. Insulated equipment grounding conductors 4 AWG and larger can be permanently reidentified at the time of installation at every point where the conductor is accessible. **Figure 250–25**

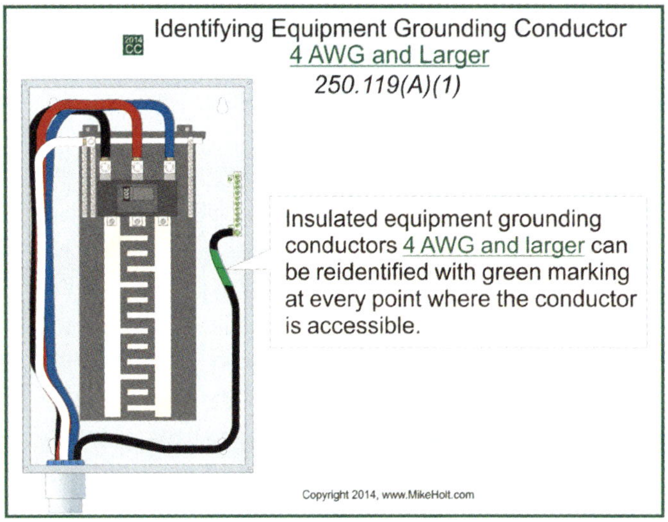

Figure 250–25

Ex: Identification of equipment grounding conductors 4 AWG and larger in conduit bodies isn't required.

(2) Identification Method. Equipment grounding conductor identification must encircle the conductor by: **Figure 250–26**

a. Removing the insulation at termination

b. Coloring the insulation green at termination

c. Marking the insulation at termination with green tape or green adhesive labels

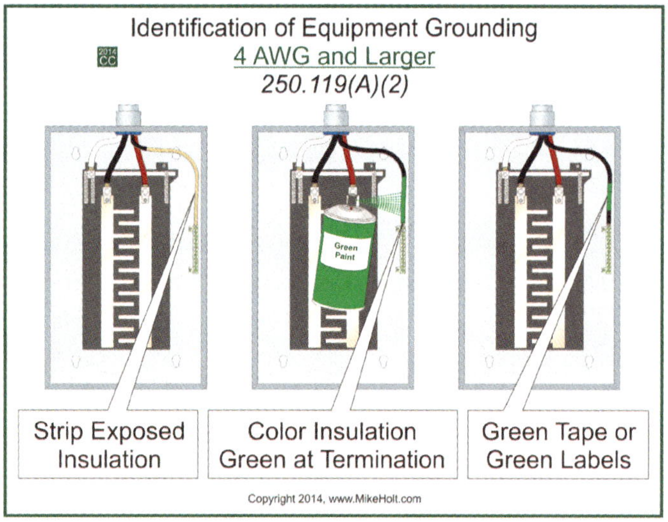

Figure 250–26

ANALYSIS: Exception 2 has been added to address green, two-conductor flexible cords. Although they're certainly less common than black cords, they do exist. If the outer jacket of the cord also serves as the individual conductor insulation (such as for Type SPT-2, also commonly called zip cord), a literal reading of the previous *Code* rules would disallow the cord from being used, since the color green can't be used for ungrounded or neutral conductors. This seems like a reasonable allowance, as a two-conductor cord is obviously not an equipment grounding conductor, so there shouldn't be any confusion by the application of the color green. The Informational Note gives a perfect example of what the exception is covering.

Exception 3 was added at the request of the traffic signal industry. While it seems odd to someone who doesn't work on these systems, the color green isn't an equipment grounding conductor for traffic signals. The green conductor is the signaling conductor that controls the green light on the traffic light...seems logical enough. This is a long-standing practice and is understood by those who work on these systems, so not allowing for this practice can actually endanger the workers who are used to the coloring schemes that are currently used.

250.119(A) was also revised to change the phrase "larger than 6 AWG" to "4 AWG and larger." Although it seems absurd, it really is easier for most people (myself included) to visualize and immediately understand "4 AWG and larger" rather than "larger than 6 AWG."

250.121 Use of Equipment Grounding Conductors

An exception to the prohibition of a combination grounding electrode conductor and equipment grounding conductor has been added.

250.121 Use of Equipment Grounding Conductors.

An equipment grounding conductor isn't permitted to be used as a grounding electrode conductor. Figure 250–27

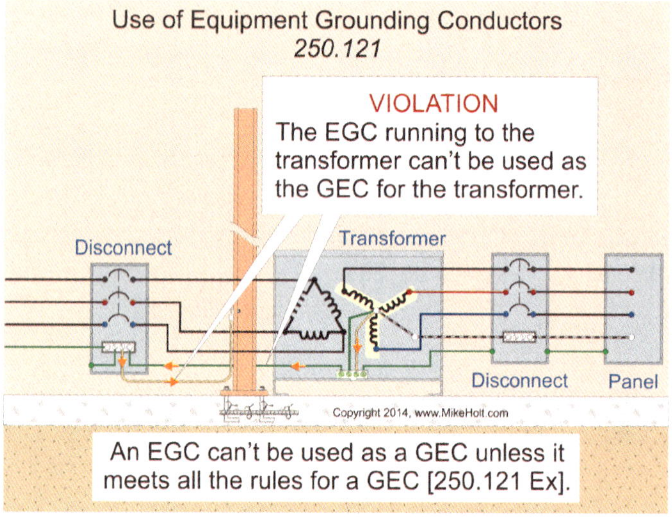

Figure 250–27

Ex: Equipment grounding conductors of the wire type can be used as a grounding electrode conductor, provided they meet all of the rules for both.

Author's Comment: For PV systems, 690.47(C) permits a combined equipment grounding/grounding electrode conductor if sized to the larger of 250.122 or 250.166 and installed in accordance with 250.64(E). Figure 250–28

ANALYSIS: This rule was added in the 2011 edition of the *Code*, and this new exception more or less removes the requirement. Most inspectors allowed one conductor to serve as both the EGC and the GEC if they met the rules for both (for example, sizing, irreversible splicing, ferrous metal enclosures, and so on). With the new exception, we're basically back to where we were in 2008.

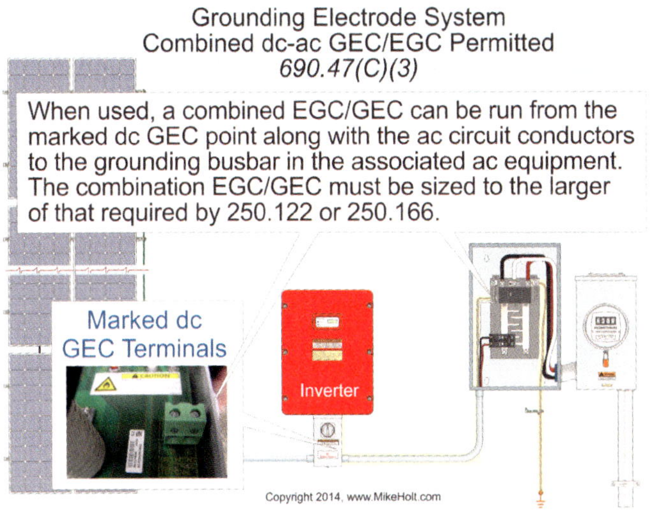

Figure 250–28

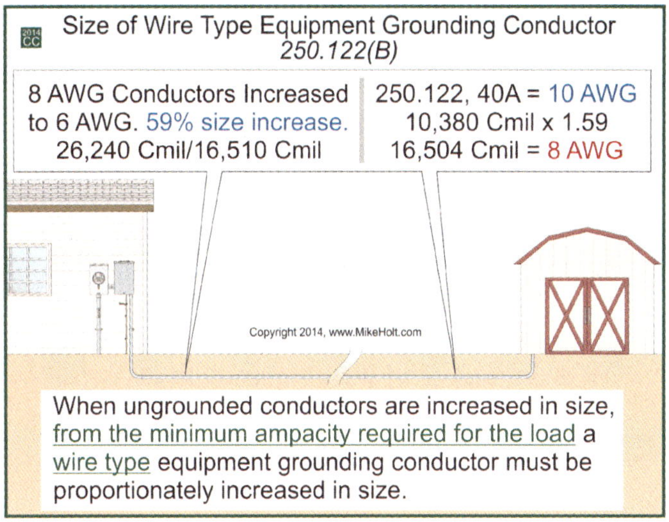

Figure 250–29

250.122 Sizing Equipment Grounding Conductor

The rule on increasing the size of the EGC has been clarified (although you may have to read it a few times to agree).

250.122 Sizing Equipment Grounding Conductor.

(B) Increased in Size. If ungrounded conductors are increased in size from the minimum ampacity that would be required for the load, wire type equipment grounding conductors must be proportionately increased in size according to the circular mil area of the ungrounded conductors.

Author's Comment: Ungrounded conductors are sometimes increased in size to accommodate conductor voltage drop, harmonic current heating, short-circuit rating, or simply for future capacity.

Question: *If the ungrounded conductors for a 40A circuit (with 75°C terminals) are increased in size from 8 AWG to 6 AWG due to voltage drop, the circuit equipment grounding conductor must be increased in size from 10 AWG to _____.* Figure 250–29

(a) 10 AWG (b) 8 AWG (c) 6 AWG (d) 4 AWG

Answer: *(b) 8 AWG*

The circular mil area of 6 AWG is 59 percent more than 8 AWG (26,240 Cmil/16,510 Cmil) [Chapter 9, Table 8].

According to Table 250.122, the circuit equipment grounding conductor for a 40A overcurrent device will be 10 AWG (10,380 Cmil), but the circuit equipment grounding conductor for this circuit must be increased in size by a multiplier of 1.59.

Conductor Size = 10,380 Cmil x 1.59
Conductor Size = 16,504 Cmil
Conductor Size = 8 AWG, Chapter 9, Table 8

Question: *If the ungrounded conductors for a 40A circuit (with 60°C terminals) are increased in size from 8 AWG to 6 AWG due to having four current-carrying conductors in a raceway, the circuit equipment grounding conductor must be increased in size from 10 AWG to _____.*

(a) An increase isn't required (b) 8 AWG
(c) 6 AWG (d) 4 AWG

Answer: *(a) An increase isn't required*

The equipment grounding conductor doesn't need to be increased in size in this example, because the 6 AWG is the smallest size ungrounded conductor allowed by the Code.

8 AWG rated 40A at 60°C x 0.80 = 32A after adjustment factors is too small for the circuit example. 6 AWG rated 55A at 60°C, is required (55A x 0.80 = 44A).

ANALYSIS: This is a requirement that's been in the *NEC* for a long time, but has also been the source of heated debates among *Code* experts. This section has stated that if the ungrounded conductor is increased in size, the EGC must be increased as well. The question is this: when the ungrounded conductor is increased *from what size*? The minimum size required to satisfy the *NEC*? The minimum size to carry the load? The minimum size to accommodate a certain voltage drop? This rule is now clear that conditions of use, such as ampacity adjustment for the number of conductors in a raceway, and temperature correction factors, aren't considered increases in size, because the ampacity of the conductor includes the conditions of its use. If a conductor, due to ampacity adjustment or temperature correction, is made larger, it's still the minimum ampacity required by the *Code*. In other words, it wasn't increased in size above the minimum required. If, however, the conductor was made larger due to voltage drop, then it was increased in size above the minimum ampacity for the load.

250.130 Replacing Nongrounding Receptacles

The allowable methods of connecting an equipment grounding conductor to replacement receptacles were increased.

Part VII. Methods of Equipment Grounding

250.130 Replacing Nongrounding Receptacles.

(C) Nongrounding Receptacle Replacement. If a nongrounding receptacle is replaced with a grounding-type receptacle from an outlet box that doesn't contain an equipment grounding conductor, the grounding contacts of the receptacle must be connected to one of the following: Figure 250–30

(1) The grounding electrode system [250.50]

(2) The grounding electrode conductor

(3) The panelboard equipment grounding terminal

(4) An equipment grounding conductor that's part of a different circuit, if both circuits originate from the same panel.

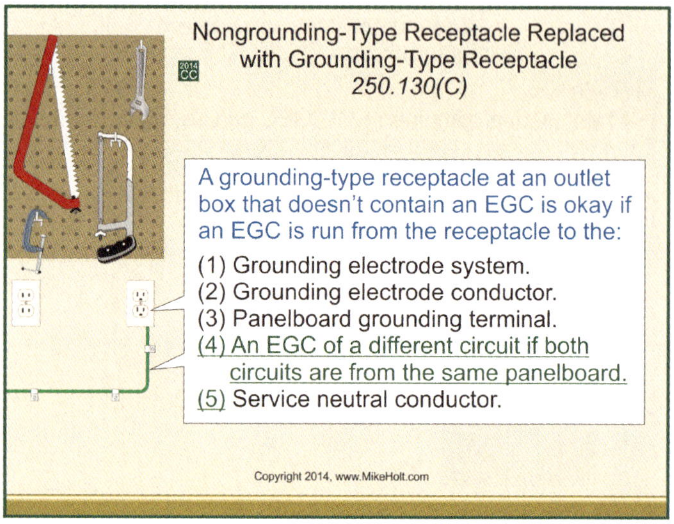

Figure 250–30

(5) The service neutral conductor

Author's Comment: Branch-circuit extensions are only permitted from an outlet box that doesn't contain an equipment grounding conductor if the receptacles on the extension have the grounding contacts connected to the grounding electrode system, grounding electrode conductor, panelboard equipment grounding terminal, or service neutral conductor in accordance with 250.130(C). Figure 250–31

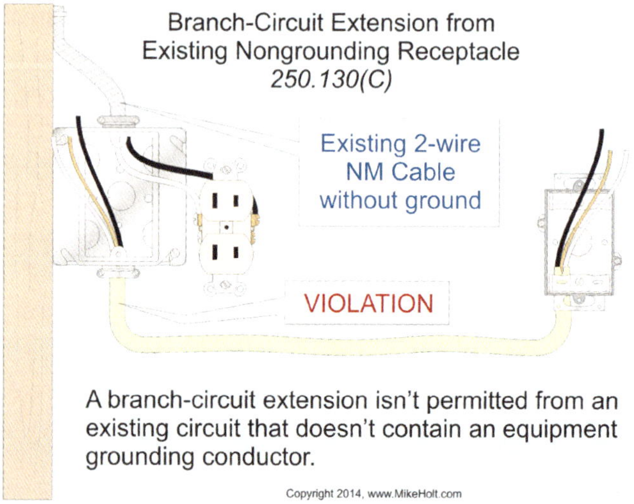

Figure 250–31

Note: A grounding-type receptacle can replace a nongrounding-type receptacle, without having the grounding terminal connected to an equipment grounding conductor, if the receptacle is GFCI protected and marked in accordance with 406.4(D)(2). **Figure 250–32**

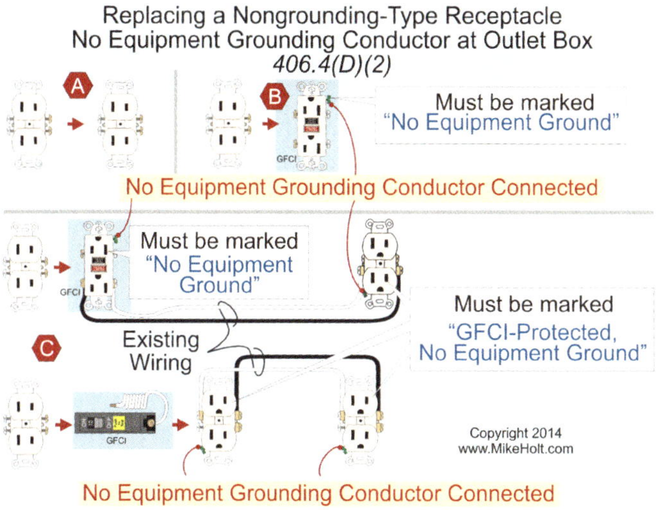

Figure 250–32

ANALYSIS: It often takes a significant amount of work to install an equipment grounding conductor in an existing building that doesn't contain any. If someone has already gone through the trouble of installing one, we should be permitted to take advantage of it. Because of how difficult this can sometimes be, the *NEC* needs to allow for as many options as possible, otherwise some installers will simply ignore the *Code* rule because it's not reasonable. This new allowance doesn't create any safety concerns, and it gives another option for increasing the safety of existing wiring.

Notes

ARTICLE 285

SURGE PROTECTIVE DEVICES (SPDS)

Introduction to Article 285—Surge Protective Devices (SPDs)

This article covers the general requirements, installation requirements, and connection requirements for surge protective devices (SPDs) rated 1kV or less that are permanently installed on premises wiring systems. The *NEC* doesn't require surge protective devices to be installed, but if they are, they must comply with this article.

Surge protective devices are designed to reduce transient voltages present on premises power distribution wiring and load-side equipment, particularly electronic equipment such as computers, telecommunications equipment, security systems, and electronic appliances.

These transient voltages can originate from a number of sources, including anything from lightning to laser printers. The best line of defense for all types of electronic equipment may be the installation of surge protective devices at the electrical service and source of power, as well as at the location of the utilization equipment. Figures 285–1 and 285–2

The intent of a surge protection device is to limit transient voltages by diverting or limiting surge current and preventing continued flow of current while remaining capable of repeating these functions [Article 100]. Figures 285–3 and 285–4

Voltage Spikes/Transients

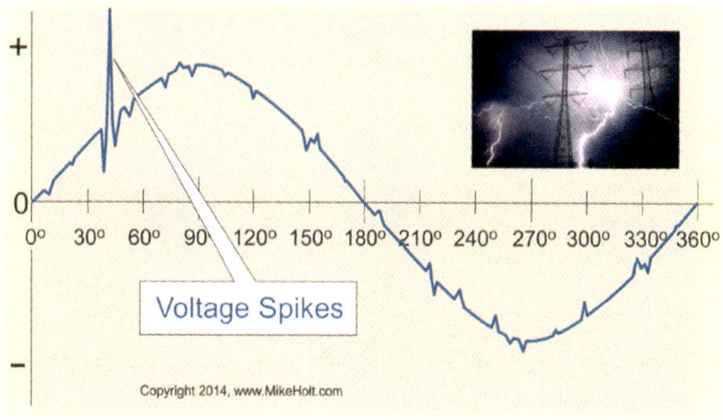

Voltage spikes/transients caused by the switching of utility power lines or power factor correction capacitors, or lightning can reach thousands of volts and amperes.

Figure 285–1

Voltage Spikes

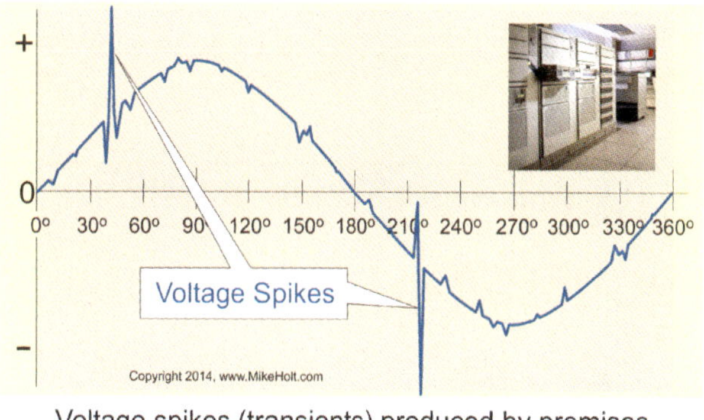

Voltage spikes (transients) produced by premises equipment such as photocopiers, laser printers, and other high reactive loads cycling off, can be in the hundreds of volts.

Figure 285–2

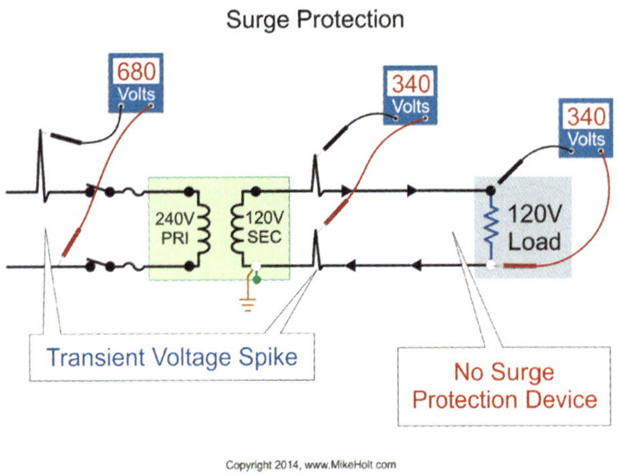

Figure 285–3

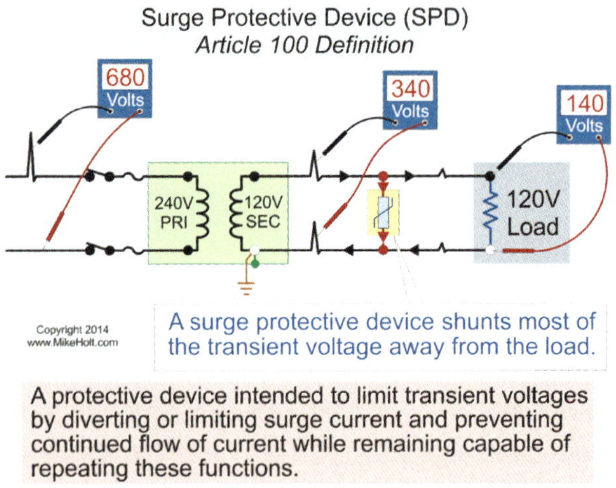

Figure 285–4

285.1 Scope

Changes throughout this article have been made to eliminate the term "TVSS."

Part I. General

285.1 Scope. This article covers the installation and connection requirements for permanently installed surge protective devices. Figure 285–5

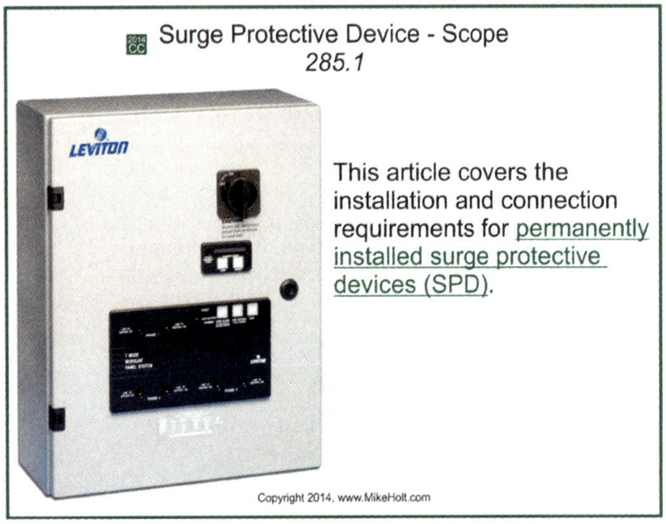

Figure 285–5

Note : Surge arresters rated less than 1,000V are known as Type 1 surge protective devices.

ANALYSIS: The term "TVSS" (transient voltage surge suppressor) was used years ago, but was changed to "SPD" (surge protective device). Over the past few *Code* cycles, the term "TVSS" has been slowly removed from the *NEC*, with the 2014 edition finishing that task.

285.13 Type 4 and Other Component Type SPDs

New text addressing Type 4 SPDs has been added.

285.13 Type 4 and Other Component Type SPDs. Type 4 component assemblies and other component type SPDs can only be installed by the manufacturer.

ANALYSIS: A Type 4 component SPD is an incomplete assembly, and isn't intended to be a field-installed product. They're only acceptable when installed as part of a listed assembly.

CHAPTER 3 WIRING METHODS AND MATERIALS

Introduction to Chapter 3—Wiring Methods and Materials

Chapter 3 covers wiring methods and materials, and provides some very specific installation requirements for conductors, cables, boxes, raceways, and fittings. This chapter includes detailed information about the installation and restrictions involved with wiring methods.

It may be because of those details that many people incorrectly apply the rules from this chapter. Be sure to pay careful attention to the details, and be sure that you make your installation comply with the rules in the *NEC*, not just completing it in the manner that you may have been taught or because "it's always been done that way." This is especially true when it comes to applying the Tables.

Violations of the rules for wiring methods found in Chapter 3 can result in problems with power quality and can lead to fire, shock, and other hazards.

The type of wiring method you'll use depends on several factors; job specifications, *Code* requirements, the environment, need, and cost are among them.

Chapter 3 begins with rules that are common to most wiring methods [Article 300]. It then covers conductors [Article 310] and enclosures [Articles 312 and 314]. The articles that follow become more specific and deal more in-depth with individual wiring methods such as specific types of cables [Articles 320 through 340] and various raceways [Articles 342 through 390]. The chapter winds up with Article 392, a support system, and the final articles [Articles 394 through 398] for open wiring.

Notice as you read through the various wiring methods that the *Code* attempts to use similar subsection numbering for similar topics from one article to the next, using the same digits after the decimal point in the section number for the same topic. This makes it easier to locate specific requirements in a particular article. For example, the rules for securing and supporting can be found in the section that ends with .30 of each article. In addition to this, you'll find a "uses permitted" and "uses not permitted" section in nearly every article.

Wiring Method Articles

- **Article 300—General Requirements for Wiring Methods and Materials.** Article 300 contains the general requirements for all wiring methods included in the *NEC*, except for signaling and communications systems, which are covered in Chapters 7 and 8.

- **Article 310—Conductors for General Wiring.** This article contains the general requirements for conductors, such as insulation markings, ampacity ratings, and conductor use. Article 310 doesn't apply to conductors that are part of flexible cords, fixture wires, or conductors that are an integral part of equipment [90.6 and 300.1(B)].

- **Article 312—Cabinets, Cutout Boxes, and Meter Socket Enclosures.** Article 312 covers the installation and construction specifications for cabinets, cutout boxes, and meter socket enclosures.

- **Article 314—Outlet, Device, Pull, and Junction Boxes, Conduit Bodies, Fittings, and Handhole Enclosures.** Installation requirements for outlet boxes, pull and junction boxes, as well as conduit bodies, and handhole enclosures are contained in this article.

Cable Articles

Articles 320 through 340 address specific types of cables. If you take the time to become familiar with the various types of cables, you'll:

- Understand what's available for doing the work.
- Recognize cable types that have special *NEC* requirements.
- Avoid buying cable that you can't install due to *Code* requirements you can't meet with that particular wiring method.

Here's a brief overview of each one:

- **Article 320—Armored Cable (Type AC).** Armored cable is an assembly of insulated conductors, 14 AWG through 1 AWG, individually wrapped with waxed paper. The conductors are contained within a flexible spiral metal (steel or aluminum) sheath that interlocks at the edges. Armored cable looks like flexible metal conduit. Many electricians call this metal cable "BX®."

- **Article 330—Metal-Clad Cable (Type MC).** Metal-clad cable encloses insulated conductors in a metal sheath of either corrugated or smooth copper or aluminum tubing, or spiral interlocked steel or aluminum. The physical characteristics of Type MC cable make it a versatile wiring method permitted in almost any location and for almost any application. The most commonly used Type MC cable is the interlocking kind, which looks similar to armored cable or flexible metal conduit.

- **Article 334—Nonmetallic-Sheathed Cable (Type NM).** Nonmetallic-sheathed cable encloses two, three, or four insulated conductors, 14 AWG through 2 AWG, within a nonmetallic outer jacket. Because this cable is nonmetallic, it contains a separate equipment grounding conductor. Nonmetallic-sheathed cable is a common wiring method used for residential and commercial branch circuits. Many electricians call this plastic-sheathed cable "Romex®."

- **Article 336—Power and Control Tray Cable (Type TC).** Power and control tray cable is a factory assembly of two or more insulated conductors under a nonmetallic sheath for installation in cable trays, in raceways, or supported by a messenger wire.

- **Article 338—Service-Entrance Cable (Types SE and USE).** Service-entrance cable can be a single-conductor or a multiconductor assembly within an overall nonmetallic covering. This cable is used primarily for services not over 600V, but is also permitted for feeders and branch circuits.

- **Article 340—Underground Feeder and Branch-Circuit Cable (Type UF).** Underground feeder cable is a moisture-, fungus-, and corrosion-resistant cable suitable for direct burial in the earth, and it comes in sizes 14 AWG through 4/0 AWG [340.104]. Multiconductor UF cable is covered in molded plastic that surrounds the insulated conductors.

Raceway Articles

Articles 342 through 390 address specific types of raceways. Refer to Article 100 for the definition of a raceway. If you take the time to become familiar with the various types of raceways, you'll:

- Understand what's available for doing the work.
- Recognize raceway types that have special *Code* requirements.
- Avoid buying a raceway that you can't install due to *NEC* requirements you can't meet with that particular wiring method.

Here's a brief overview of each one:

- **Article 342—Intermediate Metal Conduit (Type IMC).** Intermediate metal conduit is a circular metal raceway with the same outside diameter as rigid metal conduit. The wall thickness of intermediate metal conduit is less than that of rigid metal conduit, so it has a greater interior cross-sectional area for holding conductors. Intermediate metal conduit is lighter and less expensive than rigid metal conduit, but it's permitted in all the same locations as rigid metal conduit. Intermediate metal conduit also uses a different steel alloy, which makes it stronger than rigid metal conduit, even though the walls are thinner.
- **Article 344—Rigid Metal Conduit (Type RMC).** Rigid metal conduit is similar to intermediate metal conduit, except the wall thickness is greater, so it has a smaller interior cross-sectional area. Rigid metal conduit is heavier than intermediate metal conduit and it's permitted to be installed in any location, just like intermediate metal conduit.
- **Article 348—Flexible Metal Conduit (Type FMC).** Flexible metal conduit is a raceway of circular cross section made of a helically wound, interlocked metal strip of either steel or aluminum. It's commonly called "Greenfield" or "Flex."
- **Article 350—Liquidtight Flexible Metal Conduit (Type LFMC).** Liquidtight flexible metal conduit is a raceway of circular cross section with an outer liquidtight, nonmetallic, sunlight-resistant jacket over an inner flexible metal core, with associated couplings, connectors, and fittings. It's listed for the installation of electrical conductors. Liquidtight flexible metal conduit is commonly called "Sealtite®" or simply "liquidtight." Liquidtight flexible metal conduit is of similar construction to flexible metal conduit, but it has an outer thermoplastic covering.
- **Article 352—Rigid Polyvinyl Chloride Conduit (Type PVC).** Rigid polyvinyl chloride conduit is a nonmetallic raceway of circular cross section with integral or associated couplings, connectors, and fittings. It's listed for the installation of electrical conductors.
- **Article 356—Liquidtight Flexible Nonmetallic Conduit (Type LFNC).** Liquidtight flexible nonmetallic conduit is a raceway of circular cross section with an outer liquidtight, nonmetallic, sunlight-resistant jacket over an inner flexible core, with associated couplings, connectors, and fittings. It's listed for the installation of electrical conductors. LFNC is available in three types:
  - **Type LFNC-A (orange).** A smooth seamless inner core and cover bonded together with reinforcement layers inserted between the core and covers.

- ◻ **Type LFNC-B (gray).** A smooth inner surface with integral reinforcement within the conduit wall.
- ◻ **Type LFNC-C (black).** A corrugated internal and external surface without integral reinforcement within the conduit wall.

- **Article 358—Electrical Metallic Tubing (EMT).** Electrical metallic tubing is a nonthreaded thinwall raceway of circular cross section designed for the physical protection and routing of conductors and cables. Compared to rigid metal conduit and intermediate metal conduit, electrical metallic tubing is relatively easy to bend, cut, and ream. EMT isn't threaded, so all connectors and couplings are of the threadless type. Today, it's available in a range of colors, such as red and blue.
- **Article 362—Electrical Nonmetallic Tubing (ENT).** Electrical nonmetallic tubing is a pliable, corrugated, circular raceway made of PVC. It's often called "Smurf Pipe" or "Smurf Tube," because it was available only in blue when it came out and at the time the children's cartoon characters "The Smurfs" were popular. It's now available in multiple colors such as red and yellow as well as blue.
- **Article 376—Metal Wireways.** A metal wireway is a sheet metal trough with hinged or removable covers for housing and protecting electrical conductors and cable, in which conductors are placed after the wireway has been installed as a complete system.
- **Article 380—Multioutlet Assemblies.** A multioutlet assembly is a surface, flush, or freestanding raceway designed to hold conductors and receptacles. It's assembled in the field or at the factory.
- **Article 386—Surface Metal Raceways.** A surface metal raceway is a metallic raceway intended to be mounted to the surface with associated accessories, in which conductors are placed after the raceway has been installed as a complete system.
- **Article 388—Surface Nonmetallic Raceways.** A surface nonmetallic raceway is intended to be surface mounted with associated accessories. Conductors are placed inside after the raceway has been installed as a complete system.

Cable Tray

- **Article 392—Cable Trays.** A cable tray system is a unit or assembly of units or sections with associated fittings that form a structural system used to securely fasten or support cables and raceways. A cable tray isn't a raceway; it's a support system for raceways, cables, and enclosures.

ARTICLE 300 GENERAL REQUIREMENTS FOR WIRING METHODS AND MATERIALS

Introduction to Article 300—General Requirements for Wiring Methods and Materials

Article 300 contains the general requirements for all wiring methods included in the *NEC*. However, the article doesn't apply to communications systems, which are covered in Chapter 8, except when Article 300 is specifically referenced in Chapter 8.

This article is primarily concerned with how to install, route, splice, protect, and secure conductors and raceways. How well you conform to the requirements of Article 300 will generally be evident in the finished work, because many of the requirements tend to determine the appearance of the installation. Because of this, it's often easy to spot Article 300 problems if you're looking for *Code* violations. For example, you can easily see when someone runs an equipment grounding conductor outside a raceway instead of grouping all conductors of a circuit together, as required by 300.3(B).

A good understanding of Article 300 will start you on the path to correctly installing the wiring methods included in Chapter 3. Be sure to carefully consider the accompanying illustrations, and refer to the definitions in Article 100 as needed.

300.1 Scope

The title and scope of Article 300 have been changed to become more accurate.

ANALYSIS: Article 300 has long been titled "Wiring Methods." Wiring methods include raceways and cables, and Article 300 certainly doesn't contain all of the rules for them. The change to "General Requirements for Wiring Methods" much more accurately describes what this article is all about.

Part I. General

300.1 Scope.

(A) Wiring Installations. Article 300 contains the general requirements for power and lighting wiring methods.

Author's Comment: The requirements contained in Article 300 don't apply to the wiring methods for signaling and communications systems, except where there's a specific reference in Chapter 7 or 8 to a rule in Article 300.

- CATV, 820.3
- Class 2 and 3 Circuits, 725.3
- Communications Cables and Raceways, 800.133(A)(2)
- Fire Alarm Circuits, 760.3

300.5 Underground Installations

The rules for cables beneath buildings have been expanded to include conductors beneath buildings. In addition, the allowable types of underground raceways for the physical protection of direct-buried conductors and cables have been increased.

300.5 Underground Installations.

(C) Cables and Conductors Under Buildings. Cables and conductors installed under a building must be installed in a raceway that extends past the outside walls of the building. Figure 300–1

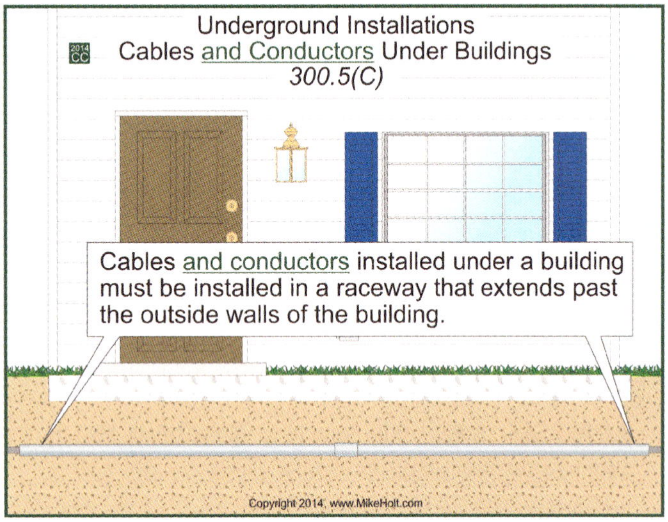

Figure 300–1

Ex 2: Type MC Cable listed for direct burial is permitted under a building without installation in a raceway [330.10(A)(5)]. Figure 300–2

ANALYSIS: While some people use the terms "cable" and "conductor" interchangeably, the *Code* does not. A cable (almost always) is an assembly of multiple conductors. Since direct-buried cables aren't permitted under a building (generally), it makes sense that direct-buried conductors aren't allowed either.

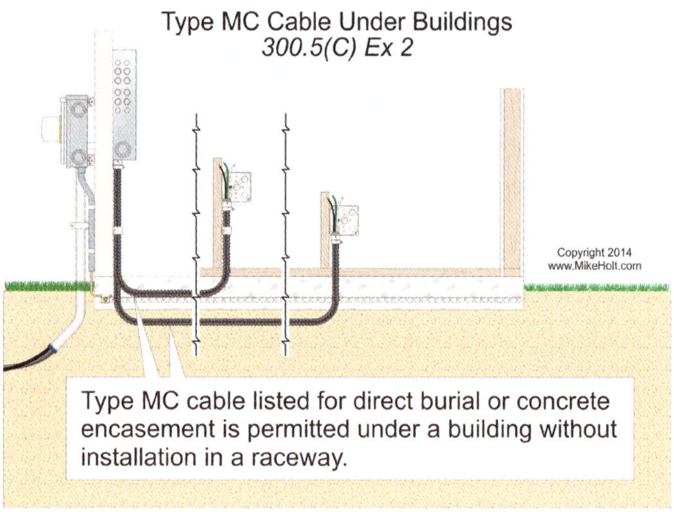

Figure 300–2

(D) Protecting Underground Cables and Conductors. Direct-buried conductors and cables such as Types MC, UF, and USE must be protected from damage in accordance with (1) through (4).

(1) Emerging from Grade. Direct-buried cables or conductors that emerge from grade must be installed in an enclosure or raceway to protect against physical damage. Protection isn't required to extend more than 18 in. below grade, and protection above ground must extend to a height of not less than 8 ft. Figure 300–3

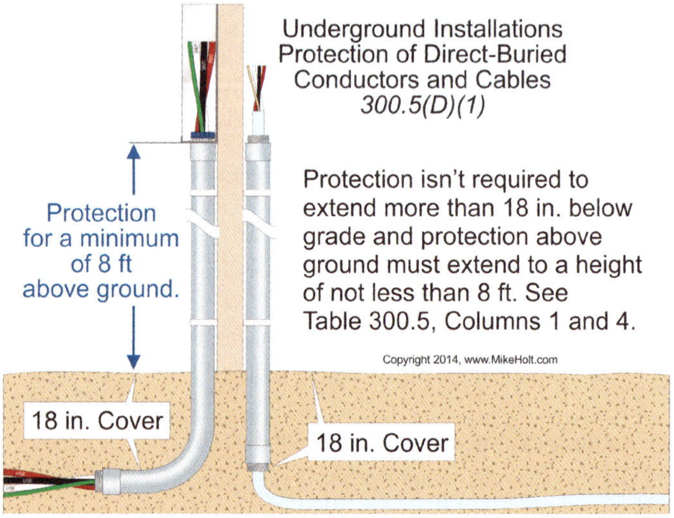

Figure 300–3

(2) Conductors Entering Buildings. Conductors that enter a building must be protected to the point of entrance.

(4) Enclosure or Raceway Damage. If direct-buried cables, enclosures, or raceways are subject to physical damage, the conductors must be installed in rigid metal conduit, intermediate metal conduit, RTRC-XW, or Schedule 80 PVC conduit.

ANALYSIS: Since the introduction of Type RTRC conduit in the *NEC*, installers have been falling in love with it. It's a very, very lightweight product, it doesn't burn when pulling ropes through it, and it costs significantly less than steel. Because it's only been allowed for a short time, there are areas in the *Code* that don't address it, and changes need to be made to add it. This is a further example.

300.6 Protection Against Corrosion and Deterioration

An Informational Note has been added to help people understand what "field-cut threads" are.

300.6 Protection Against Corrosion and Deterioration. Raceways, cable trays, cablebus, cable armor, boxes, cable sheathing, cabinets, elbows, couplings, fittings, supports, and support hardware must be suitable for the environment. Figure 300–4

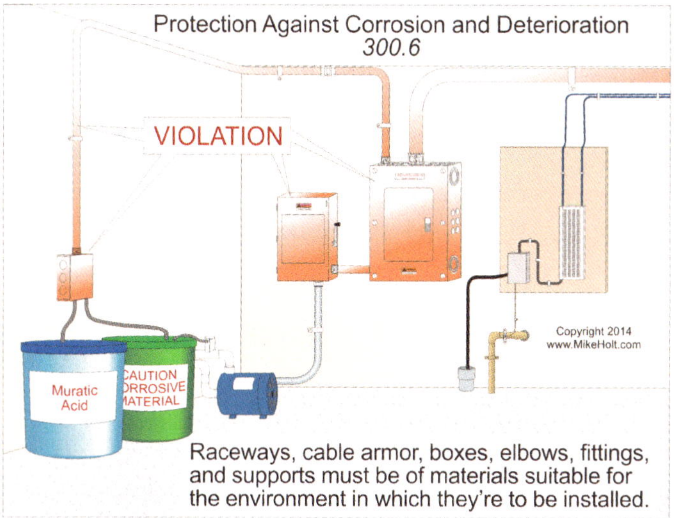

Figure 300–4

(A) Ferrous Metal Equipment. Ferrous metal raceways, enclosures, cables, cable trays, fittings, and support hardware must be protected against corrosion by a coating of listed corrosion-resistant material. Where conduit is threaded in the field, the threads must be coated with an approved electrically conductive, corrosion-resistant compound, such as cold zinc.

Note: Field-cut threads are those threads that are cut anywhere other than at the factory.

Author's Comment: Nonferrous metal raceways, such as aluminum rigid metal conduit, don't have to meet the provisions of this section.

ANALYSIS: Well I guess that clears that up!

300.22 Wiring in Ducts Not for Air Handling, Fabricated Ducts for Environmental Air, and Other Spaces for Environmental Air (Plenums)

Cable ties in plenum spaces are now discussed.

300.22 Wiring in Ducts Not for Air Handling, Fabricated Ducts for Environmental Air, and Other Spaces for Environmental Air (Plenums). The provisions of this section apply to the installation and uses of electrical wiring and equipment in ducts used for dust, loose stock, or vapor removal; ducts specifically fabricated for environmental air, and spaces used for environmental air (plenums).

(C) Other Spaces Used for Environmental Air (Plenums). This section applies to spaces used for air-handling purposes, but not fabricated for environmental air-handling purposes, Figure 300–5. This requirement doesn't apply to habitable rooms or areas of buildings, the prime purpose of which isn't air handling.

Note 1: The spaces above a suspended ceiling or below a raised floor used for environmental air are examples of the type of space to which this section applies. Figure 300–6

Note 2: The phrase "other space used for environmental air (plenums)" correlates with the term "plenum" in NFPA 90A, *Standard for the Installation of Air-Conditioning and Ventilating Systems*, and other mechanical codes where the ceiling is used for return air purposes, as well as some other air-handling spaces.

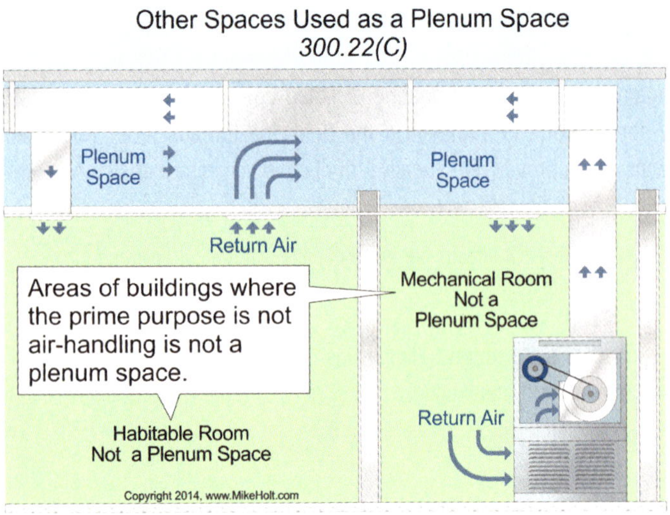

Figure 300–5

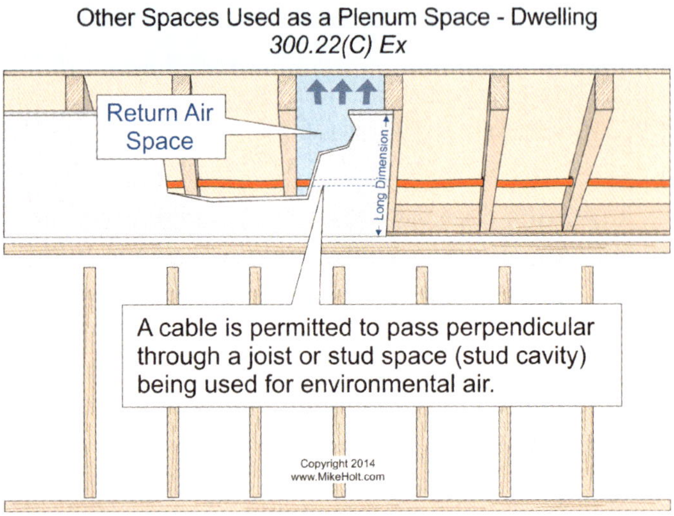

Figure 300–7

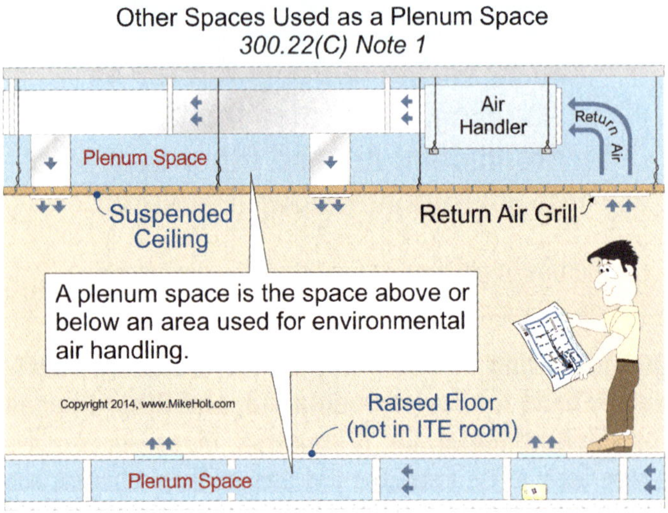

Figure 300–6

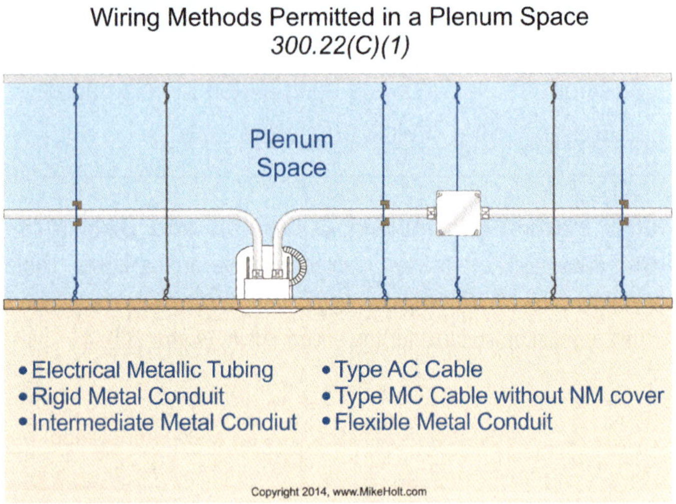

Figure 300–8

Ex: In a dwelling unit, this section doesn't apply to the space between joists or studs where the wiring passes through that space perpendicular to the long dimension of that space. Figure 300–7

(1) Wiring Methods. Electrical metallic tubing, rigid metal conduit, intermediate metal conduit, armored cable, metal-clad cable without a nonmetallic cover, and flexible metal conduit can be installed in plenum spaces. If accessible, surface metal raceways or metal wireways with metal covers can be installed in a plenum space. Figure 300–8

Cable ties for securing and supporting must be listed as having adequate fire resistant and low smoke producing characteristics. **Figure 300–9**

Author's Comments:

- PVC conduit [Article 352], electrical nonmetallic tubing [Article 362], liquidtight flexible conduit, and nonmetallic cables aren't permitted to be installed in spaces used for environmental air because they give off deadly toxic fumes when burned or superheated.

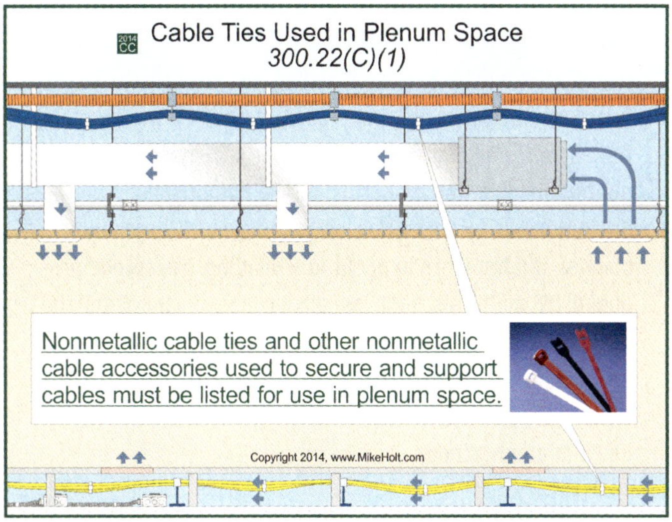

Figure 300–9

- Plenum-rated control, signaling, and communications cables and raceways are permitted in plenum spaces: Figure 300–10
  - CATV, 820.179(A)
  - Communications, 800.21
  - Control and Signaling, Table 725.154
  - Fire Alarm, 760.7
  - Optical Fiber Cables and Raceways, 770.113(C)
  - Sound Systems, 640.9(C) and Table 725.154
- Any wiring method suitable for the condition can be used in a space not used for environmental air-handling purposes. Figure 300–11

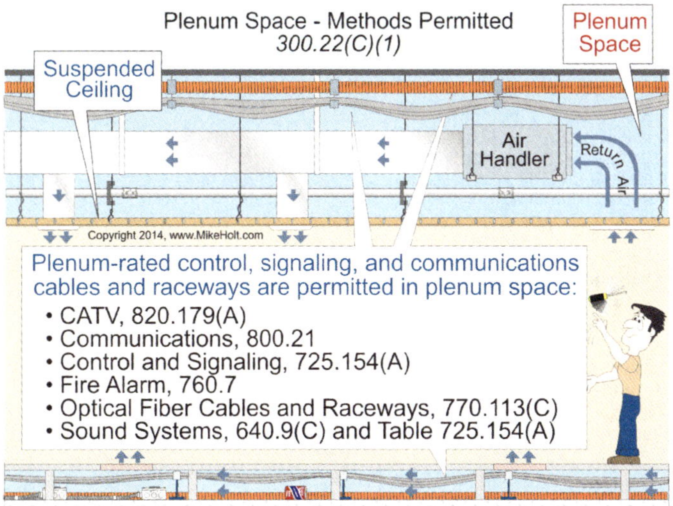

Figure 300–10

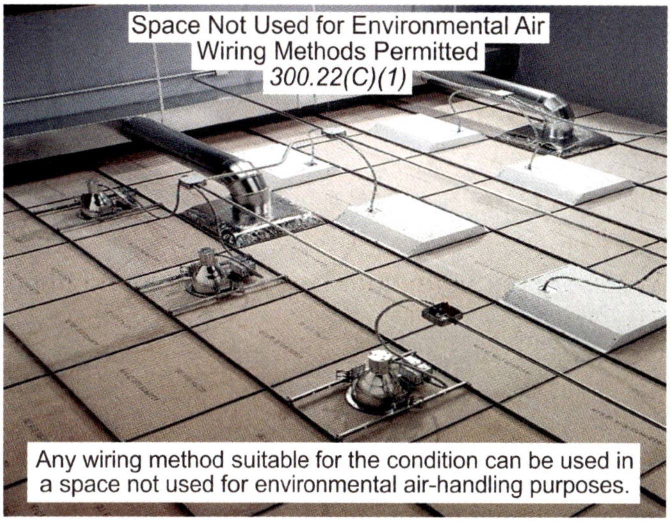

Figure 300–11

(2) Cable Tray Systems.

(a) Metal Cable Tray Systems. Metal cable tray systems can be installed to support the wiring methods and equipment permitted by this section. Figure 300–12

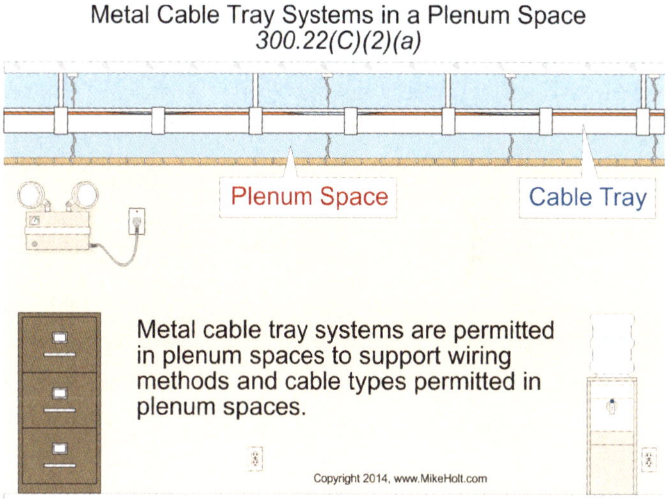

Figure 300–12

(3) Equipment. Electrical equipment with metal enclosures is permitted to be installed in plenum spaces.

Author's Comment: Examples of electrical equipment permitted in plenum spaces are air-handlers, junction boxes, and dry-type transformers; however, transformers must not be rated over 50 kVA when located in hollow spaces [450.13(B)]. Figure 300–13

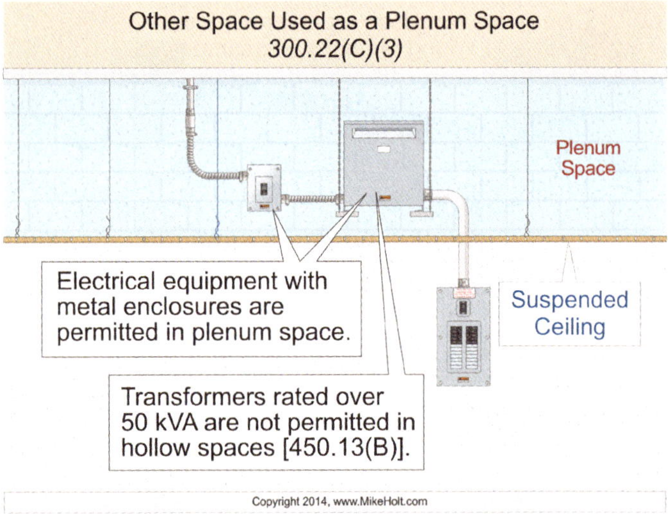

Figure 300–13

ANALYSIS: Plenum spaces, such as those commonly found above a suspended ceiling or beneath a raised floor, use the open air space as a method of transporting the air in a building. Because this air is recycled throughout the building, the properties of any combustible material are regulated by this *Code* as well as by the mechanical code(s). If a fire were to occur in a building, the smoke produced by materials such as plastic can incapacitate the occupants very quickly. While cable ties don't add a lot of fuel to a fire, they do add to the problem, and it all adds up if it's not regulated. These cable ties must now be listed for use in plenum spaces.

ARTICLE 310 CONDUCTORS FOR GENERAL WIRING

Introduction to Article 310—Conductors for General Wiring

This article contains the general requirements for conductors, such as insulation markings, ampacity ratings, and conditions of use. Article 310 doesn't apply to conductors that are part of flexible cords, fixture wires, or to conductors that are an integral part of equipment [90.7 and 300.1(B)].

People often make mistakes in applying the ampacity tables contained in Article 310. If you study the explanations carefully, you'll avoid common errors such as applying Table 310.15(B)(17) when you should be applying Table 310.15(B)(16).

Why so many tables? Why does Table 310.15(B)(17) list the ampacity of 6 THHN as 105 amperes, while Table 310.15(B)(16) lists the same conductor as having an ampacity of only 75 amperes? To answer that, go back to Article 100 and review the definition of ampacity. Notice the phrase "conditions of use." These tables set a maximum current value at which premature failure of the conductor insulation shouldn't occur during normal use, under the conditions described in the tables.

The designations THHN, THHW, RHH, and so on, are insulation types. Every type of insulation has a limit to how much heat it can withstand. When current flows through a conductor, it creates heat. How well the insulation around a conductor can dissipate that heat depends on factors such as whether that conductor is in free air or not. Think about what happens when you put on a sweater, a jacket, and then a coat—all at the same time. You heat up. Your skin can't dissipate heat with all that clothing on nearly as well as it dissipates heat in free air. The same principal applies to conductors.

Conductor insulation also fails with age. That's why we conduct cable testing and take other measures to predict failure and replace certain conductors (for example, feeders or critical equipment conductors) while they're still within design specifications. But conductor insulation failure takes decades under normal use—and it's a maintenance issue. However, if a conductor is forced to exceed the ampacity listed in the appropriate table, and as a result its design temperature is exceeded, insulation failure happens much more rapidly—often catastrophically. Consequently, exceeding the allowable ampacity of a conductor is a serious safety issue.

310.15 Conductor Ampacity

Several changes to this section include removing the dwelling unit table, dealing with the rooftop issue, and clarifying the bundling rules.

310.15 Conductor Ampacity.

Author's Comment: According to Article 100, "ampacity" means the maximum current, in amperes, a conductor can carry continuously, where the temperature of the conductor won't be raised in excess of its insulation temperature rating. Figure 310–1

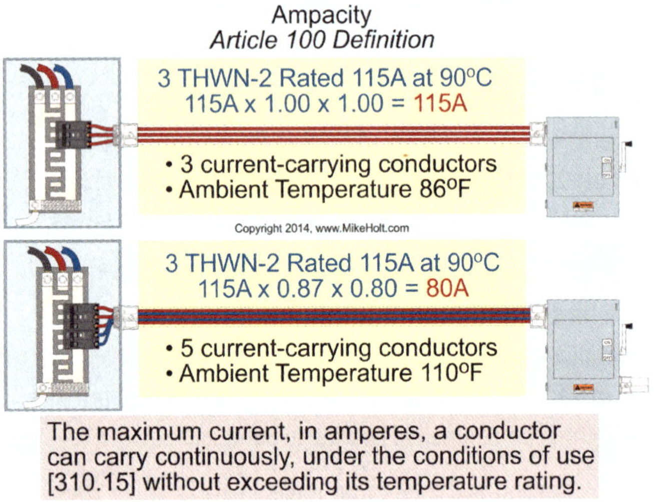

Figure 310–1

(A) General Requirements.

(1) Tables for Engineering Supervision. The ampacity of a conductor can be determined either by using the tables in accordance with 310.15(B), or under engineering supervision as provided in 310.15(C).

> **Note 1:** Ampacities provided by this section don't take voltage drop into consideration. See 210.19(A) Note 4, for branch circuits and 215.2(D) Note 2, for feeders.

(2) Conductor Ampacity—Lower Rating. Where more than one ampacity applies for a given circuit length, the lowest value must be used. Figure 310–2

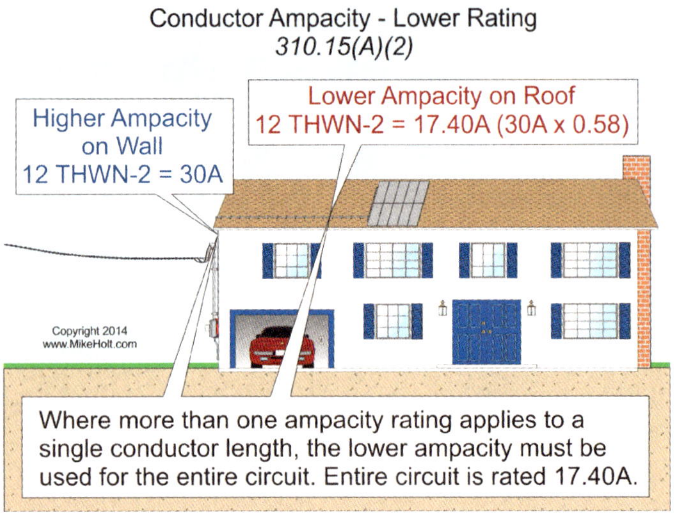

Figure 310–2

Ex: When different ampacities apply to a length of conductor, the higher ampacity is permitted for the entire circuit if the reduced ampacity length doesn't exceed 10 ft and its length doesn't exceed 10 percent of the length of the higher ampacity. Figures 310–3 and 310–4

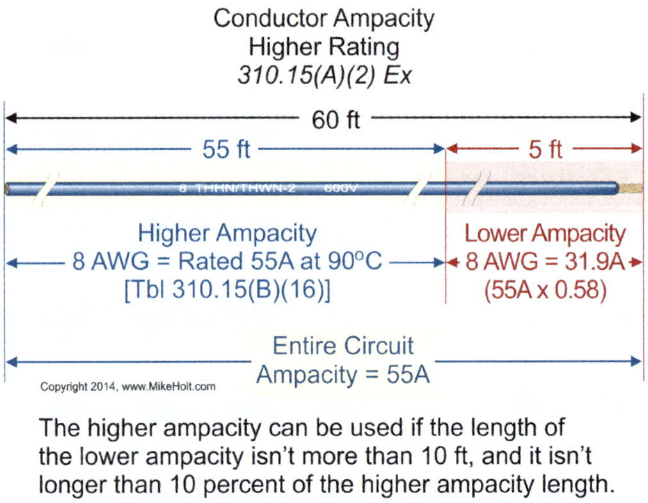

Figure 310–3

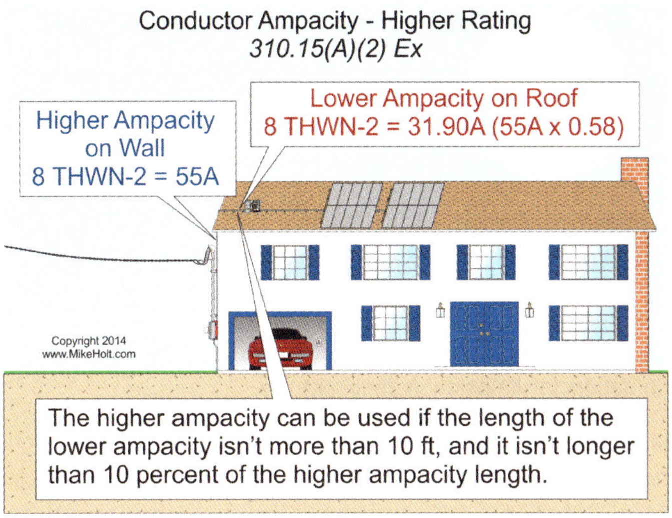

Figure 310–4

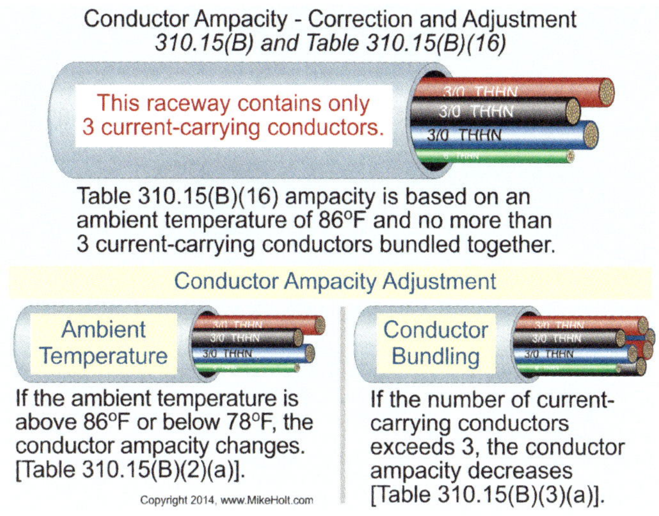

Figure 310–5

(3) Insulation Temperature Limitation. Conductors must not be used where the operating temperature exceeds that designated for the type of insulated conductor involved.

Note 1: The insulation temperature rating of a conductor [Table 310.104(A)] is the maximum temperature a conductor can withstand over a prolonged time period without serious degradation. The main factors to consider for conductor operating temperature include:

(1) Ambient temperature may vary along the conductor length as well as from time to time [Table 310.15(B)(2)(a)].

(2) Heat generated internally in the conductor—load current flow.

(3) The rate at which generated heat dissipates into the ambient medium.

(4) Adjacent load-carrying conductors have the effect of raising the ambient temperature and impeding heat dissipation [Table 310.15(B)(3)(a)].

Note 2: See 110.14(C)(1) for the temperature limitation of terminations.

(B) Ampacity Table. The allowable conductor ampacities listed in Table 310.15(B)(16) are based on conditions where the ambient temperature isn't over 86°F, and no more than three current-carrying conductors are bundled together. Figure 310–5

The temperature correction and adjustment factors apply to the conductor ampacity, based on the temperature rating of the conductor insulation in accordance with Table 310.15(B)(16). Figure 310–6

(2) Conductor Ampacity Ambient Temperature Correction. When conductors are installed in an ambient temperature other than 78°F to 86°F, the ampacities listed in Table 310.15(B)(16) must be corrected in accordance with the multipliers listed in Table 310.15(B)(2)(a). Figure 310–7

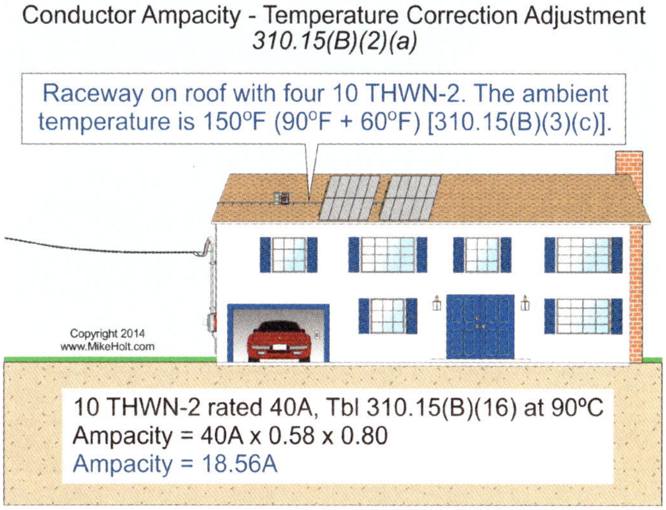

Figure 310–6

Question: *What's the corrected ampacity of 3/0 THHN conductors if the ambient temperature is 108°F?*

(a) 173A (b) 196A (c) 213A (d) 241A

Answer: *(b) 196A*

Conductor Ampacity [90°C] = 225A
Correction Factor [Table 310.(B)(2)(a)] = 0.87
Corrected Ampacity = 225A x 0.87
Corrected Ampacity = 196A

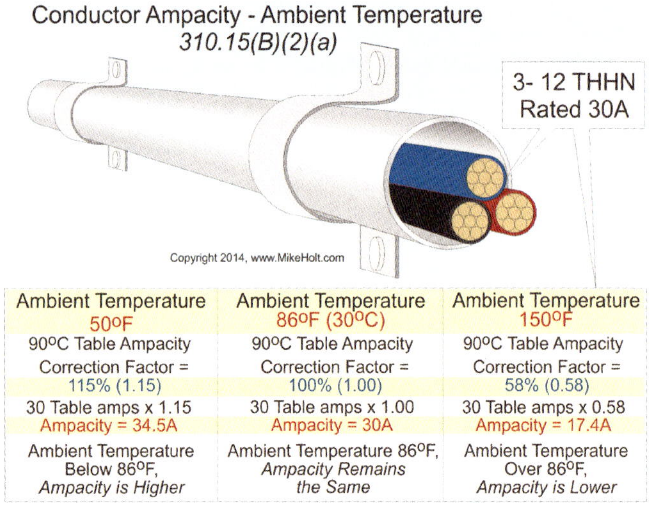

Figure 310–7

Table 310.15(B)(2)(a) Ambient Temperature Correction

Ambient Temperature °F	Ambient Temperature °C	Correction Factor 75°C Conductors	Correction Factor 90°C Conductors
50 or less	10 or less	1.20	1.15
51–59°F	11–15°C	1.15	1.12
60–68°F	16–20°C	1.11	1.08
69–77°F	21–25°C	1.05	1.04
78–86°F	26–30°C	1.00	1.00
87–95°F	31–35°C	0.94	0.96
96–104°F	36–40°C	0.88	0.91
105–113°F	41–45°C	0.82	0.87
114–122°F	46–50°C	0.75	0.82
123–131°F	51–55°C	0.67	0.76
132–140°F	56–60°C	0.58	0.71
141–149°F	61–65°C	0.47	0.65
150–158°F	66–70°C	0.33	0.58
159–167°F	71–75°C	0.00	0.50
168–176°F	76–80°C	0.00	0.41
177–185°F	81–85°C	0.00	0.29

Question: *What's the corrected ampacity of 3/0 THWN conductors if the ambient temperature is 108°F?*

(a) 164A (b) 196A (c) 213A (d) 241A

Answer: *(a) 164A*

Conductor Ampacity [75°C] = 200A
Correction Factor [Table 310.(B)(2)(a)] = 0.82
Corrected Ampacity = 200A x 0.82
Corrected Ampacity = 164A

(3) Conductor Ampacity Adjustment.

(a) Four or More Current-Carrying Conductors. Where four or more current-carrying power conductors are in a raceway longer than 24 in. [310.15(B)(3)(a)(3)], or where cables are bundled for a length longer than 24 in., the ampacity of each conductor must be reduced in accordance with Table 310.15(B)(3)(a).

Table 310.15(B)(3)(a) Conductor Ampacity Adjustment for More Than Three Current-Carrying Conductors

Number of Conductors[1]	Adjustment
4–6	0.80 or 80%
7–9	0.70 or 70%
10–20	0.50 or 50%
21–30	0.45 or 50%
31–40	0.40 or 40%
41 and above	0.35 or 35%

[1]*Number of conductors is the total number of conductors, including spare conductors, including spare conductors, adjusted in accordance with 310.15(B)(5) and (B)(6). It doesn't include conductors that can't be energized at the same time.*

Author's Comment: Conductor ampacity reduction is required when four or more current-carrying conductors are bundled because heat generated by current flow isn't able to dissipate as quickly as when there are three or fewer current-carry conductors. Figures 310–8 and 310–9

(1) Conductor ampacity adjustment of Table 310.15(B)(3)(a) doesn't apply to conductors installed in cable trays, 392.80 applies.

(2) Conductor ampacity adjustment of Table 310.15(B)(3)(a) doesn't apply to conductors in raceways having a length not exceeding 24 in. Figure 310–10

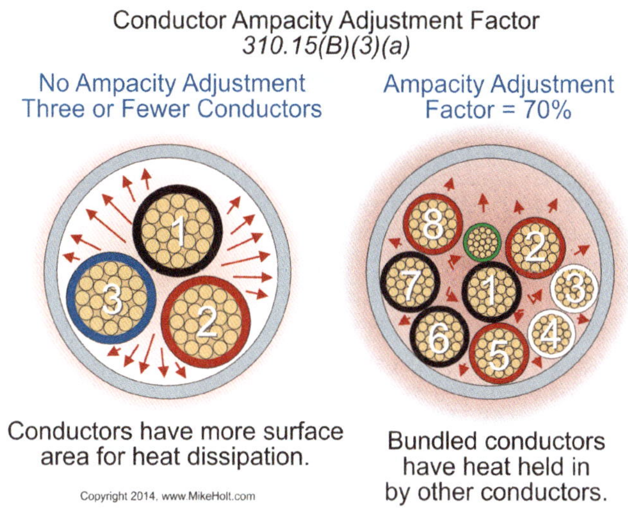

Figure 310–8

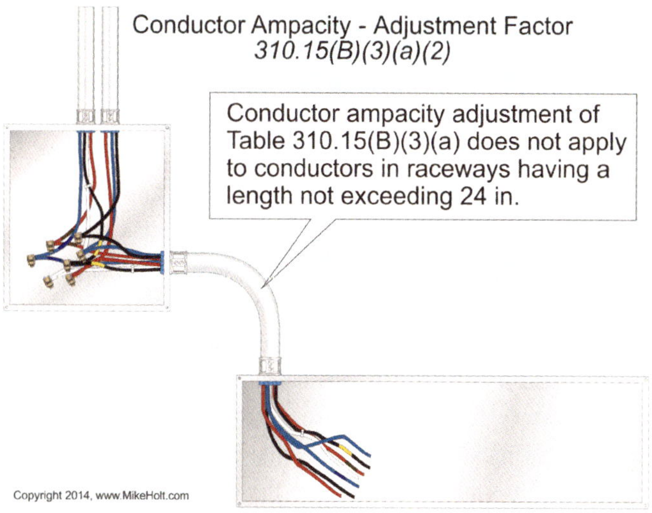

Figure 310–10

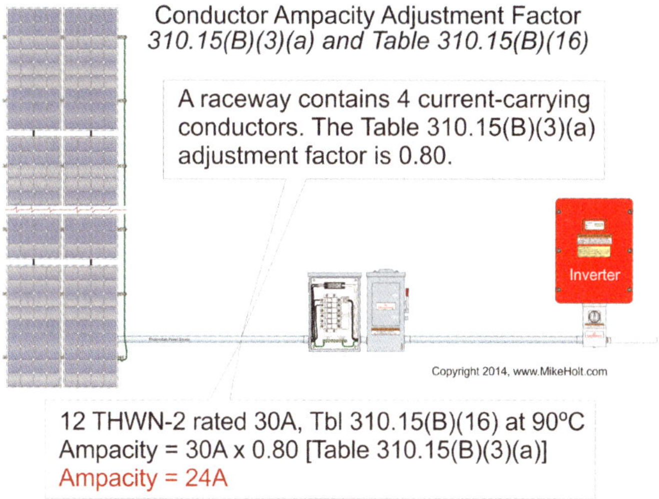

Figure 310–9

(4) Conductor ampacity adjustment of Table 310.15(B)(3)(a) doesn't apply to conductors within Type AC or Type MC cable under the following conditions: Figure 310–11

(a) The cables don't have an outer jacket,

(b) Each cable has no more than three current-carrying conductors,

(c) The conductors are 12 AWG copper, and

(d) No more than 20 current-carrying conductors (ten 2-wire cables or six 3-wire cables) are installed without maintaining spacing for a continuous length longer than 24 in.

(5) Ampacity adjustment of 60 percent applies to conductors within Type AC or Type MC cable without an overall outer jacket under the following conditions:

(b) The number of current-carrying conductors exceeds 20.

(c) The cables are stacked or bundled longer than 24 in. without spacing being maintained.

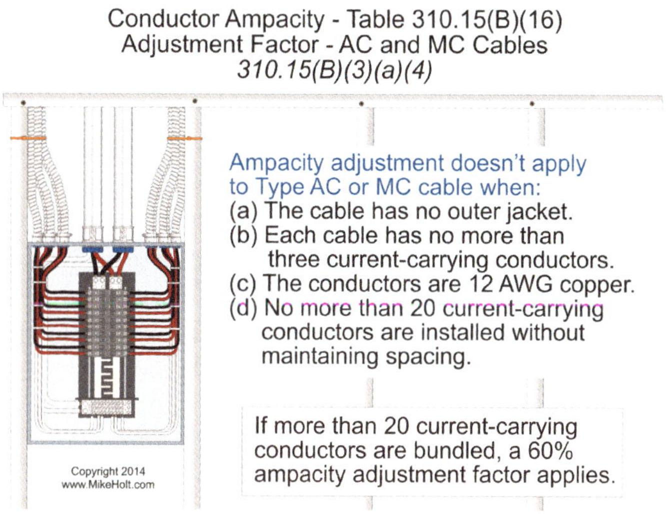

Figure 310–11

ANALYSIS: The 2011 edition of the *NEC* made an attempt to clarify the rules for ampacity adjustment as they pertain to spare conductors and other conductors that weren't clearly addressed in the rule. The attempt didn't quite work, because the title of the table, the table note, and the *Code* text seemed to argue with each other. By adding the note at the bottom of Table 310.15(B)(3)(a), it is clear that spare conductors are counted for ampacity adjustment, due to the fact that they'll probably be used eventually, and it would be a difficult sell to a customer to convince them that simply terminating these conductors to equipment suddenly makes every wire in the raceway undersized. In order to avoid that argument, the conductor is counted immediately upon installation.

Conductors that can't be energized simultaneously are also now discussed in the table. Consider a set of 3-way switches. One switch is fed by the supply conductor, while the other switch feeds the luminaire. Between these switches are two conductors, often referred to as "travelers." Regardless of the position of either switch, one of the travelers will be energized, and the other will not. If you change the position (up or down) of either switch, you'll change which of the travelers is energized, but in no case can you possibly energize both. Due to this, there's no reason to count both conductors in the ampacity adjustment, as only one of them will be adding heat.

(c) Raceways and Cables Exposed to Sunlight on Rooftops. When applying ampacity adjustment correction factors, the ambient temperature adjustment contained in Table 310.15(B)(3)(c) is added to the outdoor ambient temperature for conductors installed in raceways or cables exposed to direct sunlight on or above rooftops to determine the applicable ambient temperature for ampacity correction factors in Table 310.15(B)(2)(a) or Table 310.15(B)(2)(b). **Figures 310–12** and **310–13**

Ex: The ampacity adjustment isn't required for conductors that are type XHHW-2.

Note 1: See the *ASHRAE Handbook—Fundamentals* (www.ashrae.org) as a source for the ambient temperatures in various locations.

Note 2: The temperature adders in Table 310.15(B)(3)(c) are based on the measured temperature rise above local climatic ambient temperatures due to sunlight heating.

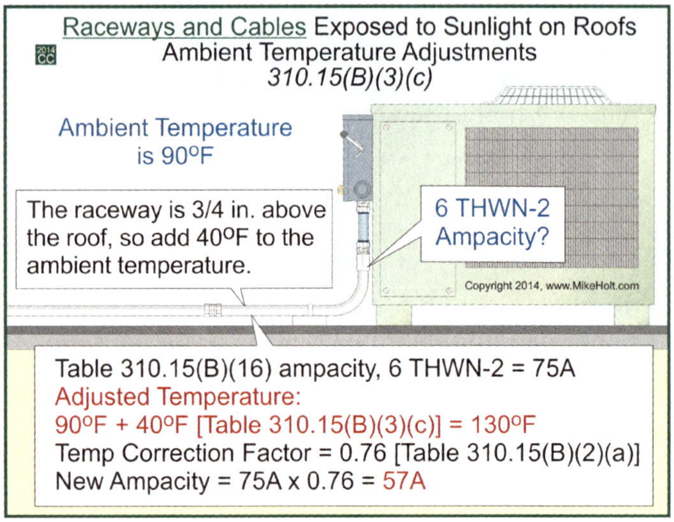

Figure 310–12

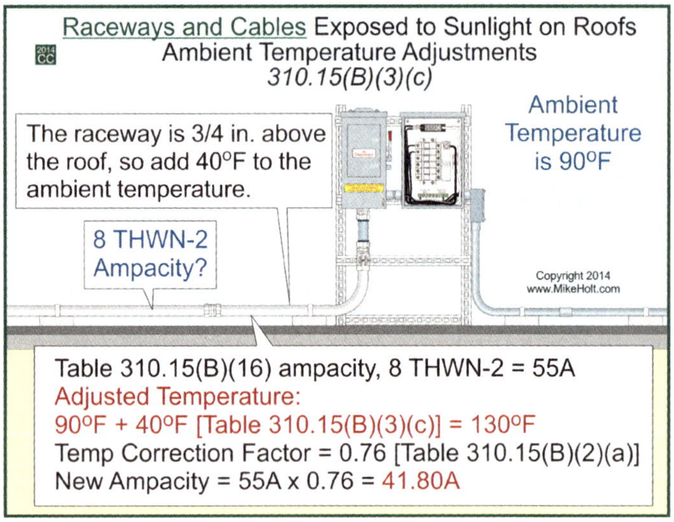

Figure 310–13

Table 310.15(B)(3)(c) Ambient Temperature Adder for Raceways or Cables On or Above Rooftops

Distance of Raceway or Cable Above Roof	C°	F°
0 to ½ in.	33	60
Above ½ in. to 3½ in.	22	40
Above 3½ in. to 12 in.	17	30
Above 12 in. to 36 in.	14	25

Author's Comment: This rule requires the ambient temperature used for ampacity correction to be adjusted where conductors or cables are installed in a raceway or cable on or above a rooftop and the raceway is exposed to direct sunlight. The reasoning is that the air inside raceways and cables that are in direct sunlight is significantly hotter than the surrounding air, and appropriate ampacity corrections must be made in order to comply with 310.10.

ANALYSIS: **Of all the *NEC* rules that have been added over the last three *Code* change cycles, this is one of the most controversial. It started as an Informational Note (actually a Fine Print Note back then), and then grew into a requirement that receives dozens of proposals every three years. New to this edition of the *NEC*, the conductors in any raceway, not just circular raceways, are required to comply with this requirement. Conductors inside of cable assemblies are also required to comply.**

A new exception for type XHHW-2 has been added as well. Testing showed that this conductor insulation type fared much better than other 90°C conductors as it relates to the impact of high temperatures. Interestingly, this data has not only resulted in the exception being added, but has generated a lot of discussion about whether or not the whole "raceways and cables on rooftops" is an issue worth having in the *Code* at all. There still haven't been any documented failures to warrant the requirement, and it appears that the *Code*-Making panel is finally willing to discuss that fact.

(5) Neutral Conductors.

(a) The neutral conductor of a 3-wire, single-phase, 120/240V system, or 4-wire, three-phase, 120/208V or 277/480V wye-connected system, isn't considered a current-carrying conductor for conductor ampacity adjustment of 310.15(B)(3)(a). Figure 310–14

(b) The neutral conductor of a 3-wire circuit from a 4-wire, three-phase, 120/208V or 277/480V wye-connected system is considered a current-carrying conductor for conductor ampacity adjustment of 310.15(B)(3)(a).

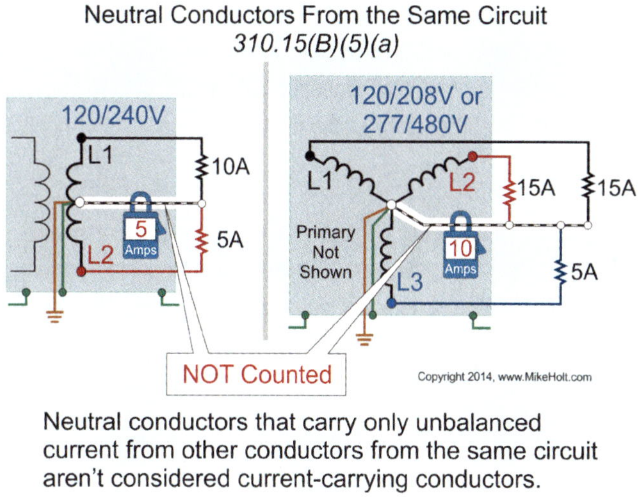

Figure 310–14

Author's Comment: When a 3-wire circuit is supplied from a 4-wire, three-phase, 120/208V or 277/480V wye-connected system, the neutral conductor carries approximately the same current as the ungrounded conductors. Figure 310–15

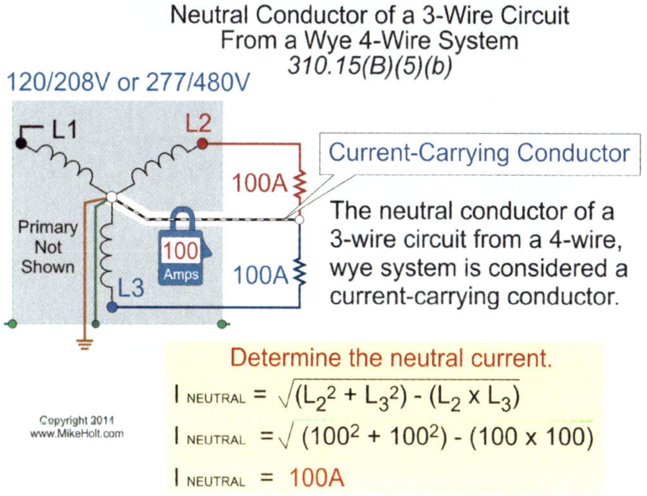

Figure 310–15

(c) The neutral conductor of a 4-wire, three-phase, 120/208V or 277/480V wye-connected system is considered a current-carrying conductor for conductor ampacity adjustment of 310.15(B)(3)(a) if more than 50 percent of the neutral load consists of nonlinear loads.

Author's Comment: Nonlinear loads supplied by a 4-wire, three-phase, 120/208V or 277/480V wye-connected system can produce unwanted and potentially hazardous odd triplen harmonic currents (3rd, 9th, 15th, and so on) that can add on the neutral conductor. To prevent fire or equipment damage from excessive harmonic neutral current, the designer should consider increasing the size of the neutral conductor or installing a separate neutral for each phase. For more information, visit www.MikeHolt.com, click on the "Technical" link, then the "Power Quality" link. Also see 210.4(A) Note, 220.61 Note 2, and 450.3 Note 2. **Figure 310–16**

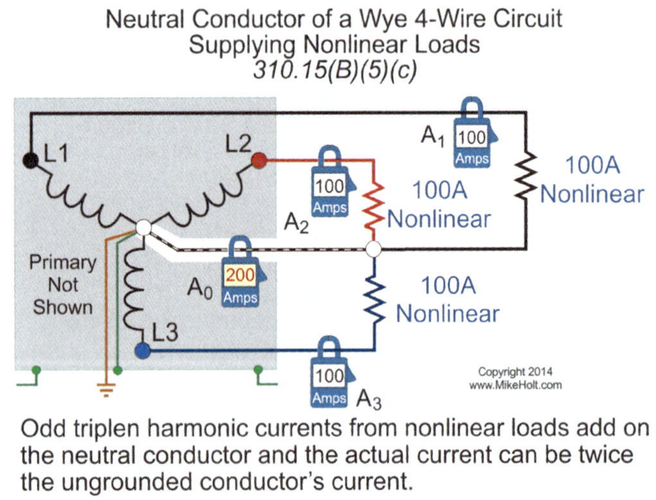

Figure 310–16

(6) Grounding Conductors. Grounding and bonding conductors aren't considered current carrying. **Figure 310–17**

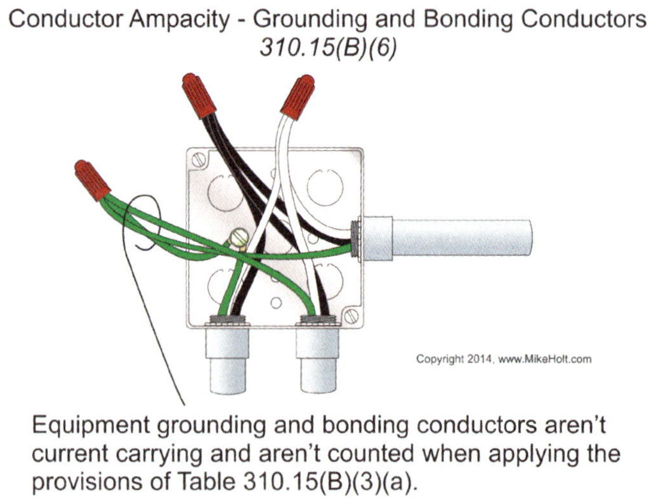

Figure 310–17

(7) 120/240V, Single-Phase Dwelling Services and Feeders. For one-family dwellings and individual dwelling units of two-family and multifamily dwellings, service and feeder conductors supplied by a single phase, 120/240V system can be sized using 310.15(B)(7)(1) through (4). **Figure 310–18**

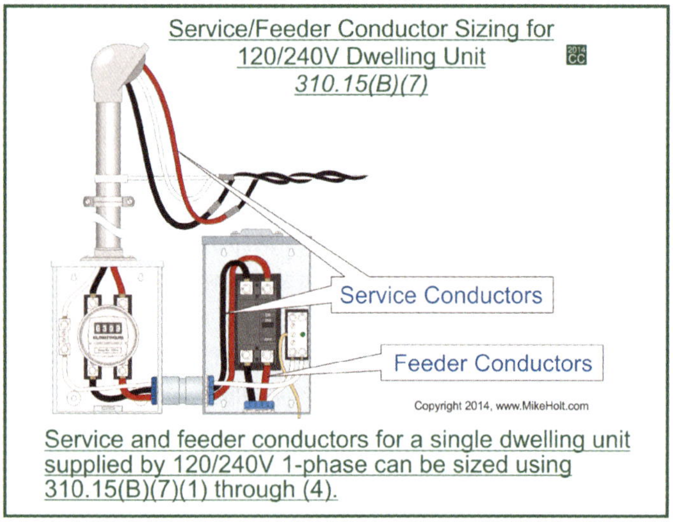

Figure 310–18

(1) Service conductors supplying the entire load of a one-family dwelling or an individual dwelling unit in a two-family or multifamily dwelling can have an ampacity of 83 percent of the service rating.

Question: *What size service conductors are required if the calculated load for a dwelling unit equals 195A, and the service disconnect is rated 200A?* **Figure 310–19**

(a) 1/0 AWG (b) 2/0 AWG (c) 3/0 AWG (d) 4/0 AWG

Answer: *(b) 2/0 AWG*

Service Conductor: 2/0 AWG rated 175A at 75°C [Table 310.15(B)(16)] (200A rated circuit breaker multiplied by 83% =166A).

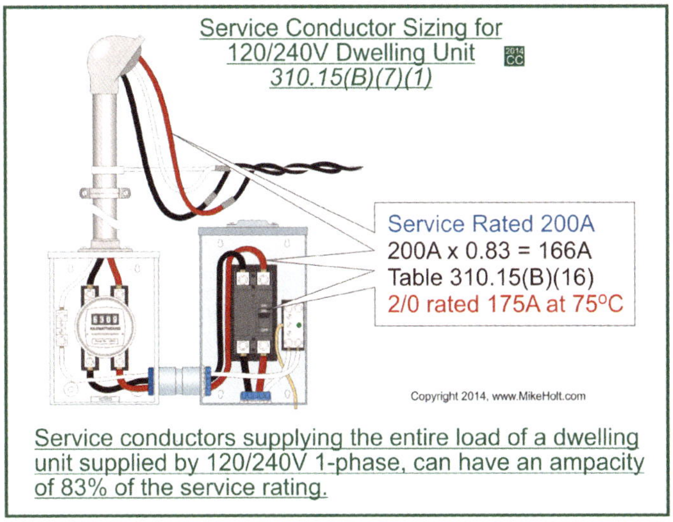

Figure 310–19

Author's Comment: 310.15(B)(7) can't be used for service conductors for two-family or multifamily dwelling buildings. **Figure 310–20**

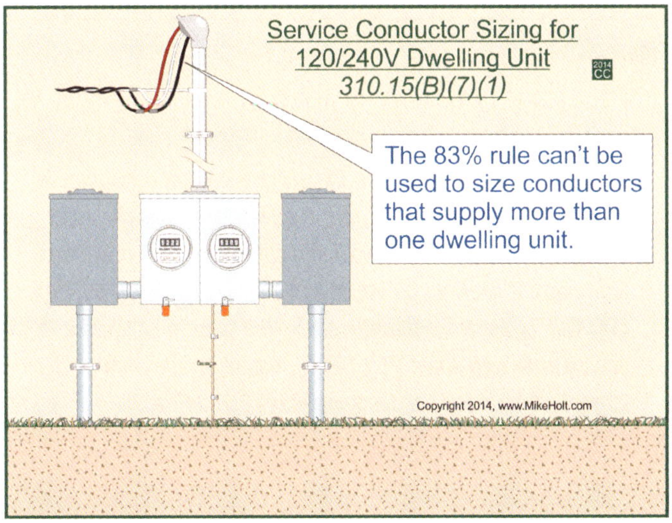

Figure 310–20

(2) For a feeder rated 100A through 400A, feeder conductors supplying a one-family dwelling, or an individual dwelling unit in a two-family or multifamily dwelling, can have an ampacity of 83 percent of the feeder rating, but only if the feeder supplies the entire load of the dwelling. **Figures 310–21** and **310–22**

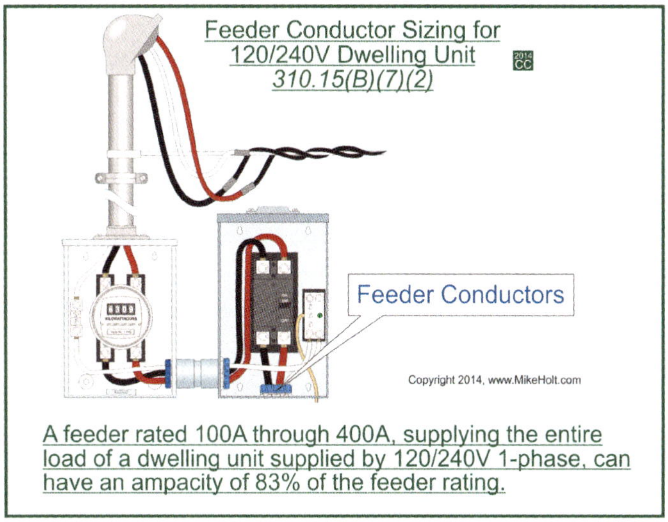

Figure 310–21

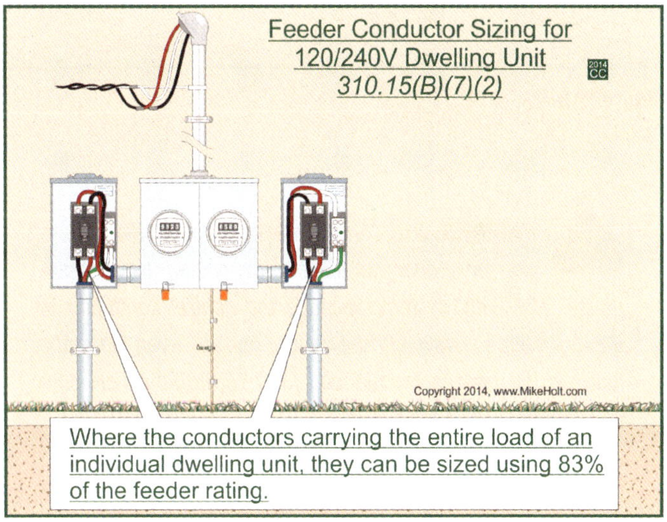

Figure 310–22

Author's Comment: 310.15(B)(7)(2) can't be used to size feeder conductors where a feeder doesn't carry the entire load of the dwelling unit.

Question: *What size feeder conductors are required if the calculated load for a dwelling unit equals 195A, the service disconnect is rated 200A, and the feeder conductors carry the entire load of the dwelling unit?* **Figure 310–23**

(a) 1/0 AWG (b) 2/0 AWG (c) 3/0 AWG (d) 4/0 AWG

Answer: *(b) 2/0 AWG*

Feeder Conductor: 2/0 AWG rated 175A at 75°C [Table 310.15(B)(16)] (200A rated circuit breaker multiplied by 83% =166A).

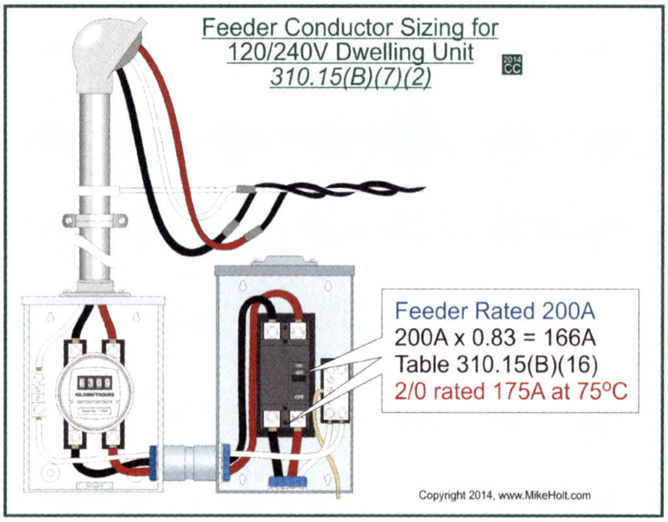

Figure 310–23

WARNING: *310.15(B)(7) doesn't apply to 3-wire service or feeder conductors connected to a three-phase, 120/208V system, because the neutral conductor in these systems always carries neutral current, even when the load on the phases is balanced [310.15(B)(5)(b)]. For more information on this topic, see 220.61(C)(1).* **Figure 310–24**

(3) Feeders for an individual dwelling unit are never required to be larger than the conductors in 310.15(B)(7)(1) or (2).

(4) Neutral conductors are sized using 220.61 and 230.42 for services and 220.61 and 215.2 for feeders. **Figure 310–25**

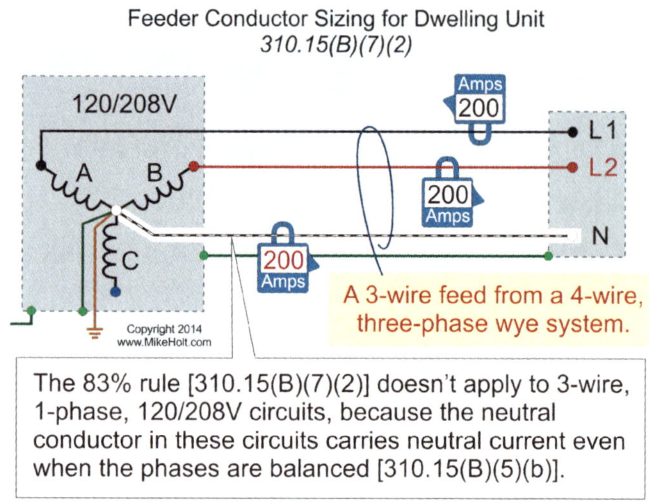

Figure 310–24

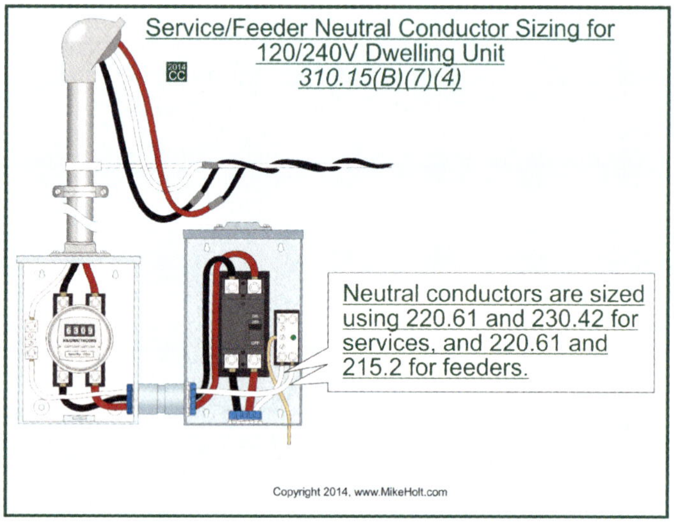

Figure 310–25

CAUTION: *Because the service neutral conductor is required to serve as the effective ground-fault current path, it must be sized so it can safely carry the maximum fault current likely to be imposed on it [110.10 and 250.4(A)(5)]. This is accomplished by sizing the neutral conductor in accordance with Table 250.102(C), based on the area of the largest ungrounded service conductor [250.24(C)(1)].*

Question: *What size neutral conductor is required if the calculated load for a dwelling unit equals 195A, the maximum unbalanced load is 100A, and the service disconnect is rated 200A with 2/0 AWG conductors?* **Figure 310–26**

(a) 6 AWG *(b) 3 AWG* *(c) 2 AWG* *(d) 1 AWG*

Answer: *(b) 3 AWG*

Neutral Conductor: 3 AWG is rated 100A at 75°C in accordance with Table 310.15(B)(16), and 310.15(B)(7)(3) doesn't allow for the 83 percent deduction for neutral conductors. In addition, 250.24(C) requires the neutral conductor to be sized no smaller than 4 AWG based on 2/0 AWG service conductors in accordance with Table 250.102(C).

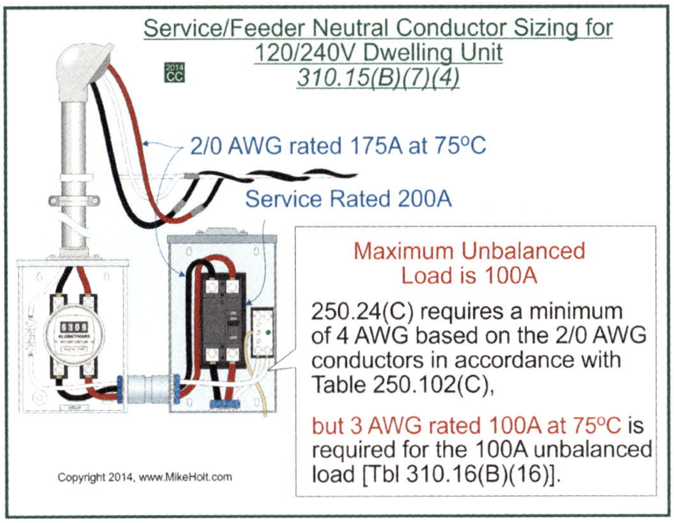

Figure 310–26

ANALYSIS: There weren't many *NEC* rules that received more proposals and public comments than this one. Up until 2008, this requirement didn't receive much thought during the *Code* change process, but then received dozens. Some proposals wanted the allowance deleted altogether while others just wanted the paragraph to be written better. The proposals that passed, however, change the allowance so that it only applies when the conductors serve the entire load of the dwelling. This idea generated dozens of proposals and comments in the 2011 edition, due to the fact that it didn't make a lot of sense (and it still doesn't). At the end of the 2011 process, it was decided that there was certainly work that needed to be done, but no one quite had the answer to fix all of the problems. Now, in 2014, the table is gone and a new 83 percent reduction has been introduced. Instead of looking at a table to determine ampacity, we get to break out the calculator as well as the *Code* book. We'll have to wait and see what happens in 2017, but it will almost certainly be changing again.

Notes

ARTICLE 312 CABINETS, CUTOUT BOXES, AND METER SOCKET ENCLOSURES

Introduction to Article 312—Cabinets, Cutout Boxes, and Meter Socket Enclosures

This article addresses the installation and construction specifications for the items mentioned in its title. In Article 310, we observed that the conditions of use have an effect on the ampacity of a conductor. Likewise, the conditions of use have an effect on the selection and application of cabinets, cutout boxes, and meter socket enclosures. For example, you can't use just any enclosure in a wet location or in a hazardous location. The conditions of use impose special requirements for these situations.

For all such enclosures, certain requirements apply—regardless of the use. For example, you must cover any openings, protect conductors from abrasion, and allow sufficient bending room for conductors.

Notice that Article 408 covers switchboards and panelboards, with primary emphasis on the interior, or "guts," while the cabinet that would be used to enclose a panelboard is covered here in Article 312. Therefore you'll find that some important considerations such as wire-bending space at terminals of panelboards are included in this article.

Article 312 covers the installation and construction specifications for cabinets, cutout boxes, and meter socket enclosures. [312.1].

312.5 Enclosures

The requirement for closing unused openings has been revised to use more easily enforceable language.

312.5 Enclosures.

(A) Unused Openings. Openings intended to provide entry for conductors must be closed in an approved manner. Figure 312–1

Author's Comment: Unused openings for circuit breakers must be closed by means that provide protection substantially equivalent to the wall of the enclosure [408.7]. Figure 312–2

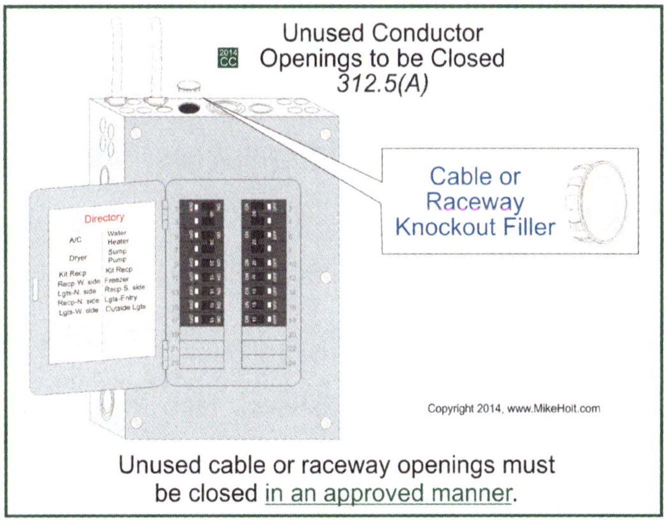

Figure 312–1

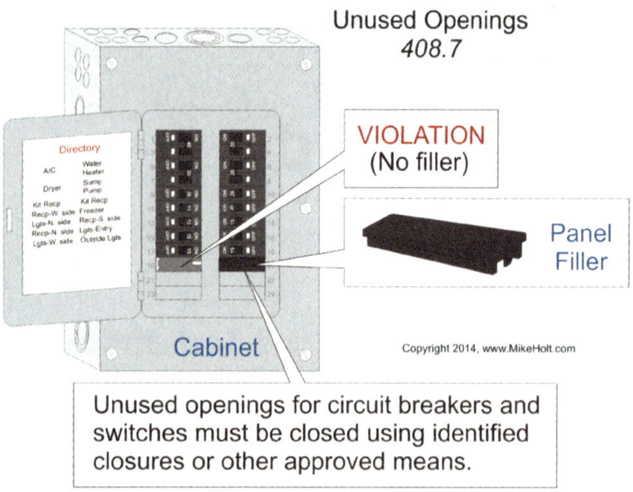

Figure 312–2

ANALYSIS: The word "adequate" is a term that should be avoided in any *Code* book, as it's far too subjective and means different things to different people. Many people talk about the fact that the *NEC* rules are often interpreted differently by various individuals. While this is true, and while it will never change, it's still worth trying to make the *Code* language less open to interpretation. Although this change doesn't completely eliminate controversy, it does decrease it. Other changes in the *NEC* that removed the word "adequate" succeeded wonderfully in removing interpretive text.

312.8 Enclosures With Splices, Taps, and Feed-Through Conductors

This section has been revised to require compliance with 110.21(B).

312.8 Enclosures With Splices, Taps, and Feed-Through Conductors. Cabinets, cutout boxes, and meter socket enclosures can be used for conductors feeding through, spliced, or tapping off to other enclosures, switches, or overcurrent devices where all of the following conditions are met:

(1) The total area of the conductors at any cross section doesn't exceed 40 percent of the cross-sectional area of the space. Figure 312–3

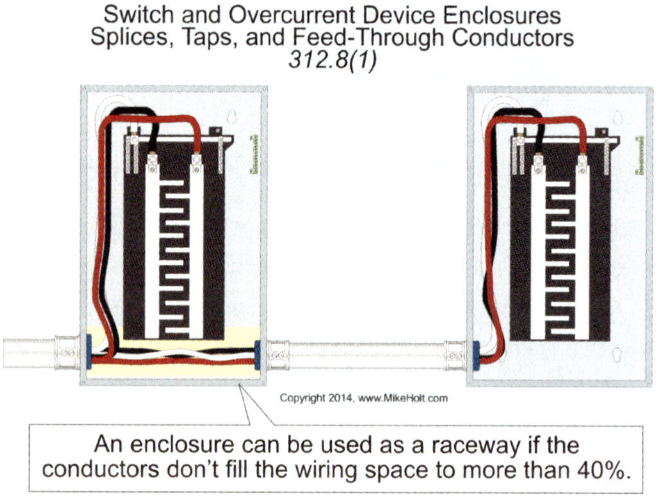

Figure 312–3

(2) The total area of conductors, splices, and taps installed at any cross section doesn't exceed 75 percent of the cross-sectional area of that space. Figure 312–4

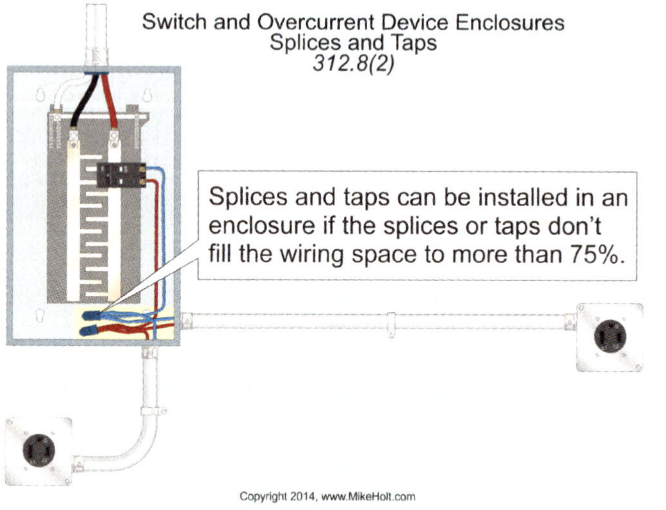

Figure 312–4

(3) A warning label that complies with 110.21(B) on the enclosure identifies the disconnecting means for feed-through conductors. Figure 312–5

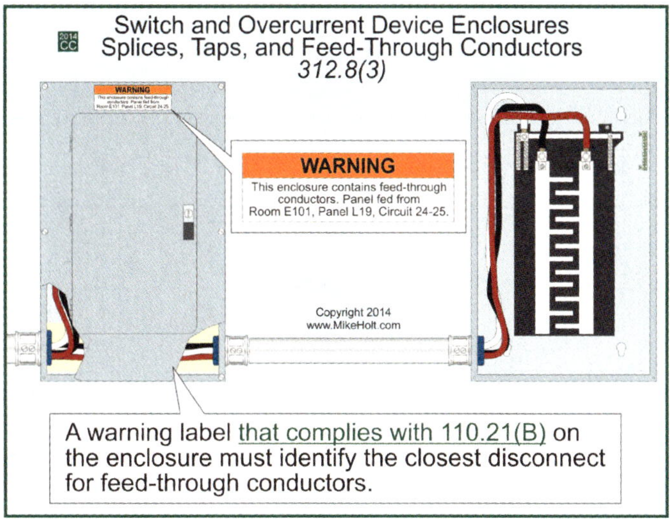

Figure 312–5

ANALYSIS: With the addition of 110.21(B), several *Code* requirements such as this one have been revised. 110.21(B) requires that field-applied labels be permanently affixed, be suitable for the environment, and not be handwritten.

Notes

ARTICLE 314 OUTLET, DEVICE, PULL, AND JUNCTION BOXES; CONDUIT BODIES; AND HANDHOLE ENCLOSURES

Introduction to Article 314—Outlet, Device, Pull, and Junction Boxes; Conduit Bodies; and Handhole Enclosures

Article 314 contains installation requirements for outlet boxes, pull and junction boxes, conduit bodies, and handhole enclosures. As with the cabinets, cutout boxes, and meter socket enclosures covered in Article 312, the conditions of use have a bearing on the type of material and equipment selected for a particular installation. If a raceway is installed in a wet location, for example, the correct fittings and the proper installation methods must be used.

This article provides guidance for selecting and installing outlet and device boxes, pull and junction boxes, conduit bodies, and handhole enclosures. The information here will help you size an outlet box using the proper cubic-inch capacity as well as calculating the minimum dimensions for larger pull boxes. There are limits on the amount of weight that can be supported by an outlet box and rules on how to support a device or outlet box to various surfaces. Article 314 will help you understand these types of rules so that your installation will be compliant with the *NEC*. As always, the clear illustrations in this article will help you visualize the finished installation.

314.15 Damp or Wet Locations

The rules on enclosures in damp and wet locations were changed to allow for field-installed drainage openings.

314.15 Damp or Wet Locations. Boxes, conduit bodies, and fittings in damp or wet locations must prevent moisture or water from entering or accumulating within the enclosure, Figure 314–1. Boxes, conduit bodies, and fittings installed in wet locations must be listed for use in wet locations.

Drainage openings can be installed in the field if they aren't larger than ¼ in. For listed drainage fittings, the holes can be larger, but must be in accordance with the manufacturer's instructions. Figure 314–2

Author's Comment: If handhole enclosures without bottoms are installed, all enclosed conductors and any splices or terminations must be listed as suitable for wet locations [314.30(C)].

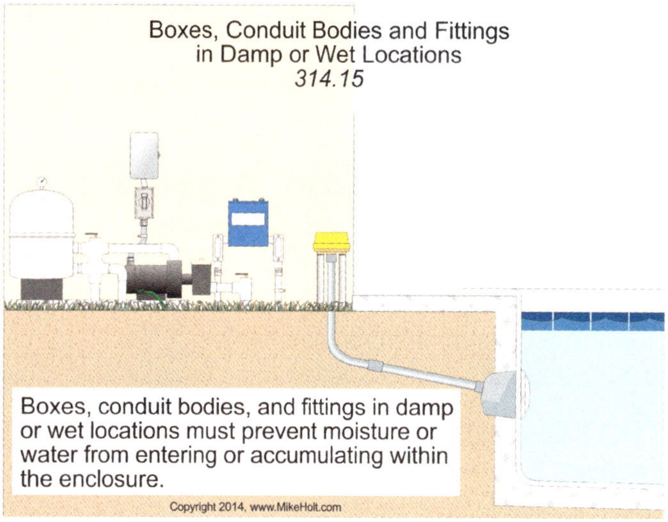

Figure 314–1

Figure 314–2

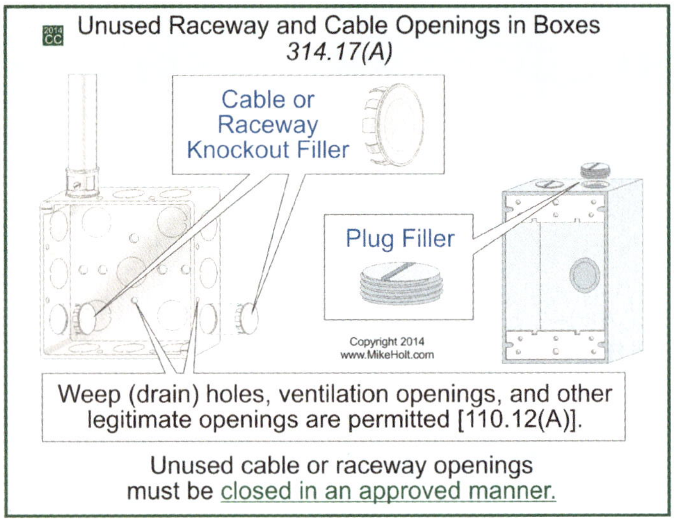

Figure 314–3

ANALYSIS: People have been drilling holes in the bottom of enclosures for years in order to facilitate drainage when the design of the box isn't good enough. Although this has been accepted by most inspectors, it hasn't been addressed in the *Code*. With the inclusion of this new text, inspectors (and installers) now have guidance about the size of holes that can be added. If holes larger than ¼ in. are needed (although I'm not sure why they would be), there must be provisions in the instructions of the enclosure that allow for it.

314.17 Conductors That Enter Boxes or Conduit Bodies

The requirements for box openings were revised to promote uniform interpretation.

314.17 Conductors That Enter Boxes or Conduit Bodies.

(A) Openings to Be Closed. Openings through which cables or raceways enter must be closed in an approved manner.

Author's Comment: Unused cable or raceway openings in electrical equipment must be effectively closed by fittings that provide protection substantially equivalent to the wall of the equipment [110.12(A)]. **Figure 314–3**

ANALYSIS: The word "adequate" is a term that should be avoided in any *Code* book, as it's far too subjective and means different things to different people. Many people talk about the fact that the *NEC* rules are often interpreted differently by various individuals. While this is true, and while it will never change, it's still worth trying to make the *Code* language less open to interpretation. Although this change doesn't completely eliminate controversy, it does decrease it. Other changes in the *NEC* that removed the word "adequate" succeeded wonderfully in removing interpretive text.

314.23 Support of Boxes and Conduit Bodies

This change clarifies which structural members are being discussed.

314.23 Support of Boxes and Conduit Bodies. Boxes must be securely supported by one of the following methods:

(B) Structural Mounting. Boxes can be supported from any structural member, or they can be supported from grade by a metal, plastic, or wood brace.

(1) Nails and Screws. Nails or screws can be used to fasten boxes, provided the exposed threads of screws are protected to prevent abrasion of conductor insulation.

(2) Braces. Metal braces no less than 0.02 in. thick and wood braces not less than a nominal 1 in. x 2 in. can support a box.

ANALYSIS: The phrase "of a building" was removed from 314.23(B). I can just hear the members of the *Code*-Making Panel voting on this rule: The word "structure" is defined in Article 100 as "that which is built or constructed." All buildings are structures. Not all structures are buildings. Does this rule apply only to the structural members of a building, and not the structural members of a structure? Or is it supposed to mean that non-structural members of other structures can't be used even though they're members that are structurally sound? Forget it—let's just delete "of a building" and talk about something else!

314.25 Covers and Canopies

This change addresses the use of noncompliant screws for mounting equipment in boxes.

314.25 Covers and Canopies.

In completed installations, a box must have a cover, faceplate, lampholder, or luminaire canopy, unless the box is covered by a luminaire in accordance with 410.24(B), Figure 314–4. Screws used for attaching covers or other equipment to the box must be machine screws that match the thread gage or size of the screw holes in the box or they must be in accordance with the manufacturer's instructions. Figure 314–5

ANALYSIS: It is, unfortunately, a common practice to use drywall screws to attach receptacles to boxes. Worse still is attaching luminaires to boxes using screws that weren't designed, tested, and listed to support them. Most people take comfort in the fact that the chandelier they're standing under was installed properly. Using screws that aren't designed to support equipment isn't only a *Code* violation, it's an unsafe practice.

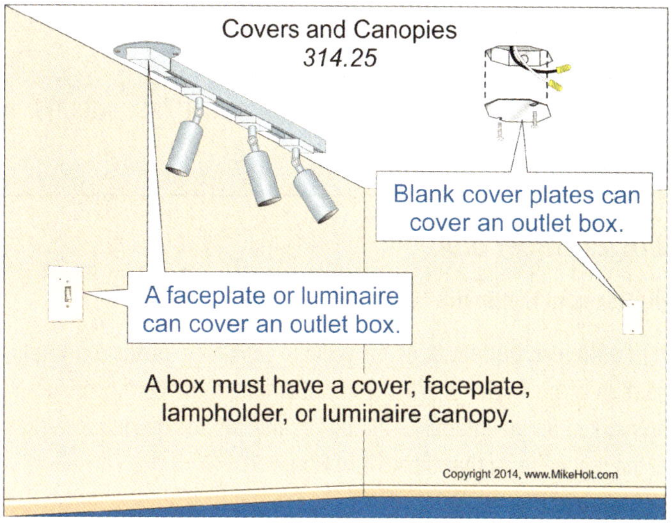

Figure 314–4

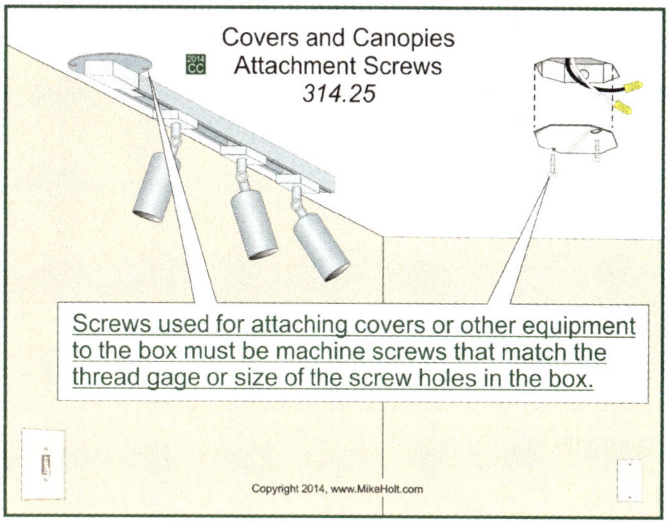

Figure 314–5

314.27 Outlet Box

The requirements for luminaire outlet box ratings have been revised...again.

314.27 Outlet Box.

(A) Boxes at Luminaire Outlets.

(1) Luminaire Outlets in or on Vertical Surfaces. Boxes for a luminaire in or on a wall or other vertical surface must be identified and be marked on the interior of the box to indicate the maximum weight of the luminaire if other than 50 lb. **Figure 314–6**

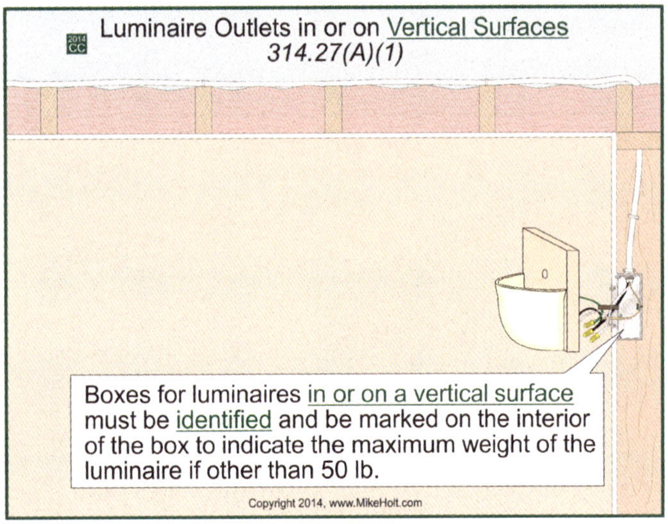

Figure 314–6

Ex: A vertically mounted luminaire weighing no more than 6 lb can be supported to a device box or plaster ring secured to a device box. **Figure 314–7**

(2) Luminaire Outlets in the Ceiling. Boxes for a luminaire in a ceiling must be designed to support a luminaire weighing a minimum of 50 lb. Luminaires weighing more than 50 lb must be supported independently of the outlet box unless the outlet box is listed and marked on the interior of the box to indicate the maximum weight the box is permitted to support. **Figure 314–8**

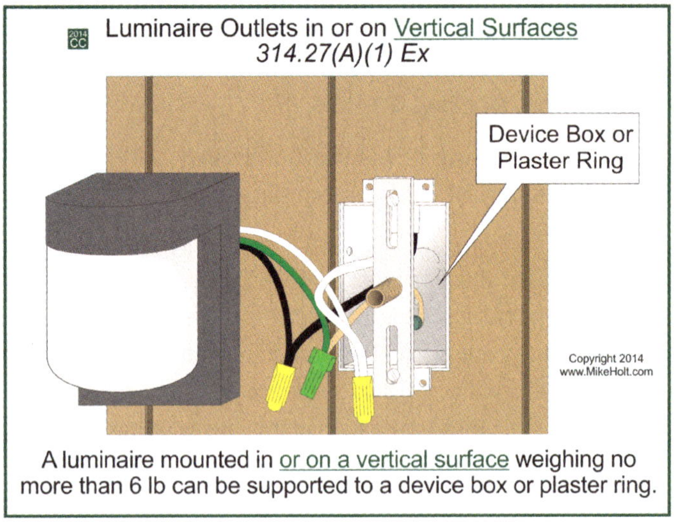

Figure 314–7

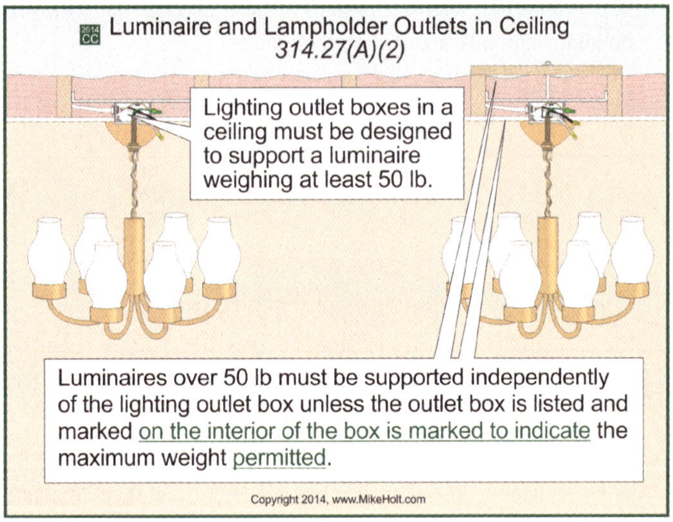

Figure 314–8

ANALYSIS: (A)(1) and its exception have been changed to clarify that luminaries installed on any vertical surface should be installed the same way, regardless of whether it's a wall or other surface.

(A)(2) has been revised to require that outlet boxes for luminaires weighing more than 50 lb be marked with the maximum weight on the inside of the box. Few will argue that this is more helpful than providing the information on the top of the box where no one can see it!

(B) Floor Box. Floor boxes must be specifically listed for the purpose. Figure 314–9

Figure 314–9

(C) Ceiling Paddle Fan Box. Outlet boxes for a ceiling paddle fan must be listed and marked as suitable for the purpose, and must not support a fan weighing more than 70 lb. Outlet boxes for a ceiling paddle fan that weighs more than 35 lb must include the maximum weight to be supported in the required marking. Figure 314–10

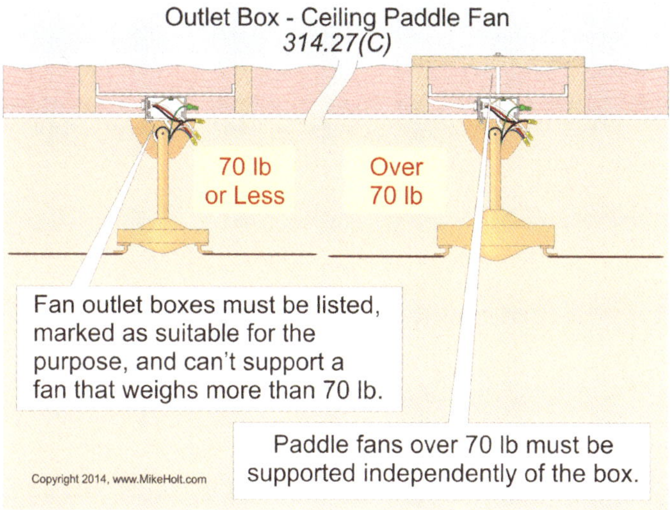

Figure 314–10

Author's Comment: If the maximum weight isn't marked on the box, and the fan weighs over 35 lb, it must be supported independently of the outlet box. Ceiling paddle fans over 70 lb must be supported independently of the outlet box.

Where spare, separately switched, ungrounded conductors are provided to a ceiling-mounted outlet box, in a location acceptable for a ceiling-suspended (paddle) fan in single-family, two-family or multi-family dwellings, the outlet box or outlet box system must be listed for the support of a ceiling-suspended (paddle) fan. Figure 314–11

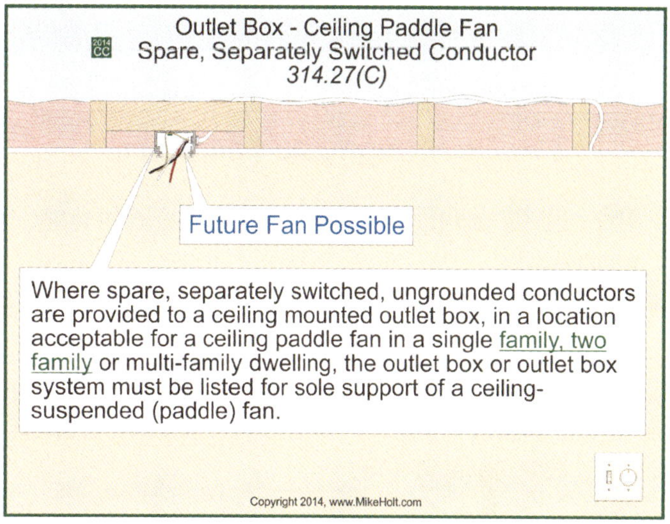

Figure 314–11

(D) Utilization Equipment. Boxes used for the support of utilization equipment must be designed to support equipment that weighs a minimum of 50 lb [314.27(A)].

Ex: Utilization equipment weighing 6 lb or less is permitted to be supported by any box or plaster ring secured to a box, provided the equipment is secured with no fewer than two No. 6 or larger screws. Figure 314–12

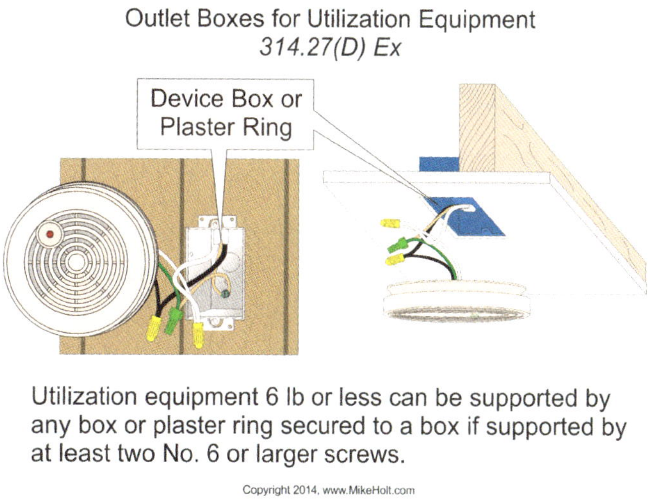

Figure 314–12

ANALYSIS: (C) has been revised to include two-family dwellings. As is often the case, when new rules are written into the *NEC*, little things are forgotten. In this example, the *Code* applied to single-family and multifamily dwellings, but not two-family dwellings. This wasn't an intentional omission, just an oversight.

314.29 Wiring to be Accessible

The rule for wiring to be accessible was editorially revised.

314.29 Wiring to be Accessible. Boxes, conduit bodies, and handhole enclosures must be installed so that the wiring is accessible without removing any part of the building or structure, sidewalks, paving, or earth. Figure 314–13

Ex: Listed boxes and handhole enclosures can be buried if covered by gravel, light aggregate, or noncohesive granulated soil, and their location is effectively identified and accessible for excavation.

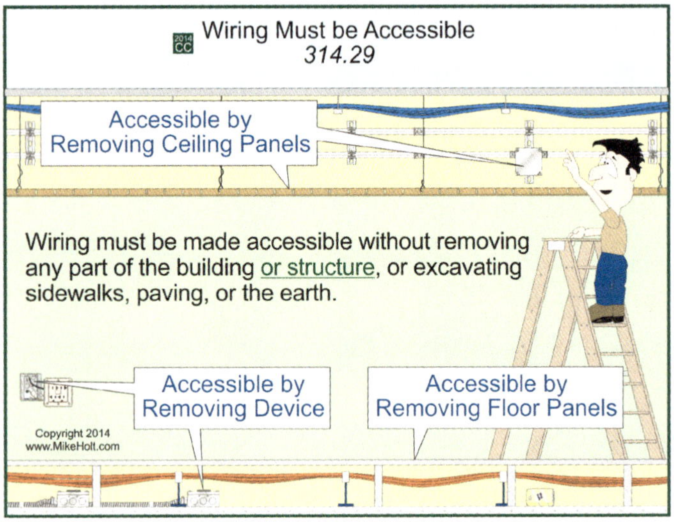

Figure 314–13

ANALYSIS: All buildings are structures. Not all structures are buildings. Here we go again.

ARTICLE 320 ARMORED CABLE (TYPE AC)

Introduction to Article 320—Armored Cable (Type AC)

Armored cable is an assembly of insulated conductors, 14 AWG through 1 AWG, individually wrapped within waxed paper and contained within a flexible spiral metal sheath. The outside appearance of armored cable looks like flexible metal conduit as well as metal-clad cable to the casual observer. This cable has been referred to as "BX®" cable over the years and used in residential wiring in some areas of the country.

320.23 In Accessible Attics or Roof Spaces

The requirements for guard strips in attics were revised to aid in uniform interpretation.

Part II. Installation

320.23 In Accessible Attics or Roof Spaces.

(A) Cables Run Across the Top of Floor Joists. Where run across the top of floor joists, or across the face of rafters or studding within 7 ft of floor or floor joists, the cable must be protected by guard strips that are at least as high as the cable. If this space isn't accessible by permanent stairs or ladders, protection is required only within 6 ft of the nearest edge of the scuttle hole or attic entrance. Figure 320–1

ANALYSIS: The word "substantial" has been removed from this requirement. Finding two people who agree entirely on what a "substantial guard strip" is would be difficult. Among the many words that shouldn't be found in the *Code* book is "substantial." Sometimes subjective terms have to be used, and the *NEC* is never going to be perfect, but terms like "substantial" should probably be removed whenever possible, as it was here.

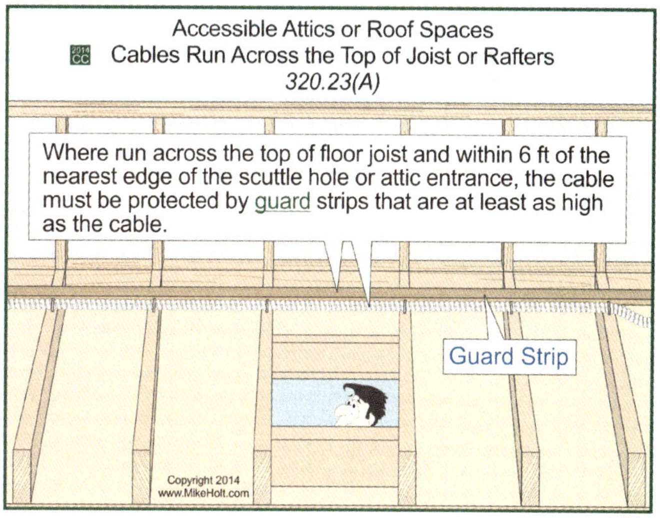

Figure 320–1

Notes

ARTICLE 330 METAL-CLAD CABLE (TYPE MC)

Introduction to Article 330—Metal-Clad Cable (Type MC)

Metal-clad cable encloses insulated conductors in a metal sheath of either corrugated or smooth copper or aluminum tubing, or spiral interlocked steel or aluminum. The physical characteristics of Type MC cable make it a versatile wiring method that you can use in almost any location, and for almost any application. The most commonly used Type MC cable is the interlocking kind, which looks similar to armored cable or flexible metal conduit. Traditional interlocked Type MC cable isn't permitted to serve as an equipment grounding conductor, therefore this cable must contain an equipment grounding conductor in accordance with 250.118(1). There's a fairly new product available called interlocked Type MC^{AP} cable that contains a bare aluminum grounding/bonding conductor running just below the metal armor, which allows the sheath to serve as an equipment grounding conductor [250.118(10)(b)].

330.10 Uses Permitted

The allowances for using MC cable in wet locations were revised.

Part II. Installation

330.10 Uses Permitted.

(A) General Uses.

(11) In wet locations, where a corrosion-resistant jacket is provided over the metal sheath and any of the following are met: **Figure 330–1**

a. The metallic covering is impervious to moisture.

b. A jacket is provided under the metal covering that's moisture resistant.

c. The insulated conductors under the metallic covering are listed for use in wet locations.

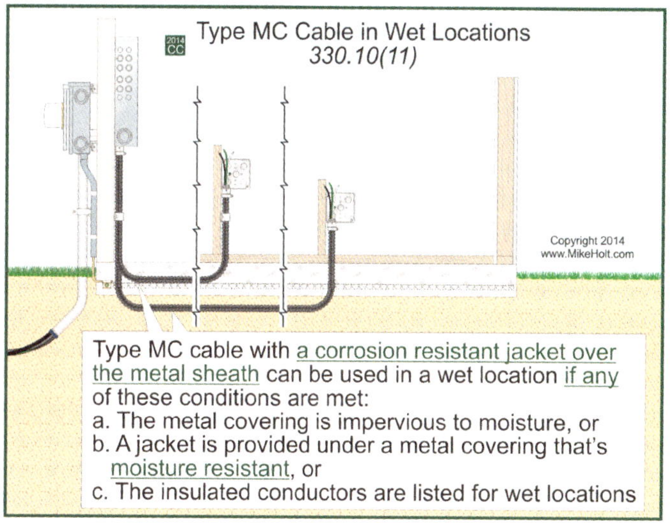

Figure 330–1

ANALYSIS: In the 2011 edition of the *Code* the metallic sheath of the cable only needed to be corrosion resistant if option "c" was being used (wet location conductors inside a corrosion-resistant metal sheath). Anytime MC cable is used in a wet location, it makes sense that the sheath should be corrosion resistant, so the language was moved from item "c" to the opening statement of the subsection, thereby requiring corrosion resistance for any MC cable used in a wet location.

Item (b) was revised to change "moisture impervious" to "moisture resistant." An impervious material is one that absolutely doesn't allow penetration of water, ever. Considering how MC cable is manufactured, this is probably an impossibility, and isn't necessary anyway.

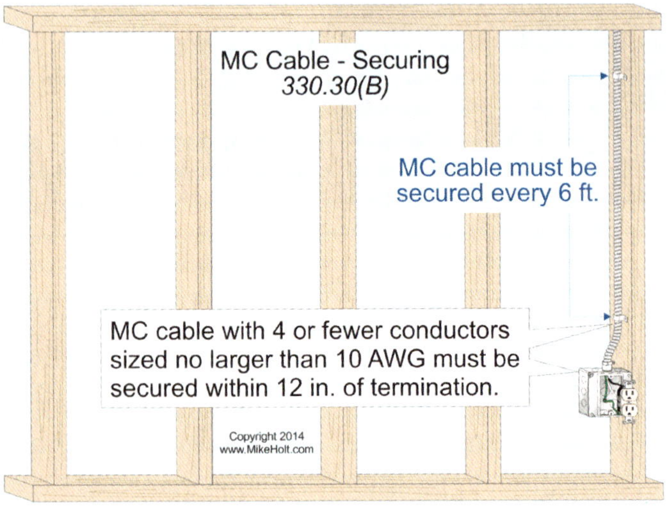

Figure 330–2

330.30 Securing and Supporting

Vertical installations of large MC cables and unsupported cables have been addressed.

330.30 Securing and Supporting.

(A) General. Type MC cable must be supported and secured by staples, cable ties, straps, hangers, or similar fittings designed and installed so as not to damage the cable.

(B) Securing. Type MC cable with four or less conductors sized no larger than 10 AWG, must be secured within 12 in. of every outlet box, junction box, cabinet, or fitting and at intervals not exceeding 6 ft. Figure 330–2

Listed cables with ungrounded conductors 250 kcmil and larger can be secured at 10-foot intervals when installed vertically.

(C) Supporting. Type MC cable must be supported at intervals not exceeding 6 ft. Cables installed horizontally through wooden or metal framing members are considered secured and supported if such support doesn't exceed 6-foot intervals. Figure 330–3

(D) Unsupported Cables. Type MC cable can be unsupported if the cable is:

(1) Fished through concealed spaces in finished buildings or structures, if support is impracticable, or

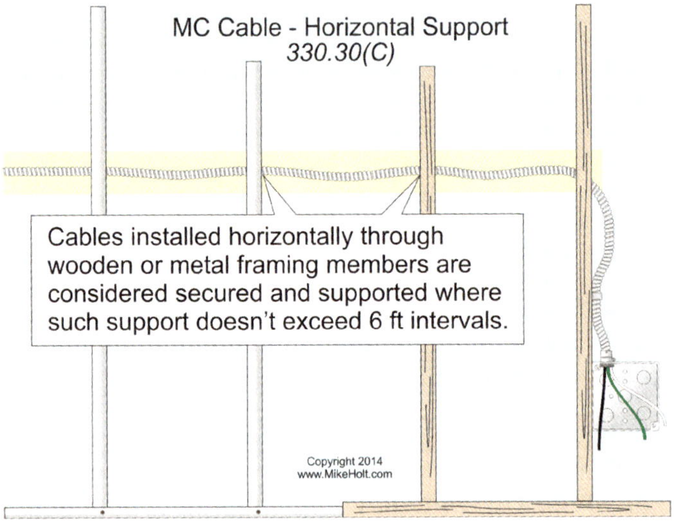

Figure 330–3

(2) Not more than 6 ft long from the last point of cable support to the point of connection to luminaires or other electrical equipment within an accessible ceiling. Type MC cable fittings are permitted as a means of cable support. Figure 330–4

(3) Of the interlocked armor type in lengths not longer than 3 ft from the last point where it's securely fastened. This applies only where the cable is used to provide flexibility for equipment that requires movement after installation, or to connect equipment where flexibility is necessary to minimize the transmission of vibration from the equipment. Figure 330–5

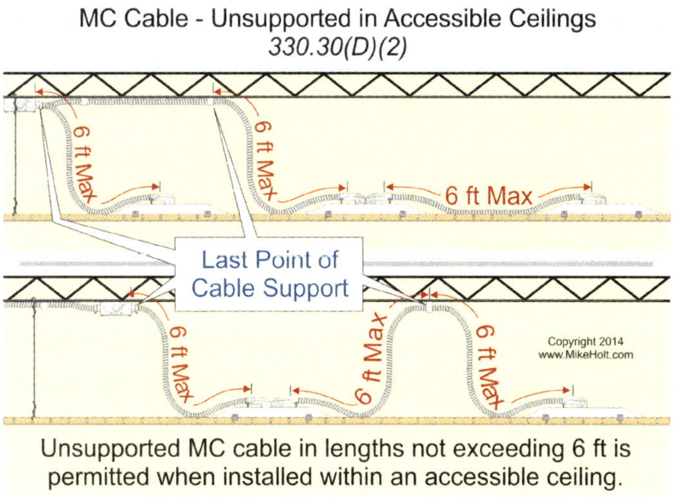

Figure 330–4

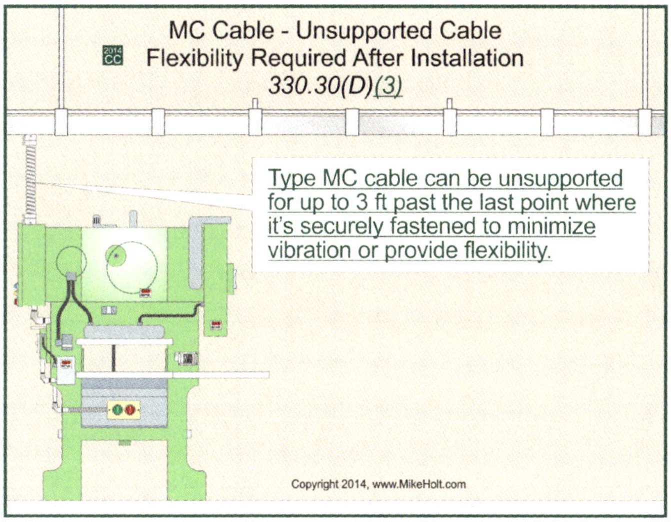

Figure 330–5

ANALYSIS: MC cables with large conductors (250 kcmil and larger) have been used in high-rise buildings, and they have an excellent track record. Due to this, the vertical securing requirements have been lessened.

Flexible metal conduit (348.30), liquidtight flexible metal conduit (350.30), and liquidtight nonmetallic conduit (356.30) have provisions for unsupported raceways similar to this new allowance for MC cable. Interlocking MC cable is very similar to those wiring methods, so it makes sense to mirror the allowance for flexible connections without support. This has, more than likely, been accepted by most inspectors who realize the logic of it.

Notes

ARTICLE 334 NONMETALLIC-SHEATHED CABLE (TYPES NM AND NMC)

Introduction to Article 334—Nonmetallic-Sheathed Cable (Types NM and NMC)

Nonmetallic-sheathed cable is flexible, inexpensive, and easily installed. It provides very limited physical protection for the conductors, so the installation restrictions are strict. Its low cost and relative ease of installation make it a common wiring method for residential and commercial branch circuits. In the field, Type NM cable is typically referred to as "Romex®."

334.10 Uses Permitted

Editorial changes to this section result in a clearer *Code* rule.

Part II. Installation

334.10 Uses Permitted. Type NM and Type NMC cables can be used in the following, except as prohibited in 334.12:

(1) One- and two-family dwellings of any height, and their attached/detached garages or storage buildings. **Figures 334–1** and **334–2**

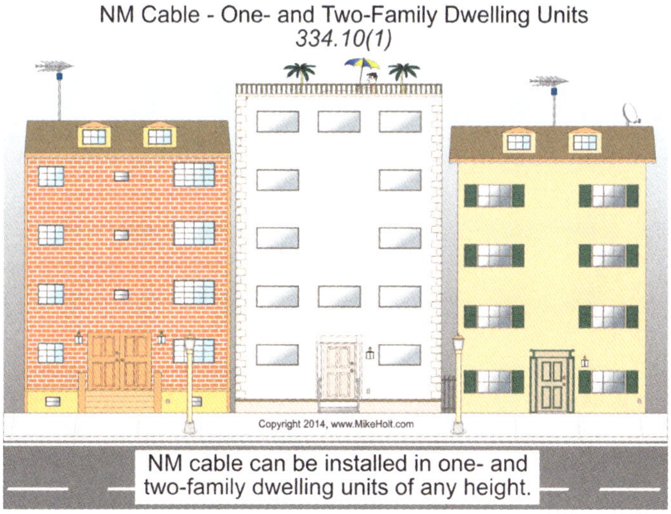

Figure 334–1

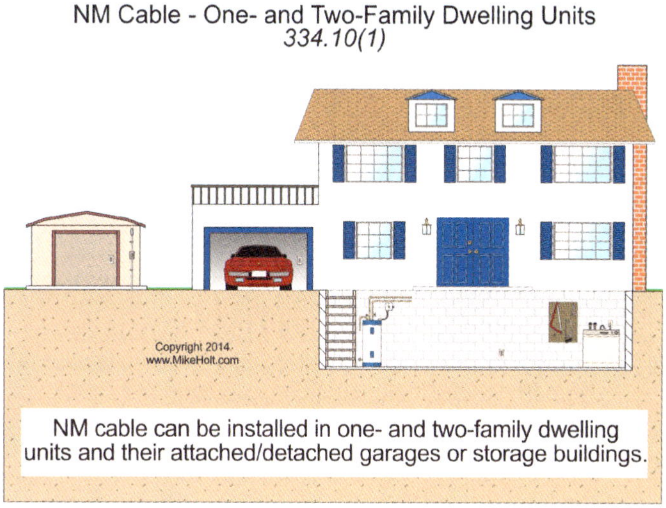

Figure 334–2

(2) Multifamily dwellings permitted to be of Types III, IV, and V construction. **Figure 334–3**

(3) Other structures permitted to be of Types III, IV, and V construction. Cables must be concealed within walls, floors, or ceilings that provide a thermal barrier of material with at least a 15-minute finish rating, as identified in listings of fire-rated assemblies. **Figure 334–4**

Author's Comment: See the definition of "Concealed" in Article 100.

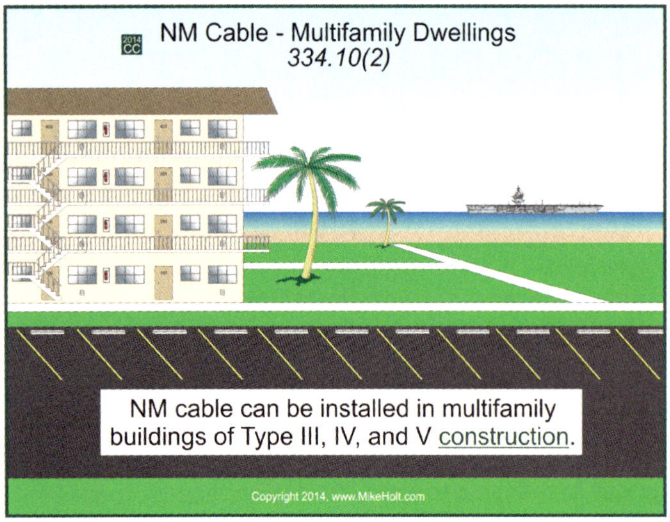

Figure 334–3

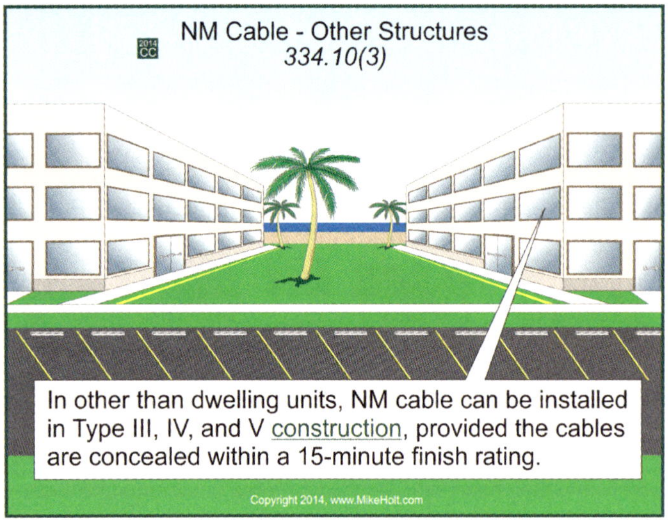

Figure 334–4

Note 1: Building constructions are defined in NFPA 220-2006, *Standard on Types of Building Construction*, the applicable building code, or both.

Note 2: See Annex E for the determination of building types [NFPA 220, Table 3-1].

ANALYSIS: The "uses permitted" and "uses not permitted" sections in the Chapter three articles have long been the subject of debate. A literal reading of the previous text seemed to allow, for example, NM cable to be used in poured concrete (see 334.12 (9)) if it was in a dwelling unit. This is hardly defensible, since the cable isn't designed for that application. With this change, the language of "except as prohibited in 334.12" has been moved from items (2) and (3) to the opening text of 334.10, making it applicable to all of 334.10. Most will agree that this change makes sense.

334.12 Uses Not Permitted

The rule on uses not permitted for NM cables was revised to correct an error.

(A) Types NM and NMC. Types NM and NMC cables aren't permitted:

(1) In any dwelling or structure not specifically permitted in 334.10(1), (2), (3), and (5).

(2) Exposed in dropped or suspended ceilings in other than one- and two-family and multifamily dwellings. Figure 334–5

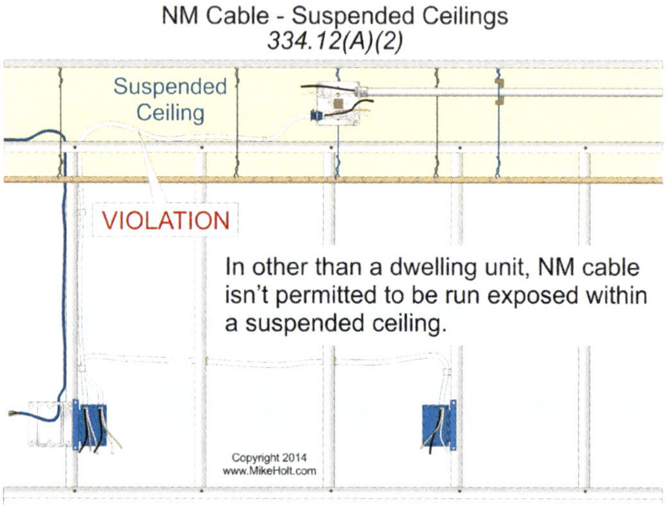

Figure 334–5

(3) As service-entrance cable.

(4) In commercial garages having hazardous locations, as defined in 511.3.

(5) In theaters and similar locations, except where permitted in 518.4(B).

(6) In motion picture studios.

(7) In storage battery rooms.

(8) In hoistways, or on elevators or escalators.

(9) Embedded in poured cement, concrete, or aggregate.

(10) In any hazardous location, except where permitted by other sections in the *Code*.

(B) Type NM. Type NM cables must not be used under the following conditions, or in the following locations:

(1) If exposed to corrosive fumes or vapors.

(2) If embedded in masonry, concrete, adobe, fill, or plaster.

(3) In a shallow chase in masonry, concrete, or adobe and covered with plaster, adobe, or similar finish.

(4) In wet or damp locations. Figure 334–6

Author's Comment: Type NM cable isn't permitted in ducts or plenum spaces [300.22], or for wiring in patient care spaces [517.13].

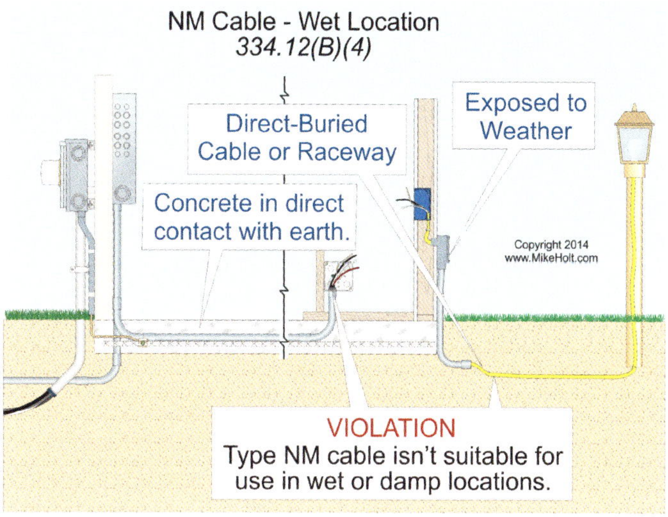

Figure 334–6

ANALYSIS: This section was revised to correct an error that occurred in 2011. Although it would be quite rare, NM cable can be used in Types I and II construction (noncombustible buildings) if it's installed in a raceway. The 2011 edition of this section didn't include a reference to 334.10(5), which is the rule that allows this. This small change in 334.12(A)(1) corrects that oversight.

Notes

ARTICLE 338 SERVICE-ENTRANCE CABLE (TYPES SE AND USE)

Introduction to Article 338—Service-Entrance Cable (Types SE and USE)

Service-entrance cable is a single conductor or multiconductor assembly with or without an overall moisture-resistant covering. This cable is used primarily for services not over 600V, but can also be used for feeders and branch circuits when the limitations of this article are observed.

338.10 Uses Permitted

Single conductor and multi-rated conductor USE is no longer subject to the 60°C rating.

Part II. Installation

338.10 Uses Permitted.

(B) Branch Circuits or Feeders.

(4) Installation Methods for Branch Circuits and Feeders. SE cable used for branch circuits or feeders must comply with (a) and (b).

(b) Exterior Installations. The cable must be supported in accordance with 334.30 and where run underground the cable must comply with Part II of Article 340.

Ex: Single conductor and multi-rated USE conductors aren't restricted to the 60°C rating required by 334.80. Figure 338–1

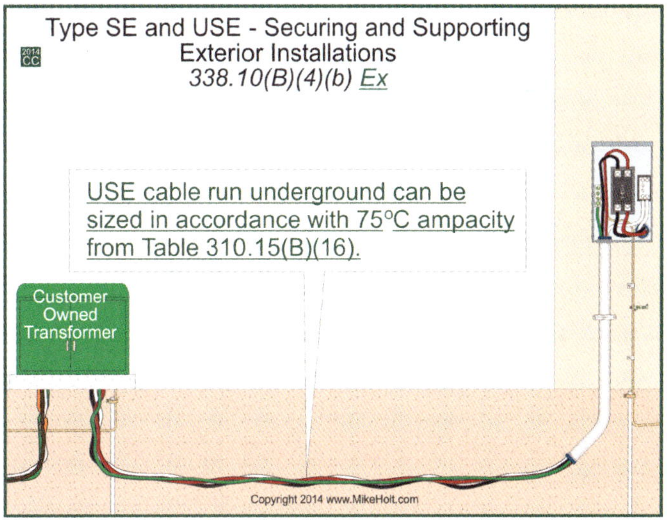

Figure 338–1

ANALYSIS: Previous editions of the *NEC* required that all USE cables installed as underground feeders and branch circuits be subject to the 60°C ampacity requirement of 340.80. This rule was added several *Code* cycles ago, but with no real technical substantiation, and therefore never should've been in the *NEC* at all. For this reason, we now have an exception for single conductor and multi-rated USE conductors.

Notes

ARTICLE 344 RIGID METAL CONDUIT (TYPE RMC)

Introduction to Article 344—Rigid Metal Conduit (Type RMC)

Rigid metal conduit, commonly called "rigid," has long been the standard raceway for providing protection from physical impact and from difficult environments. The outside diameter of rigid metal conduit is the same as intermediate metal conduit. However, the wall thickness of rigid metal conduit is greater than intermediate metal conduit; therefore the interior cross-sectional area is smaller. Rigid metal conduit is heavier and more expensive than intermediate metal conduit, and it can be used in any location. Rigid metal conduit is manufactured in both galvanized steel and aluminum; the steel type is much more common.

344.30 Securing and Supporting

The securing requirements for Rigid Metal Conduit have been changed into a list format.

Part II. Installation

344.30 Securing and Supporting. Rigid metal conduit must be installed as a complete system in accordance with 300.18 [300.10 and 300.12], and it must be securely fastened in place and supported in accordance with (A) and (B).

(A) Securely Fastened. RMC must be secured in accordance with one of the following:

(1) Fastened within 3 ft of each outlet box, junction box, device box, cabinet, conduit body, or other conduit termination. Figure 344–1

Author's Comment: Fastening is required within 3 ft of terminations, not within 3 ft of each coupling.

(2) When structural members don't permit the raceway to be secured within 3 ft of a box or termination fitting, the raceway must be secured within 5 ft of the termination. Figure 344–2

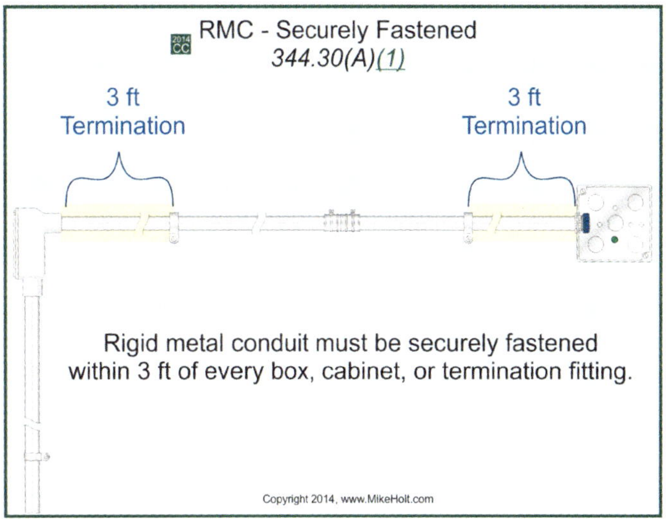

Figure 344–1

(3) Conduits aren't required to be securely fastened within 3 ft of the service head for an above-the-roof termination of a mast. Figure 344–3

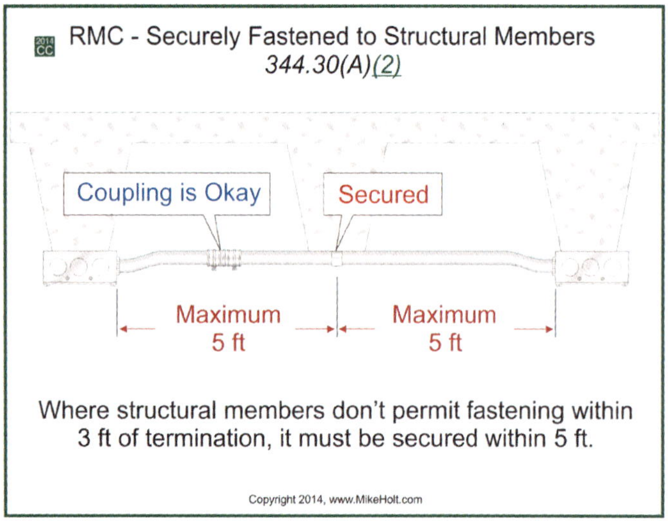

Figure 344–2

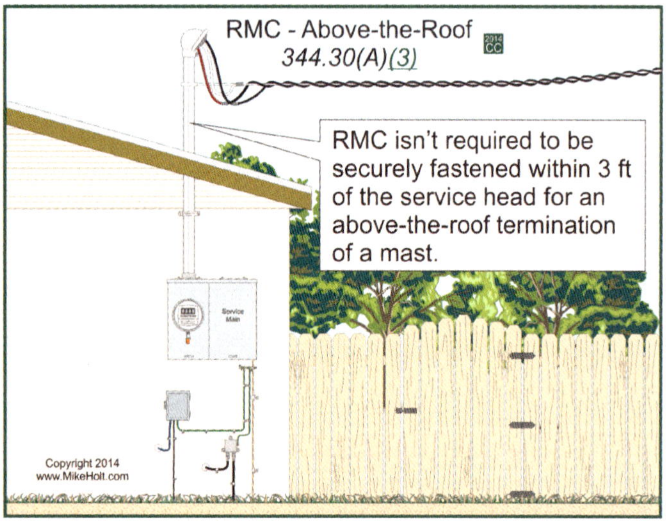

Figure 344–3

ANALYSIS: Although this change certainly isn't going to change the world, it improves the *NEC*. Over the last few *Code* cycles, a real effort has been made to change long paragraphs into itemized lists. While it may seem odd, considering that the requirements don't change, converting these paragraphs into lists really does go a long way toward enhancing the usability of the *NEC*.

Perhaps the best example of how lists work better than paragraphs is comparing the 2011 edition of 312.8 to the 2008 edition. The issue of splicing in a cabinet that contains a panelboard was confusing for many *Code* users for many years. Without changing any rules, the issue became crystal clear in 2011. How was this achieved? By putting exactly the same rules into an itemized list.

344.100 Construction

The characteristics of Rigid Metal Conduit have been relocated to a new 344.100.

Part III. Construction Specifications

344.100 Construction. RMC is constructed as one of the following:

(1) Steel (with or without protective coatings)

(2) Aluminum

(3) Red brass

(4) Stainless steel.

ANALYSIS: In order to provide consistency with other Chapter three wiring method articles, this new section has been created. No new information has been provided, since the added language is really just relocated from the definition that was in 344.2.

ARTICLE 348 FLEXIBLE METAL CONDUIT (TYPE FMC)

Introduction to Article 348—Flexible Metal Conduit (Type FMC)

Flexible metal conduit (FMC), commonly called "Greenfield" or "flex," is a raceway of an interlocked metal strip of either steel or aluminum. It's primarily used for the final 6 ft or less of raceways between a more rigid raceway system and equipment that moves, shakes, or vibrates. Examples of such equipment include pump motors and industrial machinery.

348.30 Securing and Supporting

The allowance for unsupported raceways has been revised, finally, to recognize a commonly accepted practice.

Part II. Installation

348.30 Securing and Supporting.

(A) Securely Fastened. Flexible metal conduit must be securely fastened by a means approved by the authority having jurisdiction within 1 ft of termination, and it must be secured and supported at intervals not exceeding 4½ ft. Figure 348–1

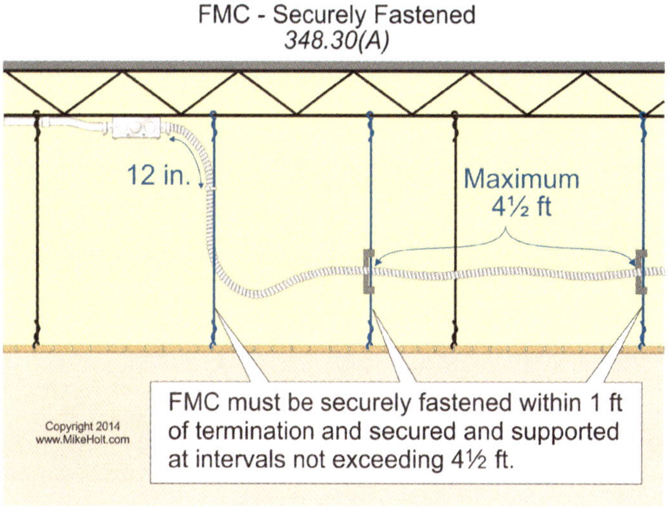

Figure 348–1

Ex 1: Flexible metal conduit isn't required to be securely fastened or supported where fished between access points through concealed spaces and supporting is impracticable.

Ex 2: If flexibility is necessary after installation, unsecured lengths from the last point the raceway is securely fastened must not exceed: Figure 348–2

(1) 3 ft for trade sizes ½ through 1¼

(2) 4 ft for trade sizes 1½ through 2

(3) 5 ft for trade sizes 2½ and larger

Ex 4: FMC to a luminaire or electrical equipment within an accessible ceiling is permitted to be unsupported for not more than 6 ft from the last point where the raceway is securely fastened. For the purposes of this exception listed fittings are considered support. Figure 348–3

(B) Horizontal Runs. Flexible metal conduit installed horizontally in bored or punched holes in wood or metal framing members, or notches in wooden members, is considered supported, but the raceway must be secured within 1 ft of terminations. Figure 348–4

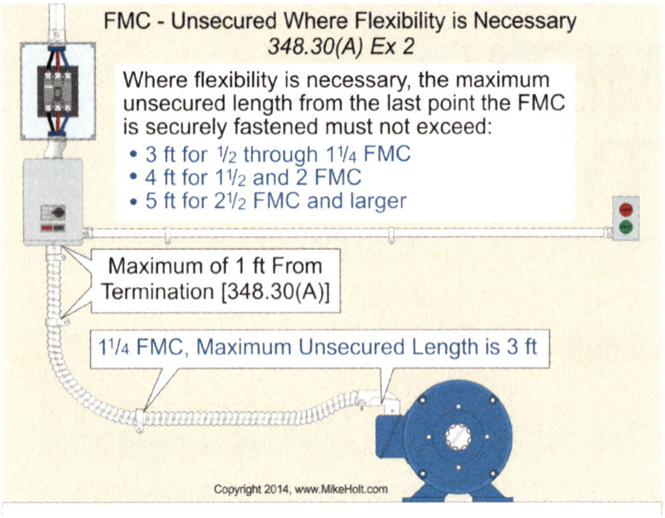

Figure 348–2

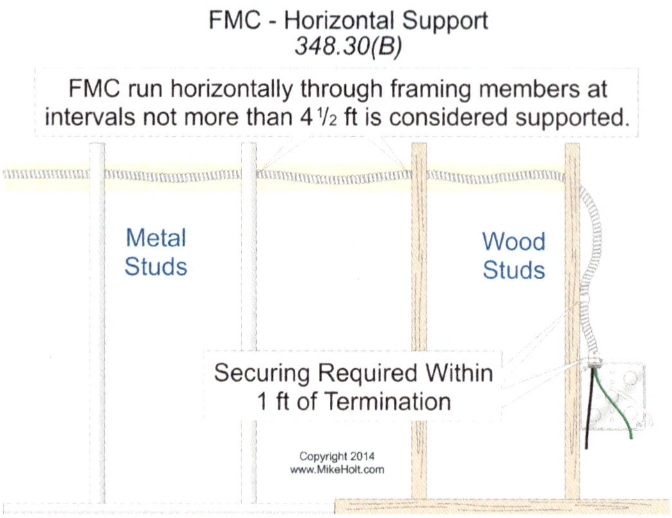

Figure 348–4

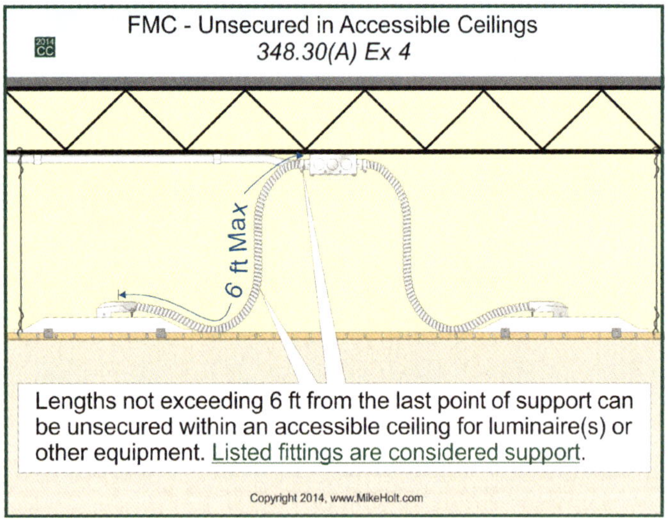

Figure 348–3

ANALYSIS: Over the last three *Code* cycles several proposals, including some from myself, have been made to try to make this allowance make sense. As previously written, a six-foot length of FMC to a luminaire in a suspended ceiling did, in fact, require support. This is due to the fact that the fitting wasn't addressed (compare this to the language in 320.30 and 330.30 for AC and MC cables, respectively). Quite often luminaires come with a six-foot length of ⅜ in. FMC attached to them, commonly known as a fixture whip. These whips, technically, required a support, although few *Code* users realized it (or cared about it). Most inspectors also either weren't aware of the rule or didn't care about it, and have allowed the FMC to go unsupported. This change makes it obvious that a six-foot length of FMC doesn't need support when it's used in a suspended ceiling.

ARTICLE 350 LIQUIDTIGHT FLEXIBLE METAL CONDUIT (TYPE LFMC)

Introduction to Article 350—Liquidtight Flexible Metal Conduit (Type LFMC)

Liquidtight flexible metal conduit (LFMC), with its associated connectors and fittings, is a flexible raceway commonly used for connections to equipment that vibrates or is required to move occasionally. Liquidtight flexible metal conduit is commonly called "Sealtight®" or "liquidtight." Liquidtight flexible metal conduit is of similar construction to flexible metal conduit, but it also has an outer liquidtight thermoplastic covering. It has the same primary purpose as flexible metal conduit, but it also provides protection from moisture and some corrosive effects.

350.30 Securing and Supporting

The allowance for unsupported raceways has been revised, finally, to recognize a commonly accepted practice.

Part II. Installation

350.30 Securing and Supporting. Liquidtight flexible metal conduit must be securely fastened in place and supported in accordance with (A) and (B).

(A) Securely Fastened. Liquidtight flexible metal conduit must be securely fastened by a means approved by the authority having jurisdiction within 1 ft of termination, and must be secured and supported at intervals not exceeding 4½ ft. Figure 350–1

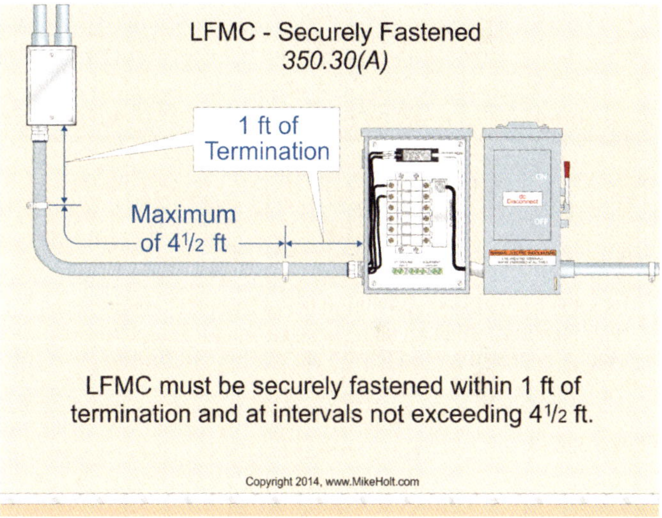

Figure 350–1

Ex 1: Liquidtight flexible metal conduit isn't required to be securely fastened or supported where fished between access points through concealed spaces and supporting is impracticable.

Ex 2: If flexibility is necessary after installation, unsecured lengths from the last point where the raceway is securely fastened must not exceed: Figure 350–2

(1) 3 ft for trade sizes ½ through 1¼

(2) 4 ft for trade sizes 1½ through 2

(3) 5 ft for trade sizes 2½ and larger

Ex 4: Lengths not exceeding 6 ft from the last point where the raceway is securely fastened can be unsecured within an accessible ceiling for luminaire(s) or other equipment. For the purposes of this exception, listed fittings are considered support. Figure 350–3

(B) Horizontal Runs. Liquidtight flexible metal conduit installed horizontally in bored or punched holes in wood or metal framing members, or notches in wooden members, is considered supported, but the raceway must be secured within 1 ft of termination.

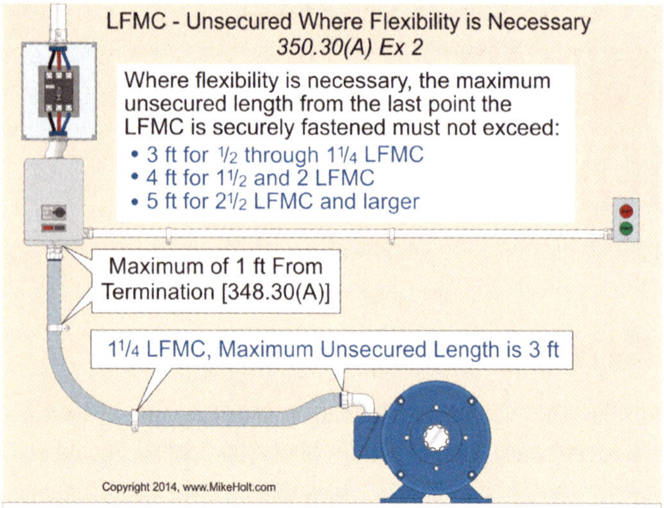

Figure 350–2

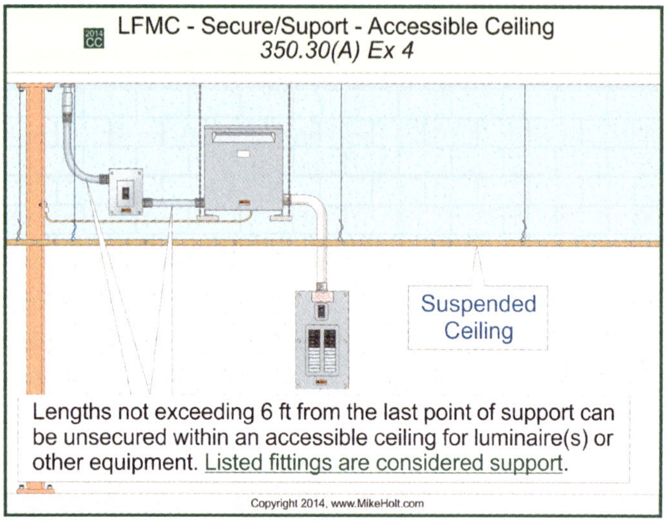

Figure 350–3

ANALYSIS: Over the last three *Code* cycles several proposals, including some from myself, have been made to try to make this allowance make sense. As previously written, a six-foot length of LFMC to a luminaire in a suspended ceiling did, in fact, require support. This is due to the fact that the fitting wasn't addressed (compare this to the language in 320.30 and 330.30 for AC and MC cables, respectively). This change makes it obvious that a six-foot length of LFMC doesn't need support when it's used in a suspended ceiling.

350.42 Fittings

The listing of fittings is now addressed in this location, and new text regarding direct-burial fittings has been added.

350.42 Fittings. Fittings used with LFMC must be listed. Angle connectors must not be concealed. Straight fittings can be buried where marked as suitable for direct burial. Figure 350–4

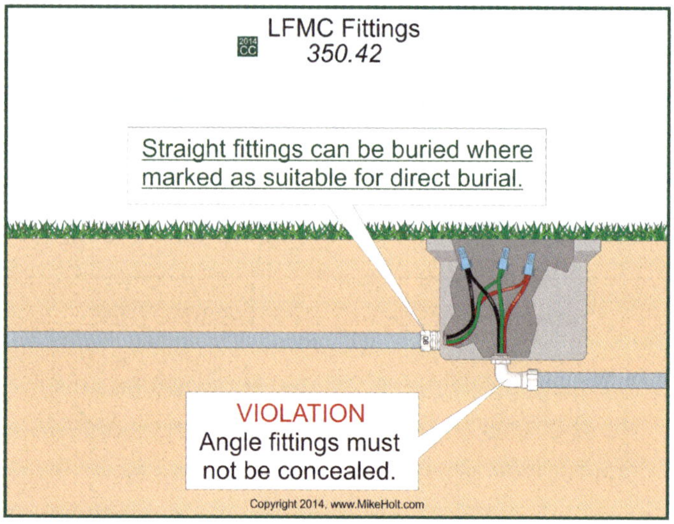

Figure 350–4

ANALYSIS: For whatever reason, the requirement of 350.6 has been copied and pasted into this section. Unlisted fittings weren't allowed before, due to 350.6, and they still aren't. New to this edition of the *NEC*, however, is an allowance for straight fittings to be buried if used in accordance with their listing. This isn't technically a change, since nothing in the previous *Code* prohibited the practice, but it certainly is more obvious now.

ARTICLE 352 RIGID POLYVINYL CHLORIDE CONDUIT (TYPE PVC)

Introduction to Article 352—Rigid Polyvinyl Chloride Conduit (Type PVC)

Rigid polyvinyl chloride conduit (PVC) is a rigid nonmetallic conduit that provides many of the advantages of rigid metal conduit, while allowing installation in areas that are wet or corrosive. It's an inexpensive raceway, and easily installed. It's lightweight, easily cut and glued together, and relatively strong. However, conduits manufactured from polyvinyl chloride (PVC) are brittle when cold, and they sag when hot. This type of conduit is commonly used as an underground raceway because of its low cost, ease of installation, and resistance to corrosion and decay.

352.2 Definition—Rigid Polyvinyl Chloride Conduit (PVC)

The definition of PVC Conduit was revised in order to comply with the *NEC* Style Manual.

352.2 Definition.

Rigid Polyvinyl Chloride Conduit (PVC). A rigid nonmetallic raceway of circular cross section with integral or associated couplings, listed for the installation of electrical conductors and cables. Figure 352–1

ANALYSIS: According to the *NEC* Style Manual, a definition shouldn't contain the term being defined. In order to satisfy this requirement, the word "conduit" (which is included in the term being defined) was changed to "raceway." Many other definitions throughout the *Code* were changed in the same manner, but they won't be discussed any further.

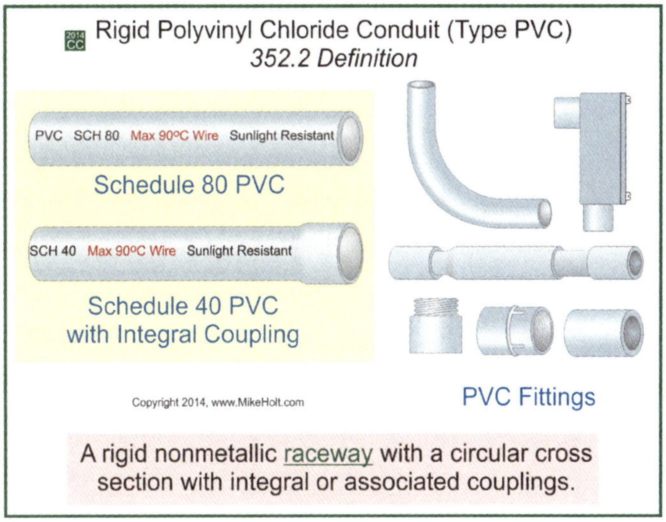

Figure 352–1

ARTICLE 356 LIQUIDTIGHT FLEXIBLE NONMETALLIC CONDUIT (TYPE LFNC)

Introduction to Article 356—Liquidtight Flexible Nonmetallic Conduit (Type LFNC)

Liquidtight flexible nonmetallic conduit (LFNC) is a listed raceway of circular cross section having an outer liquidtight, nonmetallic, sunlight-resistant jacket over an inner flexible core with associated couplings, connectors, and fittings.

356.30 Securing and Supporting

The allowance for unsupported raceways has been revised, finally, to recognize a commonly accepted practice.

Part II. Installation

356.30 Securing and Supporting. LFNC-B (gray color) must be securely fastened and supported in accordance with one of the following:

(1) The conduit must be securely fastened at intervals not exceeding 3 ft, and within 1 ft of termination when installed in lengths longer than 6 ft. Figure 356–1

(2) Securing or supporting isn't required if it's fished, installed in lengths not exceeding 3 ft at terminals if flexibility is required, or installed in lengths not exceeding 6 ft for tap conductors to luminaires, as permitted in 410.117(C).

(3) Horizontal runs of liquidtight flexible nonmetallic conduit installed horizontally in bored or punched holes in wood or metal framing members, or notches in wooden members, are considered supported, but the raceway must be secured within 1 ft of termination.

(4) Securing or supporting of LFNC-B (gray color) isn't required if installed in lengths not exceeding 6 ft from the last point where the raceway is securely fastened for connections within an accessible ceiling to luminaire(s) or other equipment. For the purposes of this allowance, listed fittings are considered support. Figure 356–2

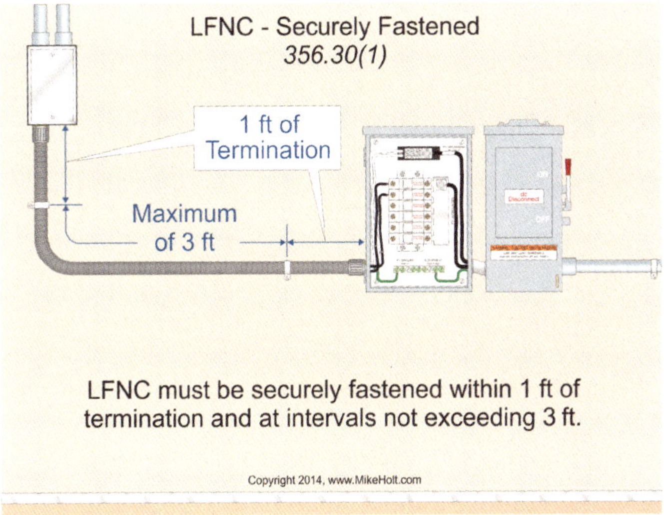

Figure 356–1

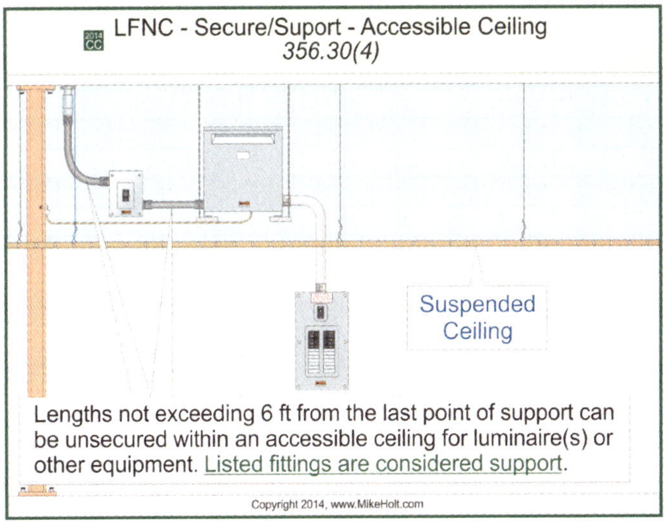

Figure 356–2

ANALYSIS: Over the last three *Code* cycles several proposals, including some from myself, have been made to try to make this allowance make sense. As previously written, a six-foot length of LFNC to a luminaire in a suspended ceiling did, in fact, require support. This is due to the fact that the fitting wasn't addressed (compare this to the language in 320.30 and 330.30 for AC and MC cables, respectively). This change makes it obvious that a six-foot length of LFNC doesn't need support when it's used in a suspended ceiling.

ARTICLE 376 METAL WIREWAYS

Introduction to Article 376—Metal Wireways

Metal wireways are commonly used where access to the conductors within a raceway is required to make terminations, splices, or taps to several devices at a single location. High cost precludes their use for other than short distances, except in some commercial or industrial occupancies where the wiring is frequently revised.

Author's Comment: Both metal wireways and nonmetallic wireways are often incorrectly called "troughs," "auxiliary gutters," "auxiliary wireways," or "gutters" in the field.

376.22 Number of Conductors and Ampacity

The requirements for ampacity adjustment in metal wireways were revised in order to create a sane rule.

Part II. Installation

376.22 Number of Conductors and Ampacity. The number of conductors and their ampacity must comply with 376.22(A) and (B).

(A) Number of Conductors. The maximum number of conductors permitted in a wireway is limited to 20 percent of the cross-sectional area of the wireway. Figures 376–1 and 376–2

Author's Comment: Splices and taps must not fill more than 75 percent of the wiring space at any cross section [376.56].

(B) Conductor Ampacity Adjustment Factors. When more than 30 current-carrying conductors are installed in any cross-sectional area of the wireway, the conductor ampacity, as listed in Table 310.15(B)(16), must be adjusted in accordance with Table 310.15(B)(3)(a). Figure 376–3

Signaling and motor-control conductors between a motor and its starter used only for starting duty aren't considered current carrying for conductor ampacity adjustment.

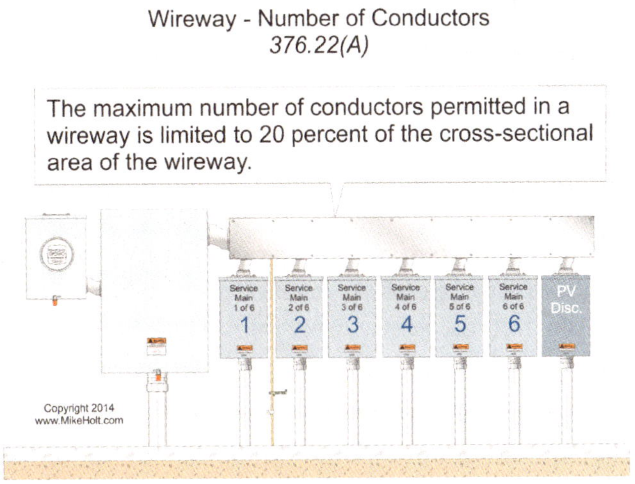

Figure 376–1

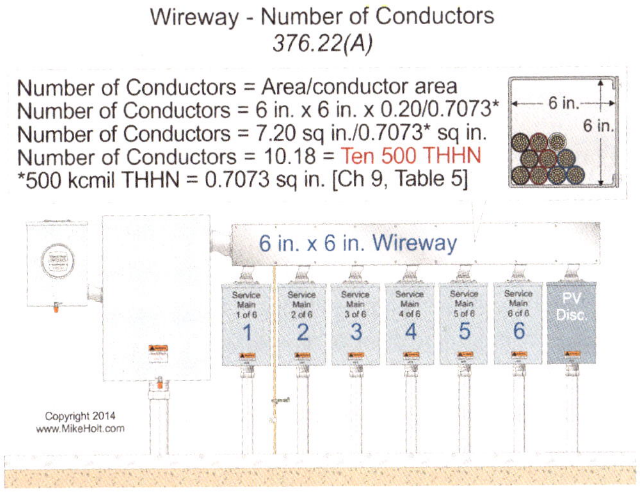

Figure 376–2

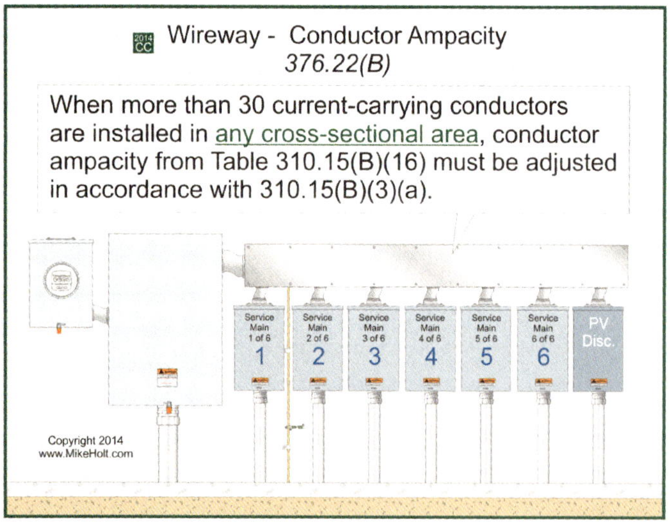

Figure 376–3

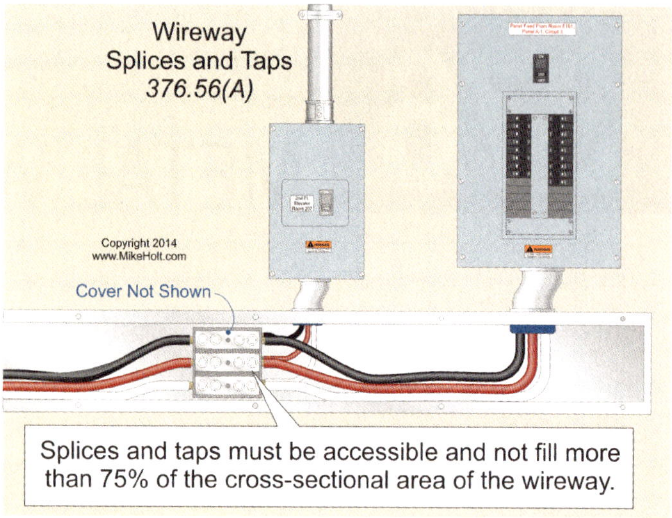

Figure 376–4

ANALYSIS: The issue of limiting the number (ampacities) of conductors in a wireway certainly makes sense. The more current-carrying conductors there are in proximity with each other, the more heat there will be. The key word here, however, is "proximity." A wireway that's 100 ft long, for example, might contain 31 current-carrying conductors. If these conductors are 10 feet away from any other conductors in the wireway, there certainly won't be any additional heating involved. It's where these conductors are in the same cross section that heat becomes a real problem. This change clarifies and solidifies this concept, and it should be a welcome change to those who desire *Code* rules that make sense.

376.56 Splices, Taps, and Power Distribution Blocks

The accessibility of the terminals for power distribution blocks in wireways has been addressed.

376.56 Splices, Taps, and Power Distribution Blocks.

(A) Splices and Taps. Splices and taps in metal wireways must be accessible, and they must not fill the wireway to more than 75 percent of its cross-sectional area. Figure 376–4

Author's Comment: The maximum number of conductors permitted in a metal wireway is limited to 20 percent of its cross-sectional area at any point [376.22(A)].

(B) Power Distribution Blocks.

(1) Installation. Power distribution blocks installed in wireways must be listed, and if they're installed on the supply side of the service disconnect they must be listed specifically for that application. Figure 376–5

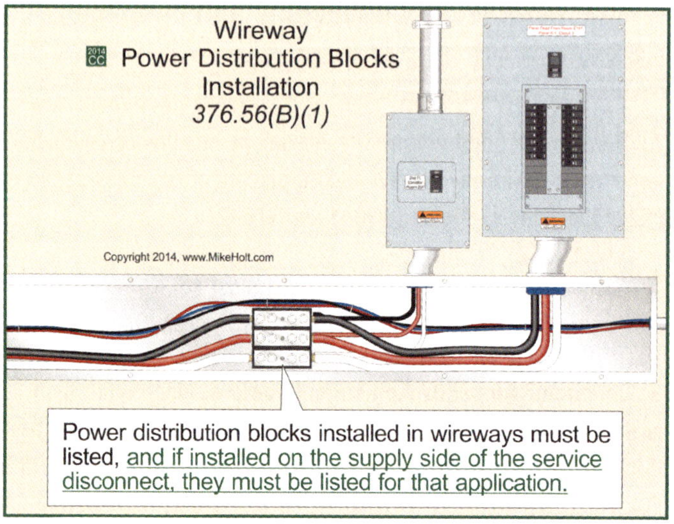

Figure 376–5

(2) Size of Enclosure. In addition to the wiring space requirements [376.56(A)], the power distribution block must be installed in a metal wireway not smaller than specified in the installation instructions of the power distribution block.

(3) Wire-Bending Space. Wire-bending space at the terminals of power distribution blocks must comply with 312.6(B).

(4) Live Parts. Power distribution blocks must not have uninsulated exposed live parts in the metal wireway after installation, whether or not the wireway cover is installed. Figure 376–6

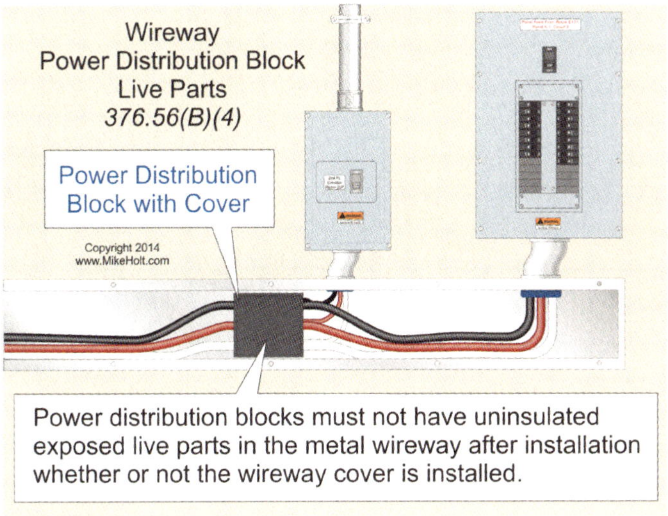

Figure 376–6

<u>**(5) Conductors.** Conductors must be installed so that the terminals of the power distribution block aren't obstructed.</u> Figure 376–7

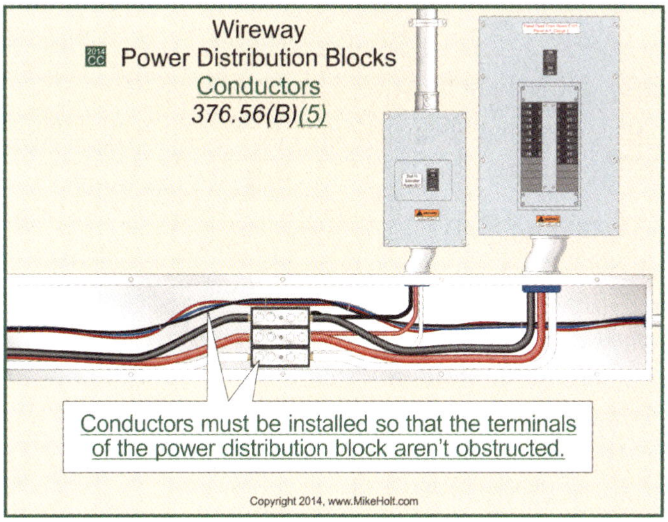

Figure 376–7

ANALYSIS: Power distribution blocks aren't, by default, listed to be used on the supply side of the service disconnect. This is information that's been in the UL White Book for quite some time, but not in the *Code*.

More often than not, a wireway with a power distribution block is also going to contain conductors that don't terminate on the block. When this is the case, the conductors must allow for the terminals of the block to be accessed. This is a difficult concept to argue against.

Notes

ARTICLE 386 SURFACE METAL RACEWAYS

Introduction to Article 386—Surface Metal Raceways

A surface metal raceway is a common method of adding a raceway when exposed traditional raceway systems aren't acceptable, and concealing the raceway isn't economically feasible. It comes in several colors, and is now available with colored or real wood inserts designed to make it look like molding rather than a raceway. A surface metal raceway is commonly known as "Wiremold®" in the field.

386.30 Securing and Supporting

The requirements for securing and supporting surface metal raceways have been revised to address fittings.

Part II. Installation

386.30 Securing and Supporting. Surface metal raceways and fittings must be supported in accordance with the manufacturer's installation instructions. Figure 386–1

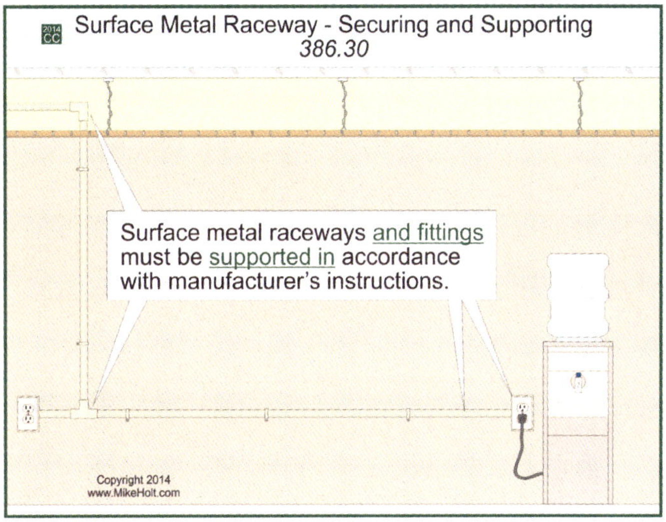

Figure 386–1

ANALYSIS: It's easy to think of fittings for surface metal raceways as just the couplings. While indeed couplings are fittings, so are the terminal boxes that are used with these systems. For example, a "fitting" that looks, smells, sounds, and feels like a box might be added so that a receptacle can be installed. What's the rule for securing and supporting this "fitting?" Does 314.23(F) for box support apply? If the answer is yes, there are going to be major problems trying to achieve *Code* compliance, as a surface metal raceway surely isn't going to be threaded into the enclosure! This change clarifies that these boxes/fittings/enclosures must be secured and supported.

Notes

ARTICLE 392 CABLE TRAYS

Introduction to Article 392—Cable Trays

A cable tray system is a unit or an assembly of units or sections with associated fittings that forms a structural system used to securely fasten or support cables and raceways. A cable tray isn't a raceway.

Cable tray systems include ladder, ventilated trough, ventilated channel, solid bottom, and other similar structures. Cable trays are manufactured in many forms, from a simple hanger or wire mesh to a substantial, rigid, steel support system. Cable trays are designed and manufactured to support specific wiring methods, as identified in 392.10(A).

392.60 Equipment Grounding Conductor

The bonding conductor size for cable trays containing only nonpower conductors has been removed.

Part II. Installation

392.60 Equipment Grounding Conductor.

(A) Metallic Cable Trays. Metallic cable trays can be used as equipment grounding conductors where continuous maintenance and supervision ensure that qualified persons service the installed cable tray system. Figure 392–1

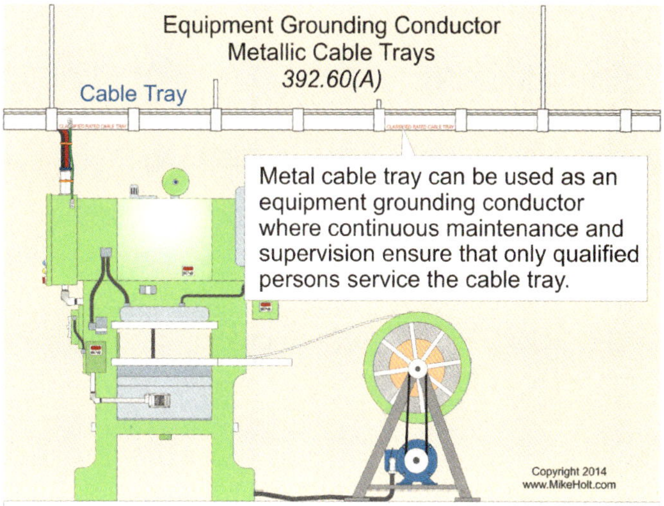

Figure 392–1

The metallic cable trays that support conductors must be bonded together to ensure that they have the capacity to conduct safely any fault current likely to be imposed in accordance with 250.96(A).

Metal cable trays containing communications, data, and signaling conductors and cables must be electrically continuous through listed connections or the use of a bonding jumper. Figure 392–2

Author's Comment: Nonconductive coatings such as paint, lacquer, and enamel on equipment must be removed to ensure an effective ground-fault current path, or the termination fittings must be designed so as to make such removal unnecessary [250.12].

ANALYSIS: The requirement to bond cable tray sections together when they contain only nonpower conductors was added in the 2011 *NEC*. This edition of the *Code* removes the requirement that a bonding jumper be 10 AWG or larger, due to the fact that there's no reason for it. In fact, there's no reason for the rule in the first place, but now it isn't quite as ridiculous as it was.

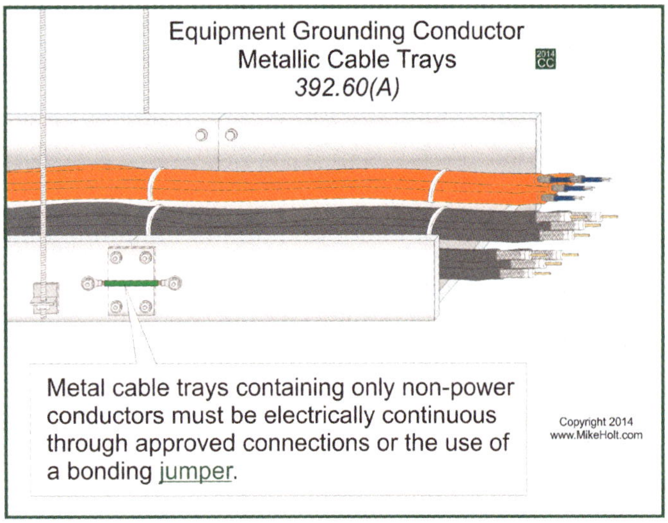
Equipment Grounding Conductor
Metallic Cable Trays
2014 CC
392.60(A)
Metal cable trays containing only non-power conductors must be electrically continuous through approved connections or the use of a bonding jumper.
Copyright 2014
www.MikeHolt.com

Figure 392–2

ARTICLE 393 LOW VOLTAGE SUSPENDED CEILING POWER DISTRIBUTION SYSTEMS

Introduction to Article 393—Low Voltage Suspended Ceiling Power Distribution Systems

Low voltage suspended ceiling power distribution systems use the ceiling grid members as electrical conductors. This allows the ceiling grid to provide power to a variety of electrical equipment; but, because of the obvious danger of energizing the ceiling grid, the voltage and current are limited to Class 2 power levels. This limitation provides safety while allowing for low energy-consuming equipment, such as speakers and audio/video equipment, to be used.

Article 393—Low Voltage Suspended Ceiling Power Distribution Systems

A new article covering "low voltage suspended ceiling power distribution systems" has been added.

ANALYSIS: These systems use the actual ceiling grid as the distribution system for low-voltage lighting. They're described in Product Category IFFA in the UL White Book. Because these systems are so new and so unusual, they have their own article. They're intended for indoor dry locations, and can include interconnecting cables and connectors.

Notes

CHAPTER 4 EQUIPMENT FOR GENERAL USE

Introduction to Chapter 4—Equipment for General Use

With the first three chapters behind you, the final chapter in the *NEC* necessary for building a solid foundation in general work is Chapter 4. This chapter helps you apply the first three to installations involving general equipment. These first four chapters follow a natural sequential progression. Each of the next four chapters—5, 6, 7, and 8—build upon the first four, but in no particular order. You need to understand all of the first four chapters to properly apply any of the next ones.

As in the preceding chapters, Chapter 4 is also arranged logically. Here are the groupings:

- Flexible cords and cables, and fixture wires.
- Switches and receptacles.
- Switchboards and panelboards.
- Lamps and luminaires.
- Appliances and space heaters.
- Motors, refrigeration equipment, generators, and transformers.
- Batteries, capacitors, and other components.

These groupings make sense. For example, motors, refrigeration equipment, generators, and transformers are all inductive equipment.

This logical arrangement of the *NEC* is something to keep in mind when you're searching for a particular item. You know, for example, that transformers are general equipment. So you'll find the *Code* requirements for them in Chapter 4. You know they're wound devices, so you'll find transformer requirements located somewhere near motor requirements.

- **Article 400—Flexible Cords and Flexible Cables.** Article 400 covers the general requirements, applications, and construction specifications for flexible cords and flexible cables.
- **Article 402—Fixture Wires.** This article covers the general requirements and construction specifications for fixture wires.
- **Article 404—Switches.** The requirements of Article 404 apply to switches of all types. These include snap (toggle) switches, dimmer switches, fan switches, knife switches, circuit breakers used as switches, and automatic switches such as time clocks, timers, and switches and circuit breakers used for disconnecting means.

- **Article 406—Receptacles, Cord Connectors, and Attachment Plugs (Caps).** This article covers the rating, type, and installation of receptacles, cord connectors, and attachment plugs (cord caps). It also covers flanged surface inlets.
- **Article 408—Switchboards and Panelboards.** Article 408 covers specific requirements for switchboards, panelboards, and distribution boards that supply lighting and power circuits.
- **Article 410—Luminaires, Lampholders, and Lamps.** This article contains the requirements for luminaires, lampholders, and lamps. Because of the many types and applications of luminaires, manufacturer's instructions are very important and helpful for proper installation. Underwriters Laboratories produces a pamphlet called the *Luminaire Marking Guide*, which provides information for properly installing common types of incandescent, fluorescent, and high-intensity discharge (HID) luminaires.
- **Article 411—Lighting Systems Operating at 30V or Less and Lighting Equipment Connected to Class-2 Power Sources.** Article 411 covers lighting systems, and their associated components, that operate at 30V or less, or that are connected to a Class 2 power source.
- **Article 422—Appliances.** This article covers electric appliances used in any occupancy.
- **Article 424—Fixed Electric Space-Heating Equipment.** Article 424 covers fixed electric equipment used for space heating. For the purpose of this article, heating equipment includes heating cable, unit heaters, boilers, central systems, and other fixed electric space-heating equipment. Article 424 doesn't apply to process heating and room air-conditioning.
- **Article 430—Motors, Motor Circuits, and Controllers.** This article contains the specific requirements for conductor sizing, overcurrent protection, control circuit conductors, motor controllers, and disconnecting means. The installation requirements for motor control centers are covered in Article 430, Part VIII.
- **Article 440—Air-Conditioning and Refrigeration Equipment.** Article 440 applies to electrically driven air-conditioning and refrigeration equipment with a motorized hermetic refrigerant compressor. The requirements in this article are in addition to, or amend, the requirements in Article 430 and others.
- **Article 445—Generators.** Article 445 contains the electrical installation requirements for generators and other requirements, such as where they can be installed, nameplate markings, conductor ampacity, and disconnecting means.
- **Article 450—Transformers.** This article covers the installation of transformers.

ARTICLE 400 FLEXIBLE CORDS AND FLEXIBLE CABLES

Introduction to Article 400—Flexible Cords and Flexible Cables

This article covers the general requirements, applications, and construction specifications for flexible cords and flexible cables. The *NEC* doesn't consider flexible cords to be wiring methods like those defined in Chapter 3.

Always use a cord (and fittings) identified for the application. Table 400.4 will help you in that regard. For example, use cords listed for a wet location if you're using them outdoors. The jacket material of any cord is tested to maintain its insulation properties and other characteristics in the environments for which it's been listed. Tables 400.5(A)(1) and 400.5(A)(2) are also important tables to turn to when looking for the ampacity of flexible cords and cables.

400.23 Equipment Grounding Conductor Identification

This section has been revised to correlate with a change made in 250.119.

400.23 Equipment Grounding Conductor Identification. A conductor intended to be used as an equipment grounding conductor must have a continuous green color or a continuous identifying marker distinguishing it from the other conductor(s). Conductors with green insulation, or green with one or more yellow stripes must not be used for an ungrounded or neutral conductor [250.119], unless they comply with 250.119 Ex 2.

ANALYSIS: Ex 2 to 250.119 has been added to address green, two-conductor flexible cords. Although they're certainly less common than black cords, they do exist. If the outer jacket of the cord also serves as the individual conductor insulation (such as for Type SPT-2, also commonly called zip cord), a literal reading of the previous *Code* rules would disallow the cord from being used, since the color green can't be used for ungrounded or neutral conductors. This seems like a reasonable allowance, since a two-conductor cord is certainly not an equipment grounding conductor, so there shouldn't be any confusion by the application of the color green.

Notes

ARTICLE 404 SWITCHES

Introduction to Article 404—Switches

The requirements of Article 404 apply to switches of all types, including snap (toggle) switches, dimmer switches, fan switches, knife switches, circuit breakers used as switches, and automatic switches, such as time clocks and timers.

404.2 Switch Connections

The requirement for having a neutral at switch locations was revised.

404.2 Switch Connections.

(C) Switches Controlling Lighting Loads. Switches controlling line-to-neutral lighting loads must have a neutral provided at the switch location, other than in the following locations:

(1) Where the conductors for switches enter the device box through a raceway that has sufficient cross-sectional area to accommodate a neutral conductor. Figure 404–1

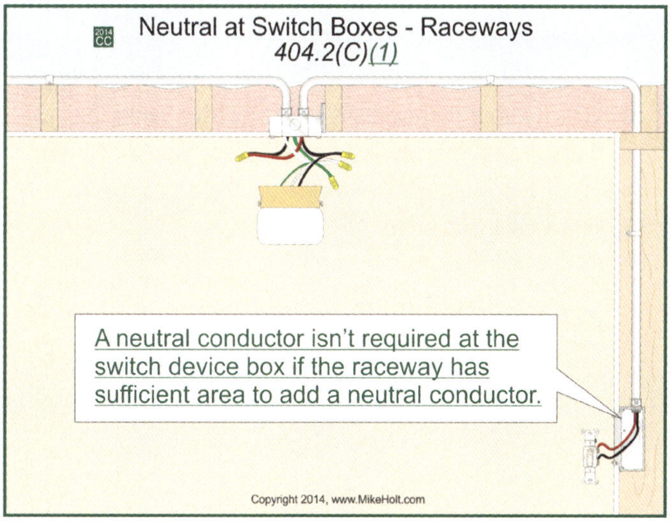

Figure 404–1

(2) Where the switch box can be accessed to add or replace a cable containing a neutral without damaging the finish of the building. Figure 404–2

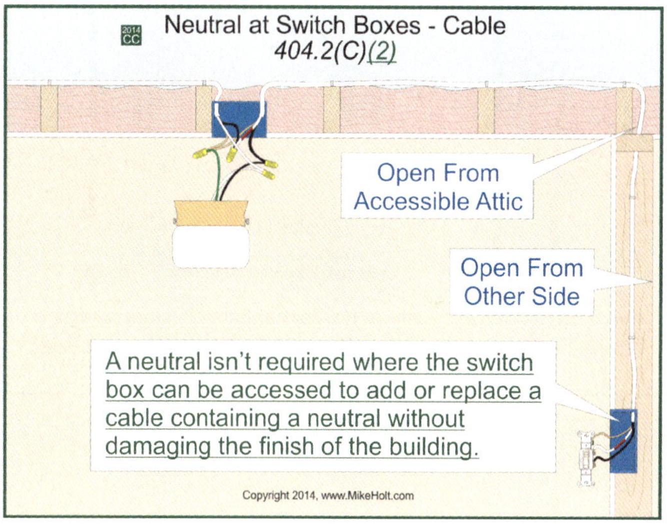

Figure 404–2

(3) Snap switches with integral enclosures [300.15(E)].

(4) Nonhabitable rooms and bathrooms. Figure 404–3

(5) For 3-way and 4-way switches, but only if the entire floor area is visible from the switches' location(s). Figure 404–4

(6) Where the lighting is controlled automatically.

(7) Switches controlling receptacles. Figure 404–5

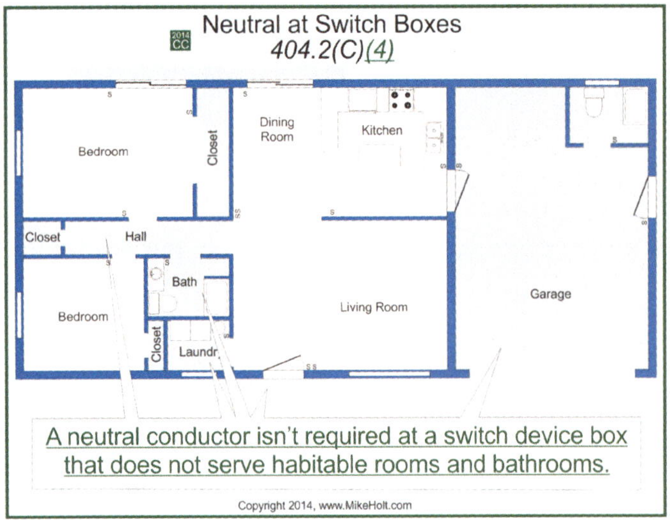

Figure 404–3

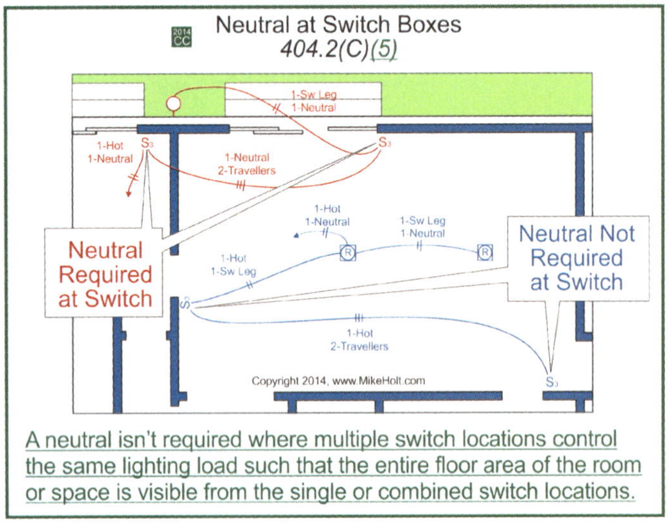

Figure 404–4

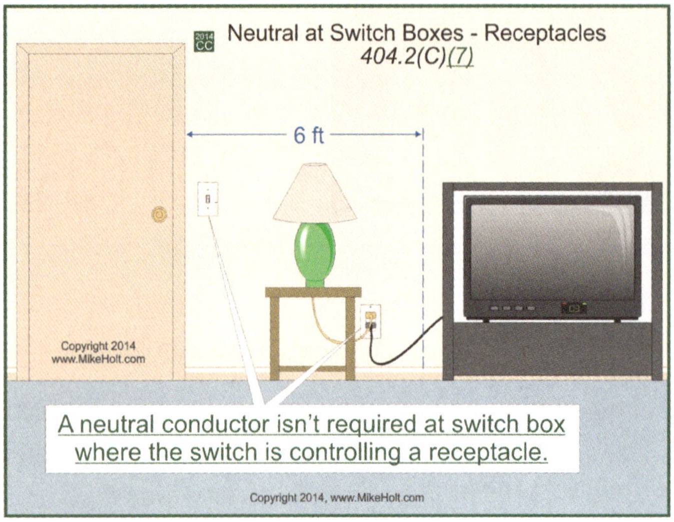

Figure 404–5

Note: The purpose of the neutral conductor is to complete a circuit path for electronic lighting control devices.

ANALYSIS: Once again, when a new, significant rule comes into the *Code*, it takes at least three more years for the *NEC* to make it logical. This isn't the fault of the people writing the *Code*, it's just that it's very difficult to anticipate every type of installation that a new rule will affect. The areas where a neutral isn't required have been greatly expanded in this edition of the *NEC*, and the existing exceptions were cleaned up dramatically as well.

The text regarding framing cavities that are "open at the top or bottom" has been removed, as even *Code* experts disagreed about what that exception meant. It's been replaced with item two, which is easier to understand, and makes more sense as well.

Additional new allowances include 3-way and 4-way switches where the switches can "see" the entire room. In these instances, an occupancy sensor would only be installed at one or the other switch, so there's no reason to require a neutral at both.

404.10 Mounting Snap Switches

Changes to this section correlate with similar changes in other articles of the *Code*.

404.10 Mounting Snap Switches.

(B) Mounting of Snap Switches. Snap switches installed in recessed boxes must have the ears of the switch yoke seated firmly against the finished wall surface. Screws for attaching a snap switch to a box must be machine screws matching the thread gage or size of the screw holes in the box, unless otherwise allowed by the manufacturer's instructions, or unless part of a listed assembly. Figure 404–6

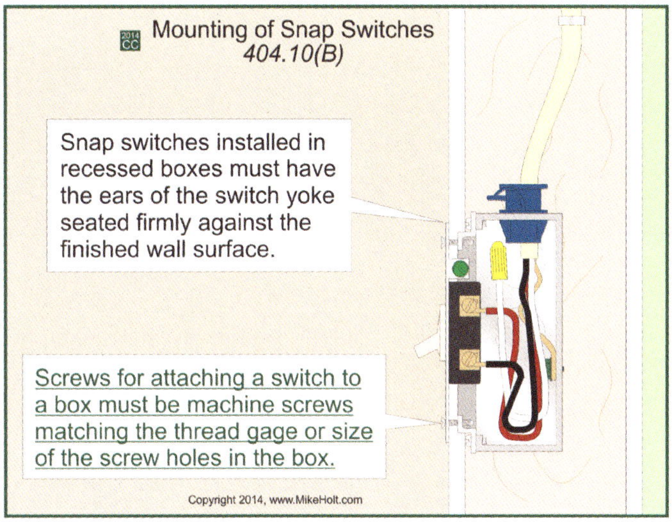

Figure 404–6

Author's Comment: In walls or ceilings of noncombustible material, such as drywall, boxes must not be set back more than ¼ in. from the finished surface. In combustible walls or ceilings, boxes must be flush with, or project slightly from, the finished surface [314.20]. There must not be any gaps more than ⅛ in. at the edge of the box [314.21].

ANALYSIS: It is, unfortunately, a common practice to use drywall screws to attach receptacles and switches to boxes. Worse still is attaching luminaires to boxes using screws that weren't designed, tested, and listed to support them. Most people take comfort in the fact that the chandelier they're standing under was installed properly. Using screws that aren't designed to support equipment isn't only a *Code* violation, it's an unsafe practice. While attaching switches to a box with the wrong screws probably isn't going to kill anyone, prohibiting the practice for all boxes provides consistency in the *NEC*.

ARTICLE 406 RECEPTACLES, CORD CONNECTORS, AND ATTACHMENT PLUGS (CAPS)

Introduction to Article 406—Receptacles, Cord Connectors, and Attachment Plugs (Caps)

This article covers the rating, type, and installation of receptacles, cord connectors, and attachment plugs (cord caps). It also addresses their grounding requirements. Some key points to remember include:

- Following the grounding requirements of the specific type of device you're using.
- Providing GFCI protection where specified by 406.4(D)(3).
- Mounting receptacles according to the requirements of 406.5, which are highly detailed.

406.3 Receptacle Rating and Type

Provisions for automatically controlled receptacles have been added.

406.3 Receptacle Rating and Type.

(E) Controlled Receptacle Marking. All nonlocking, 125V, 15A and 20A receptacles that have an automatic means to remove power from the outlet for energy management or building automation must be marked with the following symbol, Figure 406–1. The symbol must be placed on the receptacle in a location that's visible after installation.

Ex: The marking isn't required for wall switch-controlled receptacles used for lighting in a dwelling [210.70(A)(1) Ex 2].

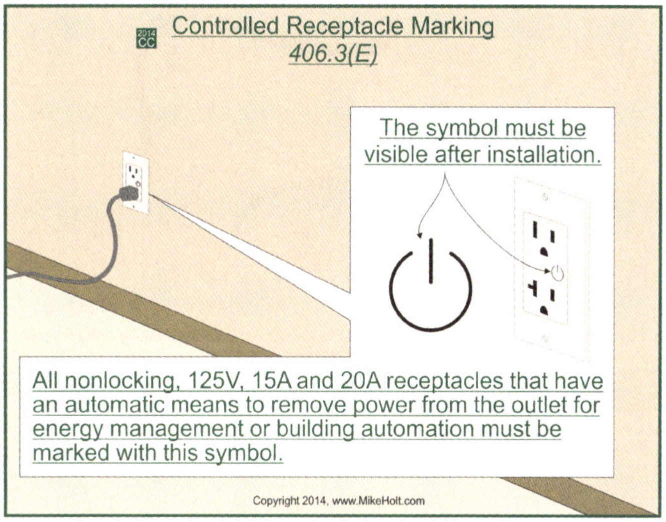

Figure 406–1

ANALYSIS: It's becoming more and more common to have receptacles in commercial buildings supplied by some sort of energy management system. These systems will de-energize receptacles at a certain time of day, such as just after quitting time. Of course, quitting time isn't the same for everybody, so the poor individual who's trying to catch up with work by staying after hours might be in a for an unpleasant surprise when his or her computer shuts off by itself! By adding this symbol, office workers might eventually figure out what it means—after they lose their work a few times.

406.4 General Installation Requirements

Editorial revisions have been made to the grounding-type receptacle rules.

406.4 General Installation Requirements.

(A) Grounding Type. Receptacles installed on 15A and 20A branch circuits must be of the grounding type, unless used for replacements as permitted in (D)(2), Figure 406–2. Single receptacles must have an ampere rating not less than the rating of the branch circuit [210.21(B)(1)], and multioutlet receptacles (such as duplex receptacles) must have a rating in accordance with Table 210.21(B)(3). Figure 406–3

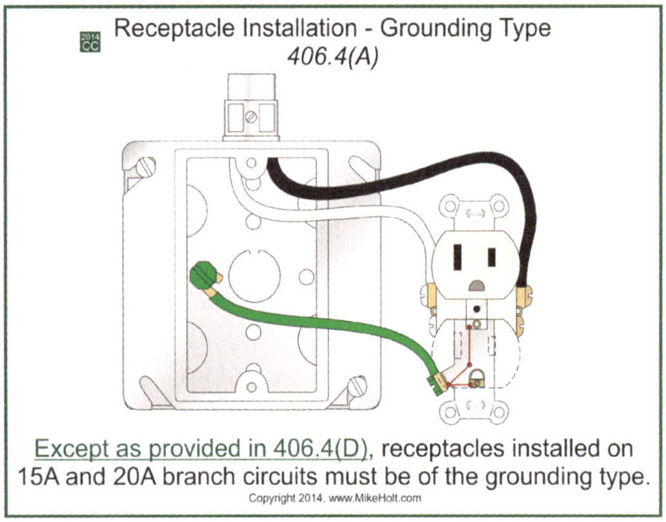

Figure 406–2

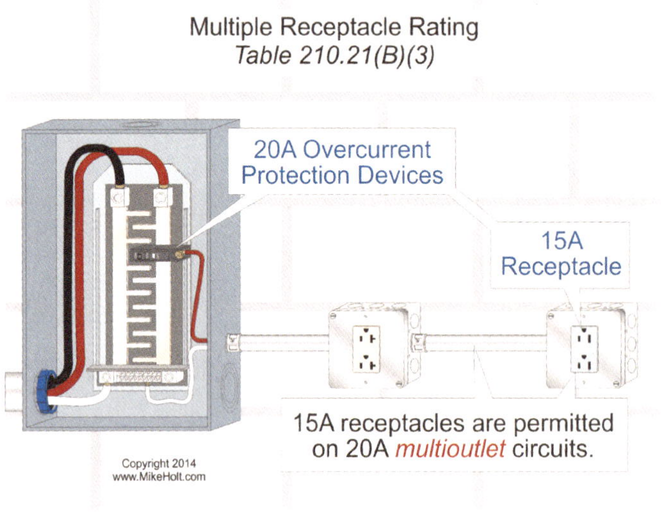

Figure 406–3

Table 210.21(B)(3) Receptacle Ratings

Circuit Rating	Receptacle Rating
15A	15A
20A	15A or 20A
30A	30A
40A	40A or 50A
50A	50A

(D) Receptacle Replacement.

(2) Nongrounding-Type Receptacles. If no equipment grounding conductor exists in the outlet box for the receptacle, such as old 2-wire Type NM cable without an equipment grounding conductor, existing nongrounding-type receptacles can be replaced in accordance with (a), (b), or (c): Figure 406–4

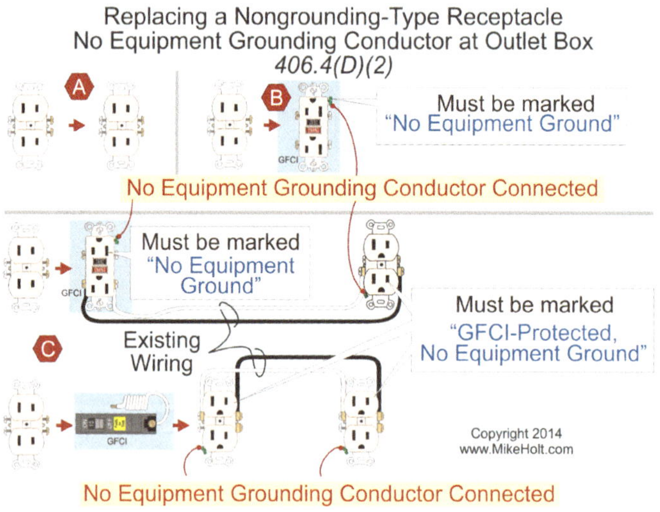

Figure 406–4

(a) Another nongrounding-type receptacle.

(b) A GFCI-type receptacle marked "No Equipment Ground."

(c) A grounding-type receptacle, if GFCI protected and marked "GFCI Protected" and "No Equipment Ground."

ANALYSIS: The exception for receptacles having to be of the grounding type was changed into positive text and was relocated to the opening statement of 406.4(A). This is just one more effort in the never-ending quest to to remove exceptions from the *National Electrical Code*.

406.5 Receptacle Mounting

Changes to this section include addressing the types of screws used for receptacles, receptacles in seating areas, receptacles in countertops, and editorial revisions.

406.5 Receptacle Mounting. Receptacles must be installed in identified outlet boxes. Screws for attaching receptacles to a box must be machine screws matching the thread gage or size of the holes in the box, or must be part of a listed assembly. Figure 406–5

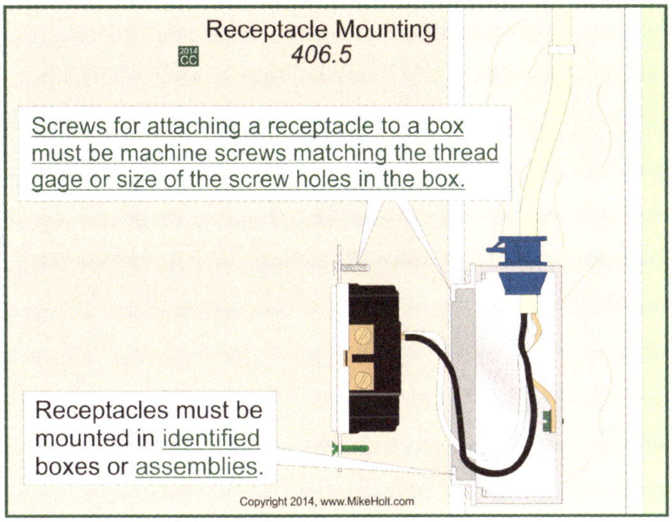

Figure 406–5

Author's Comment: The position of the ground terminal of a receptacle isn't specified in the *NEC*. The ground terminal can be up, down, or to the side. Proposals to specify the mounting position of the ground terminal have been rejected through many *Code* cycles. For more information on this subject, visit www.MikeHolt.com. Figure 406–6

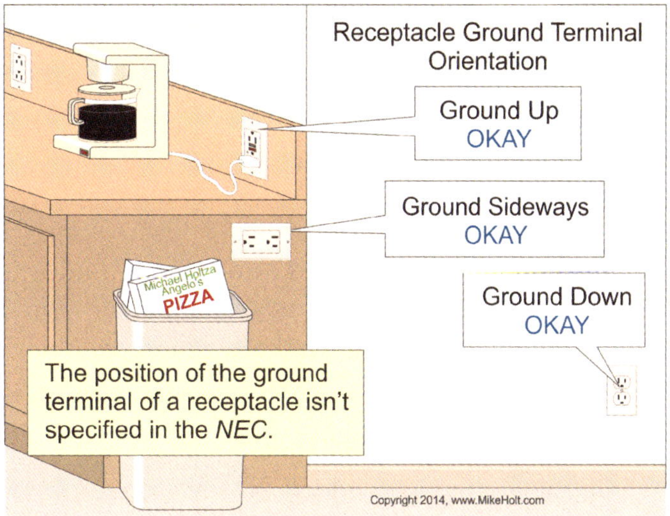

Figure 406–6

ANALYSIS: It is, unfortunately, a common practice to use drywall screws to attach receptacles and switches to boxes. Worse still is attaching luminaires to boxes using screws that weren't designed, tested, and listed to support them. Most people take comfort in the fact that the chandelier they're standing under was installed properly. Keeping in mind that receptacles are subjected to the force of pushing and pulling against them, using the wrong screw can end up resulting in a receptacle becoming unattached from the box. Using screws that aren't designed to support equipment isn't only a *Code* violation, it's an unsafe practice. While attaching receptacles to a box with the wrong screws probably isn't going to kill anyone, prohibiting the practice for all boxes provides consistency in the *NEC*.

(E) Receptacles in Countertops and Similar Work Surfaces. Receptacles must not be installed in a face-up position in countertops or similar work surface areas, unless they're part of a listed assembly for countertop surfaces. Figure 406–7

Author's Comment: Receptacle outlet assemblies listed for the application can be installed in dwelling unit kitchen and bathroom countertops [210.52(C)(5) and 210.52(D)].

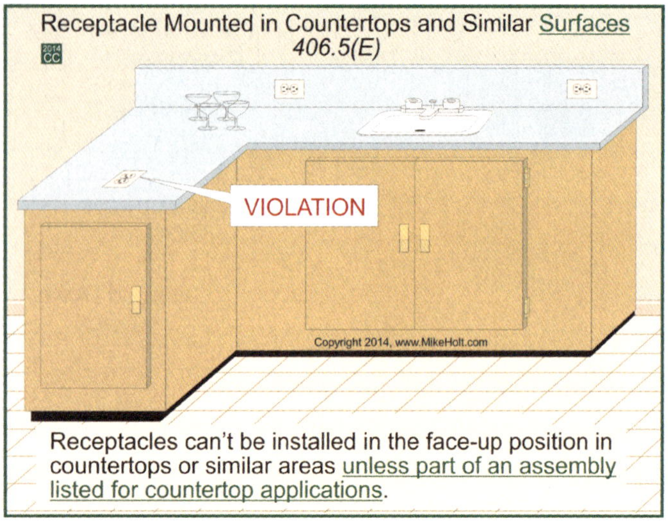

Figure 406–7

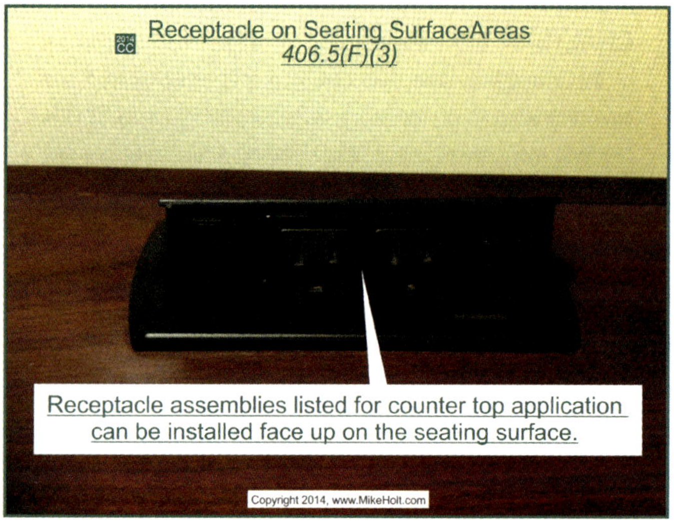

Figure 406–8

ANALYSIS: Subsection (E) was revised to prohibit receptacles from being installed face up in any countertop. Previous editions of the *Code* prohibited this practice as well, but only in dwelling units. Thinking back on a service call I did on a face-up receptacle in a commercial kitchen, I'm glad to see this change because if it had been in place years ago, one of the worst memories that I have as an electrician could have been avoided. Alas.

(F) Receptacles in Seating Areas and Similar Surfaces. Receptacles must not be installed in a face-up position in seating areas or similar surfaces, unless the receptacle is:

(1) Part of a listed furniture power distribution unit,

(2) Part of a listed furnishing,

(3) Listed for use in countertops, or Figure 406–8

(4) Installed in a listed floor box.

ANALYSIS: A new subsection (F) has been added to provide requirements for receptacles in seating areas and similar locations. It makes sense that a person sitting on a receptacle should be sitting on something that's been tested and listed for the load of a human's backside, even though human backsides aren't all created equal. The issue that may come up with this rule, however, is whether or not it applies to floor receptacles. Is this requirement talking about seating areas, as in physically sitting on the receptacle, or is it talking about seating areas, such as in an assembly hall? This change isn't intended to cover floor receptacles. Floor boxes are typically listed without the receptacle, so they aren't a listed assembly; rather, they're an assembly of listed parts.

406.9 Receptacles in Damp or Wet Locations

The requirement for an "extra-duty outlet box hood" has been expanded.

406.9 Receptacles in Damp or Wet Locations.

(B) Wet Locations.

(1) 15A and 20A Receptacles. All 15A and 20A receptacles installed in a wet location must be within an enclosure that's weatherproof when an attachment plug is inserted. Figure 406–9

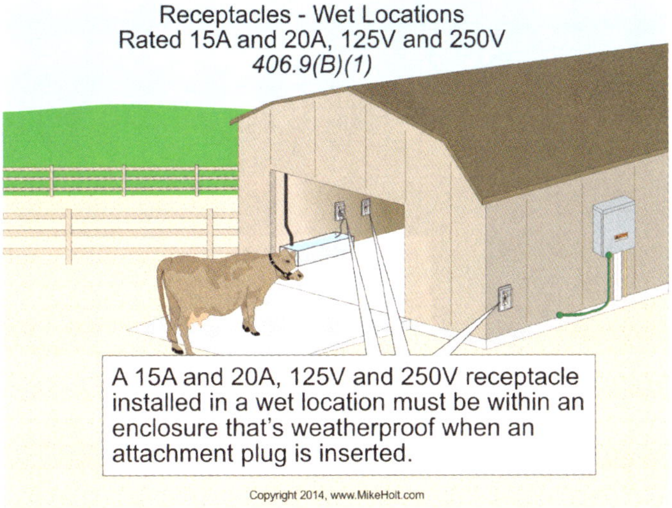

Figure 406–9

Outlet box hoods must be listed and must be identified for "extra-duty" use. Figure 406–10

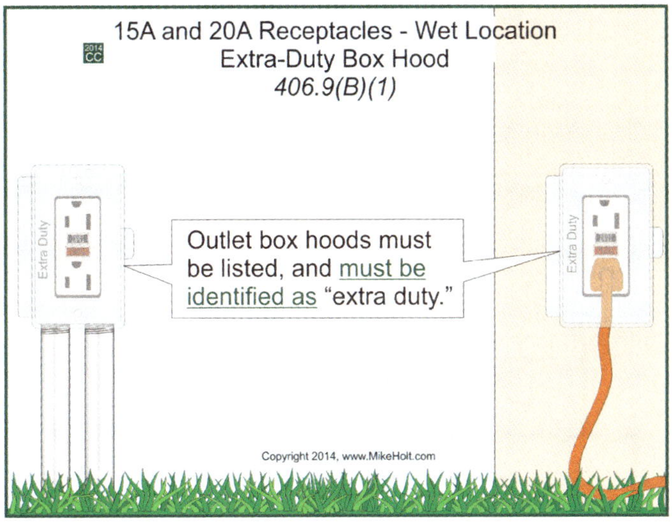

Figure 406–10

All nonlocking type 15A and 20A, 125V and 250V receptacles in a wet location must be listed as weather resistant. Figure 406–11

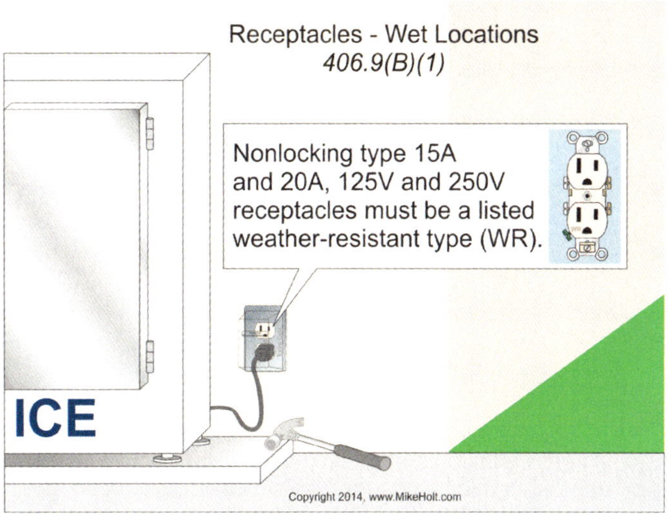

Figure 406–11

Author's Comment: Exposed plastic surface material of weather-resistant receptacles must have UV resistance to ensure that deterioration from sunlight doesn't take place, or that it's minimal. In testing, receptacles are subjected to temperature cycling from very cold to very warm conditions, and then subjected to additional dielectric testing. The rapid transition from the cold to warm temperatures will change the relative humidity and moisture content on the device, and the dielectric test ensures that this won't create a breakdown of the insulation properties.

Ex: Receptacles rated 15A and 20A that are subjected to routine high-pressure washing spray may have an enclosure that's weatherproof when the attachment plug is removed.

Author's Comment: A wet location is an area subject to saturation with water, as well as unprotected locations that are exposed to weather [Article 100]. Figure 406–12

(2) Other Receptacles. Receptacles rated 30A or more installed in a wet location must comply with (a) or (b).

(a) Wet Location Covers. A receptacle that's in a wet location, where the load isn't attended while in use, must be installed in an enclosure that's weatherproof when an attachment plug is inserted.

(b) Damp Location Covers. A receptacle installed in a wet location that will only be used while someone is in close proximity to it, such as one used with portable tools, can have an enclosure that's weatherproof when the attachment plug is removed and the cover is closed.

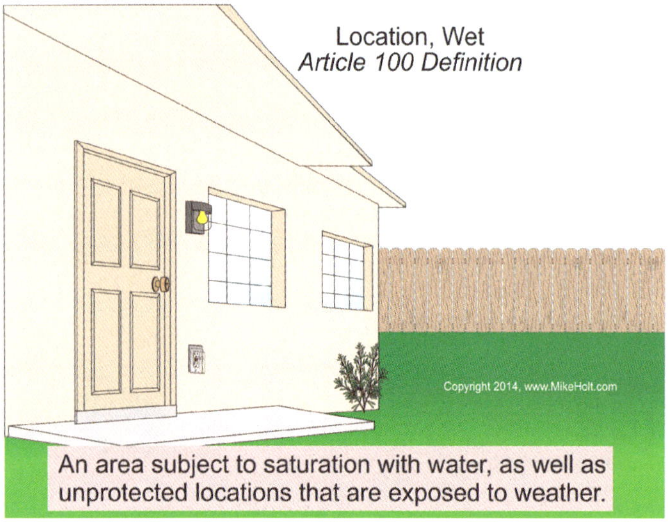

Figure 406–12

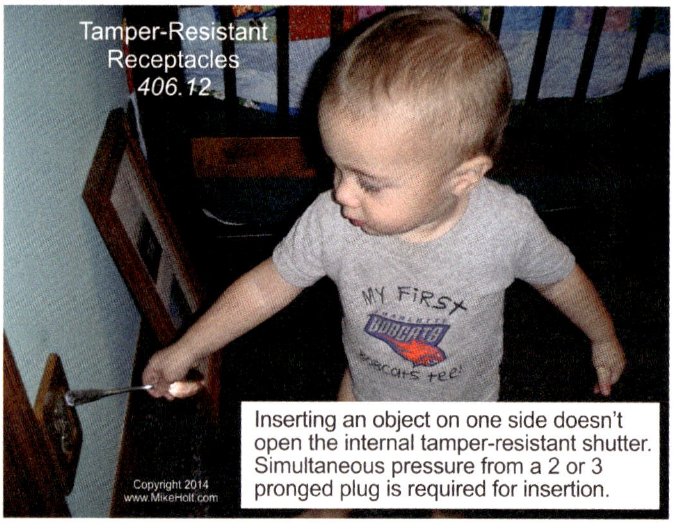

Figure 406–13

ANALYSIS: Anyone who's honest with themselves will agree that today's weatherproof covers (also known as "bubble covers" or "in-use covers") are nothing short of absurd. Typical in-use covers have a very bad habit of breaking if a person so much as looks at them, so now the *Code* is requiring the "extra-duty" variety of these abominations. The 2011 *NEC* introduced the concept of the extra-duty covers (although they aren't defined), and required them for receptacles supported from grade in nondwelling applications. By expanding the requirement to all wet locations, we should expect to see fewer broken covers.

406.12 Tamper-Resistant Receptacles

The requirements for tamper-resistant receptacles have been lumped into one section.

406.12 Tamper-Resistant Receptacles. Tamper-resistant receptacles must be installed in the following areas:

Author's Comment: On a tamper-resistant receptacle, inserting an object into one side of the receptacle doesn't open the internal tamper-resistant shutter. Simultaneous pressure from a two or three pronged plug is required for insertion. Figure 406–13

(A) Dwelling Units. All nonlocking type 15A and 20A, 125V receptacles in the following areas of a dwelling unit [210.52] must be listed as tamper resistant. Figure 406–14

- Wall Space—210.52(A)
- Small-Appliance Circuit—210.52(B)
- Countertop Space—210.52(C)
- Bathroom Area—210.52(D)
- Outdoors—210.52(E)
- Laundry Area—210.52(F)
- Garage and Outbuildings—210.52(G)
- Hallways—210.52(H)

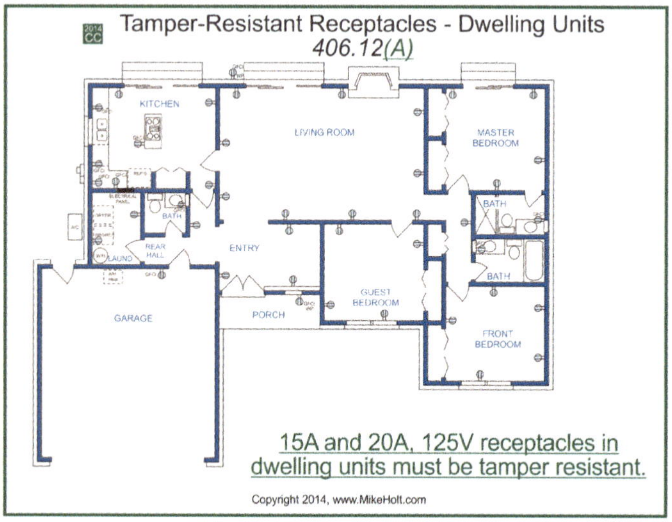

Figure 406–14

(B) Hotel and Motel Guest Rooms and Guest Suites. All Nonlocking type 15A and 20A, 125V receptacles in guest rooms and guest suites must be listed as tamper resistant.

(C) Child Care Facilities. Nonlocking type 15A and 20A, 125V receptacles in child care facilities must be listed as tamper resistant.

> **Author's Comment:** A child care facility is a building/structure or portions thereof used for educational, supervision, or personal care services for five or more children seven years in age or less [406.2].

Ex: Receptacles in the following locations aren't required to be tamper resistant:

(1) Receptacles located more than 5½ ft above the floor.

(2) Receptacles that are part of a luminaire or appliance.

(3) A receptacle located within dedicated space for an appliance that in normal use isn't easily moved from one place to another.

(4) Nongrounding receptacles used for replacements as permitted in 406.4(D)(2)(a).

ANALYSIS: The 2008 *NEC* introduced us to the concept of tamper-resistant receptacles, and specified the locations where the devices were required. At that time, there were no exceptions. In 2011, guest rooms and guest suites, as well as child care facilities, were added to the *Code*. Some exceptions were also added, but they were only applicable to the requirements for dwelling units. It seems that if receptacles need not be tamper resistant in some locations of dwellings, they shouldn't be required in the same areas of nondwellings. By combining all of the rules into one section, the exceptions become applicable to all of the areas requiring these receptacles.

406.15 Dimmer-Controlled Receptacles

A new allowance for dimmer-controlled receptacles has been added.

406.15 Dimmer-Controlled Receptacles. Receptacles supplying lighting loads must not be connected to a dimmer switch unless the plug/receptacle combination is a nonstandard configuration type specifically listed and identified for each such unique combination. Figure 406–15

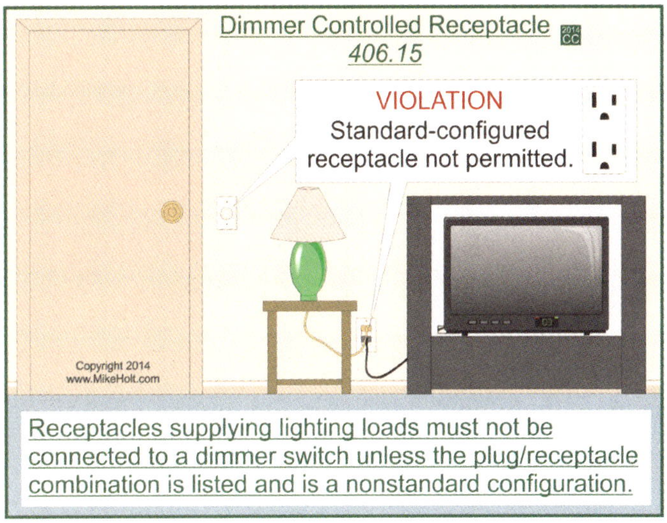

Figure 406–15

ANALYSIS: Connecting your floor lamp to a dimmer-controlled receptacle might seem like a good idea, but plugging your LED TV into the same receptacle probably isn't (unless you're doing a science experiment). The average home owner may not realize this, or, if they do, they may not remember that a particular receptacle is controlled by a dimmer switch. In order to prevent damage to equipment, the *Code* didn't allow receptacles to be connected to a dimmer switch [404.14(E)] until now. If the receptacle and plug are nonstandard, the receptacle can be dimmed, since there's no risk of someone plugging in a piece of equipment that can become damaged.

ARTICLE 408 SWITCHBOARDS AND PANELBOARDS

Introduction to Article 408—Switchboards and Panelboards

Article 408 covers the specific requirements for switchboards and panelboards that control power and lighting circuits. Some key points to remember:

- One objective of Article 408 is that the installation prevents contact between current-carrying conductors and people or equipment.
- The circuit directory of a panelboard must clearly identify the purpose or use of each circuit that originates in the panelboard.
- You must understand the detailed grounding and overcurrent protection requirements for panelboards.

408.4 Field Identification

The requirement for labeling circuits with their purpose was editorially revised.

408.4 Field Identification.

(A) Circuit Directory or Circuit Identification. All circuits, and circuit modifications, must be legibly identified as to their clear, evident, and specific purpose. Spare positions that contain unused overcurrent devices must also be identified. Identification must include an approved amount of detail to allow each circuit to be distinguished from all others, and the identification must be on a circuit directory located on the face or inside of the door of the panelboard. See 110.22. Figure 408–1

Author's Comment: Circuit identification must not be based on transient conditions of occupancy, such as Steven's, or Brittney's bedroom. Figure 408–2

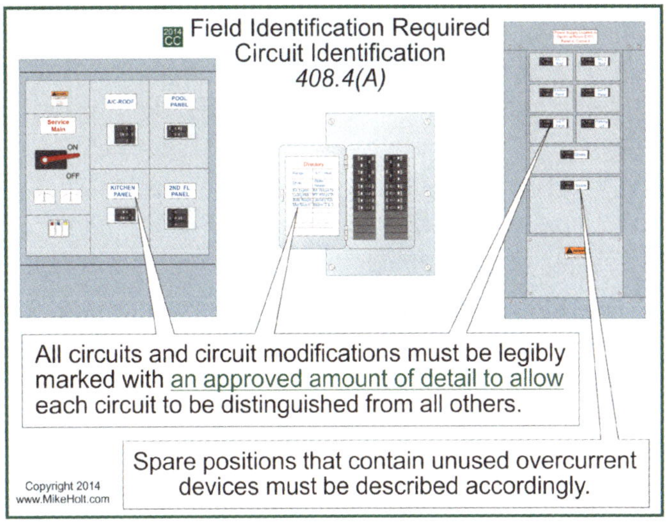

Figure 408–1

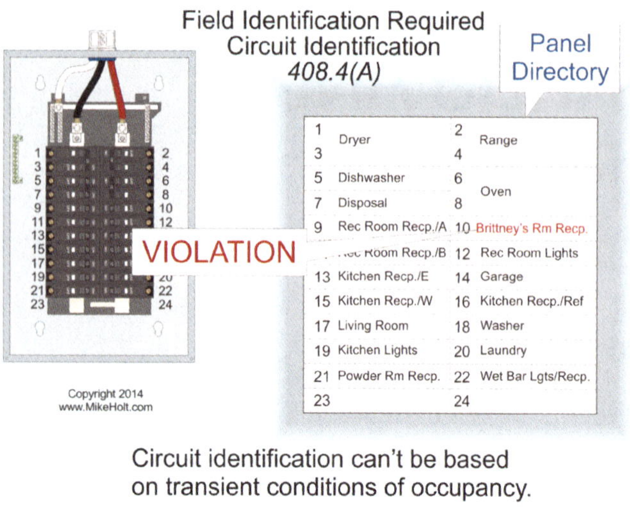

Figure 408–2

ANALYSIS: The *NEC* Style Manual contains a list of terms that shouldn't be used in the *Code*. The term "sufficient" is on the naughty list, so proposals were made throughout the *NEC* to remove it where possible. "Approved" is the term now used, which is clearly defined and not subject to as much debate (maybe).

ARTICLE 410 LUMINAIRES, LAMPHOLDERS, AND LAMPS

Introduction to Article 410—Luminaires, Lampholders, and Lamps

This article covers luminaires, lampholders, lamps, decorative lighting products, and lighting accessories for temporary seasonal and holiday use, including portable flexible lighting products, and the wiring and equipment of such products and lighting installations. Even though Article 410 is highly detailed, it's broken down into 16 parts. The first five are sequential, and apply to all luminaires, lampholders, and lamps:

- **Part I. General**
- **Part II. Location**
- **Part III. Boxes and Covers**
- **Part IV. Supports**
- **Part V. Equipment Grounding Conductors**

The first five parts contain mostly mechanical information, and aren't not hard to follow or absorb. Part VI, Wiring, ends the sequence. The seventh, ninth, and tenth parts provide requirements for manufacturers to follow—use only equipment that conforms to these requirements. Part VIII provides requirements for installing lampholders. The rest of Article 410 addresses specific types of lighting.

Author's Comment: Article 411 addresses "Lighting Systems Operating at 30 Volts or Less."

410.6 Listing Required

Lighting retrofit kits must now be listed.

Part I. General

410.6 Listing Required. Luminaires, lampholders, and retrofit kits must be listed.

ANALYSIS: Changing fluorescent luminaires into LED luminaires is a practice that's gaining more and more momentum. These conversions are often done with a hodgepodge of different pieces of equipment instead of a listed kit. This can result in components with differing voltage and current ratings, and may end in catastrophe. With this change, it's hoped that these hazards will be minimized.

410.10 Luminaires in Specific Locations

A new rule prohibits luminaires near roof decking.

Part II. Luminaire Locations

410.10 Luminaires in Specific Locations.

(F) Luminaires Installed in or Under Roof Decking. Luminaires installed under metal-corrugated sheet roof decking must be installed at least 1½ in. from the lowest surface of the roof decking measured from the bottom of the decking to the top of the luminaire.

ANALYSIS: The 2008 *NEC* added a requirement in 300.4(E) that ensures raceways won't be damaged by the roofing screws used in conjunction with these roofing systems. In 2011 that requirement was expanded to protect boxes as well, for the same reason. New to this edition of the *Code*, luminaires must now also be protected. As is often the case, when a new rule is written (300.4), it takes a few *NEC* cycles for it to really become solidified. Only time will tell what the 2017 *Code* will have to say about this, but one thing is sure: some piece of equipment that needs the same protection is probably still being forgotten. It's important to remember that the *NEC* is a living document, and will never be perfect, but those involved in deciding what to change try harder for perfection than most people think.

410.130 General

The exception for a "qualified person" has been removed from the requirement for a luminaire disconnect.

Part XII. Electric-Discharge Lighting

410.130 General.

(G) Disconnecting Means.

(1) General. In indoor locations, other than dwellings and associated accessory structures, fluorescent luminaires that utilize double-ended lamps (typical fluorescent lamps) and contain ballasts that can be serviced in place must have a disconnecting means. Figure 410–1

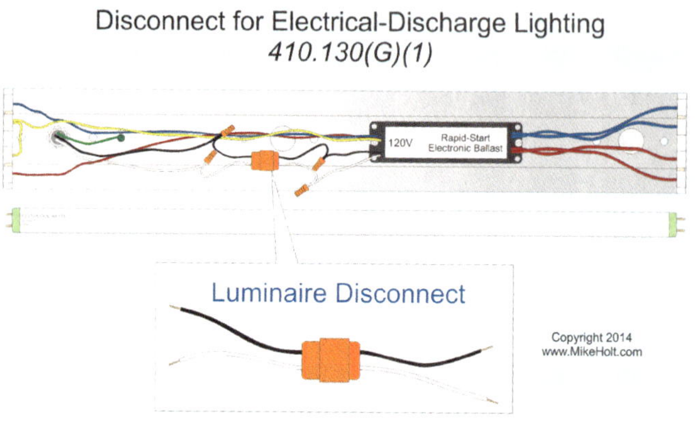

In indoor locations, other than dwellings and associated accessory structures, fluorescent luminaires that utilize double-ended lamps and contain ballasts must have a disconnecting means.

Figure 410–1

For existing installed luminaires, a disconnecting means must be added at the time a ballast is replaced. Figure 410–2

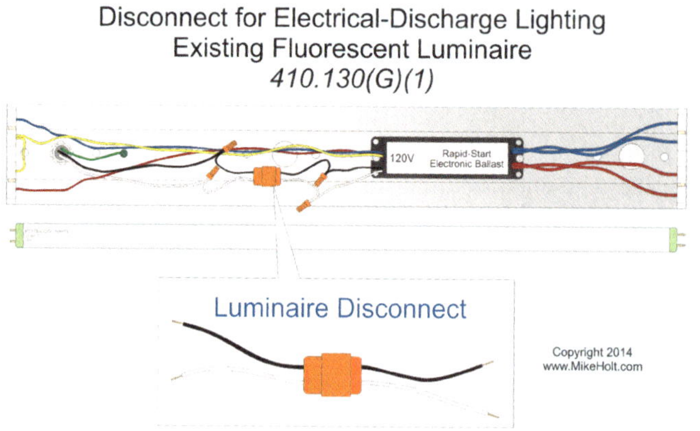

For existing installed fluorescent luminaires without disconnecting means, a disconnecting means must be added when a ballast is replaced.

Figure 410–2

Author's Comment: Changing the ballast while the circuit feeding the luminaire is energized has become a regular practice because a local disconnect isn't available.

Ex 2: A disconnecting means isn't required for the emergency illumination required in 700.16.

Ex 3: For cord-and-plug-connected luminaires, an accessible separable connector, or an accessible plug and receptacle, is permitted to serve as the disconnecting means.

Ex 4: If more than one luminaire is installed and is supplied by a branch circuit that isn't of the multiwire type, a disconnecting means isn't required for every luminaire; but, only when the light switch for the space ensures that some of the luminaires in the space will still provide illumination.

(2) Multiwire Branch Circuits. When connected to multiwire branch circuits, the fluorescent luminaire disconnect must simultaneously break all circuit conductors of the ballast, including the neutral conductor.

Author's Comment: This rule requires the disconnecting means to open "all circuit conductors of a multiwire branch circuit," including the neutral conductor. If the neutral conductor in a multiwire circuit isn't disconnected at the same time as the ungrounded conductors, a false sense of security can result in an unexpected shock from the neutral conductor.

(3) Location. The fluorescent luminaire disconnecting means must be accessible to qualified persons, and if the disconnecting means is external to the luminaire, it must be a single device and must be located in sight from the luminaire.

ANALYSIS: The requirement for a local disconnect in these luminaires is to ensure that people can change ballasts without having to do it while the luminaire is energized. Electricians who are honest with themselves will admit that changing ballasts in an energized luminaire was considered "just part of the job" for many years. This safety enhancement has probably already saved numerous lives and countless injuries...that is, unless you worked in an industrial establishment. Why should they have less stringent safety requirements? They don't anymore.

410.151 Installation

What used to be an Informational Note is now part of the *Code* text.

Part XIV. Track Lighting

410.151 Installation.

(B) Circuit Rating. The connected load on a lighting track must not exceed the rating of the track, and an overcurrent device whose rating exceeds the rating of the track must not supply the track. Figure 410–3

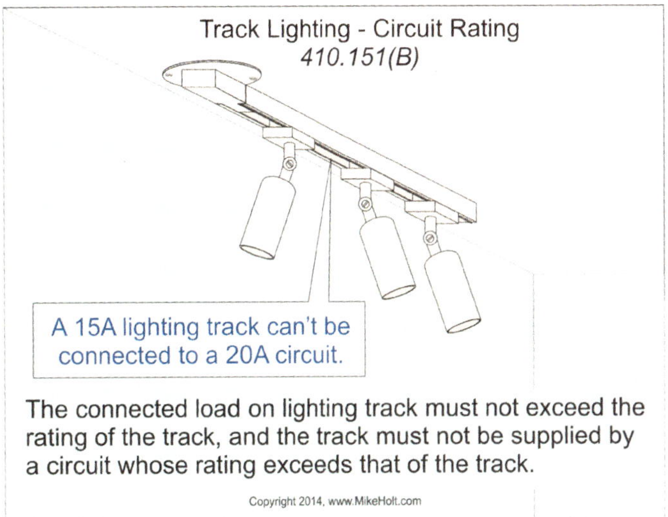

Figure 410–3

The feeder or service load calculations of 220.43(B) don't limit the number of feet of track on a circuit, nor do they limit the number of luminaires mounted on an individual track. Figure 410–4

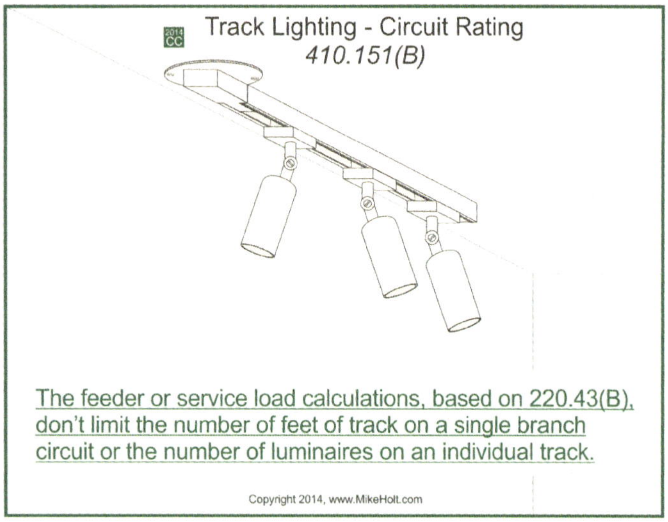

Figure 410–4

ANALYSIS: The calculations in 220.43(B) do not, and never have, limited the installation of track lighting. Although the *Code* stated this in the form of an Informational Note, some people still, somehow, didn't believe it (using the justification that Informational Notes are informational only). By putting the same statement in the actual body of the *NEC*, perhaps the (nonexistent) issue will be cleared up.

ARTICLE 411

LIGHTING SYSTEMS OPERATING AT 30V OR LESS AND LIGHTING EQUIPMENT CONNECTED TO CLASS-2 POWER SOURCES

Introduction to Article 411—Lighting Systems Operating at 30V or Less and Lighting Equipment Connected to Class-2 Power Sources

Article 411 provides the requirements for lighting systems operating at 30V or less, which are often found in such applications as landscaping, kitchen over-the-counter lighting, commercial display lighting, and museums. Don't let the half-page size of Article 411 give you the impression that 30V lighting isn't something you need to be concerned about. These systems are limited in their voltage, but the current rating can be as high as 25A, which means they're still a potential source of fire. Installation of these systems is widespread and becoming more so.

Many of these systems now use LEDs, and 30V halogen lamps are also fairly common. All 30V lighting systems have an ungrounded secondary circuit supplied by an isolating transformer. These systems have restrictions that effect where they can be located, and they can have a maximum supply breaker size of 25A.

Article 411—Lighting Systems Operating at 30V or Less and Lighting Equipment Connected to Class-2 Power Sources

The title of this article, its scope, and some of the rules, has been revised to address Class 2 power supplies.

411.1 Scope. Article 411 covers the installation of lighting systems that operate at 30V or less, as well as their associated components. This article also covers lighting equipment connected to a Class 2 power source. Figure 411–1

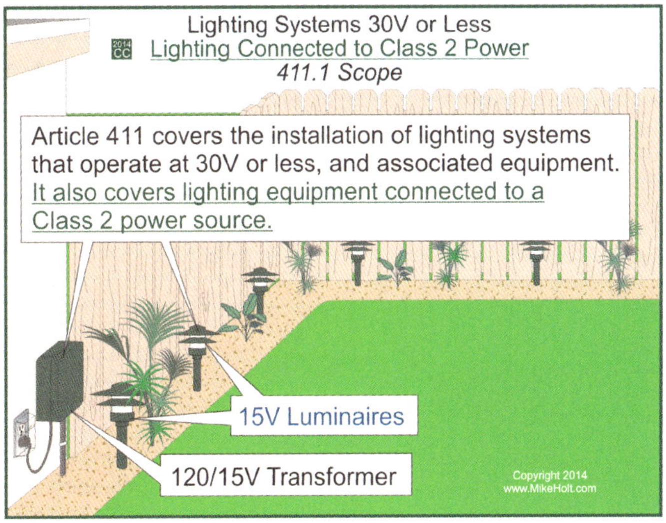

Figure 411–1

411.3 Low-Voltage Lighting Systems.

(A) General. Lighting systems operating at 30V or less must consist of an isolating power supply, low-voltage luminaires, and their associated equipment. The secondary side of the transformer must be rated 25A and 30V maximum. Figure 411–2

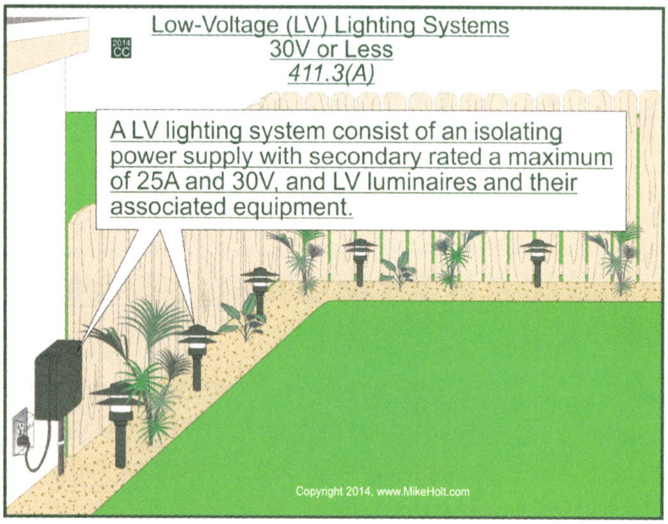

Figure 411–2

(B) Class 2 Systems. Listed Class 2 systems must meet the power requirements described in Table 11(A) or (B) in Chapter 9 of the *Code*.

ANALYSIS: This Article received extensive revisions to address Class 2 power supplies, and to make the article more user friendly. Class 2 power supplies are inherently safe, due to the voltage and current limitations that they have (see Table 11 in Chapter 9 for more information). Because of this, they're a popular choice for low-voltage lighting systems, yet the *NEC* hasn't done much of a job addressing them. With changes made in this *Code* cycle the document contains more information on Class 2 power sources, including a requirement that the power supplies be listed. The text found in 411.3(A) was formerly found in a definition in 411.2 (for lighting systems operating at 30V or less). That definition has been removed, because it was more like a set of rules than a definition.

ARTICLE
422 APPLIANCES

Introduction to Article 422—Appliances

Article 422 covers electric appliances used in any occupancy. The meat of this article is contained in Parts II and III. Parts IV and V are primarily for manufacturers, but you should examine appliances for compliance before installing them. If the appliance has a label from a recognized labeling authority (for example UL), it complies [90.7].

422.5 Ground-Fault Circuit-Interrupter (GFCI) Protection

A new requirement regarding the accessibility of GFCI devices has been added.

Part I. General

422.5 Ground-Fault Circuit-Interrupter (GFCI) Protection. GFCI devices required in this article must be readily accessible. Figure 422–1

Figure 422–1

ANALYSIS: In order to provide consistency with other *Code* sections, such as 210.8, this section has been added. By ensuring that the GFCI device is in a readily accessible location (a location that doesn't require a person to remove or climb over obstacles or resort to using portable ladders), the GFCI can be tested on a monthly basis as indicated in the instructions for the device.

I'm not quite sure how the GFCI discussed in 422.51 (which is required to be part of the cord of a vending machine) is going to be readily accessible unless the vending machine is located adjacent to (not in front of) the receptacle serving it. That ought to anger some architects (and business owners whose vending machines may now be unplugged by mischievous children or adults)!

422.16 Flexible Cords

The requirements for waste disposals were revised to close a loophole.

Part II. Branch-Circuit Requirements

422.16 Flexible Cords.

(B) Specific Appliances.

(1) In-Sink Waste (Garbage) Disposals. A flexible cord is permitted for an in-sink waste disposal if:

(1) The cord has a grounding-type attachment plug.

(2) The cord length is at least 18 in. and no longer than 3 ft.

(3) The in-sink waste disposal receptacle is located to avoid damage to the cord.

(4) The in-sink waste disposal receptacle is accessible.

ANALYSIS: The *NEC* previously called this piece of equipment an "electrically operated kitchen waste disposer." As used in that manner, the word "kitchen" is describing the equipment itself, not the location of the equipment. Some users of the *Code* believed that these requirements applied only if this piece of equipment was installed in a kitchen. While those people were incorrect, we might as well just end the argument before it has a chance to continue. By using the real name of these products, the argument is moot (if it weren't already).

422.19 Space for Conductors

The rules requiring adequate space for conductors have been added to this article.

422.19 Space for Conductors. Canopies of ceiling-suspended (paddle) fans and their outlet boxes must comply with the free space requirements of 314.16. Figure 422–2

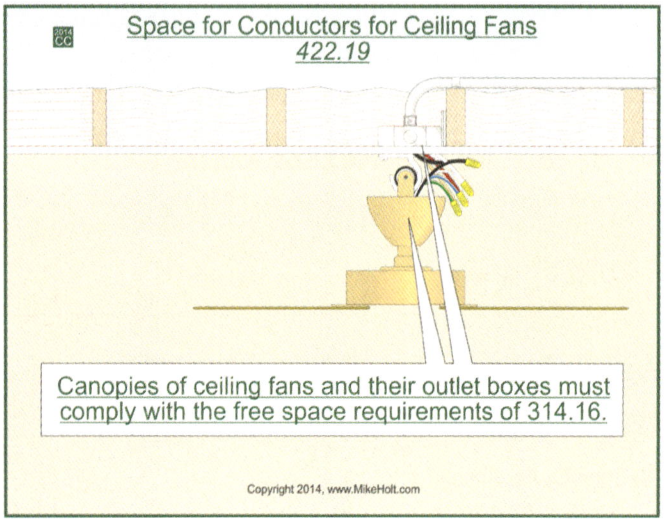

Figure 422–2

ANALYSIS: Although this rule is already found in Article 410, it's been added here because if the fan doesn't contain luminaires or lampholders, Article 410 doesn't apply.

422.20 Outlet Boxes to Be Covered

The rule requiring a cover for outlet boxes has been added to this article.

422.20 Outlet Boxes to Be Covered. In a completed installation, fan outlet boxes must have a cover unless covered by a ceiling-suspended (paddle) fan canopy.

ANALYSIS: Although this rule is already found in Article 410, it's been added here because if the fan doesn't contain luminaires or lampholders, that article doesn't apply.

422.21 Covering of Combustible Material at Outlet Boxes

The rule addressing combustible material at outlet boxes has been added to this article.

422.21 Covering of Combustible Material at Outlet Boxes. Any combustible ceiling finish exposed between the edge of a ceiling-suspended (paddle) fan canopy or fan and an outlet box must be covered with noncombustible material. Figure 422–3

ANALYSIS: Although this rule is already found in Article 410, it's been added here because if the fan doesn't contain luminaires or lampholders, that article doesn't apply.

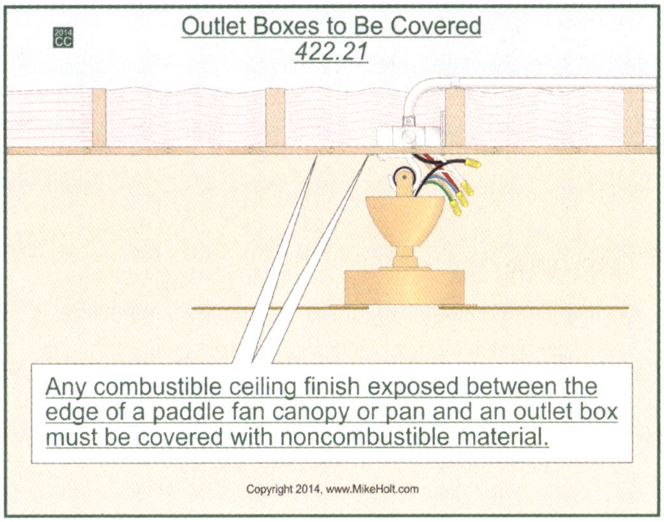

Figure 422–3

422.23 Tire Inflation and Automotive Vacuum Machines

A new rule requiring GFCI protection for tire inflation and automotive vacuum cleaners has been added.

422.23 Tire Inflation and Automotive Vacuum Machines. Tire inflation machines and automotive vacuum machines that are provided for public use must be GFCI protected. Figure 422–4

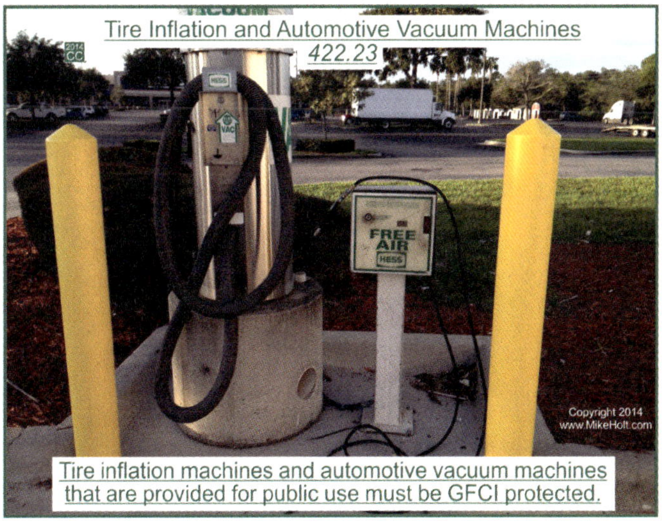

Figure 422–4

ANALYSIS: Automotive vacuums and tire inflation machines are typically found outdoors, where the person using one will be on concrete, dirt, asphalt, or other surface that can serve as a ground-fault current path. Add in the fact that these surfaces are often covered in rain water or snow and you have an electrical accident in the making. This change was added to the *Code* because of a real-world event involving an electric shock. While a GFCI device may not prevent the shock from happening, it will typically prevent such a shock from being a fatal one.

422.51 Vending Machines

Hard-wired vending machines are now discussed in this section.

Part III. Disconnect

422.51 Vending Machines.

(A) Cord-and-Plug-Connected. Cord-and-plug-connected vending machines must include a GFCI that's identified for portable use as an integral part of the attachment plug, or within 12 in. of the attachment plug. Older machines that aren't so equipped must be connected to a GFCI-protected outlet. Figure 422–5

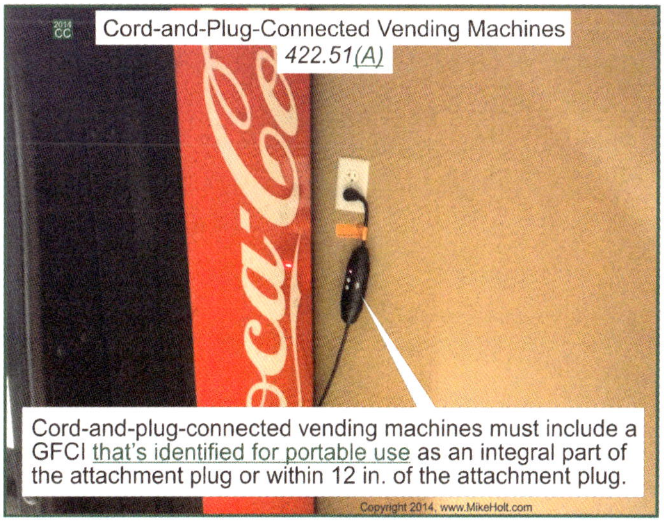

Figure 422–5

(B) Other than Cord-and–Plug-Connected. Vending machines that aren't cord-and-plug-connected must be GFCI protected. Figure 422–6

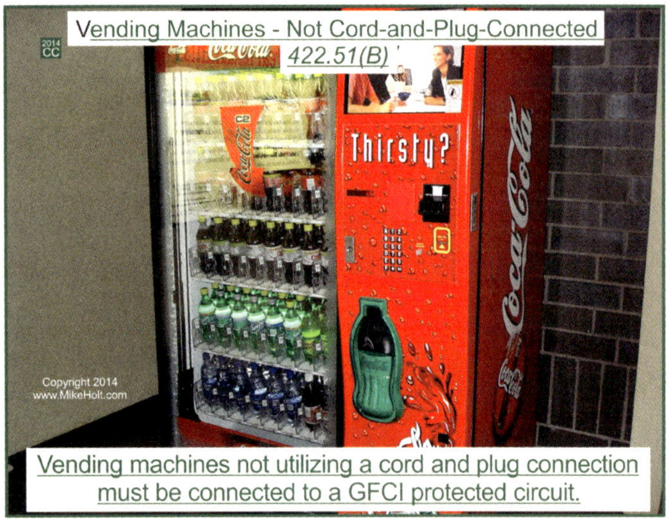

Figure 422–6

Author's Comment: Because electric vending machines are often located in damp or wet locations in public places, and are used by people standing on the ground, reliance on an equipment grounding conductor for protection against electrocution is insufficient.

ANALYSIS: The manner in which a vending machine is connected to electricity (cord and plug versus hard wired) is hardly relevant when discussing electric shock. Although no documented incidents were cited to drive this new requirement, it seems that not having this language was an inadvertent oversight in the last few *Code* editions.

ARTICLE 430 MOTORS, MOTOR CIRCUITS, AND CONTROLLERS

Introduction to Article 430—Motors, Motor Circuits, and Controllers

Article 430 contains the specific rules for conductor sizing, overcurrent protection, control circuit conductors, controllers, and disconnecting means for electric motors. The installation requirements for motor control centers are covered in Part VIII, and air-conditioning and refrigeration equipment are covered in Article 440.

Article 430 is one of the longest articles in the *NEC*. It's also one of the most complex, but motors are also complex equipment. They're electrical and mechanical devices, but what makes motor applications complex is the fact that they're inductive loads with a high-current demand at start-up that's typically six, or more, times the running current. This makes overcurrent protection for motor applications necessarily different from the protection employed for other types of equipment. So don't confuse general overcurrent protection with motor protection—you must calculate and apply them differently using the rules in Article 430.

You might be uncomfortable with the allowances for overcurrent protection found in this article, such as protecting a 10 AWG conductor with a 60A overcurrent protection device, but as you learn to understand how motor protection works, you'll understand why these allowances aren't only safe, but necessary.

430.102 Disconnect Requirement

The exception for having a controller disconnect remote from the controller has been revised for consistency with similar *Code* rules.

Part IX. Disconnecting Means

430.102 Disconnect Requirement.

(B) Motor Disconnect. A motor disconnect must be provided in accordance with (B)(1) or (B)(2). Figure 430–1

(1) Separate Motor Disconnect. A disconnecting means is required for each motor, and it must be located in sight from the motor location and the driven machinery location.

(2) Controller Disconnect. The controller disconnecting means [430.102(A)] can serve as the disconnecting means for the motor, if the disconnect is located in sight from the motor location.

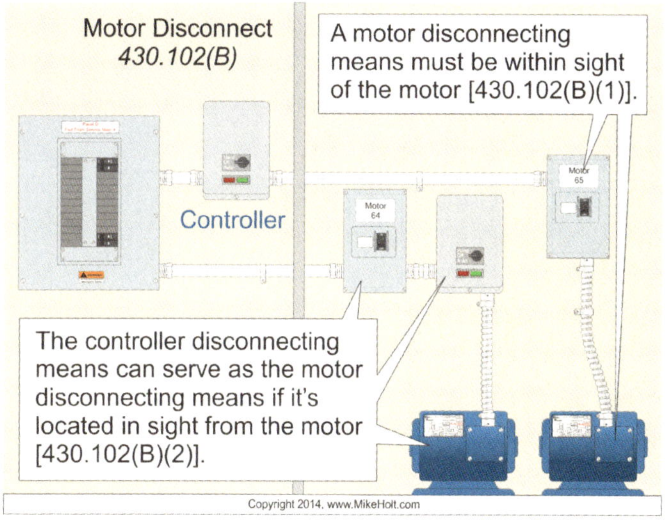

Figure 430–1

Ex to (1) and (2): A motor disconnecting means isn't required under either condition (a) or (b), if the controller disconnecting means [430.102(A)] is lockable, as described in 110.25. Figure 430–2

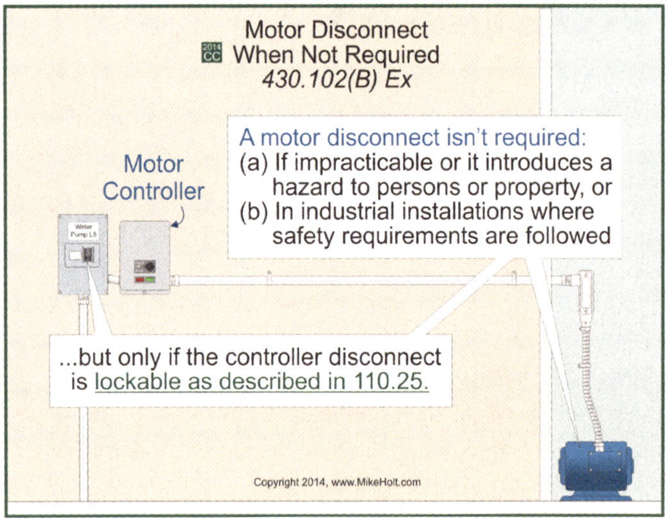

Figure 430–2

(a) If locating the disconnecting means is impracticable or introduces additional or increased hazards to persons or property.

(b) In industrial installations, with written safety procedures, where conditions of maintenance and supervision ensure only qualified persons will service the equipment.

Note 2: For information on lockout/tagout procedures, see NFPA 70E, *Standard for Electrical Safety in the Workplace.*

ANALYSIS: In an effort to create a more consistent *Code*, a new section 110.25 was added. This section contains the rules for disconnecting means that aren't within sight of their equipment. By referring to it, we no longer have different rules that cover the same thing spread throughout the *NEC*.

ARTICLE 440 AIR-CONDITIONING AND REFRIGERATION EQUIPMENT

Introduction to Article 440—Air-Conditioning and Refrigeration Equipment

This article applies to electrically driven air-conditioning and refrigeration equipment. The rules in this article add to, or amend, the rules in Article 430 and other articles.

Each equipment manufacturer has the motor for a given air-conditioning unit built to its own specifications. Cooling and other characteristics are different from those of nonhermetic motors. For each motor, the manufacturer has worked out all of the details and supplied the correct protection, conductor sizing, and other information on the nameplate. So when wiring an air conditioner, trust the information on the nameplate and don't try to over-complicate the situation. The math for sizing the overcurrent protection and conductor minimum ampacity has already been done for you.

440.14 Location

The allowance for having an air-conditioner disconnect remote from the equipment has been revised for consistency with similar *Code* rules.

Part II. Disconnecting Means

440.14 Location. A disconnecting means for air-conditioning or refrigeration equipment must be located within sight from and readily accessible from the equipment. Figures 440–1 and 440–2

Author's Comment: According to Article 100, "within sight" means that it's visible and not more than 50 ft from one to the other.

The disconnecting means can be mounted on or within the air-conditioning equipment, but it must not be located on panels designed to allow access to the equipment, or where it will obscure the equipment nameplate. Figure 440–3

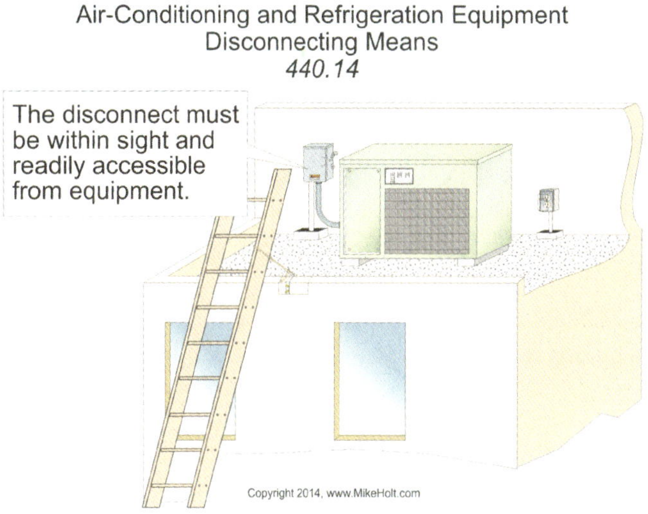

Figure 440–1

Ex 1: A disconnecting means isn't required to be within sight from the equipment, if the disconnecting means is lockable, as described in 110.25, and if the equipment is essential to an industrial process in a facility that has written safety procedures, and where the conditions of maintenance and supervision ensure only qualified persons service the equipment.

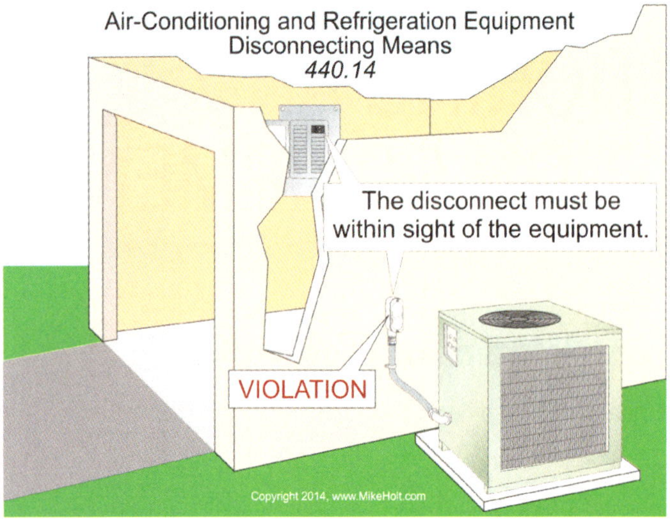

Figure 440–2

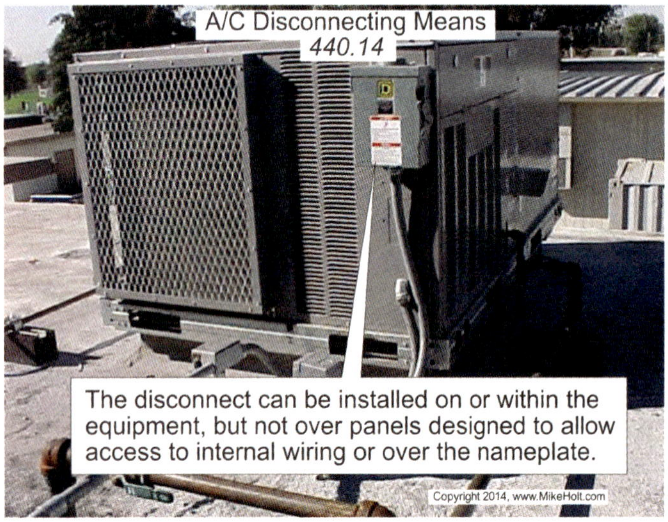

Figure 440–3

Ex 2: An accessible attachment plug and receptacle can serve as the disconnecting means.

Author's Comment: The receptacle for the attachment plug isn't required to be readily accessible.

ANALYSIS: In an effort to create a consistent *Code*, a new section 110.25 was added. This section contains the rules for disconnecting means that aren't within sight of their equipment. By referring to it, we no longer have different rules that cover the same thing spread throughout the *NEC*.

ARTICLE 445 GENERATORS

Introduction to Article 445—Generators

This article contains the electrical installation, and other requirements, for generators. These requirements include such things as where generators can be installed, nameplate markings, conductor ampacity, and disconnecting means.

Generators are basically motors that operate in reverse—they produce electricity when rotated, instead of rotating when supplied with electricity. Article 430, which covers motors, is the longest article in the *NEC*. Article 445, which covers generators, is one of the shortest. At first, this might not seem to make sense. But you don't need to size and protect conductors to a generator. You do need to size and protect them to a motor.

Generators need overload protection, and it's necessary to size the conductors that come from the generator. But these considerations are much more straightforward than the equivalent considerations for motors. Before you study Article 445, take a moment to read the definition of "Separately Derived System" in Article 100.

445.11 Marking

Additional marking requirements for generators have been added.

445.11 Marking. Each generator must be provided with a nameplate indicating the manufacturer's name, rated frequency, number of phases, rating in kilowatts or kilovolt amperes, volts and amperes corresponding to the rating, RPM, insulation class and rated ambient temperature or rated temperature rise, and time rating.

Nameplates for portable generators rated more than 15 kW and for all stationary generators must also give the power factor, the subtransient and transient impedances, insulation system class, and time rating.

All generators must be marked by the manufacturer indicating whether or not the generator neutral is bonded to the generator frame. Where the bonding of a generator is modified in the field, additional marking must be provided to indicate whether or not the generator neutral is bonded to the generator frame. Figure 445–1

Figure 445–1

ANALYSIS: A relaxation to the marking requirements for small (less than 15kW) portable generators was made, recognizing that the average homeowner doesn't need to know (and doesn't care to know) what the power factor and the subtransient vs. transient impedance (whatever that means) is.

With the changes made to 590.6 in the 2011 edition of the *Code*, the bonding of the generator neutral to its frame is becoming a major point of contention. As William Shakespeare so eloquently stated, "To bond or not to bond, that is the question."* If only the answer were a simple one. If the generator is used for temporary wiring, in accordance with Article 590, the generator frame must be bonded to the neutral; otherwise the GFCIs on it won't work. If the same generator is plugged into a house with a solid neutral transfer switch, the neutral mustn't be bonded to the frame, or the GFCIs will trip instantly and the homeowner will be literally left in the dark. Considering this, it would be helpful to know whether it's bonded or not without having to rip into the generator. The new marking requirements should make this a bit easier, although they certainly aren't going to be of any real value to the average homeowner.

*Alright, maybe Shakespeare didn't quite say it that way, but I'm sure that's what was really on his mind.

445.16 Bushings

The requirement for bushings in generator enclosures has been clarified.

445.16 Bushings. Where field-installed wiring passes through an opening in an enclosure, box, or barrier, a bushing must be installed to protect the conductors from sharp edges. The bushing must have smooth, well-rounded surfaces. Figure 445–2

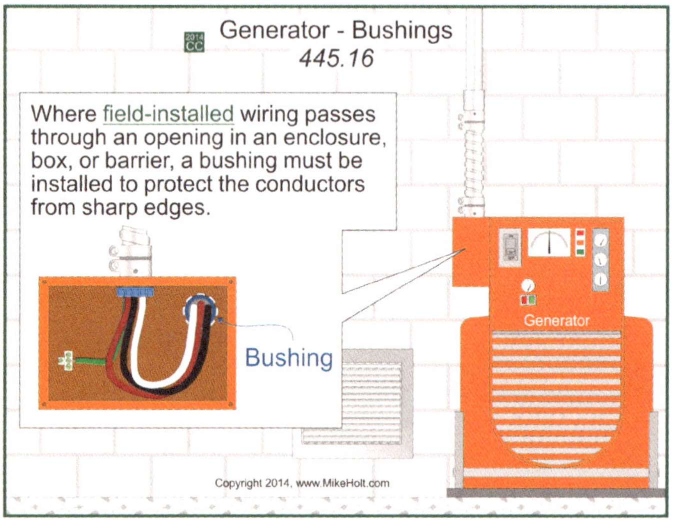

Figure 445–2

ANALYSIS: Few will argue that a grommet or bushing should be installed when wires go through a metal hole in an enclosure. In previous editions of the *Code*, it wasn't clear if this requirement was for the manufacturer, the person installing it, or both. With this change it becomes clear that this rule is for electricians, not manufacturers. The internal factory wiring is part of the product, and is subject to the testing and listing requirements of the product standard. Internal factory wiring should already be safe if it's listed.

445.20 Ground-Fault Circuit Interrupter Protection for Receptacles on 15 kW or Smaller Portable Generators

A new rule requires GFCI protection for receptacles on small portable generators.

445.20 Ground-Fault Circuit Interrupter Protection for Receptacles on 15 kW or Smaller Portable Generators. All 125V, single-phase, 15A and 20A receptacles that are a part of a 15 kW or smaller portable generator must be GFCI protected, or have a feature that will disable the 125V receptacle when the 125/250V locking receptacle is in use. If the generator doesn't contain a 125/250V locking receptacle, this section doesn't have to be followed. Figure 445–3

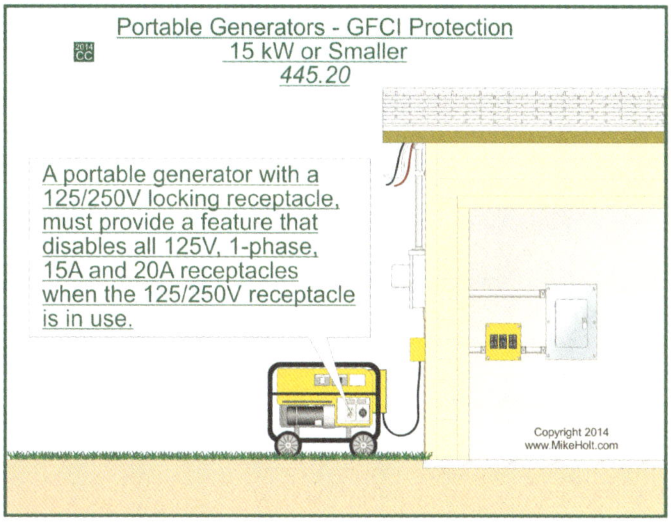

Figure 445–3

Author's Comment: 590.6 can supplement and/or modify the rules in Chapters 1 through 4 [90.3]. 590.6 mandates that the receptacle this rule allows to be disabled (the 125V, 15A or 20A receptacle) be GFCI protected. Due to this, if a generator is manufactured using the allowance to disable the 125V receptacle, it can't be used on a jobsite!

ANALYSIS: In order to create harmony with 590.6, this rule requires GFCI protection for these small generators. This is a major point of contention in the electrical industry. Please refer to the analysis contained in 445.11 for more information. The option of disabling the receptacle gives the generator manufacturers more options in their designs while not sacrificing safety. The idea behind this is that GFCI protection is really only needed on a grounded system (a system where the neutral is bonded to metal parts of equipment).

When a generator is being used to power up a house, it's connected to a grounded system (the house), and therefore GFCI protection becomes necessary. When it's used in this manner, people don't use the 125V receptacle on the generator, they use the 250V, 30A receptacle. When this is the case, the generator manufacturer can disable the 125V receptacle, resulting in safe usage of the generator (by not allowing someone to use the receptacle that isn't GFCI protected).

If the generator isn't connected to a house, but rather is being used as a stand-alone system (such as while camping or tailgating at a University of Utah football game) the generator is an ungrounded system (assuming the neutral isn't bonded to the frame). In an ungrounded system, GFCI protection isn't necessary.

ARTICLE 450 TRANSFORMERS

Introduction to Article 450—Transformers

Article 450 opens by saying, "This article covers the installation of all transformers." Then it lists eight exceptions. So what does Article 450 really cover? Essentially, it covers power transformers and most kinds of lighting transformers.

A major concern with transformers is preventing overheating. The *Code* doesn't completely address this issue. Article 90 explains that the *NEC* isn't a design manual, and it assumes that the person using the *Code* has a certain level of expertise. Proper transformer selection is an important part of preventing it from overheating.

The *NEC* assumes you've already selected a transformer suitable to the load characteristics. For the *Code* to tell you how to do that would push it into the realm of a design manual. Article 450 then takes you to the next logical step—providing overcurrent protection and the proper connections. But this article doesn't stop there; 450.9 provides ventilation requirements, and 450.13 contains accessibility requirements.

Part I of Article 450 contains the general requirements such as guarding, marking, and accessibility, Part II contains the requirements for different types of transformers, and Part III covers transformer vaults.

450.10 Grounding and Bonding

Transformers are now required to have a place to terminate grounding and bonding conductors.

Part I. General

450.10 Grounding and Bonding.

(A) Dry-Type Transformer Enclosures. Where separate equipment grounding conductors and supply-side bonding jumpers are installed, a terminal bar for these conductors must be installed inside the enclosure. The terminal bar must not cover any ventilation openings. Figure 450–1

Ex: Where a dry-type transformer is equipped with wire-type connections (leads), the terminal bar isn't required.

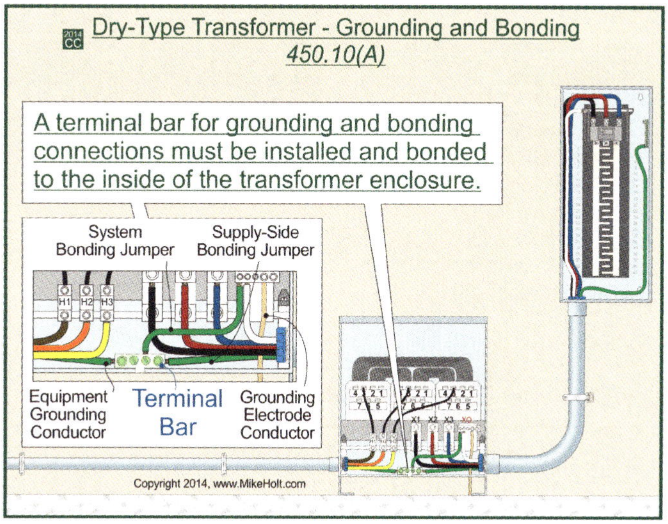

Figure 450–1

ANALYSIS: When you consider the number of green and bare wires that are typically found in a transformer, it's really a wonder that this rule hasn't been in the *Code* for 100 years. The primary conductors supplying the transformer will usually contain an equipment grounding conductor. The secondary conductors will include a supply-side bonding jumper. There will (typically) be a system bonding jumper inside the transformer. There will also be (typically) a grounding electrode conductor in the transformer. Wouldn't it be nice if there was a place to terminate these wires?

450.11 Marking

The nameplate requirements for transformers have been changed into a list format.

450.11 Marking.

(A) General. Transformers must have a nameplate that provides the following information: Figure 450–2

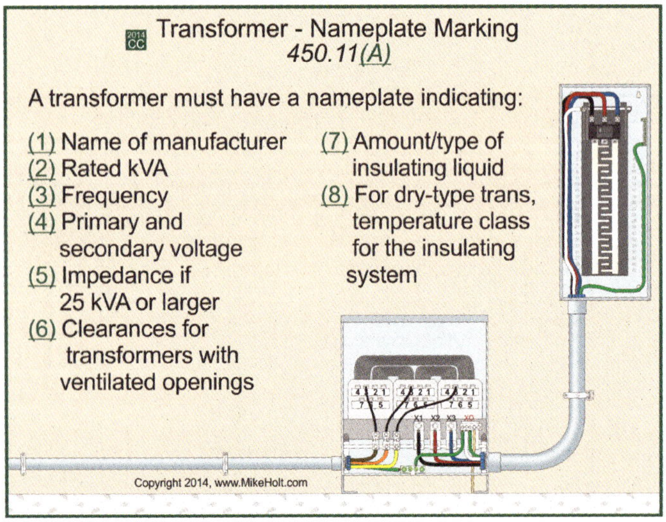

Figure 450–2

(1) The name of the manufacturer

(2) Rated kilovolt-amperes

(3) Frequency

(4) Primary and secondary voltage

(5) The impedance of transformers 25 kVA and larger

(6) Required clearances for transformers with ventilating openings

(7) The amount and kind of insulating liquid where used

(8) For dry-type transformers, the temperature class for the insulation system.

(B) Source Marking. A transformer can be supplied at the secondary voltage if allowed in the manufacturer's instructions.

ANALYSIS: A simple side-by-side comparison of the 2011 and 2014 editions of this section will convince nearly anyone that lists are better than long paragraphs.

New to this *Code* edition is the text regarding secondary voltage-supplied transformers. Many people don't realize that transformers are only suitable to be supplied at the secondary voltage if the transformer is marked for this application. For example, a transformer that's marked as 480V primary, 208V secondary can't be wired with a 208V primary and 480V secondary. According to UL 1561, only transformers marked in this manner can be installed this way.

450.14 Disconnecting Means

The allowance for having a transformer disconnect remote from the equipment has been revised for consistency with similar *Code* rules.

450.14 Disconnecting Means. A disconnect is required to disconnect all transformer ungrounded primary conductors, unless the transformer is Class 2 or Class 3, Figure 450–3. The disconnect must be located within sight of the transformer, unless the location of the disconnect is field marked on the transformer and the disconnect is lockable, as described in 110.25. Figure 450–4

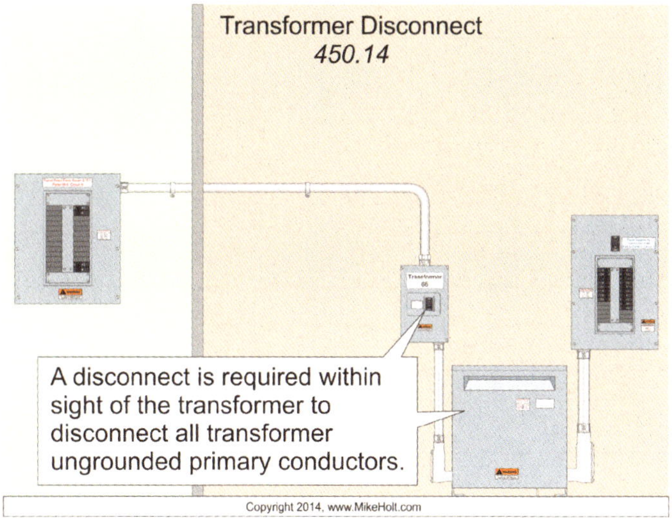

Figure 450–3

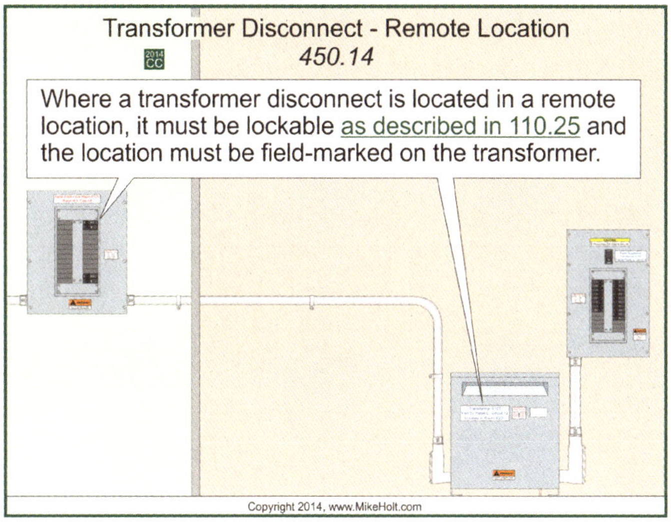

Figure 450–4

Author's Comment: Within sight means that it's visible and not more than 50 ft from one to the other [Article 100].

ANALYSIS: In an effort to create a consistent *Code*, a new section 110.25 was added. This section contains the rules for disconnecting means that aren't within sight of their equipment. By referring to it, we no longer have different rules that cover the same thing spread throughout the *NEC*.

Notes

CHAPTER 5

SPECIAL OCCUPANCIES

Introduction to Chapter 5—Special Occupancies

Chapter 5, which covers special occupancies, is the first of three *NEC* chapters that deals with special topics.

Chapters 6 and 7 cover special equipment, and special conditions, respectively. Remember, the first four chapters of the *Code* are sequential and form a foundation for each of the subsequent three chapters. Chapter 8 covers communications systems and isn't subject to the requirements of Chapters 1 through 7 except where the requirements are specifically referenced in Chapter 8.

What exactly is a "Special Occupancy?" It's a location where the facility or use of the physical facility creates specific conditions that require additional measures to ensure the "practical safeguarding of people and property" purpose of the *NEC*, as put forth in Article 90.

The *Code* groups these logically, as you might expect. Here are the general groupings:

- Environments that pose classified hazards. Articles 500 through 510.
- Specific types of facilities that pose classified hazards. Articles 511 through 516—Examples include motor fuel-dispensing facilities, aircraft hangars, and bulk storage plants.
- Facilities that pose evacuation difficulties. Articles 517 through 525—Examples include hospitals, theaters, and carnivals.
- Motion picture related facilities. Articles 530 and 540.
- Specific types of buildings. Articles 545 through 553—Examples include park trailers and floating buildings.
- Marinas and boatyards. Article 555.
- Temporary installations. Article 590.

Many people struggle to understand the requirements for special occupancies, mostly because of the narrowness of application. However, if you study the illustrations and explanations here, you'll clearly understand them.

- **Article 500—Hazardous (Classified) Locations.** A hazardous (classified) location is an area where the possibility of fire or explosion exists due to the presence of flammable or combustible gases or vapors, combustible dusts, or ignitable fibers/flyings.

- **Article 501—Class I Hazardous (Classified) Locations.** A Class I hazardous (classified) location is an area where flammable or combustible gases or vapors or flammable liquids may present the hazard of a fire or explosion.

- **Article 502—Class II Hazardous (Classified) Locations.** A Class II hazardous (classified) location is an area where the possibility of fire or explosion may exist due to combustible dust.

- **Article 503—Class III Hazardous (Classified) Locations.** Class III locations are hazardous because fire or explosion risks may exist due to ignitable fibers/flyings. This includes materials such as cotton and rayon, which are found in textile mills and clothing manufacturing plants. It can also include establishments and industries such as sawmills and woodworking plants. There are no "Group" classifications for Class III locations as there are for Class I and Class II locations.

- **Article 511—Commercial Garages, Repair, and Storage.** These occupancies include locations used for service and repair operations in connection with self-propelled vehicles (including, but not limited to, passenger automobiles, buses, trucks, and tractors) in which petroleum-based chemicals (volatile organic compounds) are used for fuel or power.

- **Article 514—Motor Fuel Dispensing Facilities.** Article 514 covers gasoline dispensing and service stations where gasoline or other volatile liquid-produced vapors or gases are transferred to the fuel tanks of self-propelled vehicles. Wiring and equipment in the area of service and repair rooms of service stations must comply with the installation requirements in Article 511.

- **Article 517—Health Care Facilities.** This article applies to electrical wiring in human health care facilities such as hospitals, nursing homes, limited-care facilities, clinics, medical and dental offices, and ambulatory care, whether permanent or movable. It doesn't apply to animal veterinary facilities.

- **Article 518—Assembly Occupancies.** Article 518 covers buildings or portions of buildings or structures specifically designed or intended for the assembly of 100 or more persons.

- **Article 525—Carnivals, Circuses, Fairs, and Similar Events.** This article covers the installation of portable wiring and equipment for temporary carnivals, circuses, exhibitions, fairs, traveling attractions, and similar functions, including wiring in or on structures.

- **Article 547—Agricultural Buildings.** Article 547 covers agricultural buildings or those parts of buildings or adjacent areas where excessive dust or dust with water may accumulate, or where a corrosive atmosphere exists.

- **Article 550—Mobile Homes, Manufactured Homes and Mobile Home Parks.** The provisions of Article 550 cover electrical conductors and equipment within or on mobile and manufactured homes, conductors that connect mobile and manufactured homes to the electrical supply, and the installation of electrical wiring, luminaires, and electrical equipment within or on mobile and manufactured homes.

- **Article 555—Marinas and Boatyards.** This article covers the installation of wiring and equipment in the areas that comprise fixed or floating piers, wharves, docks, and other areas in marinas, boatyards, boat basins, boathouses, and similar locations used, or intended to be used, for the purpose of repair, berthing, launching, storing, or fueling of small craft and the mooring of floating buildings. It doesn't apply to docks or boathouses for single-family dwelling units.

- **Article 590—Temporary Installations.** Article 590 covers temporary power and lighting for construction, remodeling, maintenance, repair, demolitions, and decorative lighting.

Many of the graphics contained in Chapter 5 use two shades of red to identify a Division location (medium red for Division 1 and lighter red to identify Division 2). In some cases, these color schemes are used as a background color to help you tell if the graphic applies to Division 1, Division 2, or both (split color background).

Notes

ARTICLE 500 HAZARDOUS (CLASSIFIED) LOCATIONS

Introduction to Article 500—Hazardous (Classified) Locations

A hazardous (classified) location is an area where the possibility of fire or explosion can be created by the presence of flammable or combustible gases or vapors, combustible dusts, or ignitable fibers/flyings. Electric arcs, sparks, and/or heated surfaces can serve as a source of ignition in such environments.

Article 500 provides a foundation for applying Article 501 (Class I Locations), Article 502 (Class II Locations), Article 503 (Class III Locations), and Article 504 (Intrinsically Safe Systems)—all of which immediately follow Article 500. This article also provides a foundation for applying Articles 510 through 516.

Before you apply any of the articles just mentioned, you must understand and apply Article 500. It's a fairly long and detailed article. You'll notice when studying Article 500 that there are many Informational Notes that you should review. Although Informational Notes aren't *NEC* requirements [90.5(C)], they contain information that should help the *Code* user to better understand the related *NEC* requirement.

A Fire Triangle (fuel, oxygen, and ignition) helps to illustrate the concept of how combustion occurs. Figure 500–1

- **Fuel.** Flammable gases or vapors, combustible dusts, and ignitable fibers/flyings.
- **Oxygen.** Air and oxidizing atmospheres.
- **Ignition.** Electric arcs or sparks, heat-producing equipment such as luminaires and motors, failure of transformers, coils, or solenoids, as well as sparks caused by metal tools dropping on metal surfaces.

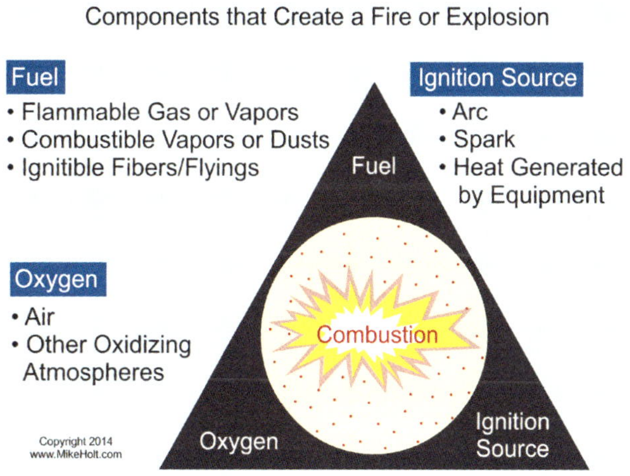

Figure 500–1

500.8 Equipment

An editorial revision has been made throughout the hazardous location articles.

500.8 Equipment.

(D) Temperature.

(1) Class I Temperature. Class I equipment must not permit the exposed equipment surface to operate at a temperature in excess of the autoignition temperature of the specific gas or vapor, as listed in Table 500.8(C).

Table 500.8(C) Classification of Maximum Surface Temperature

Maximum °C	Temperature °F	Identification Number
450	842	T1
300	572	T2
280	536	T2A
260	500	T2B
230	446	T2C
215	419	T2D
200	392	T3
180	356	T3A
165	329	T3B
160	320	T3C
135	275	T4
120	248	T4A
100	212	T5
85	185	T6

Author's Comment: This is accomplished by ensuring that the temperature marking on the equipment (especially luminaires and motors) doesn't exceed the autoignition temperature of the specific gas or vapor to be encountered.

(2) Class II Temperature. Class II equipment must not permit the exposed equipment surface to operate at a temperature in excess of the autoignition temperature of the specific dust, as listed in 500.8(C).

Author's Comment: This is accomplished by ensuring that the temperature marking on the equipment (especially luminaires) doesn't exceed the autoignition temperature of the specific dust to be encountered.

ANALYSIS: The phrase "autoignition temperature" has been used throughout various industry standards for many years, while for whatever reason the *NEC* has used "ignition temperature." This change correlates the *Code* with the standards that help drive the *NEC*, such as NFPA 497 and NFPA 499. This change is editorial only, and doesn't add or remove any technical requirements. Similar changes were made wherever the term "ignition temperature" was used.

ARTICLE 501 CLASS I HAZARDOUS (CLASSIFIED) LOCATIONS

Introduction to Article 501—Class I Hazardous (Classified) Locations

If sufficient flammable or combustible gases, vapors, or liquids are, or may be, present to produce an explosive or ignitable mixture, you have a Class I location. Examples of such locations include some fuel storage areas, certain solvent storage areas, grain processing (where hexane is used), plastic extrusion where oil removal is part of the process, refineries, and paint storage areas.

Article 500 contained a general background on hazardous (classified) locations as well as describing the differences between Class I, II, and III locations and the differences between Division 1 and Division 2 in each of the three classifications.

Article 501 contains the actual Class I, Division 1 and Division 2 installation requirements, including wiring methods, seals, and specific equipment requirements.

501.10 Wiring Methods

Changes made to this section address optical fiber cable, TC-ER cable, MC cable, and elevator cable.

Part II. Wiring

501.10 Wiring Methods.

(A) Class I, Division 1. Figure 501–1

(1) General. Only the following wiring methods are permitted within a Class I, Division 1 location.

(a) Threaded rigid metal conduit, or intermediate metal conduit, with explosionproof fittings.

(b) MI cable terminated with fittings listed for the location.

(c) In industrial establishments with restricted public access where only qualified persons will service the installation, MC-HL cable listed for use in Class I, Zone 1, or Division 1 locations, with a gas/vaportight continuous corrugated metallic sheath, an overall jacket of suitable polymeric material, a separate equipment grounding conductor(s) in accordance with 250.122, and terminated with fittings listed for the application. Such cable must comply with Part II of Article 330. Figure 501–2

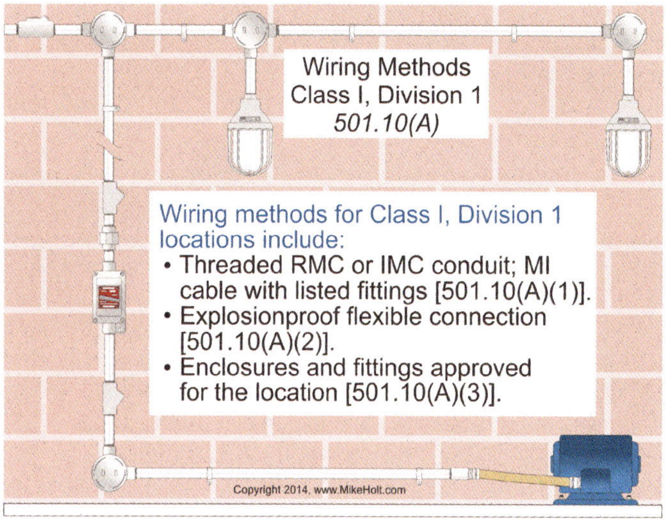

Figure 501–1

Author's Comment: Article 100 defines a "Qualified Person" as one who has skills and knowledge related to the construction and operation of the equipment and has received safety training on the hazards involved.

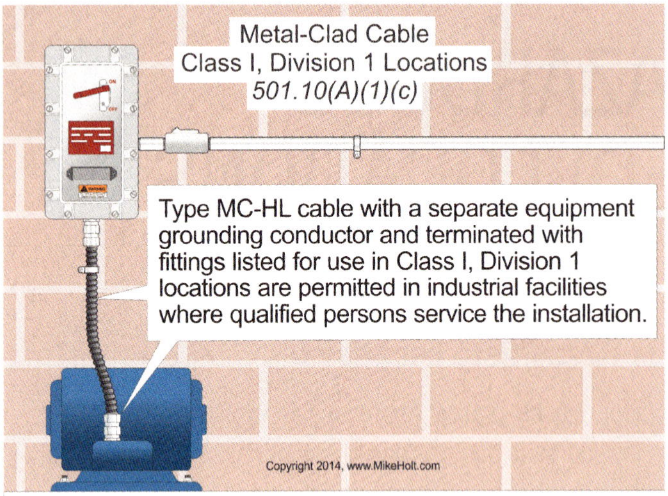

Figure 501–2

(d) In industrial establishments with restricted public access where only qualified persons will service the installation, ITC-HL cable terminated with fittings listed for the location.

(e) Types OFNP, OFCP, OFNR, OFCR, OFNG, OFCG, OFN, and OFC optical fiber cables can be installed in raceways [501.10(A)], and must be sealed in accordance with 501.15. Figure 501–3

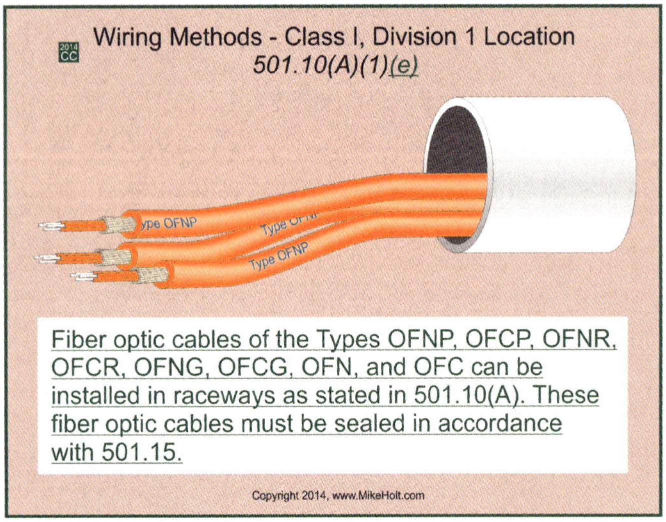

Figure 501–3

ANALYSIS: 770.3(A) states that optical fiber cables can be used in a hazardous location, yet this section was silent on the issue. In order to harmonize the two articles, an ad hoc team was created with members of different *Code*-Making panels and other industry representatives. Their efforts resulted in the addition of this text.

(2) Flexible Wiring. When necessary for vibration or movement, the following are permitted to be used:

(1) listed flexible fittings,

(2) flexible cords in accordance with 501.140,

(3) in industrial applications with restricted access, TC-ER-HL cable with listed fittings.

(3) Boxes and Fittings. Boxes and fittings must be approved by the authority having jurisdiction for Class I, Division 1 locations.

(B) Class I, Division 2.

(1) General. Only the following wiring methods are permitted within a Class I, Division 2 location. Figure 501–4

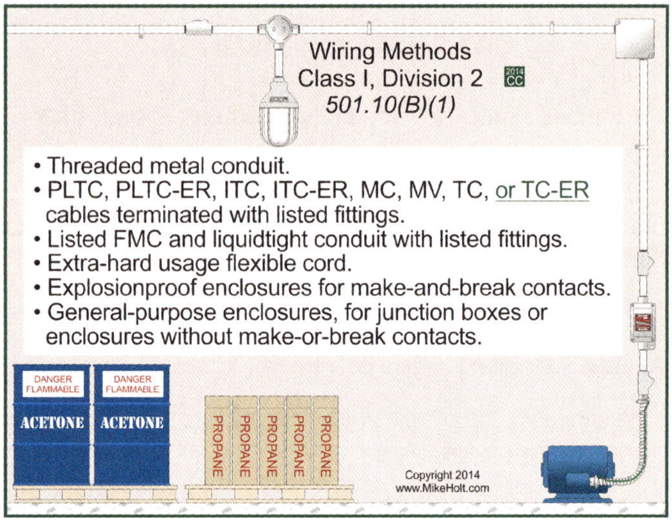

Figure 501–4

(1) Wiring methods permitted in Class I, Division 1 locations [501.10(A)].

(2) Enclosed gasketed busways and enclosed gasketed wireways.

(3) PLTC and Type PLTC-ER cable terminated with listed fittings in accordance with Article 725.

(4) ITC and ITC-ER cable terminated with listed fittings as permitted in 727.4.

(5) Types MC, MV, or TC, or TC-ER cables including installation in cable tray systems and terminated with listed fittings.

ANALYSIS: TC-ER Cable is tray cable (TC) that's allowed for exposed runs (ER). ER cables must pass crush and impact tests that other tray cables don't need to pass. Because this cable is more robust than regular TC cable, it seems logical that it should be permitted in this section.

(6) Where metallic conduit doesn't provide sufficient corrosion resistance, reinforced thermosetting resin conduit and Schedule 80 PVC conduit can be used, but only in industrial establishments where maintenance and supervision ensure that only qualified persons service the installation.

(7) Types OFNP, OFCP, OFNR, OFCR, OFNG, OFCG, OFN, and OFC optical fiber cables can be installed in cable trays or raceways [501.10(B)], and must be sealed in accordance with 501.15. Figure 501–5

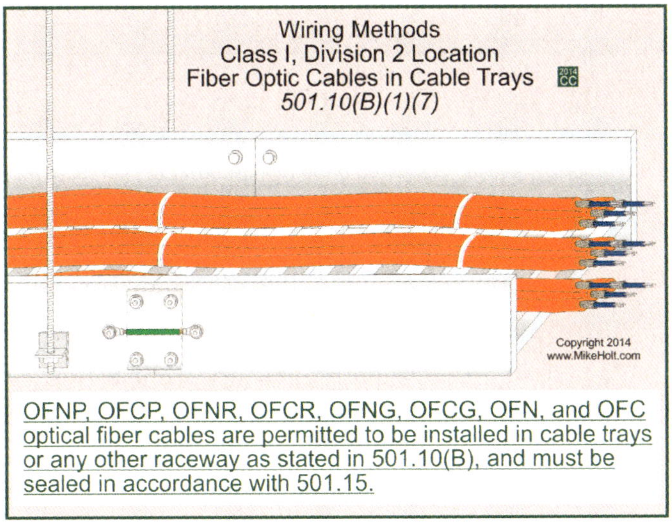

Figure 501–5

(2) Flexible Wiring. If flexibility is necessary, the following wiring methods are permitted: Figure 501–6

(1) Listed flexible metal fittings.

(2) Flexible metal conduit with listed fittings.

(3) Interlocked Type MC cable with listed fittings.

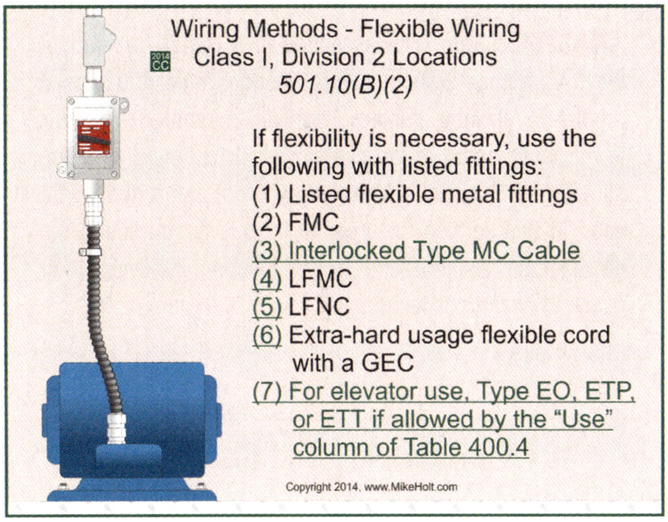

Figure 501–6

ANALYSIS: Item (3) has been added, allowing for interlocking armor Type MC cable if terminated with listed fittings. Considering that Flexible Metal Conduit is already allowed, it makes sense to allow this cable too. The construction of FMC and interlocked MC are so similar that there's no reason to allow one and not the other.

(4) Liquidtight flexible metal conduit with listed fittings.

(5) Liquidtight flexible nonmetallic conduit with listed fittings.

(6) Flexible cords listed for extra-hard usage, containing an equipment grounding conductor, and terminated with listed fittings.

Author's Comments:

- See the definition of "Grounding Conductor, Equipment" in Article 100.
- If flexible cords are used, they must comply with 501.140.

Note: See 501.30(B) for equipment grounding requirements where flexible conduit is used.

(7) For elevator use, type EO, ETP, or ETT elevator cable can be used if the "Use" column of Table 400.4 allows it, and if terminated with listed fittings.

ANALYSIS: Item (7) was added in a rather roundabout way. A proposal was made to change Table 400.4 as it relates to elevator cables. This was submitted because, in the table, some of the cables were mentioned as being allowed in hazardous locations, yet not permitted to be used in this section! In order to fix this contradiction the cables have been added to this section, allowing their usage in hazardous locations.

501.15 Raceway and Cable Seals

Changes made to the sealing requirements have been made to include optical fiber cables, and editorial revisions have been made.

501.15 Raceway and Cable Seals.

Note: Raceway and cable seals must be installed to: **Figure 501–7**

- Minimize the passage of gases and vapors from one portion of electrical equipment to another through the raceway or cable.
- Minimize the passage of flames from one portion of electrical equipment to another through the raceway or cable.
- Limit internal explosions to within the explosionproof enclosure.

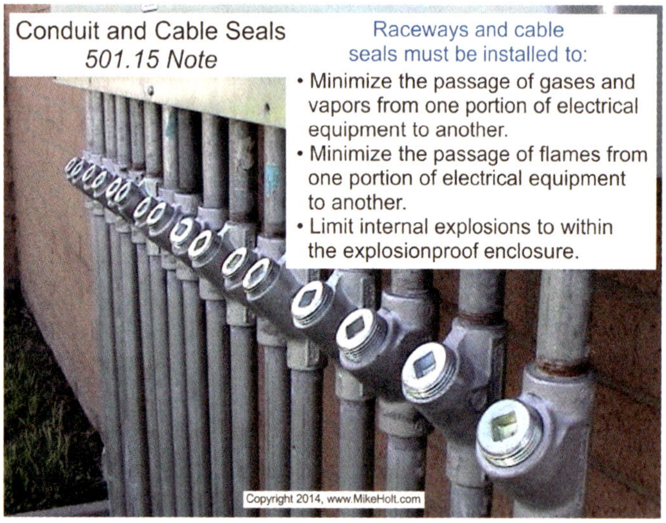

Figure 501–7

(A) Raceway Seal—Class I, Division 1. In Class I, Division 1 locations, raceway seals must be located as follows:

(1) Entering Enclosures. A raceway seal is required in each raceway that enters an explosionproof enclosure if either (1) or (2) apply:

(1) A raceway seal fitting must be installed in each raceway that enters an explosionproof enclosure that contains make-and-break contacts. A seal must also be provided where the enclosure contains equipment that operates at over 80 percent of the autoignition temperature of the gas or vapor in the area. The seal fitting must be installed within 18 in. of the explosionproof enclosure. **Figure 501–8**

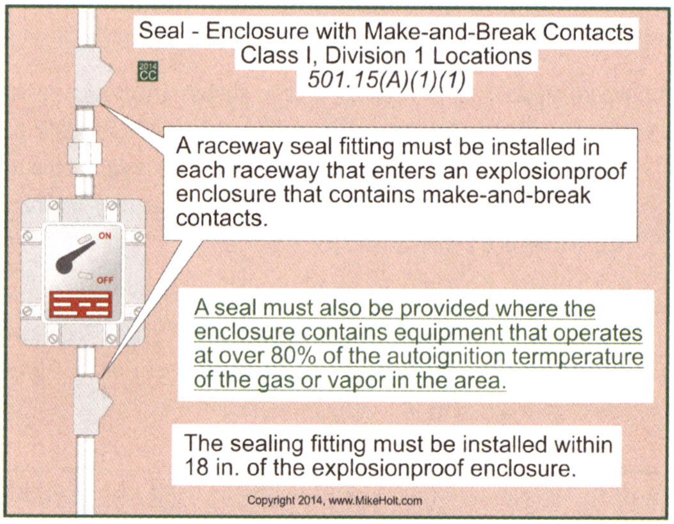

Figure 501–8

Ex: A raceway seal isn't required if the make-and-break contacts are:

a. within a hermetically sealed chamber

b. immersed in oil in accordance with 501.115(B)(1)(2)

c. enclosed within a factory-sealed explosionproof chamber

(2) A raceway seal fitting isn't required for trade size ½, ¾, 1, 1¼, or 1½ raceways that enter an explosionproof enclosure that doesn't contain any make-and-break contacts (junction and splice boxes). An example is an enclosure that only contains terminals, splices, or taps. However, a trade size 2 or larger raceway that enters any explosionproof enclosure must have a raceway seal fitting installed within 18 in. of the explosionproof enclosure [501.15(A)(1)(1)].

Author's Comment: An explosionproof enclosure that contains trade size 2 and larger raceways, as well as smaller diameter raceways only requires a raceway seal for those that are trade size 2 or larger. **Figure 501–9**

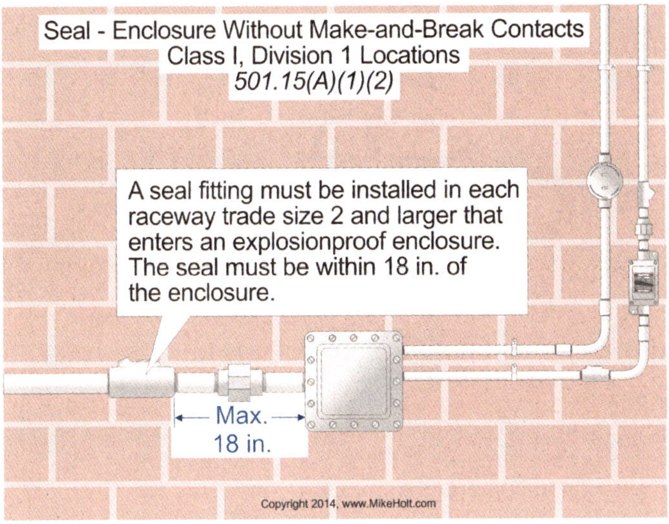

Figure 501–9

Only explosionproof unions, couplings, reducers, elbows, capped elbows, and conduit bodies are permitted between the raceway seal and the explosionproof enclosure. Figure 501–10

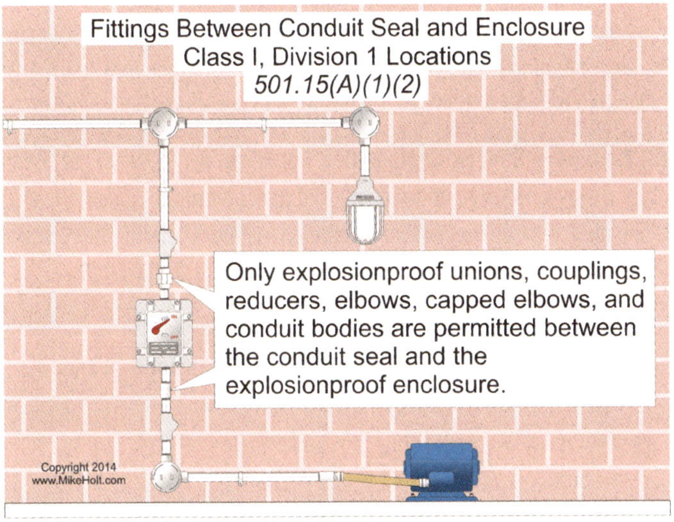

Figure 501–10

(2) Pressurized Enclosures. A raceway seal fitting must be installed in each raceway that isn't pressurized where the raceway enters a pressurized enclosure. The raceway seal fitting must be installed within 18 in. for each raceway that terminates to the pressurized enclosure.

(3) Between Explosionproof Enclosures. A single raceway seal is permitted between two explosionproof enclosures containing make-and-break contacts if the raceway seal fitting is located not more than 18 in. from either explosionproof enclosure. Figure 501–11

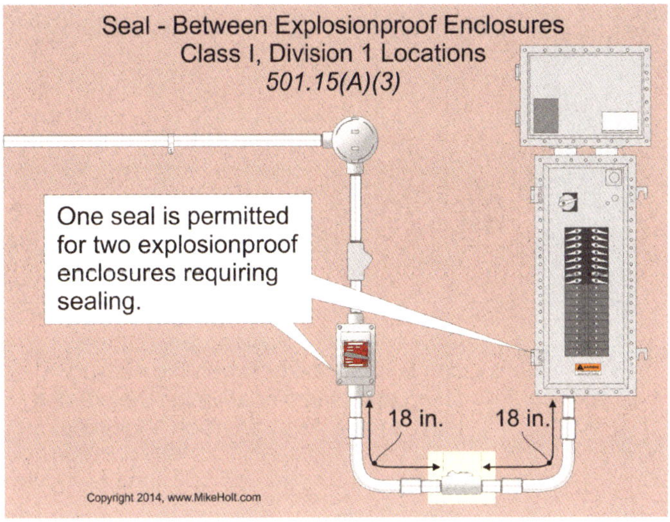

Figure 501–11

(4) Class I, Division 1, Boundary Seal. A raceway seal fitting must be installed in each raceway that leaves a Class I, Division 1 location within 10 ft of the Class I, Division 1 location on either side of the boundary. Figure 501–12

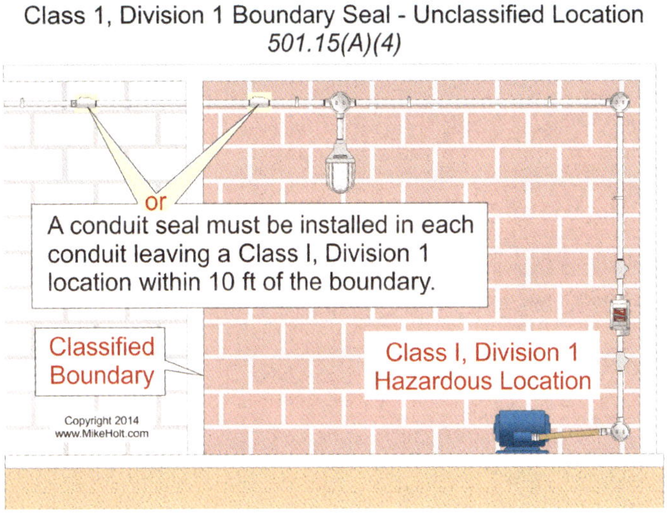

Figure 501–12

There must be no fitting, except a listed explosionproof reducer, between the seal fitting and the point at which the raceway leaves the Class I, Division 1 location. Figure 501–13

Ex 1: A raceway boundary seal fitting isn't required for a raceway that passes unbroken through the Class I, Division 1 area with no fittings less than 1 ft beyond the boundary. Figure 501–14

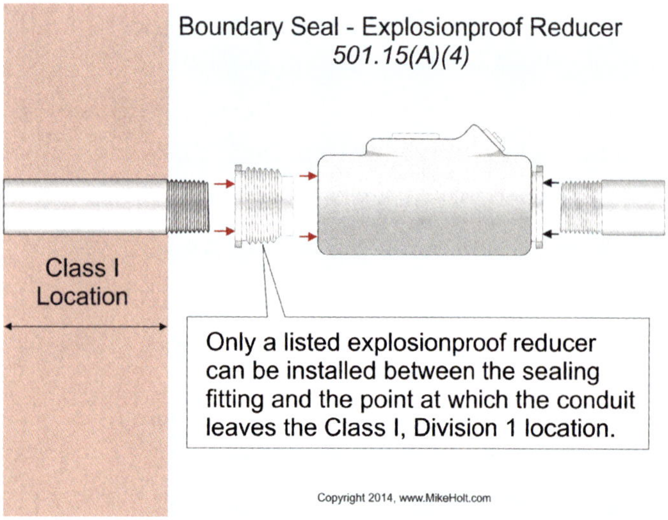

Figure 501–13

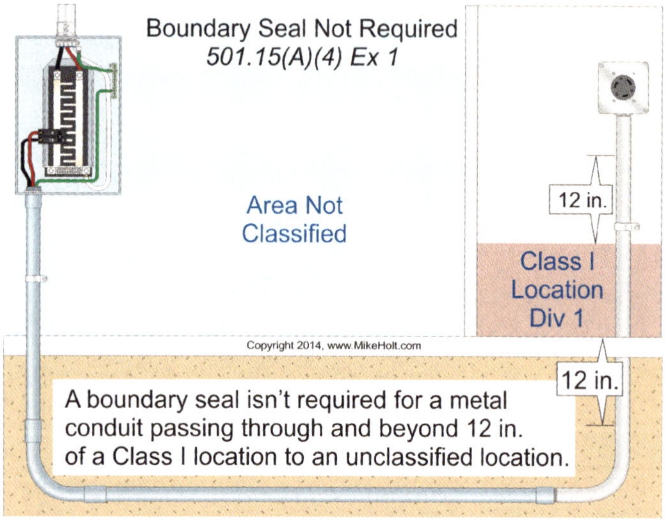

Figure 501–14

Ex 2: If the raceway boundary is below grade, the raceway seal can be located above grade, after the raceway emerges from below grade. Figure 501–15

(B) Raceway Seal—Class I, Division 2. In Class I, Division 2 locations, raceway seals must be located as follows:

(1) Enclosures with Make-and-Break Contacts. A raceway seal fitting must be installed in each raceway that enters an enclosure that must be explosionproof and that contains make-and-break contacts. The seal fitting must be installed within 18 in. of the explosionproof enclosure.

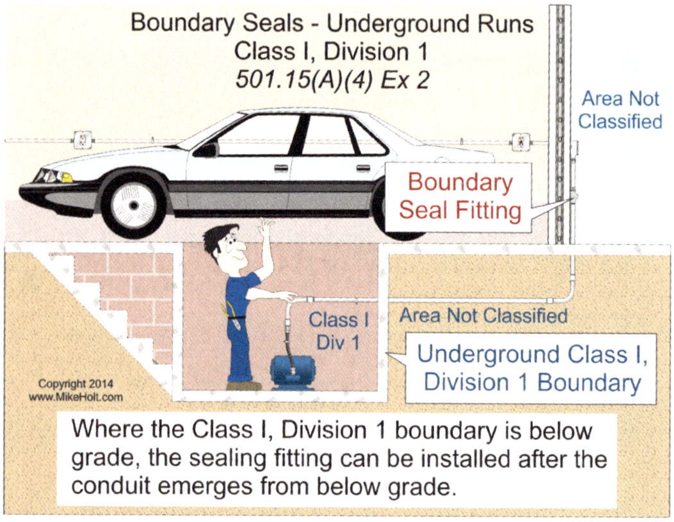

Figure 501–15

Ex: A raceway seal isn't required if the make-and-break contacts are contained within a hermetically sealed chamber or immersed in oil in accordance with 501.115(B)(1)(2), or enclosed within a factory-sealed explosionproof chamber.

A single raceway seal is permitted between two explosionproof enclosures containing make-and-break contacts, if the raceway seal fitting is located not more than 18 in. from either explosionproof enclosure.

(2) Boundary Seal at Unclassified Location. A raceway seal fitting must be installed in each raceway that passes from a Class I, Division 2 location into an unclassified location within 10 ft of the Class I, Division 2 area on either side of the boundary. Figure 501–16

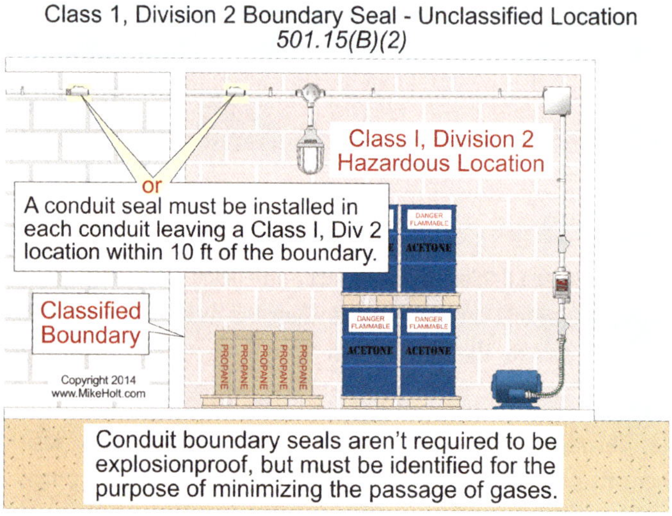

Figure 501–16

Except for listed reducers at the raceway seal, there must be no union, coupling, box, or fitting between the raceway seal and the point at which the raceway leaves the Division 2 location.

Raceway boundary seals aren't required to be explosionproof, but must be identified for the purpose of minimizing the passage of gases under normal operating conditions, and they must be accessible. See Figure 501–16

Author's Comments:

- See the definition of "Accessible" as it relates to wiring methods.
- The raceway boundary seal at unclassified locations is to minimize the passage of gases or vapors, not to contain explosions in the raceway system.

Ex 1: A raceway boundary seal fitting isn't required for a raceway that passes through the Class I, Division 2 area unbroken with no fittings less than 1 ft beyond the boundary to an unclassified location.

Ex 2: A raceway boundary seal fitting isn't required for raceways that terminate at an outdoor unclassified location for cable trays, cablebus, ventilated busways, MI cable, or open wiring.

Ex 3: A boundary seal fitting isn't required for a raceway that passes from an enclosure or room that's unclassified as a result of pressurization into a Class I, Division 2 location.

(C) Raceway Seal—Installation Requirements. If explosionproof sealing fittings are required in Class I, Division 1 and 2 locations, they must comply with the following: Figure 501–17

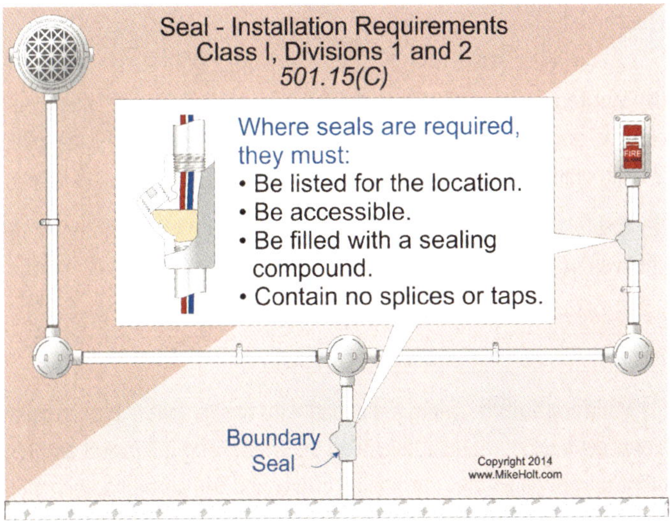

Figure 501–17

Ex: Boundary seals for Class 1 Division 2 locations aren't required to be explosionproof [501.15(B)(2)].

(1) Fittings. Raceway seal fittings must be listed for the specific sealing compounds and Class I location.

(2) Compound. The raceway seal compound must be mixed and installed in accordance with manufacturer's instructions so it minimizes the passage of gases and vapors through the seal.

Author's Comment: The sealing compound must be from the same manufacturer as the raceway seal.

(3) Thickness of Compounds. Except for listed cable sealing fittings, the minimum thickness of the raceway seal compound must not be less than the trade size of the seal fitting, but in no case less than ⅝ in.

(4) Splices and Taps. Splices and taps must not be made within a raceway seal fitting.

(6) Number of Conductors or Optical Fiber Cables. The conductor or optical fiber tube area must not exceed 25 percent of the cross-sectional area of rigid metal conduit, unless the seal fitting is identified for a higher percentage fill. Figure 501–18

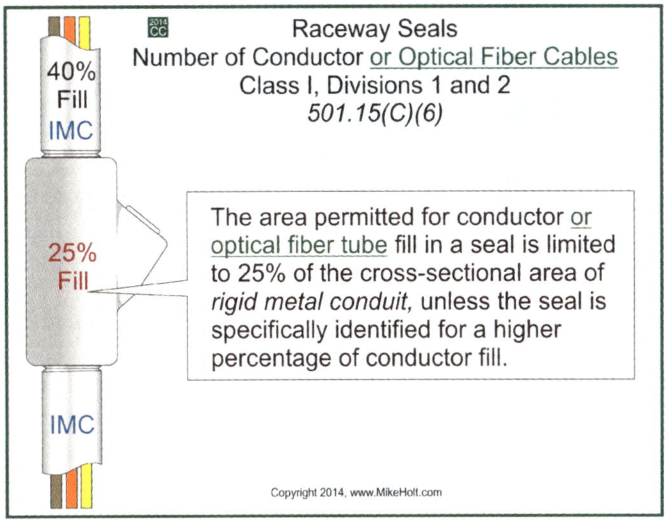

Figure 501–18

Author's Comment: The cross-sectional area of intermediate metal conduit is approximately 7 percent greater than that of rigid metal conduit because the wall thickness of intermediate metal conduit is less than rigid metal conduit. If the cross-sectional area of intermediate metal conduit is used for conductor fill calculations, the 25 percent of "rigid metal conduit conductor fill" can be exceeded.

(D) Cable Seal—Class I, Division 1. In Class I, Division 1 locations, cable seals must be located as follows:

(1) Terminations. MC-HL cable is inherently gas/vaportight by the construction of the cable, but the termination fittings must permit the sealing compound to surround each individual insulated conductor to minimize the passage of gases or vapors. Figure 501–19

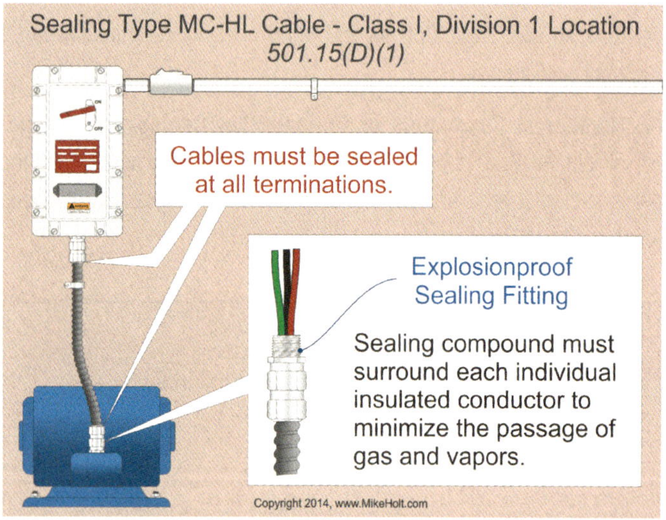

Figure 501–19

Ex: The removal of shielding material or the separation of the twisted pairs isn't required within the raceway seal fitting. Figure 501–20

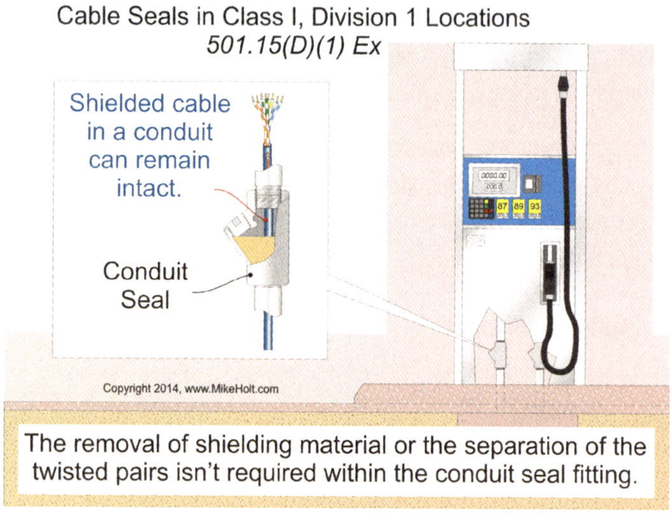

Figure 501–20

(2) Multiconductor Cable Within a Raceway. Raceways containing cables must be sealed after removing the jacket and any other coverings so that the sealing compound surrounds each individual insulated conductor <u>or optical fiber tube</u> in a manner so as to minimize the passage of gases and vapors.

Ex: The removal of shielding material or the separation of the twisted pairs isn't required within the raceway seal fitting. Figure 501–21

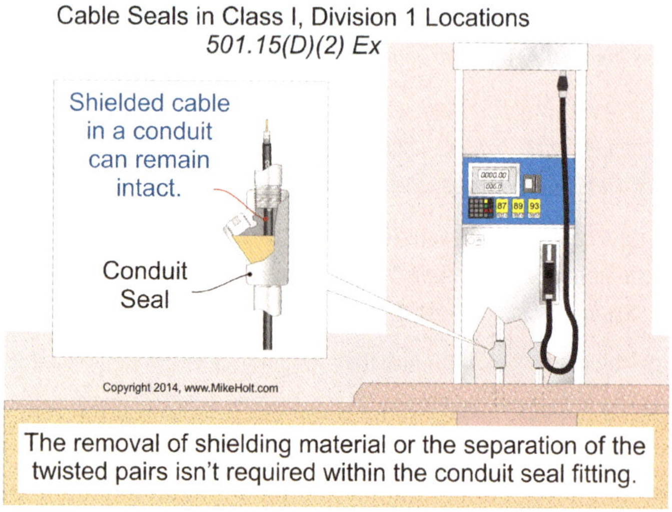

Figure 501–21

(3) Multiconductor Cables Within a Raceway. Each multiconductor cable in a raceway is considered to be a single conductor if the cable is incapable of transmitting gases or vapors through the cable core.

(E) Cable Seal—Class I, Division 2. In Class I, Division 2 locations, cable seals must be located as follows:

<u>*Ex: Seals aren't required in a Class 1 Division 2 location if the cable has an unbroken gas or vaportight sheath.*</u>

(1) Multiconductor Cable. Multiconductor cables that enter an explosionproof enclosure must be sealed after removing the jacket and any other coverings so that the sealing compound will surround each individual insulated conductor in a manner so as to minimize the passage of gases and vapors.

Multiconductor cables or optical fiber cables installed in a raceway must be sealed in accordance with 501.15(D)(2) or (3).

Ex 2: The removal of shielding material or the separation of the twisted pairs isn't required within the cable seal fitting.

(4) Cable Seal—Boundary. Cables without a gas/vaportight continuous sheath must be sealed at the boundary of the Class I, Division 2 location in a manner so as to minimize the passage of gases or vapors into an unclassified location.

ANALYSIS: In order to completely address the installation requirements for optical fiber cable in hazardous locations, an ad hoc team was created with members of different *Code*-Making panels and other industry representatives. The changes made in this section more clearly discuss the requirements for the sealing of optical fiber cables. The entire section was also editorially revised in an effort to use complete sentences and to be more grammatically correct.

501.30 Grounding and Bonding

The requirements for grounding and bonding in Class 1 locations have been clarified.

501.30 Grounding and Bonding. Because of the explosive conditions associated with electrical installations in hazardous (classified) locations [500.5], electrical continuity of metal parts of equipment and raceways must be ensured by 501.30(A) and 501.30(B). This is required regardless of the voltage of the circuit.

(A) Bonding. The locknut can't be depended on for bonding purposes; bonding jumpers with proper fittings or other approved means of bonding must be used. Such means of bonding apply to all intervening raceways, fittings, boxes, and enclosures between Class I locations and the point of grounding for service equipment. Figures 501–22 and 501–23

Author's Comment: Regardless of the circuit voltage, electrical continuity of metal parts of equipment and raceways in hazardous (classified) locations must be ensured by bonding-type locknuts, bushings, wedges, or bushings with bonding jumpers [250.92(B)(4)]; whether or not equipment grounding conductors of the wire type are installed in the raceway [250.100].

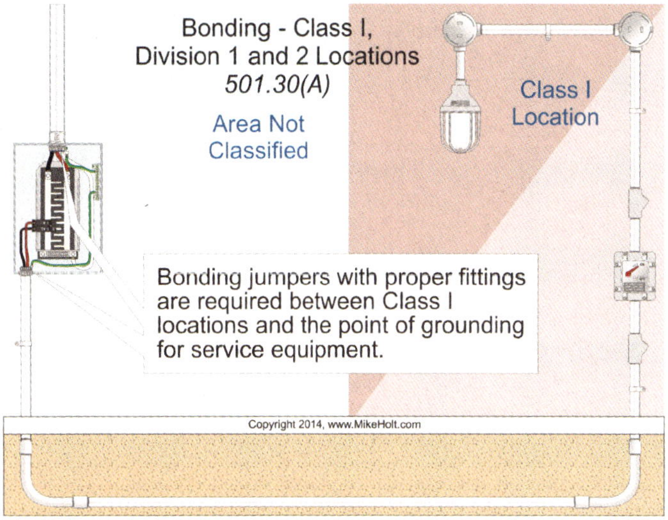

Figure 501–22

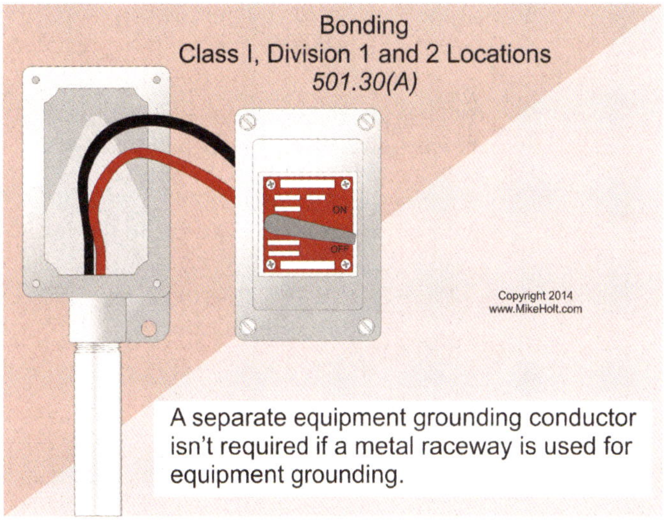

Figure 501–23

(B) Bonding—Flexible Raceway. Flexible metal conduit and liquidtight flexible metal conduit must have an equipment bonding jumper of the wire type installed in accordance with 250.102. Figure 501–24

Author's Comment: Bonding jumpers are sized in accordance with Table 250.122, based on the rating of the overcurrent device [250.102(D)], and where installed outside of a raceway, the length of bonding jumpers must not exceed 6 ft and they must be routed with the raceway [250.102(E)(2)]. Figure 501–25

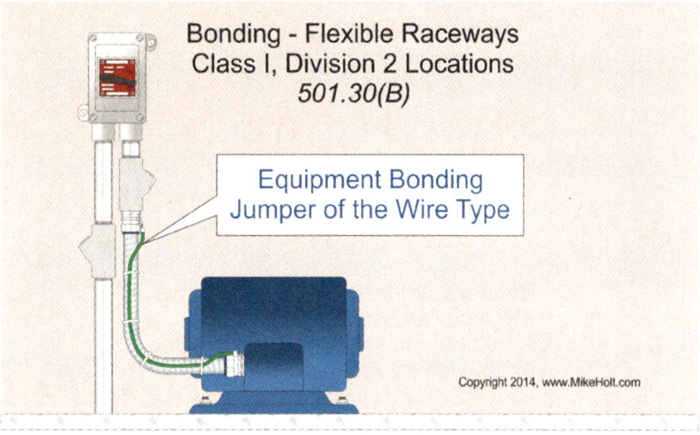

Flexible metal or liquidtight flexible conduit must have an internal or external equipment bonding jumper of the wire type installed in accordance with 250.102.

Figure 501–24

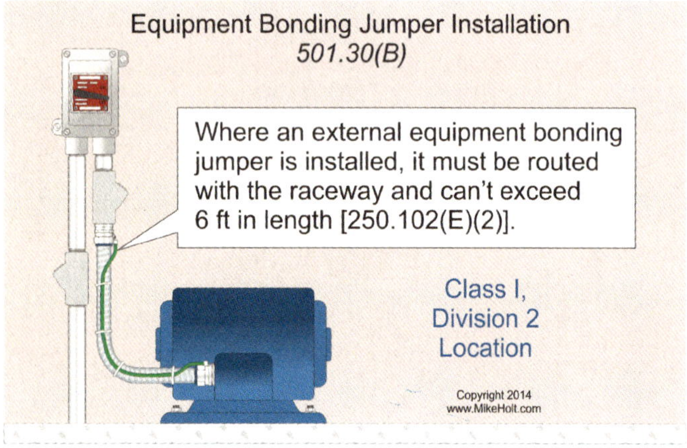

The equipment bonding jumper is sized using 250.122 based on the rating of the branch-circuit overcurrent device.

Figure 501–25

ANALYSIS: The whole concept of the hazardous location articles is to ensure that fires and explosions don't occur due to electrical equipment. Fires can occur in these locations during normal operating conditions, and the risk is magnified during abnormal conditions. An example of one of these abnormal conditions is a ground fault. Because a ground fault can create arcing, bonding is taken extra seriously in these locations. The change made to the section clarifies that the bonding required by this section applies regardless of the voltage of the circuit, as even a low-voltage or low-current arc can create enough heat to ignite the surrounding environment.

501.145 Receptacles and Attachment Plugs

Changes to this section make it clear that receptacles must be part of the building wiring.

Part III. Equipment

501.145 Receptacles and Attachment Plugs.

(A) Receptacles. Receptacles must be part of the premises wiring, unless they're part of a temporary portable assembly [501.140(A)(5)]. Figure 501–26

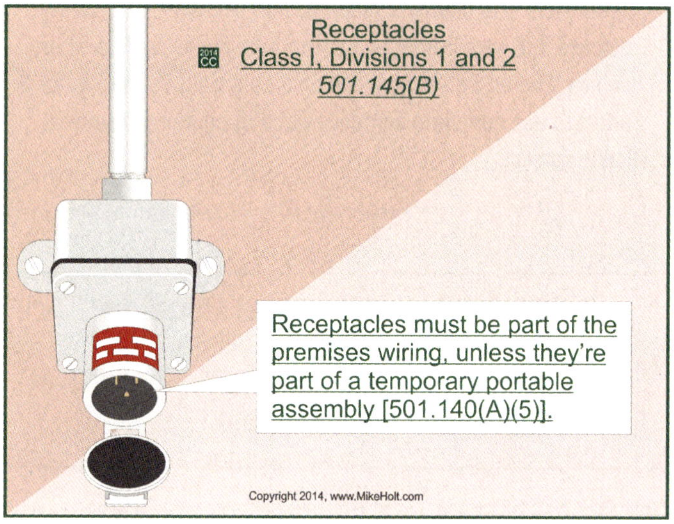

Figure 501–26

(B) Attachment Plugs. Attachment plugs must provide for the connection of an equipment grounding conductor and be identified for Class I locations. Figure 501–27

Author's Comments:

- See the definitions of "Attachment Plug" and "Receptacle" in Article 100.
- Receptacles listed for Class I locations can be any of the following types:
  - *Interlocked Switch Receptacle.* This receptacle contains a built-in rotary switch interlocked with the attachment plug. The switch must be off before the attachment plug can be inserted or removed.

- *Manual Interlocked Receptacle.* The attachment plug is inserted into the receptacle, and then it's rotated to operate the receptacle switching contacts.
- *Delayed Action Receptacle.* This receptacle requires an attachment plug and receptacle constructed so that an electrical arc will be confined within the explosionproof chamber of the receptacle.

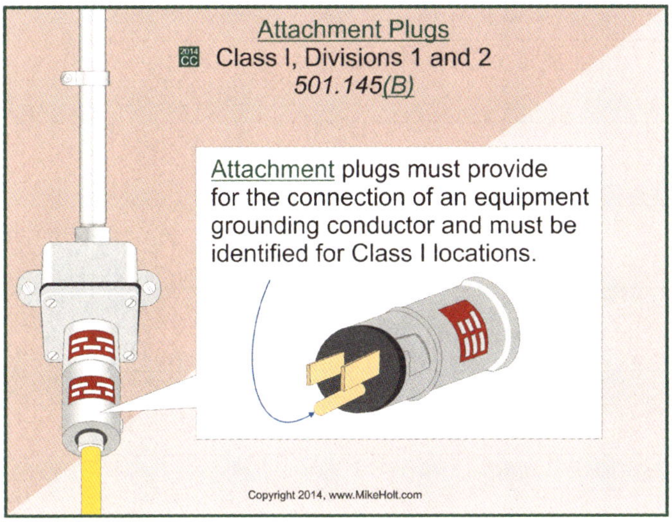

Figure 501–27

ANALYSIS: The use of makeshift assemblies of cords, plugs, and receptacles is never a great idea, but when used in a hazardous location it creates a deadly situation. Hazardous locations are classified as such because, as the name implies, they're more hazardous than a typical location. The introduction of a spark in one of these locations can have catastrophic results, including fire and explosion. By ensuring that receptacles used in a hazardous location are part of the premises wiring, the likelihood of these accidents occurring is greatly reduced.

ARTICLE 502 CLASS II HAZARDOUS (CLASSIFIED) LOCATIONS

Introduction to Article 502—Class II Hazardous (Classified) Locations

If an area has combustible dust present, it may be classified as a Class II location.

Examples of such locations include flour mills, grain silos, coal bins, wood pulp storage areas, and munitions plants.

Article 502 follows a logical arrangement similar to that of Article 501 and provides guidance in selecting equipment and wiring methods for Class II locations, including distinctions between Class II Division 1 and Class II Division 2 requirements.

502.10 Wiring Methods

Changes to this section address optical fiber cables, cord connectors, and elevator cables.

Part II. Wiring

502.10 Wiring Methods.

(A) Class II, Division 1.

(1) General. The following wiring methods can be installed in a Class II, Division 1 location: Figure 502–1

(1) Threaded rigid metal conduit or threaded intermediate metal conduit.

(2) MI cable terminated with fittings listed for the location.

(3) In industrial establishments with restricted public access where only qualified persons will service the installation, MC-HL cable listed for use in Class II, Division 1 locations, with a gas/vaportight continuous corrugated metallic sheath, an overall jacket of suitable polymeric material, a separate equipment grounding conductor(s) in accordance with 250.122, and terminated with fittings listed for the application.

(4) Types OFNP, OFCP, OFNR, OFCR, OFNG, OFCG, OFN, and OFC optical fiber cables can be installed in raceways [502.10(A)], and must be sealed in accordance with 502.15. Figure 502–2

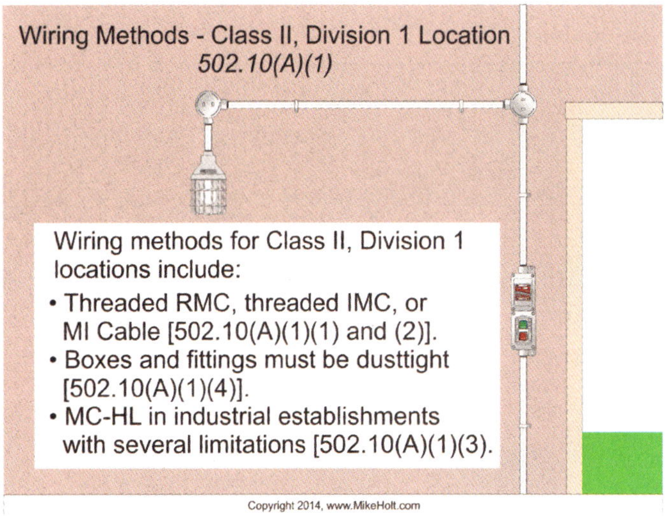

Figure 502–1

ANALYSIS: 770.3(A) states that optical fiber cables can be used in a hazardous location, yet this section was silent on the issue. In order to harmonize the two articles, an ad hoc team was created with members of different *Code*-Making panels and other industry representatives. Their efforts resulted in the addition of this text.

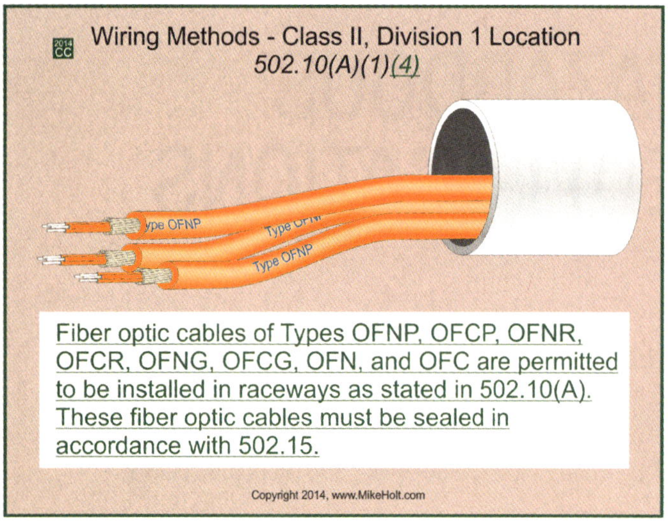

Figure 502–2

(2) Flexible Wiring. If flexibility is necessary, any of the following wiring methods are permitted in a Class II, Division 1 location: Figure 502–3

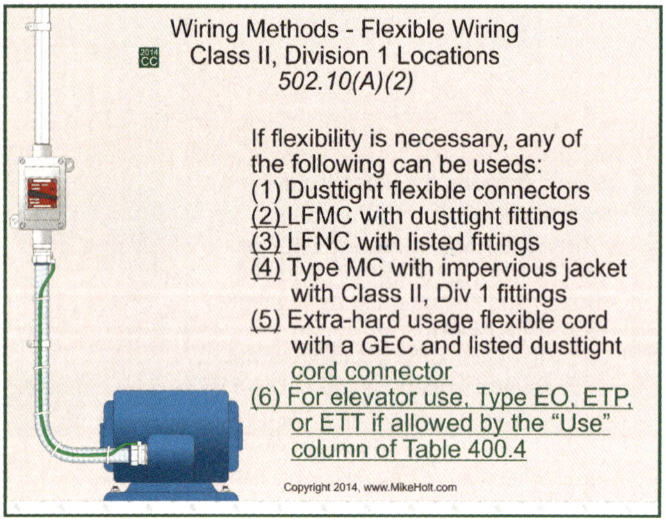

Figure 502–3

(1) Dusttight flexible connectors.

(2) Liquidtight flexible metal conduit with listed dusttight fittings.

(3) Liquidtight flexible nonmetallic conduit with listed fittings.

(4) Type MC cable with an impervious jacket and termination fittings listed for Class II, Division 1 locations.

(5) Flexible cords listed for extra-hard usage, containing an equipment grounding conductor and terminated with listed dusttight cord connectors. The flexible cord must be installed in accordance with 502.140.

(6) For elevator use, type EO, ETP, or ETT elevator cable can be used if the "Use" column of Table 400.4 allows it, and if terminated with listed dusttight fittings.

Note: See 502.30(B) for the equipment grounding requirements where flexible conduit is used.

ANALYSIS: Item (6) was added in a rather roundabout way. A proposal was made to change Table 400.4 as it relates to elevator cables. This was submitted because, in the table, some of the cables were mentioned as being allowed in hazardous locations, yet not permitted to be used in this section! In order to fix this contradiction the cables have been added to this section, allowing their usage in hazardous locations. Similar changes were made in 502.10(B) for Class II, Division 2 locations.

502.130 Luminaires

The provisions for luminaires in a Class II, Division I location were editorially revised, and now include additional marking requirements.

Part III. Equipment

502.130 Luminaires.

(A) Class II, Division 1. Luminaires must comply with the following:

(1) Marking. Each luminaire must be identified for the location and clearly marked to indicate the type and maximum wattage of the lamp for which the luminaire is designed. Figure 502–4

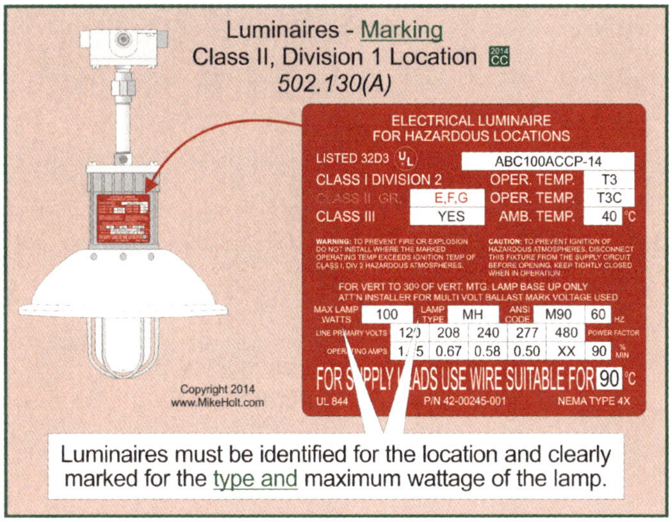

Figure 502–4

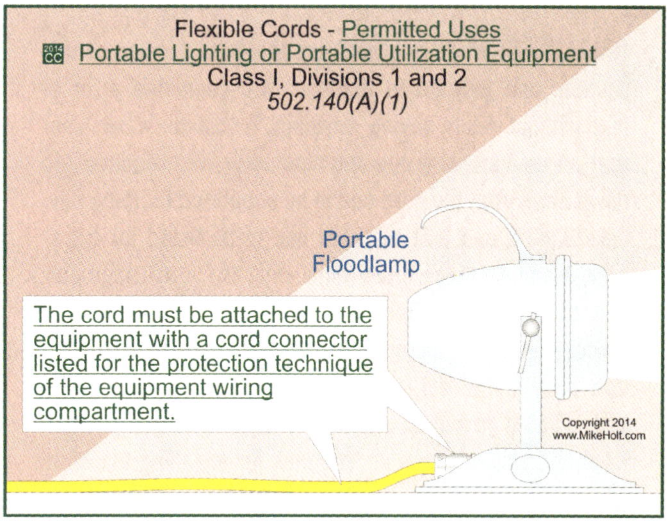

Figure 502–5

ANALYSIS: The title of 502.130 is "Luminaires," so having the title of (A)(1) be "Luminaires" as well doesn't exactly help the *Code* user. By changing the title to "Marking," the *NEC* becomes a more logical document. Changes such as these certainly don't change the world, but anytime we can make the *Code* an easier to use document we probably should.

In addition to the maximum wattage of the lamp being marked on the luminaire, the *NEC* now requires that the type of lamp be indicated as well. Most *Code* users will agree that this change makes good sense, as knowing the wattage doesn't really help if you don't know what type of lamp to use in the first place.

502.140 Flexible Cords

The rules for flexible cords have been changed to try to mirror 501.140.

502.140 Flexible Cords.

(A) Permitted Uses. Flexible cord is permitted for:

(1) Portable Lighting or Portable Utilization Equipment. The cord must be attached to the equipment with a cord connector listed for the protection technique of the equipment wiring compartment, such as dust-ignition proof. An attachment plug-in meeting the requirements of 502.140(B)(4) must also be used. Figure 502–5

(2) Where allowed by 502.10(A)(2), flexible cord can be used in an industrial establishment where conditions of maintenance and engineering supervision ensure that only qualified persons install and service the installation. The cord must be protected from damage by a suitable guard.

(3) The extension within a suitable raceway between the submersible pump in a wet-pit and the power source.

(4) Electric mixers intended for travel into and out of open-type mixing tanks or vats.

(5) Temporary portable assemblies consisting of receptacles, switches, and other devices listed for the location.

(B) Installation. Where flexible cords are used, the cords must comply with all of the following:

(1) Be of a type listed for extra-hard usage,

(2) Contain an equipment grounding conductor,

(3) Be supported in such a manner that there will be no tension on the terminal connections, and

(4) In Division 1 locations, the cord must terminate with a cord connector listed for the location or a listed cord connector installed with a seal listed for the location. In Division 2 locations, the cord must be terminated with a listed dusttight cord connector.

(5) Where 502.140(A)(5) is applied, cords must be of continuous length from the power source to the temporary portable assembly and from the temporary portable assembly to the utilization equipment.

ANALYSIS: When one analyzes the 2011 version of this section, one will notice that the *NEC* contained a lot of text without really saying anything. It told the *Code* user that an equipment grounding conductor was required (no news here), that the cord had to be supported (nothing new here either), and that the cord had to be listed for extra-hard usage. Of these three items, only the hard-usage part was of any real value, since the other two aren't optional anyway. With the changes in this edition of the *NEC*, we now have some real meat to this section. (A) provides us with a list of permitted uses (noticeably absent in previous editions), and (B) gives us the rules for installing the cord, which were mostly found in 2011. Another benefit of this change is that it nearly mirrors 501.140. When two installation practices are as similar as these are, it makes good sense for their rules as similar as possible as well.

502.145 Receptacles and Attachment Plugs

Changes to this section make it clear that receptacles must be part of the building wiring.

502.145 Receptacles and Attachment Plugs. Receptacles and attachment plugs must be identified for the location in which they're being used.

(A) Class II, Division 1.

(1) Receptacles. In Class II, Division 1 locations, receptacles must be part of the premises wiring. Figure 502–6

(2) Attachment Plugs. Attachment plugs must provide for connection of the circuit equipment grounding conductor of the flexible cord.

(B) Class II, Division 2.

(1) Receptacles. In Class II, Division 2 locations, receptacles must be part of the premises wiring.

(2) Attachment Plugs. Attachment plugs must provide for connection of the circuit equipment grounding conductor. Figure 502–7

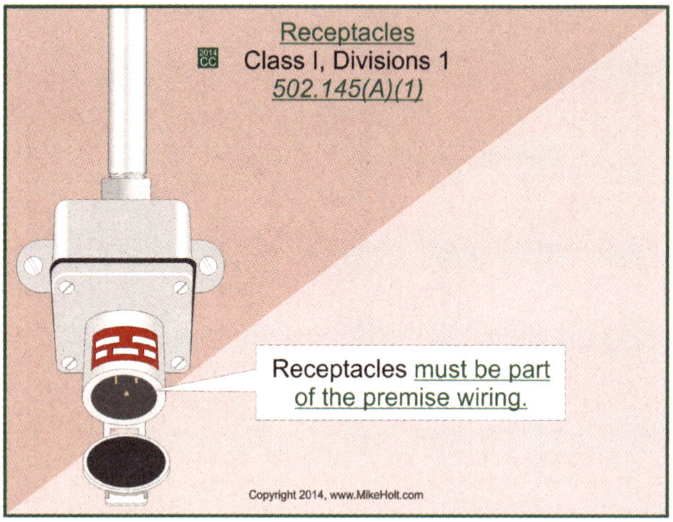

Figure 502–6

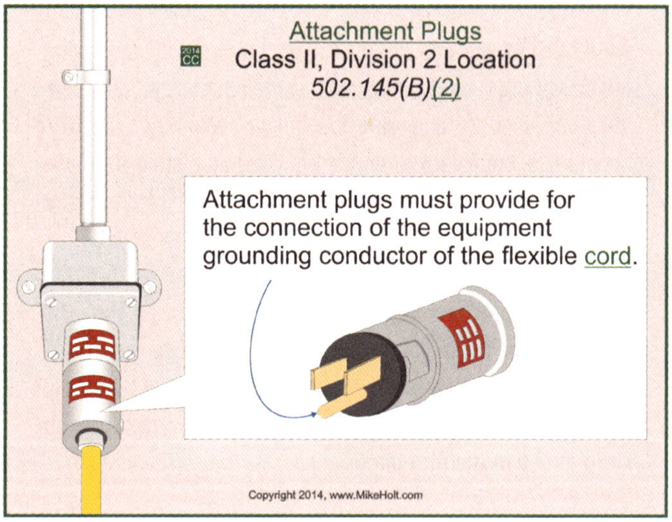

Figure 502–7

ANALYSIS: The use of makeshift assemblies of cords, plugs, and receptacles is never a great idea, but when used in a hazardous location it creates a deadly situation. Hazardous locations are classified as such because, as the name implies, they're more hazardous than a typical location. The introduction of a spark in one of these locations can have catastrophic results, including fire and explosion. By ensuring that receptacles used in a hazardous location are part of the premises wiring, the likelihood of these accidents occurring is greatly reduced.

ARTICLE 503 CLASS III HAZARDOUS (CLASSIFIED) LOCATIONS

Introduction to Article 503—Class III Hazardous (Classified) Locations

The Class III location scope is cumbersome, and many people have a hard time grasping what it means. If you have easily ignitable fibers/flyings present, you may have a Class III location. Examples of such locations include sawmills, textile mills, and fiber processing plants. In many cases, the distinction between Class II and Class III locations may be simply the size of the particles. The definition of "Combustible Dust" in Article 500 defines it based on the size of the particles, so the same material (such as sawdust) may be subject to Article 503 if the predominant material is "larger" than the definition.

503.10 Wiring Methods

Elevator cable is now permitted in a Class III location.

ANALYSIS: A proposal was made to change Table 400.4 as it relates to elevator cables. This was submitted because, in the table, some of the cables were mentioned as being allowed in hazardous locations, yet not permitted to be used in this section! In order to fix this contradiction the cables have been added, allowing their usage in hazardous locations.

Part II. Wiring

503.10 Wiring Methods. The wiring methods permitted in Class III locations include:

(A) Class III, Division 1 Location.

(6) For elevator use, type EO, ETP, or ETT elevator cable can be used if the "Use" column of Table 400.4 allows it, and if terminated with listed dusttight fittings.

Notes

ARTICLE 514 MOTOR FUEL DISPENSING FACILITIES

Introduction to Article 514—Motor Fuel Dispensing Facilities

The portion of a facility where fuel is stored and dispensed into the fuel tanks of motor vehicles and marine craft, or into approved containers must comply with Article 514.

What's most striking about this article is the large table that makes up about half of it. This table doesn't provide any electrical requirements, list any electrical specifications, or address any electrical equipment. What it does tell you is how to classify a motor fuel dispensing area based on the equipment contained therein. The rest of this article contains specific provisions, and refers to other articles that must be applied.

Author's Comment: Diesel fuel isn't a flammable liquid. Therefore, diesel dispensing equipment and associated wiring aren't required to comply with the hazardous (classified) location requirements of Article 514 [514.3(A)].

514.3 Classification of Locations

Marina and boatyard fuel dispensing facilities are now included in this section, instead of Article 555 (Marinas and Boatyards).

514.3 Classification of Locations.

(C) Motor Fuel Dispensing Stations in Boatyards and Marinas.

(1) General. Electrical wiring and equipment must be installed on the side of the wharf, pier, or dock opposite from the fuel piping system. Figure 514–1

Figure 514–1

ANALYSIS: In previous editions of the *Code*, the hazardous location requirements for marinas and boatyards were found in Article 555. It seems like a coin flip on which is the better location—514 or 555. Article 514 contains the rules for fuel, but Article 555 contains the rules for marinas and boatyards. Either location probably results in the same amount of usability, but by moving the requirements here to Article 514 any proposals are now handled by the fuel dispensing people (*Code*-Making Panel 14) instead of the boat people (*Code*-Making Panel 19). This seems logical, since Panel 14 is better equipped to deal with rules involving hazardous locations.

Notes

ARTICLE 517 HEALTH CARE FACILITIES

Introduction to Article 517—Health Care Facilities

Health care facilities differ from other types of buildings in many important ways. Article 517 is primarily concerned with those parts of health care facilities where patients are examined and treated. Whether those facilities are permanent or movable, they still fall under this article. However, Article 517 wiring and protection requirements don't apply to business offices or waiting rooms. They don't apply to animal veterinary facilities either.

Article 517 contains many specialized definitions that only apply to health care facilities. While you don't need to be able to quote these definitions, you should have a clear understanding of what the terms mean. As you study Parts II and III, keep in mind the special requirements of hospitals and why these requirements exist. The requirements in Parts II and III are highly detailed and not intuitively obvious. These are three of the main objectives of Article 517, Parts II and III:

- Maximize the physical and electromagnetic protection of wiring by requiring metal raceways.
- Minimize electrical hazards by keeping the voltage potential between patients' bodies and medical equipment low. This involves many specific steps, beginning with 517.11.
- Minimize the negative effects of power interruptions by establishing specific requirements for essential electrical systems.

Part IV addresses gas anesthesia stations. The primary objective of Part IV is to prevent ignition. Part V addresses X-ray installations and really has two main objectives:

- Provide adequate ampacity and protection for the branch circuits.
- Address the safety issues inherent in high-voltage equipment installations.

Part VI provides requirements for low-voltage communications systems, such as fire alarms and intercoms. The primary objective there is to prevent compromising those systems with inductive couplings or other sources of interference. Part VII provides requirements for isolated power systems; the main objective is to keep them actually isolated.

Be aware that the *NEC* is just one of the standards that apply to health care locations, and there may be additional requirements from other standards and special requirements for sophisticated equipment.

517.2 Definitions—Patient Care Space

"Patient care areas" are now "patient care spaces." Other associated changes have been made as well.

Part I. General

517.2 Definitions.

Patient Care Space. The area in a health care facility where patients are intended to be examined or treated.

Author's Comment: "Patient Care Space" is further broken down into four specific types of spaces. **Figure 517–1**

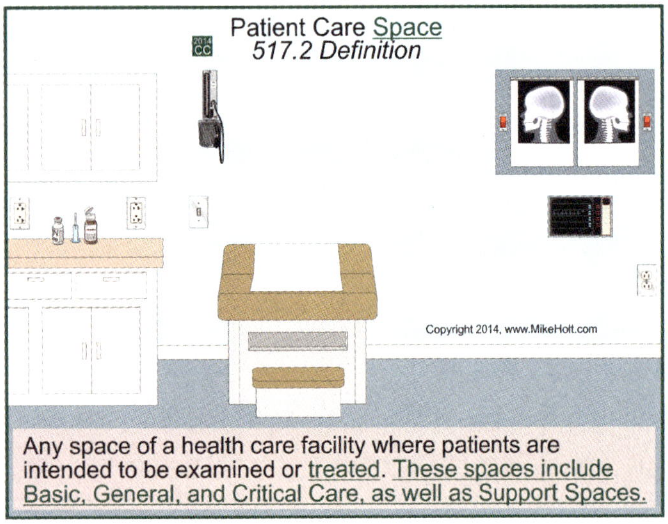

Figure 517–1

Basic Care Space. An area where failure of equipment or a system isn't likely to cause injury to the patients or caregivers.

General Care Space. An area where failure of equipment or a system is likely to cause minor injury to patients or caregivers. **Figure 517–2**

Critical Care Space. An area where failure of equipment or a system is likely to cause major injury or death to patients or caregivers.

Support Space. An area where failure of equipment or a system isn't likely to have a physical impact on patients or caregivers.

Note 1: The governing body of the facility determines room usage in accordance with the type of patient care anticipated. Business offices, corridors, lounges, day rooms, dining rooms, or similar areas aren't classified as patient care spaces.

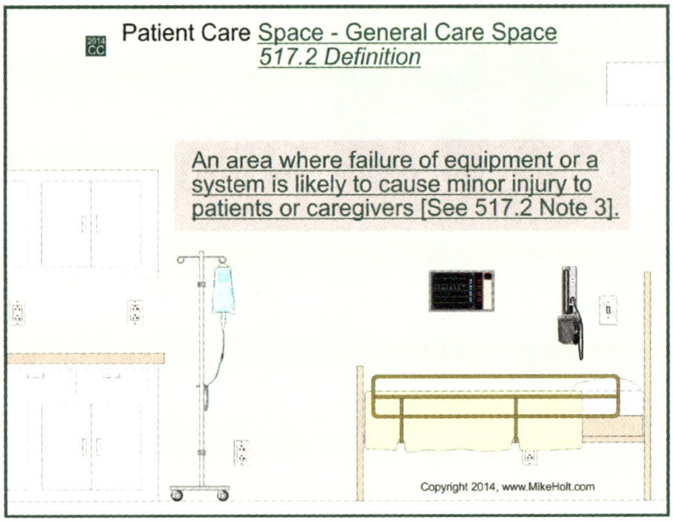

Figure 517–2

Note 2: Basic care spaces are where basic medical and dental care, examinations, and treatment occur.

Note 3: General care spaces are areas such as patient bedrooms, examining rooms, treatment rooms, clinics, and similar areas in which it's intended that the patient come in contact with ordinary appliances such as a nurse call system, electric beds, examining lamps, telephones, and entertainment devices.

Note 4: Critical care spaces include special care units, intensive care units, coronary care units, angiography laboratories, cardiac catheterization laboratories, delivery rooms, operating rooms, and similar areas in which patients are intended to be subjected to invasive procedures and connected to line-operated, electromedical devices.

ANALYSIS: **NFPA 99 *(Health Care Facilities Code)* contains the design requirements for buildings within its scope (health care facilities). Definitions of terms are the responsibility of that document. When NFPA 99 changes a definition, it's changed in the *NEC* as well. It's worth noting that, other than the titles of the terms, not much changed in the definition. What used to be known as a "general care area" is what most *Code* users deal with in areas other than hospitals. These areas are now subdivided into two terms, "basic care spaces" and "general care spaces." While this may (or may not) matter in NFPA 99, it doesn't appear to make a real difference in the *NEC*.**

There are still instances of the phrase "patient care area" in the *NEC*. This was accidentally left in the *Code*, and all were supposed to be replaced with "patient care space."

517.16 Isolated Ground Receptacles

The prohibition on isolated ground receptacles has been lessened.

517.18 General Care Areas

The number of receptacles at patient bed locations has been increased.

Part II. Wiring and Protection

517.16 Isolated Ground Receptacles. Receptacles having insulated grounding terminals (isolated ground receptacles) [250.146(D)] aren't allowed in a patient care vicinity. Figure 517–3

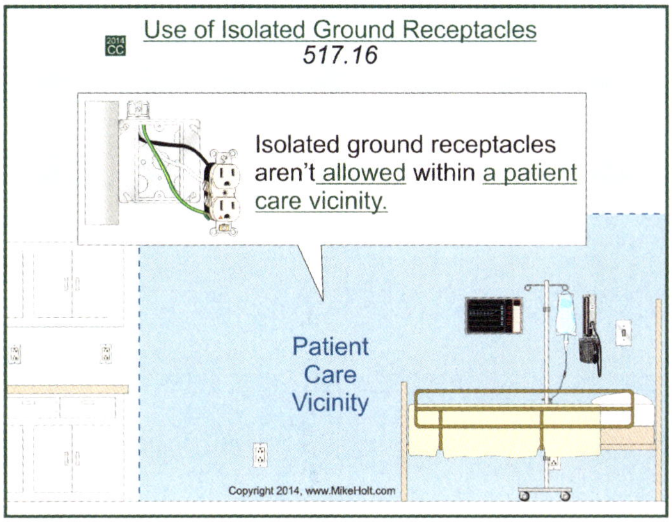

Figure 517–3

ANALYSIS: A change made in the 2011 *NEC* prohibited the use of isolated ground (IG) receptacles in patient care spaces. When using an IG receptacle in a patient care space, the entire concept of 517.13 is pointless, because the redundancy afforded by that section is lost. With the loss of the dual equipment grounding conductor required in 517.13, the patient is put in a much more vulnerable position as it relates to electric shock. The change in this edition of the *Code* ensures that equipment the patient can come in contact with isn't connected to an IG receptacle.

517.18 General Care Areas.

(B) Hospital Grade Receptacles. Inpatient sleeping beds or procedure table beds must be provided with a minimum of eight hospital grade receptacles (single, duplex, quadplex, or any combination of the three). Figure 517–4

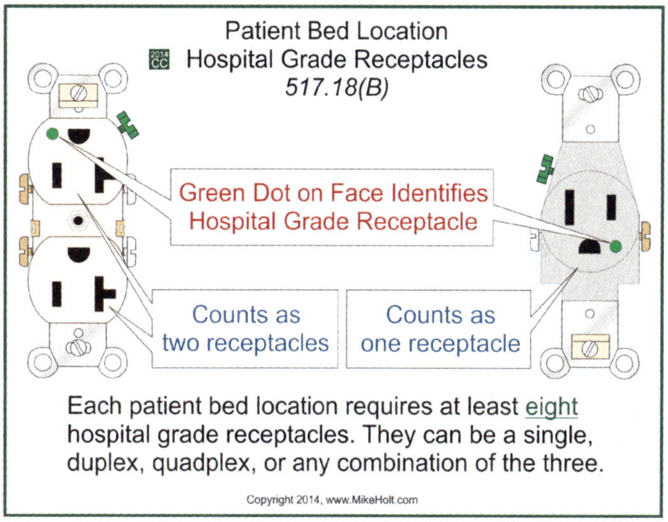

Figure 517–4

Author's Comment: "Hospital grade" receptacles aren't required in treatment rooms of clinics, medical and dental offices, or outpatient facilities because these locations don't have a "patient bed location" as defined in 517.2. Figure 517–5

ANALYSIS: NFPA 99, *The Health Care Facilities Code*, is the document that deals with the design and functionality of the electrical system in health care facilities. Because the number of receptacles isn't an electrical safety issue, they're under the jurisdiction of that document. NFPA 99 was revised to mandate eight receptacles in these locations, so the *NEC* has been changed to match those requirements.

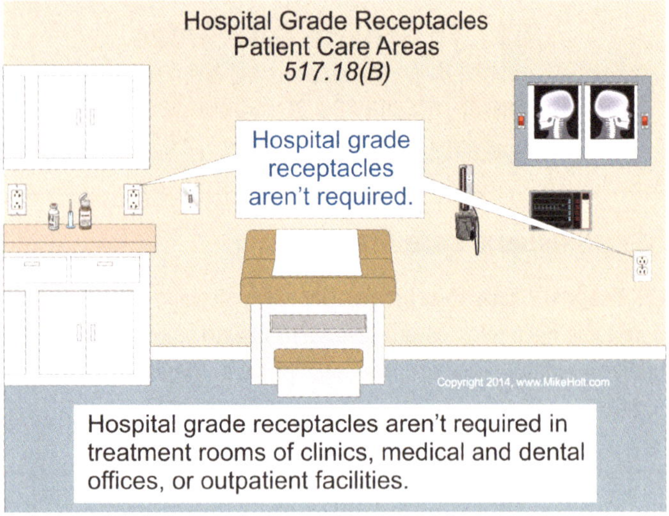
Hospital Grade Receptacles
Patient Care Areas
517.18(B)
Hospital grade receptacles aren't required.
Copyright 2014, www.MikeHolt.com
Hospital grade receptacles aren't required in treatment rooms of clinics, medical and dental offices, or outpatient facilities.

Figure 517–5

ARTICLE

525 CARNIVALS, CIRCUSES, FAIRS, AND SIMILAR EVENTS

Introduction to Article 525—Carnivals, Circuses, Fairs, and Similar Events

Article 525 covers the installation of portable wiring and equipment for carnivals, circuses, exhibitions, fairs, traveling attractions, and similar functions [525.1]. At first glance, a couple of questions arise. "Aren't these just like assembly occupancies? Why do we need Article 525 if Article 518 covers the same thing?"

Yes, these locations are similar to assembly occupancies [Article 518], but they're not the same. In fact, there are two big differences:

- Article 525 applications are temporary, while Article 518 occupancies aren't.
- Article 518 doesn't cover amusement rides and attractions, while Article 525 does.

You may want to compare these two articles to see if you can spot other similarities and differences between them. Doing so will help you understand both articles better.

525.32 Equipment Grounding Conductor Continuity Assurance

This section was revised to use defined terms.

Part IV. Grounding and Bonding

525.32 Equipment Grounding Conductor Continuity Assurance. The continuity of the circuit equipment grounding conductor for portable electrical equipment must be verified each time the equipment is connected.

Author's Comment: Verification of the circuit equipment grounding conductor is necessary to ensure electrical safety. This rule doesn't specify how it's verified, what circuits are required to be verified, how the verification is recorded, or who's required or qualified to perform the verification.

ANALYSIS: The term "grounding conductor" was removed from the *Code* in 2011. The definition of that term really didn't make any sense, and it became a "catch-all" for any conductor that's green or bare. An example of that issue was in this section. Previously, it referred to checking the continuity of the "grounding conductor." Reading this rule in context, it's obvious that the equipment grounding conductor is the conductor being discussed, but through years of misusing the terms, this section held onto the wrong one. This change not only deletes a term that's no longer used, but also makes it clear which conductor the *NEC* is talking about.

ARTICLE 547 AGRICULTURAL BUILDINGS

Introduction to Article 547—Agricultural Buildings

Two factors have a tremendous influence on the lifespan of agricultural equipment: dust and moisture.

Dust gets into mechanisms and causes premature wear. But with electricity on the scene, dust adds two other dangers: fire and explosion. Dust from hay, grain, and fertilizer is highly flammable. Litter materials, such as straw, are also highly flammable. Excrement from farm animals may cause corrosive vapors that eat at mechanical equipment and wiring methods and can cause electrical equipment to fail. For these reasons, Article 547 includes requirements for dealing with dust and corrosion.

Another factor to consider in agricultural buildings is moisture, which causes corrosion. Water is present for many reasons, including wash down. Thus, this article has requirements for dealing with wet and damp environments, and also includes other rules. For example, you must install equipotential planes in all concrete floor confinement areas of livestock buildings containing metallic equipment accessible to animals and likely to become energized.

Livestock animals have a low tolerance to small levels of stray electrical current, which can cause loss of milk production and, at times, livestock fatality. As a result, the *NEC* contains specific requirements for an equipotential plane in buildings that house livestock.

547.2 Definitions—Equipotential Plane

The definition of "equipotential plane" has been revised for accuracy.

547.2 Definitions.

Equipotential Plane. An equipotential plane is an area where wire mesh or other conductive elements are embedded in or placed under concrete, and are bonded to the electrical system to minimize voltage differences within the plane, between the plane and electrical equipment, and between the plane and the earth [547.10(B)]. **Figure 547–1**

ANALYSIS: If you want to *prevent* stray voltage from developing within a plane, you have one (and only one) option: Remove any and all sources of electricity from the building. If you want to *minimize* stray voltage, you install an equipotential plane. This change mirrors the language found in 680.26(A), which is more accurate.

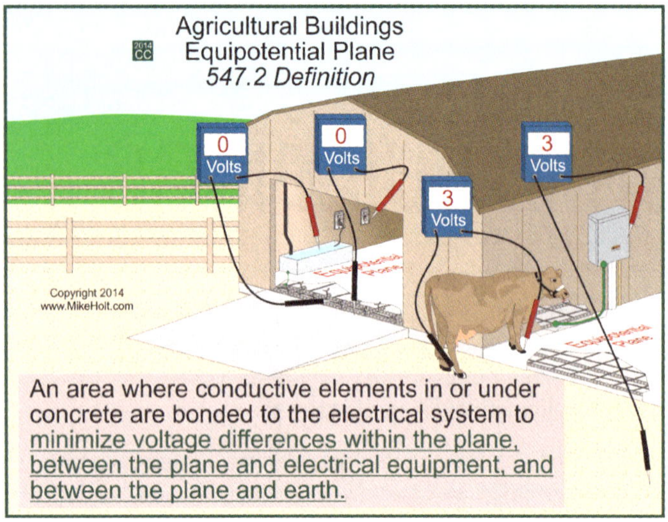

Figure 547–1

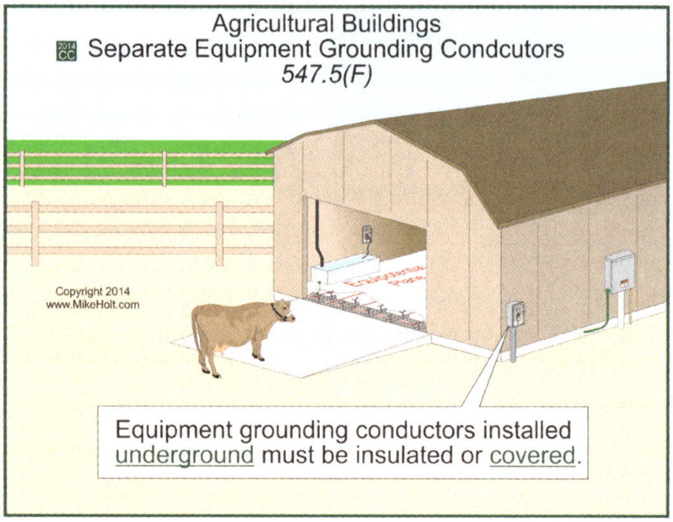

Figure 547–2

547.5 Wiring Methods

Copper equipment grounding conductors are no longer required for agricultural buildings.

547.5 Wiring Methods.

(F) Separate Equipment Grounding Conductor. An equipment grounding conductor for circuits in agricultural buildings must be insulated or covered when installed underground. Figure 547–2

ANALYSIS: After studying the corrosive effects of the various items found in agricultural buildings (methane gas, ammonia, carbon dioxide, hydrogen sulfide, and so forth), it was determined that aluminum conductors perform as well as copper conductors. With this new information, the *Code* now allows aluminum equipment grounding conductors to be used.

ARTICLE 555 MARINAS AND BOATYARDS

Introduction to Article 555—Marinas and Boatyards

Water levels aren't constant. Ocean tides rise and fall, while lakes and rivers vary in depth in response to rain. To provide power to a marina or boatyard, you must allow for these variations in water level between the point of use and the power source. Article 555 addresses this issue.

This article begins with the concept of the electrical datum plane. You might think of it as the border of a "demilitarized zone" for electrical equipment. Or, you can think of it as a line that marks the beginning of a "no man's land" where you simply don't place electrical equipment. Once you determine where this plane is, don't locate transformers, connections, or receptacles below that line.

555.2 Definitions—Marine Power Outlet

The definition of "marine power outlet" was revised to omit needless words.

555.2 Definitions.

Marine Power Outlet. An assembly that can include equipment such as receptacles, circuit breakers, fused switches, fuses, watt-hour meters, and panelboards for marine use. Figure 555–1

Author's Comment: This definition is necessary for the application of shore power receptacles [555.19(A)(1)] and disconnecting means [555.17(B)].

ANALYSIS: "Panelboard" is the term used throughout the *Code*, so the term "distribution panelboard" in this definition was revised by deleting one of its two words. You get two guesses to figure out which one it was.

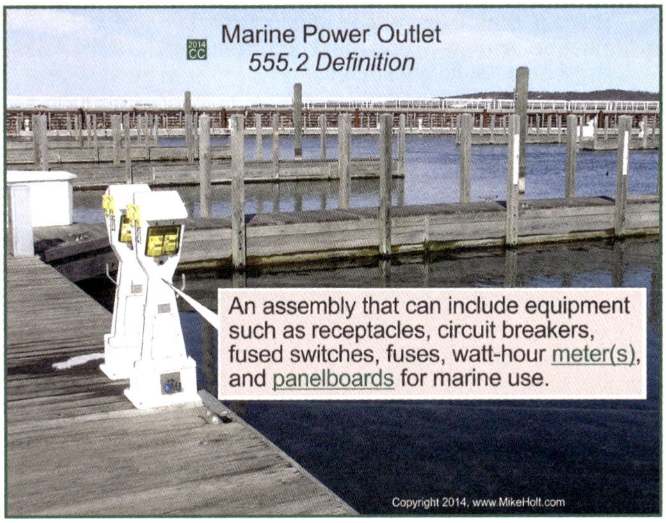

Figure 555–1

555.15 Grounding

Copper equipment grounding conductors are no longer required.

555.15 Grounding.

(B) Equipment Grounding Conductor. An insulated equipment grounding conductor is required for circuits. **Figure 555–2**

Figure 555–2

(C) Size of Equipment Grounding Conductor. The insulated equipment grounding conductor must be sized in accordance with 250.122, but not smaller than 12 AWG.

ANALYSIS: It seems that aluminum still has the negative stigma attached to it that developed in the 1960s and '70s. Not only have installation practices improved since then, but the conductors themselves have as well. New and better alloys are used in the manufacture of aluminum conductors, and they have an excellent track record. Furthermore, the effects of sea water and fresh water on aluminum conductors are minor. With this change aluminum equipment grounding conductors are now allowed.

ARTICLE

590 TEMPORARY INSTALLATIONS

Introduction to Article 590—Temporary Installations

It's a common misconception that temporary wiring represents a lower standard than that of other wiring. In truth, it merely meets a different standard. The same rules of workmanship, ampacity, and overcurrent protection apply to temporary installations as to others.

So, how is a temporary installation different? In one sense, it does represent a lower standard. For example, you can use Type NM cable rather than raceway-enclosed wiring without any limitations based on the type of construction, and you don't have to put splices in boxes. You must remove a temporary installation upon completion of the purpose for which it was installed. If the temporary installation is for holiday displays, it can't last more than 90 days.

Article 590 addresses the practicality and execution issues that are inherent in temporary installations, thereby making them less time consuming to install.

590.4 General

New text for cords and cables has been added.

590.4 General.

(J) Support. Cable assemblies and flexible cords must be supported at intervals that ensure protection from physical damage. Support must be in the form of staples, cable ties, straps, or other similar means designed not to damage the cable or cord assembly. Cords and cables, other than extension cords, aren't allowed on the floor or the ground when they're used as branch circuits or feeders. Figure 590–1

> **Author's Comment:** The support requirement for temporary cables is determined by the authority having jurisdiction, based on the jobsite conditions [590.2(B)].

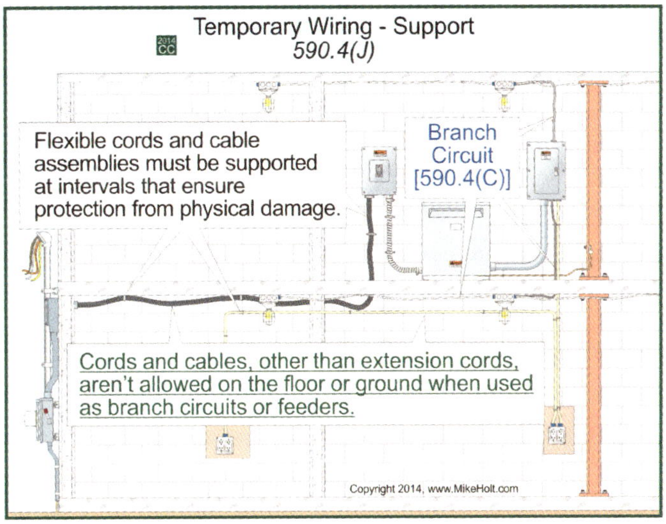

Figure 590–1

Vegetation must not be used for the support of overhead branch circuit or feeder conductors. Figure 590–2

Ex: Vegetation can be used to support decorative lighting if strain-relief devices, tension take-up devices, or other means approved by the authority having jurisdiction are used to prevent damage to conductors from the movement of the live vegetation.

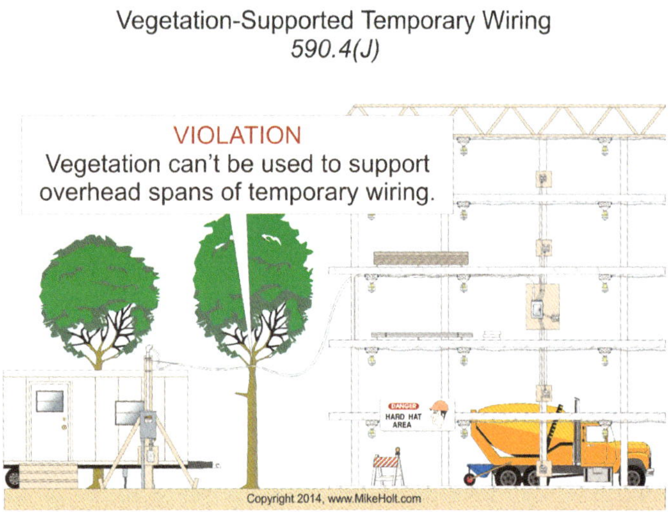

Figure 590–2

ANALYSIS: Prohibiting cords and cables from being on the floor is a result of trying to coordinate *Code* requirements with OSHA requirements. It's important to realize that this rule doesn't prohibit extension cords from being on the ground or floor (which would be impossible to enforce or even comply with), but it does prohibit cables, such as NM cable or SE cable, from being there.

590.6 Ground-Fault Protection for Personnel

Listed cord sets can provide the GFCI protection required by 590.6(A)(1).

590.6 Ground-Fault Protection for Personnel.

(A) Receptacle Outlets. Ground-fault protection for personnel is required for temporary wiring used for construction, remodeling, maintenance, repair, or demolition of buildings, structures, or equipment, from power derived from an electric utility company or from an on-site generated power source.

(1) Receptacles Not Part of Permanent Wiring. GFCI protection is required for 15A, 20A, and 30A, 125V receptacle outlets that aren't a part of the permanent wiring of the building/structure used by personnel. Listed cord sets or adapters that incorporate listed GFCI protection can be used to meet this requirement. Figure 590–3

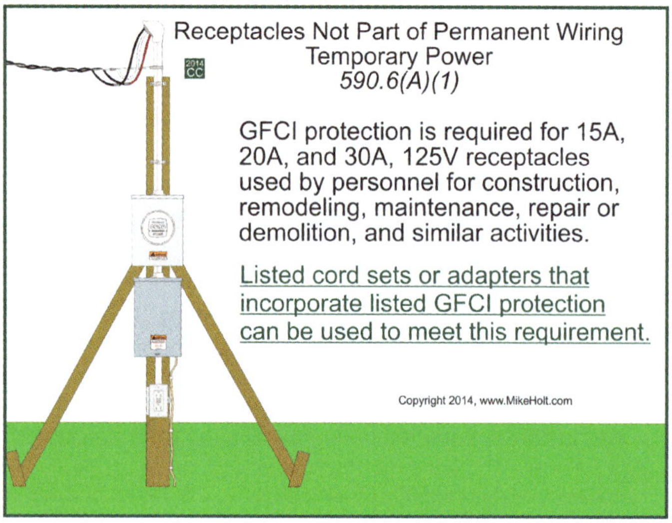

Figure 590–3

ANALYSIS: This allowance is already permitted in 590.6(A)(2) and (A)(3), but was missing from (A)(1). This change simply corrects that error.

CHAPTER 6 SPECIAL EQUIPMENT

Introduction to Chapter 6—Special Equipment

Chapter 6, which covers special equipment, is the second of three *NEC* chapters that deal with special topics. Chapters 5 and 7 focus on special occupancies, and special conditions respectively. Remember, the first four chapters of the *Code* are sequential and form a foundation for each of the subsequent three. Chapter 8 covers communications systems and isn't subject to the requirements of Chapters 1 through 7 except where the requirements are specifically referenced in Chapter 8.

What exactly is "Special Equipment?" It's equipment that, by the nature of its use, construction, or by its unique nature creates a need for additional measures to ensure the "safeguarding of people and property" mission of the *NEC*, as stated in Article 90.

The *Code* groups the articles in this chapter logically, as you might expect. Here are the general groupings:

- Prefabricated items that are assembled in the field. Articles 600 through 605. These are signs, manufactured wiring systems, and office furnishings.
- Lifting equipment. Articles 610 and 620. Cranes, hoists, elevators, dumbwaiters, wheelchair lifts, and escalators are included.
- Electric vehicle charging systems. Article 625.
- Electric welders. Article 630.
- Equipment for creating or processing information. Article 645 covers computers (information technology) and Article 646 pertains to portable (modular) data centers.
- X-ray equipment. Article 660.
- Process and production equipment. Articles 665 through 675. Induction heaters, electrolytic cells, electroplating, and irrigation machines are included.
- Swimming Pools, Fountains, and Similar Installations. Article 680.
- "New Energy" Technologies. Article 690 covers solar PV systems, Article 692 addresses fuel cells, and Article 694 pertains to small wind systems.
- Fire pumps. Article 695.

Author's Comment: The NFPA also produces a fire pump standard. It's NFPA 20, *Standard for the Installation of Stationary Pumps for Fire Protection.*

It's important to remember that Chapter 6 addresses only the minimum safety requirements for the special equipment it covers and that, in most cases, other standards also apply. The *NEC* isn't meant as a substitute for those other standards. So before you begin work on any of this special equipment, first obtain the standards written for it. If you're not sure what standards apply, contact the manufacturer for assistance.

- **Article 600—Electric Signs and Outline Lighting.** This article covers the installation of conductors and equipment for electric signs and outline lighting as defined in Article 100. Electric signs and outline lighting include all products and installations that utilize neon tubing, such as signs, decorative elements, skeleton tubing, or art forms.
- **Article 604—Manufactured Wiring Systems.** Article 604 covers field-installed manufactured wiring systems used for branch circuits, remote-control circuits, signaling circuits, and communications circuits in accessible areas. The components of a listed manufactured wiring system can be assembled at the jobsite.
- **Article 620—Elevators, Escalators, and Moving Walks.** This article covers electrical equipment and wiring used in connection with elevators, dumbwaiters, escalators, moving walks, wheelchair lifts, and stairway chair lifts.
- **Article 625—Electric Vehicle Charging System.** An electrically-powered vehicle needs a dedicated charging circuit. And that's where Article 625 comes in. It provides the requirements for the electrical equipment needed to charge automotive-type electric and hybrid vehicles, including cars, bikes, and buses.
- **Article 640—Audio Signal Processing, Amplification, and Reproduction Equipment.** Article 640 covers equipment and wiring for audio signal generation, recording, processing, amplification and reproduction, distribution of sound, public address, speech input systems, temporary audio system installations, and electronic musical instruments such as electric organs, electric guitars, and electronic drums/percussion.
- **Article 645—Information Technology Equipment.** This article applies to equipment, power-supply wiring, equipment interconnecting wiring and grounding of information technology equipment and systems, including terminal units in an information technology equipment room.
- **Article 646—Modular Data Centers.** Article 646 applies to portable data centers, which are typically used when a facility needs more data equipment that it currently has. Modular data centers vary greatly in size, and are typically not permanent facilities.
- **Article 680—Swimming Pools, Spas, Hot Tubs, Fountains, and Similar Installations.** This article covers the installation of electric wiring and equipment that supplies swimming, wading, therapeutic and decorative pools, fountains, hot tubs, spas, and hydromassage bathtubs, whether permanently installed or storable.
- **Article 690—Solar Photovoltaic (PV) Systems.** The provisions of this article will be covered in a separate, standalone textbook, *Changes to the NEC 2014—Solar PV Systems Edition.* For more information call 888.632.2633.

ARTICLE 600 ELECTRIC SIGNS AND OUTLINE LIGHTING

Introduction to Article 600—Electric Signs and Outline Lighting

One of the first things you notice when entering a strip mall is that there's a sign for every store. Every commercial occupancy needs a form of identification, and the standard method is the electric sign; thus, 600.5 requires a sign outlet for the entrance of each tenant location. Article 600 requires a disconnecting means within sight of a sign unless it can be locked in the open position.

> **Author's Comment:** Article 100 defines an electric sign as any "fixed, stationary, or portable self-contained, electrically illuminated utilization equipment with words or symbols designed to convey information or attract attention."

Another requirement is height. Freestanding signs, such as those that might be erected in a parking lot, must be located at least 14 ft above vehicle areas unless they're protected from physical damage.

Neon art forms or decorative elements are subsets of electric signs and outline lighting. If installed and not attached to an enclosure or sign body, they're considered skeleton tubing for the purpose of applying the requirements of Article 600. However, if that neon tubing is attached to an enclosure or sign body, which may be a simple support frame, it's considered a sign or outline lighting subject to all of the provisions that apply to signs and outline lighting, such as 600.3, which requires the product to be listed.

600.3 Listing

Retrofit kits must now be listed, and instructions must now be included with signs.

Part I. General

600.3 Listing. Electric signs, section signs, retrofit kits, and outline lighting—fixed, mobile, or portable—regardless of voltage, must be listed and installed in accordance with the listing instructions, which must be included with the sign, except as permitted in (A) or (B). Figure 600–1

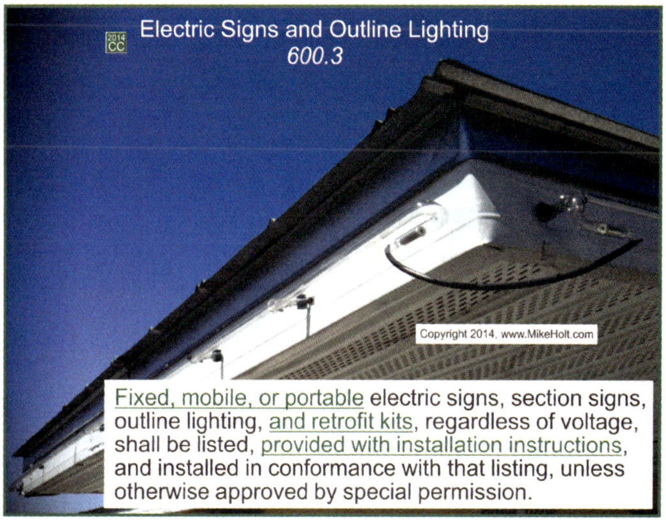

Figure 600–1

(A) Field-Installed Skeleton Tubing. Field-installed skeleton tubing isn't required to be listed.

(B) Outline Lighting. Field-installed outline lighting isn't required to be listed if wired in accordance with Chapter 3.

ANALYSIS: With energy conservation being taken more seriously than perhaps ever before, retrofitting luminaires into higher efficiency models, such as LEDs, has become quite popular. Although an LED luminaire certainly uses less energy, they aren't any safer from a shock or fire perspective if they're installed incorrectly. In an effort to ensure that a bunch of mix-and-match components aren't used for retrofits, the *Code* is requiring the use of a listed retrofit assembly.

Although following instructions has historically been a problem for the male gender of our species, it's still important. Following instructions is infinitely easier, however, if you actually possess them! This change will mandate that manufacturers provide instructions for their products, and hopefully they'll be read and followed by those in the field.

600.4 Markings

The requirement to mark equipment with language regarding instructions has been expanded.

600.4 Markings.

(E) Section Signs. All signs, outline lighting, skeleton tubing systems and retrofit kits must be marked to indicate that field-wiring and installation instructions are required.

Ex: Portable, cord-connected signs aren't required to be marked.

ANALYSIS: It's important to follow the instructions that are included with any electrical equipment. The requirement that manufacturers mark their equipment to state that instructions are included is intended to inform an inspector that there are instructions that will help him or her perform the inspection. This concept holds true not only for section signs (as required in 2011), but outline lighting, retrofit kits, and skeleton tubing as well.

600.6 Disconnecting Means

The location of the sign disconnect is now addressed.

600.6 Disconnecting Means. Each circuit for a sign, outline lighting system, or skeleton tubing must be controlled by an externally-operable switch or circuit breaker that will open all ungrounded conductors, Figure 600–2. Where the circuit is a multiwire branch circuit, the switch or circuit breaker must open all ungrounded conductors of the circuit simultaneously.

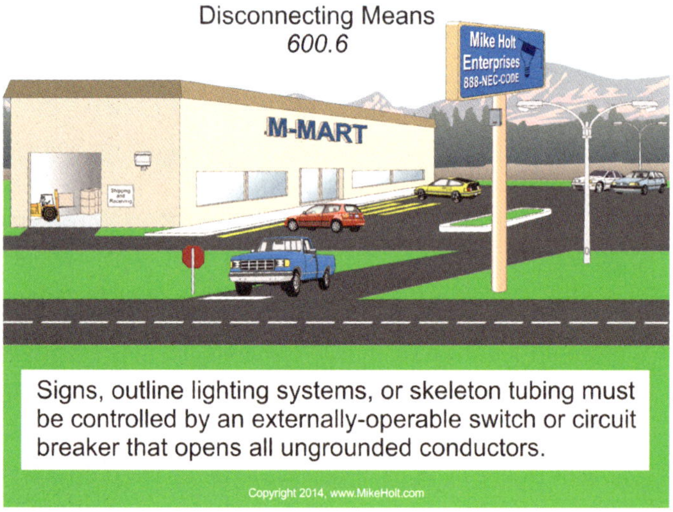

Figure 600–2

(A) Location.

(1) At Point of Entry to a Sign Enclosure. The disconnect must be located at the point where the conductors for a sign or outline lighting system enter a sign enclosure or pole, and it must disconnect all conductors of the circuit. Figure 600–3

Ex: The disconnect isn't required when the conductors are in a raceway and pass through the sign.

(2) Within Sight of Sign. The disconnecting means must be within sight of the sign or outline lighting system. Figure 600–4

If the disconnecting means is out of the line of sight from any section of the sign or outline lighting able to be energized, the disconnecting means must be lockable, as described in 110.25. Figure 600–5

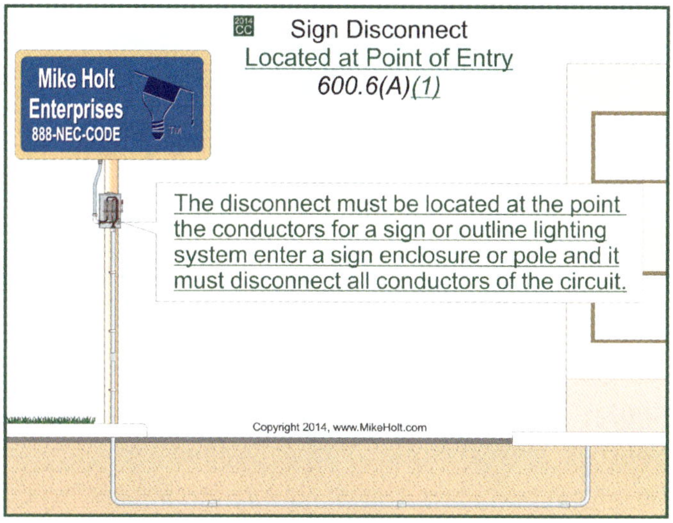

Figure 600–3

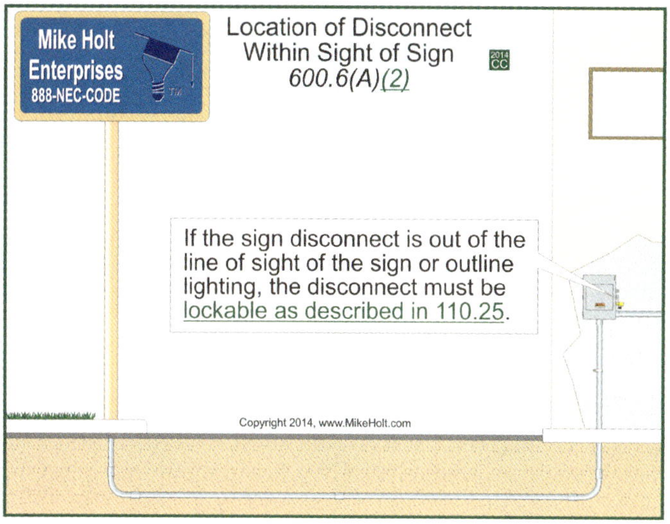

Figure 600–5

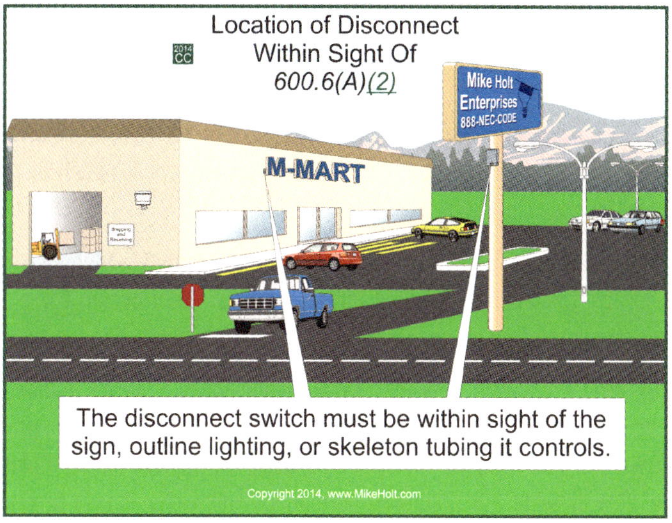

Figure 600–4

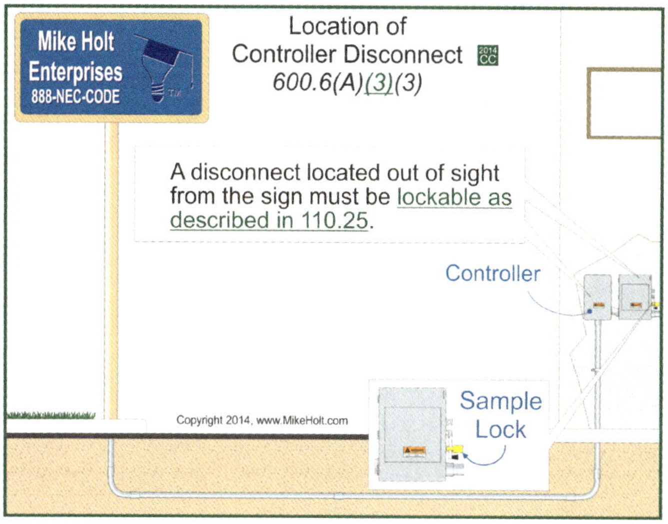

Figure 600–6

Author's Comment: According to Article 100, "within sight" means that it's visible and not more than 50 ft from one to the other.

(3) Within Sight of the Controller. Signs or outline lighting systems operated by electronic or electromechanical controllers located external to the sign or outline lighting system must have the disconnecting means installed in accordance with (1) through (3):

(1) Located within sight of or in the same enclosure with the controller.

(2) Be capable of disconnecting the sign or outline lighting and the controller from all ungrounded supply conductors.

(3) Be lockable, as described in 110.25. Figure 600–6

ANALYSIS: Although signs have had disconnect requirements for quite some time, its physical location has been a gray area of the *Code*. By ensuring that the disconnect is installed at the point that the conductors enter the sign, installers can rest assured that all of the conductors inside the enclosure are de-energized. According to the submitter of this proposal, who represents the International Sign Association, sign disconnects are often installed in odd locations, which results in some of the conductors in the enclosure remaining energized with the switch in the off position. This change should enhance worker safety, which is always something worth doing.

600.7 Grounding and Bonding

The requirements for connection to an equipment grounding conductor have been revised to include skeleton tubing.

600.7 Grounding and Bonding.

(A) Grounding.

(1) Equipment Grounding. Metal equipment of signs, outline lighting systems, and skeleton tubing must be connected to the circuit equipment grounding conductor of the supply circuit using an equipment grounding conductor recognized in 250.118. Figure 600–7

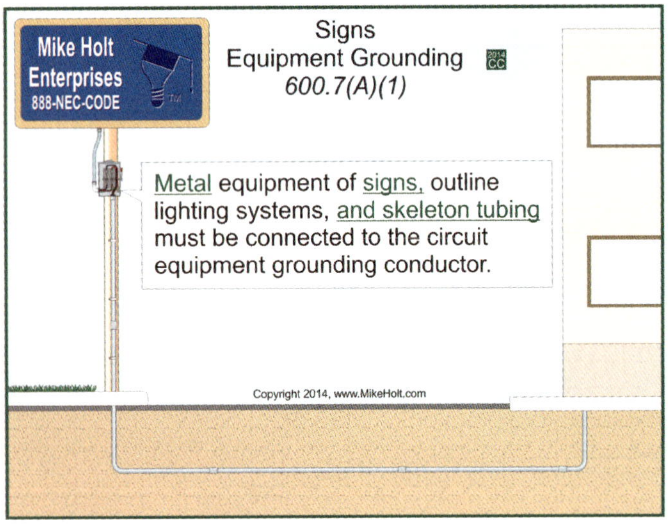

Figure 600–7

ANALYSIS: Skeleton tubing can operate at over 1,000 volts, yet there was no rule discussing the connection to an equipment grounding conductor in previous editions of this rule. Obviously the metal parts of these systems are dangerous (deadly) if energized, so they're now included in the requirement.

This section was also cleaned up editorially by changing the phrase, "Signs and metal equipment of outline lighting systems..." to "Metal equipment of signs, outline lighting, and skeleton tubing systems..." That helps make it clear that metal parts are the issue here, not the nonconductive surfaces, lamps, or similar components.

600.21 Ballasts, Transformers, Class 2 Power Sources, and Electronic Power Supplies

The location requirements for transformers and similar equipment now include Class 2 power supplies. Enclosures for these pieces of equipment are now addressed as well.

600.21 Ballasts, Transformers, Class 2 Power Sources, and Electronic Power Supplies. Ballasts, transformers, electronic power supplies, and Class 2 Power Sources must be self-contained or enclosed in a listed sign body or listed separate enclosure.

(A) Accessibility. Ballasts, transformers, Class 2 power sources, and electronic power supplies must be accessible and must be securely fastened in place.

(B) Location. The secondary conductors from ballasts, transformers, Class 2 power sources, and electronic power supplies must be as short as possible.

(D) Working Space. A working space not less than 3 ft high by 3 ft wide by 3 ft deep is required for each ballast, transformer, Class 2 power source, and electronic power supply if not installed in a sign.

(E) Attic Locations. Ballasts, transformers, Class 2 power sources, and electronic power supplies are permitted in attics and soffits, provided there's an access door and a passageway not less than 3 ft high by 22½ in. wide with a suitable permanent walkway at least 1 ft wide to the point of entry for each component.

At least one lighting outlet that contains a switch or is controlled by a wall switch must be installed at the usual point of entry to these spaces. The lighting outlet must be located at or near the equipment requiring servicing.

(F) Suspended Ceilings. Ballasts, transformers, electronic power supplies, and Class 2 power sources can be above a suspended ceiling, provided the enclosures are securely fastened in place and don't use the suspended-ceiling grid for support. Ballasts, transformers, and electronic power supplies installed above a suspended ceiling must not be connected to the branch-circuit wiring by a flexible cord. Figure 600–8

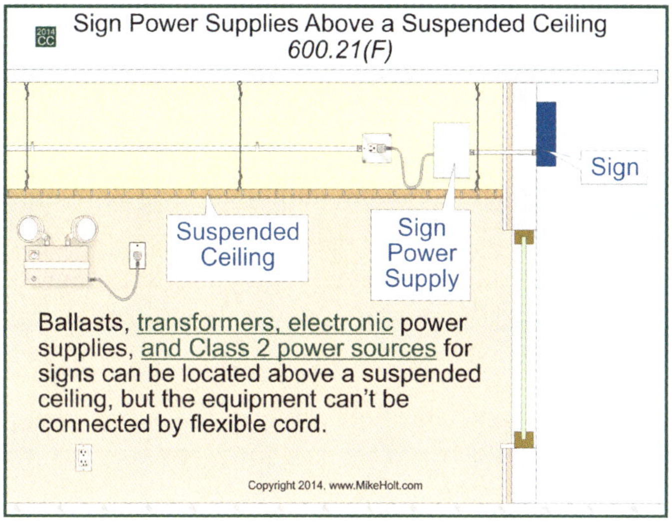

Figure 600–8

Author's Comment: 400.8(2) and (5) prohibit flexible cords from being installed through, or above, a suspended ceiling.

ANALYSIS: In previous editions of the *Code*, there were no rules that required an enclosure for a sign's power supply. The product standard for signs (UL 48) requires that power supplies be contained in some sort of an enclosure, but the *Code* was silent on the issue. Because product standards aren't free, and are often quite expensive, the average installer or inspector won't have them. By including the requirements in the *NEC* the rules are now available to any *Code* user.

Class 2 power supplies are now discussed in this section. Class 2 circuits are considered safe as they relate to fire and shock (see the definition of Class 2 circuit in 725.2). While the output of a Class 2 power supply is safe, the input side of the power supply is usually 120V, which isn't safe. Because of the dangers involved with working near 120V equipment, the rules discussed here for location, working space, access, and so on, have been expanded to include Class 2 power supplies.

ARTICLE 620 ELEVATORS, ESCALATORS, AND MOVING WALKS

Introduction to Article 620—Elevators, Escalators, and Moving Walks

With the exception of dumbwaiters, the equipment covered by Article 620 moves people. Thus, a major concept in this article is that of keeping people separate from electrical power. That's why, for example, 620.3 requires live parts to be enclosed. Article 620 consists of 10 parts:

- **Part I—General.** This part provides the scope of the article, definitions, and voltage limitations.
- **Part II—Conductors.** The single-line diagram of Figure 620.13 shown in the *NEC* book illustrates how the requirements of Part II work together.
- **Part III—Wiring.** This addresses wiring methods and branch-circuit requirements for different equipment.
- **Part IV—Installation of Conductors.** This covers conductor fill, supports, and related items.
- **Part V—Traveling Cables.** Installation, suspension, location, and protection of cables that move with the motion of the elevator or lift are all covered.
- **Part VI—Disconnecting Means and Control.** The requirements vary with the application.
- **Part VII—Overcurrent Protection.** While most of this part refers to Article 430, it does include additional requirements, such as providing selective coordination.
- **Part VIII—Machine and Control Rooms and Spaces.** The primary goal here is the prevention of unauthorized access.
- **Part IX—Equipment Grounding Conductor.** While most of this part refers to Article 250, it includes additional requirements as well. For example, 15A and 20A, 125V receptacles in certain locations must be GFCI protected.
- **Part X—Emergency and Standby Systems.** This deals with regenerative power and with the need for a disconnecting means that can disconnect an elevator from both the normal power system and the emergency or standby system.

620.51 Disconnecting Means

The disconnecting means requirements have been revised for consistency with other *Code* rules.

Part VI. Disconnecting means and Control

620.51 Disconnecting Means. A disconnecting means must be provided with a means to simultaneously disconnect all ungrounded main power-supply conductors for each unit.

(A) Type. The disconnecting means must be an externally operable fused motor-circuit switch or circuit breaker that's lockable, as described in 110.25. Figure 620–1

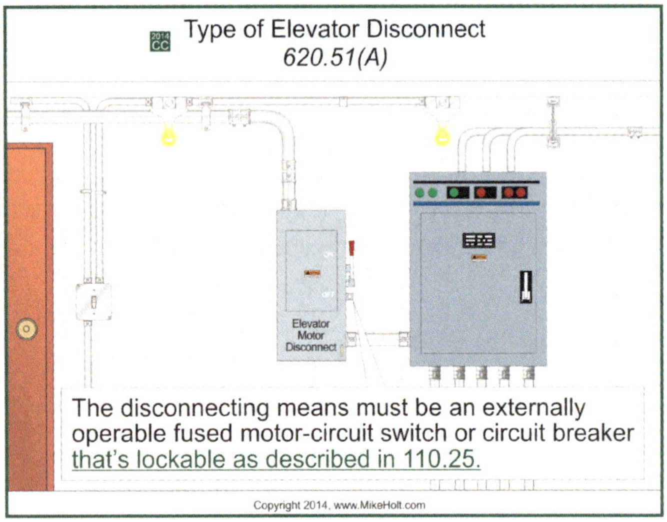

Figure 620–1

Note: See ASME A17/CSA B44, *Safety Code for Elevators and Escalators*, for additional information for the disconnecting means.

ANALYSIS: When different *NEC* articles have the same requirements it's nearly impossible to make them all say the same thing. The rules for equipment requiring a disconnect can be found in nearly every article of the *Code*. In order for all of the rules to say the same thing, you have to have one rule, and it has to cover all of the requirements. 110.25 was added to achieve the goal of consistency throughout the *NEC*, and by requiring compliance with it in this rule we have a consistent *Code*.

ARTICLE 640 AUDIO SIGNAL PROCESSING, AMPLIFICATION, AND REPRODUCTION EQUIPMENT

Introduction to Article 640—Audio Signal Processing, Amplification, and Reproduction Equipment

If you understand the three major goals of Article 640, you'll be able to better understand and apply the requirements. These three goals are to:

- Reduce the spread of fire and smoke.
- Comply with other articles.
- Prevent shock. This article includes several requirements, such as specifics in the mechanical execution of work, and requirements when audio equipment is located near bodies of water to reduce shock hazards peculiar to audio equipment installations.

In addition, Article 640 distinguishes between permanent and temporary audio installations. Part II provides requirements for permanent installations, and Part III provides requirements for temporary installations.

640.1 Scope

The scope of this article has been revised to clarify what it does and doesn't cover.

Part I. General

640.1 Scope.

(A) Covered. Article 640 covers equipment and wiring for audio distribution of sound and public address systems, including temporary audio system installations.

Note: Permanently installed distributed audio system locations include, but aren't limited to, restaurants, hotels, business offices, commercial and retail sales environments, churches, and schools. Temporary installations include, but aren't limited to, auditoriums, theaters, stadiums, and outdoor events such as fairs, festivals, circuses, public events, and concerts.

(B) Not Covered. This article doesn't cover fire and burglary alarms.

ANALYSIS: Article 760 covers fire alarms and Article 725 covers signaling circuits for burglar alarms. Some *Code* users have struggled with this, because a fire alarm horn is certainly an audible device, and Article 640 covers audio stuff. Previous editions of the *NEC* contained a note in this section telling us that fire and burglar alarms aren't covered here, but why should it be a note instead of part of the scope? This change corrects the issue by moving that language into enforceable text.

640.10 Audio Systems Near Bodies of Water

An editorial revision should help clarify the rules regarding audio equipment near swimming pools and similar bodies of water.

640.10 Audio Systems Near Bodies of Water. Audio systems near bodies of water, either natural or artificial, are subject to the restrictions in (A) and (B).

Note: See 680.27(A) for the requirements of underwater audio equipment near pools, spas, and hot tubs.

(A) Branch-Circuit Power. Audio system equipment supplied by a branch circuit must not be placed horizontally within 5 ft of the inside wall of a pool, spa, hot tub, fountain, or tidal high-water mark. Figure 640–1

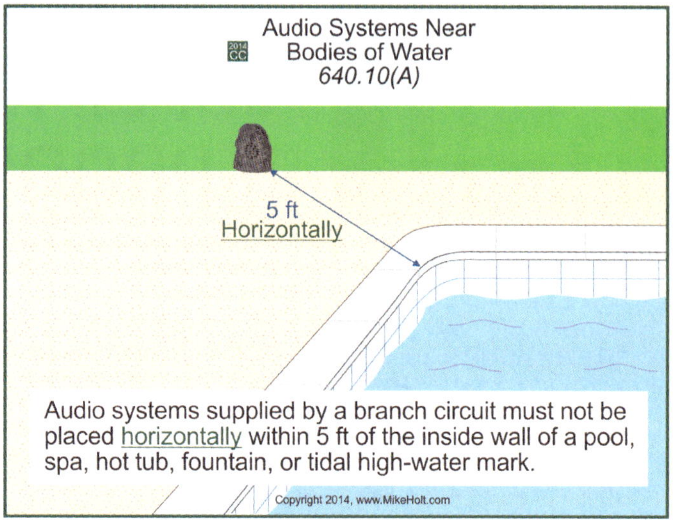

Figure 640–1

ANALYSIS: Although the word "laterally" is defined as, basically, "side-to-side," there was confusion over the term. By using the word "horizontally" the confusion should be minimized, as that term is used throughout the *Code*.

ARTICLE 645 INFORMATION TECHNOLOGY EQUIPMENT

Introduction to Article 645—Information Technology Equipment

One of the unique things about Article 645 is the requirement for a shutoff switch readily accessible from the exit doors of information technology equipment rooms [645.10]. This requirement seems to be wrong on its face because it allows someone to shut power to the IT room off from a single point. So despite having a UPS and taking every precaution against a power outage, the IT system is still vulnerable to a shutdown from a readily accessible switch at the principal exit doors.

What was the *Code*-Making Panel thinking of when they added this requirement? They were thinking of fire and rescue teams. Having a means to shut down the power and disconnect the batteries before entering the IT room during a fire allows the rescue team to use fire hoses and other equipment without risking contact with energized equipment. Yes, there's loss of IT function during the shutdown, but if the room needs fire and rescue teams, loss of the IT function is the least of its problems at that time. The shutdown allows the rescue of people and property. A breakaway lock can protect the IT room from inadvertent shutdown via this switch.

What about the rest of Article 645? The major goal is to reduce the spread of fire and smoke. The raised floors common in IT rooms pose additional challenges to achieving this goal, so this article devotes a fair percentage of its text to raised floor requirements. Fire-resistant walls, separate HVAC systems, and other requirements further help to achieve this goal.

645.14 System Grounding

A new section for separately derived systems has been added.

645.14 System Grounding. Separately derived systems must comply with 250.30. Power supplies within listed IT equipment that supply IT equipment through receptacles or cables aren't considered separately derived systems.

ANALYSIS: This section was added in order to make 645.15 (having to do with the equipment grounding conductor) a bit easier to understand. In previous editions of the *Code*, there was information about the equipment grounding conductor (EGC), then information about separately derived systems, then more information on the EGC. This change goes a long away in cleaning up this part of the article.

Notes

ARTICLE 646 MODULAR DATA CENTERS

Introduction to Article 646 Modular Data Centers

Modular data centers are a portable method of providing or increasing data center capacity. They consist of communications and power equipment, such as servers, and networking and cooling equipment. They can be shipped to a customer anywhere they're needed.

The most common type is the "containerized" or "portable modular" data center which is a typical shipping container that holds data center equipment and is placed at the customer's site.

Article 646—Modular Data Centers

A new article for modular data centers has been created.

ANALYSIS: With the always growing demand for data capacity, modular units are often being used when additional data capacity and functionality are needed. These units are portable, and vary greatly in size. This new article contains very little that isn't already required elsewhere in the *NEC*, but will probably change dramatically over the next few *Code* cycles.

Article 646 Modular Data Centers

This article covers modular data centers, which are prefabricated units, enclosing racks or cabinets of IT equipment, as well as support equipment, such as electrical service and distribution equipment and HVAC systems [646.2].

Notes

ARTICLE 680 SWIMMING POOLS, SPAS, HOT TUBS, FOUNTAINS, AND SIMILAR INSTALLATIONS

Introduction to Article 680—Swimming Pools, Spas, Hot Tubs, Fountains, and Similar Installations

The requirements contained in Article 680 apply to the installation of electrical wiring and equipment for swimming pools, spas, hot tubs, fountains, and hydromassage bathtubs. The overriding concern of Article 680 is to keep people and electricity separated.

This article is divided into seven parts. The various parts apply to certain types of installations, so be careful to determine which parts of this article apply to what and where. For instance, Part I and Part II apply to spas and hot tubs installed outdoors, except as modified in Part IV. In contrast, hydromassage bathtubs are only covered by Part VII. Read the details of this article carefully so you'll be able to provide a safe installation.

- **Part I—General.**
- **Part II—Permanently Installed Pools.** Installations at permanently installed pools must comply with both Parts I and II of this article.
- **Part III—Storable Swimming Pools, Storable Spas, and Storable Hot Tubs.** Installations of storable pools, storable spas, and storable hot tubs must comply with Parts I and III of Article 680.
- **Part IV—Spas and Hot Tubs.** Spas and hot tubs must comply with Parts I and IV of this article; outdoor spas and hot tubs must also comply with Part II in accordance with 680.42.
- **Part V—Fountains.** Parts I and II apply to permanently installed fountains. If they have water in common with a pool, Part II also applies. Self-contained, portable fountains are covered by Article 422, Parts II and III.
- **Part VI—Pools and Tubs for Therapeutic Use.** Parts I and VI apply to pools and tubs for therapeutic use in health care facilities, gymnasiums, athletic training rooms and similar installations. If they're portable appliances, then Article 422, Parts II and III apply.
- **Part VII—Hydromassage Bathtubs.** Part VI applies to hydromassage bathtubs, but no other parts of Article 680 do.

680.2 Definitions—Storable Swimming Pool

The definition for "storable pool" has been expanded.

Part I. General Requirements for Pools, Spas, Hot Tubs, and Fountains

680.2 Definitions.

Author's Comment: The requirements contained in Part I of Article 680 apply to permanently installed pools [680.20], storable pools [680.30], spas and hot tubs [680.42 and 680.43], and fountains [680.50].

Storable Swimming Pool or Storable/Portable Spas and Hot Tubs. An aboveground pool, or spa, or hot tub with a maximum water depth of 42 in. **Figure 680–1**

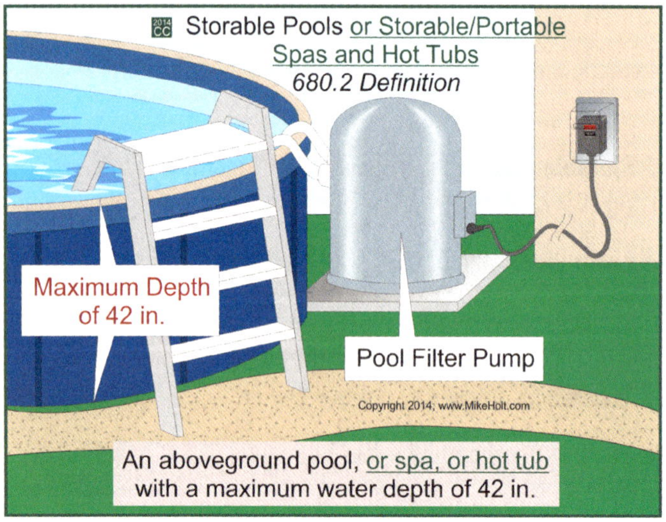

Figure 680–1

Author's Comment: Storable pools are sold as a complete package that consists of the pool walls, vinyl liner, plumbing kit, and pump/filter device. Underwriters Laboratories, Inc. (UL) requires the pump/filter units to have a minimum 25 ft cord to discourage the use of extension cords.

ANALYSIS: Portable spas and hot tubs have been available for quite some time, but somehow weren't clearly addressed in this article. In order to clarify which rules govern their installation, this definition was revised to include portable or storable spas and hot tubs. Similar changes were made in Part III of this article to correlate with these changes.

680.8 Overhead Conductor Clearance

The requirements for overhead clearances were revised to catch up with changes made in 2011.

680.8 Overhead Conductor Clearance. Overhead conductors must meet the clearance requirements contained in Table 680.8. The clearance is measured from the maximum water level.

(A) Overhead Power Conductors. Permanently installed swimming pools, storable pools, outdoor spas, outdoor hot tubs, fountains, diving structures, observation stands, towers, or platforms near overhead service conductors and other overhead conductors must not be placed within the clearances contained in the *NEC*, Table 680.8(A). **Figure 680–2**

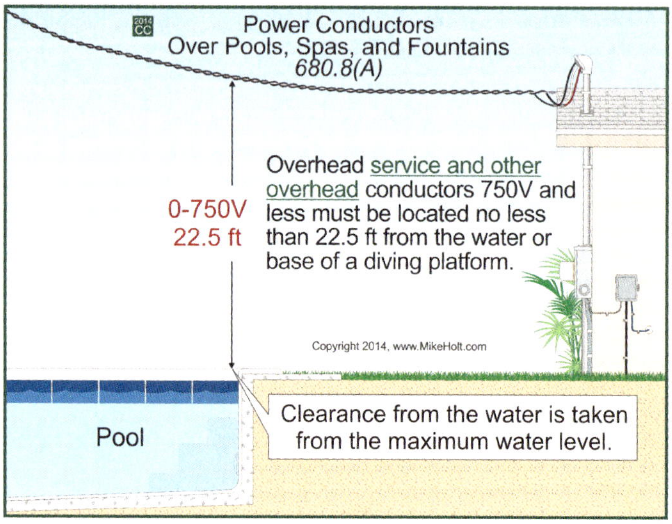

Figure 680–2

Author's Comment: This rule doesn't prohibit utility-owned overhead service-drop conductors from being installed over a permanently installed pool, storable pool, outdoor spa, outdoor hot tub, or fountain [90.2(B)(5)]. It does prohibit a permanently installed pool, storable pool, outdoor spa, outdoor hot tub, or fountain from being installed under an existing service drop that isn't at least 22½ ft above the water.

ANALYSIS: It's nearly impossible to make a global change throughout the *NEC* and not miss a few things. In 2011, the *Code* made changes to "service" related terms, such as service drop, service conductors, service point, and so forth. These terms are used in nearly every article of the *NEC*, and trying to catch all of them in one try is nearly impossible. When these changes occurred in 2011, the different committees and individuals involved did a truly remarkable job of catching almost every instance of these terms, but this is one that was missed.

680.11 Equipment Rooms and Pits

A change to this section attempts to remove interpretation.

680.11 Equipment Rooms and Pits. Permanently installed pool, storable pool, outdoor spa, outdoor hot tub, or fountain equipment must not be located in rooms or pits that don't have drainage <u>that prevents</u> water accumulation during normal operation or filter maintenance. Figure 680–3

ANALYSIS: The *NEC* Style Manual contains a list of terms that shouldn't be used in the *Code*. The term "adequate" is on the that list, so proposals were made throughout the *NEC* to remove it where possible. By deleting this word, it doesn't appear that anything has really changed.

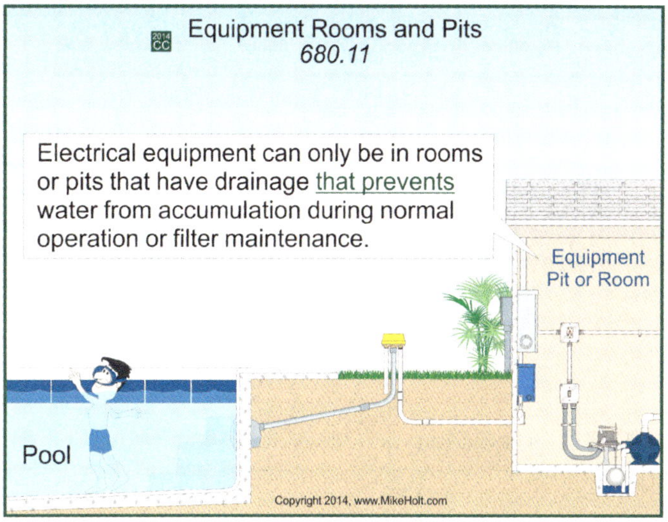

Figure 680–3

680.12 Maintenance Disconnecting Means

Fountains are now included in the disconnecting means requirements.

680.12 Maintenance Disconnecting Means. A maintenance disconnecting means is required for the permanently installed pool, storable pool, outdoor spa, outdoor hot tub, <u>or fountain equipment</u>, other than lighting, for these water bodies.

The maintenance disconnecting means must be readily accessible and located within sight and at least 5 ft from the permanently installed pool, storable pool, outdoor spa, outdoor hot tub, <u>or fountain equipment</u> unless separated from the open water by a permanently installed barrier that provides a 5-foot reach path or greater. This horizontal distance is measured from the water's edge along the shortest path required to reach the disconnecting means. Figure 680–4

Author's Comment: According to Article 100, "within sight" means that it's visible and not more than 50 ft from one to the other.

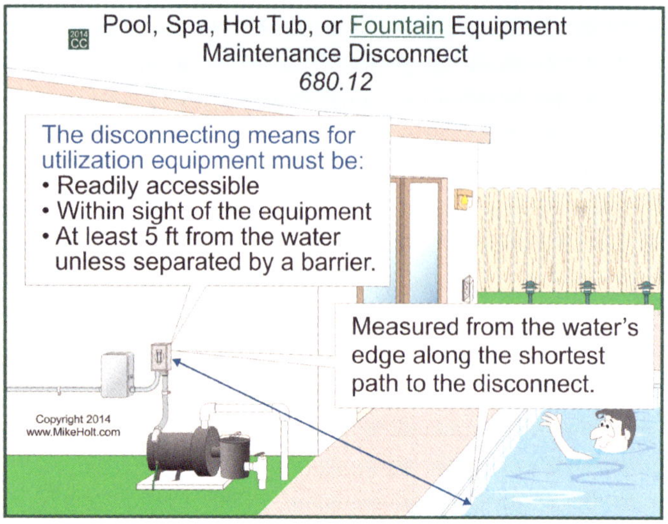

Figure 680–4

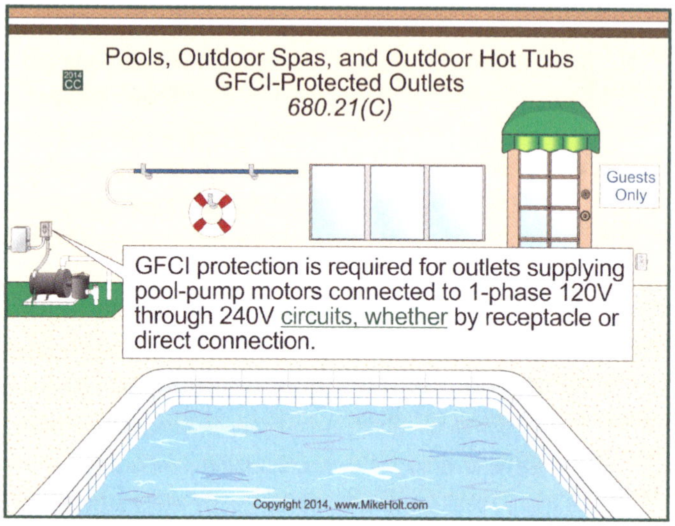

Figure 680–5

ANALYSIS: This rule, like many others, requires a disconnecting means for equipment so that personnel performing work on the equipment can do so safely. Interestingly, nearly every type of equipment discussed in this article was included in this section, except fountains. This was probably just an oversight, so fountains have now been added here.

680.21 Motors

The requirement for GFCI protection of swimming pool motors has been expanded.

Part II. Permanently Installed Pools, Outdoor Spas, and Outdoor Hot Tubs

680.20 General. The installation requirements contained in Part I and Part II apply to permanently installed pools [680.20], spas and hot tubs [680.42 and 680.43].

680.21 Motors.

(C) GFCI Protection. GFCI protection is required for outlets supplying pool pump motors connected to single-phase, 120V through 240V branch circuits, whether by receptacle or by direct connection. Figure 680–5

ANALYSIS: Previous editions of the *Code* required GFCI protection for swimming pool motors if the circuit supplying the motor was 15A or 20A. It's pretty tough to argue that the swimming pool should have less protection if it's fed by a larger circuit (in fact, most will say that it's impossible to argue that point). Due to this apparent flaw in logic, the *NEC* has been changed to mandate GFCI protection for the motor regardless of the circuit ampacity, provided that the motor is on a 120V through 240V circuit.

680.22 Lighting, Receptacles, and Equipment

The requirement for a locking-type receptacle has been removed, and the rule for providing a convenience receptacle has been expanded.

680.22 Lighting, Receptacles, and Equipment.

(A) Receptacles.

(1) Required Receptacle Location. One 15A or 20A, 125V receptacle must be located not less than 6 ft and not more than 20 ft from the inside walls of a permanently installed pool, outdoor spa, or outdoor hot tub. This receptacle must be located not more than 6½ ft above the floor, platform, or grade level serving the permanently installed pool, outdoor spa, or outdoor hot tub. Figure 680–6

Figure 680–6

(2) **Circulation System.** Receptacles for permanently installed pool, outdoor spa, and outdoor hot tub motors, or other loads directly related to the circulation system must be located not less than 10 ft from the inside walls of a permanently installed pool, outdoor spa, or outdoor hot tub, or not less than 6 ft from the inside walls of a permanently installed pool, outdoor spa, or outdoor hot tub if they meet all of the following conditions: Figure 680–7

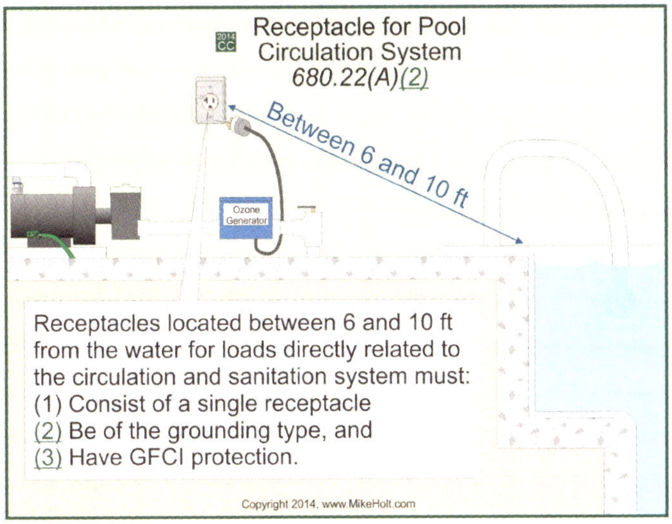

Figure 680–7

(1) Consist of a single receptacle

(2) Be of the grounding type

(3) Have GFCI protection

(3) **Other Receptacles.** Receptacles not for motors or other loads directly related to the circulation system must be not less than 6 ft from the inside walls of a permanently installed pool, outdoor spa, or outdoor hot tub. Figure 680–8

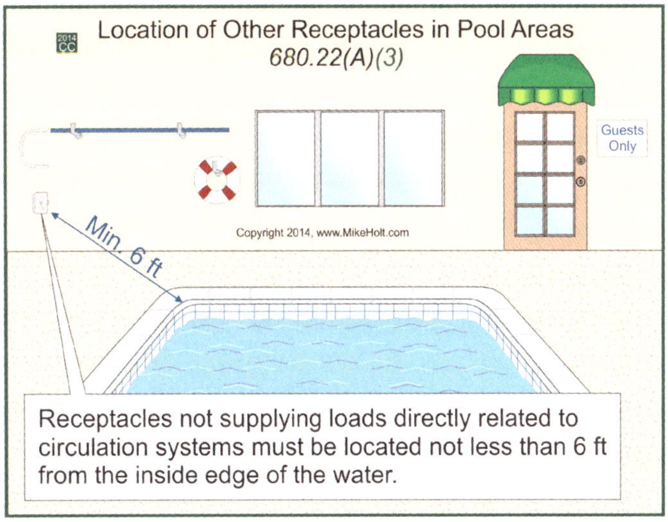

Figure 680–8

ANALYSIS: Previous editions of the *Code* required a receptacle within 20 ft of a swimming pool, but only if the pool was installed at a dwelling unit. The requirement for a convenience receptacle within 20 ft of a pool is intended to provide a way for people to use electricity for all sorts of items without having to resort to an extension cord. For example, if I'm having a pool party in my backyard, I may want to plug in a radio to listen to music. By providing a receptacle within 20 ft of the pool, we can ensure that the radio will remain a safe distance away from it. If we don't have this receptacle an extension cord will probably be used, and there will be no way of preventing the people from placing the radio right next to the pool, where (especially if alcohol is involved), it will likely end up in the water. While this scenario is easy to visualize in a residential environment, it can certainly happen in a commercial setting as well. With the *Code* now requiring this receptacle for commercial pools [680.22(A)(1)] we can avoid this potentially deadly scenario.

A change that was made to 680.22(A)(2) is quite subtle, and probably won't be noticed by most people. The receptacle for a pool circulation system must be 10 ft from the pool, unless it's a GFCI-protected, singular, grounding type, and (previously) locking-type. If these criteria are met, the receptacle can be as close as 6 ft from the pool. Other receptacles (that aren't for the circulation system) can already be 6 ft from the pool and don't need to be of the locking type [680.22(A)(2)], so why does this one have to be a locking-type receptacle? Well, it no longer does.

ANALYSIS: Once again, when new rules find themselves in the *Code*, it takes a couple of years to fill in all of the gaps. In 2011 the *NEC* introduced us to the concept of the "low-voltage contact limit." These luminaires are safer than others due to their voltage limitations and should therefore have fewer restrictions. This change will allow these luminaires to be installed less than 5 ft from the pool.

680.22 Lighting, Receptacles, and Equipment

Low-voltage luminaires are now addressed in this section.

680.22 Lighting, Receptacles, and Equipment.

(B) Luminaires and Ceiling Fans.

(6) Low-Voltage Luminaires. Listed luminaires that don't require grounding, and that meet the low-voltage contact limit, can be less than 5 ft from the inside walls of the pool. Figure 680–9

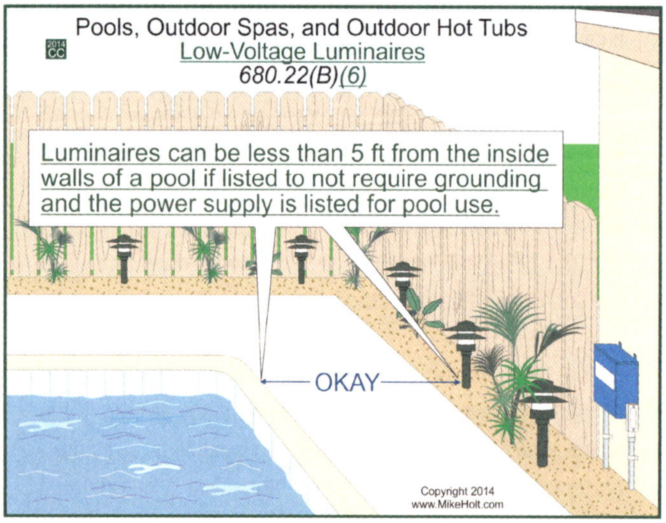

Figure 680–9

Author's Comment: The Low-Voltage Contact Limit is defined in 680.2.

680.26 Equipotential Bonding

The requirement to "bond" pool water has been editorially revised.

680.26 Equipotential Bonding.

(C) Pool Water. Pool water must have an electrical connection to one of the bonded parts described in 680.26(B), or the pool water must be in contact with a corrosion-resistant surface that's at least 9 sq in., bonded in accordance with 680.26(B). This corrosion-resistant surface must also be located in an area where it won't be dislodged or damaged during normal pool usage. Figures 680–10 and 680–11

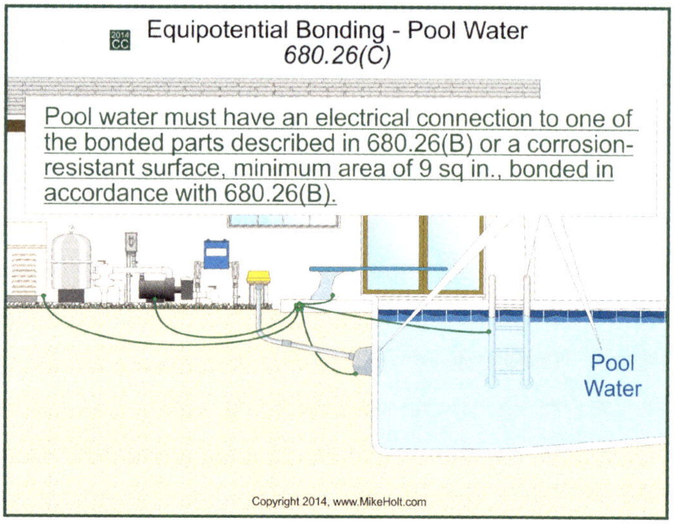

Figure 680–10

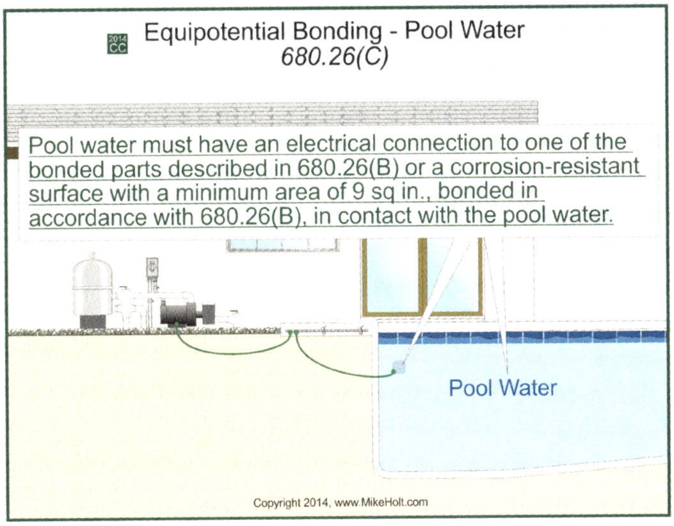

Figure 680–11

ANALYSIS: Previous editions of the *NEC* stated that the pool water must be "bonded." Because "bonded" is a defined term, people had a hard time understanding what the requirement in this section was really trying to say. This change gets rid of the idea of "bonding the water" altogether, and while not making any real difference, it gets rid of a misuse of defined terms. This change also dictates that the item making contact with the pool water must be in an area that isn't going to get dislodged in the pool. This seems like a good idea, and adds a common sense requirement to a *Code* section that can use all of the help it can get.

Article 680—Part III. Storable Swimming Pools, Storable Spas, and Storable Hot Tubs

Changes to the title and subsequent sections clarify what this Part of the article applies to.

Part III. Storable Swimming Pools, Storable Spas, and Storable Hot Tubs

680.30 General. Electrical installations for storable pools, storable spas, and storable hot tubs must also comply with Part I of Article 680.

Author's Comment: The requirements contained in Part I of Article 680 include the locations of switches, receptacles, and luminaires.

ANALYSIS: Portable spas and hot tubs have been available for quite some time, but somehow weren't clearly addressed in this article. In order to clarify which rules govern their installation, the definition of storable pool was revised to include portable or storable spas and hot tubs. Similar changes were made in Part III of this article to correlate with this change.

680.42 Outdoor Installations

The bonding requirements for outdoor spas and hot tubs have been revised (again), and wiring method requirements have been expanded.

Part IV. Spas and Hot Tubs

680.42 Outdoor Installations. Electrical installations for outdoor spas or hot tubs must comply with Parts I and II of this article, except as permitted in (A) or (B).

(B) Bonding. Bonding is permitted by mounting equipment to a metal frame or base. Metal bands that secure wooden staves aren't required to be bonded.

Bonding of perimeter surfaces [680.26(B)(2)] isn't required for spas and hot tubs if the spa or hot tub meets all of the following:

(1) Listed as a self-contained spa for aboveground use.

(2) Not identified as suitable only for indoor use.

(3) Installed in accordance with the manufacturer's instructions and located on or above grade.

(4) The top rim must be at least 28 in. above all perimeter surfaces that are within 30 in. measured horizontally from the spa or hot tub. Nonconductive external steps for entry to the spa can't be used to reduce or increase the rim height measurement.

ANALYSIS: The equipotential bonding requirements for an outdoor spa or hot tub have been puzzling at best for a long time. Changes to 680.42(B) were made in an effort to clarify what the rules are for these pieces of equipment. The bonding requirements for spas and hot tubs are the same as the requirements for swimming pools, other than the perimeter surface allowances that were added by this change. The common installation of an aboveground spa or hot tub doesn't result in any real danger from nearby conductive surfaces, unless the top of the spa or hot tub is less than 28 in. from the surface. When it's that low, a person can have one foot in the water and another on a concrete (or similar) floor, and be in a dangerous predicament should the water be (or become) energized.

(C) Interior Wiring for Outdoor Spas or Hot Tubs. Any Chapter 3 wiring method containing a copper equipment grounding conductor insulated or enclosed within the outer sheath of the wiring method and not smaller than 12 AWG is permitted in the interior of a dwelling unit for the connection to motor, heating, and control loads that are part of a self-contained spa or hot tub, or a packaged spa or hot tub equipment assembly. Figure 680–12

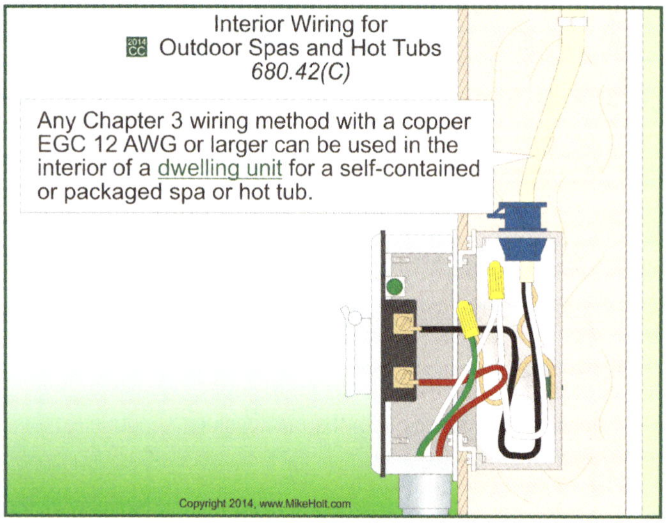

Figure 680–12

Wiring to an underwater light must comply with 680.23 or 680.33.

ANALYSIS: Subsection (C) was modified to allow two-family dwelling units to take advantage of the allowances of this subsection. If the spa or hot tub is installed in a location other than a dwelling unit, the requirements of 680.21(A) requiring RMC, IMC, PVC, EMT, or Type MC cable listed for the location apply.

680.43 Indoor Installations

A new exception for dwelling unit wiring methods for indoor spas and hot tubs has been added for consistency with the rest of the article.

680.43 Indoor Installations. Electrical installations for an indoor spa or hot tub must comply with Parts I and II of Article 680, except as modified by this section. Indoor installations of spas or hot tubs can be connected by any of the wiring methods contained in Chapter 3.

Ex 2: The equipotential bonding requirements for perimeter surfaces contained in 680.26(B)(2) don't apply to a listed self-contained spa or hot tub installed above an indoor finished floor.

Ex 3: The allowances in 680.42(C) for dwelling units can be used.

ANALYSIS: Article 680 is one of the most difficult articles in the *NEC* to navigate. The *Code* user must be very careful to remember which Part of the article they're in. The rule we're currently discussing is found in Part IV, which begins at 680.40 and ends at 680.44. 680.40 tells us that Parts I and IV apply to spas and hot tubs. So, pools and hot tubs must comply with 680.40 through 680.44 (Part IV), as well as 680.1 through 680.12 (Part I). Easy enough, right? Not so fast. 680.42 says that outdoor installations have to comply with Part II as well, which goes from 680.20 through 680.27, unless modified by 680.42(A) or (B). Frustrated yet? It gets worse. Indoor installations must also comply with 680.20 through 680.27 (Part II of the article), except as modified in 680.43! Now that you're an expert at how Article 680 works, please tell me what wiring methods are permitted for indoor spas or hot tubs*. The new exception will save you the headache of trying to figure it out.

*Any Chapter 3 wiring method containing a copper equipment grounding conductor insulated or enclosed within the outer sheath of the wiring method and not smaller than 12 AWG is allowed [680.42(C)].

680.57 Signs in or Adjacent to Fountains

The GFCI requirements for signs in or near fountains have been revised for accuracy.

Part V. Fountains

680.57 Signs in or Adjacent to Fountains.

(B) GFCI Protection of Sign Equipment. Each branch circuit or feeder that supplies a sign installed within a fountain, or within 10 ft of the fountain edge, must be GFCI protected [680.57(A)]. Figure 680–13

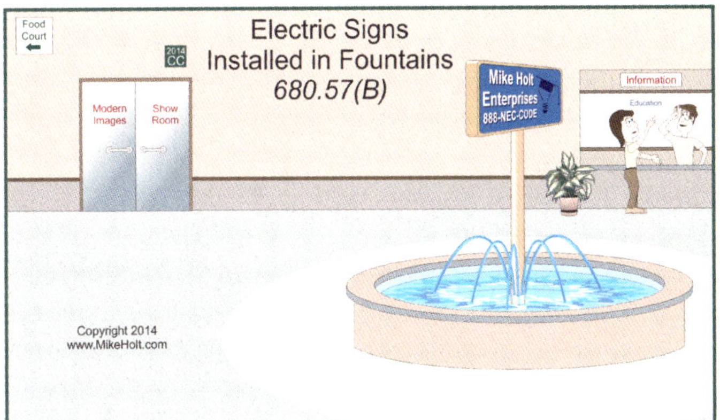

Each branch circuit or feeder that supplies a sign installed within a fountain, or within 10 ft of the fountain edge, must be GFCI protected [680.57(A)].

Figure 680–13

ANALYSIS: Previous versions of this text required GFCI protection for all circuits supplying signs that were in or near a fountain. While this sounds good on the surface, it's actually not quite practical. A signaling circuit, or a communications circuit, feeding a sign isn't going to have GFCI protection, nor should it. It will be interesting to see how many times this mistake occurs in the *Code*, because I, for one, never noticed this one.

680.74 Equipotential Bonding

The strange requirement for bonding hydromassage tub motors has been revised, again.

Part VII. Hydromassage Bathtubs

680.74 Equipotential Bonding. Both metal piping systems and grounded metal parts in contact with the circulating water must be bonded to the hydromassage circulating pump motor that isn't double insulated with an 8 AWG or larger bare copper conductor. Figure 680–14

Both metal piping systems and grounded metal parts in contact with the circulating water must be bonded to the hydromassage circulating pump motor that's not double insulated with an 8 AWG or larger bare solid copper conductor.

Figure 680–14

Where the metal piping systems or grounded metal parts in contact with the circulating water is present with a double-insulated motor, an 8 AWG or larger bare copper conductor must be provided at the hydromassage circulating motor with sufficient length to terminate on a replacement non-double-insulated pump motor. Figure 680–15

Hydromassage Bathtub - Bonding Jumper
680.74

The 8 AWG or larger solid copper equipotential BJ must be long enough to terminate on a replacement non-double-insulated pump, and must terminate to the EGC of the branch circuit of the motor when a double-insulated circulating pump is used.

Figure 680–15

The metal piping to the motor bonding jumper isn't required to be attached to any panelboard, service equipment, or electrode.

ANALYSIS: The requirement for bonding applies only if you have two things: (1) a motor that isn't double insulated, and (2) a metallic water piping system. If you have both of these, you need to bond them together. If either of these two items is missing, you can't possibly bond them together, since one of them is nonexistent. This concept has been difficult for some people to wrap their heads around, so this change was made. We'll see if it helps.

CHAPTER 7 SPECIAL CONDITIONS

Introduction to Chapter 7—Special Conditions

Chapter 7, which covers special conditions, is the third of the *NEC* chapters that deal with special topics. Chapters 5 and 6 cover special occupancies, and special equipment, respectively. Remember, the first four chapters of the *Code* are sequential and form a foundation for each of the subsequent three chapters. Chapter 8 covers communications systems and isn't subject to the requirements of Chapters 1 through 7 except where the requirements are specifically referenced there.

What exactly is a "Special Condition?" It's a situation that doesn't fall under the category of special occupancies or special equipment, but creates a need for additional measures to ensure the "safeguarding of people and property" mission of the *NEC*, as stated in 90.1(A).

The *Code* groups these logically, as you might expect. Here are the general groupings:

- Power systems—Articles 700, 701, and 702. Article 700 addresses emergency systems, Article 701 applies to legally required standby systems, and Article 702 covers optional standby systems.
- Interconnected power sources—Article 705. This primarily has to do with generators or PV systems used for on-site power generation.
- Low-voltage, limited energy systems—Articles 725 through 770. Examples include control, signaling, instrumentation, fire alarm systems, and optical fiber installations.

- **Article 700—Emergency Systems.** The requirements of Article 700 apply only to the wiring methods for "Emergency Systems" that are essential for safety to human life and required by federal, state, municipal, or other regulatory codes. When normal power is lost, emergency systems must be capable of supplying emergency power in 10 seconds or less.

- **Article 701—Legally Required Standby Systems.** Legally required standby systems provide electrical power to aid in firefighting, rescue operations, control of health hazards, and similar operations, and are required by federal, state, municipal, or other regulatory codes. When normal power is lost, legally required standby systems must be capable of automatically supplying standby power in 60 seconds or less, instead of the 10 seconds or less required of emergency systems.

- **Article 702—Optional Standby Systems.** Optional standby systems are intended to protect public or private facilities or property where life safety doesn't depend on the performance of the system. These systems are typically installed to provide an alternate source of electrical power for such facilities as industrial and commercial buildings, farms, and residences, and to serve loads that, when stopped during any power outage, can cause discomfort, serious interruption of a process, or damage to a product or process. Optional standby systems are intended to supply on-site generated power to loads selected by the customer, either automatically or manually.
- **Article 725—Remote-Control, Signaling, and Power-Limited Circuits.** Article 725 contains the requirements for remote-control, signaling, and power-limited circuits that aren't an integral part of a device or appliance.
    - **Remote-Control Circuit.** A circuit that controls other circuits through a relay or solid-state device. For example, a circuit that controls the coil of a motor starter or lighting contactor is one type of remote-control circuit.
    - **Signaling Circuit.** A circuit that supplies energy to an appliance or device that gives a visual and/or audible signal. Circuits for doorbells, buzzers, code-calling systems, signal lights, annunciators, burglar alarms, and other indication or alarm devices are examples of signaling circuits.
- **Article 760—Fire Alarm Systems.** This article covers the installation of wiring and equipment for fire alarm systems. They include fire detection and alarm notification, voice communications, guard's tour, sprinkler waterflow, and sprinkler supervisory systems.
- **Article 770—Optical Fiber Cables and Raceways.** Article 770 covers the installation of optical fiber cables, which transmit signals using light for control, signaling, and communications. It also contains the installation requirements for raceways that contain optical fiber cables, and rules for composite cables (often called "hybrid" cables in the field) that combine optical fibers with current-carrying metallic conductors.

ARTICLE 700 EMERGENCY SYSTEMS

Introduction to Article 700—Emergency Systems

Emergency systems are legally required, often as a condition of an operating permit for a given facility. The authority having jurisdiction makes the determination as to whether such a system is necessary for a given facility and what it must entail. Sometimes, it simply provides power for exit lighting and exit signs upon loss of the main power or in the case of fire. Its purpose isn't to provide power for normal business operations, but rather to provide lighting and controls essential for human life safety.

The general goal is to keep the emergency operation as reliable as possible. The emergency system must be able to supply all emergency loads simultaneously. When the emergency supply also supplies power for other nonemergency loads, the emergency loads take priority over the others, and those other loads must be subject to automatic load pickup and load shedding to support the emergency loads if the emergency system doesn't have adequate capacity and rating for all loads simultaneously.

As you study Article 700, keep in mind that emergency systems are essentially lifelines for people. The entire article is based on keeping those lifelines from breaking.

700.8 Surge Protection

A new rule requiring an SPD on emergency systems has been added.

Part I. General

700.8 Surge Protection. A listed SPD must be installed for all emergency system panelboards and switchboards. Figure 700–1

ANALYSIS: A surge protective device is now required on emergency system panelboards and switchboards. Because damage to the emergency system from a surge can result in a tragedy, this extra protection is warranted.

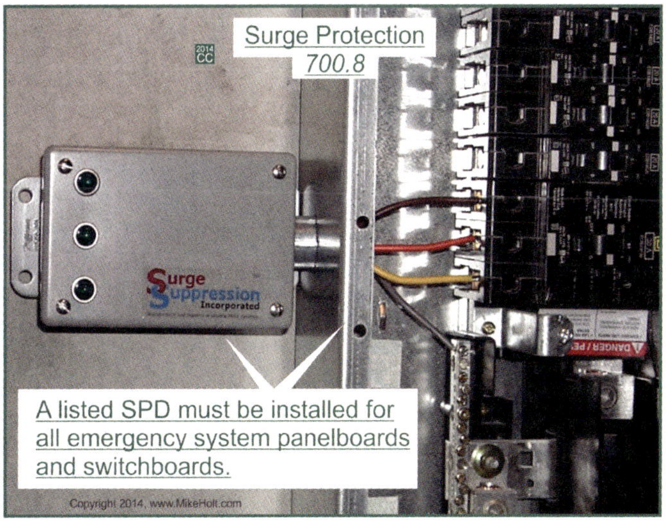

Figure 700–1

700.12 General Requirements

The disconnect requirement for generators supplying a building or structure was revised for clarity, and the circuiting requirements for unit equipment have also been revised.

Part III. Sources of Power

700.12 General Requirements. In the event of failure of the normal supply to the building/structure, emergency power must be available within 10 seconds. Emergency equipment must be designed and located so as to minimize the hazards that might cause complete failure due to flooding, fires, icing, and vandalism. The emergency power supply must be one of the following:

(B) Generator Set.

(6) Outdoor Generator Sets. If a generator located outdoors is equipped with a readily accessible disconnecting means located within sight of the building/structure in accordance with 445.18, an additional disconnecting means isn't required on or at the building/structure for the generator feeder conductors that serve or pass through the building/structure. Figure 700–2

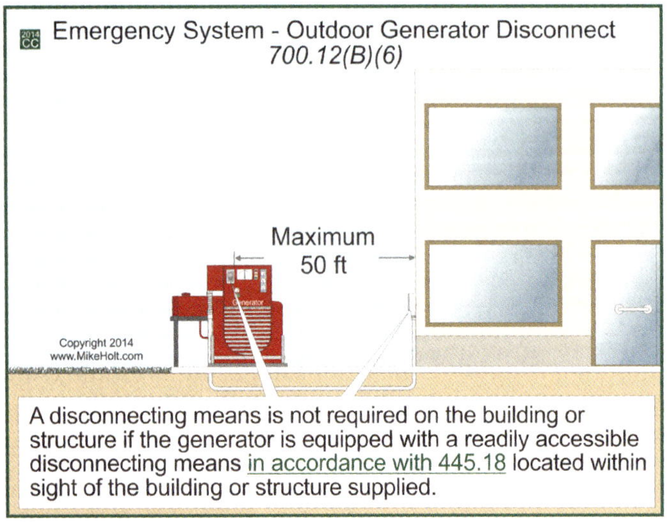

Figure 700–2

Author's Comment: According to Article 100, "within sight" means that it's visible and not more than 50 ft from one to the other.

Ex: Where conditions of maintenance and supervision ensure that only qualified persons will monitor and service the installation and where documented safe switching procedures are established and maintained for disconnection, the generator disconnecting means isn't required to be located within sight of the building or structure served.

ANALYSIS: This change was made in order to clarify the requirements of a building or structure supplied by a generator. In previous editions of the *Code*, there was some debate about the disconnect having to meet the requirements of 225.36, which required it to be listed as "suitable for use as service equipment." In this edition of the *NEC*, this section was revised to clarify the requirements, but, as it turns out, it's no longer necessary. The "suitable for use as service equipment" requirement has been removed from 225.36, so the whole discussion is now moot.

(F) Unit Equipment.

(1) Components of Unit Equipment. Individual unit equipment (an emergency lighting battery pack) must consist of the following: Figure 700–3

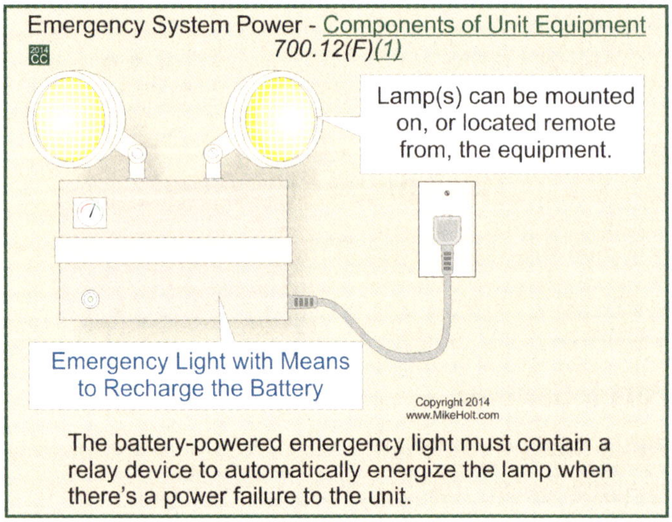

Figure 700–3

(1) A rechargeable battery,

(2) A battery charging means,

(3) Provisions for one or more lamps mounted on the equipment, or terminals for remote lamps (or both), and

(4) A relaying device arranged to energize the lamps automatically upon failure of the supply to the unit equipment.

(2) Installation Requirements for Unit Equipment. The installation of unit equipment must meet the following:

(2) Emergency lighting battery pack equipment must be permanently fixed in place. Flexible cord-and-plug connection (a locking receptacle isn't required) is permitted for emergency lighting battery pack equipment designed for this purpose, provided the cord doesn't exceed 3 ft in length.

(3) The branch-circuit wiring that supplies emergency lighting battery pack equipment must be the same branch-circuit wiring that supplies the normal lighting in the area, but the emergency lighting battery pack equipment must be connected ahead of any local switches. Figure 700–4

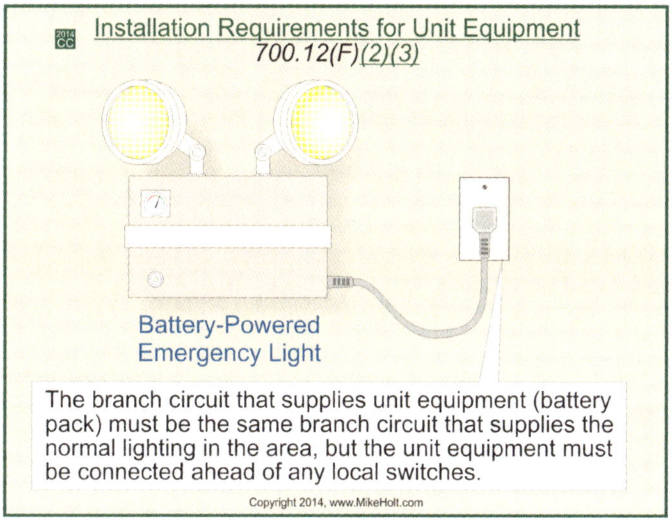

Figure 700–4

Ex: In a separate and uninterrupted area supplied by at least three normal lighting circuits that aren't a multiwire branch circuit, a separate branch circuit for unit equipment is allowed if it originates from the same panelboard as the normal lighting circuits and is provided with a lock-on feature.

Author's Comment: There are two reasons why the emergency lighting battery packs must be connected ahead of the switch controlling the normal area lighting: (1) in the event of a power loss to the lighting circuit, the emergency battery lighting packs will activate and provide emergency lighting for people to exit the building, and (2) the emergency lighting battery packs won't turn on when the switch controlling normal lighting is turned off.

CAUTION: *Individual unit equipment must not be connected to the emergency circuit, because it won't operate when normal power is lost, since the equipment is being supplied by the emergency power system*

(4) The branch circuit that feeds the emergency lighting battery pack equipment must be clearly identified at the distribution panel in accordance with 110.22(A) and 408.4.

(6) Power for remote heads providing the exterior lighting of an exit door can be supplied by the unit equipment serving the area immediately inside the exit door.

ANALYSIS: Although very little changed as a result of this revision, we do have a better *Code*. Previous editions of the *NEC* found this requirement seemingly having two parts of text written by two different groups. The first part of the text was a nice, concise list of items from one to four. The rest of the rule was a whole lot of text without any list items to break up the rule. This revision results in a *Code* rule that's easier to use and understand.

The exception regarding the circuiting of unit equipment was revised to address multiwire branch circuits. The general idea of the circuiting requirement (that the unit equipment be on the same circuit as the normal lights) is in the *NEC* to ensure that nobody can turn off the unit equipment without unintentionally notifying the occupants. Imagine being in a large assembly room with five hundred people, none of whom are very familiar with the setting (such as in a Mike Holt seminar). Imagine further that Mike tries an electrical experiment that trips the circuit breaker serving some receptacles in the room, and is too embarrassed to tell the maintenance staff. Probably not a big deal, but what if the emergency lights were on that circuit too? The emergency lights (unit equipment such as bug eyes) would turn on, but nobody would notice because the regular lights would still be on. In the meantime the batteries would drain, and there would be no emergency lighting until somebody turned that tripped breaker back on. Fortunately, such an installation is prohibited by this rule. The unit equipment must be on the lighting circuit serving the room, that way if Mike trips the breaker, all of the lights will go out, the emergency lights will turn on, and the breaker will have to be reset to make the room usable. The exception allows us to use a dedicated circuit for the emergency lights (unit equipment) if the room is so big that three or more circuits provide the normal lighting to the area. When this occurs, a breaker locking the circuit to the unit equipment in the "On" (closed) position must be used to ensure that nobody can shut it off. Because a multiwire branch circuit must have a simultaneous disconnect [210.4(B)], the normal lighting could be turned off via a single ground fault (if the breaker is a three pole). This change now requires the three normal circuits to not share a neutral.

700.16 Emergency Illumination

A new requirement for emergency illumination of some electrical equipment has been added.

Part IV. Circuits for Lighting and Power

700.16 Emergency Illumination. Emergency lighting systems must be designed and installed so that the failure of any individual lighting element, such as the burning out of a lamp, won't leave in total darkness any space that requires emergency illumination.

Author's Comment: This means that a single remote head is never sufficient for an area. A minimum of two lighting heads is always required. This is why individual unit equipment (sometimes called "lunchboxes" in the field) always has two lighting heads.

When an emergency system is installed, emergency illumination must be provided to illuminate the service or building disconnecting means, if the disconnect is located indoors. Figure 700–5

ANALYSIS: This new requirement was put into the *Code* so that an injured electrician can be located by emergency response personnel. Many of us in the electrical industry have seen pictures or videos of an unfortunate electrician who was the victim of an arc flash or arc blast at the service or building disconnect. When these incidents occur, the main disconnect is probably going to trip, resulting in a severely injured electrician laying in complete darkness waiting for emergency response. With this change, the first responders will not only have the lighting required to find the victim, but will also have lighting to perform whatever type of medical aid the incident warrants.

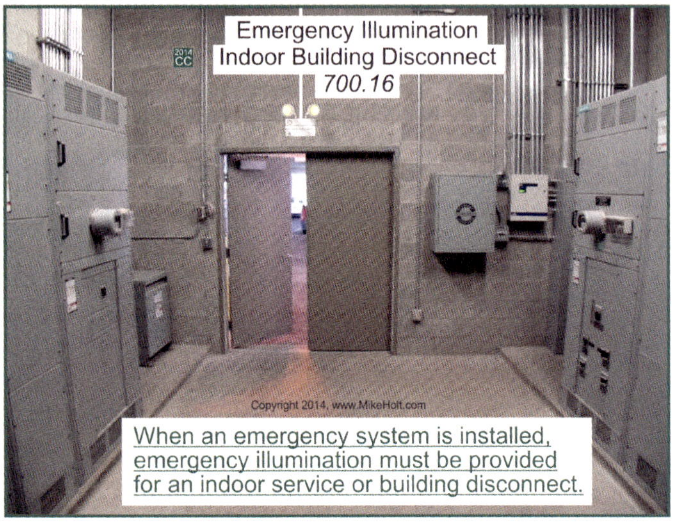

Figure 700–5

700.19 Multiwire Branch Circuits

A new requirement prohibits multiwire branch circuits on emergency systems.

700.19 Multiwire Branch Circuits. Multiwire branch circuits aren't allowed for emergency systems. Figure 700–6

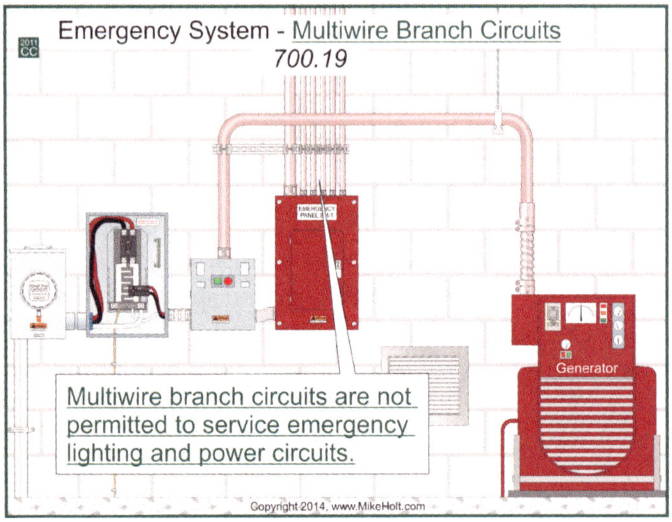

Figure 700–6

ANALYSIS: Multiwire branch circuits are required to have a simultaneous disconnect at the circuit breaker [210.4(B)]. Although single-pole breakers with handle ties can be used, many people choose to use two- or three-pole breakers instead. When using multipole breakers, a single fault or even an overload will shut off all of the circuits attached to that breaker. While this is certainly an inconvenience in most instances, it's downright hazardous if these circuits are providing emergency power or emergency lighting. This new requirement avoids the problem by prohibiting these circuits from being multiwire branch circuits.

700.27 Ground-Fault Protection of Equipment

The allowance for omitting ground-fault protection of equipment for emergency systems has been clarified.

Part VI. Overcurrent Protection

700.27 Ground-Fault Protection of Equipment. The alternate power supply for emergency power systems isn't required to have ground-fault protection of equipment, but 700.6(D) requires ground-fault indication. If ground-fault protection of equipment is provided, and the equipment automatically disconnects during the fault, the indication isn't required.

ANALYSIS: This rule doesn't prohibit GFPE on an emergency system power source, it just makes it optional. If GFPE is provided, there's no reason to have the indication discussed in 700.6(D), since the "indication" of a ground fault will be the breaker tripping off. If, however, the GFPE is omitted, the indication is required. This has always been the intent of the rule, but it's much clearer now.

700.28 Selective Coordination

The selective coordination of the system must now be designed by an engineer or similarly qualified person.

700.28 Selective Coordination. Overcurrent devices for emergency power systems must be selectively coordinated with all supply-side overcurrent devices. The design must be made by an engineer or similarly qualified person, and it must be documented and made available to the AHJ.

Author's Comment: Selective coordination means the overcurrent protection scheme confines the interruption to a particular area rather than to the whole system. For example, if a short circuit or ground fault occurs with selective coordination, the only breaker/fuse that will open is the one protecting just the branch circuit involved. Without selective coordination, an entire floor of a building can go dark. See Article 100 for the definition of the term "Coordination, Selective."

ANALYSIS: Since its inception in 2005, few *Code* rules have had as many proposals as this one (for both emergency and legally required standby systems). Very few of these proposals pass since most of them seek to reduce the safety requirements. This change, however, makes the requirement a bit more stringent, as it now requires the design of the system to be engineered by someone who knows what they're doing. This was probably already occurring, but now an inspector or plans examiner has a rule they can hang their hat on if the design is beyond the competency of the designer.

ARTICLE 701 LEGALLY REQUIRED STANDBY SYSTEMS

Introduction to Article 701—Legally Required Standby Systems

In the hierarchy of electrical systems, Article 700 Emergency Systems receives first priority. Taking the number two spot are Legally Required Standby Systems, which fall under Article 701. Legally required standby systems must supply standby power in 60 seconds or less after a power loss, instead of the 10 seconds or less required for emergency power systems.

Article 700 basically applies to systems or equipment required to protect people who are in an emergency and trying to get out, while Article 701 basically applies to systems or equipment needed to aid the people responding to the emergency. For example, Article 700 lighting provides an exit path. But, Article 701 might control the elevator used by fire fighters to reach the applicable floor.

701.12 General Requirements

The disconnect requirements for generators supplying a building or structure were revised for clarity.

Part III. Sources of Power

701.12 General Requirements. If the normal supply fails, legally required standby power must be available within 60 seconds. The supply system for the legally required standby power supply must be one of the following:

(B) Generator Set.

(5) Outdoor Generator Sets. If a generator located outdoors is equipped with a readily accessible disconnecting means located within sight of the building/structure, in accordance with 445.18, an additional disconnecting means isn't required on or at the building/structure for the generator feeder conductors that serve or pass through the building/structure. Figure 701–1

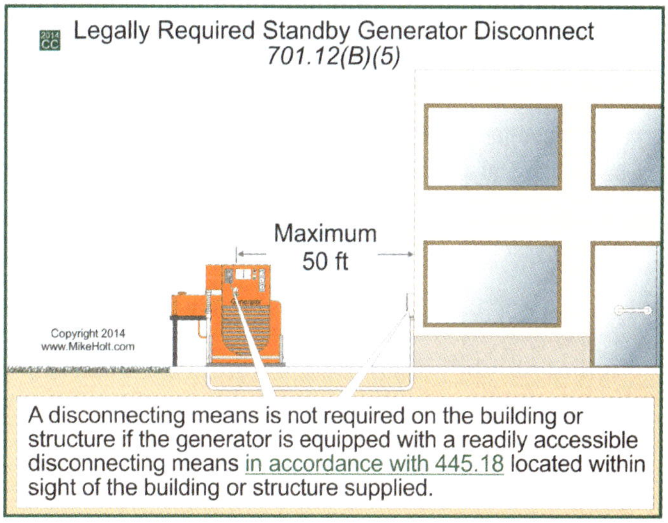

Figure 701–1

Author's Comment: According to Article 100, "within sight" means that it's visible and not more than 50 ft from one to the other.

ANALYSIS: This change was made in order to clarify the requirements of a building or structure supplied by a generator. In previous editions of the *Code*, there was some debate about the disconnect having to meet the requirements of 225.36, which required it to be listed as "suitable for use as service equipment." In this edition of the *NEC*, this section was revised to clarify the requirements, but, as it turns out, it's no longer necessary. The "suitable for use as service equipment" requirement has been removed from 225.36, so the whole discussion is now moot.

701.26 Ground-Fault Protection of Equipment

The allowance for omitting ground-fault protection of equipment for legally required standby systems has been clarified.

Part IV. Overcurrent Protection

701.26 Ground-Fault Protection of Equipment. The alternate source for legally required standby systems isn't required to have ground-fault protection of equipment but 701.6(D) requires ground-fault indication. If ground-fault protection of equipment is provided, and the equipment automatically disconnects during the fault, the indication isn't required.

ANALYSIS: This rule doesn't prohibit GFPE on a legally required standby system power source, it just makes it optional. If GFPE is provided, there's no reason to have the indication discussed in 701.6(D), since the "indication" of a ground fault will be the breaker tripping off. If, however, the GFPE is omitted, the indication is required. This has always been the intent of the rule and it's much clearer now.

701.27 Selective Coordination

The selective coordination of the system must now be designed by an engineer or similarly qualified person.

701.27 Selective Coordination. Overcurrent devices for legally required standby systems must be selectively coordinated with all supply-side overcurrent devices. The design must be made by an engineer or similarly qualified person, and it must be documented and made available to the AHJ.

Author's Comment: See the definition of "Coordination, Selective" in Article 100.

ANALYSIS: Since its inception in 2005, few *Code* rules have had as many proposals as this one (for both emergency and legally required standby systems). Very few of these proposals pass since most of them seek to reduce the safety requirements. This change, however, makes the requirement a bit more stringent, as it now requires the design of the system to be engineered by someone who knows what they're doing. This was probably already occurring, but now an inspector or plans examiner has a rule they can hang their hat on if the design is beyond the competency of the designer.

ARTICLE 702 OPTIONAL STANDBY SYSTEMS

Introduction to Article 702—Optional Standby Systems

Taking third priority after Emergency and Legally Required Systems, Optional Standby Systems protect public or private facilities or property where life safety doesn't depend on the performance of the system. These systems aren't required for rescue operations.

Suppose a glass plant loses power. Once glass hardens in the equipment—which it will do when process heat is lost—the plant is going to suffer a great deal of downtime and expense before it can resume operations. An optional standby system can prevent this loss.

You'll see these systems in facilities where loss of power can cause economic loss or business interruptions. Data centers can lose millions of dollars from a single minute of lost power. A chemical or pharmaceutical plant can lose an entire batch from a single momentary power glitch. In many cases, the lost revenue can't be recouped.

This article also applies to the installation of optional standby generators in homes, farmsteads, small businesses, and many other applications where standby power isn't legally required.

702.7 Signs

A new sign is now required at flanged inlets used for the connection of generators for optional standby systems.

Part I. General

702.7 Signs.

(C) Power Inlet. Where a power inlet is used for a temporary connection to a portable generator, a warning sign must be placed near the inlet, stating either:

WARNING—FOR CONNECTION OF A SEPARATELY DERIVED (BONDED NEUTRAL) SYSTEM ONLY

OR

WARNING—FOR CONNECTION OF A NONSEPARATELY DERIVED (FLOATING NEUTRAL) SYSTEM ONLY

Figure 702–1

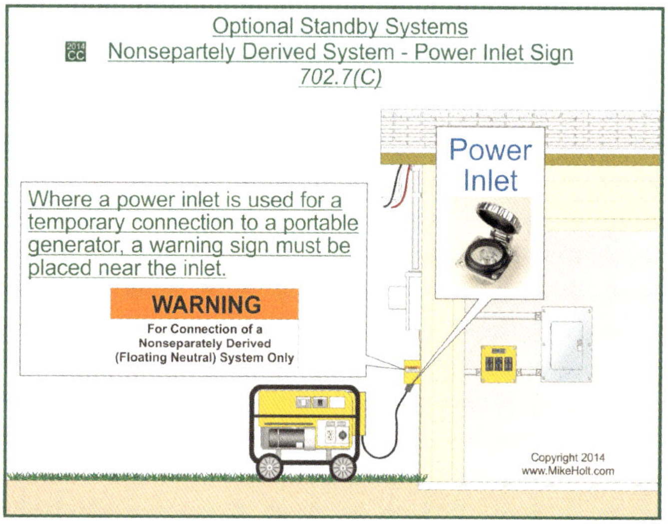

Figure 702–1

ANALYSIS: The manner in which a transfer switch is wired is what determines how you wire the generator. If the transfer switch has a solid (unswitched) neutral, the generator isn't separately derived (which means the neutral of the generator must not be connected to the frame, and a grounding electrode isn't required). If the transfer switch switches the neutral, the generator is a separately derived system (which means the neutral of the generator must be connected to the frame, and a grounding electrode is required). In order to ensure that the correct type of generator is plugged into a building, we now must have a label at the flanged inlet letting people know how the transfer switch is wired.

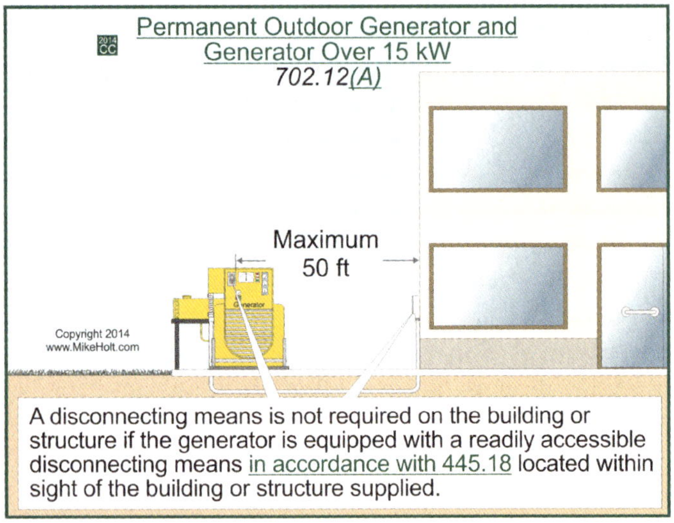

Figure 702–2

702.12 Outdoor Generator Sets

The disconnect requirements for generators supplying a building or structure were revised for clarity, and a new requirement for portable generators has been added.

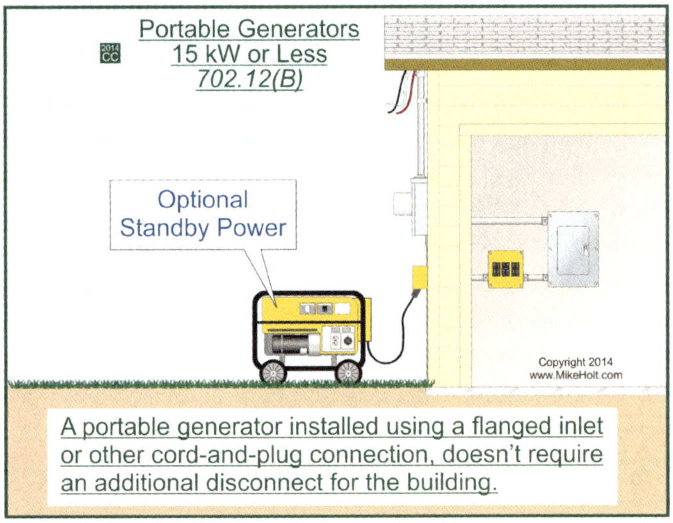

Figure 702–3

Part II. Circuit Wiring

702.12 Outdoor Generator Sets.

(A) Permanent Generators and Generators Larger than 15kW. If a generator located outdoors is equipped with a readily accessible disconnecting means located within sight of the building/structure, in accordance with 445.18, an additional disconnecting means isn't required on or at the building/structure for the generator feeder conductors that serve or pass through the building/structure. Figure 702–2

Author's Comment: According to Article 100, "within sight" means that it's visible and not more than 50 ft from one to the other.

(B) Portable Generators 15 KW or Less. Where a portable generator, rated 15 kW or less, is installed using a flanged inlet or other cord-and-plug type connection, an additional disconnecting means isn't required for the building. Figure 702–3

ANALYSIS: The change in (A) was made in order to clarify the requirements of a building or structure supplied by a generator. In previous editions of the *Code*, there was some debate about the disconnect having to meet the requirements of 225.36, which required it to be listed as "suitable for use as service equipment." In this edition of the *NEC*, this section was revised to clarify the requirements. As it turns out, it's no longer necessary. The "suitable for use as service equipment" requirement has been removed from 225.36, so the whole discussion is now moot.

A new subsection (B) has been added to address small portable generators. It's very common, especially in residential buildings, to plug a generator into the house using some combination of cords, attachment plugs, receptacles, inlets, and so on. When this is the case, a disconnect isn't required for the house, since unplugging the generator will do the same thing as a disconnect. I guess the *Code* had to say it...

Notes

ARTICLE 725 REMOTE-CONTROL, SIGNALING, AND POWER-LIMITED CIRCUITS

Introduction to Article 725—Remote-Control, Signaling, and Power-Limited Circuits

Circuits that fall under Article 725 are remote-control, signaling, and power-limited circuits that aren't an integral part of a device or appliance. This article includes circuits for burglar alarms, access control, sound, nurse call, intercoms, some computer networks, some lighting dimmer controls, and some low-voltage industrial controls.

Let's take a quick look at the types of circuits:

- A remote-control circuit controls other circuits through a relay or solid-state device, such as a motion-activated security lighting circuit.
- A signaling circuit provides output that's a signal or indicator, such as a buzzer, flashing light, or annunciator.
- A power-limited circuit is a circuit supplied by a transformer or other power source that limits the amount of power to provide safety from electrical shock and/or fire ignition.

The purpose of Article 725 is to allow for the fact that these circuits "are characterized by usage and power limitations that differentiate them from electrical power circuits" [725.1 Note]. This article provides alternative requirements for minimum conductor sizes, overcurrent protection, insulation requirements, wiring methods, and materials.

Article 725 consists of four parts. Part I provides general information, Part II pertains to Class 1 circuits, Part III addresses Class 2 and Class 3 circuits, while Part IV focuses on listing requirements. The key to understanding and applying each of these parts is in knowing the voltage and energy levels of the circuits, the wiring method involved, and the purpose(s) of the circuit.

725.3 Other Articles

Conductors and cables under the scope of this article now must comply with the rules for corrosive, damp, and wet locations, as well as the rules for conductors with other systems.

Part I. General

725.3 Other Articles. Only those sections contained in Article 300 specifically referenced below apply to Class 1, 2, and 3 circuits.

Author's Comment: Boxes or other enclosures aren't required for Class 2 or Class 3 splices or terminations because Article 725 doesn't reference 300.15, which contains those requirements. Figure 725–1

(K) Installation of Conductors with Other Systems. Raceways for the use of conductors and cables aren't permitted to contain nonelectrical components, such as pipes or tubes for steam, water, air, gas, drainage, and so forth [300.8]. Figure 725–2

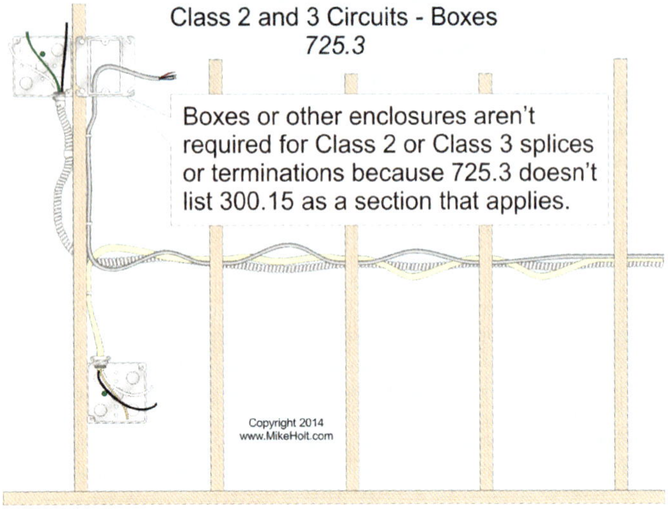

Figure 725–1

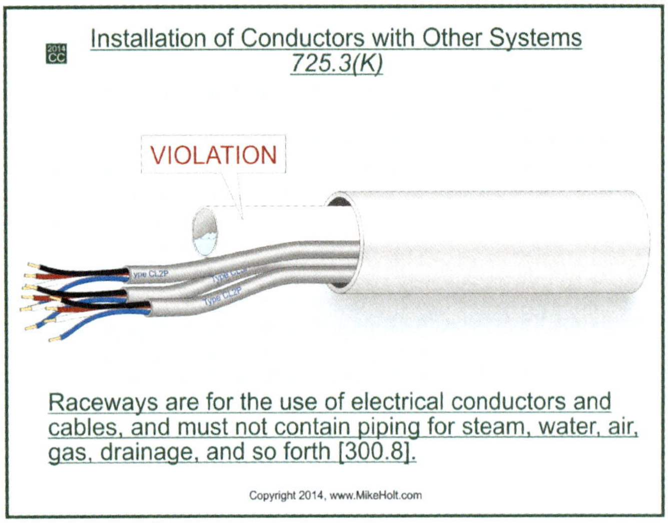

Figure 725–2

ANALYSIS: Does the *Code* have to tell you that you shouldn't put a steam pipe inside of an electrical raceway? I guess so.

(L) Corrosive, Damp, or Wet Locations. Where installed in corrosive, damp, or wet locations, conductors and cables must be identified for the location, in accordance with 110.11 and 310.10(G). Conductors and cables installed in underground raceways, or in raceways aboveground in wet locations, must also be identified for wet locations, in accordance with 300.5(B). Where corrosion may occur, the requirements of 300.6 must be used.

ANALYSIS: Although Class 2 and Class 3 circuits don't present much of a hazard from the perspective of fire and shock, conductors and cables should still be installed in accordance with the manufacturer's design in mind. Cables that aren't designed to be installed in a wet location, for example, won't kill anyone if they deteriorate, but will still cause the owner to spend money repairing an installation that he or she probably thought they had already paid enough for. It's worth remembering that the intent of the *Code* isn't only protecting people from fire and shock, but property as well [90.1(A)].

725.135 Installation of Class 2, Class 3, and PLTC Cables

A new section dealing with the allowed cable types has been added.

Part III. Class 2 and Class 3 Circuit Requirements

725.135 Installation of Class 2, Class 3, and PLTC Cables. Installation of Class 2, Class 3, and PLTC cables must comply with 725.135(A) through (M).

(A) Listing. Class 2, Class 3 and PLTC cables installed in buildings must be listed.

(C) Plenum spaces. The following cables can be used in plenum spaces as described in 300.22(C):

(1) Types CL2P and CL3P cables

(2) Types CL2P and CL3P cables installed in plenum communications raceways

(3) Types CL2P and CL3P cables and plenum communications raceways supported by open metallic cable trays or cable tray systems

(4) Types CL2P, CL3P, CL2R, CL3R, CL2, CL3, CL2X, CL3X, and PLTC cables installed in raceways that are installed in accordance with 300.22(C)

(H) Cable Trays. Cables installed in outdoor cable trays outdoors must be Type PLTC.

The following cables are allowed in cable trays inside buildings:

(1) Types CM CL2P, CL3P, CL2R, CL3R, CL2, CL3, and PLTC cables

(2) Types CL2P, CL3P, CL2R, CL3R, CL2, CL3, and PLTC cables installed in:

a. Plenum communications raceways

b. Riser communications raceways

c. General-purpose communications raceways

(K) Other Building Locations. The following cables are allowed in building locations other than the locations covered in 725.135(B) through (I):

(1) Types CL2P, CL3P, CL2R, CL3R, CL2, CL3 and PLTC cables

(2) A maximum of 10 ft of exposed Type CL2X in nonconcealed spaces

(3) A maximum of 10 ft of exposed Type CL3X in nonconcealed spaces

(4) Types CL2P, CL3P, CL2R, CL3R, CL2, CL3, and PLTC cables installed in:

a. Plenum communications raceways

b. Plenum cable routing assemblies

c. Riser communications raceways

d. Riser cable routing assemblies

e. General-purpose communications raceways

f. General-purpose cable routing assemblies

(5) Types CL2P, CL3P, CL2R, CL3R, CL2, CL3, CL2X, CL3X and PLTC cables installed in raceways recognized in Chapter 3

(6) Type CMUC undercarpet communications cables installed under carpet

(M) One- and Two-Family dwellings. The following cables are allowed in one- and two-family dwellings in locations other than the locations covered in 725.135 (B) through (I):

(1) Types CL2P, CL3P, CL2R, CL3R, CL2, CL3 and PLTC cables

(2) Type CL2X less than ¼ in. in diameter

(3) Type CL3X less than ¼ in. in diameter

(4) Communications cables and Types CL2P, CL3P, CL2R, CL3R, CL2, CL3 and PLTC cables installed in:

a Plenum communications raceways

b. Plenum cable routing assemblies

c. Riser communications raceways

d. Riser cable routing assemblies

e. General-purpose communications raceways

f. General-purpose cable routing assemblies

(5) Types CL2P, CL3P, CL2R, CL3R, CL2, CL3, CL2X, CL3X, and PLTC cables installed in raceways recognized in Chapter 3

(6) Type CMUC undercarpet communications cables installed under carpet

ANALYSIS: In order to make this article more similar to the Chapter 8 articles, this new section has been added. Most of this information was in 725.154, which is now just a table.

725.139 Conductors of Different Circuits in the Same Cable, Enclosure, Cable Tray, Raceway, or Cable Routing Assembly

Cable routing assemblies are now included in the requirements for conductors and cables in raceways, enclosures, and cable trays.

725.139 Conductors of Different Circuits in Same Cable, Enclosure, Cable Tray, Raceway, or Cable Routing Assembly.

(A) Class 2 Conductors. Class 2 circuit conductors can be in the same cable, cable routing assembly, enclosure, or raceway with other Class 2 circuit conductors.

(B) Class 3 Conductors. Class 3 circuit conductors can be in the same cable, cable routing assembly, enclosure, or raceway with other Class 3 circuit conductors.

(C) Class 2 Conductors with Class 3 Conductors. Class 2 conductors are permitted within the same cable, cable routing assembly, enclosure, or raceway with Class 3 circuit conductors, provided the Class 2 circuit conductors use a Class 3 wiring method in accordance with 725.179.

Author's Comment: Listed Class 2 cables have 150V insulation, whereas listed Class 3 cables are rated 300V [725.179(G)].

(D) Class 2 and Class 3 Circuits with Communications Circuits.

(1) Classified as Communications Circuits. Class 2 and Class 3 conductors can be within the same cables with communications conductors in listed communications cables if installed in accordance with Article 800 [800.113 and 800.133(A)(1)(b)]. Figure 725–3

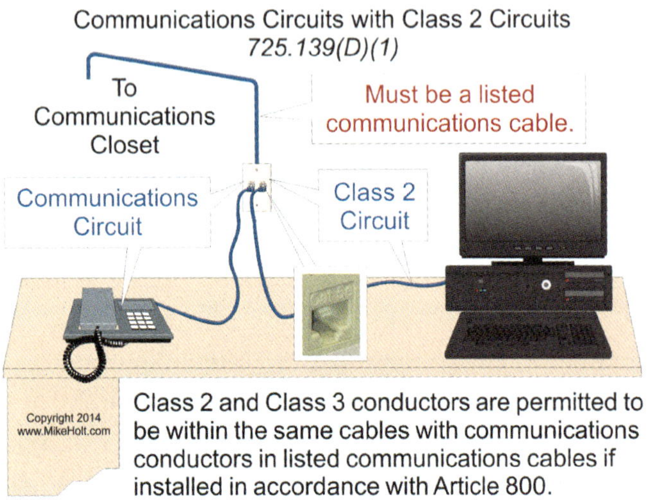

Figure 725–3

Author's Comments:

- A common application of this requirement is when a single communications cable is used for both voice communications and data.
- Listed Class 2 cables have 150V insulation [725.179(G)], whereas listed communications cables have a voltage rating of 300V [800.179].

(E) Class 2 or Class 3 Cables with Other Cables. Class 2 or Class 3 jacketed cables can be in the same enclosure, cable tray, raceway, or cable routing assembly as jacketed cables of any of the following: Figure 725–4

(1) Power-limited fire alarm circuits in compliance with Article 760.

(2) Nonconductive and conductive optical fiber cables in compliance with Article 770.

(3) Communications circuits in compliance with Article 800.

(4) Coaxial cables in compliance with Article 820.

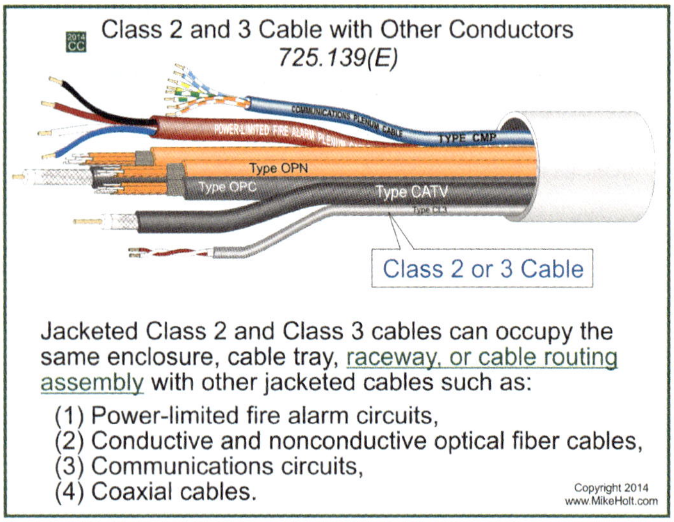

Figure 725–4

(F) Class 2 or Class 3 Circuits with Audio System Circuits. Audio output circuits [640.9(C)] using Class 2 or Class 3 wiring methods [725.136 and Table 725.154] aren't permitted in any enclosure, cable routing assembly, raceway, or cable with conductors of electric light or power circuits. However, audio output circuits utilizing Class 1 wiring methods [725.46] can be mixed with power circuits if the two systems are functionally associated with each other [725.48(B)(1)].

Author's Comment: The concern is that a fault from audio amplifier circuits to a Class 2 and Class 3 circuit has the potential of creating a hazard by disrupting the operation of alarm systems and remote-control circuits for safety-control equipment.

ANALYSIS: Cable routing assemblies are still a fairly new concept in the *Code*, so the rules for them are still rather inconsistent. This section was revised to include cable routing assemblies with raceways and enclosures. Several changes in Articles 725 through 840 have been made to introduce cable routing assemblies, but they won't all be mentioned in this textbook. All of the changes were made for the same reason.

725.154 Applications of Class 2 and Class 3 Cables

A new table and revised text should greatly clarify the requirements for Class 2 and Class 3 cables.

ANALYSIS: When the *Code* contains a requirement that's as long as this one was, it's often best to just create a giant table to illustrate the rules. Those who are familiar with Articles 800 and 820 will recognize this new table, as it borrows from the concept presented there.

725.154 Applications of Class 2 and Class 3 Cables. Class 2 and Class 3 cables must comply with the requirements of (A) through (G), as indicated in Table 725.154.

Notes

ARTICLE 760 FIRE ALARM SYSTEMS

Introduction to Article 760—Fire Alarm Systems

Article 760 covers the installation of wiring and equipment for fire alarm systems, including circuits controlled and powered by the fire alarm control panel. These include fire detection and alarm notification, voice communications, guard's tour, sprinkler waterflow, and sprinkler supervisory systems. NFPA 72, *National Fire Alarm Code* provides other fire alarm system requirements.

760.3 Other Articles

The requirements for fire alarm cables in corrosive, damp, or wet locations have been slightly expanded.

760.3 Other Articles. Only those sections of Article 300 specifically referenced in this section apply to fire alarm circuits and equipment and must comply with (A) through (G) as follows:

(D) Corrosive, Damp, or Wet Locations. Fire alarm circuits installed in corrosive, damp, or wet locations must be identified for use in the operating environment [110.11]; must be of materials suitable for the environment in which they're to be installed; and must be of a type suitable for the application [300.5(B), 300.6, 300.9, and 310.10(G)].

ANALYSIS: By referring to 300.5(B) and 300.9, it's now clear that fire alarm conductors and cables must be identified for use in a wet location if installed in an underground raceway [300.5(B)], or in an aboveground raceway that's in a wet location [300.9]. Although you could have argued that the *Code* already said this through reference to 110.11, why even have the argument? This change shuts the door on possible misapplication.

760.32 Fire Alarm Circuit Cables Extending Beyond a Building

The requirements for fire alarm circuits extending beyond a building were greatly expanded.

760.32 Fire Alarm Circuit Cables Extending Beyond a Building. If fire alarm circuit conductors extend beyond a building, they must be installed in accordance with Parts II, III, and IV of Article 800, and they must also be installed in accordance with Part I of Article 300.

ANALYSIS: Previous editions of this section required that power-limited fire alarm circuits extending beyond a building comply with Parts II, III, and IV of Article 800 *or* Part I of Article 300. This has been changed to now require compliance with all of them. This seems to make sense, since complying with Part I of Article 300 certainly doesn't give you the type of protection given by Part III of Article 800 (primary protection devices) or the grounding requirements of Part IV of Article 800. On the other hand, complying with just Article 800 doesn't give you some of the protection discussed in Part I of Article 300 (like the underground cover requirements of 300.5).

760.135 Installation of PLFA Cables in Buildings

A new section dealing with the installation of PLFA cable has been added.

Part III. Power-Limited Fire Alarm (PLFA) Circuits

760.135 Installation of PLFA Cables in Buildings. Installation of power-limited fire alarm cables in buildings must comply with 760.135(A) through (J).

(A) Listing. PLFA cables installed in buildings must be listed.

(C) Other Spaces used For Environmental Air (Plenums). The following cables can be used in plenum spaces as described in 300.22(C):

(1) Type FPLP cables

(2) Type FPLP cables installed in plenum communications raceways

(3) Type FPLP and FPLP-CI cables supported by open metallic cable trays or cable tray systems

(4) Types FPLP, FPLR, and FPL cables installed in raceways that are installed in compliance with 300.22(C)

(H) Other Building Locations. The following cables are permitted to be installed in building locations other than the locations covered in 770.113(B) through (H):

(1) Types FPLP, FPLR, and FPL cables

(2) Types FPLP, FPLR, and FPL cables installed in:

a. Plenum communications raceways

b. Plenum cable routing assemblies

c. Riser communications raceways

d. Riser cable routing assemblies

e. General-purpose communications raceways

f. General-purpose cable routing assemblies

(3) Types FPLP, FPLR, and FPL cables installed in a raceway of a type recognized in Chapter 3

ANALYSIS: In order to make this article more similar to the Chapter 8 articles, this new section has been added. Most of this information was in 760.154, which is now just a table.

760.139 Power-Limited Fire Alarm Circuits, Class 2, Class 3, and Communications Circuits

Cable routing assemblies are now included in the requirements for conductors and cables in raceways, enclosures, and cable trays.

760.139 Power-Limited Fire Alarm Circuits, Class 2, Class 3, and Communications Circuits.

(A) Two or More Circuits. Power-limited fire alarm circuits, communications circuits, or Class 3 circuits can be in the same cable, enclosure, cable tray, raceway, or cable routing assembly. Figure 760–1

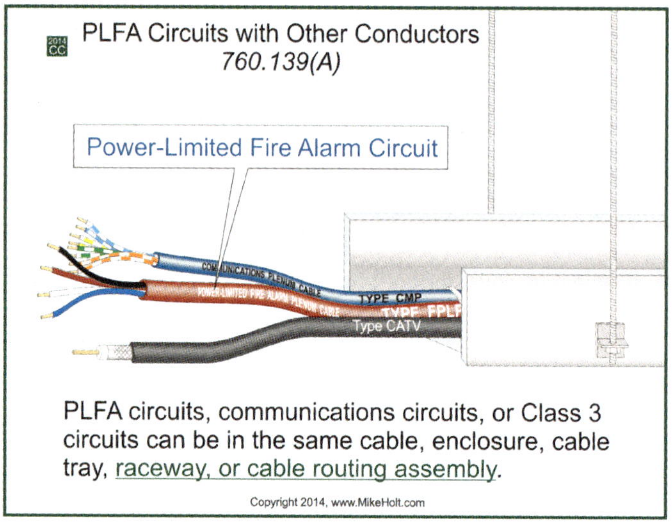

Figure 760–1

(B) PLFA and Class 2 Circuits. Class 2 circuits can be within the same cable, cable routing assembly, enclosure, cable tray, or raceway as conductors of power-limited fire alarm circuits provided the Class 2 circuit conductor insulation isn't less than that required for the power-limited fire alarm circuit.

Author's Comment: Listed Class 2 cables have a voltage rating of 150V [725.179(G)], whereas listed power-limited fire alarm cables have a voltage rating of 300V [760.179(C)].

(D) Audio System Circuits and Power-Limited Fire Alarm Circuits. Audio system circuits [640.9(C)] using Class 2 or Class 3 wiring methods must not be installed in the same cable, cable routing assembly, cable tray, or raceway with power-limited fire alarm conductors or cables.

Author's Comment: The concern is that a fault from audio amplifier circuits to fire alarm circuits has the potential to create a hazard by disrupting the operation of fire alarm systems. However, this restriction doesn't apply to the voice annunciation audio circuits supplied and controlled from a fire alarm panel and commonly required in high-rise buildings and similar applications.

ANALYSIS: Cable routing assemblies are still a fairly new concept in the *Code*, so the rules for them are still rather inconsistent. This section was revised to include cable routing assemblies with raceways and enclosures. Several changes in Articles 725 through 840 have been made to introduce cable routing assemblies, but they won't all be mentioned in this textbook. All of the changes were made for the same reason.

760.154 Applications of Power-Limited Fire Alarm Cables (PLFA)

A new table and revised text should greatly clarify the requirements for fire alarm cables.

760.154 Applications of Power-Limited Fire Alarm Cables (PLFA). PLFA cables must meet the requirements of Table 760.154, or the substitutions allowed in 760.154(A).

ANALYSIS: When the *Code* contains a rule that's as long as this one was, it's often best to just create a giant table to illustrate the rules. Those who are familiar with Articles 800 and 820 will recognize this new table, as it borrows from the concept presented there.

As with the rest of this article, this section now addresses cable routing assemblies.

Notes

ARTICLE 770 OPTICAL FIBER CABLES AND RACEWAYS

Introduction to Article 770—Optical Fiber Cables and Raceways

Article 770 provides the requirements for installing optical fiber cables and special raceways for optical fiber cables. It also contains the requirements for composite cables, often called "hybrid," that combine optical fibers with current-carrying conductors.

While we normally think of Article 300 in connection with wiring methods, you only need to use the Article 770 methods for optical fiber cables, except where it makes specific references to Article 300 [770.3]. For instance, in 770.113, reference is made to 300.22, which applies when installing optical fiber cables and optical fiber raceways in ducts and plenum spaces.

This article doesn't refer to 300.15, so boxes aren't required for splices or terminations of optical fiber cable. Note 1 to 770.48 states that splice cases and terminal boxes are typically used as enclosures for splicing or terminating optical fiber cables.

Article 90 states that the *NEC* isn't a design guide or installation manual. Thus, Article 770 doesn't deal with the performance of optical fiber systems. For example, it doesn't mention cable bending radii. It doesn't explain how to install and test cable safely either, but that doesn't mean you should look into an optical fiber cable, even if you can't see any light coming through it. Light used in these circuits usually isn't visible, but it can still damage your eyes.

770.2 Definitions—Innerduct

A new definition of "innerduct" has been added to this article.

Part I. General

770.2 Definitions.

Innerduct. A nonmetallic raceway placed within a larger raceway. Figure 770–1

ANALYSIS: What can I say? It's a tube inside another tube.

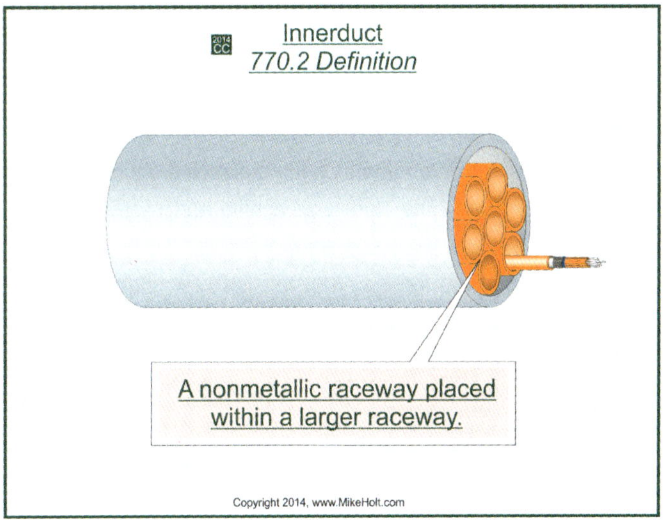

Figure 770–1

770.2 Definitions—Optical Fiber Cable

The definition of "optical fiber cable" was revised to omit needless words, and to address field-assembled cables.

770.2 Definitions.

Optical Fiber Cable. A factory assembly or field assembly of optical fibers having an overall covering. Figure 770–2

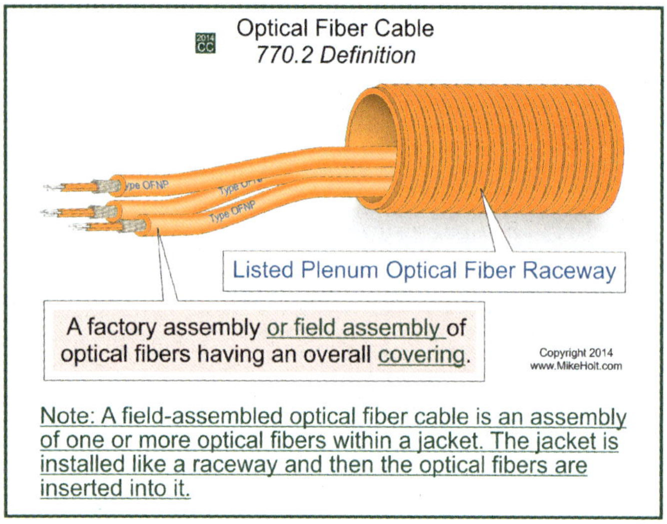

Figure 770–2

Note: A field-assembled optical fiber cable is an assembly of one or more optical fibers within a jacket. The jacket is installed like a raceway, and then the optical fibers are inserted into it.

ANALYSIS: The definition was revised, and the Informational Note added, to address field-assembled optical fiber cable assemblies. The Note was copied and pasted from the UL White Book (Product Category QAZD).

While fibers do indeed "transmit light for control, signaling and communications," is there any reason to include that in the definition? Apparently not, because they have now been deleted.

770.2 Definitions—Point of Entrance

The definition of "point of entrance" was revised to remove needless words.

770.2 Definitions.

Point of Entrance. The point within a building at which the optical fiber cable emerges from an external wall, from a concrete floor slab, or from a rigid metal conduit or an intermediate metal conduit.

ANALYSIS: In an effort to simplify definitions, a task group was created to review all of the definitions from Articles 770 through 840. This change is one of the results of that effort. Definitions need to be clear and accurate, and most people will agree that they should be as short as possible while still conveying the necessary information.

770.12 Innerduct

The term "optical fiber raceway" has been changed to "communications raceway."

770.12 Innerduct. Listed communications raceways can be installed as innerduct in any Chapter 3 raceway. Figure 770–3

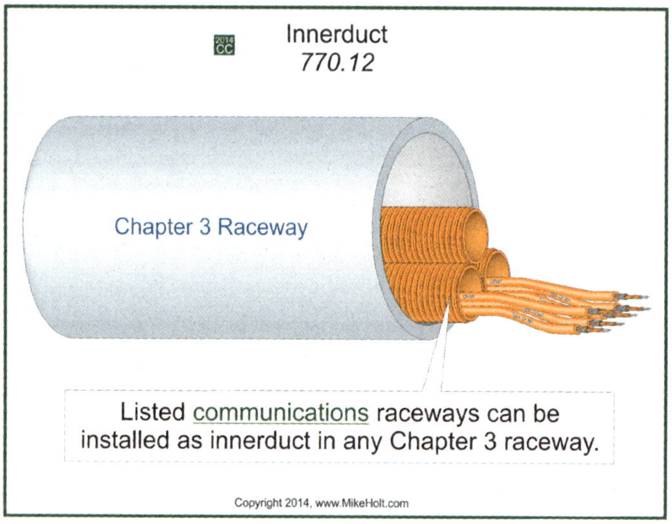

Figure 770–3

ANALYSIS: In an effort to make all of the limited-energy *Code* articles say the same thing, the term "communications raceway" is being used wherever possible. Let's see what happens in three years when we revisit this issue yet again…

770.24 Mechanical Execution of Work

Cable ties are now required to be listed for use in plenums.

770.24 Mechanical Execution of Work. Equipment and cabling must be installed in a neat and workmanlike manner. Exposed cables must be supported by the structural components of the building so that the cable won't be damaged by normal building use. Such cables must be secured by straps, staples, hangers, cable ties, or similar fittings designed and installed in a manner that won't damage the cable. Figure 770–4

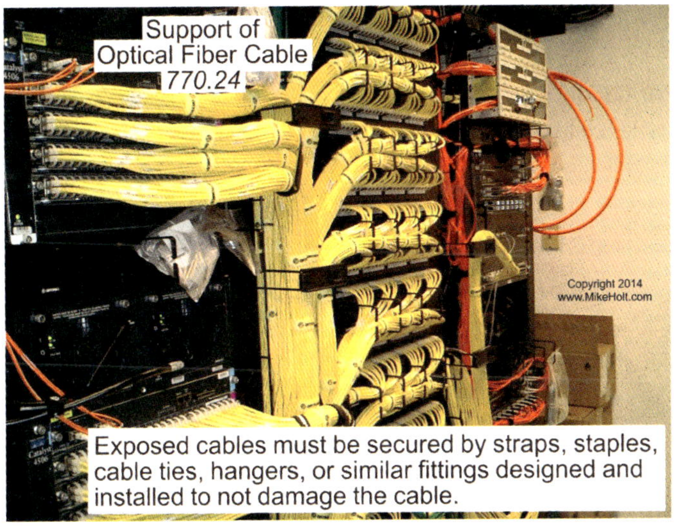

Figure 770–4

Communications raceways and cable assemblies must be securely fastened in place and the ceiling-support wires or ceiling grid must not be used to support optical fiber raceways or cables [300.11]. Figure 770–5

Author's Comment: Raceways and cables can be supported by independent support wires attached to the suspended ceiling in accordance with 300.11(A).

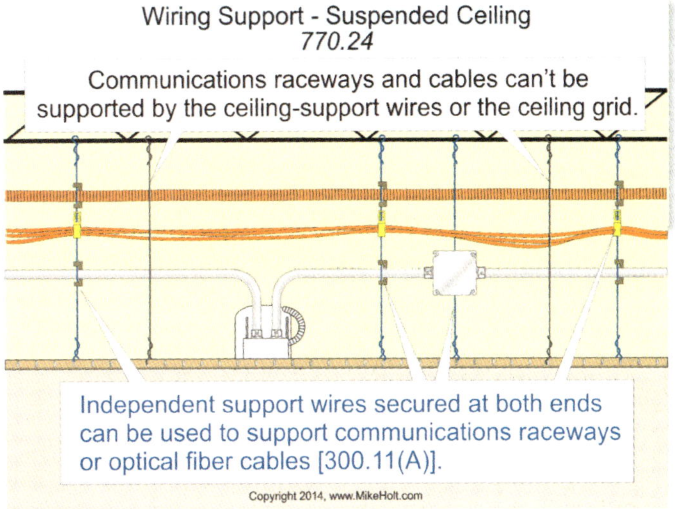

Figure 770–5

Cables installed through or parallel to framing members or furring strips must be protected where they're likely to be penetrated by nails or screws by installing the wiring method so it isn't less than 1¼ in. from the nearest edge of the framing member or furring strips, or is protected by a 1/16 in. thick steel plate or the equivalent [300.4]. Figure 770–6

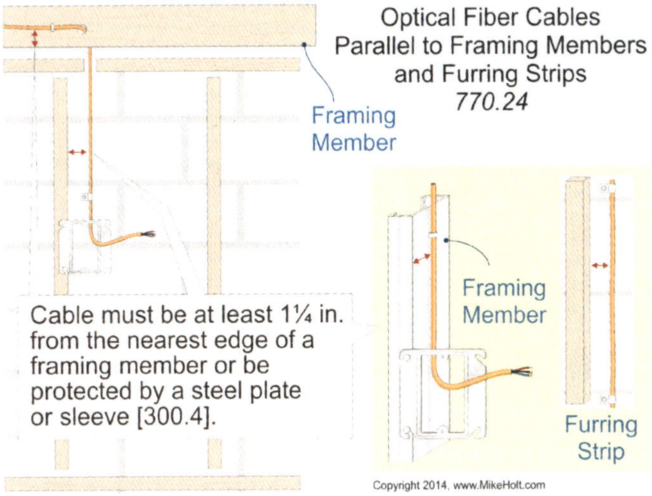

Figure 770–6

Cable ties used to secure or support optical fiber cables in plenums must be listed for use in plenums. Figure 770–7

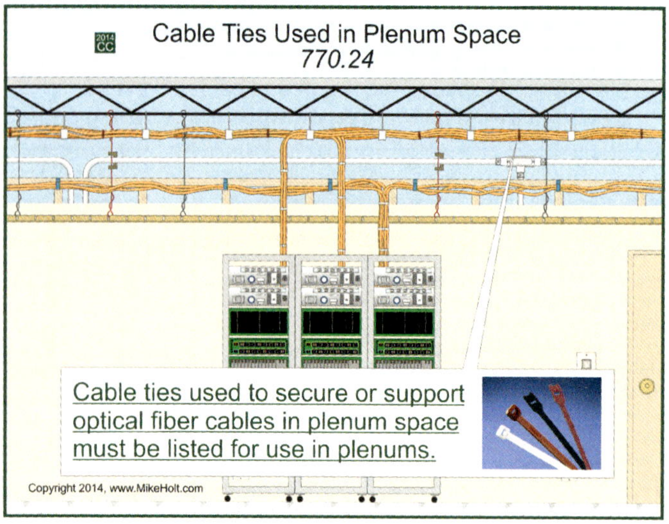

Figure 770–7

Note 1: Accepted industry practices are described in ANSI/NECA/BICSI 568, *Standard for Installing Commercial Building Telecommunications Cabling* and ANSI/NECA/FOA 301, *Standard for Installing and Testing Fiber Optic Cables.* **Figure 770–8**

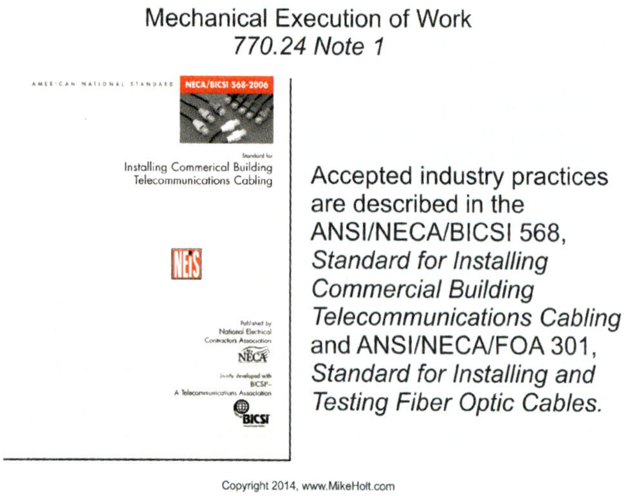

Figure 770–8

Author's Comment: For more information about these standards, visit http://www.NECA-NEIS.org/.

Note 2: See NFPA 90A-2009, *Standard for the Installation of Air-Conditioning and Ventilating Systems*, for discrete combustible components installed in accordance with 300.22(B) and (C).

ANALYSIS: Plenum spaces, such as those found above some suspended ceilings, contain the air that you breathe. It makes sense that the *Code* restricts the types of items that are in them. Cable ties may be small, but there also might be thousands of them in a plenum, and they do add up. If the plenum space has a fire inside it, the smoke will be breathed by the occupants who are trying to escape. Nonplenum-rated materials release more toxic fumes than their plenum-rated counterparts, and that's the last thing anyone running out of a burning building needs to be dealing with.

770.48 Unlisted Cables Entering Buildings

The types of raceways used with unlisted cables entering buildings were revised into a list format.

Part II. Cables Outside and Entering Buildings

770.48 Unlisted Cables Entering Buildings.

(A) Conductive and Nonconductive Cables. Unlisted optical fiber cables can be installed in building spaces, other than risers, ducts, or plenum spaces, if the length of the optical fiber cable measured from its point of entrance doesn't exceed 50 ft and the optical fiber cable terminates in an enclosure.

Note 2: The point of entrance is defined as the point within a building at which the optical fiber cable emerges from an external wall, from a concrete floor slab, or from a rigid metal conduit or an intermediate metal conduit connected by a grounding conductor to an electrode in accordance with 770.100 [110.2].

(B) Nonconductive Cables in Raceway.

Unlisted nonconductive optical fiber cables can enter the building if installed in any of the following raceways:

(1) Intermediate metal conduit (IMC)

(2) Rigid metal conduit (RMC)

(3) Rigid polyvinyl chloride conduit (PVC)

(4) Electrical metallic tubing (EMT)

ANALYSIS: Lists work better than long paragraphs. They just do.

770.49 Metallic Entrance Conduit Grounding

A new section discussing the grounding of raceways entering buildings has been added.

770.49 Metallic Entrance Conduit Grounding. Rigid metal conduit (RMC) or intermediate metal conduit (IMC) containing optical fiber entrance cable must be connected to a grounding electrode in accordance with 770.100(B).

ANALYSIS: With the change to the definition of "point of entrance" in 770.2 this new section became necessary. It technically isn't anything new, because the definition discussed this, but definitions aren't supposed to contain requirements.

770.110 Raceways and Cable Routing Assemblies for Optical Fiber Cables

Requirements for cable routing assemblies have been added.

Part V. Installation Methods Within Buildings

770.110 Raceways and Cable Routing Assemblies for Optical Fiber Cables.

(A) Types of Raceways.

(1) Chapter 3 Raceways. Optical fiber cables can be installed in any Chapter 3 raceways in accordance with the requirements of Chapter 3.

(2) Communications Raceways. Optical fiber cables can be installed in a listed communications raceway in accordance with 362.24 through 362.56. Figure 770–9

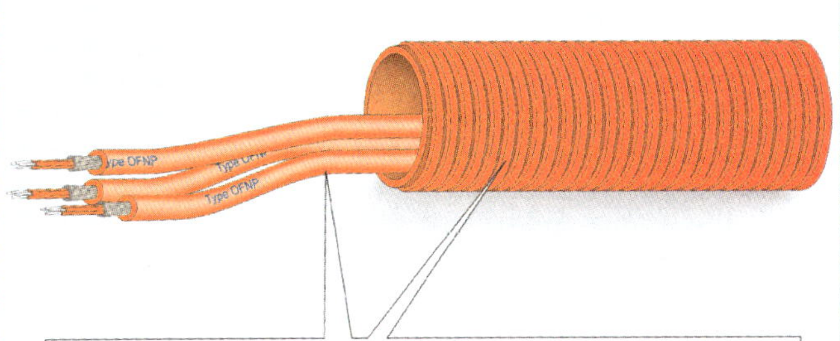

Figure 770–9

Author's Comment: In other words, listed communications raceways must be installed according to the following ENT rules:

- 362.24 Bending radius
- 362.26 Maximum total bends between pull points, 360 degrees
- 362.28 Trimmed to remove rough edges
- 362.30 Support every 3 ft, within 3 ft of any enclosure
- 362.48 Joints between tubing, fittings, and boxes

(B) Raceway Fill for Optical Fiber Cables.

(1) Without Electric Light or Power Conductors. If optical fiber cables are installed in a raceway without current-carrying conductors, the raceway fill tables of Chapter 9 don't apply.

(2) Nonconductive Optical Fiber Cables With Electric Light or Power Conductors. If nonconductive optical fiber cables are installed with electrical conductors in a raceway, the raceway fill tables of Chapter 3 and Chapter 9 apply. Figure 770–10

(C) Cable Routing Assemblies. Optical fiber cables can be installed in cable routing assemblies in accordance with 800.113 and Table 800.154(c). They must also be supported in accordance with the following:

(1) Horizontal Support. Where installed horizontally, cable routing assemblies must be supported every 3 ft, and at each end or joint, unless listed otherwise. Supports can never exceed 10 ft.

(2) Vertical Support. Where installed vertically, cable routing assemblies must be securely supported every 4 ft, unless listed otherwise, and must not have more than one joint between supports.

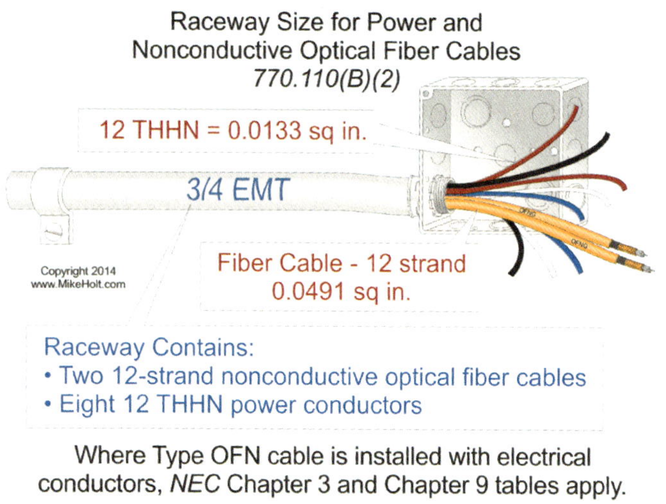

Figure 770–10

ANALYSIS: With the growing popularity of cable routing assemblies, new requirements have been added throughout the *NEC*. This section contains the support requirements for cable routing assemblies, and simply refers the *Code* user to 800.113 and Table 800.154(c) to address the plenum, riser, general use, (and so forth) issues.

770.113 Installation of Optical Fiber Cables

Cable routing assemblies and optical fiber raceways are no longer discussed in 770.113.

770.113 Installation of Optical Fiber Cables.

(A) Listing. Optical fiber cables installed within buildings must be listed.

Ex: Unless the length of the cable from its point of entrance, doesn't exceed 50 ft as permitted by 770.48.

Author's Comment: The *NEC* doesn't require outside or underground cable to be listed, but the cable must be approved by the authority having jurisdiction as suitable for the application in accordance with 90.4, 90.7, and 110.2.

(C) Plenum Spaces. The following cables are permitted in plenum spaces described in 300.22(C): **Figure 770–11**

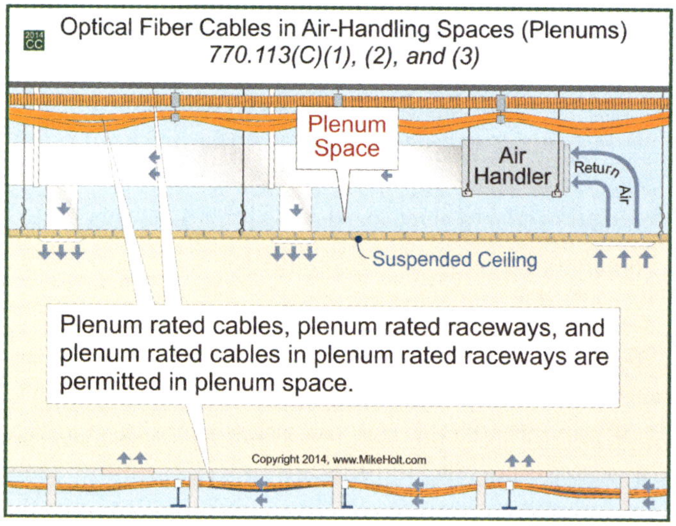

Figure 770–11

(1) Types OFNP and OFCP cables

(2) Types OFNP and OFCP cables installed in listed plenum raceways

(3) Types OFNP and OFCP cables supported by open metallic cable trays or cable tray systems

(4) Types OFNP, OFCP, OFNR, OFCR, OFNG, OFCG, OFN, and OFC cables installed in raceways in accordance with 300.22(C).

(H) Cable Trays. The following cables can be installed in cable trays:

(1) Types OFNP, OFCP, OFNR, OFCR, OFNG, OFCG, OFN, and OFC

(2) Types OFNP, OFCP, OFNR, OFCR, OFNG, OFCG, OFN, and OFC installed in communications raceways

(J) Other Building Locations. The following cables are permitted in the spaces not described in (B) through (I):

(1) Types OFNP, OFCP, OFNR, OFCR, OFNG, OFCG, OFN, and OFC

(2) Types OFNP, OFCP, OFNR, OFCR, OFNG, OFCG, OFN, and OFC installed in communications raceways

(3) Types OFNP, OFCP, OFNR, OFCR, OFNG, OFCG, OFN, and OFC installed in a Chapter 3 type raceway

ANALYSIS: Previous editions of the *Code* addressed optical fiber raceways in this article. Optical fiber raceways are actually communications raceways, so, in an effort to simplify the *Code*, the term "communications raceway" is used throughout the *Code*, instead of every article from 770 to 840 having their own type of raceway (which were are the same raceway anyway). This is similar to a change that was made in Article 820 in the 2011 edition of the *NEC*, which most people agreed was a change for the better.

770.133 Installation of Optical Fiber Cables

A few housekeeping-type changes have been made to this section, dealing with the installation of optical fiber cables.

770.133 Installation of Optical Fiber Cables.

(A) With Power Conductors. Optical fibers are permitted within the same composite cable with power circuits, if the functions of the optical fibers and the electrical conductors are associated.

Nonconductive optical fiber cables are permitted to occupy the same cable tray or raceway with conductors for electric light, power, and Class 1 circuits. Figure 770–12

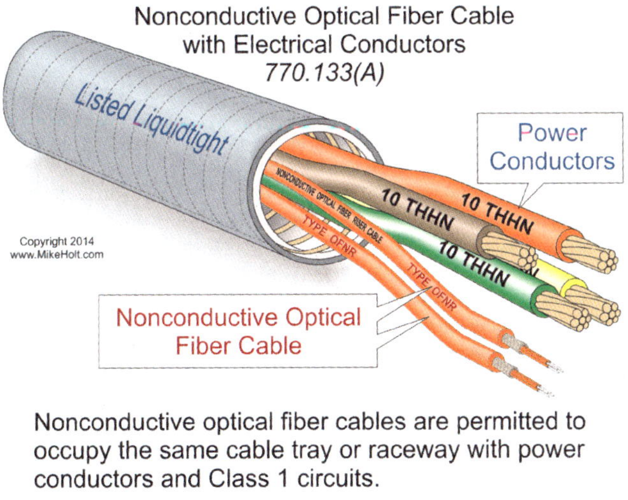

Figure 770–12

Nonconductive optical fiber cables can't occupy a cabinet, outlet box, panel, or similar enclosure housing the electrical terminations of an electric light, power, or Class 1 circuit.

Ex 1: Nonconductive optical fiber cables are permitted to occupy the same cabinet, outlet box, panel, or similar enclosure housing the electrical terminations of an electric light, power, or Class 1 circuit, if the nonconductive optical fiber cable is functionally associated with the electric light, power, or Class 1 circuit.

(B) With Communications Cables. Optical fiber cables can be in the same raceway, cable tray, box, enclosure, or cable routing assembly, with conductors of any of the following: Figure 770–13

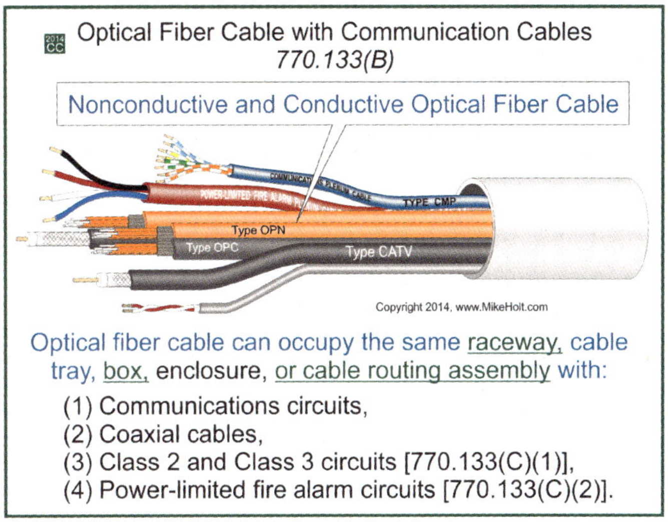

Figure 770–13

(1) Communications circuits in accordance with Parts I and V of Article 800.

(2) Coaxial cables in accordance with Parts I and V of Article 820.

(C) With Other Circuits. Optical fiber cables can be in the same raceway, cable tray, box, cable routing assembly, or enclosure with conductors of any of the following:

(1) Class 2 and Class 3 circuits in accordance with Parts I and III of Article 725 or in accordance with Article 645.

(2) Power-limited fire alarm circuits in accordance with Parts I and III of Article 760.

(D) Support of Cables. Optical fiber cables aren't permitted to be strapped, taped, or attached to the exterior of any raceway as a means of support. Figure 770–14

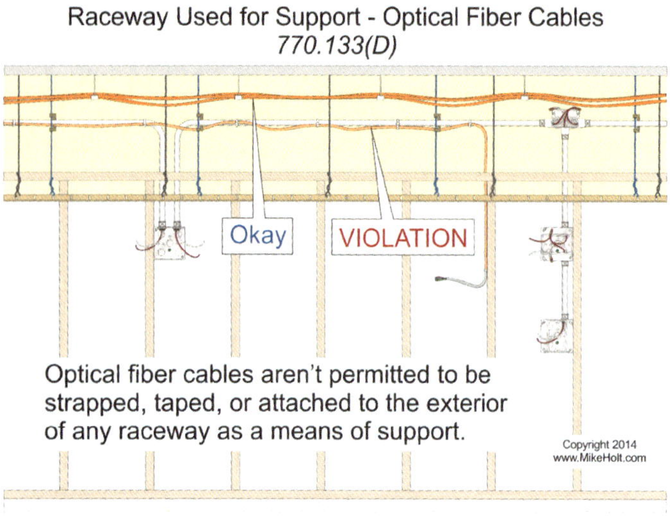

Figure 770–14

ANALYSIS: (B) and (C) have been revised to clarify that optical fiber cables can share boxes and cable routing assemblies with communications circuits and coaxial cables. Although it was probably already allowed by inspectors, the *NEC* didn't come right out and say it was permitted. Changes such as these are intended to make a better *Code*, and to remove arguments in the field, so most people will agree that these changes are worthwhile.

(B)(1) and (B)(2) contained a reference to the wrong Parts of Articles 800 and 820. Part IV of these articles, which is what the *NEC* used to refer to, deals with grounding, whereas Part V deals with installation methods.

CHAPTER 8 COMMUNICATIONS SYSTEMS

Introduction to Chapter 8—Communications Systems

Chapter 8 of the *National Electrical Code* covers the wiring requirements for communications systems such as telephones, radio and TV antennas, satellite dishes, closed-circuit television (CCTV), and cable TV (CATV), as well as network-powered and broadband-powered communications systems. **Figure 1**

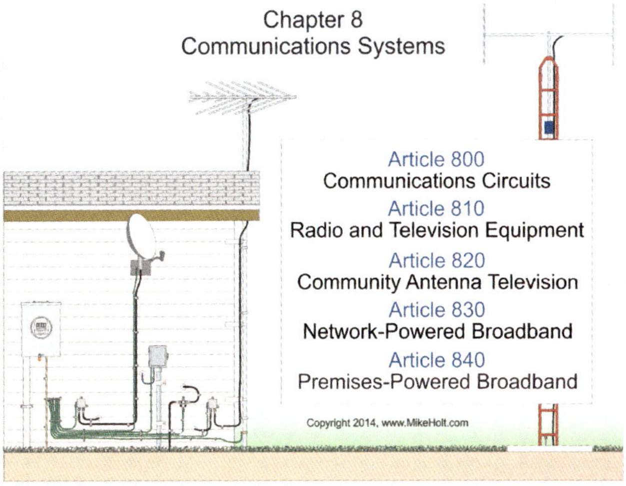

Figure 1

Communications systems aren't subject to the general requirements contained in Chapters 1 through 4 or the special requirements of Chapters 5 through 7, except where a Chapter 8 rule specifically refers to one of those chapters [90.3]. Also, installations of communications equipment under the exclusive control of communications utilities located outdoors, or in building spaces used exclusively for such installations, are exempt from the *NEC* [90.2(B)(4)]. **Figure 2**

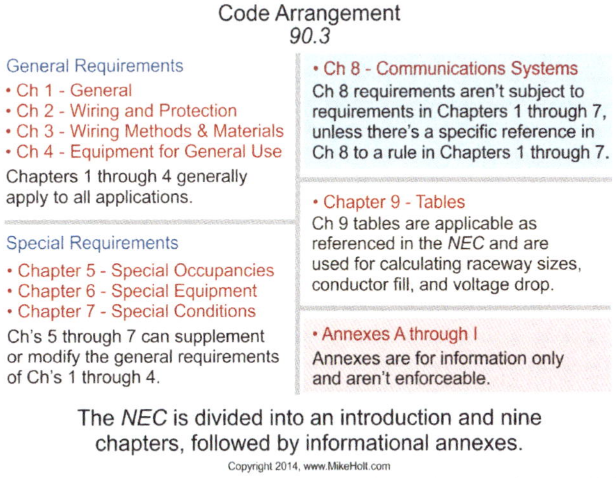

Figure 2

- **Article 800—Communications Circuits.** Article 800 covers the installation requirements for telephone wiring and for other related telecommunications purposes such as computer local area networks (LANs), and outside wiring for fire and burglar alarm systems connected to central stations.

- **Article 810—Radio and Television Equipment.** This article covers antenna systems for radio and television receiving equipment, amateur radio transmitting and receiving equipment, and certain features of transmitter safety. It also includes antennas such as multi-element, vertical rod and dish, and the wiring and cabling that connects them to the equipment.

- **Article 820—Community Antenna Television (CATV) and Radio Distribution Systems.** Article 820 covers the installation of coaxial cables to distribute limited-energy high-frequency signals for television, cable TV, and closed-circuit television (CCTV), which is often used for security purposes. It also covers the premises wiring of satellite TV systems where the dish antenna is outside and covered by Article 810.

ARTICLE 800 COMMUNICATIONS CIRCUITS

Introduction to Article 800—Communications Circuits

This article has its roots in telephone technology. Consequently, it addresses telephone and related systems that use twisted-pair wiring. Here are a few key points to remember about Article 800:

- Don't attach incoming communications cables to the service-entrance power mast.
- It's critical to determine the "point of entrance" for these circuits.
- Ground the primary protector as close as practicable to the point of entrance.
- Keep the grounding electrode conductor for the primary protector as straight and as short as possible.
- If you locate communications cables above a suspended ceiling, route and support them to allow access via ceiling panel removal.
- Keep these cables separated from lightning protection circuits.
- If you install communications cables in a Chapter 3 raceway, you must do so in conformance with the *NEC* requirements for the raceway system.
- Special labeling and marking provisions apply—follow them carefully.

Note: The term "Grounding Conductor" previously used in this article has been replaced by either "Bonding Conductor" or "Grounding Electrode Conductor (GEC)" where applicable to more accurately reflect the application and function of the conductor.

Author's Comment: For Articles 800, 810, and 820, the difference between a "bonding conductor" and a "grounding electrode conductor" is where they terminate. The bonding conductor terminates at the intersystem bonding termination; the grounding electrode connects to the power grounding electrode system [250.50]. Figures 800–1 and 800–2

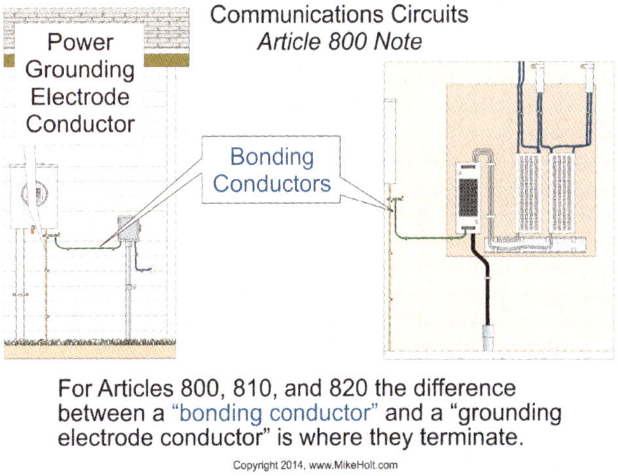

Figure 800–1

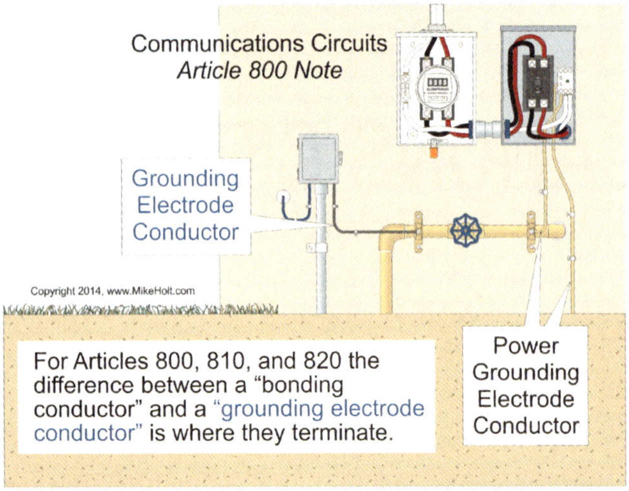

Figure 800–2

ANALYSIS: Because optical fiber cable installers and communications cable installers may not read each other's *Code* articles, this definition has been copied and pasted into 800.2 from 770.2. It's the same definition, and now it's in both places. What's innerduct, you might ask? It's a tube inside another tube.

800.2 Definitions—Innerduct

The definition of "innerduct" has been copied into Article 800.

800.2 Definitions.

Innerduct. A nonmetallic raceway placed within a larger raceway. Figure 800–3

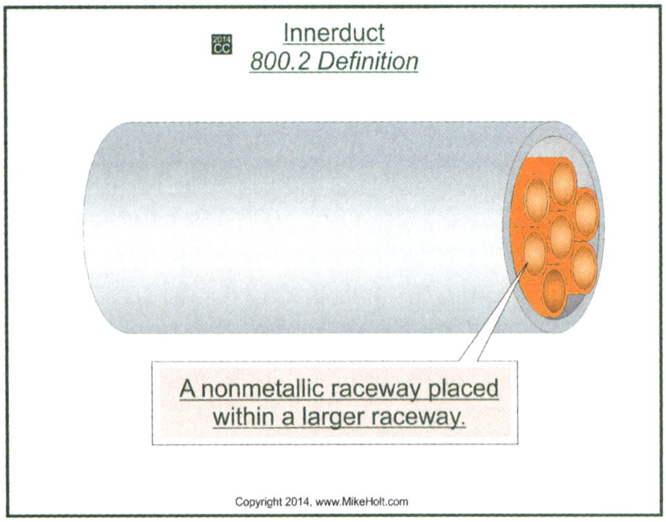

Figure 800–3

800.2 Definitions—Point of Entrance

The definition of "point of entrance" was revised for brevity.

800.2 Definitions.

Point of Entrance. The point within a building at which the communications cable emerges from an external wall, from a concrete floor slab, or from a rigid metal conduit (RMC) or an intermediate metal conduit (IMC). Figure 800–4

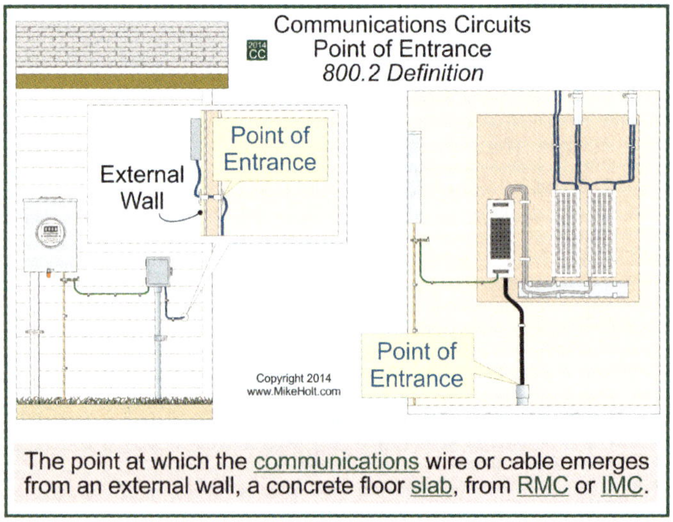

Figure 800–4

ANALYSIS: Definitions aren't supposed to contain requirements. Although the deleted text ("connected by a bonding conductor or grounding electrode in accordance with 800.100(B)") doesn't seem to be a requirement, it can be construed as such. A task group was created to create some sanity in the definitions of the limited-energy *Code* articles, and this change was one of the results.

800.12 Innerduct

A new allowance for innerduct has been added.

800.12 Innerduct. Listed communications raceways can be installed as innerduct in any Chapter 3 raceway. Figure 800–5

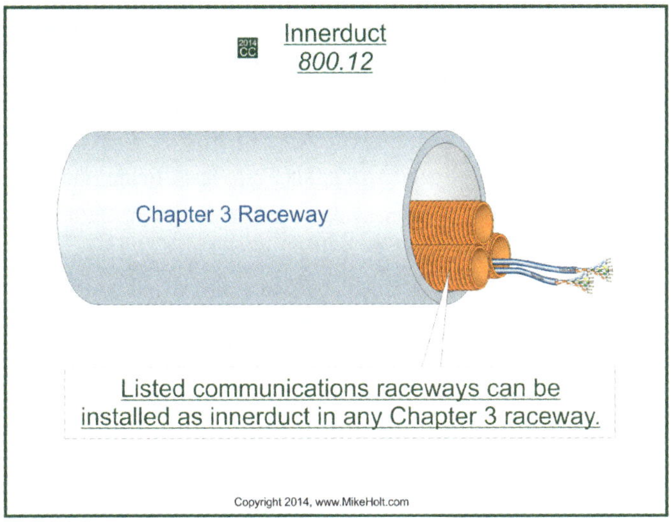

Figure 800–5

ANALYSIS: The concept of innerduct has been in the *Code* for a while, but interestingly enough, it was only in Article 770 for optical fiber cables [770.12]. There's certainly no hazard in using it for communications circuits, so the allowance has been added here in Article 800.

800.24 Mechanical Execution of Work

Cable ties are now required to be listed for use in plenums.

800.24 Mechanical Execution of Work. Equipment and communications cabling must be installed in a neat and workmanlike manner. Exposed communications cables must be supported by the structural components of the building so that the communications cable won't be damaged by normal building use. Cables must be secured with straps, staples, cable ties, hangers, or similar fittings designed and installed so as not to damage the communications cable. Figure 800–6

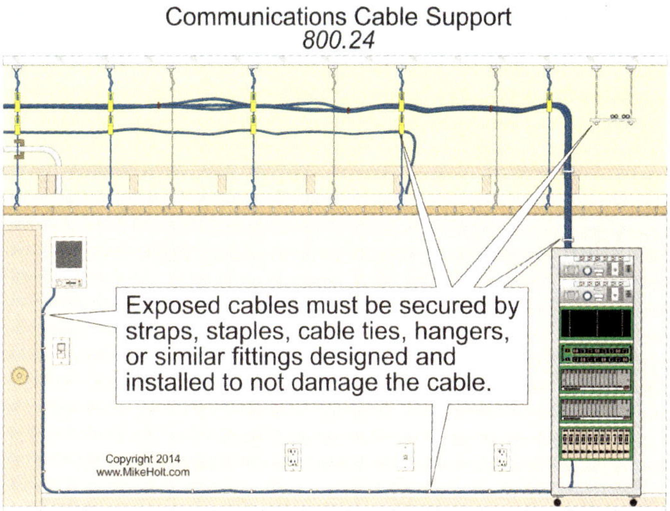

Figure 800–6

Communications raceways and communications cable assemblies must be securely fastened in place and ceiling-support wires or the ceiling grid must not be used to support communications raceways or communications cables [300.11]. Figure 800–7

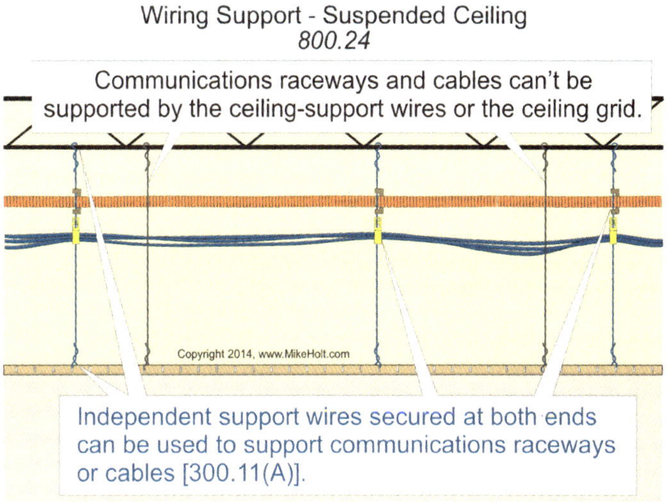

Figure 800–7

Author's Comment: Raceways and cables can be supported by independent support wires attached to the suspended ceiling in accordance with 300.11(A).

Cables installed parallel to framing members or furring strips must be protected where they're likely to be penetrated by nails or screws, by installing the wiring method so it isn't less than 1¼ in. from the nearest edge of the framing member or furring strips, or is protected by a 1⁄16 in. thick steel plate or the equivalent [300.4(D)]. Figure 800–8

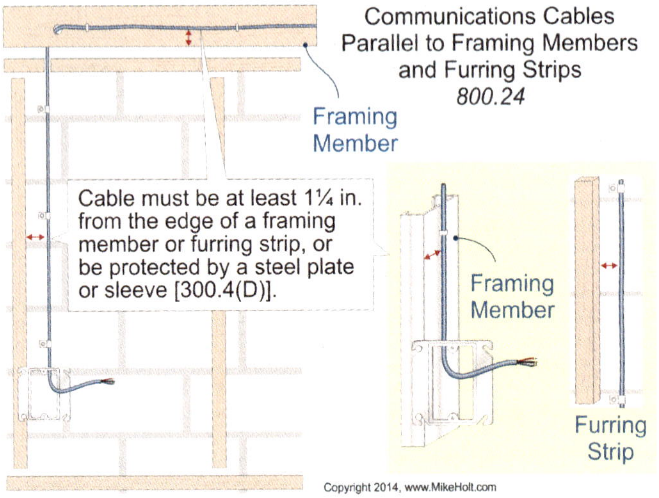

Figure 800–8

Cable ties used to secure or support communications cables in plenums must be listed for use in plenums. Figure 800–9

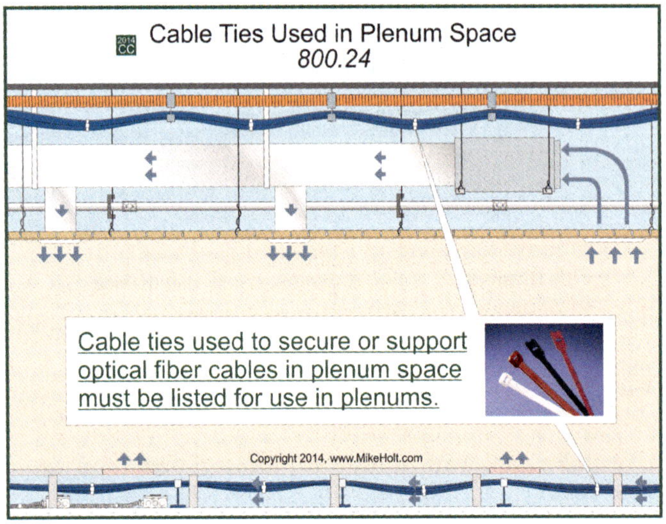

Figure 800–9

Note 1: Accepted industry practices are described in ANSI/NECA/BICSI 568, *Standard for Installing Commercial Building Telecommunications Cabling*, ANSI/TIA 569, *Commercial Building Standard for Telecommunications Pathways and spaces*, ANSI/TIA 570, *Residential Telecommunications Infrastructure*, and other ANSI standards.

Author's Comment: For more information about these standards, visit http://www.NECA-NEIS.org/.

Note 2: See NFPA 90A-2009, *Standard for the Installation of Air-Conditioning and Ventilating Systems*, for discrete combustible components installed in accordance with 300.22(B) and (C).

ANALYSIS: A plenum space, such as those found above some suspended ceilings, contains the air that you breathe. It makes sense that the *Code* restricts what types of items are in it. Cable ties may be small, but there also might be thousands of them in a plenum, and they do add up. If the plenum space has a fire inside of it, the smoke will be breathed by the occupants who are trying to escape. Nonplenum-rated materials release more toxic fumes than their plenum-rated counterparts, and that's the last thing anyone running out of a burning building needs to be dealing with.

800.49 Metallic Entrance Conduit Grounding

A new section discussing the grounding of raceways entering buildings has been added.

PART II. Cables Outside and Entering Buildings

800.49 Metallic Entrance Conduit Grounding. Rigid metal conduit (RMC) or intermediate metal conduit (IMC) containing communications entrance cable must be connected to a grounding electrode in accordance with 800.100(B). Figure 800–10

ANALYSIS: With the change to the definition of "point of entrance" in 800.2 this new section became necessary. It technically isn't anything new, because the definition discussed this, but definitions aren't supposed to contain requirements.

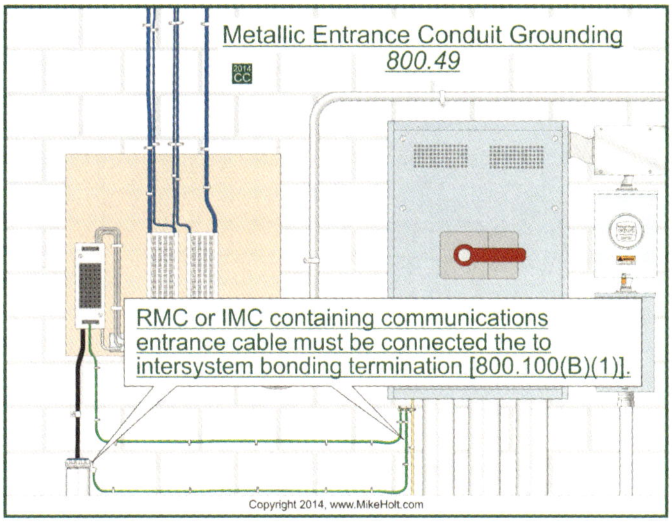

Figure 800–10

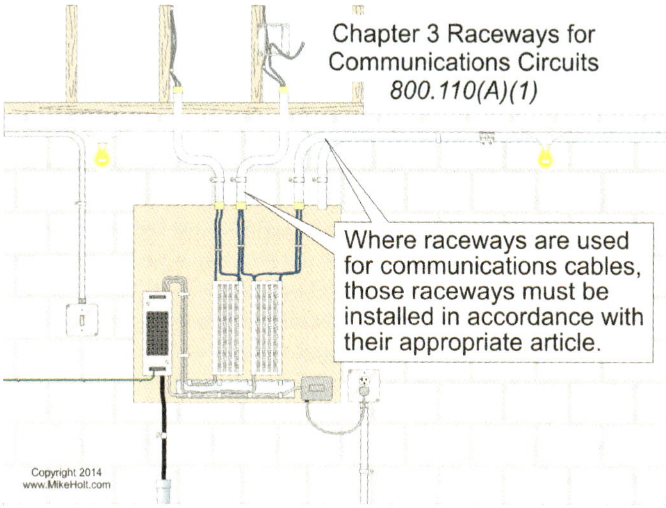

Figure 800–11

800.110 Raceways and Cable Routing Assemblies for Communications Wires and Cables

Requirements for cable routing assemblies have been added.

Part V. Installation Methods Within Buildings

800.110 Raceways and Cable Routing Assemblies for Communications Wires and Cables.

(A) Types of Raceways.

(1) Chapter 3 Raceways. Communications cables can be installed in any Chapter 3 raceway in accordance with the requirements of Chapter 3. Figure 800–11

(2) Communications Raceways. Communications cables can be installed in a listed communications raceway. If communications cables are installed in a listed communications nonmetallic raceway, the raceway must be installed in accordance with 362.24 through 362.56. Figure 800–12

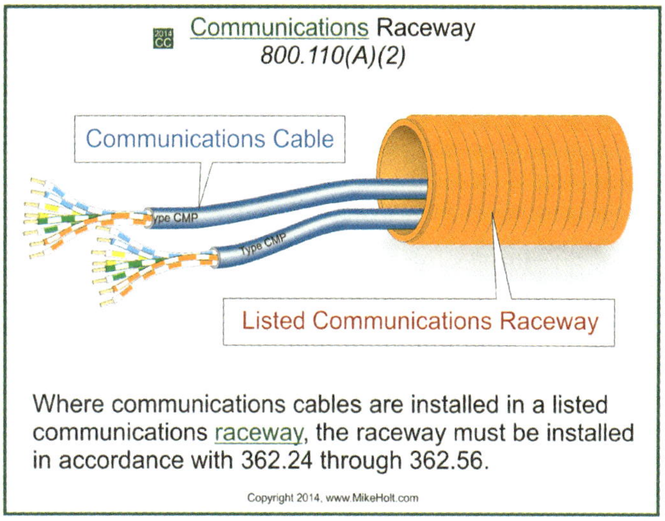

Figure 800–12

Author's Comment: In other words, listed communications raceways must be installed in accordance with the following rules for ENT:

- 362.24 Bending radius
- 362.26 Maximum total bends between pull points, 360 degrees
- 362.28 Trimmed to remove rough edges
- 362.30 Supported every 3 ft, and within 3 ft of any enclosure
- 362.48 Joints between tubing, fittings, and boxes

(B) Raceway Fill for Communications Wires and Cables. Raceway fill limitations of 300.17 don't apply to communications cables installed in a raceway.

(C) Cable Routing Assemblies. Communications cables can be installed in cable routing assemblies in accordance with 800.113 and Table 800.133. They must also be supported in accordance with the following:

(1) Horizontal Support. Where installed horizontally, cable routing assemblies must be supported every 3 ft, and at each end or joint, unless listed otherwise. Supports can never exceed 10 ft.

(2) Vertical Support. Where installed vertically, cable routing assemblies must be supported every 4 ft, unless listed otherwise, and must not have more than one joint between supports.

ANALYSIS: With the growing popularity of cable routing assemblies, new requirements have been added throughout the *NEC*. This section contains the support requirements for cable routing assemblies, and simply refers the *Code* user to 800.113 to address the plenum, riser, general use, (and so on) issues.

800.113 Installation of Communications Cables, Communications Raceways, and Cable Routing Assemblies

Cable routing assemblies are now included in this section, which covers the installations of communications cables and raceways.

800.113 Installation of Communications Cables, Communications Raceways, and Cable Routing Assemblies.

(A) Listing. Communications cables, raceways, and cable routing assemblies installed within buildings must be listed.

Ex: Unless the length of the cable from its point of entrance doesn't exceed 50 ft as permitted by 800.48.

(C) Plenum Spaces. The following cables and raceways are permitted in plenum spaces as described in 300.22(C): Figure 800–13

(1) Type CMP cables

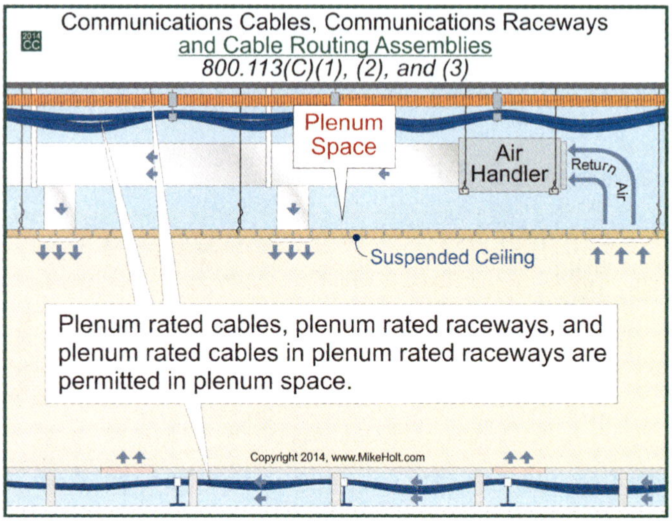

Figure 800–13

(2) Listed plenum communications raceways

(3) Type CMP cables installed in plenum raceways

(4) Types CMP cables and plenum communications raceways supported by open metallic cable trays or cable tray systems

(5) Types CMP, CMR, CMG, CM, and CMX cables installed in raceways in accordance with 300.22(C) Figure 800–14

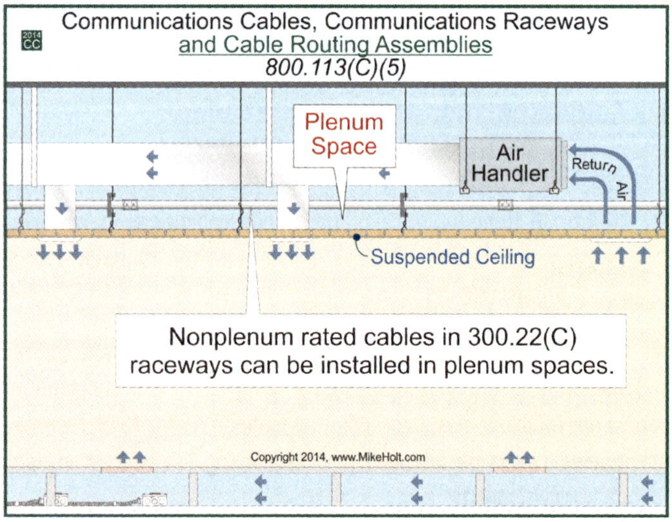

Figure 800–14

(H) Cable Trays. The following cables and raceways can be installed in cable trays:

(1) Types CMP, CMR, CMG, and CM cables

(2) Communications raceways

(3) Types CMP, CMR, CMG, and CM cables installed in communications raceways

(J) Other Building Locations.

(1) Types CMP, CMR, CMG, and CM cables

(2) A maximum of 10 ft of exposed Type CMX cable in nonconcealed spaces

(3) Communications raceways

(4) Cable routing assemblies

(6) Types CMP, CMR, CMG, and CM cables installed in communications raceways

(7) Listed communication wires and Types CMP, CMR, CMG, CM, and CMX cables and installed in a Chapter 3 raceway

(L) One- and Two-Family Dwellings. The following cables and raceways can be installed in one- and two-family dwellings in locations other than the locations covered in 800.113(B) through (F):

(1) Types CMP, CMR, CMG, and CM cables

(2) Type CMX cable less than ¼ in. in diameter

(3) Plenum, riser, and general-purpose communications raceways installed in accordance with 800.110

(4) Cable routing assemblies

(6) Types CMP, CMR, CMG, and CM cables installed in plenum, riser, or general-purpose communications raceways

(7) Listed communication wires and Types CMP, CMR, CMG, CM, and CMX cables and installed in a raceway of a type included in Chapter 3

ANALYSIS: This change is yet another example of cleaning up the rules for cable routing assemblies by consolidating them all into one location. There's no sense in having the same rules copied and pasted throughout the *Code* book, so this will hopefully create a better *NEC*.

800.133 Installation of Communications Cables

A few housekeeping-type changes dealing with the installation of communications cables have been made to this section.

800.133 Installation of Communications Cables.

(A) Separation from Power Conductors.

(1) In Raceways, Cable Routing Assemblies, Cable Trays, and Enclosures. Figure 800–15

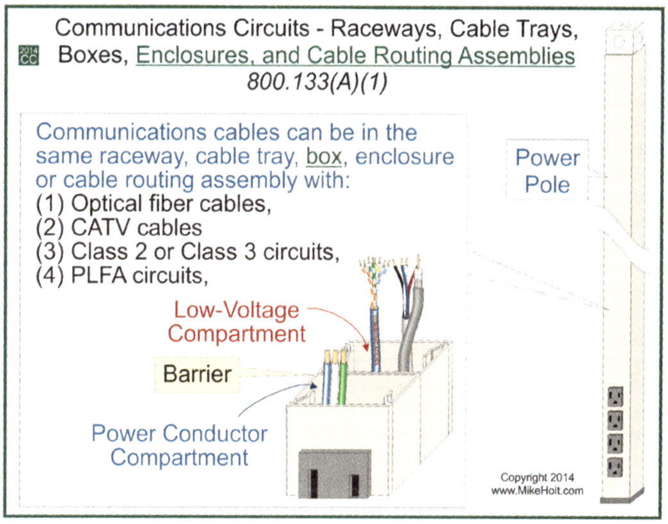

Figure 800–15

(a) With Optical Fiber Cables. Communications cables can be in the same raceway, cable tray, cable routing assembly, or enclosure with conductors of any of the following:

(1) Optical fiber cables in accordance with Parts I and V of Article 770.

(2) Coaxial cables in accordance with Parts I and V of Article 820.

(b) With Other Circuits. Communications cables can be in the same raceway, cable tray, cable routing assembly, or enclosure with conductors of any of the following:

(1) Class 2 and Class 3 circuits in accordance with Article 645 or Parts I and III of Article 725.

(2) Power-limited fire alarm circuits in accordance with Parts I and III of Article 760.

(c) Class 2 and Class 3 Circuits. Communications conductors can be within the same cable with Class 2 or Class 3 conductors, provided that communications cables in accordance with Article 800 are used [725.139(D)(1)]. Figure 800–16

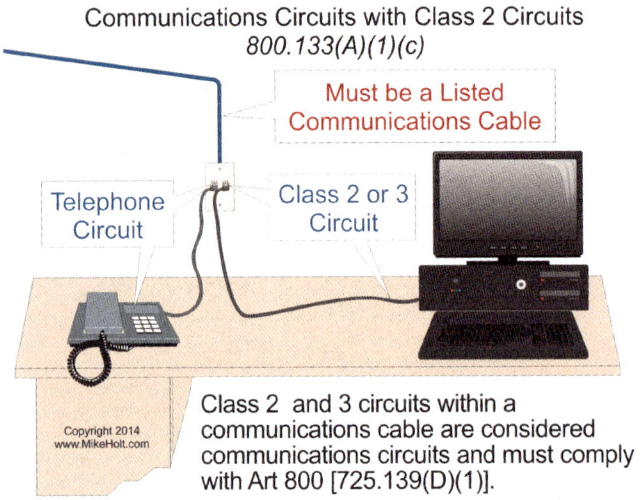

Figure 800–16

Author's Comments:

- A common application of this requirement is when a single cable is used for both voice communications and data.
- Listed Class 2 cables have a voltage rating of 150V [725.179(G)], whereas communications cables have a voltage rating of 300V [800.179].

(d) With Power Conductors in Same Raceway or Enclosure. Communications conductors must not be placed in any raceway, compartment, outlet box, junction box, or similar fitting with conductors of electric power or Class 1 circuits.

Ex 1: Communications circuits can be within the same enclosure with conductors of electric power and Class 1 circuits, where separated by a permanent barrier or listed divider.

Author's Comment: Separation is required to prevent a fire or shock hazard that can occur from a short between the communications circuits and the higher-voltage circuits.

Ex 2: Communications conductors can be mixed with power conductors if the power circuit conductors are only introduced to supply power to communications equipment. The power circuit conductors must maintain a minimum ½ in. separation from the communications circuit conductors.

ANALYSIS: 800.133 deals with the installation of communications cables. Although 800.133(A)(1) contained rules regarding cable routing assemblies, the title of the section didn't reflect it. The title of 800.133(A)(1) was revised to include cable routing assemblies.

800.133(A)(1)(a), which contains installation requirements, contained references to the wrong Parts of Articles 770 and 820 in previous editions. Part IV of these articles, which is what the *Code* used to refer to, deals with grounding, whereas Part V (the correct Part) deals with installation methods.

800.154 Applications of Communications Cables, Communications Raceways, and Cable Routing Assemblies

Cable routing assemblies are now addressed in the permitted applications table(s).

800.154 Applications of Communications Cables, Communications Raceways, and Cable Routing Assemblies.

Listed communications cables, raceways, and cable routing assemblies can be installed as indicated in Tables 800.154(a), (b), and (c), as limited by 800.113, and cable substitutions may be made in accordance with Table 800.154(d). Figure 800–17

ANALYSIS: Once again, the *Code* is trying to get all of the rules for cable routing assemblies in Article 800. I'm not quite sure why adding these two new tables [800.154(b) and 800.154(c)] with no new information will be helpful, however.

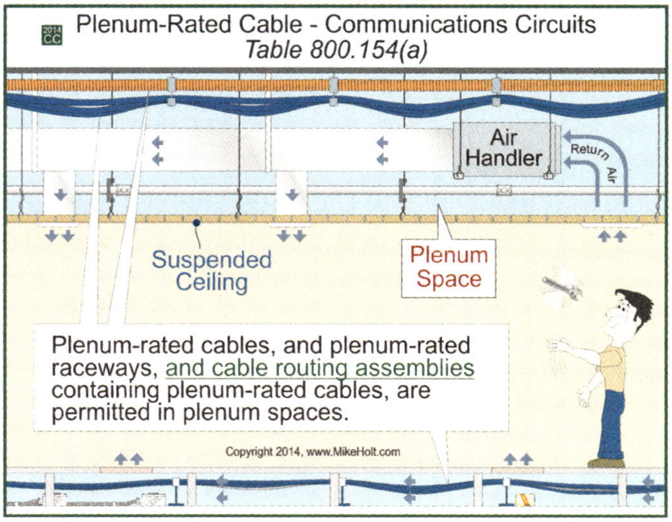

Figure 800–17

Notes

ARTICLE 810 RADIO AND TELEVISION EQUIPMENT

Introduction to Article 810—Radio and Television Equipment

This article covers transmitter and receiver equipment—and the wiring and cabling associated with that equipment. Here are a few key points to remember about Article 810:

- Avoid contact with conductors of other systems.
- Don't attach antennas or other equipment to the service-entrance power mast.
- If the mast isn't grounded properly, voltage surges caused by nearby lightning strikes can destroy it.
- Keep the bonding conductor or grounding electrode conductor as straight as practicable, and protect it from physical damage.
- If the mast isn't bonded properly, you risk flashovers and possible electrocution.
- Keep in mind that the purpose of bonding is to prevent a difference of potential between metallic objects and other conductive items, such as swimming pools.
- Clearances are critical, and Article 810 contains detailed clearance requirements. For example, it provides separate clearance requirements for indoor and outdoor locations.

810.6 Antenna Lead-In Protectors

A new section requiring antenna lead-in surge protectors to be listed has been added.

Part I. General

810.6 Antenna Lead-In Protectors. Antenna lead-in surge protectors must be listed, and must be grounded in accordance with 810.21.

ANALYSIS: Although they aren't required to be installed, antenna lead-in surge protectors are sometimes used by those desiring extra protection for their equipment. Because these devices are subject to high-energy lightning surges they're required to be listed. An unlisted piece of equipment trying to deal with the massive amount of induced energy from lightning can result in fire or personnel injury.

810.7 Grounding Devices

A new requirement for listed fittings has been added.

810.7 Grounding Devices. Fittings used to connect bonding jumpers or grounding electrode conductors to equipment must be listed.

ANALYSIS: There are quite a few sections in this article that require the grounding or bonding of cables or equipment, yet none of them really discuss the fittings used. This new requirement will ensure that proper devices are employed, which ultimately adds to the overall safety of the installation.

ARTICLE 820 COMMUNITY ANTENNA TELEVISION (CATV) AND RADIO DISTRIBUTION SYSTEMS

Introduction to Article 820—Community Antenna Television (CATV) and Radio Distribution Systems

This article focuses on the distribution of television and radio signals within a facility or on a property via cable, rather than their transmission or reception via antenna. These signals are limited energy, but they're high frequency.

- As with Article 800, you must determine the "point of entrance" for these circuits.
- Ground the incoming coaxial cable as close as practicable to the point of entrance.
- If coaxial cables are located above a suspended ceiling, route and support them to allow access via ceiling panel removal.
- Clearances are critical, and Article 820 contains detailed clearance requirements. For example, it requires at least 6 ft of clearance between coaxial cable and lightning conductors.
- If the building or structure has an intersystem bonding termination, the bonding conductor must be connected to it.
- If you use a separate grounding electrode, you must run a bonding jumper to the power grounding system.

820.2 Definitions—Point of Entrance

The definition of "point of entrance" was revised for brevity.

820.2 Definitions.

Point of Entrance. The point within a building where the coaxial cable emerges from an external wall, from a concrete floor slab, or from a rigid metal conduit or an intermediate metal conduit. Figure 820–1

ANALYSIS: Definitions aren't supposed to contain requirements. Although the deleted text ("connected by a bonding conductor or grounding electrode in accordance with 820.100(B)") doesn't seem to be a requirement, it can be construed as such. A task group was created to create some sanity in the definitions of the limited-energy *Code* articles, and this change was one of the results.

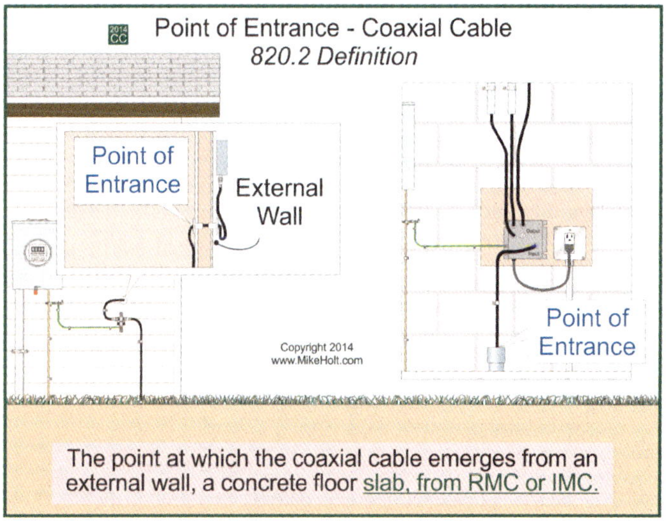

Figure 820–1

820.24 Mechanical Execution of Work

Cable ties are now required to be listed for use in plenums.

820.24 Mechanical Execution of Work. Equipment and coaxial cabling must be installed in a neat and workmanlike manner. Exposed coaxial cables must be supported by the structural components of the building so that the coaxial cable won't be damaged by normal building use. Coaxial cables must be secured by straps, staples, cable ties, hangers, or similar fittings designed and installed so as not to damage the coaxial cable. Figure 820–2

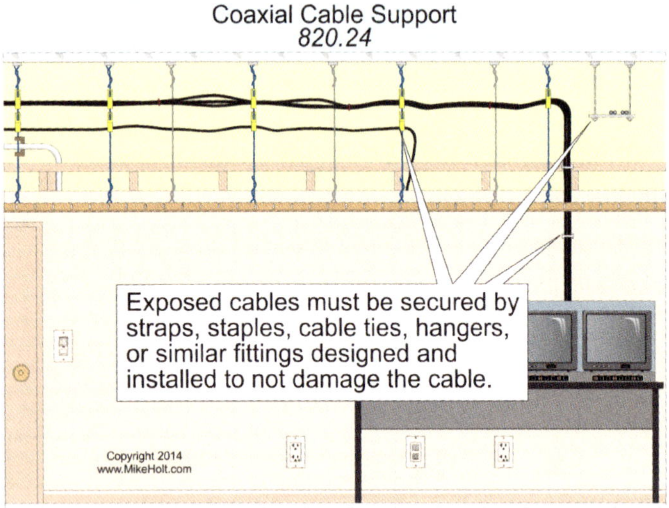

Figure 820–2

Raceways that contain coaxial cables must be securely fastened in place. Ceiling-support wires or the ceiling grid must not be used to support raceways or coaxial cables [300.11]. Figure 820–3

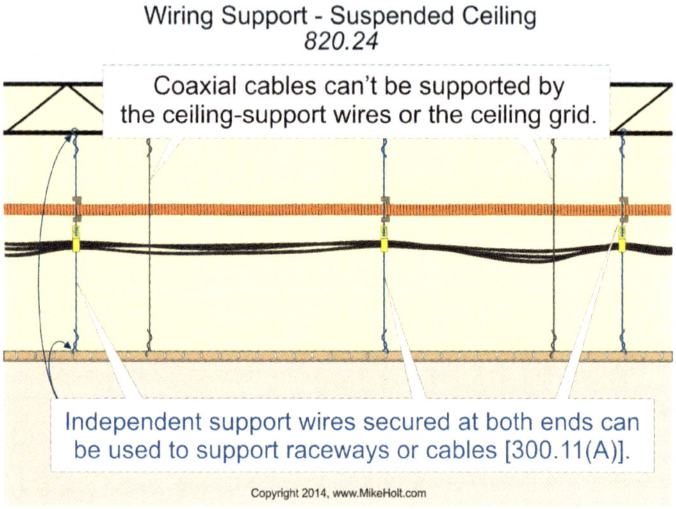

Figure 820–3

> **Author's Comment:** Raceways and coaxial cables can be supported by independent support wires attached to the suspended ceiling in accordance with 300.11(A).

Coaxial cables installed through or parallel to framing members or furring strips must be protected where they're likely to be penetrated by nails or screws, by installing the coaxial cables so they aren't less than 1¼ in. from the nearest edge of the framing member or furring strips, or by protecting the coaxial cable with a 1⁄16 in. thick steel plate or the equivalent [300.4(D)]. Figure 820–4

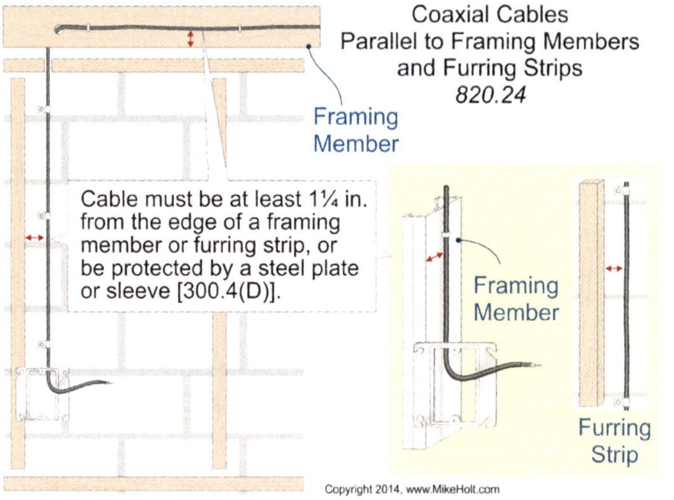

Figure 820–4

Cable ties used to secure or support coaxial cables in plenums must be listed for use in plenums.

> **Note 1:** Accepted industry practices are described in ANSI/NECA/BICSI 568, *Standard for Installing Commercial Building Telecommunications Cabling*, ANSI/TIA 568, *Part 1 General Requirements Commercial Building Telecommunications Cabling Standard*, ANSI/TIA 569, *Commercial Building Standard for Telecommunications Pathways and Spaces*, ANSI/TIA 570, *Residential Telecommunications Infrastructure*, and other ANSI-approved standards.

> **Author's Comment:** For more information about these standards, visit http://www.NECA-NEIS.org/.

> **Note 2:** See NFPA 90A-2009, *Standard for the Installation of Air-Conditioning and Ventilating Systems*, for discrete combustible components installed in accordance with 300.22(B) and (C).

ANALYSIS: A plenum space, such as those found above some suspended ceilings, contains the air that you breathe. It makes sense that the *Code* restricts what types of items are in it. Cable ties may be small, but there also might be thousands of them in a plenum, and they do add up. If the plenum space has a fire inside of it, the smoke will be breathed by the occupants who are trying to escape. Nonplenum-rated materials release more toxic fumes than their plenum-rated counterparts, and that's the last thing anyone running out of a burning building needs to be dealing with.

820.49 Metallic Entrance Conduit Grounding

A new section discussing the grounding of raceways entering buildings has been added.

Part II. Coaxial Cables Outside and Entering Buildings

820.49 Metallic Entrance Conduit Grounding. Rigid metal conduit (RMC) or intermediate metal conduit (IMC) containing entrance coaxial cable must be connected to a grounding electrode in accordance with 820.100(B). **Figure 820–5**

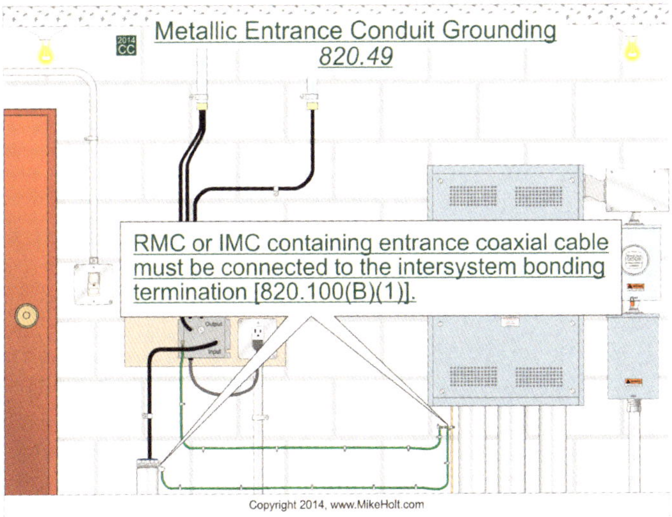

Figure 820–5

ANALYSIS: With the change to the definition of "point of entrance" in 820.2 this new section became necessary. It technically isn't anything new, because the definition discussed this, but definitions aren't supposed to contain requirements.

820.110 Raceways for Coaxial Cables

Requirements for cable routing assemblies have been added.

Part V. Installation Methods Within Buildings

820.110 Raceways for Coaxial Cables.

(A) Types of Raceways.

(1) Chapter 3 Raceways. Coaxial cables can be installed in any Chapter 3 raceway in accordance with the requirements of Chapter 3. **Figure 820–6**

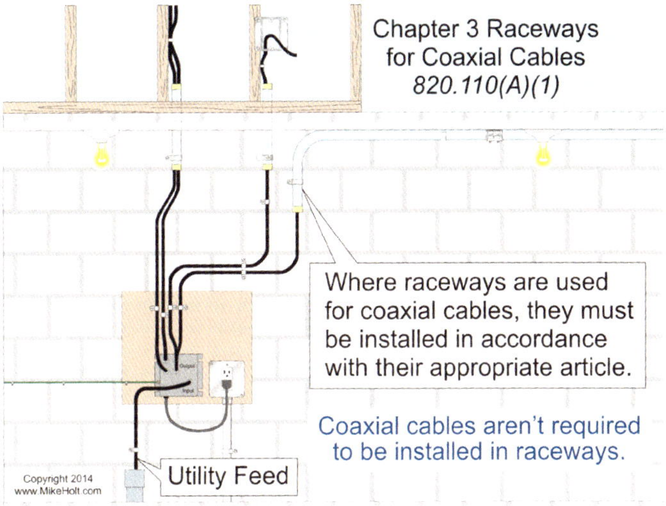

Figure 820–6

(2) Communications Raceways. Coaxial cables can be installed in listed communications raceways. If coaxial cables are installed in a listed communications raceway, the raceway must be installed in accordance with 362.24 through 362.56. **Figure 820–7**

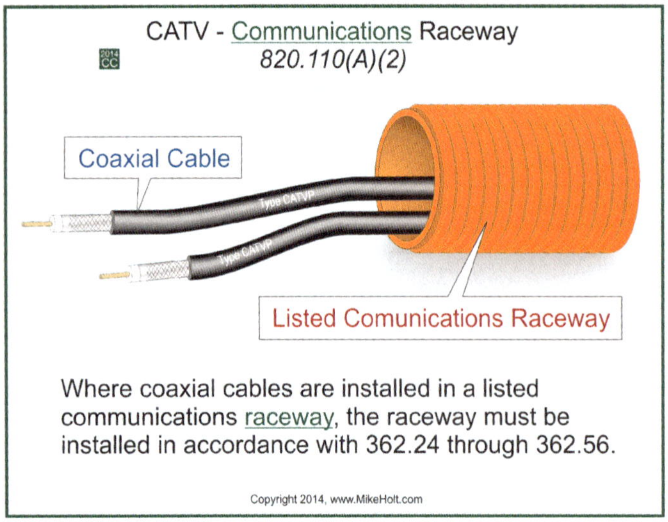

Figure 820–7

Author's Comment: In other words, listed coaxial raceways must be installed in accordance with the following rules for ENT:

- 362.24 Bending radius
- 362.26 Maximum total bends between pull points, 360 degrees
- 362.28 Trimmed to remove rough edges
- 362.30 Supported every 3 ft, and within 3 ft of any enclosure
- 362.48 Joints between tubing, fittings, and boxes

(B) Raceway Fill for Coaxial Cables. Raceway fill limitations of 300.17 don't apply to coaxial cables installed in a raceway.

(C) Cable Routing Assemblies. Communications cables can be installed in cable routing assemblies in accordance with 800.113. They must also be supported in accordance with the following:

(1) Horizontal Support. Where installed horizontally, cable routing assemblies must be supported every 3 ft, and at each end or joint, unless listed otherwise. Supports can never exceed 10 ft.

(2) Vertical Support. Where installed vertically, cable routing assemblies must be securely supported every 4 ft, unless listed otherwise, and must not have more than one joint between supports.

ANALYSIS: With the growing popularity of cable routing assemblies, new requirements have been added throughout the *NEC*. This section contains the support requirements for cable routing assemblies, and simply refers the *Code* user to 800.113 to address the plenum, riser, general use, (and so forth) issues.

ANNEX J
ADA STANDARDS FOR ACCESSIBLE DESIGN

Introduction to Annex J— ADA Standards for Accessible Design

Informative annexes aren't part of the requirements of the *Code*, but are included for informational purposes only. Although annexes aren't enforceable parts of the *Code*, the provisions in this annex are often required in commercial buildings and multifamily dwellings where accessibility for disabled persons is mandated by the building code.

Annex J—ADA Standards for Accessible Design

A new Annex J relating to accessibility for disabled persons has been created.

J.2 Protrusion Limits. Objects installed between 27 in. and 80 in. above the floor must not protrude from the wall (or similar surface) more than 4 in.

J.6 Forward Reach.

Author's Comment: Forward reach is used when the wheelchair uses a forward approach to the item (reaching in front of the wheelchair to reach an item).

J.6.1 Unobstructed. Where a forward reach is unobstructed, the high forward reach is 48 in. maximum, and the low forward reach is 15 in. minimum above the finish floor or ground.

Author's Comment: Unobstructed reach is the typical environment. This means that, generally speaking, items such as receptacles, switches, thermostats, and similar items must be between 15 in. and 48 in. above the floor.

J.6.2 Obstructed. Where a forward reach is over an obstruction, the high forward reach is 48 in. maximum where the reach depth (such as the depth of a kitchen countertop) is 20 in. or less. Where the reach depth exceeds 20 in., the high forward reach is 44 in. maximum, and the reach depth is 25 in. maximum.

Author's Comment: Obstructions can include nearly anything, but perhaps the easiest thing to visualize is countertop receptacles. The countertop obstructs a person's reach if they're in a wheelchair, which results in them not being able to reach as high.

J.7 Side Reach.

Author's Comment: Side reach is used when the wheelchair uses a parallel approach to the item (leaning across the side of the wheelchair to reach an item).

J.7.1 Unobstructed. Where a parallel approach to an item is used, and the reach isn't obstructed, the high side reach is 48 in. maximum, and the low side reach is 15 in. minimum above the finished floor.

J.7.2 Obstructed. Where a parallel approach to an item is used, and the high side reach is over an obstruction, the height of the obstruction can be 34 in. maximum, and the depth of the obstruction can be 24 in. maximum. The high side reach is 48 in. maximum for a reach depth of up to 10 in. Where the reach depth is more than 10 in., the high side reach is 46 in. maximum for a reach depth of 24 in. maximum.

ANALYSIS: Most commercial buildings and multifamily dwellings need to be constructed to meet the Americans with Disabilities Act. This can be done by following the *Americans with Disabilities Act Accessibility Guidelines* (ADAAG), or the ICC A117.1 *Accessible and Usable Buildings and Facilities*. Both of these documents contain information that's pertinent to electrical installations. This includes mounting heights for things such as receptacles, switches, and thermostats, as well as limitations on protruding objects like wall sconce luminaires. Annex J was added to let *Code* users know of some of these requirements. Annex J certainly isn't an all-inclusive list of the requirements for accessibility to disabled persons, but it does include the most common requirements about which electricians and electrical engineers need to know.

If you're in a wheelchair, you're obviously limited by how far you can reach. Due to this, receptacles and switches must be mounted between 15 in. and 48 in. above the floor. What if you're visually impaired and use a cane? One of the more dangerous things that you could encounter is an object that sticks out from the wall (like a wall sconce) that's mounted high enough that your cane won't detect it, but low enough so your face will! For this reason, objects must only stick out from the wall to 4 in., if that object is mounted between 27 in. and 80 in. above the floor (next time you're in a commercial building look at how many things violate this, like drinking fountains and fire extinguishers).

CHANGES TO THE NEC 2014 FINAL EXAM

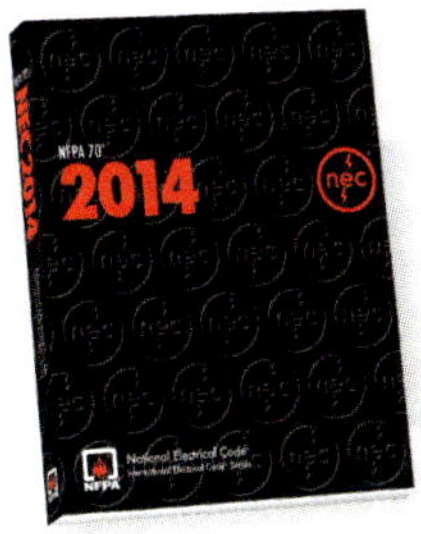

Please use the 2014 *Code* book to answer the following questions.

Article 90. Introduction

1. The *Code* isn't a design specification standard or instruction manual for the untrained and unqualified.

   (a) True
   (b) False

CHAPTER 1. GENERAL

Article 100. Definitions

2. Capable of being reached quickly for operation, renewal, or inspections without resorting to portable ladders or the use of tools is known as _____.

   (a) accessible (as applied to equipment)
   (b) accessible (as applied to wiring methods)
   (c) accessible, readily
   (d) all of these

3. A cable routing assembly is composed of single or connected multiple channels as well as associated fittings, forming a structural system to ______ high densities of wires and cables, typically communications wires and cables, optical fiber and data (Class 2 and Class 3) cables.

   (a) support
   (b) route
   (c) protect
   (d) a and b

4. Communications equipment includes equipment and conductors used for the transmission of _____.

   (a) audio
   (b) video
   (c) data
   (d) any of these

5. A communications raceway is an enclosed channel of nonmetallic materials designed for holding communications wires and cables in _____ applications.

   (a) plenum
   (b) riser
   (c) general-purpose
   (d) all of these

6. Wires are considered _____ if rendered inaccessible by the structure or finish of the building.

   (a) inaccessible
   (b) concealed
   (c) hidden
   (d) enclosed

7. The selection and installation of overcurrent devices so that an overcurrent condition will be localized and restrict outages to the circuit or equipment affected, is called "_____."

   (a) overcurrent protection
   (b) interrupting capacity
   (c) selective coordination
   (d) overload protection

8. A unit of an electrical system, other than a conductor, that carries or controls electric energy as its principal function is a(n) "______."

(a) raceway
(b) fitting
(c) device
(d) enclosure

9. An effective ground-fault current path is an intentionally constructed, low-impedance electrically conductive path designed and intended to carry fault current from the point of a ground fault on a wiring system to ______.

(a) ground
(b) earth
(c) the electrical supply source
(d) none of these

10. When the term "exposed," as it applies to live parts, is used in the *Code*, it refers to ______.

(a) being capable of being inadvertently touched or approached nearer than a safe distance by a person
(b) parts that are not suitably guarded, isolated, or insulated
(c) wiring on, or attached to, the surface or behind panels designed to allow access
(d) a and b

11. A ground-fault current path is an electrically conductive path from the point of a ground fault through normally noncurrent-carrying conductors, equipment, or the earth to the ______.

(a) ground
(b) earth
(c) electrical supply source
(d) none of these

12. Examples of ground-fault current paths include any combination of conductive materials including ______.

(a) equipment grounding conductors
(b) metallic raceways
(c) metal water and gas piping
(d) all of these

13. The installed conductive path(s) that provide(s) a ground-fault current path and connects normally noncurrent-carrying metal parts of equipment together and to the system grounded conductor or to the grounding electrode conductor, or both, is known as a(n) ______.

(a) grounding electrode conductor
(b) grounding conductor
(c) equipment grounding conductor
(d) none of these

14. Lighting track is a manufactured assembly and its length may not be altered by the addition or subtraction of sections of track.

(a) True
(b) False

15. Lighting track is a manufactured assembly designed to support and ______ luminaires that are capable of being readily repositioned on the track.

(a) connect
(b) protect
(c) energize
(d) all of these

16. A ______ location is protected from weather and not subject to saturation with water or other liquids.

(a) dry
(b) damp
(c) wet
(d) moist

17. Premises wiring includes ______ wiring from the service point or power source to the outlets.

(a) interior
(b) exterior
(c) underground
(d) a and b

18. Equipment enclosed in a case or cabinet with a means of sealing or locking so that live parts cannot be made accessible without opening the enclosure is said to be "______."

(a) guarded
(b) protected
(c) sealable
(d) lockable

19. A(n) _____ system is an electrical source, other than a service, having no direct connection(s) to circuit conductors of any other electrical source other than those established by grounding and bonding connections.

(a) separately derived
(b) classified
(c) direct
(d) emergency

20. A value assigned to a circuit or system for the purpose of conveniently designating its voltage class, such as 120/240V, is called "_____ voltage."

(a) root-mean-square
(b) circuit
(c) nominal
(d) source

Article 110. Requirements for Electrical Installations

21. Many terminations and equipment are marked with _____, or have that information included in the product's instructions.

(a) an etching tool
(b) a removable label
(c) a tightening torque
(d) the manufacturer's initials

22. Electrical equipment such as switchboards, switchgear, panelboards, industrial control panels, meter socket enclosures, and motor control centers, that are in other than dwelling units, and are likely to require _____ while energized, shall be field or factory marked to warn qualified persons of potential electric arc flash hazards.

(a) examination
(b) adjustment
(c) servicing or maintenance
(d) any of these

23. Where required by the *Code*, markings or labels on all electrical equipment shall contain voltage, current, wattage, or other ratings with sufficient durability to withstand _____.

(a) the voltages encountered
(b) painting and other finishes applied
(c) the environment involved
(d) any lack of planning by the installer

24. _____ in other than dwelling units must be legibly field marked with the maximum available fault current, including the date the fault-current calculation was performed and be of sufficient durability to withstand the environment involved.

(a) Service equipment
(b) Sub panels
(c) Motor control centers
(d) all of these

25. Field markings of maximum available fault current at a service are not required in industrial installations where conditions of maintenance and supervision ensure that only qualified persons service the equipment.

(a) True
(b) False

26. For equipment rated 800A or more that contains overcurrent devices, switching devices, or control devices; and where the entrance to the working space has a personnel door less than 25 ft from the working space, the door shall _____.

(a) open either in or out with simple pressure and shall not have any lock
(b) open in the direction of egress and be equipped with listed panic hardware
(c) be equipped with a locking means
(d) be equipped with an electronic opener

27. All switchboards, panelboards, and motor control centers shall be _____.

(a) located in dedicated spaces
(b) protected from damage
(c) in weatherproof enclosures
(d) a and b

28. To guard live parts operating at 50V must be guarded by being ______.

(a) located in a room accessible only to qualified persons
(b) located on a balcony accessible only to qualified persons
(c) elevated 8 ft or more above the floor or other working surface for 50V to 300V
(d) any of these

CHAPTER 2. WIRING AND PROTECTION

Article 200. Use and Identification of [Neutral] Grounded Conductors

29. An insulated grounded conductor of ______ or smaller shall be identified by a continuous white or gray outer finish, or by three continuous white or gray stripes along its entire length on other than green insulation.

(a) 8 AWG
(b) 6 AWG
(c) 4 AWG
(d) 3 AWG

30. If used for single-pole, 3-way or 4-way switch loops, the reidentified conductor with white or gray insulation or three continuous white or gray stripes can be used for the supply to the switch but not as a return conductor from the switch to the outlet.

(a) True
(b) False

Article 210. Branch Circuits

31. The GFCI protection required by 210.8(A), (B), (C), and (D) must be ______.

(a) the circuit breaker type only
(b) accessible
(c) readily accessible
(d) concealed

32. GFCI protection shall be provided for all 15A and 20A, 125V receptacles installed within 6 ft of all dwelling unit sinks located in ______.

(a) laundry rooms
(b) bathrooms
(c) dens
(d) all of these

33. All 15A and 20A, 125V receptacles installed in other than dwelling unit garages, service bays, and similar areas where ______ is/are to be used must be GFCI protected, unless located in vehicle exhibition halls and showrooms.

(a) electrical diagnostic equipment
(b) electrical hand tools
(c) portable lighting equipment
(d) all of these

34. All 15A or 20A, 120V branch circuits that supply outlets or devices in dwelling unit kitchens, family rooms, dining rooms, living rooms, parlors, libraries, dens, bedrooms, sunrooms, recreation rooms, closets, hallways, laundry areas, or similar rooms or areas shall be AFCI protected by a listed arc-fault circuit interrupter.

(a) True
(b) False

35. Where branch circuit wiring in a dwelling unit is modified, replaced, or extended in any of the areas specified in 210.12(A), the branch circuit must be protected by ______.

(a) a listed combination AFCI located at the origin of the branch circuit
(b) a listed outlet branch-circuit AFCI located at the first receptacle outlet of the existing branch circuit
(c) a GFCI circuit breaker or receptacle
(d) a or b

36. The receptacle outlet for a dwelling unit bathroom must be located on a ______ adjacent to the basin or basin counter surface, or on the side or face of the basin cabinet, and never more than 12 in. below the top of the basin.

(a) wall
(b) partition
(c) light fixture
(d) a or b

37. At least one receptacle outlet not more than _____ above a balcony, deck, or porch shall be installed at each balcony, deck, or porch that is attached to and accessible from a dwelling unit.

(a) 3 ft
(b) 6½ ft
(c) 8 ft
(d) 24 in.

38. For a one-family dwelling, at least one receptacle outlet shall be installed in each _____.

(a) basement
(b) attached garage
(c) detached garage or accessory building with electric power
(d) all of these

39. Where a portion of the dwelling unit basement is finished into one or more habitable rooms, each separate unfinished portion shall have a receptacle outlet installed.

(a) True
(b) False

40. Foyers with an area greater than _____ sq ft must have a receptacle located in each wall space 3 ft or more in width unbroken by doorways, windows next to doors that extend to the floor, and similar openings.

(a) 40
(b) 60
(c) 80
(d) 100

41. At least one 125V, 15A or 20A receptacle outlet shall be installed within 18 in. of the top of a show window for each _____ linear ft, or major fraction thereof, of show-window area measured horizontally at its maximum width.

(a) 10
(b) 12
(c) 18
(d) 24

Article 215. Feeders

42. The minimum feeder conductor ampacity must be no less than the noncontinuous load plus _____ percent of the continuous load, and not less than the maximum load after the application of adjustment and correction factors.

(a) 80
(b) 100
(c) 125
(d) 150

43. Feeder neutral conductors shall be permitted to be sized at _____ percent of the continuous and noncontinuous load.

(a) 80
(b) 100
(c) 125
(d) 150

44. The feeder conductor ampacity shall not be less than that of the service conductors where the feeder conductors carry the total load supplied by service conductors with an ampacity of _____ or less.

(a) 30A
(b) 55A
(c) 60A
(d) 100A

Article 225. Outside Branch Circuits and Feeders

45. Where a mast is used for overhead branch-circuit or feeder conductor support, it shall be of adequate strength or be supported by braces or guy wire to withstand safely the strain imposed by the conductors.

(a) True
(b) False

Article 230. Services

46. Service conductors installed in overhead masts on the outside surface of the building traveling through the eave, but not the wall, of that building are considered to be outside of the building.

(a) True
(b) False

47. The minimum point of attachment of overhead service conductors to a building shall not be less than _____ above finished grade.

(a) 8 ft
(b) 10 ft
(c) 12 ft
(d) 15 ft

48. Where conduits are used as service masts, hubs shall be _____ for use with service entrance equipment.

(a) identified
(b) approved
(c) of a heavy-duty type
(d) listed

49. Ungrounded service-entrance conductors shall be sized not less than _____ percent of the continuous load, plus 100 percent of the noncontinuous load.

(a) 100
(b) 115
(c) 125
(d) 150

Article 250. Grounding and Bonding

50. Ground clamps and fittings that are exposed to physical damage shall be enclosed in _____.

(a) metal
(b) wood
(c) the equivalent of a or b
(d) none of these

51. Ungrounded alternating current systems from 50V to less than 1,000V must be legibly marked "Caution: Ungrounded System—Operating _____ Volts Between Conductors" at _____ of the system, with sufficient durability to withstand the environment involved.

(a) the source
(b) the first disconnecting means
(c) every junction box
(d) a or b

52. The grounding electrode conductor shall be connected to the grounded service conductor at the _____.

(a) load end of the service drop
(b) load end of the service lateral
(c) service disconnecting means
(d) any of these

53. Grounding electrode conductors of the wire type shall be _____.

(a) solid
(b) stranded
(c) insulated or bare
(d) any of these

54. Where service equipment consists of more than one enclosure, grounding electrode conductor connections shall be permitted to be _____.

(a) multiple individual grounding electrode conductors
(b) one grounding electrode conductor at a common location
(c) a common grounding electrode conductor and taps
(d) any of these

55. Ferrous metal raceways and enclosures for grounding electrode conductors shall be electrically continuous from the point of attachment to cabinets or equipment to the grounding electrode.

(a) True
(b) False

56. What is the minimum size copper supply-side bonding jumper for a service raceway containing 4/0 THHN aluminum conductors?

(a) 6 AWG aluminum
(b) 4 AWG aluminum
(c) 4 AWG copper
(d) 3 AWG copper

57. A wire type equipment grounding conductor is permitted to be used as a grounding electrode conductor if it meets all the requirements of Parts II, III, and IV of Article 250.

(a) True
(b) False

58. When ungrounded circuit conductors are increased in size from the minimum size that has sufficient ampacity for the intended installation, the equipment grounding conductor must be proportionately increased in size according to the _____ of the ungrounded conductors.

(a) ampacity
(b) circular mil area
(c) diameter
(d) none of these

Article 285. Surge Protective Devices

59. Surge arrestors 1,000V or less are also known as Type 1 surge protective devices (SPDs).

(a) True
(b) False

CHAPTER 3. WIRING METHODS AND MATERIALS

Article 310. Conductors for General Wiring

60. Where conductors are installed in raceways or cables exposed to direct sunlight on or above rooftops, the ambient temperature shall be increased by _____ where the conduits are less than ½ in. from the rooftop.

(a) 30°F
(b) 40°F
(c) 50°F
(d) 60°F

Article 312. Cabinets, Cutout Boxes, and Meter Socket Enclosures

61. Openings in cabinets, cutout boxes, and meter socket enclosures through which conductors enter shall be _____.

(a) closed in an approved manner
(b) made using concentric knockouts only
(c) centered in the cabinet wall
(d) identified

Article 314. Outlet, Device, Pull, and Junction Boxes; Conduit Bodies; Fittings; and Handhole Enclosures

62. _____ can be used to fasten boxes to a structural member using brackets on the outside of the enclosure.

(a) Nails
(b) Screws
(c) Bolts
(d) a and b

63. A vertically mounted luminaire weighing not more than _____ can be supported to a device box or plaster ring with no fewer than two No. 6 or larger screws.

(a) 4 lb
(b) 6 lb
(c) 8 lb
(d) 10 lb

64. _____ shall be installed so that the wiring contained can be rendered accessible without removing any part of the building or structure or, in underground circuits, without excavating sidewalks, paving, or earth.

(a) Boxes
(b) Conduit bodies
(c) Handhole enclosures
(d) all of these

Article 320. Armored Cable (Type AC)

65. When Type AC cable is run across the top of a floor joist in an attic without permanent ladders or stairs, guard strips within _____ of the scuttle hole or attic entrance shall protect the cable.

(a) 3 ft
(b) 4 ft
(c) 5 ft
(d) 6 ft

Article 348. Flexible Metal Conduit (Type FMC)

66. FMC to a luminaire or electrical equipment within an accessible ceiling is permitted to be unsupported for not more than 6 ft from the last point where the raceway is securely fastened, including securing by listed FMC fittings.

(a) True
(b) False

Article 376. Metal Wireways

67. The ampacity adjustment factors in 310.15(B)(3)(a) shall be applied to a metal wireway only where the number of current-carrying conductors in any cross section of the wireway exceeds _____.

(a) 30
(b) 40
(c) 50
(d) 60

68. Power distribution blocks installed in metal wireways on the line side of the service equipment shall be listed for the purpose.

(a) True
(b) False

Article 386. Surface Metal Raceways

69. Surface metal raceways and associated fittings shall be supported _____.

(a) in accordance with the manufacturer's installation instructions
(b) at intervals appropriate for the building design
(c) at intervals not exceeding 4 ft
(d) at intervals not exceeding 8 ft

Article 392. Cable Trays

70. Metal cable trays containing only non-power conductors (such as communication, data, and signal conductors and cables) must be electrically continuous through approved connections or the use of a(n) _____.

(a) grounding electrode conductor
(b) bonding jumper
(c) equipment grounding conductor
(d) grounded conductor

CHAPTER 4. EQUIPMENT FOR GENERAL USE

Article 404. Switches

71. Switches controlling line-to-neutral lighting loads must have a grounded conductor provided at the switch location unless the _____.

(a) conductors enter the device box through a raceway that has sufficient area to accommodate a grounded conductor
(b) box enclosing the switch is accessible for the installation of an additional or replacement cable without removing finish materials
(c) lighting consists of all fluorescent fixtures with integral disconnects for the ballasts
(d) a or b

Article 406. Receptacles, Cord Connectors, and Attachment Plugs (Caps)

72. Receptacles in countertops and similar work surfaces shall not be installed ______, unless listed as receptacle assemblies for countertop applications.

(a) in the sides of cabinets
(b) in a face-up position
(c) on GFCI circuits
(d) on the kitchen small-appliance circuit

73. When 15A and 20A receptacles are installed in a wet location, the outlet box ______ must be listed for extra-duty use.

(a) sleeve
(b) hood
(c) threaded entry
(d) mounting

Article 410 Luminaires, Lampholders, and Lamps

74. In indoor locations other than dwellings and associated accessory structures, fluorescent luminaires that utilize double-ended lamps (typical fluorescent lamps) and contain ballast(s) that can be serviced in place must have a disconnecting means except for ______.

(a) emergency illumination required in 700.16.
(b) cord-and-plug-connected luminaires with accessible plugs and receptacles
(c) industrial establishments with restricted public access and written procedures and conditions of maintenance and supervision
(d) a and b

75. A 120V section of lighting track that is continuously loaded shall not exceed 12 ft in length, in accordance with 220.43(B).

(a) True
(b) False

Article 411. Lighting Systems Operating at 30 Volts or Less and Lighting Equipment Connected to Class-2 Power Sources

76. A lighting system covered by Article 411 shall have a power supply output rated not more than ______ and not more than 30V.

(a) 15A
(b) 20A
(c) 25A
(d) 30A

Article 422. Appliances

77. An in-sink waste disposer can be cord-and-plug-connected, but the cord shall not be less than 18 in. or more than ______ in length.

(a) 30 in.
(b) 36 in.
(c) 42 in.
(d) 48 in.

78. Cord-and-plug-connected vending machines manufactured or remanufactured on or after January 1, 2005 shall include a ground-fault circuit interrupter identified for portable use as an integral part of the attachment plug or in the power-supply cord within 12 in. of the attachment plug. Older vending machines not incorporating integral GFCI protection shall be ______.

(a) remanufactured
(b) disabled
(c) connected to a GFCI-protected outlet
(d) connected to an AFCI-protected circuit

Article 430. Motors, Motor Circuits and Controllers

79. The motor disconnecting means shall not be required to be in sight from the motor and the driven machinery location, provided ______.

    (a) the controller disconnecting means is lockable, in accordance with 110.25
    (b) locating the motor disconnecting means within sight of the motor is impractical
    (c) locating the motor disconnecting means within sight of the motor introduces additional or increased hazards to people or property
    (d) all of these

Article 440. Air-Conditioning and Refrigeration Equipment

80. Where the air conditioner disconnecting means is not within sight from the equipment, the disconnecting means must be ______.

    (a) guarded
    (b) exposed
    (c) lockable
    (d) elevated

Article 450. Transformers

81. For transformers, other than Class 2 and Class 3, a means is required to disconnect all transformer ungrounded primary conductors. The disconnecting means must be located within sight of the transformer unless the disconnect ______.

    (a) location is field marked on the transformer
    (b) is lockable in accordance with 110.25
    (c) is nonfusible
    (d) a and b

CHAPTER 5. SPECIAL OCCUPANCIES

Article 501. Class I Hazardous (Classified) Locations

82. Wiring methods and materials permitted in Class I, Division 1 locations include ______.

    (a) threaded rigid metal or threaded steel IMC
    (b) flexible fittings listed for Class I, Division 1 locations
    (c) boxes approved for Class I, Division 1 locations
    (d) all of these

83. ______ are among the wiring methods permitted within a Class I, Division 2 location.

    (a) Enclosed gasketed busways and enclosed gasketed wireways
    (b) PLTC and Type PLTC-ER cable and ITC and ITC-ER cable terminated with listed fittings
    (c) Types MC, MV, OFNP, OFCP, OFC, or TC cables including installation in cable tray systems and terminated with listed fittings
    (d) all of these

84. In a Class I, Division 2 location, if flexibility is necessary, ______ are some of the wiring methods that are permitted.

    (a) listed flexible metal fittings
    (b) flexible metal conduit, liquidtight flexible metal conduit and liquidtight nonmetallic conduit, all with listed fittings
    (c) interlocked armor Type MC cable with listed fittings
    (d) all of these

85. The cross-sectional area of the conductors or optical fiber tubes permitted in a sealing fitting shall not exceed ______ percent of the cross-sectional area of RMC of the same trade size.

    (a) 25
    (b) 50
    (c) 100
    (d) 125

86. In Class I locations, attachment plugs shall be of the type providing for ______ a flexible cord and shall be identified for the location.

    (a) sealing compound around
    (b) quick connection to
    (c) connection to the equipment grounding conductor of
    (d) none of these

Article 502. Class II Hazardous (Classified) Locations

87. Luminaires installed in Class II, Division 1 locations shall be identified for the location and shall be clearly marked to indicate the ______.

(a) maximum wattage and type of lamps for which they're designed
(b) minimum conductor size
(c) maximum overcurrent protection permitted
(d) all of these

Article 517. Health Care Facilities

88. The patient care space is any portion of a health care facility where patients are intended to be ______.

(a) examined
(b) treated
(c) registered
(d) a or b

89. The patient care space of a health care facility does not typically include business offices, corridors, lounges, day rooms, dining rooms, or similar areas.

(a) True
(b) False

90. In health care facilities, receptacles with insulated grounding terminals, as described in 250.146(D) shall be permitted in a patient care vicinity.

(a) True
(b) False

91. Each general care area patient bed location shall be provided with a minimum of ______ receptacle(s), which can be single, duplex, or any combination of these.

(a) two
(b) four
(c) six
(d) eight

Article 525. Carnivals, Circuses, Fairs, and Similar Events

92. The continuity of the equipment grounding conductor system used to reduce electrical shock hazards at carnivals, circuses, fairs, and similar events shall be verified each time that portable electrical equipment is connected.

(a) True
(b) False

Article 547. Agricultural Buildings

93. The purpose of the equipotential plane in agricultural buildings or adjacent areas is to minimize differences in voltage within the plane, as well as between planes, grounded equipment, and the earth.

(a) True
(b) False

94. Where an equipment grounding conductor is installed underground within an agricultural building, it shall be a(n) ______ conductor.

(a) insulated or covered
(b) copper
(c) bare
(d) any of these

Article 555. Marinas and Boatyards

95. A ______ is an enclosed assembly that can include receptacles, circuit breakers, fused switches, fuses, watt-hour meter(s), panelboards and monitoring means approved for marine use.

(a) marine power receptacle
(b) marine outlet
(c) marine power outlet
(d) any of these

96. The equipment grounding conductor at a marina is required to be an insulated copper conductor for all circuits.

(a) True
(b) False

Article 590. Temporary Installations

97. GFCI protection is required for 15A, 20A, and 30A, 125V receptacle outlets that are installed or existing as part of the permanent wiring of the building/structure when used during construction or remodeling. Listed cord sets or adapters that incorporate listed GFCI protection for portable use can be used to meet this requirement.

    (a) True
    (b) False

CHAPTER 6. SPECIAL EQUIPMENT

Article 600. Electric Signs and Outline Lighting

98. Fixed, mobile, or portable electric signs, section signs, outline lighting, and retrofit kits shall be _____.

    (a) approved by special permission
    (b) listed
    (c) identified for the location
    (d) a or b

99. Electric signs (other than portable, cord-connected signs), outline lighting, skeleton tubing systems, and retrofit kits shall be marked to indicate that field wiring and _____ are required.

    (a) listing
    (b) labeling
    (c) inspection
    (d) installation instructions

100. Where the disconnecting means is out of the line of sight from any section of a sign or outline lighting able to be energized, the disconnecting means must be _____ in the open position.

    (a) secured
    (b) bolted
    (c) lockable
    (d) none of these

101. For a sign, outline lighting system, or skeleton tubing system, the equipment grounding conductor size shall be in accordance with _____, based on the rating of the overcurrent device protecting the conductors supplying the sign or equipment.

    (a) 250.66
    (b) 250.122
    (c) 310.13
    (d) 310.16

102. A working space not less than 3 ft high by 3 ft wide by _____ deep is required for each ballast, transformer, electronic power supply, and Class 2 power source where not installed in a sign.

    (a) 2 ft
    (b) 3 ft
    (c) 4 ft
    (d) 6 ft

103. Ballasts, transformers, electronic power supplies, and Class 2 power sources for signs can be located above a suspended ceiling, provided the enclosures _____.

    (a) are securely fastened in place
    (b) don't use the suspended-ceiling grid for support
    (c) a or b
    (d) a and b

Article 620. Elevators, Escalators, and Moving Walks

104. The disconnecting means for an elevator or escalator shall be an enclosed externally operable circuit breaker or fused motor circuit switch that is _____.

    (a) capable of interrupting six times the locked-rotor current
    (b) lockable
    (c) inherently protected
    (d) suitable for use as service equipment

Article 640. Audio Signal Processing, Amplification, and Reproduction Equipment

105. Audio system equipment supplied by branch-circuit power shall not be located within _____ horizontally of the inside wall of a pool, spa, hot tub, fountain, or tidal high-water mark.

(a) 18 in.
(b) 2 ft
(c) 5 ft
(d) 10 ft

Article 680. Swimming Pools, Spas, Hot Tubs, Fountains, and Similar Installations

106. Insulated overhead service conductors that are cabled together with a bare messenger and operate at not over 750 volts-to-ground shall maintain a _____ clearance in any direction to the water level of swimming pools, fountains, and similar installations.

(a) 14 ft
(b) 16 ft
(c) 20 ft
(d) 22½ ft

107. Electric swimming pool equipment can be installed in pits where drainage prevents water accumulation during abnormal operation.

(a) True
(b) False

108. Outlets supplying pool pump motors connected to single-phase 120V through 240V branch circuits, whether by receptacle or by direct connection, shall be provided with _____ protection for personnel.

(a) AFCI
(b) GFCI
(c) a or b
(d) a and b

109. A 125V receptacle shall be installed a minimum of 6 ft and a maximum of 20 ft from the inside wall of a permanently installed pool.

(a) True
(b) False

110. Grounding-type GFCI-protected receptacles of the single type for motors related to the circulation and sanitation system of a pool can be located not less than _____ from the inside walls of the pool.

(a) 3 ft
(b) 6 ft
(c) 8 ft
(d) 12 ft

111. Both metal piping systems and all grounded metal parts in contact with the circulating water of a hydromassage bathtub shall be bonded together using a(n) _____ solid copper bonding jumper not smaller than 8 AWG.

(a) insulated
(b) covered
(c) bare
(d) any of these

CHAPTER 7. SPECIAL CONDITIONS

Article 700. Emergency Systems

112. If a generator for emergency system power located outdoors is equipped with a readily accessible disconnecting means in accordance with 445.18, and the disconnecting means is located within sight (within 50 ft) of the building/structure, an additional disconnecting means isn't required on or at the building/structure for the generator feeder conductors that serve or pass through the building/structure.

(a) True
(b) False

Article 702. Optional Standby Systems

113. Where a generator for an optional standby system is installed outdoors and equipped with a readily accessible disconnecting means located ______, an additional disconnecting means is not required where ungrounded conductors serve or pass through the building or structure.

   (a) inside the building or structure
   (b) within sight of the building or structure
   (c) inside the generator enclosure
   (d) a or c

Article 725. Remote-Control, Signaling, and Power-Limited Circuits

114. Audio system circuits using Class 2 or Class 3 wiring methods, are not permitted in the same cable, raceway, or cable routing assembly with ______.

   (a) other audio system circuits
   (b) Class 2 conductors or cables
   (c) Class 3 conductors or cables
   (d) b or c

Article 760. Fire Alarm Systems

115. Cables and conductors of two or more power-limited fire alarm circuits can be installed in the same cable, enclosure, cable tray, raceway, or cable routing assembly.

   (a) True
   (b) False

116. Audio system circuits using Class 2 or Class 3 wiring methods shall not be installed in the same cable, raceway, or cable routing assembly with ______.

   (a) other audio system circuits
   (b) power-limited fire alarm conductors or cables
   (c) a or b
   (d) none of these

Article 770. Optical Fiber Cables and Raceways

117. An optical fiber cable is a factory assembly or field assembly of one or more optical fibers having a(n) ______ covering.

   (a) conductive
   (b) nonconductive
   (c) overall
   (d) metallic

118. The point of entrance of an optical fiber installation is the point ______ at which the optical fiber cable emerges from an external wall, from a concrete floor slab, from rigid metal conduit, or from intermediate metal conduit.

   (a) outside a building
   (b) within a building
   (c) on the building
   (d) none of these

119. Conductive optical fiber cables can occupy the same cable tray, raceway, box, enclosure, or cable routing assembly with conductors for electric light, power, and Class 1 circuits.

   (a) True
   (b) False

CHAPTER 8. COMMUNICATIONS SYSTEMS

Article 800. Communications Circuits

120. The point of entrance of a communications circuit is the point ______ at which the communications cable emerges from an external wall, from a concrete floor slab, from RMC, or from IMC.

   (a) outside a building
   (b) within a building
   (c) on the building
   (d) none of these

121. Communications wires, communications cables, communications raceways, and cable routing assemblies installed in buildings shall be listed except for up to 50 ft past the point of entry as allowed by 800.48.

   (a) True
   (b) False

Article 820. Community Antenna Television (CATV) and Radio Distribution Systems

122. The point of entrance of a CATV coaxial cable is the point ______ at which the coaxial cable emerges from an external wall, from a concrete floor slab, from rigid metal conduit (RMC). or from intermediate metal conduit (IMC).

    (a) outside a building
    (b) within a building
    (c) on the building
    (d) none of these

Notes

Notes

INDEX

Description	Page
A	
Accessible, Readily (Readily Accessible)	8
ADA Standards for Accessible Design	321
Adjustable Speed Drive System	9
Adjustable Speed Drive	8
Agricultural Buildings—Equipotential Plane	239
Agricultural Buildings—Wiring Methods	240
Air-Conditioning and Refrigeration Equipment—Disconnect	197
Antenna Grounding Devices	315
Antenna Lead-In Protectors	315
Appliances—Flexible Cords	191
Appliances—Ground-Fault Circuit-Interrupter (GFCI) Protection	191
Appliances—Outlet Boxes to Be Covered	192
Appliances—Space for Conductors	192
Arc-Fault Circuit-Interrupter Protection	49
Arc-Flash Hazard Warning	25
Armored Cable (Type AC)	135
Attics or Roof Spaces	135
Audio Signal, Processing, Amplification, and Reproduction Equipment	255
Audio Systems Near Bodies of Water	256
Available Fault Current	27
B	
Bonding Conductors and Jumpers	92
Bonding in Hazardous (Classified) Locations	92
Box Support	130
Boxes in Damp or Wet Locations	129
Branch Circuits	43
Branch-Circuit, Feeder, and Service Calculations	65
C	
Cabinets, Cutout Boxes, and Meter Socket Enclosures	125
Cable Routing Assembly	9
Cable Trays—Equipment Grounding Conductor	163
Carnivals, Circuses, Fairs, and Similar Events—Grounding Conductor Continuity	237
CATV—Mechanical Execution of Work	318
CATV—Metallic Entrance Conduit Grounding	319
CATV—Point of Entrance	317
CATV—Raceways for Coaxial Cables	319
Class 2 and Class 3 Cables	289
Class 2, Class 3, and PLTC Cables	286
Class I Hazardous Locations—Grounding and Bonding	221
Class I Hazardous Locations—Raceway and Cable Seals	216
Class I Hazardous Locations—Receptacles and Attachment Plugs	222
Class I Hazardous Locations—Wiring Methods	213
Class II Hazardous Locations—Flexible Cords	227
Class II Hazardous Locations—Luminaires	226
Class II Hazardous Locations—Receptacles and Attachment Plugs	228
Class II Hazardous Locations—Wiring Methods	225
Class III Hazardous Locations—Wiring Methods	229
Combustible Material at Outlet Boxes	192
Communications Cable Installation	311
Communications Cables and Raceways Application	312
Communications Cables, Communications Raceways, and Cable Routing Assemblies	310
Communications Circuits—Innerduct Definition	306
Communications Circuits—Innerduct	307
Communications Circuits—Mechanical Execution of Work	307
Communications Circuits—Metallic Entrance Conduit Grounding	308
Communications Circuits—Point of Entrance	306
Communications Circuits—Raceways and Cable Routing Assemblies	309
Communications Equipment	10
Communications Raceway	10

Description	Page
***C** (continued)*	
Communications Systems	303
Concealed	11
Conductor Ampacity	114
Conductor Sizing	52
Conductor Termination and Splicing	24
Conductors for General Wiring	113
Conduit Bodies	130
Control Circuit	11
Coordination (Selective)	12
Covers and Canopies	131
D	
Definitions	7
Device	13
Dimmer-Controlled Receptacles	181
Dwelling Unit Receptacle Outlet Requirements	54
E	
Effective Ground-Fault Current Path	13
Electric-Discharge Lighting	14
Electric-Discharge Lighting—General	186
Electric-Discharge Lighting—Installation	187
Electric Signs and Outline Lighting —Ballasts, Transformers, Class 2 and Electronic Power Supplies	250
Electric Signs and Outline Lighting—Disconnecting Means	248
Electric Signs and Outline Lighting—Grounding and Bonding	250
Electric Signs and Outline Lighting—Listing	247
Electric Signs and Outline Lighting—Markings	248
Electric Vehicle Branch Circuit	51
Electrical Service Areas	58
Elevators, Escalators, and Moving Walks—Disconnecting Means	254
Emergency Systems—Multiwire Branch Circuits	276
Emergency Systems—General Requirements	274
Emergency Systems—-Ground-Fault Protection of Equipment	277
Emergency Systems—Illumination	276
Emergency Systems—Selective Coordination	277
Emergency Systems—Surge Protection	273
Equipment for General Use	167
Equipment Grounding Conductor Sizing	97
Equipment Grounding Conductors	96
Exposed (as applied to live parts)	15
F	
Feeders	61
Feeders—Minimum Rating	61
Fire Alarm Systems—Circuit Cables Extending Beyond a Building	291
Flexible Cords—Equipment Grounding Conductor Identification	169
Flexible Metal Conduit—Securing and Supporting	149
G	
General Care Areas	235
General Lighting	66
General Requirements for Wiring Methods and Materials	107
Generators—Bushings	200
Generators—GFCI Protection	201
Generators—Marking	199
GFCI Protection	45
Grounded Conductors	39
Ground-Fault Current Path	15
Grounding and Bonding	83
Grounding and Bonding—Service Equipment	85
Grounding Conductor Identification	94
Grounding Conductor, Equipment (EGC)	16
Grounding Electrode Conductor Installation	86
Grounding Electrode Conductor Sizing	89
Grounding Electrode Conductor	85
Grounding Electrode Termination	90
Grounding Termination	83
Grounding—Protection of Fittings	84
Guarding Live Parts	36
H	
Hazardous (Classified) Locations—Equipment	212
Health Care Facilities	233
Hermetic Refrigerant Motor-Compressor	17
Hydromassage Bathtub Equipotential Bonding	269

Description	Page

I

Description	Page
Identification of Disconnecting Means	27
Information Technology Equipment—System Grounding	257
Intersystem Bonding Termination	17
Isolated Ground Receptacles	235

L

Description	Page
Legally Required Standby Systems—General Requirements	279
Legally Required Standby Systems—Ground-Fault Protection of Equipment	280
Legally Required Standby Systems—Selective Coordination	280
Lighting Systems Operating at 30V or Less and Class-2 Power Sources	189
Lighting Track (Track Lighting)	17
Liquidtight Flexible Metal Conduit—Fittings	152
Liquidtight Flexible Metal Conduit—Securing and Supporting	151
Liquidtight Flexible Nonmetallic Conduit—Securing and Supporting	155
Location, Damp	18
Lockable Disconnecting Means	28
Low Voltage Suspended Ceiling Power Distribution Systems	165
Luminaires—Listing Required	185
Luminaires—Specific Locations	186

M

Description	Page
Marinas and Boatyards—Grounding	242
Marine Power Outlet	241
Markings	26
Masts as Supports	69
Metal Wireways—Number of Conductors and Ampacity	157
Metal Wireways—Splices, Taps, and Power Distribution Blocks	158
Metal-Clad Cable—Securing and Supporting	138
Metal-Clad Cable—Uses Permitted	137
Modular Data Centers	259
Motors—Disconnect Requirement	195
Motor Fuel Dispensing Facilities Classification of Locations	231
Multiwire Branch Circuits	44

N

Description	Page
Neutral Conductor Identification	41
Neutral Conductors	40
Nonmetallic-Sheathed Cable—Uses Not Permitted	142
Nonmetallic-Sheathed Cable—Uses Permitted	141

O

Description	Page
Optical Fiber Cable Installation	300
Optical Fiber Cables	296
Optical Fiber Cables—Mechanical Execution of Work	297
Optical Fiber Cables—Metallic Entrance Conduit Grounding	299
Optical Fiber Cables—Point of Entrance	296
Optical Fiber Cables—Raceways and Cable Routing Assemblies	299
Optical Fiber Cables and Conductors	301
Optical Fiber Cables and Raceways	295
Optical Fiber Cables—Unlisted Cables Entering Buildings	298
Optical Fiber Cables—Innerduct Definition	295
Optical Fiber Cables—Innerduct	296
Optional Standby Systems—Outdoor Generator Sets	282
Optional Standby Systems—Signs	281
Outlet Box	132
Outlet, Device, Pull, and Junction Boxes	129
Outside Branch Circuits and Feeders	69
Overcurrent Protection Location in Circuit	80

P

Description	Page
Patient Care Space	234
Permissible Loads, Individual Branch Circuits	53
Plenum Space	109
PLFA Cables in Buildings	292
Pool Equipotential Bonding	266
Pool Lighting, Receptacles, and Equipment	264
Pool Motors	264
Pools, Spas, Hot Tubs, and Fountains—Disconnecting Means	263
Pools, Spas, Hot Tubs, and Fountains—Equipment Rooms and Pits	263
Pools, Spas, Hot Tubs, and Fountains—Overhead Conductor Clearance	262
Power-Limited Fire Alarm Cables (PLFA)	293

Description	Page
P *(continued)*	
Power-Limited Fire Alarm Circuits, Class 2, Class 3, and Communications Circuits	292
Premises Wiring	18
Protection Against Corrosion and Deterioration	109
Purpose of the *NEC*	2
R	
Raceway	19
Raceway Seal	71
Radio and Television Equipment	315
Receptacle—Rating and Type	175
Receptacle—General Installation Requirements	176
Receptacle—Mounting	177
Receptacles in Damp or Wet Locations	178
Remote-Control, Signaling, and Power-Limited Circuits—Mixing	287
Replacing Nongrounding Receptacles	98
Requirements for Electrical Installations	23
Retrofit Kit	20
Rigid Metal Conduit Construction	148
Rigid Metal Conduit—Securing and Supporting	147
Rigid Polyvinyl Chloride Conduit Definition	153
S	
Sealable Equipment	20
Separately Derived System	20
Services—Point of Attachment	75
Service Conductors Considered Outside a Building	74
Service Masts Used as Supports	75
Service Size and Rating	77
Service-Entrance Cable—Uses Permitted	145
Services	73
Show Windows	58
Signs in or Adjacent to Fountains	269
Spaces About Electrical Equipment	29
Special Conditions	271
Special Equipment	245
Special Occupancies	207
Splices, Taps, and Feed-Through Conductors	126
Storable Pools, Spas, and Hot Tubs—Indoor Installations	268
Storable Pools, Spas, and Hot Tubs—Outdoor Installations	267
Storable Swimming Pool	262
Surface Metal Raceways—Securing and Supporting	161
Surge Protective Devices (SPDs)	101
Swimming Pools, Spas, Hot Tubs, Fountains, and Similar Installations	261
Switch Connections	171
Switch Mounting	173
Switchboards and Panelboards—Field Identification	183
T	
Tamper-Resistant Receptacles	180
Temporary Installations—GFCI	244
Tire Inflation and Automotive Vacuum Machines	193
Transformers—Disconnecting Means	204
Transformers—Grounding and Bonding	203
Transformers—Marking	204
U	
Underground Installations	108
Ungrounded Systems—50V to 1,000V	84
V	
Vending Machines	193
Voltage, Nominal	21
W	
Wiring and Protection	37
Wiring Methods and Materials	103
Wiring to be Accessible	134